Professional Visual Basic 6 Web Programming

Jerry Ablan
Tom Barnaby
Pierre Boutquin
Matt Brown
Charles Caison
Richard Harrison
Jeffrey Hasan
Matthew Reynolds
Dmitriy Slosberg
Michael Lane Thomas
Thearon Willis
Paul Wilton

Wrox Press Ltd. ®

Professional Visual Basic 6
Web Programming

© 1999 Wrox Press

Published by Wrox Press Ltd. Arden House,1102 Warwick Road,
Acocks Green, Birmingham, B27 6BH
Printed in USA
ISBN 1-861002-22-X

Credits

Authors
Jerry Ablan
Tom Barnaby
Pierre Boutquin
Matt Brown
Charles Caison
Richard Harrison
Jeffrey Hasan
Matthew Reynolds
Dmitriy Slosberg
Michael Lane Thomas
Thearon Willis
Paul Wilton

Development Editors
Dominic Lowe
Greg Pearson

Additional Material
Chris Ullman
Tim Waters

Cover
Chris Morris

Technical Reviewers
Robert Chang
John Granade
Joe Sutphin

Managing Editor
Chris Hindley

Editors
Andrew Polshaw
Jeremy Beacock
Soheb Siddiqi

Design/Layout
Tom Bartlett
Mark Burdett
David Boyce
William Fallon
Jonathan Jones
John McNulty

Index
Andrew Criddle

About the Authors

Jerry Ablan

Jerry Ablan is a Web developer with several years experience

Tom Barnaby

Tom has been working with computers for over 13 years. He started in grade school working on the venerable TI-99/4A and his education continued into college where he studied Computer Science. After graduating, Tom embarked on a career which has run the gamut of the programming experience – from system level programming with C and UNIX, to client/server systems with C++ and NT, and finally to Web Development with Visual Basic. Along the way, Tom has designed and developed 4GL, ERP, and data warehouse applications.

Tom's teaching career began in 1995 with an "Intro to UNIX" evening course at a local community college. Since then, he has gradually moved into instructing full-time, developing and teaching courses in Visual Basic, C++, OOA/D, and MFC.

Pierre Boutquin

To Sandra.

Pierre Boutquin is a Senior Analyst in the corporate treasury of a major Canadian bank, where he helps develop leading-edge market risk management software. He has over a decade of experience implementing PC-based computer systems with in-depth knowledge of object-oriented analysis and design, Visual Basic, Visual C++, and SQL. He most recently co-authored "Visual Basic 6 SuperBible" and "Visual Basic 6 Interactive Course", published by The Waite Group. He has also contributed material on COM and SQL for other books. Pierre's spare time is mainly owned by Koshka and Sasha, his two adorable Burmese cats. While petting them, he often thinks how nice it would be to find more time and get back into chess or keep up with news from Belgium, his native country. You can reach him at boutquin@hotmail.com.

I would like to thank Greg Pearson and all the other Wrox associates for the opportunity to work with them. Jeremy Beacock, Soheb Siddiqi and Andrew Polshaw are all appreciated for their help in making me look like an accomplished writer. Most importantly, I must acknowledge the enthusiastic encouragement I receive from my wife Sandra. Without her, I surely would have faltered in my writing efforts. Finally, I must also thank my colleagues in Corporate Treasury for their support and friendship.

Matt Brown

Matt Brown is a technical consultant and trainer for DBBasics in Raleigh North Carolina. He lives with his vivacious wife Karen and his children: Matthew, Erin, and Dominic. In his spare time he enjoys sleeping, reading, eating large quantities of meat, long walks and sunsets. In his spare time he resents having to shave and bathe, but does so on a regular basis. Among Matt's favorite authors are Robert Silverberg, Ayn Rand, and Guy Gavriel Kay. Matt wishes to make mention of and thank: Gary Kohan, Tim Waters, and his father Al Brown. You can send email to Matt at Mattbr@hotmail.com.

Charles Caison

Charles Caison is an instructor with DBBasics Corporation (`http://www.dbbasics.com`). He has been involved in Windows development since 1992. He is a contributing author to Visual Basic Programmer's Journal, Windows NT magazine, Microsoft Interactive Developer and other industry publications. He also speaks at Microsoft Developer Days and other industry events. You can reach him at `charlesc@dbbasics.com`.

Richard Harrison

Richard is a Microsoft Certified Solution Developer and a senior consultant for a major global IT services company. He has recently been specialising in Microsoft Internet architectures and helping organisations to use these technologies to build mission critical Web solutions.

Jeffrey Hasan

Jeff is a Lead Software Engineer with the Rare Medium Group in Los Angeles, California, where he is responsible for architecting and implementing leading-edge e-commerce sites for Fortune 100 companies and .com startups. He is experienced with NT/IIS web application development using Active Server Pages, Visual Basic and SQL Server. He a regular contributor to several magazines, writing articles on VB, ASP, ADO, COM and any other acronym he can think of. Jeff's chronic travel bug has most recently taken him from the rainforests of Costa Rica to the Karakoram mountains of Northern Pakistan.

Matthew Reynolds

Matthew Reynolds is a developer, architect and evangelist of Web-based applications running on Microsoft Internet technologies. He is also Senior Editor for ASPWatch.com. He lives in Phoenix, Arizona and London, England on no fixed schedule.

Dmitriy Slosberg

Dmitriy Shlosberg has many years of experience in the field. He worked as a contractor for the past 3 years developing enterprise solutions for the HealthCare, financial, educational, and security industry and is currently a CEO of Impera Software Corp, where he is currently working on a new enterprise e-commerce solution.

Michael Lane Thomas

Michael Lane Thomas has just got a job with Microsoft, and is too busy to write a proper bio!

Thearon Willis

A senior consultant with 19 years of IT experience, Thearon is currently a consultant for an International Insurance company providing Web programming services. His Web development tools of choice are ASP, Dynamic HTML, Visual Basic and SQL Server. Thearon lives in Charlotte, North Carolina with his wife and daughter.

To my wife Margie for her patience and understanding while I write yet another book, I love you very much.

Paul Wilton

Being a History and Politics graduate and Law post graduate the obvious career move was to programming. However a misspent youth in and out of computer book stores and programming in BBC Basic and Z80 assembler gave some head start.

After an initial start as a Visual Basic applications programmer he found himself pulled into the net and has spent the last 18 months helping create internet and intranet solutions.

Currently he is developing web based systems primarily using Visual Basic 6 and SQL Server 7 along with other numerous technologies.

Lots of love to my fiancée Catherine who ensures my sanity chip remains plugged in.

Table of Contents

Chapter 2: Windows DNA - a framework for building applications   35

Chapter 6: Dynamic HTML Applications 171

Chapter 7: Integrating Web Browsing Using the WebBrowser Objects 201

Chapter 9: Building Server Components in Visual Basic   309

Chapter 10: Advanced Visual Basic Server Components   347

Chapter 11: Interfacing With Server Services in Visual Basic   403

Chapter 16: A Guide to XML   575

Case Study 1 : Message Board Part 1   627

Introduction

What Does this Book Cover?

Over the past five years, the internet has gone from the preserve of academics to the cutting edge of business. A large part of this has been driven by the growth of the Web, with its graphical browsers and high media profile. Even so, there are considerable advantages to using the internet as a programming medium, and Microsoft have worked hard at finding ways of applying Visual Basic skills gained in traditional application development to the internet. In this book, we're going to explore these methods, focusing on how you can use your Visual Basic skills to program the web.

In particular, we'll be looking at the following areas:

> - Introducing Internet Application development
> - Client side programming
> - Server Side Programming
> - Data handling on the Internet

Let's discuss each of these sections in a little more depth.

Introducing Internet Application development

In this introductory section, we'll examine the internet's history and discuss its infrastructure. We'll look at the advantages and disadvantages of developing for the web, and introduce you to the tools and techniques that are available to you as a Visual Basic programmer. Most importantly, we'll discuss the architecture and design considerations you need to bear in mind when you start designing for the web.

> ➢ Web Fundamentals
> ➢ Windows DNA Application Framework
> ➢ Building Windows DNA Applications

Programming the client

One of the limiting factors in the growth of the internet was, for a long time, the inflexibility of the early browsers. Essentially, they were designed to display simple text files, marked up with HTML. While this was fine for research and simple publishing, it was not suitable for the transfer or retrieval of business information, or for providing interactive, intelligent applications that allow users to carry out useful tasks, or simply have fun. Gradually, however, browser potential has increased as Microsoft and Netscape, loosely (and occasionally ineffectually!) shepherded by the World Wide Web Consortium, have introduced various technologies to take browsers beyond simple display. We've focused specifically on those techniques that can be directly leveraged by a Visual Basic programmer:

> ➢ Client-Side Programming with Visual Basic
> ➢ Building Client-Side ActiveX Controls
> ➢ DHTML Applications
> ➢ Integrating Web Browsing Using the WebBrowser Objects

The final chapter in this section is not directly about programming the client; instead it covers how you can add web browsing to your applications, to take advantage of the flexibility of the Internet while still maintaining complete design control over the client.

Server side programming

As you'll discover, although client-side programming with Visual Basic is very powerful, it also has some significant disadvantages. In this section, we'll move on to looking at techniques for dynamically generating HTML on the server, sending it out to clients, and processing information that the clients return. We'll begin by looking at Microsoft's Active Server Pages, which is the foundation of Microsoft server-side development, and then go on to explore the techniques which use Active Server Pages as a delivery mechanism for your Visual Basic skills.

> ➢ Understanding ASP
> ➢ Server Components
> ➢ Advanced Server Components
> ➢ Interfacing With Server Services
> ➢ Intro to Web Classes & IIS Apps
> ➢ Basics of Web Classes & IIS Apps
> ➢ Advanced Web Classes Techniques

Datahandling on the Web

To finish off our introduction to web programming, we're going to glance briefly at data-handling on the web. The first technique will be an introduction to the **Remote Data Services** (**RDS**) which offer a powerful method of manipulating data on the client, using a combination of client-side and server-side components. Then we'll take a look at the next wave of web technology, **XML** – the **eXtensible Markup Language**

> ➢ Meet RDS
> ➢ A Guide to XML

Case Study

Finally, we've rounded out the book with four case studies that look at the different aspects of programming for the web. All the case studies showcase several different techniques, and provide real world application of the methods we've studied throughout the book.

Who is this Book For?

If you've already picked this book up, then you probably have the most important knowledge you'll need already – a solid understanding of Visual Basic. We expect you to have some knowledge of Visual Basic's related skills, and in particular a reasonable familiarity with **ADO**, and how to use it to access databases.

This book isn't intended to teach you how to write your first web page, so we're assuming you already know HTML. In any case, if you can master Visual Basic, you should have no trouble picking up HTML, from any one of the wide range of HTML tutorials around; Wrox's own HTML 4.0 Programmer's Reference (ISBN 1-861001-56-8) gives a no-nonsense introduction.

Apart from that, all you need is a desire to learn how to add the internet to your programming repertoire!

Technology Requirements

We've assumed that you either use or have access to a machine with NT4.0 installed. You'll need Service Pack 5 (the most current update at the time of printing) and Option Pack 4 installed as well. Option Pack 4 gives you Internet Information Server 4.0 and Active Server Pages 2.0, the standard set-up on which we've based this book.

> *You can install Personal Web Server on a Windows 95 or 98 machine, or peer-to-peer Web Services on NT workstation to get Active Server Pages 2.0. We haven't covered these however, and, although you will be able to run the code, you should refer to Microsoft's documentation or to Wrox's Beginning Active Server Pages for more details.*

For the client, we're assuming Internet Explorer 5.0. Installing IE5.0 will automatically add the ADO 2.1 library, and IE5 is essential for the chapters which discuss XML. If you choose to use IE4.1, then you will need to install ADO 2.1 separately. You can download it from the Microsoft Data webpage, HTTP://WWW.MICROSOFT.COM/DATA/

If you want to be able to run all the code, you should also have access to a SQL Server 7.0 database. It need not necessarily be installed on your development machine, but you will need administrator privileges. You will also need the sample databases supplied with SQL Server. The code we've supplied will run with SQL Server 6.5, or even Access at a pinch, but you should be prepared to do some tweaking.

For programming itself, we naturally expect you to have Visual Basic 6.0 installed, along with the most up to date Service Pack for Studio 6.0 (currently 3, and available from http://msdn.microsoft.com/vbasic/). You will also need a good HTML editor – Visual Interdev 6.0 is the most obvious choice, since it integrates well with VB – but there are a range of other packages with varying degrees of sophistication and ASP and VB support. Homestead4.0 and Drumbeat2000 are popular choices. You'll also find a simple text editor – Notepad is fine – useful for quick checks and fixes.

To summarise, the optimal set up is:

> NT 4.0, with Service Pack 5 and Option Pack 4
> Internet Explorer 5.0
> ADO 2.1
> SQL Server 7.0 (SP2)
> Visual Basic 6.0 (SP3)
> Visual Interdev 6.0 (SP3)
> Notepad

Conventions

We have used a number of different styles of text and layout in the book to help differentiate between the different kinds of information. Here are examples of the styles we use and an explanation of what they mean:

Advice, hints, and background information comes indented and italicized, like this.

Important information comes in boxes like this.

Bullets are also indented, and appear with a little box marking each new bullet point, like this:

> **Important Words** are in a bold type font
> Words that appear on the screen in menus like the File or Window are in a similar font to the one that you see on screen
> Keys that you press on the keyboard, like *Ctrl* and *Enter*, are in italics
> Code has several fonts. If it's a word that we're talking about in the text, for example when discussing the For...Next loop, it's in a bold font. If it's a block of code that you can type in as a program and run, then it's also in a gray box:

```
Set oCars = CreateObject("WCCCars.Cars")
    Set recCars = oCars.GetAll(RegistryRestore("Showroom", "Not Set"))
```

> ➢ Sometimes you'll see code in a mixture of styles, like this:

```
If IsMissing(ConnectionString) Then
        varConn = RegistryRestore("Showroom", "Not Set")
    Else
        varConn = ConnectionString
    End If
```

The code with a white background is code we've already looked at and that we don't wish to examine further.

These formats are designed to make sure that you know what it is you're looking at. We hope they make life easier.

Tell Us What You Think

We've worked hard on this book to make it useful. We've tried to understand what you're willing to exchange your hard-earned money for, and we've tried to make the book live up to your expectations.

Please let us know what you think about this book. Tell us what we did wrong, and what we did right. This isn't just marketing flannel: we really do huddle around the email to find out what you think. If you don't believe it, then send us a note. We'll answer, and we'll take whatever you say on board for future editions. The easiest way is to use email:

feedback@wrox.com

You can also find more details about Wrox Press on our web site. There, you'll find the code from our latest books, sneak previews of forthcoming titles, and information about the authors and editors. You can order Wrox titles directly from the site, or find out where your nearest local bookstore with Wrox titles is located.

Customer Support

If you find a mistake, please have a look at the errata page for this book on our web site first. If you can't find an answer there, tell us about the problem and we'll do everything we can to answer promptly! Appendix L outlines how can you can submit an errata in much greater detail. Just send us an email:

support@wrox.com

or fill in the form on our web site:

http://www.wrox.com/Contacts.asp

1

Web Fundamentals

For a long time now, Microsoft has promoted their vision of "Information at Your Fingertips" so that a user can operate more efficiently. It was during his keynote speech at COMDEX in 1990 that Bill Gates introduced this concept and discussed his expectations of the future. He painted a picture of the consequences that desktop computer technology would have in many areas of everyday life.

Four years later, Bill Gates gave another COMDEX speech updating his original theme. While he talked about the effects of the recent rapid changes in the technology, there was still no reference to what no doubt has caused the biggest revolution in the IT industry since the PC ... the Internet.

Microsoft's D-Day awakening to the Internet wasn't until December 1995 when they publicly acknowledged its significance and announced an overall Internet strategy. Later in March 1996 at their Professional Developers Conference, Microsoft delivered a promise to use Internet standards to extend and embrace existing IT infrastructures and to deliver a more effective computing environment. This would be achieved by producing a comprehensive set of technologies, products, services and tools that would seamlessly integrate desktops, LANs, legacy systems, GroupWare applications and the public Internet.

While Microsoft joined the Internet game relatively late, they rapidly gained momentum and have since released an incredible range of innovative Internet products. These products have provided users with rich Internet experiences, and organizations with the mechanisms to develop business critical Internet solutions that are secure, robust, high performing and scaleable.

The most recent vision of Microsoft's strategy for delivering their "Information at Your Fingertips" goal was unveiled at the Professional Developers Conference in September 1997. It was announced that Microsoft's future strategy would be based on delivering an architectural framework for creating modern, open, scaleable, multi-tier distributed Windows applications using both the Internet and client/server technologies – this was to be known as the **Windows Distributed interNet Applications Architecture** or Windows DNA.

The roadmap for the delivery of Windows DNA meant that its introduction would be evolutionary and not revolutionary. It would build on current investments in technologies, hardware, applications and skills. Many of the services detailed in Windows DNA had been around for a number of years – however, Windows DNA was the formalization of the framework and a blueprint for the future. Fundamental to Windows DNA is Windows 2000 (previously known as Windows NT 5.0), which is not targeted for delivery until late 1999. However, some of the key Windows DNA components are available now and supplied in the Windows NT 4.0 Option Packs and Internet Explorer 5.

A crucial part of Microsoft's Windows DNA arsenal is their comprehensive portfolio of development products. Most notable is Visual Studio (current version 6.0), which in its Enterprise edition includes all of the Microsoft programming languages, development tools and documentation. The aim of the latest releases of these development products is to address Windows DNA by reducing the differences between the development of Internet applications and of more traditional client/server environments. Without doubt, the most popular programming language is Visual Basic and, as we shall see throughout this book, the latest version (Visual Basic 6.0) meets the DNA objectives in full.

In this chapter, we'll preview the key concepts of Web technologies in order to provide a foundation for each of the topics discussed throughout the book. In particular we shall look at:

> Why the Web and Internet technologies are so popular and the reasons that many businesses are now basing their IT strategies upon them

> The fundamentals of Web technologies, covering the key concepts that the remainder of the book will assume the reader understands

> How various Microsoft technologies have overcome some of the problems of the early Web methods to improve the user experience and enable business critical applications to be deployed over the Web

So let us start by discussing why Web technologies are so popular and understand fully why their wide acceptance is not just due to media hype.

Why Web Technology?

Although the Internet has existed in various forms since the late 1960s, it is only over the last few years that it has become widely known and utilized. In such a very short period of time, it has caused major changes in information technology, business processes, communications and the way many people spend their leisure time. It is probable that no other significant invention or technology has been embraced by so many so quickly, or has had the potential to change our future lifestyle so dramatically. To compare its growth, consider that the World Wide Web attained 50 millions users in four years – it took radio 38 years and television 13 years to reach similar penetration.

To understand the main reasons for the rapid adoption of Web technologies, we need to comprehend the effects of two important and independent issues that are driving future Information Technology directions – one is business led and the other is technical. In the next couple of sections we shall discuss:

> ➢ the critical issues facing organizations as they adjust to address the changing market forces and do business in the 21st century

> ➢ the convergence of computing and communications, and discuss the evolution of IT system architectures

IT Strategy for the Millennium

As we approach the millennium, today's senior management is faced with the unique problems of ensuring that their organizations can meet the challenges caused by the rapidly changing market place.

To survive, it is vital that their organizations have an effective IT strategy to enable competitive advantage by providing productivity improvements, increased customer satisfaction, mechanisms for new and enhanced revenue streams and timely access to key data for effective business decisions. In addition, the IT infrastructure must provide flexibility and allow the business to react quickly to change and when potential opportunities are recognized.

Another term recently coined by Microsoft is the **Digital Nervous System** and this provides a great analogy. In a human, it is the web of nerves and synapses that enables the body to have the information that it needs, when it needs it, to unconsciously perform its various complex tasks. Similarly, any competitive company must have a healthy IT infrastructure (i.e. 'digital' nervous system) that provides good information flow, allows it to perform its tasks in an efficient manner and that allows the business to respond quickly to the frequently changing market dynamics.

Processing Islands in the Enterprise

For many years, organizations have accomplished their business goals by exploiting their technology base in the following three dimensions:

> ➢ Data Processing – these are the core IT systems that control the fundamental business processes in an organization; examples can include Accounting, Stock Control, Order Processing, Job Tracking, etc. Many types of technologies, from large mainframes to client/server architectures have been applied to these business critical systems and most of these still have a part to play in today's IT infrastructures.

> ➢ Personal Productivity – the huge popularity of the PC and the Integrated Office suites has forever changed the way individual employees work with information and has often changed business practices and strategies. These tools have dramatically increased productivity, streamlined operations and made IT more cost effective.

> ➢ Collaboration – the use of communications and GroupWare software has enabled both organizations and individuals to work in partnership and teams. Such systems can scale to thousands of users across the enterprise enabling businesses to redefine their operations for further advantage and reduced costs.

However, many of these benefits do not come without high cost. Each of these dimensions typically has their own infrastructures and businesses have been faced with the complex problem of building 'information bridges' between the different systems and applications – building systems that span all dimensions has been historically difficult. Furthermore, having multiple technology infrastructures always results in additional costs for software, hardware, support and training.

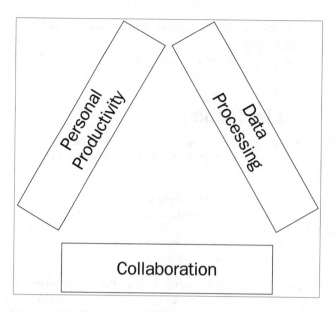

Integrating the Enterprise

Over the years, software vendors have offered various architectures in an attempt to integrate the various distributed environments within an organization. Unfortunately such solutions have never provided the complete seamless integration and flexibility that a business demands. At long last, there now seems to be light at the end of the tunnel as it appears that using distributed computing frameworks based on Web technologies provide the key to fulfilling these requirements. The rapid adoption of Internet standards by every significant IT vendor has provided for the complete integration of the various distributed environments and different infrastructures within an organization.

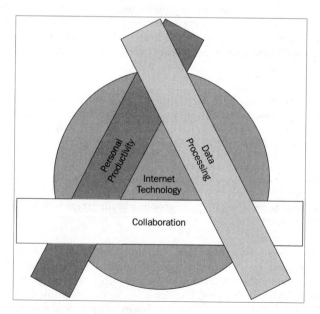

The first serious use of Web technology within business was for the implementation of **Intranets**. Intranets take full advantage of the open industry standards and the familiar Web browser/server software, originally devised for the Internet, to provide employees with access to corporate information and processes. However, whereas the Internet is open to all, an Intranet is closed and has strict user access controls enforced.

Many companies are now taking advantage of Intranets to make it more efficient for their staff to locate and process information, and to collaborate with each other. The Web browser approach enables a consistent user interface and provides a single view of all company information irrespective of its native file format or the type of data source. For most organizations their business information is key and many have huge amounts of investment in existing data systems and electronic documents – mechanisms enabling the leverage of such valuable knowledge in the organization can have considerable impact on business performance.

Extending the Enterprise

A digital nervous system is not just about moving information around inside a company but also out to customers, partners and suppliers. The recent advances in networking means that both private and public networks (and in particular the Internet) can be exploited to extend the Enterprise to include external parties. Many businesses are now finding that their infrastructures are becoming intelligently intertwined with each other to form **Extranets** that are large 'Virtual Enterprises', and which frequently comprise many different organizations.

As an example, consider the manufacturing supply chain; before the goods reach the end customer, numerous organizations are involved along the chain from handling the raw materials, through the manufacturing process, and on to distribution and retail. Each of these organizations can achieve faster delivery times and reduce their inventory costs if they handle their business processes electronically.

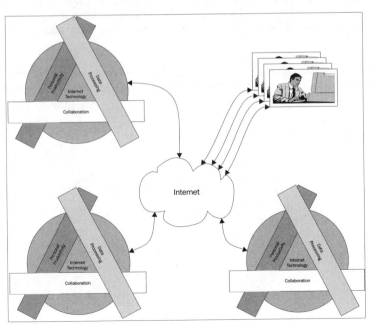

Business partners and customers work together to form a single, distributed, 'Virtual Enterprise'.

Let us now take a look at some of the technical aspects of this change.

The Evolution of IT System Architectures

Over the next few sections we shall be looking at the evolution of IT architectures and see how the pursuit of an optimal solution has led us to using an infrastructure based on Web technologies. Hopefully by the end of this discussion, you shall start to agree that the compulsion to move to using Web architectures is irresistible.

So we shall start with a short history lesson...

The Early Days – Centralized Computing

In the 1960s and 70s, the computers adopted by businesses were expensive mainframes that used simple monochrome terminals with keyboards to access the applications and the databases. These resources were located centrally on the mainframe and processing times was shared or 'time-sliced' between the various users.

Such terminals are now often referred to as 'dumb terminals' since they could not perform any of the processing logic – they were text based and only capable of displaying screen forms comprising of information received from the central system or entered by the user. The keyboards had a designated button for 'submission' in which all of the information entered into the screen form would be sent to the central system for subsequent processing such as validation and database access.

As time passed on, the hardware technology evolved and many small businesses migrated towards the use of cheaper minicomputers and UNIX super-microcomputers. These systems relied on a new generation of dumb terminals but they were typically no smarter than their predecessors. Such systems would intercept every user key-press and then instantaneously generate the appropriate screen interaction.

This early model of computing was centralized –the business processing, data management and screen presentation was all controlled by the central systems with just the user interaction handled by the terminal devices.

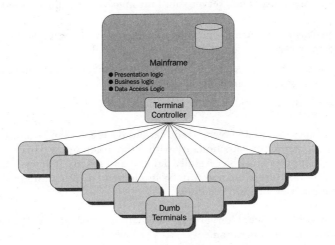

PC Networking: Moving Towards Decentralization

Over time, further advances in hardware, software and networking enabled the computer systems to move from a centralized shared logic based architecture to a network of workstations and servers.

The first personal computers and local area networks appeared in the early 1980s. Applications that exploited this new model were based on file sharing and various XBase products such as dBase, FoxPro and Clipper popularized this approach. In such systems, all the data is downloaded from a central file server and operated upon by application logic that is totally resident on the workstation. File sharing systems worked well for small amounts of data and small populations of users. However, as the momentum for PC networking grew, the capacity of such applications became strained and an alternative approach was required – the solution came from using an application architecture known as client/server computing.

Client/Server Computing

Client/server involves breaking up the system functionality into distinct manageable layers that can be independently developed, deployed across multiple machines and that use a communication mechanism to allow the different layers to co-operate.

This approach is regarded as an enabling technology that can implement systems across an organization in a modular and flexible manner. It allows for the distribution of applications away from single machines located in isolated departments to an implementation across the enterprise. For example, it is now possible for one person in customer services to access all corporate systems (subject to any security restrictions that may have been imposed)– gone are the old days of annoying transfers between the different representatives in each department.

It is common to find that most client/server solutions involve the following independent layers:

> **Presentation logic** – this handles how the user interacts with the application; usually implemented by providing an easy to use graphical user interface (GUI)

> **Business logic** – this handles the mechanics (or business rules) of the application, the processes that reflect the everyday functions of the business

> **Data access logic** – this handles the storage and retrieval of data

The development of these separate layers needs careful design and an accurate definition of the distinct boundaries to ensure that functionality within the different layers is not intertwined. Interfaces between the layers must be carefully defined and strictly followed. Encapsulating the logic in this fashion ensures that future changes can be implemented without impacting the other layers and this enables both reusability and reliability.

There are many variations to client/server implementation; we shall now look at the three principle architectures that are put into operation.

Two Tier Client/Server

The first generation of client/server systems was an evolution of the file sharing applications mentioned above. With these applications, the central file server is replaced with a specialized **relational database management system** (RDBMS). Such databases can offer high transaction rates at a fraction of the costs associated with mainframes. When the client (a workstation application typically using a screen-based form or GUI) needs to act upon data, it makes a request via the network to the database server – the database then processes the request and returns just the data appropriate to the client's needs.

When compared to the file sharing application (which returned the complete file), this client/server architecture dramatically reduces network traffic. In addition, today's databases provide many features that enable the development of advanced multi-user applications – for example, allowing multiple users to access and update the same set of data.

Because the processing is split between distinct layers – the workstation and the database server – such architectures are referred to as being **two-tier client/server architecture**.

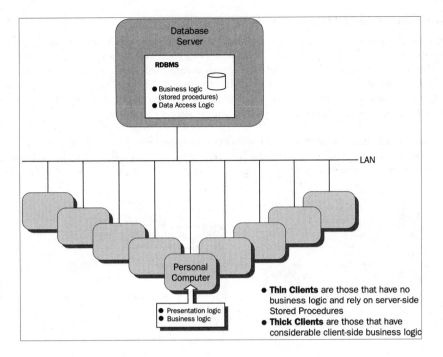

This approach became very popular as it was found that sophisticated systems could be implemented quickly (and thus cheaply) using development tools like Visual Basic and **rapid application development** (RAD) techniques.

However, as expectations increased it was found that this architecture had certain limitations and problems, including the following:

> the database requests can generate large result sets; the performance of two-tier architectures is found to rapidly deteriorate as networking bottlenecks occur when an optimum number of users is exceeded

> the architecture imposes substantial processing on the client, since both the business and the presentation logic are implemented here; this means workstations with powerful CPUs and large amounts of disk and memory may be required

> each workstation session requires a separate database connection; this can drain resources on the database server – for example, Microsoft SQL Server requires 37K of memory for each user connection (and this is much lower than many other vendor's RDBMSs)

> deploying the business rules on the client can lead to high costs of deployment and support; if the logic changes, the effort in updating software on numerous workstations can be excessive

So whilst two-tier client/server is justifiable for small workgroup applications, it is now generally agreed that this approach offers a poor solution since it does not provide the flexibility or scalability for large-scale applications deployed across the corporate enterprise.

Three Tier Client/Server

Drawing on the lessons learnt from the two-tier systems, an increase in application performance and a notable reduction in network traffic can be be achieved by inserting an additional tier in the middle, between the workstation and the database server, to create three tiers. Because the programmer can then make changes to the internal structure of the database, the way the client presents information, and most importantly to the middle tier, without affecting the other two layers, the architecture is far more modular and thus far easier to adapt to business's ever changing needs.

This approach is known as a **three-tier client/server architecture**. The middle layer is called the application server and is used to handle the business logic of the system. The workstation is now only responsible for handling the presentation logic. As before, the database server handles the data access logic.

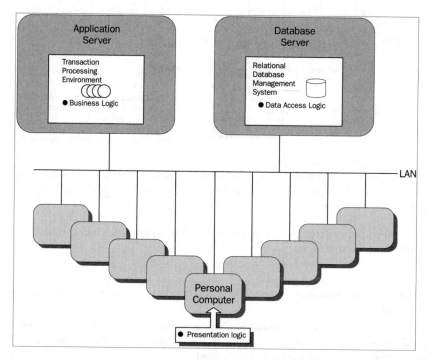

It is possible for the application server and database server to physically reside on the same machine – and in many cases this can provide an optimum solution. However, for it to be recognized as three-tier, distinct logical boundaries or interfaces must exist between the two layers to ensure the advantages of the architecture are achieved.

Multi Tier Client/Server

A further extension to three-tier solutions is the **multi-tier**, also called **n-tier**, architecture. These solutions are the most flexible and scaleable and build on all the advantages of the three-tier architecture.

In a multi-tier client/server solution, the business logic is partitioned and distributed over several machines. As requirements change during a system's lifetime, this partitioning and deployment can be reviewed and amended with minimal impact. Furthermore, additional tiers are included to support multiple databases and other services such as message queues, legacy systems, data warehouses, communication middleware and so on.

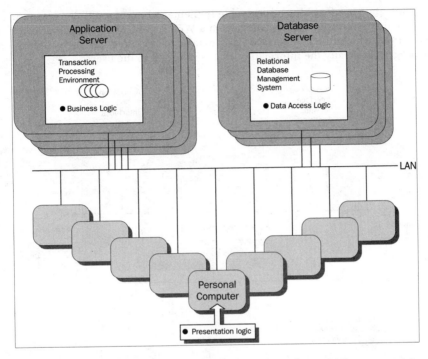

By enabling the distribution of the workload over many CPUs (using either symmetric multiprocessing or massively parallel processing cluster technology), it is obvious how scalable solutions can be delivered. Sometimes the distribution of the logic over separate geographical regions can be considered to achieve optimum performance; for example, to locate processes at the sites where it limits the amount of slow network communications performed.

> **symmetric multiprocessing (SMP)** is an architecture allowing processing to be undertaken by multiple CPUs that share a common operating system and memory
>
> **massively parallel processing (MPP)** is an architecture that coordinates the overall processing of a complex task by breaking it up and allowing each part to be undertaken by a separate system (single CPU or SMP) using its own operating system and memory.

Unfortunately, three-tier and multi-tier client/server solutions are not trivial to implement. There are more tasks to undertake and more complex issues to address than when building two-tier systems. A strong understanding of the multi-tier client/server development techniques and an appreciation of the potential pitfalls are vital. Once this experience has been acquired and the problems mastered, the rewards are solutions that are more flexible, provide greater scalability and are easier to support.

Web Technologies: Centralized Computing but with a Twist

Just as we were beginning to get used to the issues of developing multi-tier architectures, the new paradigm of Web Technologies arrived to direct interest from the traditional client/server architectures.

The Web architecture is a flexible and scaleable implementation of multi-tier computing and uses a Web browser (client) to retrieve information from a Web server. The Web server can interface with application servers which in turn interfaces with databases, enabling our Web applications to determine programmatically the information that is returned to the user.

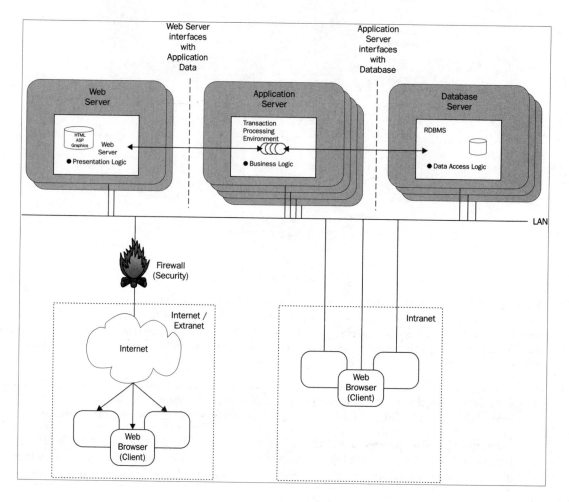

In the simplest scenario, the three processing layers may reside on the same machine, as shown below.

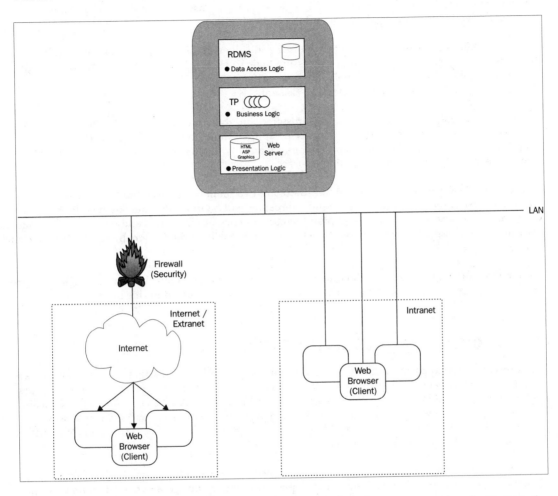

Many people confuse the terms Internet and Web or consider the two as equivalent but in fact, the two are very distinct. It is important to recognize that the Web is not a network but an application that operates over networks using a communications protocol called **HTTP (Hyper Text Transfer Protocol)**.

Most documents retrieved over the Web contain **HTML (Hyper Text Markup Language)**, which is a page description language that defines both the data content of the document and information on how the information should be displayed (or **rendered**) by the Web browser. Modern Web browsers support the display of multimedia within the retrieved HTML documents – including text, graphics, sound, video – and **hyperlinks** in which items on the document are linked to other Web resources. By clicking on a hyperlink, the Web browser automatically navigates to the target document.

We can now see how the Web based data access model has traveled a full 360 degrees back to an apparently centralized computing model. The twist however, is in this model, instead of accessing a single mainframe, the client is now accessing geographically distributed applications resident on multiple servers interconnected by networking technologies.

The great thing about this Web architecture is that it solves the several problems with traditional client/server. By restricting the client processing logic to HTML it is possible to develop a single universal application that can be deployed across different types of platforms, whether Windows, Mac, one of the Unix flavors, or something else entirely.

In addition, all client logic is centrally administered and dynamically deployed – this means that any bug fixes or enhancements will automatically be applied the next time the user accesses the application. This avoids the process of having to manually deploy software on every desktop, which can be very costly on a large population of users.

So recapping on what we have seen so far, there are two main messages to take with us as we proceed. Firstly, the next hugely successful companies will be those that quickly enable the next generation of business systems that exploit the convergence of computers and networking for business advantage. Secondly, it will be the Web technologies that will be the key enabler in their search for prosperity.

In the next section we shall introduce some of the basics concepts about Web technologies that are prerequisite knowledge in order to understanding the topics discussed in this book.

Web Technology Fundamentals

The recent rapid expansion of the Internet has led many people to think that the Internet is a new innovation. Most people are surprised to learn that it has actually been around a number of years after starting life off in the late 1960's as a research project called **ARPANET** (Advanced Research Projects Agency Network). At the time of the Cold War, the US Department of Defense was concerned that their communications infrastructure could be wiped out by a single nuclear strike on their central military computer systems.

The objective of the ARPANET project was to investigate the development of a decentralized computer network such that each node is of equal importance and an unexpected malfunction or deletion of a node does not affect the resilience of the network. Should a network node be taken out of service (for any reason), the network dynamically adjusts its routing configuration to use alternative paths to ensure that the information is successfully delivered to its intended destination.

The ARPANET network later opened up to education establishments and commercial organizations. It has since adopted a suite of protocols called the **Internet Protocol Suite** or as more commonly known **TCP/IP**.

The network then became known as the **Internet** and this took its name from being a collection of interconnected networks. Now, the Internet has grown to encompass a huge number of autonomous networks. Recent estimates have suggested that there will be over 100,000,000 computers on the Internet very early into the new millennium.

TCP/IP Networking

The Internet Protocol Suite includes a number of standard communications protocols; however, the two most common protocols are:

> **Internet Protocol** (IP) – this is used to route a packet of data from node to node across the network

> **Transmission Control Protocol** (TCP) – this is used to create a point-to-point communication channel and ensures that the information is delivered error free and in the correct order that it was originally transmitted

It is these two main protocols that give the suite its more common name, TCP/IP.

TCP/IP Protocol Stack

The following diagram shows how TCP/IP exists in a stack of networking protocols that provides the communications functionality.

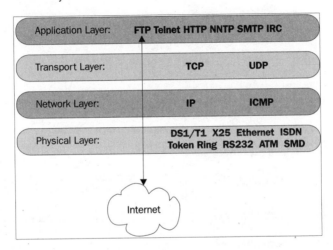

There are a number of application protocols that can operate above the TCP/IP layers and applications that use these can operate simultaneously. Common examples include Web (HTTP), Electronic Mail (SMTP), Chat (IRC), File Transfer (FTP), Newsgroup Bulletin Boards (NNTP) and Terminal Emulation for accessing traditional mainframes (Telnet).

Network Addresses

Every computer that is connected to an IP network is uniquely identified by a value, known as its **IP address**. An IP address is written and spoken as a sequence of four 8-bit decimal numbers, separated by the dot character, for example:

194.27.254.189

An IP network may be a single network of just a few computers, such as an Intranet, or it could be a complex interconnected set of independent networks – an example of the latter case is the Internet. The IP address must uniquely identify both the network, and the computer within the network. There are four different ways in which this 32-bit block can be broken down into the **network address** and the **host address** – these four decompositions are defined by the **class types** A, B, C and D; these are shown in the table below:

Class Type	Range of Network Addresses	Example
A	1 to 126	100 123 200 65 — Network/Host
B	128.xxx to 191.xxx	132 45 245 189 — Network/Host
C	192.xxx.xxx to 223.xxx.xxx	194 27 254 189 — Network/Host
D	224.xxx.xxx.xxx to 254.xxx.xxx.xxx	N/A Used for broadcasting (multicasting) Individual machines are not specified.

The rapid growth of the Internet has led to a shortage of IP addresses – no one could have anticipated the Internet when the protocol was first devised. The next version of the Internet Protocol (IPv6) will provide relief to this problem by lengthening the IP address from 32 bits to 128 bits. This version is also frequently referred to as **IPng** (IP Next Generation).

With certain Internet applications, it is possible to identify a computer on an IP network by using a logical name, for example:

```
http://www.wrox.com/
```

When this happens, the Internet application must first resolve this logical name (i.e. www.wrox.com) to its corresponding IP address by communicating with another predefined server called a **DNS** (Domain Name System). This server returns the associated IP address by means of a lookup database, that maps logical domain names to IP addresses, or by communicating onwards with other DNS servers for the IP address to be resolved.

Don't worry about the leading `http://` prefix in the above example – we shall be discussing this shortly.

Port Numbers

There is another important number that must be considered when communicating over an IP network; this is called the **port number**. A port number is used to distinguish between the individual networking applications that are running simultaneously above the TCP/IP protocol stack.

Port numbers for standard TCP/IP services are often referred to as **well-known** port numbers; here are some examples:

> 21   – File Transfer Protocol (FTP) ... File Transfer

> 23   – Telnet ... Terminal Emulation

> 25   – Simple Mail Transfer Protocol (SMTP) ... Electronic Mail (E-Mail)

> 80   – Hypertext Transfer Protocol (HTTP) ... Web / WWW

> 119 – Network News Transfer Protocol (NNTP) ... Newsgroups / Forums

> 194 – Internet Relay Chat (IRC) ... Conferencing

Server processes are associated with a fixed port and the client must know the port in order to connect with the network service.For example, a Web server will normally be listening for connections on port 80 (the `http` well-known port number) – a Web browser will use this port number by default when attempting to connect to the remote computer.

Uniform Resource Locator

All information that can be accessed over the Internet must be uniquely identified using a reference that is called a **URL** (Uniform Resource Locator). The naming scheme involves three concatenated items as follows:

```
<protocol> :// <machine id> / <local name>
```

where:

Item	Description
`<protocol>`	identifies the application protocol used to retrieved the resource
`<machine id>`	identifies the server on which the resource is located – this is either an IP address (a unique sequence of four 8 bit numbers e.g. `204.148.170.3`) or a domain name (e.g. `www.wrox.com`)
`<local name>`	identifies the resource on the server and can include a directory structure which the server must interpret. Can point to a default resource if one not specified.

As an example, consider:

```
http://www.microsoft.com/sitebuilder/whatsnew.htm
```

This will use the `http` protocol to retrieve a file from the machine `www.microsoft.com` (which is resolved to an IP address of `207.46.131.137`). The Web server maps the identifier `sitebuilder/whatsnew.htm` onto a local filename that is then returned to the originator of the request.

The World Wide Web

Along with e-mail, the most popular and commonly used Internet service is the Web. Recapping from what we discussed earlier, the Web architecture is based on a client/server model and uses a client-side Web browser to retrieve data files (documents, graphics, etc.) from a Web server. This server may be located on our own local network or half way around the world on the Internet's **World Wide Web** (WWW).

> **Important!** Many people confuse the terms WWW and Internet or consider the two as equivalent, but in fact they are very distinct. It is important to recognize that the Web is not a network but an application that operates over networks using TCP/IP protocols.

In our earlier discussions we mentioned HTTP and HTML – we shall now investigate these further.

Hyper Text Transfer Protocol (HTTP)

To retrieve a Web resource, the user either specifies a URL in the Web browser's address field or clicks on a hyperlink in a document that has a URL associated with it. As we have already seen, the URL determines how to access the Web resource by specifying a protocol, server address and the local name.

The Web browser specifies the details of the required document in an **HTTP Request** message. The Web server receives this request and after processing it completes the operation by either returning the document or an error in the **HTTP Response** message. If the operation is successful, the Web browser will determine if there are any other embedded resources within the document, such as images, and if so fires off further requests for the additional information required for completing the page rendering.

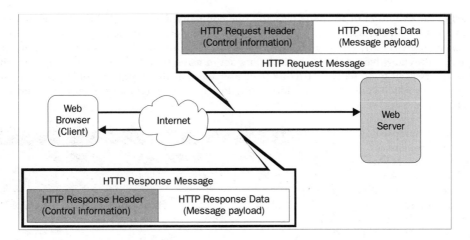

HyperText Markup Language (HTML)

HyperText Markup Language (HTML) is a page description language for defining the content of hypertext documents that are displayed in a format established by the Web browsers rendering scheme. HTML files are typically suffixed with either .htm or .html.

An HTML document contains a series of **tags** and text that define the structure and content of the document. A tag is a reserved keyword that is delimited by the < and > characters. Some tags (but not all) can appear in both start and end formats with the latter proceeded by a forward slash e.g. <I> and </I> to start and end italic formatting.

Some tags also include **attributes** that further qualify the meaning – for example:

```
<font face = "Times New Roman">
```

is used to specify the typeface of the subsequent text.

Several elements should always be included in HTML documents and this is illustrated in the following basic HTML document skeleton:

```
<HTML>
<HEAD>
<TITLE>
    Document Title
</TITLE>
</HEAD>
<BODY>
    Document content
</BODY>
</HTML>
```

When the Web was first established the HTML documents that traveled the Internet originated from research and academic circles. Such documents were typically textual and could be nicely formatted using a minimal number of tags. Then graphic designers got involved and they cared more about visual effects, compelling images and fancy fonts than document content.

This led to the evolution of aesthetic tags and one company, Netscape, led the way with a number of their own tags. Unfortunately, this proprietary approach meant that the original concept of platform independence for HTML across all browsers was lost. The life of a Web Designer became much more complex as they now had to think about the impact of using such tags. This meant considering the commercial risks of potentially restricting their user base, or the designers could generate more complex pages which contain simpler formatting instructions should a browser not support a particular tag.

These screen dumps show a more comprehensive example of some HTML. They demonstrate an HTML Editor from a Web management and authoring system called Microsoft FrontPage. The tabs at the base of the screen allow the page author to switch between editing the page and previewing what it would look like when rendered by a Web browser.

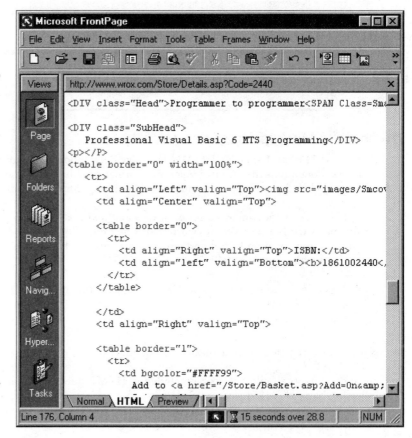

First Generation Web Applications

The first generation Web browsers were only capable of handling text and simple multimedia such as images and sound. Information from a user could be captured by means of simple HTML forms and transmitted to the Web server. These early Web pages are now often called **static pages** since they lack the facilities for user interaction that we are accustomed to from typical PC software.

The problem with static pages is that their contents is fixed, and so can not be adjusted depending on the identity of the user or from information stored in backend databases and applications. The solution to this was to extend the functionality of Web servers by means of the **Common Gateway Interface** (CGI). This enabled the contents of a page to be generated dynamically by a program typically written in the C programming language or a scripting language such as Perl.

With CGI, the Web page contents could be dynamically generated and personalized for the user and constructed from information stored centrally. But unfortunately, CGI applications are a poor solution for this activity – this is because each CGI HTTP request will cause a new process to be spawned, and after the request has been handled, the process is killed. In a heavily hit site, the repetition of process creations and database openings imposes an excessive overhead on system resources.

Another disadvantage of CGI is that HTML tags have to be hard coded into C `printf` statements and it is usually difficult to visualize the Web page until the CGI process is actually invoked and the results are displayed in a browser. This does not provide an optimum development process and compares poorly with some of the latest tools that do provide a WYSIWYG Web development environment.

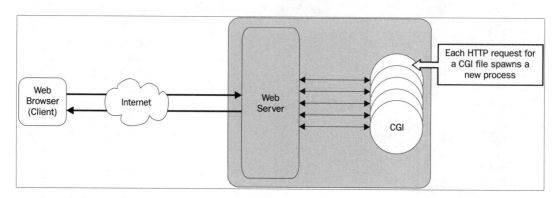

Next Generation Web Applications

The next generation of Web applications addressed these limitations by providing facilities for **active pages** that enabled user interaction and an architecture designed for high performance, secure, robust and scaleable distributed computing solutions.

Client-side: Dynamic HTML/Scripting/Components

The latest generation of Web browsers – such as **Microsoft Internet Explorer 4.0 / 5.0** – have provided a great improvement over their early counterparts through their support for downloaded software components, scripting languages and advanced HTML capabilities.

Software components embedded within Web pages can be written using high level languages such as Visual Basic, Visual C++ and Java. This enables sophisticated functionality unavailable with the relatively primitive HTML. Furthermore, such components can establish direct TCP/IP connections with other distributed components (i.e. the business logic tier) and avoid using the Web server – thus enabling a true distributed computing environment.

Scripting languages can be included within a Web page, and act as the software glue to allow the different entities within a Web page to interact. Such items include the HTML intrinsic controls (such as edit boxes and lists), the objects exposed by the Web browser and any embedded software components.

The use of script logic in our pages allows the client to become **event-driven**. As an example, script code can be used to detect an event being fired by one control (a button click) and this can then invoke a method on another control (such as starting the playback of a video control). The most commonly used scripting languages for the Web are VBScript (a subset of Visual Basic) and JavaScript.

Previously, once an HTML page had been rendered on the screen its contents could only be changed if a request was made to the Web server for a page refresh. This process could take at best a few seconds and so severely impairing the users interactivity. The latest Web browsers now support a new generation of HTML called **Dynamic HTML** (DHTML) that allows all of the HTML elements on a Web page to be manipulated using script logic. Now changes to a Web page can be made, on the fly, without any need for time and network consuming HTTP communication.

> **At the time of writing, Internet Explorer is the only browser that supports VBScript and embedded software components written in Visual Basic and Visual C++. Thus these technologies are only suitable for Intranets and Extranets where you can impose restrictions over the type of browser that may access your Web pages. If you need to reach the maximum audience possible on the Internet, then you must avoid any scripting and software components in your Web pages. A frequent compromise is to restrict access to just Internet Explorer (3.0 or later) or Netscape Navigator (3.0 or later) as the vast majority of Internet users employ these browsers. JavaScript and Java is the common denominator across all of these browsers.**

Alternative mechanisms for developing server extensions were created which addressed the performance pitfalls of using the traditional CGI processes. For example, several Web servers – including **Microsoft Internet Information Server** (**IIS**) – support the Internet Server Application Programming Interface (**ISAPI**). This enables the programmable logic to be compiled into Dynamic Link libraries and reside within the Web server's process space – such logic can be loaded, once and for all, on first demand. ISAPI is much more efficient than CGI because client requests do not spawn new processes.

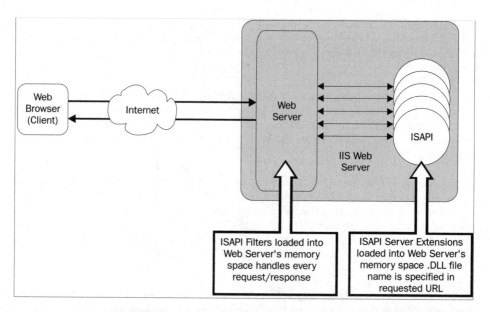

ISAPI programs are typically written using Visual C++. Fortunately for many, there is an easier method to extend Web applications but still gain from the benefits that ISAPI offers – this simplicity comes from **Microsoft Active Server Pages** (**ASP**). To use ASP, however, you must run these pages on Microsoft Internet Information Server, or its scaled down Windows 98 implementation, Personal Web Server.

ASP builds on top of the ISAPI infrastructure to provide a server-side application framework.

An Active Server Page is a file with a .ASP suffix that contains both HTML syntax and server-side script logic. When the Web server receives an HTTP request for the ASP document, an output HTML file is generated for the response using a combination of both the HTML static information plus any HTML that is generated dynamically by the server-side script logic. Several scripting languages are available for use in ASP applications but the one most commonly used (including throughout this book) is VBScript.

The real power of ASP comes from its ability to very easily interact with other objects (such as the built-in utility ASP objects, multi-tier client/server business objects, middleware to access databases and legacy systems, Microsoft BackOffice components, etc.).

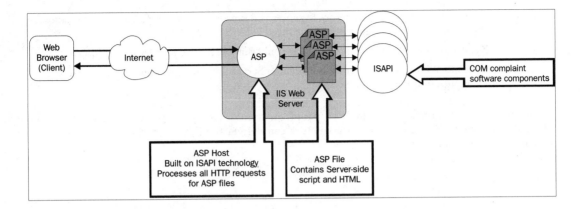

It is crucial that you do not get confused between Dynamic HTML (DHTML) and dynamically generated Web pages. DHTML is the feature that enables every HTML element in a web page to be programmatically controlled using client-side script logic.

Dynamically generated web pages are those that are programmatically created, on the fly, at the Web server (typically by means of ASP / ISAPI / CGI and by using information about the user and/or interfacing with server-side components, databases, etc.)

Summary

That concludes our discussion on Web fundamentals and the subsequent topics will assume that you are now familiar with the following basic concepts:

- Web technologies are built on a standard communications protocol called TCP/IP.
- The WWW (an application) and Internet (a network) are not interchangeable terms.
- HTTP is an application protocol that operates above the TCP/IP stack and is used to retrieve Web resources.
- An Intranet is an implementation of Web technologies operating over a TCP/IP network that is restricted to employees only. An Extranet is where a corporate TCP/IP network has been opened up to allow access by business partners to specific areas of an internal Web site.
- Every computer on the TCP/IP network is uniquely identified by an IP address.
- Network server applications are assigned to operate on a specific well-known port number.
- Every Web resource is uniquely identified by its URL.
- HTML is a page description language for defining the content of hypertext documents.

> ➤ Microsoft's Web browser is Internet Explorer and it provides support for downloaded software components, scripting languages and advanced HTML capabilities.

> ➤ VB software components and VBScript are only suitable for use in Internet Explorer

> ➤ Microsoft's Web server is Internet Information Server and this can support sophisticated multi-tier Web applications that are built using Active Server Pages.

Now that we can appreciate why the Web paradigm is increasingly important, we shall start to look at how the Microsoft Windows DNA infrastructure can deliver the flexible digital nervous system that business now demands.

Windows DNA - a framework for building applications

During the opening discussion to this chapter, we introduced Microsoft's architectural framework called the Windows Distributed interNet Applications Architecture (Windows DNA). One of the main objectives of Windows DNA is to synthesize the differences between developing software for the Windows platform and for the Internet, and to provide a development model that capitalizes on the best features from each approach to provide a unified solution.

Some of the key features to this new development model are:

➤ Windows DNA integrates these two different worlds by enabling computers to interoperate and co-operate equally well across both private and public networks using protocols that conform to open industry standards.

➤ Windows DNA applications are designed around a loosely coupled distributed architecture. This involves breaking the solution into the following distinct layers: presentation logic, business logic and data access logic. These layers are then deployed in an optimum manner across multiple tiers.

➤ Windows DNA provides a set of standard services to handle components, communications, scripting, user interface (DHTML), transactions, message queuing, security, directory services, data access, systems management and high availability. By providing these core features 'out of the box', developers can concentrate on their application rather than basic infrastructure and so can bring innovative solutions to market quicker and at a lower cost.

➤ Windows DNA applications can take advantage of an efficient just-in-time software delivery model; this allows central management to reduce the overall cost of ownership and ensures that the users are always running the latest version of the software. For example, Office 2000 can be set up centrally so that it will install itself on a desktop by deploying only the appropriate components for the profile of the user. If another person (with a different profile) then uses the same desktop, Office will then automatically deploy (if necessary) any additional components that they are entitled to. Also, if a component gets updated or accidentally deleted, this will be automatically detected and will re-deploy that component.

> ➤ Windows DNA fully embraces an open approach to Internet computing, and supports numerous standards approved by bodies such as the World Wide Web Consortium (W3C) and the Internet Engineering Task Force (IETF).

> ➤ Windows DNA provides for mobile computing; when such applications are operating disconnected from the network and central systems, they should still provide as much functionality as possible but degrade gracefully where this is not possible.

> ➤ Windows DNA will continue to evolve and take advantage of many new technologies, however it will always ensure that existing investments in skills, systems and information will be preserved.

It is the intention of Microsoft to deliver the different parts of Windows DNA over a number of years with many of the key features being supplied as part of Windows 2000 (previously NT5.0). However, as we shall see throughout this book, many of the features of Windows DNA are available today on Windows NT 4.0 when enhanced with the Windows NT 4.0 Option Pack and the Visual Studio 6.0 development environment.

In this chapter we shall investigate the key components and development methodologies provided by the Windows DNA superstructure. In particular we shall look at:

> ➤ the Windows DNA Server Platform provided by the Windows NT/2000 operating system plus a number of application services

> ➤ the advantages of using software components and why this approach is fundamental when building solutions with Microsoft products

> ➤ the Microsoft initiatives to provide easy access to data irrespective of its format or the location where it resides

> ➤ how to ensure the integrity of our data by means of transactions

> ➤ how to protect our systems by employing security measures

So let's start by putting Windows NT under the microscope.

The Windows DNA Server Platform

Bill Gates first conceived Windows NT in 1988 when he announced that Microsoft would develop an operating system that was portable, secure, scalable, extensible, open, and internationalizable. These goals meant that Windows NT could be converted to run on a number of different hardware platforms and operate in a number of languages and character sets, all with minimal changes to the core code. In addition, it could provide support for symmetric multiprocessing (SMP), that is run on machines with multiple CPUs.

To design Windows NT, Microsoft hired the much-regarded David Cutler who had worked on a number of operating systems, including the PDP-11 and VAX, at Digital Equipment Corporation. The ideal operating system initially dreamt by Bill Gates and David Cutler was code-named Cairo. The full objectives have proven to be very difficult and tormenting to achieve and the ideas of Cairo have recently changed from being an actual product release to just a philosophy.

After five years of development, Windows NT was released; it was delivered in two versions NT 3.1 and NT Advanced Server 3.1. The 3.1 tag indicates that the roots of its user interface were from Windows 3.1; but that is where the similarities stopped.

In late 1994, Microsoft clarified the roles of the two versions by changing their names to give a clear indication of their purpose. Windows NT became Windows NT Workstation 3.51 and Windows NT Server 3.51. Whilst being based on the same core code, the internal scheduling of tasks was optimized so that one functions best as a desktop operating system and the other as a robust enterprise level multi-purpose network operating system.

In 1996, NT version 4.0 (Workstation and Server) was released and included many new features; in addition, it adopted the user interface from Windows 95.

Windows 2000 will be Microsoft's next step towards Cairo and will bring many advantages in the areas of system management, application infrastructure, networking and communications, and information sharing and publishing. Windows 2000 will be available in the following versions:

> Windows 2000 Professional will be the mainstream operating system for the business desktop

> Windows 2000 Server will to be the mainstream network operating system designed for small to medium enterprise application deployments, it will support up to two-way symmetric multi-processing.

> Windows 2000 Advanced Server will be a more powerful application server designed for database-intensive work and will include integrated clustering and load balancing services, it will support up to four-way symmetric multi-processing and large physical memories.

> Windows 2000 Datacenter Server will be the most powerful server operating system optimized for large scale data warehouses, online transaction processing and complex simulations, it will support up to 16-way symmetric multi-processing and up to 64GB of physical memory.

Windows DNA Application Services

Microsoft has made available a number of products and components that work together with Windows NT to form a single coherent infrastructure that delivers a comprehensive business solution. Furthermore, the familiar and consistent approach found throughout these products considerably reduces training and support costs.

The products include:

> Internet Information Server (IIS) – provides Internet services including Web (HTTP), File Transfer (FTP), News Groups (NNTP) and Email (SMTP). It is designed for ease of use, scalability, portability, security, and extensibility, and it provides a powerful environment for the next generation of line-of-business applications.

> Active Server Pages (ASP) – provides a server side scripting mechanism to implement extensions to the IIS Web services.

> Transaction Server (MTS) – provides the infrastructure needed for multi-tier client server solutions. It includes facilities to share resources, manage transactions and administrate component deployment.

> Message Queue Server (MSMQ) – provides store and forward asynchronous communications to achieve reliable message delivery. It handles network outages and heterogeneous networking architectures.

> Index Server – provides search engine facilities to identify documents that contain specific text.

> Exchange Server - provides an integrated system for email, personal and group scheduling, electronic forms, and groupware applications.

> SQL Server - provides a large-scale relational database management system designed specifically for distributed client-server computing. There is also a 'light' version known as MSDE (Microsoft Data Engine) that is suitable for a maximum of 5 simultaneous connections.

> Systems Management Server (SMS) - provides a centralized management tool for software distribution, hardware/software inventory and diagnostic facilities.

> SNA Server - provides facilities for interfacing with legacy IBM and other host systems using SNA communication protocols.

> Proxy Server - provides Internet access to the corporate desktop in a secure manner. It also enables the caching of popular Web pages to improve performance

> Commercial Internet System - Provides facilities for Internet communities. It includes servers for membership, personalization, billing, white pages, chat, mail, newsgroups, user locator, content replication, and information retrieval.

> Site Server - provides a Web site environment for the deployment, implementation and analysis of Intranets and business critical Web sites. There is also a Commerce Edition suitable for electronic commerce sites.

> NetShow Server - provides streaming media services for Video and Audio broadcasting (called netcasting).

> Cluster Server - provides clustering facilities allowing multiple NT nodes to combine to provide high availability and scalability.

> Terminal Server - provides Windows applications to diverse desktop hardware through terminal emulation.

> Certificate Server - provides facilities for the generation and distribution of digital certificates (which we shall meet later in this chapter when we discuss security).

At the heart of Windows NT and the above products is the Microsoft Component Object Model (COM), which is the glue that binds together the different parts of Windows DNA. COM is the most widely used component software model in the computer industry and is used on over 150 million computer systems throughout the world. The use of COM makes the development of complex applications and systems integration tasks much simpler than any other alternative approach.

We shall now discuss why component software provides the most cost effective development approach and investigate the COM technologies in a bit more depth.

Software Components

Reaffirming our earlier discussions, exploiting information technology for business advantage has become critical for companies to lower the cost of doing business and obtaining competitive advantage. However, the software industry in its early years had become renowned for failing to deliver many projects on time or to budget. Furthermore, organizations were finding this new generation of advanced software costly to support and difficult to enhance. Such code was often poorly designed and written in an unstructured fashion with different bits of logic intertwined. This made it difficult to understand and very risky to change; even what might appear to be a minor amendment could easily and unknowingly cause severe repercussions throughout the system.

IT managers recognized that new software techniques were required to overcome the problems of complexity, increase the production rate of robust software, and re-use existing proven code. One powerful technique that delivers this goal is component based software and this is fundamental when building solutions with Microsoft products.

Component based software is a development process that emulates the construction processes used by many more established industries. For example, the majority of today's car manufacturers build vehicles from hundreds of components parts supplied from a large number of external companies. Each individual part would have been designed, manufactured and passed through quality checks as a separate isolated process undertaken by the part supplier. By delegating responsibility for many of these low level complexities, a car manufacturer can concentrate on their core business – that is designing and building cars that are more reliable and brought to market quickly due to a short development cycle ... the exact goal that every software company wants to achieve.

The software industry can now build systems in a similar manner by selecting a number of best of breed software components. These components can then be glued together, using a software technology like COM, to allow them to co-operate together to form a single integrated solution. The system designers and integration team must have confidence that the functionality of the component behaves as published but they do not need to worry about the complexities of the internal processing logic.

For many items of functionality, we can purchase 'off-the-shelf' software components from one the numerous software vendors that specialize in the market of reusable components. Alternatively, if our requirements are unique, then we can develop our own components using a suitable development tool such as Visual Basic. In fact, this will be one of the major themes throughout this book.

Component Object Model

The Component Object Model (COM) is software technology that allows applications to be built from binary software components. It provides a comprehensive framework that allows software components to be plugged together to co-operate even if they have been written by different vendors, at different times using different tools / languages and, if the objects are located in the same process, same machine or distributed over multiple machines. Put simply, COM provides the 'software plumbing' between software objects and insulates the component developer from such complexities

The original specification of COM always allowed for co-operating objects to be located on different machines but this was not implemented until Windows NT 4.0 and was then called Distributed COM (**DCOM**). Because of this, in reality DCOM and COM are now the same animals. DCOM is layered on top of the DCE (**Distributed Computing Environment**) RPC (**Remote Procedure Call**) specifications.

The following diagram shows how objects use COM/DCOM to co-operate even across process and machine boundaries.

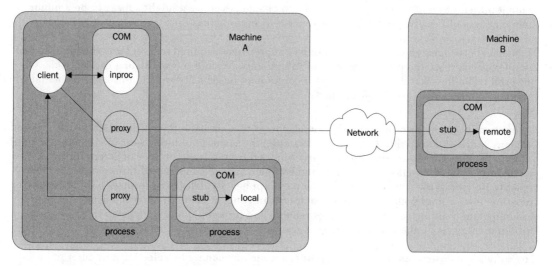

Whilst COM was not originally a committee-driven standard, it has since become an open market-driven technology that is now fully published from the lowest level communications protocols to the highest-level API functions. In addition, Microsoft has donated ownership of the technology's specifications to an open industry association working under the auspices of The Open Group – to promote the common adoption of these core technologies.

COM is now ubiquitous and available on a number of platforms including the following:

> IBM MVS, IBM OS/400, IBM AIX, Siemens Nixdorf, HP/UX, Linux 2.0 (Intel), Sun Solaris, SCO UnixWare, Compaq / Digital Unix, Compaq Digital Open VMS,

For more information, check out:

Solaris –

    http://www.microsoft.com/ActiveX/resource/solaris.asp

Compaq/Digital –
    http://www.unix.digital.com/com/
    http://www.openvms.digital.com/openvms/products/dcom/

Software AG -
    http://www.softwareag.com/corporat/solutions/entirex/entirex.htm

ActiveX

When Microsoft released their first set of Internet tools in March 1996, they announced ActiveX technology – which in all truth was just a catchy new name devised by the Microsoft marketing machine for specific parts of their existing COM technology. ActiveX has to be one of the most misunderstood and naively used expressions in the Internet technology arena. Many people get confused about ActiveX because it does not mean just one thing. More precisely, ActiveX encompasses an ever-growing series of technologies, each of which defines the interfaces between the software components to implement some particular functionality. For the Internet and Windows DNA, examples include:

> ActiveX Scripting – enables script logic to be included in the downloaded Web page or used on the server to generate the page content

> ActiveX Controls – enable client components to be incorporated within a web page and dynamically downloaded as needed

> ActiveX Documents– enable the browser to support non HTML documents (such as Microsoft Office documents)

> ActiveX Data Objects – enable an easy and flexible mechanism to get at data that can be located in a number of different types of data stores

> ActiveX Server Components – enable the IIS Web Server to interface to other server software components

To most Internet users, the ActiveX technologies work seamlessly and transparently, and they just experience the effects of these rich technologies; it is irrelevant to them whether it is ActiveX or "voodoo magic" that is operating under the covers. However, to the Web application developer ActiveX provides an unrivalled set of tools for creating dynamic Web solutions that releases the full potential of Microsoft's powerful Web platform.

> **Important! Currently, the only Web browser to natively support ActiveX technologies is Internet Explorer (v3.0 onwards). If you use these technologies on the Web then you may be severely restricting the number of visitors to your site. In Intranet and Extranet solutions – where you can impose restrictions on the Web browser – this is not such a problem. Using ActiveX technologies on the server is perfectly acceptable in all cases because ASP can send standard platform independent HTML to the client.**

Software Component Characteristics

A software component can be defined as a combination of data and code that may act on that data, which together can be considered as a single unit. An object, of which there may be many, is a created instance of a software component.

The data and code associated to the component defines everything that the component represents (state) and what it can do (behavior). These characteristics are specified by the software component's definition; this can comprise of:

> Properties – these are the attributes of the object that are available for access, update or both from an external client that is using the object

> Methods – these are functions that can be invoked from an external client that is using the object, sometimes methods will take arguments

> Events – these are signals which are fired when a specific action or interesting state occurs; these signals are detected and acted upon by the external client

A software component may expose many properties and methods. Properties and methods that operate together to perform a specific task are often grouped together and referred to as an object's ingoing interface. Events that occur are grouped in an object's outgoing interface. A software component will frequently support more than one interface and each interface is given a name, which by convention will normally begin with a 'I' character; for example, IUnknown.

To help clarify this, lets look at a 'real world' example of a component that controls a Car.

Cars are very complex machines and so different interfaces are likely to be implemented to handle each of the different parts ... lets consider just one of its possible interfaces. The interface to handle the car's fuel might be called IFuelTank.

IFuelTank would have a series of methods, properties and events; examples might include:

Properties: FuelLevel   Amount of fuel in fuel tank

Method: FillTank   Add fuel until tank is full

Events: TankFull   Fired when the FuelLevel is at a maximum
               TankLow   Fired when FuelLevel reaches below 10% of maximum.
               TankEmpty   Fired when FuelLevel reaches zero

Some interfaces are standard and are published by software vendors; for example, Microsoft's ActiveX specifications define many standard interfaces. Published interfaces cannot be changed. If software developers write their software to conform to standard interfaces, then their software can communicate and cooperate with other software conforming to such interfaces if required.

Universal Data Access

Reiterating again the message from our earlier discussions, a principal aim from Microsoft's early days has been to put "Information at Your Fingertips" and enable businesses to exploit their data in order to gain maximum business advantage. As a result, demands were put on the Microsoft designers and developers to provide Windows DNA with a leading set of data access technologies and we shall now discuss how they have reacted to this challenge with a strategy known as Universal Data Access (UDA). This is a Windows DNA initiative to deliver both standards and software technologies for data access.

In the past, data access mechanisms (such as ODBC - Microsoft's first open data access technology) have assumed that the data is stored in structured relational databases. However, businesses today also store their information in a number of other different data stores including office suite documents (Word, Excel, etc.), text files, multimedia files (video, audio, graphics), email systems, directory services, project management tools and so on. We can now start to see why the word *'Universal'* in UDA was chosen.

Some major database vendors now supply "universal databases" that provide some support for data in non-traditional formats such as those listed above. However this approach forces the data to be migrated into their database engine and, as a result, can be expensive and not practical when the data is normally distributed in a complex fashion across a large corporate enterprise.

The alternative strategy used by Microsoft UDA is to provide simple, consistent and highly efficient mechanisms for accessing data irrespective of its format or the location where it resides, and without any need for the data to be transformed or duplicated.

OLEDB & Active Data Objects

As part of the UDA solution, Microsoft has provided two software layers referred to as OLEDB and Active Data Objects (ADO). Naturally, both of these layers expose COM interfaces and so they can easily be plugged into our own applications as shown below.

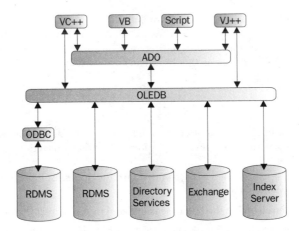

From this diagram we can see that we can access data using either OLEDB or ADO.

OLEDB is designed to be the COM compliant successor to ODBC but in addition also addresses the need to support data stored in non-relational data stores. However, also notice that OLEDB can sit above ODBC and so may seamlessly be used with all of the numerous databases that are already ODBC compliant. With time, most database vendors will support OLEDB natively as the direct approach will be more efficient.

ADO works at a higher level than OLEDB and avoids many of the complexities that a programmer working at the OLEDB needs to consider. In particular, it provides support for ActiveX clients, like the ActiveX Scripting engine, making it ideal for use in ASP. ADO provides a simpler object model and enables data access code to be developed with minimal effort. It is designed to be the only interface that most programmers will need to understand to access data.

The database examples in this book will be using the simple ADO rather than OLEDB.

> Some readers may be familiar with the older RDO and DAO data access
> mechanisms, and indeed these do have similarities with ADO. However, it is
> Microsoft's intention that ADO will eventually replace both RDO and DAO.

ADO also provides some useful features when working with Web architectures in which there may be no permanent or error free connection between the client and the server. It includes support for a facility called the Remote Data Service (RDS) in which the data may be disconnected and stored or manipulated on the client; any changes to the data can then be reapplied to the server at a later time.

OLEDB, ADO, RDS and ODBC are collectively known as the Microsoft Data Access Components (MDAC) and at the time of writing, the current version was MDAC v2.1. The latest version for download and its associated information can be obtained from:
http://www.microsoft.com/data

For business critical systems, an organization must be able to rely on its data and protect it from operating failures. Data integrity relies on software services that prevent files and data stores from being left in a corrupted state should system, network or application failures occur. We shall now discuss how Windows DNA addresses this by means of transactions.

Transactions

A transaction is a group of independent actions that when considered as a whole, form a 'single item of work'. When working with databases, it is important that a transaction has the following properties:

> > Atomicity – all updates to a database under a transaction must be either committed or get rolled back to their previous state

> > Consistency – ensures that the database is updated in the correct manner

> > Isolation – uncommitted transactional results are not seen by other pending transactions

> > Durability – once a transaction is committed, it will persist even if failures occur

These properties are often referred to by the acronym **ACID**.

The use of transactions with older two-tier client / server architectures is simple to implement. Database updates that are processed within a transaction must be bound by calls to functions with the database engine – typically these are called **Begin Transaction** and **Commit Transaction**. If a failure of any sort is programmatically detected, the database can be reverted to its original state by another called – typically **Rollback Transaction** or **Abort Transaction**. If a system crash occurs, pending transactions can be identified and the integrity of the database recovered, when the system restarts.

With the demands of Internet and distributed computing, life gets more complex as we need to be able to co-ordinate transactions over multi-tier architectures with multiple data sources (including relational databases, legacy systems and message queuing systems). The implementation of a distributed transactional system can be very complicated without some assistance.

A generic solution to this problem is software known as a transaction processing monitor (TPM). With such systems, the client's request for business logic processing is sent to the TPM, which is then responsible for routing the request to the appropriate service and ensuring the correct fulfillment of the operation, in other words, ensuring the transaction's ACID. Additional features provided by such solutions include load balancing / dynamic configuration, central resource monitoring and security.

As we might expect, Windows DNA provides exactly this kind of service, and, by means of Microsoft Transaction Server,provides us with the infrastructure needed to address these requirements.

Microsoft Transaction Server

Microsoft Transaction Server (MTS) is a transaction processing environment that is designed for the management of distributed component based applications. It provides an easy to use programming model that extends COM and simplifies the development of secure, robust, scaleable, and high performance solutions.

The functionality within MTS addresses many of the complex issues that previously developers had to consider themselves when building multi-tier computing architectures. It manages automatically all threading issues, object pooling, the sharing of resources, security access controls and the handling of transaction context across objects. This all means that developers can concentrate totally on their own business logic as the underlying plumbing and infrastructure is handled for them.

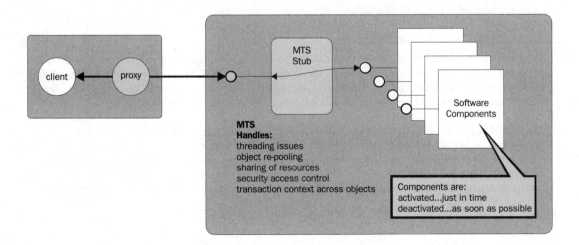

Performance and Scalability

With standard COM, a created object will exist until either the client deletes the object or the client processing it is terminated. This can obviously result in a heavily used server-centric application needing a large number of components to be created, putting an excessive drain on precious systems resources.

To improve performance and scalability, MTS provides what is known as 'just in time' activation and 'as soon as possible' deactivation. This feature enables clients to hold on to references to objects but the objects become 'deactivated' for the period of time when their services are not required. When a client needs the services of an object, MTS will try to assign one from its pool of deactivated objects (if available) before resorting to the instantiation of a new object (if none available). This increases performance and scalability because:

> ➤ Only a few objects need to be instantiated since they can be shared over many clients thus reducing the demand on system resources.

> ➤ Objects can be initialized and waiting on standby, enabling them to react immediately to any client request.

It is well known that establishing database connections is a notoriously expensive operation and in large systems can result in unacceptable performance levels. Another advantage of MTS is that it provides resource dispensers to recycle valuable system resources in a similar fashion to the way it recycles objects.

For example, an ODBC resource dispenser is available which recycles database connections. When an ODBC database connection is no longer required, MTS just deactivates the connection rather than closing it. When a component requires an ODBC database connection, MTS will first try to assign a connection that it has in its pool of deactivated connections. A new ODBC database connection is only established if the pool of available connections is empty.

Distributed Transaction Coordinator

When MTS is installed, another service called the Distributed Transaction Co-ordinator (DTC) is also installed and configured to start up when the system is booted. DTC is responsible for managing the transactions across networks and works by co-operating with the database's resource manager –the part of the database that is responsible for ensuring the integrity of the database.

DTC monitors any MTS Components that are configured to support transactions. If any such component reports a failure to MTS, then the DTC will automatically handle the database rollback. With a single component operating on a single database this would be a simple task for us to program. However, MTS and DTC really come into their own when a transaction involves multiple components operating in a multi-tier distributed environment and spanning multiple databases.

Consider the following example where a 'transfer' transaction consists of crediting one account and debiting another. We must ensure that either both database transactions occur, or no database transactions occur – otherwise money will have been created or lost.

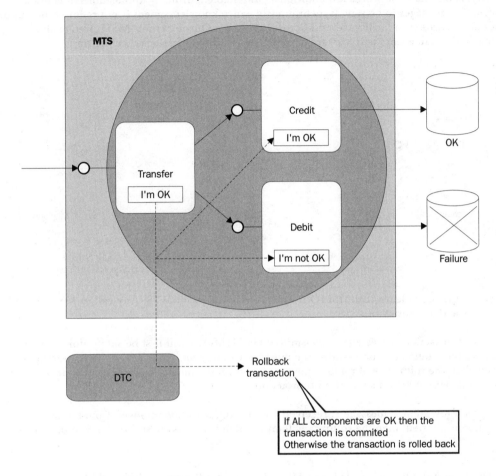

MTS

Credit

I'm OK

OK

Transfer

I'm OK

Debit

I'm not OK

Failure

DTC

Rollback transaction

If ALL components are OK then the transaction is commited
Otherwise the transaction is rolled back

Message Queuing

One of the downsides of building business critical distributed systems that operate over the Internet or WANs is that these networks are notoriously unreliable. For many applications, it is often sufficient for messages to be sent asynchronously –an acknowledgement is not required in real time. Windows DNA offers a facility called Microsoft Message Queue Server (MSMQ) to enable an efficient and reliable store and forward asynchronous communications mechanism.

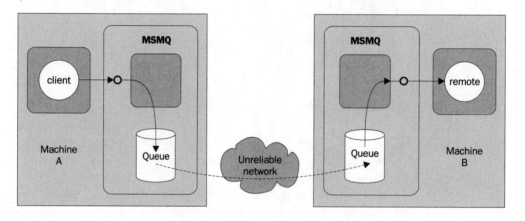

It is not surprising to learn that MSMQ is tightly integrated with MTS. Any call to MSMQ can be part of any active transaction.

If within a transaction, a message is transmitted via MSMQ, it will first be safely stored in queue. If the transaction completes successfully, the message will be sent. However, if the transaction is aborted, then the rollback will remove the message from the queue – a receiver will never get a message that is sent within an aborted transaction.

If within a transaction, a message is received via MSMQ, it will be removed from the queue. If the transaction is aborted, then the rollback will ensure that the message still remains in the queue and so is not lost.

> For more information on MTS and MSMQ, check out Professional MTS/MSMQ, ISBN 1-861001-46-0, from Wrox Press. Details of the objects, methods, and properties relating to these technologies are available in the appendices at the end of this book.

Security

Security is an important concern with Windows DNA applications, and in particular those that involve the public Internet. Scare stories of break-ins at high profile Internet sites, attacks on vital Internet services, impersonation of important organizations, invasion of personal privacy and tales of electronic commerce fraud makes attractive headlines and so frequently appear the computer industry press. From this it is not surprising that one of the biggest concerns that businesses have about using the latest networking technologies is for the security of their systems.

Good security is achieved by the creation of sound policies, the employment of appropriate security technologies, the consistent monitoring of all practices and a general awareness of trends in the security arena. Fortunately most of the scare stories could have been avoided if the organizations involved had understood fully the security practices and software technology that is available

When Microsoft developed their vision of Windows NT for the enterprise, their intention was that security should be treated as paramount – so security features were designed into the foundations of the operating system. This enables any organization to layer its security options in an appropriate combination, which is specifically suited to combat the perceived risk of that organization. All Microsoft products and operating system extensions that form part of the Windows DNA vision (such as COM, MTS, IIS, BackOffice, and so on), are tightly integrated with Windows NT security and share the same security features and administration tools.

Strong levels of security were built into the core of Windows NT in order to meet and exceed a certifiable security standard, the C2 security guidelines required by the U.S. Department of Defense's security evaluation criteria. Compliance with the C2 security standard was originally only required for government organizations, but many commercial organizations have demanding corporate security needs and recognize the value of the enhanced security that such systems offer.

Internet Security

The **Internet Security Framework** (ISF) is a white paper that was published by Microsoft towards the end of 1996 and it explained their strategy to support a set of security technologies designed for online communications and electronic business. Since this document was released, Microsoft has delivered extensive security architecture for the Windows DNA based on industry standards. It includes certificate services, secure communication channels, payment protocols and cryptographic support.

Internet Information Server Access Controls

The IIS Web service facilities are built upon the Windows NT security model. This means that all files and directories that may be accessed over the Web are protected by Windows NT file permissions. All users accessing the Web service are either given guest access or are authenticated against the Windows NT security database, and then given appropriate access to the various objects.

When IIS is installed, it creates an anonymous user account called IUSR_sysname where sysname is the computer name of the Windows NT system. Normally a user will access a Web site anonymously, and in this case will operate under the security context of the IUSR_sysname account. This means that access is restricted to those Web resources with the file permissions allocated to the IUSR_sysname account.

If the user requests a resource for which the IUSR_sysname user account does not have the appropriate permissions, then IIS will deny the request and inform the originator what authentication methods it supports. The server can then request the user's credentials – logon name and password – and then submit this information in another request for the Web resource. The user information is then authenticated against the Windows NT security database and provided that the user has been granted suitable permissions to access the resource, the resource will be returned; otherwise the request is again denied.

IIS supports two authentication methods; these are the Basic Authentication and the Windows NT Challenge/Response mechanism. The main difference between Basic Authentication and Windows NT Challenge/Response is that the latter does not send the password information across the network. Currently Internet Explorer is the only Web browser to support Windows NT Challenge/Response.

Another possible use for Internet Explorer's Windows NT Challenge/Response capabilities is within an Intranet environment and where a user has already logged on to a Windows domain.

When IIS denies an anonymous request and Windows NT Challenge/Response authentication is enabled, IE will first attempt to use the user's domain credentials in the authentication process. Only if this fails will the user be prompted for their credentials. This will happen automatically and transparently to the user thus improving their user experience and providing seamless integration with the existing infrastructure.

Secure Channels

The IIS Web service supports a security technology called secure channels, which provides a point to point network connection that enables the following features:

> Authentication – one end point of an established communications session can request information to identify the other end point.

> Non-repudiation – a message sender cannot falsely claim that they did not send the message.

> Privacy – messages in transit are encrypted; so the contents cannot be inspected if intercepted

> Integrity – messages in transit cannot be tampered with; otherwise protocol violation will occur

The secure channels technology encompasses a number of industry standard security protocols; the one that is most commonly supported by most Web browsers is **Secure Socket Layer** (**SSL 2.0 / SSL 3.0**).

Digital certificates

Secure channels rely on another security technology that is called digital certificates. A digital certificate contains the details of an individual or an organization in a format that is defined by a standard called X.509 version 3. Digital certificates may be exchanged when a secured channel is established and this allows each party to determine the identity of the other.

But what is there to stop anybody from creating a false certificate, and pretending that they are someone else? The solution to this problem is **Certificate Authorities** (**CAs**), who are responsible for the issuing of digital certificates. A CA is a commonly known trusted third party, responsible for verifying both the contents and ownership of a certificate. Examples of Certificate Authorities include VeriSign, Thawte, GTE and Entrust.

With Microsoft Certificate Server we can become the Certificate Authority and manage the generation and distribution of digital certificates for our own communities of users, such as our customer base (Internet), business partners (Extranets) and employees (Intranets).

Authenticode

Now that the Web has become 'Active', executable logic can be automatically delivered to our desktop in a variety of different forms such as browser scripts, ActiveX controls, Java applets, batch files, macros attached to documents from office suite products and normal .EXE executables. Because this logic can originate from an unknown source, there is obviously the scope for something really malicious to be downloaded and cause irrevocable damage.

When we purchase software in the high street – such as the Microsoft Flight Simulator – we have confidence that the product is safe to install on our machines for two reasons. Firstly it has been developed by a software vendor that we trust and secondly, it is shrink-wrapped and so we believe that it has not been tampered with since leaving Microsoft's manufacturing site. Similarly, for the downloadable Web executable logic we need similar protection using. accountability and electronic shrink-wrapping.

The solution from Microsoft is Authenticode, which enables users and software publishers to create a trust relationship between themselves. By using Authenticode, a software publisher use a digital certificate to sign their code when they make it available for downloaded.

When Internet Explorer downloads executable logic, it checks that the software has not been tampered with and uses the digital signature to ascertain the originator of the code, which it then notifies to the user. The user is then given the option of either accepting the code or canceling the operation. If the user does not trust the origin of the code, then they should, without hesitation, reject the code.

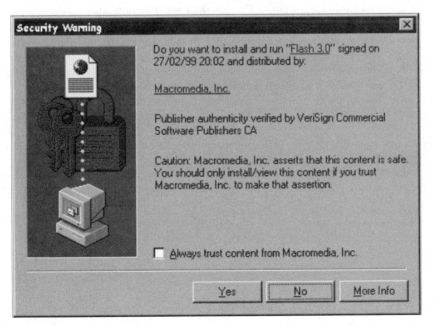

Summary

In this chapter we have investigated Windows DNA – the name that Microsoft is calling their framework that addresses the convergence of personal computers and the Web / networking technologies. We have seen how it provides complete support for the ActiveX and Internet standards that enables developers to integrate HTML, scripting, components, and transactions to build powerful, scaleable and highly available applications that can run over the Internet and across the corporate enterprise.

The key points to this chapter are:

> Windows DNA is Microsoft's architectural framework for developing software for the Windows platform and for the Internet. It provides a development model that capitalizes on the best features from each technology to provide a unified solution. It provides a set of core services that frees the developers from the complexity of programming infrastructure and allows them to concentrate on delivering business solutions.

> Developing component-based software overcomes many problems of today's complex systems; it increases the production rate of robust software and enables the re-use existing proven code.

> The Microsoft Component Object Model (COM) is the most widely used component software model in the computer industry and is fundamental in building Windows DNA solutions. ActiveX is a name given to many technologies based on COM.

> The key building blocks to Windows DNA are:

  – The core server platform – Windows NT 4 / 2000, plus various extensions such as Windows NT 4.0 Option pack, BackOffice and so on
  – Component based software using COM technologies to simplify systems integration and aid software reuse
  – Universal Data Access to enable information to flow by providing reliable and high performance access to data irrespective of the type of data source
  – The use of transactions to provide data integrity
  – The application of security measures to ensure that a system can be trusted.

The final message from this chapter is that many people are claiming that the "Internet will change everything", ... well that's wrong, it already has! So let's not get left behind. We shall now move swiftly on and see how we can exploit Visual Basic and the Web to their full extent, starting in the next chapter with a look at how we can use Visual Basic as the 'enabler' to deliver our Windows DNA solutions.

3

An Overview of Building Windows DNA Applications with Visual Basic

Since the main focus of this book is on Visual Basic Web programming, it's time now to investigate how we can use Visual Basic technologies to enable the integration of HTML, scripting, components, and transactions to build powerful, scaleable and highly available applications that run across the Internet and corporate enterprise. The latest release – Visual Basic 6.0 – fully addresses the new Web paradigm and provides the most productive tools for building Windows DNA applications.

The nature of the Windows DNA platform means that there are a number of different techniques and locations for deploying our Visual Basic developed logic. The different types of executable logic that we shall be considering in this book are shown below:

- ActiveX Scripting – Visual Basic Script
- ActiveX Controls
- WebClasses
- Dynamic HTML Applications
- ActiveX Server Components
- ActiveX Documents
- Traditional Windows Clients

The locations for each of these technologies are shown in the diagram below, showing how some of the items operate in the client-side, others operate on the server-side and one, VBScript, operates on both.

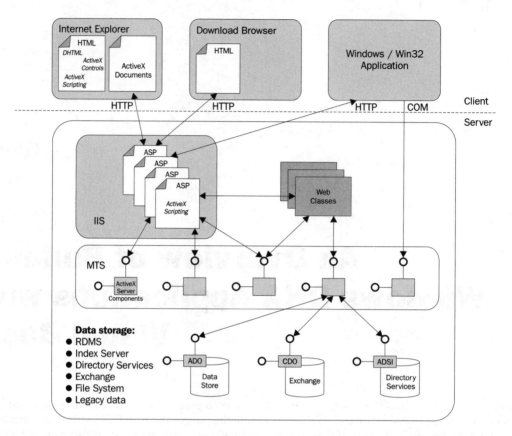

In this chapter we shall consider each one of these topics in turn and discuss the role that Visual Basic has to play. For each, we shall briefly consider a simple example that, although not particularly challenging, will set the scene and give a flavor of what is possible.

ActiveX Scripting – Visual Basic Script

Earlier, when we discussed *'Next Generation Web applications'* we saw that scripting languages can be used on both the client-side (IE handling Web pages) and the server-side (IIS invoking Active Server Pages). In both cases, scripting is used to act as the software glue that integrates software components and controls the actions required when events firing are detected. Script logic is interpreted and there is no concept of compiling the scripts.

Rather than develop specific script processing logic for both IE and ASP, Microsoft has used ActiveX technologies to provide a generic and flexible framework for adding any scripting language to any application. The ActiveX Scripting architecture allows **script hosts** (such as IE, ASP or our own application) to invoke scripting services within **script engines** (such as VBScript, JavaScript or our own scripting language). The ActiveX Scripting specifications define the COM interfaces that a script host and script engine must support; thus the hosts and engines can be supplied from different software vendors that conform to the specification.

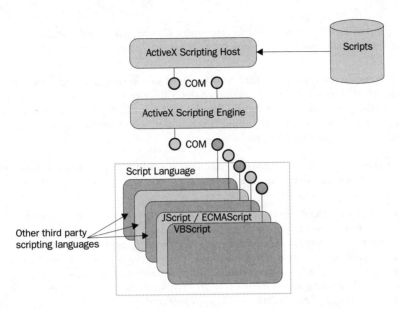

Visual Basic Script (VBScript) is a popular script language and will be used throughout this book. VBScript is a subset of Visual Basic for Applications (VBA, as used by the Microsoft Office Products), which in turn is a subset of the popular Visual Basic. Most readers familiar with VB should be able to quickly grasp this lightweight scripting version of the language. Note that the normal Visual Basic development tool is not suitable for editing VBScript logic – instead, the most productive tool is the Visual InterDev development environment.

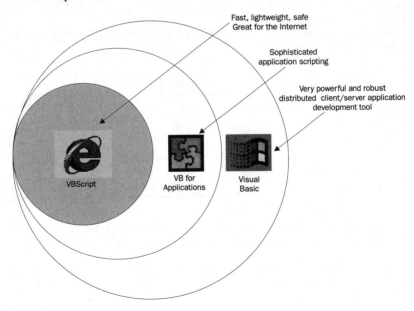

A VBScript reference guide is available in Appendix D, and Microsoft's online documentation is available at `http://msdn.microsoft.com/scripting/`

Web developers frequently complain that their clever client-side script logic can easily be viewed and copied once downloaded. The most recent version of the VBScript engine (version 5.0) enables a BASE64 simple encoding algorithm to be applied to the VBScript code. This means that when a Web page source code is viewed, the script logic appears scrambled which makes it awkward (though not impossible) for anyone to inspect and re-use.

We shall now look at two examples of VBScript, one that is client-side executed in Internet Explorer and the other server-side executed by the ASP host.

Remember that Internet Explorer (v3.0 onwards) is currently the only browser to support VBScript and so its use on the Web is likely to restrict the number of visitors to your site. However, VBScript is more frequently used with Intranets and Extranets where you can usually impose restrictions of the Web browser that may be used. If you require script logic to be used in a Web solution then you should consider using JavaScript (and don't encode it!). There's a short JavaScript tutorial in Appendix D, and O'Reilly's JavaScript: The Definitive Guide is just that.

Example – IE Client-side VBScript

Our client-side scripting example illustrates how we can detect the user interacting with the Web page and then execute a routine. The Web page contains a button that when clicked fires a routine to display Hello World.

The `onclick` attribute within the `<INPUT>` tag defines the actions that are invoked when the user clicks on the button; in our example we call a routine named `clicked()`.

```
<INPUT id=butClickMe type=button value="Click me"
    onclick="call clicked()">
```

> **Note: The code in the** `onclick` **attribute is actually JavaScript because this is the default and no language attribute was specified to override this. This illustrates that it is possible to combine more than one scripting language in the same page.**

The routine `clicked()` is defined with the `<SCRIPT>` and `</SCRIPT>` tags – which specifies that the scripting language is VBScript.

```
<SCRIPT LANGUAGE=VBSCRIPT>
<!--
  sub clicked
    msgbox "Hello world"
  end sub
//-->
</SCRIPT>
```

The HTML code in its entirety is as follows:

```
<HTML>
<HEAD>
<META NAME="GENERATOR" Content="Microsoft Visual Studio 6.0">
<TITLE>Wrox's Web Programming with VB6</TITLE>

<STYLE>
BODY {FONT-FAMILY: Arial; BACKGROUND-COLOR: pink; }
</STYLE>

<SCRIPT LANGUAGE=VBSCRIPT>
<!--
sub clicked
    msgbox "Hello world"
end sub
//-->
</SCRIPT>
</HEAD>

<BODY>
<H1>Client-side VBScript ... in action</H1>
<P><INPUT id=butClickMe type=button value="Click me"
       onclick="call clicked()"></P>
</BODY>
</HTML>
```

Example – ASP Server-side VBScript

In Chapter 1 we introduced Active Server Pages and saw that they are files with a `.ASP` suffix that contain both HTML syntax and server-side script logic. When the Web server receives an HTTP request for the ASP document, an output HTML file is generated for the response using a combination of both the HTML static information plus any HTML that is generated dynamically by the server-side script logic.

In our next scripting example, we shall demonstrate how we can use an ASP server-side script to dynamically generate Web content. Our script logic will interface with a Microsoft product called Membership & Personalization (M&P) Server to identify a Web user and to retrieve their name. The response that is sent to the client is then able to give a personalized greeting.

The script logic in an ASP file that is to be executed server-side is identified by being within either:

➢   `<%` and `%>` marks, or

➢   `<SCRIPT RUNAT=Server>` and `</SCRIPT>` tags (note – if the `RUNAT` attribute is omitted then the script is executed client side)

Whilst it is not important to worry about the actual details of the M&P processing, notice that a software component is created using `Server.CreateObject` and then ASP invokes various methods on the object to perform the required actions.

```
Set User = Server.CreateObject("Membership.UserObjects")
User.BindAs "", gMemUserScriptID, gMemUserPassword
```

This is typical of ASP processing where the main functionality is performed by other components and ASP is simply used as the software glue to integrate the different components and pass the results back to the Web browser.

The ASP code in its entirety is as follows:

```
<%@ Language=VBScript %>
<HTML>

<HEAD>
<META NAME="GENERATOR" Content="Microsoft Visual Studio 6.0">
<TITLE>Wrox's Web Programming with VB6</TITLE>
```

```
<STYLE>
BODY {FONT-FAMILY: Arial;BACKGROUND-COLOR: wheat; }
</STYLE>

<%
gMemUserPassword = "password"
gMemUserScriptID = "cn=administrator,ou=members,o=HarrisonMembership"
Set User = Server.CreateObject("Membership.UserObjects")
User.BindAs "", gMemUserScriptID, gMemUserPassword
vFirstName = User.givenName
vSurname = User.sn
%>

<SCRIPT LANGUAGE=VBSCRIPT>
<!--
sub clicked
    msgbox "Hello " & "<% = vFirstName %>" & " " & "<% = vSurname %>"
end sub
//-->
</SCRIPT>

</HEAD>

<BODY>
<H1>Server-side & Client-side VBScript ... in action</H1>
<P><INPUT id=butClickMe type=button value="Click me"
        onclick="call clicked()"></P>
</BODY>

</HTML>
```

We shall study VB Script on the client in detail in Chapters 4 and 5 and ASP and VBScript in Chapter X (on the server).

ActiveX Controls

ActiveX Controls are software components that can 'package' a specific item of functionality and be hosted within a parent application (known as an ActiveX Control Container) such as Internet Explorer (version 3.0 and later). This enables our Web pages to include advanced functionality that cannot be accommodated with standard HTML and scripting. Examples of ActiveX controls include video/audio (Windows Media Player) and animation (e.g. Macromedia Shockwave), which are installed with the Full version of Internet Explorer.

> **ActiveX controls are the next generation of OLE Custom eXtension/controls (OCXs 32 bit applications) and Visual Basic eXtension controls (VBXs) (16 bit applications).**

ActiveX controls can expose properties and methods, and fire events; these may be combined with some script logic in our Web page to provide interactivity between the user and the control.

For example, our Web page could have a video control and a button; the script logic could detect the button click and then invoke the control's `Play` methods:

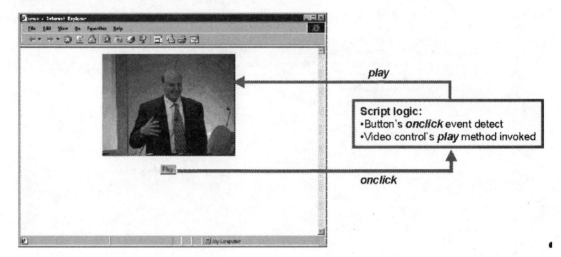

One great feature of ActiveX controls is that they can be referenced in the Web page so that the Web browser will automatically download and install them if needed; such as when either the client does not have the control or the installed control is an earlier version. This approach contrasts greatly with Netscape's plug-ins, which is the alternative approach for embedding complex functionality into an area within the Web browser. The installation of a plug-in is not automatic and involves invoking an application setup utility followed by restarting the browser.

Using the Authenticode security technologies that we discussed in Chapter 2, the user can have confidence of the software publisher of the control and that it has not been tampered with since it was released.

ActiveX controls can be written in any of the COM compliant programming languages, including Visual C++, Visual J++ (Java) and, of course, Visual Basic. They must be compiled in the native machine code of the client's target platform, which means that if we are to support multiple platforms, then we must produce a separate version for each.

> Remember again, that Internet Explorer is currently the only Web browser that supports ActiveX technologies. Using them on the Internet will restrict the number of users that can use your Web pages.

Example – ActiveX Control

Our next example shows an ActiveX control that takes over an area of the Web page and displays a smiley face. When the user clicks the Click Here text, it responds with a Hello World speech balloon.

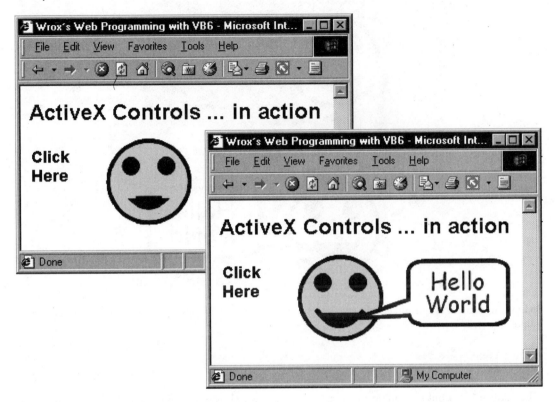

We start in the VB development environment by specifying that we want to create an ActiveX Control project.

ActiveX
Control

The Form for the project contains the following two images:

Image1

Image2

When the control is initialized, the event `UserControl_Initialize` is called. This event will make Image1 appear:

```
Image1.Visible = True
Image2.Visible = False
```

The control has a public function called `SayHello`, which is exposed by COM. The function must be declared as public so that it can be invoked from outside the object. When called, it first makes Image2 appear:

```
Image1.Visible = False
Image2.Visible = True
```

A delay of 3 seconds is then established:

```
PauseTime = 3
start = Timer
Do While Timer < start + PauseTime
    DoEvents
Loop
```

And finally the normal face is restored

```
Image1.Visible = False
Image2.Visible = True
```

The ActiveX control is embedded into our Web page using the <OBJECT> tag. This specifies the required version of the control and the name of the cabinet file that contains the files required to install the control. A wizard called the **Package and Deployment Wizard**, which we discuss in Chapter 6 is used to package and compress the control plus the information required to install the control, into a .CAB file.

```
<OBJECT id=HelloCtrl classid=CLSID:FBDC6779-E4A0-11D2-943D-00104B4F37A4
     codeBase=Hello.CAB#version=1,0,0,0 height=124 width=264>
</OBJECT>
```

The Web page also includes a text item with an onclick attribute. If the user clicks on the text, the SayHello method on our ActiveX control is invoked and the user will see the **Hello World** speech balloon appear.

```
<H3 id=txtClickHere onclick="HelloCtrl.SayHello()">
  Click Here</H3>
```

The VB ActiveX control code in its entirety is as follows:

```
Private Sub UserControl_Initialize()
   Image1.Visible = True
   Image2.Visible = False
End Sub
Public Function SayHello() As Variant

   Image1.Visible = False
   Image2.Visible = True

   PauseTime = 3
   start = Timer
   Do While Timer < start + PauseTime
      DoEvents
   Loop

   Image1.Visible = True
   Image2.Visible = False

End Function
```

and the HTML page that displays the results looks like this:

```
<HTML>

<HEAD>
<META NAME="GENERATOR" Content="Microsoft Visual Studio 6.0">
<TITLE> Wrox's Web Programming with VB6</TITLE>

<STYLE>
BODY {FONT-FAMILY: Arial;BACKGROUND-COLOR: silver; }
</STYLE>

</HEAD>

<BODY>
<H1>ActiveX Controls ... in action</h1>
```

```
<TABLE>
<TR>
    <TD>
    <H3 id=txtClickHere onclick="HelloCtrl.SayHello()">
    Click Here</H3>
    </TD>

    <TD>
    <OBJECT id=HelloCtrl classid=CLSID:FBDC6779-E4A0-11D2-943D-00104B4F37A4
        codeBase=Hello.CAB#version=1,0,0,0
        height=124 width=264>
    </OBJECT>
    </TD>
</TR>
</TABLE>

</BODY>

</HTML>
```

We shall study ActiveX Controls in detail in Chapter 5.

WebClasses

Visual Basic 6.0 introduces a new type of VB project called a **WebClass**, which provides another alternative for dynamically generating web pages. A Visual Basic WebClass is a server-side software component that is responsible for handling HTTP Requests from a Web browser and generating the HTML that is then returned in the HTTP Response. For each WebClass, VB generates one ASP file. This ASP file contains just a few lines of script that is used to call the WebClass; this is shown in the diagram below.

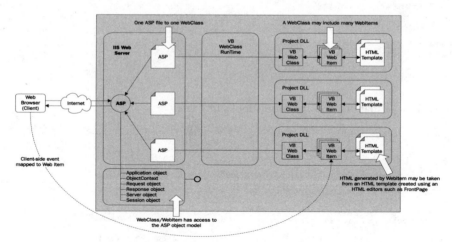

A WebClass is invoked from the Web browser by specifying a URL that references its corresponding ASP file. The ASP is just a few lines of code that passes control onto the WebClass

A WebClass includes a number of modules called **WebItems**, which are responsible for generating the text (normally HTML) to be returned. There are two types of WebItems:

> ➤ HTML Templates WebItems – these return chunks of HTML taken from files that can be created using HTML editors such as Microsoft FrontPage. Non-standard HTML tags can be included in the templates that will fire the `ProcessTag` event enabling the WebItem to apply some business rules and replace the tag with meaningful data.

> ➤ Custom WebItems – these return chunks of HTML using a series of programmatic statements.

WebItems may expose routines that act as event handlers and can be made to fire in response to actions occurring on the Web browser; for example, the user clicking on an image or an item of text. When this happens, the Web page logic requests a URL that specifies the ASP file for the WebClass and has some parameters tacked onto the end of the URL to identify the WebItem and the event handler.

Visual Basic 6.0 includes a WebClass visual designer to help manipulate HTML Templates and map Web browser events to WebItem event handlers.

Example – WebClasses

The following WebClass example demonstrates the replacement processing and the mapping of a client-side event to a server-side event handler.

The first screen will display a welcome message that is appropriate for the time of day. When the user clicks on a hyperlink in the page, the server-side WebClass is called to generate the next Web page.

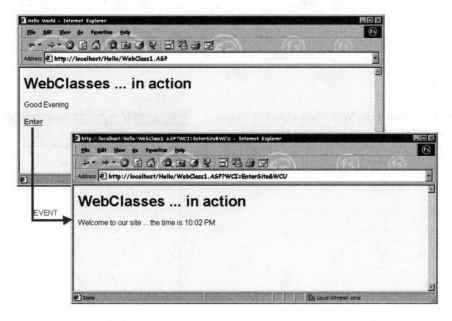

We start by specifying that we want an IIS Application project.

IIS Application

When a WebClass is first invoked, the first function that is always called is `WebClass_Start`. In our example, we specify that the WebItem to process the HTTP request is called `Greeting`.

```
Set NextItem = Greeting
```

This causes the `Greeting_Respond` routine to be called, which dumps out the HTML in the template file that was assigned to the `Greeting` WebItem.

```
Greeting.WriteTemplate
```

But notice that the template includes a bit of nonstandard HTML, as below:

```
<WC@GREETING>Greeting</WC@GREETING>
```

The `WC@` prefix in the tag means that this section of the HTML content is to be replaced. To handle this, the `Greeting_ProcessTag` event is automatically called and the replacement tag is passed as a parameter. For the `WC@GREETING` tag, the section of HTML is replaced (using the `TagContents` parameter) with a greeting that is appropriate for the time of day.

```
If TagName = "WC@GREETING" Then
   TheHour = Hour(Time())
   If TheHour < 12 Then
      TagContents = "Good Morning"
   ElseIf TheHour > 18 Then
      TagContents = "Good Evening"
   Else
      TagContents = "Good Day"
   End If
End If
```

Using the Visual Basic WebClass visual designer we can connect the event of a user clicking on the **Enter** text to the WebItem event handler called `EnterSite_Respond`.

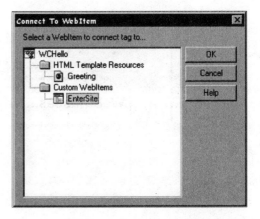

This 'Connect to WebItem' operation sets the HTML anchor to reference the required WebItem in the URL.

```
<A HREF="WebClass1.ASP?WCI=EnterSite&WCU"><H4>Enter</H4></A>
```

When the user clicks on the Enter text, the ASP file `WebClass1.asp` is called and this in turn routes the HTTP request on to the `EnterSite_Respond` event handler.

Whereas `Greeting_Respond` delivered an HTML template, the `EnterSite_Respond` routine takes an alternative approach. Instead, this WebItem generates the HTML in the HTTP Response using a series of `Response.Write` statements.

```
Response.Write "<HTML><HEAD>"
Response.Write "<STYLE>"
Response.Write "   BODY {FONT-FAMILY: Arial; & _
                    BACKGROUND-COLOR: lightyellow; }"
Response.Write "</STYLE>"
Response.Write "</HEAD><BODY>"
Response.Write "<H1>WebClasses ... in action</H1>"
Response.Write "Welcome to our site ... the time is " & _
            Format(Now, "hh:mm AM/PM")
Response.Write "</BODY></HTML>"
```

The VB WebClass code in its entirety is as follows:

```
Option Explicit
Option Compare Text
Private Sub Greeting_ProcessTag(ByVal TagName As String, TagContents As String,
SendTags As Boolean)
    Dim TheHour
    If TagName = "WC@GREETING" Then
        TheHour = Hour(Time())
        If TheHour < 12 Then
            TagContents = "Good Morning"
        ElseIf TheHour > 18 Then
            TagContents = "Good Evening"
        Else
            TagContents = "Good Day"
        End If
    End If
End Sub
Private Sub Greeting_Respond()
    Greeting.WriteTemplate
End Sub
Private Sub EnterSite_Respond()
    Response.Write "<HTML><HEAD>"
    Response.Write "<STYLE>"
    Response.Write "   BODY {FONT-FAMILY: Arial;" & _
                    "BACKGROUND-COLOR: lightyellow; }"
    Response.Write "</STYLE>"
    Response.Write "</HEAD><BODY>"
    Response.Write "<H1>WebClasses ... in action</H1>"
    Response.Write "Welcome to our site ... the time is " & _
            Format(Now, "hh:mm AM/PM")
    Response.Write "</BODY></HTML>"
End Sub
Private Sub WebClass_Start()
    Set NextItem = Greeting
End Sub
```

and the HTML template for the `Greeting` WebItem is:

```
<HTML>

<HEAD>
<META NAME="GENERATOR" Content="Microsoft FrontPage 3.0">
<TITLE>Wrox's Web programming With VB6</TITLE>

<STYLE>
BODY {FONT-FAMILY: Arial; BACKGROUND-COLOR: lightyellow; }
</STYLE>

</HEAD>

<BODY>

<H1>WebClasses ... in action</H1>

<P><WC@GREETING>Greeting</WC@GREETING>
<A><H4>Enter</H4></A>
</BODY>

</HTML>
```

We shall study WebClasses in detail in Chapters 12 to 14.

Dynamic HTML Applications

As we know from our earlier discussions, the early generation of Web browsers could only render static documents. To change the display, time and network intensive communication with the Web server was required in order to get a page refresh.

As from version 4.0 of Internet Explorer, all of the HTML elements on a Web page can be manipulated *'on the fly'* by means of a technology known as Dynamic HTML (DHTML). This browser provides a comprehensive **Document Object Model** (DOM) that allows all tags and attributes in a Web page to be programmatically accessed and amended using a scripting language such as VBScript. Thanks to DHTML we can enable dynamic user interaction and reduce the load on the Web server.

Visual Basic 6.0 has introduced a new type of VB project called a **DHTML Application** that offers us an alternative approach to using the scripting language to develop logic to manipulate the IE DOM and handle user interactions.

> **Important!** As with ActiveX technologies, when we use this technology we are restricting ourselves to the latest versions of Internet Explorer and so limiting the number of Internet users that can view our pages. The W3C have published a DOM specification which hopefully one day all browser vendors will support in its entirety ... until then, we can only live in expectation of the glorious world of browser compatibility.

A Visual Basic DHTML Application produces two separate items:

> ➤ a client-side software component (an ActiveX Control without any user interface)
> ➤ a collection of HTML pages

The control is embedded within the Web pages and has full programmatic access to the document object model. The two items operate together to perform the presentation layer functionality.

The advantages of using the DHTML Application approach as opposed to including script logic in the HTML page include:

> ➤ the software component is compiled and so runs faster
> ➤ the deployed logic is in a binary format and so cannot easily be examined and ripped off
> ➤ the application can be developed using our familiar and powerful VB development environment

Visual Basic 6.0 includes a DHTML Application page designer to create the HTML Web pages and to identify the tags that can be manipulated by the code.

Example – Dynamic HTML

In this next DHTML Application example we shall display a HELLO sign and then rotate it in three dimensions.

There are also two buttons that allow the speed of the rotation to be altered.

We start by specifying that we want a DHTML Application project.

DHTML
Application

The HELLO sign is displayed by using a Microsoft ActiveX control called the Structure Graphics Control that is supplied as part of Internet Explorer. This uses vector graphics that are commands and a coordinate system to reproduce an image; typical commands being Draw a Line, Draw a Shape, Fill With a Color, Display Text, and so on. By using these methods it is often possible to generate graphical effects that are much more lightweight than using equivalent JPG or GIF graphics files.

To get our sign, we specify the vector commands as parameters to the control.

```
<OBJECT classid=CLSID:369303C2-D7AC-11D0-89D5-00A0C90833E6
    height=100 id=sgHelloSign width=100 VIEWASTEXT>
  <PARAM NAME="SourceURL" VALUE="">
  <PARAM NAME="CoordinateSystem" VALUE="0">
  <PARAM NAME="MouseEventsEnabled" VALUE="-1">
  <PARAM NAME="HighQuality" VALUE="0">
  <PARAM NAME="PreserveAspectRatio" VALUE="-1">
  <PARAM NAME="Line0001" VALUE="SetLineColor(255,255,255)">
  <PARAM NAME="Line0002" VALUE="SetFillColor(255,0,0,0,255)">
  <PARAM NAME="Line0003" VALUE="SetFillStyle(1)">
  <PARAM NAME="Line0004" VALUE="SetLineStyle(1,0)">
  <PARAM NAME="Line0005" VALUE="Polygon(
        8,-45,15,-15,45,15,45,45,15,45,-15,15,-45,-15,-45,-45,-15)">
  <PARAM NAME="Line0006" VALUE="SetFont('Arial',24,500,0,0,0)">
  <PARAM NAME="Line0007" VALUE="SetLineColor(255,255,255)">
  <PARAM NAME="Line0008" VALUE="SetFillColor(255,255,255,255,0,0)">
  <PARAM NAME="Line0009" VALUE="Text('HELLO',-35,5)">
</OBJECT>
```

In addition, the HTML references another object – this is our DHTML Application object. The ClassID for the object is inserted automatically by the Visual Basic development environment.

```
<!--METADATA TYPE="MsHtmlPageDesigner" startspan-->
  <object id="DHTMLPage1"
    classid="clsid:A97E9A15-E601-11D2-943F-00104B4F37A4"
    width=0 height=0>
  </object>
<!--METADATA TYPE="MsHtmlPageDesigner" endspan-->
```

The DHTML Application has access to all of the items in the Web page and the Web browser's `window` object.

When the Web page has been loaded, the `BaseWindow_onload` event is called. First a variable called `vTimer` that is used to store the delay between each frame of the rotation, is initialized and then displayed on the Web page.

```
vTimer = 50
txtTimer.innerText = vTimer
```

Then a timer is kicked off. We specify that when the timer expires, the VBScript routine named `DoRotate` in our DHTML Application object should be called.

```
Call BaseWindow.setTimeout("call DHTMLPage1.DoRotate()", vTimer, "VBScript")
```

So let's look at `DoRotate()`. First, the next frame in the rotation of the sign is done by calling the Structure Graphics Control's `Rotate()` method.

```
Call sgHelloSign.Rotate(3, 2, 1)
```

Then, the same timer as before is restarted, and this whole process is continually repeated.

The speed of the rotation is handled by amending the value of `vTimer` when either the **Faster** or **Slower** buttons are clicked; these user actions are picked up by the `butFaster_onclick` and `butSlower_onclick` event handlers.

The DHTML Application code in its entirety is as follows:

```
Dim vTimer

Private Sub BaseWindow_onload()
    vTimer = 50
    txtTimer.innerText = vTimer
    Call BaseWindow.setTimeout("call DHTMLPage1.DoRotate()", vTimer, "VBScript")
End Sub

Public Function DoRotate() As Variant
    Call sgHelloSign.Rotate(3, 2, 1)
    Call BaseWindow.setTimeout("call DHTMLPage1.DoRotate()", vTimer, "VBScript")
End Function

Private Function butFaster_onclick() As Boolean
    If vTimer > 2 Then
        vTimer = vTimer - 2
    End If
    txtTimer.innerText = vTimer
End Function

Private Function butSlower_onclick() As Boolean
    If vTimer < 200 Then
        vTimer = vTimer + 2
    End If
    txtTimer.innerText = vTimer
End Function
```

The HTML page looks like this:

```
<HTML>

<HEAD>
<TITLE>Hello World</TITLE>

<STYLE>
BODY {FONT-FAMILY: Arial;BACKGROUND-COLOR: lightblue; }
.SPEED {CURSOR: Hand; BACKGROUND-COLOR: blue; COLOR: white}
</STYLE>

</HEAD>

<BODY>

<!--METADATA TYPE="MsHtmlPageDesigner" startspan-->
    <object id="DHTMLPage1"
       classid="clsid:A97E9A15-E601-11D2-943F-00104B4F37A4"
       width=0 height=0>
    </object>
<!--METADATA TYPE="MsHtmlPageDesigner" endspan-->

<H1>Dynamic HTML ... in action</H1>
<TABLE>

    <TR><TD align=middle>
      <OBJECT classid=CLSID:369303C2-D7AC-11D0-89D5-00A0C90833E6
            height=100 id=sgHelloSign width=100 VIEWASTEXT>
      <PARAM NAME="SourceURL" VALUE="">
      <PARAM NAME="CoordinateSystem" VALUE="0">
      <PARAM NAME="MouseEventsEnabled" VALUE="-1">
      <PARAM NAME="HighQuality" VALUE="0">
      <PARAM NAME="PreserveAspectRatio" VALUE="-1">
      <PARAM NAME="Line0001" VALUE="SetLineColor(255,255,255)">
      <PARAM NAME="Line0002" VALUE="SetFillColor(255,0,0,0,0,255)">
      <PARAM NAME="Line0003" VALUE="SetFillStyle(1)">
      <PARAM NAME="Line0004" VALUE="SetLineStyle(1,0)">
      <PARAM NAME="Line0005" VALUE="Polygon(
            8,-45,15,-15,45,15,45,45,15,45,-15,15,-45,-15,-45,-45,-15)">
      <PARAM NAME="Line0006" VALUE="SetFont('Arial',24,500,0,0,0)">
      <PARAM NAME="Line0007" VALUE="SetLineColor(255,255,255)">
      <PARAM NAME="Line0008" VALUE="SetFillColor(255,255,255,255,0,0)">
      <PARAM NAME="Line0009" VALUE="Text('HELLO',-35,5)">
    </OBJECT>
    </TD>

    <TD align=middle width=150>
      <INPUT type="button" value="Faster" id=butFaster>
      <INPUT type="button" value="Slower" id=butSlower>
      <BR><BR>
      Timer = <SPAN id=txtTimer>value</SPAN>
    </TD></TR>

</TABLE>

</BODY>

</HTML>
```

We shall study Dynamic HTML Applications in detail in Chapter 6.

ActiveX Server Components

An ActiveX Server Component is a non-visual COM compliant software component that is executed on the server and used to perform specific business rules.

When we are developing complex ASP applications we must remember that the server-side script logic is interpreted VBScript or JavaScript. When we start to develop really complex Web applications, Web server performance starts to slow as it interprets the script logic. Furthermore, the scripting languages have limited-functionality when compared to the capabilities of Visual Basic 6.0.

The recommended solution for ASP Web applications is to minimize the amount of script and to develop or reuse existing ActiveX Server Components for the business logic. The ASP logic is then restricted to generating the presentation layer (i.e. the HTML tags) and synchronizing the information flow between the components. Alternatively, using WebClasses (called from ASP) to handle the presentation layer and to call on the ActiveX Server Components for the business logic can optimize Web applications further.

ActiveX Server Components may be configured to run within the MTS environment. We discussed earlier how this simplifies the development of transaction-based applications and can improve on the performance and scalability of our systems.

Example – ActiveX Server Components

Our next example uses an ActiveX Server Component to generate the welcome text for a Web page. The component reads the text from a database and uses a passed 'language' parameter as a key to the database retrieval query.

> *The example uses ADO, which is the standard data access mechanism provided by Windows DNA. ADO is a large topic and outside the scope of a DNA/VB overview chapter. In fact whole books can be written on the subject such as Wrox's ADO 2.0 Programmers Reference Guide and the Wrox book Professional ADO / RDS Programming.*

We start by specifying that we want an ActiveX DLL project.

ActiveX DLL

Using the Visual Basic **Properties** window, we set the name of the project to `HelloAxCtrl` and the name if the class to `XHello`.

The function that may be called to perform the action is called `GetWelcome`. Since this must be exposed to callers from outside the component, we must specify that it is `Public`.

```
Public Function GetWelcome(ByVal vLanguage As Variant) As Variant
```

First, the SQL statement to get the text from the database is set up using the passed language parameter.

```
Let vSQL = "Select Message FROM WelcomeMsg " & _
           "WHERE LanguageId = '" & vLanguage & "';"
```

Next an ADO Recordset object is instantiated. An ADO Recordset is probably the most used object with the ADO object model and is used to examine and manipulate data from a data store.

```
Set oRs = CreateObject("ADODB.Recordset")
```

We then invoke the query by calling the `open` method on the ADO Recordset object

```
oRs.MaxRecords = 1
oRs.Open vSQL, vDbConn, , , adCmdText
```

Then the welcome can be retrieved from the ADO Resultset returned from query.

```
vWelcome = oRs.Fields("Message")
```

Finally, we tell MTS that everything was successful and then return the Welcome text as the result of the function call.

```
objMTSContext.SetComplete
GetWelcome = vWelcome
```

The ASP logic determines the required language from a URL parameter

```
vLanguage = Request.QueryString("Language")
```

It then instantiates the component by using a ProgId based on the component's project and class names, i.e. `HelloAxCtrl.XHello`

```
Set obj = Server.CreateObject("HelloAxCtrl.XHello")
```

Next the `GetWelcome` method can be invoked to obtain the **Welcome** text.

```
vHello = obj.GetWelcome(vLanguage)
```

Finally, the result is returned back in the HTTP response.

```
<H4><% = vHello %><H4>
```

The MTS Component code in its entirety is as follows:

```
Implements ObjectControl
Private Const vDbConn As Variant = "DSN=Welcome;"
Private oRs As ADODB.Recordset
Private objMTSContext As ObjectContext
Private Function ObjectControl_CanBePooled() As Boolean
    ObjectControl_CanBePooled = True
End Function
Private Sub ObjectControl_Deactivate()
    Set objMTSContext = Nothing
    Set oRs = Nothing
End Sub
Private Sub ObjectControl_Activate()
    On Error GoTo ActivateErr
    Set objMTSContext = GetObjectContext()
    Exit Sub
ActivateErr:
End Sub
Public Function GetWelcome(ByVal vLanguage As Variant) As Variant
    On Error GoTo GetWelcomeErr

    Dim vSQL As Variant
    Dim vWelcome As Variant

    Let vSQL = "Select Message FROM WelcomeMsg " & _
        "WHERE LanguageId = '" & vLanguage & "';"

    Set oRs = CreateObject("ADODB.Recordset")
    oRs.MaxRecords = 1
    oRs.Open vSQL, vDbConn, , , adCmdText

    vWelcome = oRs.Fields("Message")

    objMTSContext.SetComplete
    GetWelcome = vWelcome
    Exit Function

GetWelcomeErr:
    Trace (Err.Description)
    objMTSContext.SetAbort
    GetWelcome = "?" & Err.Description

End Function
```

The ASP code is this:

```
<HTML>

<HEAD>
<TITLE>Hello World</TITLE>

<STYLE>
BODY {FONT-FAMILY: Arial;BACKGROUND-COLOR: peachpuff; }
</STYLE>

</HEAD>

<BODY>
<H1>ActiveX Server Components ... in action<h1>
<%
   Dim vLanguage,vHello,obj
   vLanguage = Request.QueryString("Language")
   Set obj = Server.CreateObject("HelloAxCtrl.XHello")
   vHello = obj.GetWelcome(vLanguage)
%>
<H4><% = vHello %><H4>
</BODY>

</HTML>
```

We shall study ActiveX Server Components in detail in Chapter 9 and MTS is covered in Chapter 11.

ActiveX Documents

An **ActiveX Document** is a file that contains some data and a reference to a server application that can allow the user to see and interact with the data. An ActiveX document can only be viewed in applications that can act as **ActiveX** Document **Containers**, example of which are Internet Explorer and the Microsoft Office Binder.

An example of an ActiveX Document is an MS Word document – this stores the content of the document and has a reference to the MS Word executable. To illustrate this, remove the file association mapping of .DOC files to MS Word (this is done via the **Folder Options** menu option from within Windows Explorer. If you double click on a .DOC file, a dialog will appear asking what file to use as there is no longer any application associated with this file type. However, try dragging and dropping the .DOC file into Internet Explorer ... you will see that the browser then takes on the MS Word personality and opens the file. Clever stuff!

> If you do delete the .DOC **file association mapping, then first make a note of the settings so that you can return your system back to the same state. Alternatively, you will have to reinstall MS Word.**

This is shown in the screen shot below, where the container is Internet Explorer but it has incorporated the MS Word menus and toolbars.

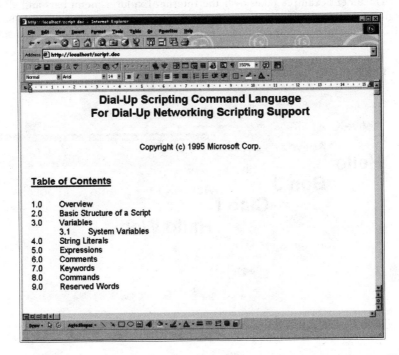

From version 5.0, Visual Basic has been able to support the development of ActiveX documents and so enables us to deploy applications and associated data over the Web.

Example – ActiveX Documents

Our ActiveX Document example takes over the Internet Explorer menu bars and allows the control over the language that the Hello World greeting is displayed in. You can see from the screen dumps below that IE now includes a menu option called Language that allows the user to select the required language.

We start by specifying that we want an ActiveX Document DLL project.

ActiveX Document
Dll

In a similar manner to developing a standard Visual Basic application, we use the VB development environment to define the application menus and create a form that contains two labels. The second label is dynamically changed to display the greeting when the user selects the language.

Clicking on an entry in the Language menu causes the mnuLang_Click event to be fired and the greeting label is amended to the appropriate message for the required language.

The ActiveX Document code in its entirety is as follows:

```
Option Explicit

Private Sub mnuLang_Click(Index As Integer)
   Select Case Index
      Case 1:
         Label2.Caption = "Hello World"
      Case 2:
         Label2.Caption = "Bon Jour"
      Case 3:
         Label2.Caption = "Hallo Welt"
      Case 4:
         Label2.Caption = "Ciao Mondo"
      Case 5:
         Label2.Caption = "Hello Mundo"
      Case 6:
         Label2.Caption = "Hola Mundo"
      Case Else:
         Label2.Caption = "?"
   End Select
End Sub
Private Sub UserDocument_Initialize()
   Label2.Caption = "Hello World"
End Sub
```

Traditional Windows Clients

When discussing the latest Visual Basic features such as WebClasses and DHTML Applications, it's easy to forget that standard Window applications can be developed to fully exploit the Web and networking technologies. We shall see that it is easy to develop such applications that can render Hypertext Markup Language (HTML) documents and use the TCP/IP protocols to retrieve and share information.

Visual Basic client applications can now operate in the multi-tier computing environments and invoke business logic stored in server-side software components. This can be done either directly using DCOM or by means of using HTTP to interface through a Web server with ASP logic. The latter is achieved through the use of the Microsoft **Internet Transfer Control** that allows Visual Basic applications to connect to and retrieve files from any Internet site that supports either the Hypertext Transfer Protocol (HTTP) or the File Transfer Protocol (FTP).

The Microsoft **Web Browser Control** is an ActiveX control that may be used on a Visual Basic form to retrieve data located on the Internet and to display Web content. It provides the same capabilities as Internet Explorer including support for DHTML, ActiveX controls, ActiveX scripting, Java applets and multimedia content (video and audio). In fact, Internet Explorer actually uses this control to render its pages and so the reason it provides the same capabilities is no coincidence.

Example DCOM

In this example, we communicate using DCOM directly to the server-side `HelloAxCtrl.XHello` component that we created earlier for deployment in MTS. The user chooses the language that is passed in the DCOM call by means of a **Language** menu.

The code to instantiate the MTS component and invoke the `GetWelcome` method is similar to the logic that we saw earlier when the task was done from an ASP script.

```
Set objHello = CreateObject("HelloAxCtrl.XHello")
lblHello.Caption = objHello.GetWelcome(vLanguage)
```

However, the main difference this time is that the target object is created on a different machine and the method call to `GetWelcome` is made across the network. The information needed by DCOM to know about the location of the component is stored in the Windows registry on the client machine. This registry configuration is done for us by running a client installation program that is created by invoking an MTS export facility.

The Standard.EXE Application code in its entirety is as follows:

```
Option Explicit

Private Sub mnuLang_Click(Index As Integer)
    Dim vLanguage
    Dim objHello As Object
    On Error GoTo errorhandler

    Select Case Index
      Case 1:
        vLanguage = "EN"
      Case 2:
        vLanguage = "FR"
      Case 3:
        vLanguage = "DE"
      Case 4:
        vLanguage = "IT"
```

```
    Case 5:
       vLanguage = "PO"
    Case 6:
       vLanguage = "ES"
    Case Else:
       vLanguage = "??"
   End Select

   Set objHello = CreateObject("HelloAxCtrl.XHello")
   lblHello.Caption = objHello.GetWelcome(vLanguage)
   Set objHello = Nothing

   Exit Sub

errorhandler:
   MsgBox "Error: " & Err.Description

End Sub
```

Example – Internet Transfer Control

Our next example uses the Internet Transfer Control to initiate an HTTP Request then displays the HTML data that is received in the HTTP Response. We shall request the Web page that we used earlier to demonstrate ActiveX Server Components. As before, the user may choose the required language by means of a Language menu. What should be shown is the HTML specific for the language selected.

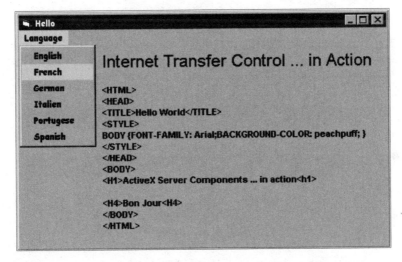

When the user has chosen their language, then, provided that there is no outstanding request, we invoke the HTTP request using the Internet Transfer Control's Execute method. This specifies the URL of the required Web resource.

```
If Not ctrlInternet.StillExecuting Then
   ctrlInternet.Execute _
      "http://harrison/hello/hello.asp?language=" & vLanguage, "GET"
End If
```

Any change of status on the Internet Transfer Control causes the `ctrlInternet_StateChanged` event to be called. The parameter that is passed gives us more information about the type of change of status. When the HTTP Response has been received, the event is called passing a state of `icResponseCompleted`.

When we detect that the HTTP Response has been received, we then extract the information out of the response using `GetChunk` and then amend a label on the form to display it to the user

```
vData = ctrlInternet.GetChunk(4096)
lblHTML.Caption = vData
```

The Standard .EXE Application code in its entirety is as follows:

```
Option Explicit

Private Sub mnuLang_Click(Index As Integer)
    Dim vLanguage
    On Error GoTo errorhandler

    Select Case Index
      Case 1:
        vLanguage = "EN"
      Case 2:
        vLanguage = "FR"
      Case 3:
        vLanguage = "DE"
      Case 4:
        vLanguage = "IT"
      Case 5:
        vLanguage = "PO"
      Case 6:
        vLanguage = "ES"
      Case Else:
        vLanguage = "??"
    End Select

    If Not ctrlInternet.StillExecuting Then
      ctrlInternet.Execute _
        "http://harrison/hello/hello.asp?language=" & vLanguage, "GET"
    End If

    Exit Sub

errorhandler:
    MsgBox "Error: " & Err.Description

End Sub
Private Sub ctrlInternet_StateChanged(ByVal State As Integer)
    Dim vHeader As Variant
    Dim vData As Variant
    On Error GoTo errorhandler
```

```
Select Case State
    Case icResponseCompleted
        vHeader = ctrlInternet.GetHeader()
        vData = ctrlInternet.GetChunk(4096)
        ctrlInternet.Cancel
        Rem MsgBox "Header: " & vHeader
        Rem MsgBox "Data: " & vData
        lblHTML.Caption = vData

    End Select

    Exit Sub

errorhandler:
    MsgBox "Error " & Err.Description

End Sub
```

Example – Web Browser Control

Our final example works in a similar manner to the previous example but this time uses the Web Browser Control to handle the HTTP Request / Response communications. In addition, this control has the ability to display the HTML on the screen.

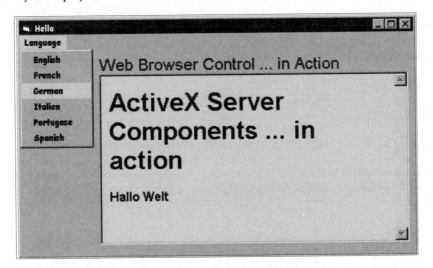

When the user has chosen their language, we invoke the HTTP Request using the Web Browser Control's `Navigate` method, which specifies the URL of the required Web resource. The control displays the HTML as soon as the HTTP Response is received.

```
ctlWB.Navigate _
    "http://harrison/hello/hello.asp?language=" & vLanguage
```

The Standard .EXE Application code in its entirety is as follows:

```
Option Explicit

Private Sub mnuLang_Click(Index As Integer)
    Dim vLanguage
    On Error GoTo errorhandler

    Select Case Index
      Case 1:
        vLanguage = "EN"
      Case 2:
        vLanguage = "FR"
      Case 3:
        vLanguage = "DE"
      Case 4:
        vLanguage = "IT"
      Case 5:
        vLanguage = "PO"
      Case 6:
        vLanguage = "ES"
      Case Else:
        vLanguage = "??"
    End Select

    ctlWB.Navigate _
      "http://harrison/hello/hello.asp?language=" & vLanguage

    Exit Sub

errorhandler:
    MsgBox "Error: " & Err.Description

End Sub
```

We will discuss MTS/DCOM in Chapter 11 and the Web Browser Control in Chapter 6.

That concludes our quick tour of the different ways of using Visual Basic for implementing our Web Applications in a Windows DNA environment.

Summary

In our lightning tour of using VB to create Windows DNA applications, we have seen that Visual Basic 6.0 and Visual Interdev 6.0 fully address the new Web paradigms and without doubt, they together provide the most productive toolset for building Windows DNA applications.

The key points to this chapter are:

> ➢ There are many facets to using VB with the Web and we have seen a variety of areas when VB logic may be implemented; in particular we have considered VB deployed at:

The Web Client
- – Web pages
- – ActiveX Controls
- – Dynamic HTML Applications
- – ActiveX Documents
- – Traditional Windows Clients

The Web Server
- – Active Server Pages
- – WebClasses
- – ActiveX Server Components

> ➢ The use of ActiveX technologies will restrict your web pages to later versions of Internet Explorer and so will restrict the number of Internet users that can use your pages.

We warned you at the top of this chapter that the pace would be fast and that we would only be considering the code in the examples at a very high level in order to give a flavor of what is possible when using VB to build Windows DNA applications. This easy life must now come to an end as it's time to drill down a lot deeper and learn how to exploit these technologies to their full potential. We shall now consider each one of these topics in much greater depth, starting in the next chapter with a look at the Web client.

4

Client-Side Programming with Visual Basic

In recent months, server-side technologies have received much of the attention in the wide world of Web development. Technologies such as Active Server Pages and VB software components handle all processing on the Web server and deliver formatted HTML–only pages to the client for display in the browser. Traditionally, the Internet has been conceived as a world of fast, powerful Web servers and slow, weak clients that can do little more than point a browser to the Web server and make simple requests. As a result, the conventional wisdom has been to have the processing burden on the server, and to keep the client thin. This approach does have its advantages. For one, server-side logic provides for a low cost of ownership, because the files need only be updated in one location. Also, thin clients receive pure HTML, and so they are not dependent on the platform that the server-side logic is deployed on.

Yet today, several factors are changing the conventional wisdom that thin clients are better, namely:

➤ Powerful client computers (home and office PCs) are equipped with high-speed chips and large stores of RAM.

➤ Limitations on how much information can be exchanged over the Web are rapidly lifting because more people now have high-speed Internet access via technologies like 56K modems, cable access, and ISDN.

➤ Improved compression technologies for audio and video files means that more dynamic content can be delivered to clients in a reasonable amount of time.

➤ **Intranets**, which bring Internet technologies to local (LAN) and wide-area (WAN) networks, are an increasingly popular corporate solution for information storage and exchange. Intranet solutions rely on sharing the processing burden between server and clients.

The need for capable and responsive client machines has grown as Web applications have become more complex, and as the demand for dynamic, interactive content has increased. Significant delays, and even timeouts, frequently result if the client has to make too many calls back to the Web server. Even a simple, non-transactional page refresh can take quite a few seconds and so cause an undesirable user experience. One or more of the following factors potentially delays client requests:

> Delays at the proxy server;

> Delays due to limited bandwidth on phone lines;

> Delays at the Web server, especially at high-traffic sites. The delay here could also be at database and application servers that are behind the web server.

> Delays on one of the network nodes on route from one ISP to another.

Some client requests can only be handled by the Web server, such as resource-intensive database requests in an e-commerce application. However, the client more efficiently handles other kinds of requests. These include validating user input, formatting database requests (to the server), and handling user-interface details. This division of labor is integral to the concept of **n-tier application architecture**, which specifies that presentation services should be kept distinct from business and data access services.

In this chapter we'll introduce some of the exciting technologies that are pushing client-side Web development to the next level. These include:

> ActiveX Scripting (e.g. VBScript)

> Client-side ActiveX controls

> XML, for delivering structured data to the Web

> COM-enabled Scriptlets (XML and ActiveX Scripting)

The Intranet Revolution

Intranets are designed to allow organizations to share information and provide services to its employees. Intranet applications are developed using Internet technologies, but they are deployed on local- (LAN) or wide-area (WAN) networks instead of the World Wide Web. Intranets are developed using a browser/server architecture that shares the processing burden between the server and the client. Data services and business services are run on Web servers (sometimes tied to dedicated database servers). Presentation-services are managed on the client-side, and a browser is used to communicate between the client machine and the Web server application.

Intranets are a popular solution for large companies, and offer the following advantages:

> TCP/IP network protocol and HTTP server/browser protocol for fast, reliable communication.

> HTML for publishing information to the Corporate Enterprise. HTML requires a short learning curve and easily integrates with server-side technologies such as ASP and CGI, and other client-side technologies such as ActiveX Scripting.

> Browser-based application front-ends can be rapidly developed using HTML, ActiveX Scripting and ActiveX controls. (Chapter 5 shows you how to create custom ActiveX controls, in case you need to extend or supplant a commercial ActiveX control).

> Intranets centralize and organize information in a manner best suited to the organization. They enable a company's key information (often distributed all over the enterprise in a number of geographical areas) to be easily and quickly located and retrieved – thus avoiding the waste of this information not being exploited or having to be reinvented.

> Because the browser interface is a familiar environment for most users, they often find Intranet applications easy to learn. By fronting many different applications with a web browser, a user gets a consistent view of all corporate applications and data sources even though behind the scenes there may be many different technologies and interfaces in use.

> Well-designed Intranets offer a secure environment where users can trust the content they receive.

Developing applications for Intranets mirrors developing for the Web, but with more advantages. Intranet applications are developed for a restricted environment. Developers know in advance the processing capabilities of the server and client machines, and can optimize the application for the environment. This luxury is usually not afforded when developing for the Web, especially when catering to the mass market, where multiple browsers and versions must be supported. The exception is where you are providing a great service that lots of people want, such as a home banking application. In this case you can afford to restrict the supported browser to Internet Explorer 4, for example, and shut out those users who don't want to go along with the restriction.

The advantages of Intranets for developers are:

> Intranets usually use one standard browser, so developers need not worry about how their scripts will be interpreted by different browsers. Of course, it is possible to have two versions of the same vendor's browser in a large enterprise where users are gradually migrating from one version of a browser to another.

> A standard browser lets developers exploit the latest client features to the full they know what the browser can support. On the Web, where numerous browsers are used, developers have to support the lowest common denominator of capabilities. This often means restricting the site to using old or outdated technologies.

> Developers know in advance how much of the processing burden can be shared between server and clients, based on machine capabilities.

> Web development technologies such as HTML and ActiveX allow for rapid client-side development. Technologies like ASP and CGI provide for development on the server-side.

Client-side technologies are very important to Intranet development because Intranet client machines can typically handle a higher processing burden than Internet client machines. Client-side technologies greatly extend server-based applications by enabling the client to provide user services, such as a graphical interface and input validation. Client-side technologies also transfer some of the processing burden from the server to the client. In this chapter we'll discuss the technologies that are available for client-side development and get you well on your way to becoming an effective Web and Intranet developer.

ActiveX Scripting

ActiveX Scripting integrates a scripting language such as VBScript or JScript into a Web browser. ActiveX Scripting depends on a scripting host and a scripting engine. The scripting engine is an in-process ActiveX component that executes the script code. The scripting engine for VBScript, for example, is the component `vbscript.dll`. The Internet Explorer browser is referred to as the ActiveX scripting host, which is a platform for running the ActiveX scripting engine. When the browser encounters a `<SCRIPT>` section it checks the `LANGUAGE` attribute and looks for an appropriate registered engine on the client. The browser calls the engine, which executes the script and returns the result.

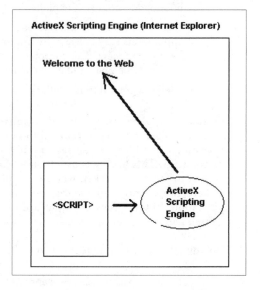

With ActiveX scripting, you can use any scripting language for which an engine is available and registered on the client. Visual Basic Scripting Edition (VBScript) is just one of several scripting languages, but it's the one we'll be covering in this chapter. VBScript is not an isolated technology, but a player in a larger framework.

Client-Side Scripting Using VBScript

Since its introduction almost three years ago, VBScript grew from a simple, lightweight interpreter with a basic collection of functions to a key player in advanced new client-side technologies like COM-enabled scriptlets and DHTML (both reviewed later in this chapter). VBScript is a subset of the Visual Basic for Applications (VBA) language, which finds wide use as a development language in products like Microsoft Word, Excel and Access. VBScript is designed to be lightweight, portable and secure. You won't find any File I/O functions in VBScript, nor can you use it to interact with the client machine's registry. You can't even make calls to API functions registered on the client, because all of these activities leave the client susceptible to file corruption, viruses and a host of other potential problems that we in the business generally classify as *bad news*. Be warned, however, that VBScript can invoke dangerous COM components that may have unwittingly been installed on the system.

What can I use VBScript for?

VBScript works alone, or in combination with other technologies to bring powerful functionality to the Web. The key uses for VBScript are:

- Validation of user input
- Scripting ActiveX Controls on a Web page
- With XML for creating COM-enabled scriptlets
- Scripting Active Server Pages (server-side only)
- In the Windows Script Host, to write macros that automate common tasks
- Scripting events in Microsoft Exchange

VBScript or JScript: Which one do I use?

This question can't be answered by touting one scripting language as being superior to the other. Your choice of scripting language really depends on your background, your personal preference, and your intended audience. As a Visual Basic programmer, you will presumably want to leverage your existing knowledge of VB into learning VBScript, which you can pick up in as little as a day. JScript, which is closer in syntax to C++, is Microsoft's implementation of the so-called ECMA scripting language standard that is set by a European standards association. JavaScript is Netscape's implementation of the ECMA standard. In short, JScript and JavaScript are two languages based on the same standard, but marketed by different companies.

If you want your Web pages to display properly in both the Internet Explorer and Netscape browsers, you should probably choose JavaScript for scripting, although VBScript is supported in Netscape via a third party plug-in, which you can download from `http://www.ncompasslabs.com`. This chapter focuses on using VBScript with Internet Explorer. Keep in mind that some of the technologies covered here, such as scriptlets and DHTML, will currently only work in Internet Explorer and many of the technologies specifically require version 5.0 of the browser; this is available for free download from Microsoft at `http://www.microsoft.com/windows/ie/download/default.asp`

Overview of VBScript

It is customary for a discussion of VBScript to commence with what VBA elements are *missing* in VBScript. In keeping with this tradition I give you the following table, which highlights important differences between VBA and VBScript. However, I prefer not to focus on the *missing* elements, because it leaves the reader with the impression that VBScript is a weak, watered-down language. In actuality, VBScript is a slim, lightweight language that is tailored to its special environment: the browser.

Category	VBA	VBScript
Arrays	Flexible array bounds. Option Base keyword.	Lower Array index only starts at zero.
Data Types	All data types available, including user-defined types.	No strict data types. Variants only.
Strings	Range of string functions.	VBScript has a superior range of string functions!
File I/O	Several File I/O functions.	No File I/O functions. Use Microsoft Scripting Library on the server-side for File I/O.
Collections	Flexible collection object.	Cannot use Add, Count, Item and Remove methods, but VBScript *can* iterate through collections of HTML and XML elements.
Objects	Flexible object creation.	Object creation is late-bound. Can define Classes as of VBScript 5.0. Supports CreateObject and GetObject for Automation.
System Objects	Screen, Printer, Err object.	Err object only.
Error Handling	Flexible error handling.	In-line error handling only with On Error Resume Next.

VBScript is embedded directly on a Web page using the `<SCRIPT>` tag, which for our purposes has a single LANGUAGE attribute that should be set to VBScript in order for the scripting host to reference the VBScript scripting engine. The general syntax for VBScript on a Web page is shown below, using a schematic example:

```
<HTML>
<HEAD>
<SCRIPT LANGUAGE="VBScript">
<!--
Dim MyGlobal
Sub MyPublicScript()
    ' Code goes here
End Sub
-->
</SCRIPT>
</HEAD>
<BODY>
<SCRIPT LANGUAGE="VBScript">
<!—
Sub window_onLoad()
    Call MyPrivateScript
End Sub
Sub MyPrivateScript()
    Call MyPublicScript
End Sub
```

```
      MsgBox "This code is worth $" & MyGlobal
-->
</SCRIPT>
</BODY>
<HTML>
```

VBScript code can be contained in procedures, as in `MyPrivateScript`, or it can be outside of any procedure, as the `MsgBox` function above illustrates. Procedures and variables that are included between `<HEAD>` tags take on a public scope and can be referenced by procedures between the `<BODY>` tags. Note that all variables in VBScript use the variant data type. No user-defined data types are allowed. This also applies to the interface of any DLL that you call from a script.

If you want to port your DLLs to VBScript, then ideally the interface should contain only variant arguments. You can bend the rules somewhat by using a small handful of strict data types as arguments, including String and Integer, but then you must apply the appropriate conversion function to any script variable that gets passed to the DLL. For example, consider the following function, taken from the `Arithmetic` class of `MathDLL`:

```
Public Function Multiply(ByVal intNum1 As Integer, ByVal varNum2 As Variant) As _
   Variant
     ' Calculate and return a result
End Function
```

This function gets called from a script as follows:

```
Dim objMath, Num1, Num2, Result
Num1 = 2
Num2 = 4

Set objMath = CreateObject("MathDLL.Arithmetic")

Result = objMath.Multiply(CInt(Num1),Num2)
```

Finally, you can use VBScript to script event procedures for HTML elements such as the `onLoad` event of a window element. In fact, Internet Explorer exposes an entire object model that can be manipulated programmatically using script (See Chapter 7). Later in this chapter we'll discuss how to use Scripting Wizard in the ActiveX Control Pad to script HTML elements. In Chapter 4 we discuss how to use DHTML to code against the Document Object Model that the browser also exposes.

VBScript does have some advantages over its full-featured cousin, VBA, most notably in the area of string manipulation. Some VBScript functions, such as `Filter` and `Join`, work directly with arrays. Whereas VBA requires you to loop through an array if you want to manipulate its elements, these VBScript functions accept the array directly, and handle the iterations for you behind the scenes.

For example, here is the `Filter` function:

```
Dim X
Dim Result(3)
X = Array("Wrox","Press","Books")
Result = Filter(X,"o") 'Result(0)="Wrox", Result(1)="Books"
```

The next table summarizes the useful string manipulation functions that were, until recently, only available in VBScript, and have been since version 2.0. However, if you have VBA 2000, then you now have access to all of these functions too. Seeing as not everyone will have the latest version, it still makes sense to include this table. Functions that accept or return arrays only deal in one-dimensional arrays. The table includes a "Nearest VBA Equivalent" column that gives you an idea of how much extra work is involved to duplicate these VBScript functions in VBA.

VBScript Function	Purpose	Nearest VBA Equivalent
Filter	Searches an array for all occurrences of a specified string. Returns an array.	Loop through each element of an array and apply InStr.
Join	Concatenates all elements of an array. Returns a string.	Loop through the array and concatenate each element in turn.
InStrRev	Works like InStr, except it will use the end of the string as the starting position for searches. It can also behave like InStr. Returns a position.	Use InStr to locate the search string, then subtract the position from the length of the string.
StrReverse	Reverse the order of characters in a string. Returns a string.	Reassemble the string while looping through it backwards.
Replace	Substitute a section of a string with another string. You can either explicitly specify the section to be replaced, or you can specify a starting position and a character count. Returns a string.	Use Mid, Left and Right functions to dissect the string, then concatenate preserved sections with the new section.
Split	Transform a single string with embedded delimiters into a one-dimensional array. Returns an array.	A reverse of the Array function. Lots of work to duplicate!

Although string manipulation functions are the most significant distinction between VBScript and older versions of VBA, there are others. VBScript now supports Regular Expressions, which take string matching to another level, as I will outline later in the chapter. For advanced file manipulation VBScript 5.0 also adds the Scripting Runtime Library, which has long been available with Active Server Pages. (I won't be discussing the Scripting Runtime Library here since it is only used for server-side scripting). Finally, VBScript has specialized formatting functions for currency and date/time (among others) to return formatted values that are localized to the server's regional system settings.

There are several excellent introductory references available for VBScript; there is also a VBScript Reference and a Tutorial in the appendices at the back of this book. You can also visit Microsoft's Scripting site for the most up-to-date VBScript language reference. With VBScript 5.0, the differences between VBA and VBScript have lessened. VBScript offers increased functionality and enhanced features, which I'll discuss next.

> **Microsoft's Scripting site is located at:**
> `http://msdn.microsoft.com/scripting`

New Features in VBScript 5.0

VBScript 5.0, which ships with Internet Explorer 5.0, takes a big leap ahead from its predecessors, bringing it up to par with JScript. VBScript 5.0 supports the following new features. The appendices at the back cover the core VBScript programming language but do not include the features below:

- ➢ Classes
- ➢ Regular Expressions
- ➢ Function-pointers
- ➢ `With...End With` statement execution
- ➢ Script Encoding

Classes

The new `Class` statement brings object-oriented capability to VBScript. Object-oriented design simplifies development by breaking complex code into simpler, smaller code components that encapsulate their logic behind a robust interface. Classes define both the interface and the implementation of the object. In Visual Basic, class definitions are contained in separate `.CLS` modules, but VBScript embeds the class definition directly on the Web page between opening and closing Class statements. Within these statements, you can define properties and methods as usual, using Public and Private statements, to distinguish public interface members from private ones. Properties can be defined using property procedures or public variables, while methods can be defined using regular procedures and functions.

There are some key differences between classes in Visual Basic versus VBScript. In Visual Basic, the interface details can be kept separate from the implementation by defining the interface in one class module, and then implementing this interface in another class module. This is not an option in VBScript. Also, Visual Basic classes can raise events, but VBScript classes cannot. VBScript classes can, however, raise errors using the `Error` object, which is useful for alerting the client to invalid input. Finally, VBScript does not support the `Friends` statement for interface members.

So what can you use classes for in VBScript? The most meaningful use is to create business objects that encapsulate business logic and validate user input. For example, you could create a business object that accepts input from an HTML form, validates it, and then performs some calculations. The form's submit button would invoke a method on a business object that assigns the input to properties and validates it in the process. If the input is valid, the object can proceed with the calculations; otherwise, the object can raise an error to the client that can be handled using an error trap.

Let's look at an example of a class called `SalaryCalculator` that calculates an adjusted salary using the inflation rate and a multiplier, which is simply a multiplication factor that is applied to the inflation rate. So if your employer really likes you, they could use this calculator to adjust your salary by 2 times inflation, where 2 is the multiplier:

```
<HTML>
<HEAD>
<SCRIPT LANGUAGE="VBScript">
<!--
Class SalaryCalculator
    Public IRate, IMultiplier
    Private varSalary

    Property Get Salary
        Salary = varSalary
    End Property

    Property Let Salary (varValue)
        If varValue >0 Then
            varSalary = varValue
        Else
            Err.Raise 6000, "salary", "Salary must be >$0."
        End If
    End Property

    Function NewSalary()
        NewSalary = varSalary*((1+(IRate*IMultiplier/100)))
    End Function
End Class
-->
</SCRIPT>
</HEAD>
```

The object interface has three properties and a single method. The properties are `Salary`, `IRate` and `IMultiplier`. The `Salary` property is implemented as a property procedure, while the other properties, for illustration purposes, are implemented as public variables. You should always use property procedures so that you can validate input and raise errors if necessary. Finally, the interface method is `NewSalary`, implemented as a public function, which is provided to calculate an adjusted salary.

The class definition is included in the `<HEAD>` section of the Web page to make it available to the entire Web page before the `<BODY>` section is interpreted. In the `<BODY>` section we create a `SalaryCalculator` object by setting an object variable reference to the class. Object references in VBScript are always late-bound, and you cannot use the As New syntax to create an object. The following code listing illustrates how to create and use the `SalaryCalculator` object using VBScript:

```
<BODY>
<SCRIPT LANGUAGE="VBScript">
<!--
Sub window_OnLoad()
    On Error Resume Next
    Dim y
    Set y = New SalaryCalculator
```

```
      y.Salary = 30000
      'Fixed values here, but you can retrieve them from an online form
      y.IRate = 4.0
      y.IMultiplier = 1.5
      If Err.Number <> 0 Then
          document.write "Error " & Err.Number & ": " & Err.Description & "<br>"
      Else
          document.write "Your current salary is " & FormatCurrency(y.Salary) & "<br>"
          document.write "The inflation rate is " & y.IRate & _
          "% and the multiplier is " & y.IMultiplier & "<br>"
          document.write "Your new salary is " & FormatCurrency(y.NewSalary)
      End If
  End Sub
  -->
  </SCRIPT>
  </BODY>
  </HTML>
```

The output to the Web page from this code listing is:

```
Your current salary is $30,000.00
The inflation rate is 4.0% and the multiplier is 1.5
Your new salary is $31,800.00
```

Error Handling in VBScript

Let's take a quick moment to discuss error handling in VBScript. As in Visual Basic, VBScript errors are exposed using the Err object, which is global in scope and does not need to be explicitly instanced. VBScript only provides in-line error handling, which means that you need to use On Error Resume Next to skip past the offending line. If you don't include this statement then a runtime error will halt execution of the script.

VBScript has no On Error Goto statement, so the error handling statements must be included with the regular code statements. As the example above illustrates, you should test the Number property of the Err object prior to running any calculations. If its value is anything other than zero, then you have an error and should take appropriate action. In this example, only the Salary property is validated. If an invalid value is assigned, then the property procedure raises an error, which changes the property values of the Error object, including the Number, Description and Source properties. Unlike with Visual Basic, this does not cause the interpreter to jump directly to an error handler, because technically, there is none.

Issues to Consider when Using Classes in VBScript

While classes are an exciting new addition to VBScript, you shouldn't use them without first considering whether it is wise to expose your class definitions to the outside world. If the class contains proprietary business logic then you should encapsulate the logic in a binary ActiveX component instead, and insert the component in the Web page. There are other advantages to using binary components. For one, they are created using languages like Visual Basic, which offer more functions to the developer than VBScript. Binary components are compiled and therefore more efficient for complex processing. Finally, you can add licensing and security certificates to a binary component, which is not an option for VBScript objects.

Regular Expressions

The new `RegExp` object brings the power of regular expressions to VBScript. Regular expression patterns are used to match an input string against a set of regular expression characters, which describe how the valid input string should look. If you've ever worked with input masks, then you've used regular expression patterns. For example, the pattern for an e-mail address like `president@whitehouse.gov`, is:

```
RegExp.Pattern = "\w+\@\w+\.\w+"
```

The `\w` mask matches any word, character or digit, including an underscore. Notice that placeholder text, such as the @ in an email address, is shown literally. The pattern for a phone number with area code, such as (610) 555-1212 is:

```
RegExp.Pattern = "\(\d{3}\)\s\d{3}\-\d{4}"
```

This example uses the `\d` mask for digits, and the `\s` mask for a space. Regular expressions help validate complex strings. You can see a full listing of special characters for patterns in the table below, which is adapted from the VBScript documentation.

Character	Description
\	Marks the next character as either a special character or a literal. For example, "n" matches the character "n". "\n" matches a newline character. The sequence "\\" matches "\" and "\(" matches "(".
^	Matches the first character of input.
$	Matches the last character of input.
*	Matches the preceding character zero or more times. For example, "zo*" matches either "z" or "zoo".
+	Matches the preceding character one or more times. For example, "zo+" matches "zoo" but not "z".
?	Matches the preceding character zero or one time. For example, "a?ve?" matches the "ve" in "never".
.	Matches any single character except a newline character.
(pattern)	Matches *pattern* and remembers the match. The matched substring can be retrieved from the resulting Matches collection, using `Item [0]...[n]`.
x|y	Matches either *x* or *y*. For example, "z|food" matches "z" or "food". "(z|f)ood" matches "zoo" or "food".

Character	Description
{n}	Matches exactly *n* times, where *n* is a nonnegative integer. For example, "p{1}" matches "pet" but not "happy".
{n,}	Matches at least *n* times, where *n* is a nonnegative integer. For example, "p{2,}" matches "happy" but not "pet".
{n,m}	Matches a character between *n* and *m* times, where *m*>n and *m* and *n* are nonnegative integers. For example, "C{2,3}" matches "ICCA" or "ICCCA" but not "ICA".
[xyz]	A character set. Matches any one of the enclosed characters. For example, "[abc]" matches the "a" in "plain".
[^xyz]	A negative character set. Matches any character not enclosed. For example, "[^abc]" matches the "p" in "plain".
[a-z]	A range of characters. Matches any character in the specified range. For example, "[a-z]" matches any lowercase alphabetic character in the range "a" through "z".
[^m-z]	A negative range of characters. Matches any character not in the specified range. For example, "[^m-z]" matches any character not in the range "m" through "z".
\b	Matches a word boundary, or, the position between a word and a space. For example, "er\b" matches the "er" in "never" but not the "er" in "verb".
\B	Matches a nonword boundary. "ea*r\B" matches the "ear" in "never early".
\d	Matches a digit character. Equivalent to [0-9].
\D	Matches a nondigit character. Equivalent to [^0-9].
\f	Matches a form-feed character.
\n	Matches a newline character.
\r	Matches a carriage return character.
\s	Matches any white space including space, tab, form-feed, etc.
\S	Matches any nonwhite space character.
\t	Matches a tab character.
\v	Matches a vertical tab character.
\w	Matches any word character or digit, including underscore.
\W	Matches any nonword character. Equivalent to "[^A-Za-z0-9_]".
\num	Matches *num*, where *num* is a positive integer. A reference back to remembered matches. For example, "(.)\1" matches two consecutive identical characters.

Here is an example of the `RegExp` object using its `Test` method:

```vbscript
<SCRIPT LANGUAGE="VBScript">
<!--
Sub window_onLoad()
    Dim email, phone
    email="president@whitehouse.gov"
    phone="(610) 555-1212"
    Call Validate(email,"\w+\@\w+\.\w+")
    Call Validate(phone,"\(\d{3}\)\s\d{3}\-\d{4}")
End Sub

Sub Validate(Input,Patrn)
    Dim TestExp
    Set TestExp = New RegExp
    TestExp.Pattern = Patrn
    TestExp.IgnoreCase = True
    If TestExp.Test(Input) Then
        MsgBox Input & " is VALID"
    Else
        MsgBox Input & " is INVALID"
    End If
End Sub
-->
</SCRIPT>
```

Pattern matches are executed using one of three methods of the `RegExp` object, which are:

- Test
- Replace
- Execute

The **Test** method uses the search string as an argument and returns `True` or `False`, depending if a valid match is found. The **Replace** method accepts two arguments, the search string and a replacement string. If a valid match is found, then the method returns the modified string; otherwise, it returns the original search string. Note that VBScript provides its own `Replace` function for substituting one string into another. This function is relatively inflexible, in that only a specific substring can be replaced, such as "blue" for "red". On the other hand, the method that is provided by the `RegExp` object allows you to substitute directly into a regular expression pattern match. For example, all e-mail matches in a sentence can be located by their regular expression pattern, and then substituted.

The properties of the `RegExp` object are:

- Pattern
- IgnoreCase
- Global

The three properties define the settings for how a regular expression search gets conducted. The **Pattern** property sets the regular expression pattern, as shown in the examples above. The **Global** property is a Boolean that sets whether the regular expression matches multiple occurrences of the expression (True), or just the first occurrence (False). By default, the Global property is True. Finally, the **IgnoreCase** property is another Boolean that sets whether the match is case-sensitive (True) or case-insensitive (False).

The Match Object and the Matches Collection

The **Execute** method of the RegExp object returns a special object called a **Match** object, which holds read-only properties that describe the results of the match. The properties of the Match object are:

➤ FirstIndex
➤ Length
➤ Value

The **FirstIndex** property holds the starting character of the match in the string. The **Length** property holds the matched string length in characters, and the **Value** property holds the actual matched string. The Execute method also creates a Matches collection object, which holds all of the Match objects that result from a single search. You need to set the Global property of the RegExp object to True in order to get more than one match in a search string.

Here is an example of the Match object and Matches collection object:

```
<SCRIPT LANGUAGE="VBScript">
<!--
Sub Match()
    Dim TestExp, Match, Matches, Result, I
    I=0
    Set TestExp = New RegExp
    TestExp.Pattern = "\w+\@\w+\.\w+"
    TestExp.IgnoreCase = True
    TestExp.Global = True
    Set Matches = TestExp.Execute("Write to: jeff@duke.edu or jeff@ucsc.edu")
    For Each Match in Matches
        I=I+1
        Result = Result & "Match " & I & " (Position "
        Result = Result & Match.FirstIndex & ") = "
        Result = Result & Match.Value & "<br>"
    Next
    document.writeln Result
End Sub
-->
</SCRIPT>
```

The code listing begins by declaring a new RegExp object called TestExp then defining its properties. The regular expression pattern is set for an e-mail address. Once these properties are set, the Execute method gets called with a string argument that contains two e-mail addresses. Recall that the Execute method returns a Matches collection, which in this example will contain two items, one for each e-mail address in the string.

The code returns this output:

```
Match 1 (Position 10) = jeff@duke.edu
Match 2 (Position 27) = jeff@ucsc.edu
```

Function Pointers

In keeping with the dynamic, event-driven nature of the Web, VBScript introduces function pointers, which are designed to work with the event handlers of DHTML objects in the Internet Explorer object model, such as the `window` and `form` objects. Using the `GetRef` function, you can assign a procedure directly to the event handler of a DHTML object. The alternative is that you would have to create a procedure for each event handler, which takes a minimum of three lines of code, with implementation. However, a function pointer sets the reference in a single line.

The following code sample illustrates no less than three function pointers for a Web page with a single command button. The pointers operate on the window `load` and `unload` events, and on the button `Click` event:

```
<HTML>
<HEAD>
<TITLE>GetRef Example</TITLE>
<SCRIPT LANGUAGE="VBScript">
<!--
    Sub LoadPointer()
       MsgBox "Loading  " & document.title, 64, "Loading Web Page"
    End Sub
    Sub UnloadPointer()
       MsgBox "Unloading  " & document.title, 64, "Unloading Web Page"
    End Sub
    Sub ClickPointer()
       MsgBox "Current Form:     " & document.forms(0).name & Chr(13) & _
          "Current Button:   " & document.forms(0).elements(0).name, 64, _
          "Web Page Info"
       End Sub
       set window.onload = GetRef("LoadPointer")
       set window.onunload = GetRef("UnloadPointer")
-->
</SCRIPT>
</HEAD>
<BODY>
<FORM NAME="InputForm">
   <INPUT NAME="cmdSubmit" TYPE="submit" VALUE="Submit Request">
   <SCRIPT LANGUAGE="VBScript">
<!--
       set InputForm.onsubmit = GetRef("ClickPointer")
-->
   </SCRIPT>

   </FORM>
</BODY>
</HTML>
```

With Statement

The `With` statement allows you to set a reference to an object once, and then make subsequent calls to its interface without continually specifying the object name. This gives script performance a boost by reducing the number of times the scripting engine has to make calls to reference the object's type library. Here is an example, using the Err object:

```
<SCRIPT LANGUAGE="VBScript">
<!--
    With Err
        If .Number <> 0 Then
            document.write "Error " & .Number & ": " & .Description & "<br>"
        End If
    End With
-->
</SCRIPT>
```

Script Encoding

Many of us learned about scripting languages and some clever techniques by viewing the source code of Web pages we find exceptionally interesting. However, many Web developers prefer not to share the fruits of their labor so easily with the outside world. The stakes are higher with scriptlets, which are components that are implemented using script. Component architectures are often proprietary in nature and need to be protected.

Script encoding transforms scriptlets, HTML, and ASP scripts into an unreadable hash that includes a calculated *check sum*, to ensure the integrity of the script. If anyone tries to alter the encoded script, then the check sum will not match the script, and it will fail to load in the browser. Internet Explorer 5.0 can interpret encoded scripts directly, although earlier versions of the browser cannot. Script is marked for encoding by setting the LANGUAGE attribute of the script in the HTML page to `<SCRIPT LANGUAGE = VBSCRIPT.ENCODE>`.

For encoding, Microsoft provides a command-line utility called **Windows Script Encoder** (Version 1.0) that is available for download from Microsoft's Windows Script Technologies site, at `http://msdn.microsoft.com/scripting/`. After downloading the executable, `sce10en.exe`, double-click on its icon to un-bundle the documentation and to add the utility to `C:\Program Files\Windows Script Encoder\screnc.exe`.

To encode a script:

Move the script into the same directory as the utility (unless you add the directory to the PATH variable in `AutoExec.bat`). Let's assume that the script is embedded along with regular HTML in a page called `Scrpt.htm`.

> Open an MS-DOS command prompt, navigate to the directory, and type the following at the command line: `screnc Scrpt.htm EncScrpt.htm` or
> `screnc /f Scrpt.htm`

The first syntax will create a separate file for the encoded script, while the second syntax will overwrite the original file. The script encoder will encode scripting code only, and plain text will be left untouched. Microsoft recommends that you add a plain-text copyright message to the top of your scripts to further deter would-be pirates.

As a final note of caution, bear in mind that encoding is not the same as encrypting. Encoding makes life a little bit awkward for the casual viewer but it won't stop those that really want to view the scripting from finding a way to do so. Source encoding is not as reliable as the binary protection provided by ActiveX controls. If the security of your script is of major concern, you might want to consider an alternative approach, such as using server-side scripts, or encapsulating the script's business logic inside a binary ActiveX control.

Handling Different Versions of VBScript

The new features available in VBScript 5.0 may be exciting, but only Internet Explorer 5.0 users (and later) are guaranteed to be running the latest scripting engine. Unfortunately, it takes time for everyone to install the latest version of a new browser. Older versions of Internet Explorer are also compatible with VBScript 5.0 as long as the client has installed the latest version of the scripting engine. Otherwise, VBScript compilation errors (pop-up message boxes) will occur if an older browser attempts to load a page with newer script features, such as an embedded Class definition. At best, the rest of the page will load smoothly after the initial error. At worst, critical business logic will fail to load, and the user will be left with a completely non-working page.

If there is any doubt about which browser version your user has, which is everywhere except in a controlled Intranet setting, then you should refrain from using statements that may fail in earlier browsers. This makes life less interesting, because the new VBScript features extend the scripting language in powerful ways. You could put some code in the onLoad() event of the script window that detects what scripting engine the user has installed. If the VBScript version is older than 5.0, you could display a message alerting the user, and then perform a redirection or otherwise. Here is an example code listing:

```
<SCRIPT LANGUAGE="VBScript">
<!--
Sub window_onLoad()
    If ScriptEngineMajorVersion < 5 Then
        MsgBox "You are using an old version of VBScript." & _
            vbCrLf & "Please download the new version before proceeding.", _
                vbExclamation
        window.Navigate("http://msdn.microsoft.com/scripting/")
    Else
        MsgBox "You are using: " & ScriptEngineVersion, vbInformation
    End If
End Sub

Function ScriptEngineVersion()
    Dim s
    s = "" ' Build string with necessary info.
    s = ScriptEngine & " Version "
    s = s & ScriptEngineMajorVersion & "."
    s = s & ScriptEngineMinorVersion & "."
    ScriptEngineVersion = s 'Return the version.
```

```
End Function
-->
</SCRIPT>
```

Using the Microsoft Script Debugger

As Visual Basic developers, we are accustomed to an integrated development environment (IDE) that provides responsive, informative tools for debugging. These tools include:

> - Breakpoints
> - Watch Expressions
> - Step-wise compilation

The Microsoft Script Debugger is a plug-in for Internet Explorer that provides the same set of familiar debugging tools for your scripting languages, and works with both VBScript and JScript. The Script Debugger not only helps you find bugs, but it's a great learning tool, because you can step through scripts a line at a time and can examine the script behavior at an easy pace.

The Script Debugger is available for download from Microsoft's Windows Script Technologies site. When you install the Script Debugger, it becomes integrated with Internet Explorer. There are two ways to launch the Script Debugger from Internet Explorer:

> - Click on View | Script Debugger | Open
> - Click on View | Script Debugger | Break at Next Statement

Alternatively, you can insert a `Stop` statement in the VBScript code, which launches the Debugger and breaks execution of the script. If your script generates an error during execution, Internet Explorer will prompt you with a dialog box that reports the error and asks if you want to debug the script. If you agree, the Script Debugger will launch into debug mode. Refreshing the script page prompts the debugger to ask you if you want to reload the page into the Debugger. If you want to continue debugging, then respond with "Yes" (you will lose any prior debugging information).

The figures below show what happens when you try and execute the last script example for handling different versions of VBScript. Before re-running the script, I edited the `If` function so that it now reads `Iff`. On loading the script, the following dialog box pops up:

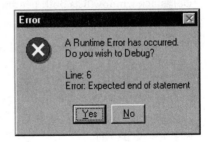

On clicking "Yes", the Microsoft Script Debugger launches, as shown below:

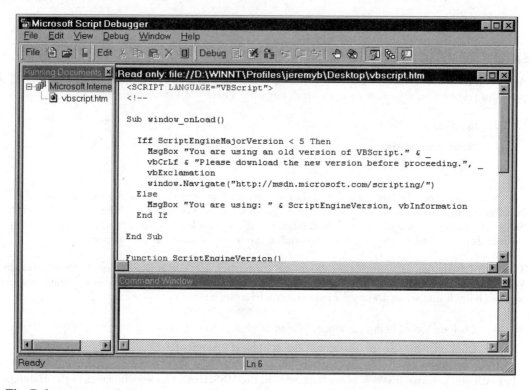

The Debugger provides menus and toolbars for accessing its debugging functions. A "Running Documents" pane shows all of the Internet Explorer windows currently open, and also shows what scripts are running. The actual script code is displayed in its own code pane. The Immediate window, or Command Window as it is called here when shown, is also available for you to query variables and execute code, just like you're used to doing in Visual Basic's IDE. Finally, (though not shown), the Call stack window lists both pending and previously called procedures in descending order in the window.

The Debug menu provides the following options:

> Continue
> Break at Next Statement
> Step Into
> Step Over
> Step Out

> ➤ Toggle Breakpoint
> ➤ Clear All Breakpoints
> ➤ Show Next Statement

The file in the Script Debugger is read-only, so once you have detected your error and are ready to fix it, open your script in an editing environment and make the change. If the Debugger is still open, it will prompt you to refresh the script. Alternatively, you can close the Debugger before editing your script, and just hope that you've caught all the errors.

If you have Visual InterDev installed, then you don't need to install the Script Debugger, because Visual InterDev will serve the same function as the Debugger. Visual InterDev is an all-around superior and much more versatile product. However, the Script Debugger is free and easy to install, which makes it a welcome addition for your Web development environment.

Introducing XML and Scriptlets

Extensible Markup Language (XML) is a new standard for describing and delivering structured data to the Web. XML is a subset of Standardized General Markup Language (SGML), which means that it uses a tag-based syntax. Whereas HTML uses tags to *display* data, XML uses tags to *describe* data. Also, while HTML uses fixed tags only, XML uses tags that are entirely custom-defined. Hence, the XML language is referred to as *extensible*. The important features of XML are:

> ➤ XML data is self-describing
> ➤ XML is extensible
> ➤ XML separates data structure from display
> ➤ XML allows granular updates

If you are looking for a detailed introduction to XML, this chapter will disappoint you, because our interest in XML is limited to the role it plays in constructing **scriptlets**, which are COM-enabled components for the Web created with XML and an ActiveX Scripting language. For detailed information on XML, see chapter 16 or visit Microsoft's Web site at `http://msdn.microsoft.com/xml`.

The Bare Essentials of XML

Let's look at a simple example of an XML script called `object.xml`, which describes the structure of the Visual Basic Error object:

```
<XML ID="ObjectModel" TYPE="text/xml">
<object-browser>
   <object>
      <name>ErrObject</name>
      <properties>
         <property>Description </property>
         <property>Number</property>
         <property>Source</property>
         <property>HelpContext</property>
         <property>HelpFile</property>
      </properties>
      <methods>
         <method>Raise</method>
         <method>Clear</method>
      </methods>
   </object>
</object-browser>
</XML>
```

The simplicity of the script is striking, and you will notice how clearly the hierarchical nature of the Error object model comes through. The unique tag names make it very easy to understand what each data element is, and how it relates to others in the hierarchy. An XML script like this one can be embedded directly in a web page, where it is referred to as a **data island**.

The XML model allows developers to create an unlimited number of custom tags to describe their data. Because XML does not dictate how the data should be displayed, the client has complete control over what data gets viewed and in what format. XML is an excellent means of delivering data from a server to a client. Once the data is on the client desktop, client-side scripts can dynamically display the data in different views without having to make repeated calls to the server.

There are several options for displaying XML data in the browser. Style sheets can be used to assign a custom style to each element in the XML object model. Here is an example of a style sheet called `objstyle.css`:

```
object {display:block;
   font-size:18pt;
   font-family:Arial;
   color:blue;
   text-align:left
   }
properties {
   font-size:14pt;
   font-family:Arial;
   color:black;
   text-align:left;
   }
methods {
   font-size:14pt;
   font-family:Arial;
   color:green;
   text-align:left;
   }
```

The style sheet is linked to the XML file by adding a style definition at the top of the XML file, as in:

```
<?xml:stylesheet href="objStyle.css" type="text/css" ?>
<XML ID="ObjectModel" TYPE="text/xml">
<object-browser>
```

Internet Explorer 5.0 is able to natively parse and display XML, so you can point this browser directly to an XML file to display it. In the case of `object.xml`, using the style sheet, the browser should display the following text:

ErrObject Description Number Source HelpFile HelpContext Raise Clear

This will probably not win any creative awards, even with the color differences you'd see on your browser, but it does illustrate the distinction between XML definition versus display. If no style sheet is specified, then the browser will display a collapsible tree-view of the XML definition that looks just like the `object.xml` code listing.

Another option for displaying XML is with Internet Explorer's Document Object Model. XML data islands are included in the document object model of the Web page, so you can use DHTML to traverse through a data island with script in the same way that you would iterate through other document elements. In the future we can expect to see new tools that will facilitate publishing XML to the Web.

This concludes our brief introduction to XML. Although you won't yet be an XML expert, you've seen enough to understand the role that XML plays in constructing scriptlets.

Scriptlets: Components for the Web

`Scriptlets` are COM-enabled, custom components designed for the Web. They are intended to bring to the Web the advantages of component-based development. As COM objects, scriptlets can provide the same services that other COM objects provide, such as Automation. There are actually two kinds of scriptlets, and it's important for you to understand the distinction between them:

➢ `DHTML Scriptlets` are user-interface components written in DHTML. With the release of Internet Explorer 5.0, Microsoft now recommends that you use `DHTML behaviors` in place of scriptlets. For more on DHTML behaviors please see Chapter 6.

➢ `Scriptlets` are general-purpose components for the Web, written in XML and ActiveX script. This is the type of scriptlet we will be discussing here.

How To Write a Scriptlet

Scriptlets are analogous to class modules in Visual Basic, which serve as blueprints for creating objects. Class modules contain:

➢ A definition of the object's interface

➢ Code implementation of the interface members.

We've seen how useful XML is for defining data structures. XML is used in a scriptlet to define the interface, while ActiveX scripting is used to code the interface implementation and business logic.

Scriptlets usually contain four XML elements:

> The <scriptlet> element, which encloses the scriptlet definition (i.e., the following three elements in this list).

> The <registration> element, which contains information for registering your scriptlet, such as the ProgID.

> The <implements> element, which specifies the COM interfaces that the scriptlet implements. For example, if the scriptlet needs to provide Automation services, then it implements the Automation handler. The interface definition is contained within the <implements> tags.

> The <script> element encloses ActiveX scripting code that implements the scriptlet's interface and the business logic.

By now we're familiar with the SalaryCalculator example from earlier in the chapter. We first introduced this example using plain vanilla VBScript. Later, we coded SalaryCalculator as a VBScript class. Now we will create a third incarnation by coding SalaryCalculator as a scriptlet.

The code listing is:

```
<SCRIPTLET>

<REGISTRATION PROGID="SalaryCalculator.Scriptlet">
</REGISTRATION>

<IMPLEMENTS ID=AUTOMATION TYPE=AUTOMATION>
    <PROPERTY NAME=SALARY INTERNALNAME=VARSALARY>
        <GET/>
        <PUT/>
    </PROPERTY>
    <METHOD NAME=NEWSALARY>
        <PARAMETER NAME=IRate/>
        <PARAMETER NAME=IMultiplier/>
    </METHOD>
</IMPLEMENTS>

<SCRIPT LANGUAGE="VBSCRIPT">

Private varSalary

function get_Salary()
    Salary=varSalary
end function

function put_Salary(varValue)
  If varValue >0 Then
     varSalary = varValue
  Else
     Err.Raise 6000, "salary", "Salary must be >$0."
  End If
end function

function NewSalary(IRate,IMultiplier)
    NewSalary = varSalary*((1+(IRate*IMultiplier/100)))
end function
```

```
</SCRIPT>
</SCRIPTLET>
```

The code listing for the scriptlet should look quite familiar to you except for some syntax differences. The first section of the code defines the component's interface, with `<PUT>` and `<GET>` tags used in place of `Property Let` and `Property Get` statements. The second section of the code contains VBScript to implement the interface. In the next section we look at how to download and use scriptlets in web pages.

Using the Scriptlet

The scriptlet is available to be called from a Web page once it has been downloaded. Scriptlets are subject to the same security restrictions that ActiveX controls are subject to. For example, a Medium security setting in Internet Explorer will ensure that the user is prompted before the scriptlet is downloaded. Here is a simple Web page that uses the `SalaryCalculator` scriptlet:

```
<HTML>
<HEAD>
<TITLE> SalaryCalculator Scriptlet </TITLE>
</HEAD>

<OBJECT ID="SalaryCalculator" TYPE="text/x-scriptlet" WIDTH=300 HEIGHT=200>
    <PARAM NAME="url" VALUE="http://myserver/SalaryCalculator.sct"></OBJECT>
```

```
<BODY>

<SCRIPT LANGUAGE="VBScript">
<!--
Sub window_OnLoad()

On Error Resume Next

Dim MyInflation, MyMultiplier

SalaryCalculator.Salary = 30000
MyInflation=5.0
MyMultiplier=1.5

If Err.Number <> 0 Then
    document.write "Error " & Err.Number & ": " & Err.Description & "<br>"
Else
    document.write "Your current salary is " &
FormatCurrency(SalaryCalculator.Salary) & _ "<br>"
    document.write "The inflation rate is " & MyInflation & "% and the multiplier
is " & _
        MyMultiplier & "<br>"
    document.write "Your new salary is " & _
FormatCurrency(SalaryCalculator.NewSalary(MyInflation, _
        MyMultiplier))
End If

End Sub
```

```
   -->
   </SCRIPT>

   </BODY>
   </HTML>
```

It can get tedious to type a scriptlet, so you may want to download the Microsoft Scriptlet Wizard, which lets you add interface members and their parameters. The Wizard will generate the scriptlet interface definition for you, but you will have to add the ActiveX scripting yourself. This wraps up our discussion of scriptlets. Go forth and create components!

Using ActiveX Controls on the Client

For serious added functionality to your Web page, you will want to use ActiveX controls. Although HTML and VBScript together can accomplish plenty, they do not match the sophistication of an ActiveX control, nor do they provide the same robustness. Client-side scripts have no access to the client's system files, whereas a registered ActiveX control potentially does. From a security perspective this may not be a good thing, but from a functionality perspective it is. Clients can take precautions to protect themselves from potentially damaging ActiveX controls. Chapter 5 covers ActiveX controls in detail, and reviews digital signing, which is a way of certifying that a control is from a trusted source and is safe to use.

Scripts do not protect their proprietary business logic as well as ActiveX controls. (Although even binary components can be reverse engineered by determined hackers to display their business logic). Script encoding in Internet Explorer 5.0 goes some way toward solving this problem, but it is not the most secure way to protect your source code. With ActiveX controls, you have many more options for protecting your intellectual property, including licensing. In addition, ActiveX controls are compiled, binary components, so the source code is not available for viewing.

In this section we will discuss how ActiveX Controls are included in a Web page. We will focus on using the ActiveX Control Pad for adding controls to a Web page. Like the Script Debugger, this tool is available for free, and works with controls in a similar fashion to its more sophisticated cousin, Visual InterDev. The Control Pad also provides a Script Wizard that makes it easy to add script to client-side ActiveX controls. This section introduces tools and concepts that will be explored further in Chapter 5.

ActiveX Out of the Box

As Visual Basic developers, we work with ActiveX controls all the time, and many of us regularly create custom controls to develop an application. ActiveX controls are reusable software components that expose a custom interface that can be manipulated programmatically. The Visual Basic Toolbox contains several intrinsic ActiveX controls that are included in Visual Basic's runtime library. The Label, PictureBox and CommandButton controls are all examples of intrinsic controls.

Visual Basic also ships with additional ActiveX controls, which are packaged in separate binary files with .OCX extensions. Many more controls ship with Visual Basic, and can be accessed from the Project | Components menu, including the **Calendar Control** and the **Microsoft Chart Control**. Some .OCX files actually contain a package of controls, such as **Microsoft Windows Common Controls 5.0** (COMCTL32.OCX), which contains eight ActiveX controls, including the TabStrip, ToolBar, StatusBar, ProgressBar, TreeView, ListView, ImageList and Slider controls.

There are many excellent ActiveX components available for use on the desktop and the Web. You can find a good selection of components in the ActiveX Gallery at http://www.microsoft.com/gallery/activex. If this selection of controls does not meet your development needs, you can find many third-party ActiveX controls available on the market. These controls are usually reasonably priced and can save you hours of development time. You also can develop your own ActiveX control. Chapter 5 outlines how to write your own ActiveX components using Visual Basic.

Hosting ActiveX Controls on a Web Page

ActiveX controls enrich static Web pages with dynamic content and improve the quality and ease-of-use of the interface that the clients see in their browser. ActiveX controls are not designed to function as stand-alone components. Instead, they must function inside a host **container**, which is any environment that implements COM and can support ActiveX controls. Examples of containers include forms in Visual Basic projects, and the Internet Explorer browser. So it should come as no surprise that many ActiveX controls function equally well on the desktop and on the Web. Each environment simply represents a different kind of host container for the control.

ActiveX components may be integrated into a Web page in one of two ways:

Directly into an HTML page using the <OBJECT> tag, for example:

```
<OBJECT CLASSID="3HGSD-000X-C10000A"
        ID="MyCalendar"
        CODEBASE="http://www.microsoft.com>
</OBJECT>
```

Or using a scripting language such as VBScript's CreateObject method:

```
CreateObject("Organizer.Calendar")
```

The HTML <OBJECT> tag's many attributes provide detailed specifications for how the Web page hosts the ActiveX control. There are attributes for everything from the control's registry GUID to coordinates that specify where the control is placed on the page. The attributes of the <OBJECT> tag are summarized in the table below:

Attribute	Description
ID	Equivalent to the Name property of the ActiveX control. It is the name that will be used to script the object and set/call its properties and methods.
CLASSID	The global unique identifer (GUID) that identifies a registered ActiveX control. The GUID is used to instance an ActiveX class.
CODEBASE	The URL location from where the browser can download the component, if it does not already exist on the client machine. The CODEBASE optionally contains a version number for the control.
DATA	Specifies a file that is used by the ActiveX control. For example, a Multimedia control uses .avi (video) and .wav (audio) files.
NAME	This attribute identifies the control if it exists inside a <FORM> and is submitted in the HTTP method.
STANDBY	Text that identifies the ActiveX control while it is downloading or instancing.
ALIGN	Specifies the placement of the ActiveX control on the Web page. Align Values include: Baseline, Center, Left, Middle, Right, TextBottom, TextMiddle and TextTop.
HEIGHT, WIDTH	Height and Width parameters in pixels.
BORDER, HSPACE, VSPACE	Border width and padding parameters.

The Internet Download Service

The **Internet Download Service** (IDS) is the process by which ActiveX controls are downloaded to a client machine and registered. When the browser opens a Web page and encounters an <OBJECT> tag, it uses the value of the CLASSID attribute to determine whether the component is already registered on the client machine, and if the version is up to date. If the ActiveX control is not found, or if it is out of date, then a new version of the control needs to be downloaded to the client machine.

The specific steps of the IDS are as follows:

> The browser encounters an <OBJECT> tag.

> The browser reads the CLASSID attribute (GUID) and checks the Windows Registry to determine if the control is already registered on the client machine, and if it is the correct version. To enable version checking, the CODEBASE attribute should contain the version information appended to the URL, as in:

```
<OBJECT
  CODEBASE=www.microsoft.com/jeff.cab#version=1,0,0,2
  ...
/OBJECT>
```

> If the control is not already registered, or if the version must be updated, then the browser makes a call to the Windows API function called GoGetClassObjectFromURL. The control's CODEBASE information is passed in the function call. The function will asynchronously download the control and register it to the client machine. (Here is a trick: You can set #version equal to -1,-1,-1,-1 to ensure that the ActiveX control is downloaded and re-registered every time the <OBJECT> tag is encountered by the browser. This ensures that you are always using the most current version of the control).

You will face potential security risks when downloading ActiveX controls from the Web, because the controls must be registered to a client machine. The IDS does not check whether the downloaded control is certified as safe. By "safe" we mean that the control comes from a trusted source and that it will not corrupt the client machine in any way. Safety screening is provided by the browser, which uses security certificates and digital certificates to screen for potentially damaging controls. This technology is discussed in further detail in Chapter 5.

Using the ActiveX Control Pad

ActiveX Controls are usually not useful until activated by setting properties and calling methods on the control. You can manipulate ActiveX Controls both at design-time (using property pages, for example) and at run-time (using script). The **ActiveX Control Pad** makes it easy for you to work with ActiveX controls, and allows you to:

> Insert ActiveX controls on a Web page

> Set properties at design–time

> Add script to manipulate the control at run-time.

The ActiveX Control Pad is available for download at:
http://msdn.microsoft.com/workshop/misc/cpad/default.asp

> To illustrate the ActiveX Control Pad, we will create a simple front-end to the SalaryCalculator class listed earlier. You will design the front-end using Microsoft Forms 2.0 ActiveX controls, which ship with Internet Explorer, and are a group of familiar user interface controls, such as textboxes and command buttons. We will use the Script Wizard to implement code in the event procedures raised by the controls.

Install the ActiveX Control Pad and run it from the Programs menu. The Control Pad opens to a new HTML page.

Select Edit | Insert ActiveX Control. You will see a dialog box with a list of available ActiveX controls:

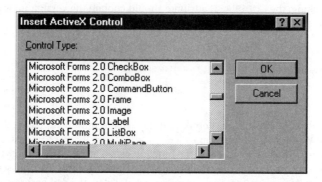

Insert a `CommandButton` control, and you will see the following entry in the HTML pane:

```
<OBJECT ID="cmdOK" CLASSID="CLSID:D7053240-CE69-11CD-A777-00DD01143C57"
    STYLE="TOP:94pt;LEFT:94pt;WIDTH:78pt;HEIGHT:16pt;TABINDEX:5;ZINDEX:5;">
        <PARAM NAME="Caption" VALUE="Calculate">
        <PARAM NAME="Size" VALUE="2752;564">
        <PARAM NAME="FontCharSet" VALUE="0">
        <PARAM NAME="FontPitchAndFamily" VALUE="2">
        <PARAM NAME="ParagraphAlign" VALUE="3">
        <PARAM NAME="FontWeight" VALUE="0">
</OBJECT>
```

Next, you should see a blue cube in the left margin of the code pane next to this code listing. If you click on this cube it will bring up the control in design-time view with its property sheet. You can set the properties here, just like in Visual Basic.

Insert two textboxes, a command button and descriptive labels, so that the layout resembles this screenshot:

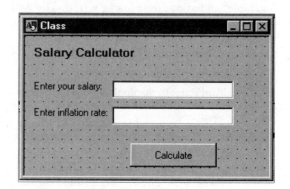

The final HTML code listing for the remaining controls (excluding the `CommandButton` control) appears below. You can read the property settings for each control directly from this listing. If we were writing this code in straight HTML, we would need to use tables to align the controls. But by using ActiveX controls, we can specify the dimensions directly in the `<OBJECT>` tag.

```
<BODY>
<OBJECT ID="Label1"
     CLASSID="CLSID:978C9E23-D4B0-11CE-BF2D-00AA003F40D0"
STYLE="TOP:8pt;LEFT:8pt;WIDTH:94pt;HEIGHT:16pt;ZINDEX:0;">
        <PARAM NAME="Caption" VALUE="Salary Calculator">
        <PARAM NAME="Size" VALUE="3316;564">
        <PARAM NAME="FontEffects" VALUE="1073741825">
        <PARAM NAME="FontHeight" VALUE="200">
        <PARAM NAME="FontCharSet" VALUE="0">
        <PARAM NAME="FontPitchAndFamily" VALUE="2">
        <PARAM NAME="FontWeight" VALUE="700">
    </OBJECT>
    <OBJECT ID="Label2"
     CLASSID="CLSID:978C9E23-D4B0-11CE-BF2D-00AA003F40D0"
STYLE="TOP:39pt;LEFT:8pt;WIDTH:70pt;HEIGHT:16pt;ZINDEX:1;">
        <PARAM NAME="Caption" VALUE="Enter your salary:">
        <PARAM NAME="Size" VALUE="2469;564">
        <PARAM NAME="FontCharSet" VALUE="0">
        <PARAM NAME="FontPitchAndFamily" VALUE="2">
        <PARAM NAME="FontWeight" VALUE="0">
    </OBJECT>
    <OBJECT ID="Label3"
     CLASSID="CLSID:978C9E23-D4B0-11CE-BF2D-00AA003F40D0"
STYLE="TOP:62pt;LEFT:8pt;WIDTH:70pt;HEIGHT:16pt;ZINDEX:2;">
        <PARAM NAME="Caption" VALUE="Enter inflation rate:">
        <PARAM NAME="Size" VALUE="2469;564">
        <PARAM NAME="FontCharSet" VALUE="0">
        <PARAM NAME="FontPitchAndFamily" VALUE="2">
        <PARAM NAME="FontWeight" VALUE="0">
    </OBJECT>
    <OBJECT ID="TxtSalary"
     CLASSID="CLSID:8BD21D10-EC42-11CE-9E0D-00AA006002F3"
STYLE="TOP:39pt;LEFT:78pt;WIDTH:109pt;HEIGHT:16pt;TABINDEX:3;ZINDEX:3;">
        <PARAM NAME="VariousPropertyBits" VALUE="746604571">
        <PARAM NAME="Size" VALUE="3845;564">
        <PARAM NAME="FontCharSet" VALUE="0">
        <PARAM NAME="FontPitchAndFamily" VALUE="2">
        <PARAM NAME="FontWeight" VALUE="0">
    </OBJECT>
    <OBJECT ID="TxtIRate"
     CLASSID="CLSID:8BD21D10-EC42-11CE-9E0D-00AA006002F3"
STYLE="TOP:62pt;LEFT:78pt;WIDTH:109pt;HEIGHT:16pt;TABINDEX:4;ZINDEX:4;">
        <PARAM NAME="VariousPropertyBits" VALUE="746604571">
        <PARAM NAME="Size" VALUE="3845;564">
        <PARAM NAME="FontCharSet" VALUE="0">
        <PARAM NAME="FontPitchAndFamily" VALUE="2">
        <PARAM NAME="FontWeight" VALUE="0">
    </OBJECT>
</BODY>
```

Now it's time to implement the `SalaryCalculator` code. Select **Tools | Script Wizard** to open the Script Wizard. On the left you see an event pane, which shows the constituent controls. Locate "cmdOK" (the `CommandButton` control), and click on the sign to view all of the event procedures for this control. Select the "`Click`" event, and toggle the "`Code View`" option button on. (Code View allows you to write customized VBScript or JavaScript, while List View does not). Your screen should appear like this:

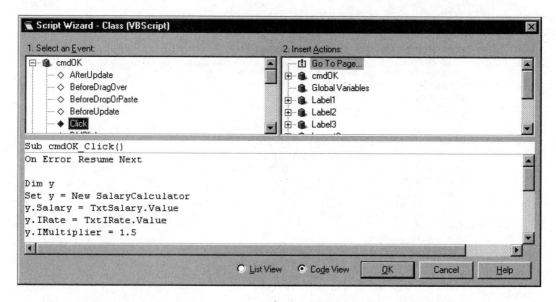

Add the following code listing to the `cmdOK_Click()` event procedure in the code pane:

```
On Error Resume Next

Dim y
Set y = New SalaryCalculator
y.Salary = TxtSalary.Value
y.IRate = TxtIRate.Value
y.IMultiplier = 1.5

If Err.Number <> 0 Then
  If Err.Number=13 Then MsgBox "Error 13: Empty input is invalid" & Chr(13) & _
    "Please enter valid input", 16, "Invalid Input"
  If Err.Number<>13 Then MsgBox "Error " & Err.Number & ": " & _
      Err.Description & Chr(13) & _
    "Please enter a valid " & Err.Source, 16, "Invalid Input"
Else
  MsgBox "Your new salary is " & FormatCurrency(y.NewSalary) & _
      ", based on an IRate of " & _
    y.IRate & "%" & Chr(13) & "and a multiplier of 1.5", 64, "New Salary"
End If
```

Close out of the Script Wizard and add the class definition to the <HEAD> section:

```
<SCRIPT LANGUAGE="VBScript">
<!--
Class SalaryCalculator
   Public IRate, IMultiplier
   Private varSalary

   Property Get Salary
      Salary = varSalary
   End Property

   Property Let Salary (varValue)
      If varValue >0 Then
         varSalary = varValue
      Else
         Err.Raise 6000, "salary", "Salary must be >$0."
      End If
   End Property

   Function NewSalary()
      NewSalary = varSalary*((1+(IRate*IMultiplier/100)))
   End Function
End Class
-->
</SCRIPT>
```

Save the HTML file as `ClassUI.htm`, then open it up in Internet Explorer. You should see the following:

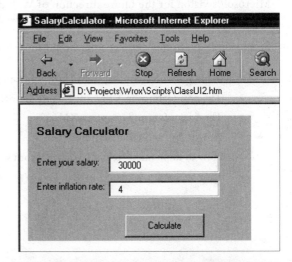

Pressing the calculate button results in:

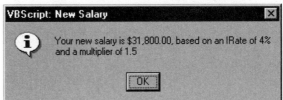

As this example shows, using the ActiveX Control Pad is more than a convenience. You will want to avoid manually inserting ActiveX controls for two good reasons:

> ➢ It is easy to mistype the CLASSID, not to mention it's tedious, and

> ➢ The Control Pad's graphical interface provides a versatile view of all the controls on a Web page, and enables you to quickly scan available control properties and methods, set property values, and implement code behind event procedures.

Keep in mind that this example is for illustrative purposes only, since you could accomplish the same thing using straight HTML. We will be revisiting the ActiveX Control Pad in Chapter 5, when we use it to add a custom control to a Web page with script.

Summary

This chapter demonstrated the many aspects to client-side programming, especially with the release of Internet Explorer 5.0, which supports several client-side technologies, including ActiveX Scripting, XML, and Scriptlets. DHTML, another important client-side technology, is covered in full in Chapter 6. These technologies are changing the traditional client-server relationship on the Web. By bringing a higher level of sophistication to the client-side, these technologies are reducing client dependence on the server. Today, Web applications do more and perform better. ActiveX is a key player in Microsoft's vision for the future direction of Web development technology. In the next chapter you'll see a start-to-finish approach for deploying ActiveX components on the Web.

So to sum it up, in this chapter you should have learned:

> ➢ What ActiveX Scripting is and how you can implement it

> ➢ The new features in VBScript 5.0 and how to implement them

> ➢ The basics for implementing XML

> ➢ How to use and write Scriptlets

> ➢ How to implement ActiveX controls from within your Web page, using scripting

> ➢ How to use the ActiveX Control Pad to place ActiveX controls into your Web page

5

Building Client-Side ActiveX Controls

ActiveX controls are software components that are used as building blocks for applications. We introduced **component based software** in Chapter 1, and discussed the advantages that this approach provides. ActiveX controls encapsulate their functionality and logic behind a programmable **public interface**. Developers can access the control's functionality by manipulating the interface. Many controls also expose a **visual interface**, such as the Calendar control, while others, such as the Timer control, do not.

ActiveX controls always operate within a **Container**, which could include a Visual Basic form or a Web browser. In fact, many controls function equally well both on the desktop and on the Web. The control itself will look and behave the same regardless of what container it is sited in. However, each container type has its own way of interacting with the control. A Web browser, for example, would use HTML and a scripting language to manipulate a control. On the desktop, the same control could be added to a Visual Basic form and manipulated with code.

Developers use controls to build their applications more quickly and efficiently, because controls save them from having to code all the functionality themselves. A good ActiveX control can contribute to an application in two ways. First, it provides out-of-the-box functionality, and a rich, programmable interface for accessing the control. Second, if the control provides a visual interface, then it contributes directly to the look and feel of the application. As with cars and electronics, the quality of an application is a direct reflection of the quality of the controls that were used to build it.

ActiveX is a key technology in the world of object-oriented programming, which has become popular among Visual Basic developers in response to a growing need to make sophisticated applications easier to develop, debug and maintain, especially by multi-person development teams. Component-based application development allows complex applications to be broken out into self-contained units of code that can be independently developed and inserted into the application framework. ActiveX components are also called **server components**, because their purpose is to respond to, and service, client requests.

A further advantage of ActiveX is that it is a language-independent technology, and components may be written and deployed in several development environments, including Visual Basic, Visual C++ and Visual J++. As we saw in Chapter 4, ActiveX COM components can also be written directly for the Web using Scriptlets (XML and VBScript together).

Understanding What ActiveX Is

It might be more appropriate to ask what ActiveX *isn't*, because these days, ActiveX appears everywhere. ActiveX is a catchall term for any reusable, binary COM component. ActiveX components are COM objects, which means that they implement standard interfaces, encapsulate their business logic and support automation requests. These components include:

> - ActiveX Controls (*.ocx)
> - ActiveX DLLs (*.dll)
> - ActiveX EXEs (*.exe)
> - ActiveX Documents (*.vbd)

ActiveX Controls are components that always operate in a container, and usually expose a visual interface. **ActiveX DLLs** are in-process components that provide classes and functions, but usually do not expose a visual interface. ActiveX DLLs are useful for when you want to encapsulate business logic, but don't need the overhead of a visual interface. **ActiveX EXEs** are out-of-process components and serve a similar function to ActiveX DLLs, except that they function as stand-alone applications. Finally, **ActiveX Documents** are complete applications that are designed to run in a browser. Visual Basic provides a wizard to migrate existing Standard EXE projects to ActiveX Document projects. ActiveX Documents allow you to quickly and easily migrate existing desktop applications to the Web.

Understanding ActiveX Controls

From this point forward, we will focus on ActiveX *controls*, as opposed to the family of components that fall under the ActiveX umbrella. ActiveX controls fall under one of three types:

> - Aggregate controls
> - Sub-classed controls
> - User controls

The **aggregate control** is the most common kind of control. Two or more existing controls combine into one control, which aggregates, or combines, the interfaces of each constituent control. The **sub-classed control** takes an existing control and extends its behavior in some way. For example, it may take a standard textbox control and add a couple of custom properties. A **user control** describes any control that does not rely on constituent or sub-classed controls. This kind of control is not common, because the development environment of Visual Basic is very control-oriented, and it's difficult to code without them.

ActiveX controls are written for developers to use in building their own applications. A compiled control is activated as soon as it is placed in a Container, such as a form or a browser. The ActiveX control is activated whether the Container is in design-time or run-time mode, but the control does not always make all of its properties equally available to write to in both modes. This might occur, for example, if the control has certain property settings that affect its performance, and which should only be manipulated by the developer at design-time. For the purposes of this discussion, we define the **user** of a control to be a developer who has added your compiled control to their project, and is accessing it both at design-time and at run-time, when they compile their own project.

The UserControl Object

When you open a new ActiveX Control project, a blank **UserControl Designer** loads to the screen. The UserControl contributes to an ActiveX control project at two levels. On the one hand, you use it to assemble the control's visual interface by adding constituent controls, just as you would add to a Visual Basic form. (Note that non-visual ActiveX controls, such as the Timer control simply have nothing added to the UserControl Designer). In addition, the UserControl is a special object whose interface is incorporated into the public interface of the new ActiveX control. The UserControl object contributes events that are raised at different stages throughout the control's lifetime. It also provides access to the control's Container by way of the Extender object, which allows the control to adopt property values that are set by the Container. The UserControl object's key interface members are:

Interface Member	Description
Initialize Event	This event fires each time an instance of the control is created. Controls are instanced in design-time, when they are added to a container (e.g., a form) and at run-time, when they are loaded.
InitProperties/ ReadProperties Events	The very first time a control is instanced, the InitProperties event fires. Usually, the initial properties are written to the PropertyBag object. The ReadProperties event fires at all subsequent times. Usually, this event contains code that retrieves initial properties from the PropertyBag object.
WriteProperties Event	This event occurs at design-time when a control instance is destroyed, prior to the Terminate event firing. This event will only fire if a property setting has changed during design-time.

Table Continued on Following Page

127

Interface Member	Description
Terminate Event	This event occurs when the control instance is destroyed. When a project is compiled, the design-time instance of the control is destroyed, and is replaced by a new, run-time instance of the control. Thus, the Terminate event fires when a project in design mode is compiled, and an Initialize event immediately follows.
AmbientChanged Event	The UserControl object provides an Ambient object, which contains properties that the Container object passes on to the control, such as BackColor. This event fires if an ambient property changes.
AsyncReadComplete Event	The UserControl object supports asynchronous downloading of data. This event fires when a download is complete.
Extender Object	This object is provided to allow the control to adopt selected Container properties.
Hyperlink Property	This property returns a Hyperlink object that provides navigation services.

In summary, the UserControl object allows an ActiveX control to respond to its environment, to interact with its Container and to manage its state. This list only touches on the detailed interface of the UserControl object.

The ActiveX Control Interface

The **ActiveX Control Interface** is a complex mix of aggregated and custom members derived from three sources:

> - Aggregated interfaces of the constituent controls
> - The UserControl Interface
> - Custom Interface members that are coded into the control

```
ActiveX Control
    ┌─────────────────────────────────────────────┐
    │                           UserControl Object  │
    │                                               │
    │   * UserControl Events:                       │
    │       *Initalize, InitProperties, ReadProperties, │
    │       WriteProperties, Terminate              │
    │   * UserControl Methods & Properties:         │
    │       *Ambient                                │
    │                                               │
    │   ┌───────────────────────────────────┐       │
    │   │ Constituent Controls              │       │
    │   │                                   │       │
    │   │   ┌─────────────────────────┐     │       │
    │   │   │ * Events                │     │       │
    │   │   │ * Methods               │     │       │
    │   │   │ * Properties            │     │       │
    │   │   └─────────────────────────┘     │       │
    │   │                                   │       │
    │   │   ┌──────────┐   ┌──────────┐     │       │
    │   │   └──────────┘   └──────────┘     │       │
    │   └───────────────────────────────────┘       │
    │                                               │
    │   ┌───────────────────────────────────┐       │
    │   │ Custom                            │       │
    │   │ * Events                          │       │
    │   │ * Methods                         │       │
    │   │ * Properties                      │       │
    │   └───────────────────────────────────┘       │
    └─────────────────────────────────────────────┘
```

ActiveX controls expose a public interface that can be manipulated by the control's user. They also have a private interface that can be manipulated internally, but which is not available for outside manipulation. However, a control may expose any private member as public, by mapping the private member to a public one. For example, consider a control with a command button that raises a private Click event. When the user of the control clicks on this button, the Click event is raised *internally* to the control, which then executes any implemented code. The user will not see the Click event unless the control raises a public event in response to the private event being raised.

For every private interface member that you choose to map as public, there are several more that you shouldn't map. Clearly, you have to make choices to avoid cluttering the public interface. As we'll see, the ActiveX Control Interface Wizard is a useful tool for selectively mapping private members as public.

An ActiveX control inherits the interfaces of its constituent controls. These contribute to the ActiveX control's private interface, and also make up its **visual interface**, which gives the user something to interact with. Some controls, such as the Timer control, do not provide a visual interface. Frequently, the control's visual interface members are mapped to public interface members, because users like to have many programming options with ActiveX controls. This requires extra work while creating the control, because each constituent control has to be mapped individually.

Most of the UserControl interface members contribute directly to the ActiveX control's public interface. The Initialize and ReadProperties events, for example, are important members of the public interface. Finally, a control can have custom interface members, such as property procedures, custom events, and functions. There is no rule as to whether custom members contribute to the ActiveX control's public or private interface. This is your choice to make, as the control's developer.

The term **abstract interface** refers to the collective set of properties, methods and events, both public and private, that describe what the object *is* and *does*. All of the members we've discussed so far contribute to the control's abstract interface. From the user's perspective, the ActiveX control presents a unified public interface. From the developer's perspective, an ActiveX control provides an abstract interface of both public and private members, which combine to provide the control's complete interface.

ActiveX controls are complicated components to create because of their peculiar, event-intensive interface, which must be implemented so that the control can function effectively in both design-time and run-time modes. But the good news is that developing controls for desktop applications does not differ much from developing for Web applications. The biggest difference is that each environment provides a different type of container, and so the options for interacting with the control are different. On the Web, for example, ActiveX controls are manipulated using a scripting language, such as VBScript. In an Excel container, Visual Basic for Applications is the available "scripting" language. This is of little importance because wherever the COM standard is supported, ActiveX controls can be used. A well-designed ActiveX control offers the user with a rich, programmable interface, but does not restrict the user to any one programming method.

ActiveX Control Creation Using Visual Basic

The software marketplace is brimming with hundreds of commercial ActiveX controls that provide many different kinds of functionality. Examples include stock ticker controls and controls that provide Internet capabilities. Most of these controls are reasonably priced and include unlimited, royalty-free run-time licenses, so you can include the control in your applications and distribute it to as many users as buy your software. Despite the choices, there are still times when you may need to develop your own custom controls.

Visual Basic provides an excellent development environment for ActiveX controls, especially Version 6.0, which we will focus on here, although I will attempt to accommodate Version 5.0 users as well. Visual Basic allows multiple projects to be added to a group and opened simultaneously. This feature is invaluable for debugging ActiveX controls, which only function inside a container. Visual Basic 6 extends your options for debugging controls by allowing you to specify how the component will be launched, whether in a browser or in another project. The Enterprise Edition of VB6 also provides a utility (not covered here) called the ActiveX Control Test Container, which lets you test individual interface members with ease.

The ActiveX Control Project Type

ActiveX controls are created in their own project type, which provides a **UserControl** instead of a form. The `UserControl` object is the base for the ActiveX control. It hosts constituent controls and contributes its interface to the public interface of the ActiveX control.

Building the Sales Analyzer ActiveX Control

Now that we've covered the theory behind ActiveX controls, it's time to create one of our own controls. The best way to understand the complicated life of an ActiveX control is to jump in and build one. As with other kinds of projects, you should not start coding until you have established the purpose of the control, and have planned out its interface. In this chapter, we'll be building a "Sales Analyzer" ActiveX control, which charts sales data. The steps involved in building the control are:

> Define the purpose of the control
> Define the control's abstract interface
> Define the control's visual interface
> Implement code behind the interface
> Debug and test the control.

Defining the Sales Analyzer Control's Purpose

To understand the purpose of the Sales Analyzer control, let's consider the following business scenario: A large food distribution company uses an AS/400 mainframe application to manage its transactions and to run nightly batch processes. Every night the system generates a summary of the previous day's sales by customer account, and exports the data as a comma-delimited text file to the company's Windows NT Web server. The next business day, employees can log on to the corporate intranet and use their browser to display the sales data. Instead of displaying hard sales numbers, the Web page contains a Sales Analyzer control to chart the data by selected customer account. Furthermore, the user is able to click on any chart point to display a summary of the sales data.

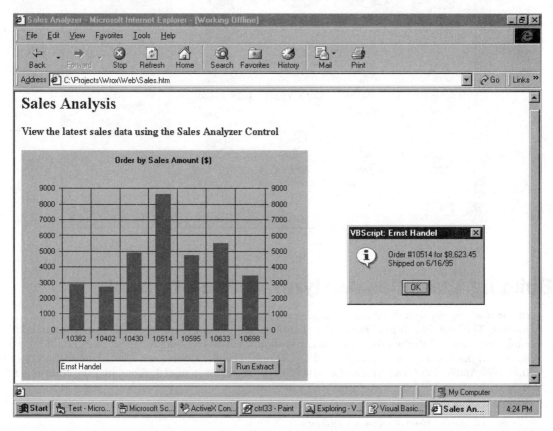

The figure shows a sample Web page containing the Sales Analyzer control, with sales data already loaded into the control. The Sales Analyzer control works as follows:

1. The control loads on the Web page, but is not yet populated with data.

2. The control exposes an `ExtractFile` property for the path to the file containing the sales data. This property should be set on the Web page using a `<PARAM>` tag.

3. The user clicks the "Run Extract" button.

4. If the extract file is valid, then the control runs private procedures that open the extract file, and loads the sales data. If the extract file is not found, then the control prompts the user to enter a valid filename.

5. Once the sales data is loaded, the user can select any customer from the drop-down combo box. The customer's sales data will automatically be charted.

6. The user can point and click on any chart point to see a summary of the sales data, including the sales order ID, the amount of the sale, and the date the merchandise was shipped.

This description of how the control works is not exactly accurate in describing how the control sends notifications the user. While it is possible for an ActiveX control embedded on a Web page to raise a message box or input box, it is not very good style. A good programming rule of thumb is to have the Container be responsible for all direct interactions with the user, which includes raising message boxes. So instead of raising message boxes, the ActiveX control should be designed to raise custom events, which can be trapped by scripting language procedures in the Web page. These procedures, in turn, determine the best way to send a notification to the user.

Step 1: Starting the Project

Developing ActiveX controls directly for the Web is not an intuitive exercise for most people, so initially we'll develop the Sales Analyzer control for the desktop. Once the control is debugged and compiled, we'll insert it on a Web page for display in a browser.

To start developing the Sales Analyzer control, we need to set up the project files as follows:

1. Open Visual Basic and choose File | New Project. Double-click the ActiveX Control icon to display the UserControl Designer.

2. Open Project | Project1 Properties and change the settings to match the screenshot below. The control's threading model must be set to single-threaded to support the Microsoft Chart Control (one of the constituent controls).

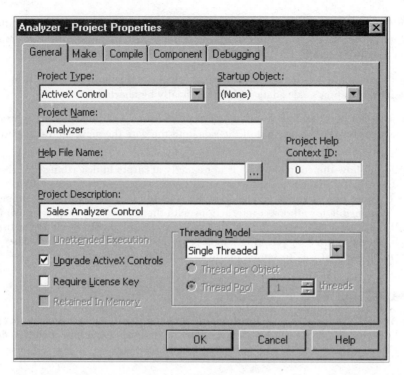

A discussion of threading is beyond the scope of this chapter, so a simple description will be adequate. The threading model determines how many threads per process are used to service requests to the ActiveX control. Apartment-threaded controls employ several threads per process, and are well-suited to Internet Explorer, which is itself multi-threaded. Single-threaded controls, however, provide only one thread per process, and so may suffer lower performance because all calls have to be handled in sequence. The general rule for VB components is to use apartment threading where possible, then all the rest is taken care of for you behind the scenes.

3. Open Project | Components and set references to the **Microsoft Chart Control** and to the **Microsoft Common Dialog Control**.

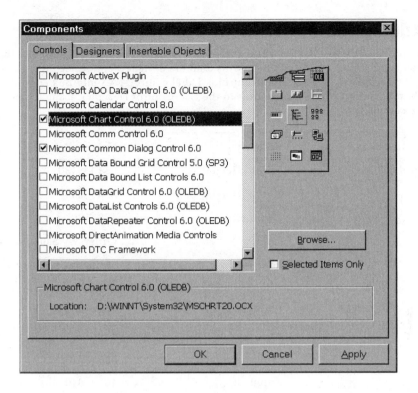

Rename `UserControl1` to `Sales`, and rename the project file to `Analyzer.vbp`.

4. Use File | Add Project to add a Standard EXE project to the Project Explorer window. This will serve as the test environment for our control before we migrate it to a web environment. Rename Project1 to Test, and save the project files in a new directory called Analyzer, using the default Group1 group project name. Make sure that you right click on Test and select the option "Set As Startup" from the pop-up menu. The Project Explorer window should now look like:

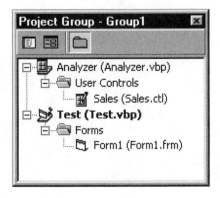

Step 2: Adding the Constituent Controls

Controls are added to the UserControl Designer in the same way as they are added to the Form Designer: you simply drag-and-drop the controls onto the designer, and resize them as needed. The Sales Analyzer control uses an MS Chart control, a Label control, a ComboBox control, and a CommandButton control. Add these controls to the UserControl Designer, using the property settings shown in the table below.

Control (Name)	Property	Value
UserControl (Sales)	Width, Height	6540, 5130
Label (lblTitle)	Width, Height	6255, 255
	Top, Left	120, 120
	Caption	Orders by Sales Amount ($)
	Font	MS Sans Serif, 8 pt, Bold
	Alignment	Center
MSChart (MSChart1)	Width, Height	6255, 4095
	Top, Left	480, 120
ComboBox (cboCustomers)	Width, Height	3855, 315
	Top, Left	4680, 840
CommandButton (cmdExtract)	Width, Height	1095, 315
	Top, Left	4680, 4800
	Caption	&Run Extract

The UserControl designer should now look like this:

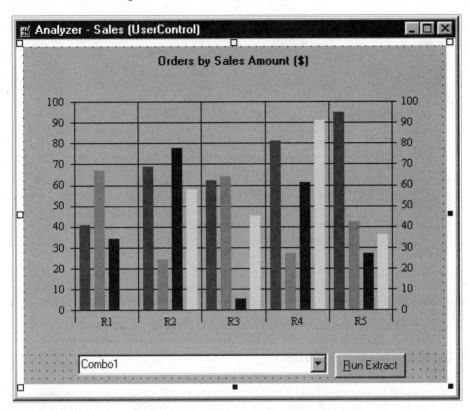

Step 3: Creating the ActiveX Control Interface

The visual interface of the Sales Analyzer control is now in place, so the next steps are:

1. Decide which interface members to implement from constituent controls

2. Code additional interface members, such as property procedures, and

3. Add property pages.

Recall that the interfaces of each of the constituent controls are aggregated into the overall ActiveX control interface. The Sales Analyzer control traps events from each of its constituent controls, so that it recognizes when the user is taking an action. We can implement code behind the event procedures of any constituent control, such as the Click event of the cmdExtract button. These interface members are private, so only the ActiveX control can respond to them, and they do not contribute to the control's public interface. If we want these private events to map to the public interface then we can do so by raising custom public events from the private event procedures. Interfaces are useful because they limit the number of ways in which a user can make requests of the ActiveX control. It is up to you, the developer, to decide which private interface members to map as public.

The public interface of the Sales Analyzer control will consist of two custom properties and two custom events:

Interface attributes	Description
`ExtractFile` property	Sets the filename and path to the extract file that contains the sales data.
`ChartType` property	Sets the chart type to a 2D-bar chart or a 3D-bar chart.
`FileStatus` event	Raised from the `cmdExtract_Click` event, which fires when the user clicks the "Run Extract" button. The event argument is a status code that indicates whether `ExtractFile` references a valid extract file.
`PointSelected` event	Raised directly from the `MSChart1_PointSelected` event, which fires when the user clicks a data point on the chart. The event arguments contain sales data specific to the selected data point.

Notice that the control's public `FileStatus` event is raised from within the private `Click` event of the `cmdExtract` constituent control. Similarly, the control's public `PointSelected` event is raised from within the private `PointSelected` event of the `MSChart1` constituent control. This is how private interface members are mapped to the public interface.

The ActiveX Control Interface Wizard

The ActiveX Control Interface Wizard is a timesaving tool for creating a public interface from an often complex, aggregated private interface. The wizard allows you to create custom members and to map private interface members of constituent controls to the public interface of the ActiveX control. The wizard's job is to auto-generate code based on your specifications. The wizard may be run any number of times, but you should always run it as soon as you have added all the constituent controls and prior to implementing any code. I have not noticed any ill effects from running the wizard against a "mature" control with lots of implemented code.

The wizard has a number of dialog boxes to work through, but it will save you lots of coding time. You can only run the wizard right after you have added the constituent controls (the visual interface) and you are ready to create the control's public interface. The wizard helps you understand the process of creating an ActiveX control interface, and how the private interface maps to the public interface. In short, the wizard is a time-saver *and* a great learning tool. The steps for using the wizard for our control are as follows:

4. In Visual Basic 6, select Add-Ins | Add-In Manager and select the wizard as shown below:

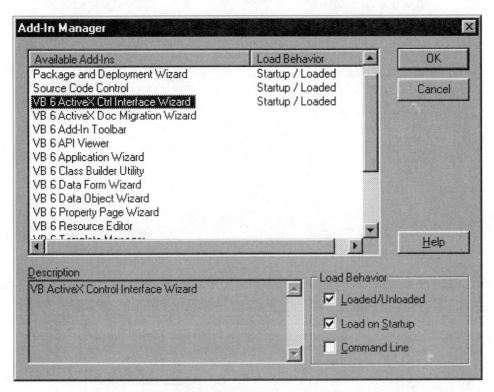

5. Next, run the wizard from Add-Ins | ActiveX Control Interface Wizard. The first dialog after the introduction in the wizard prompts you to select interface members of constituent controls that you want to add to the main control's public interface. Remove all of the members, since we want to custom create our own interface.

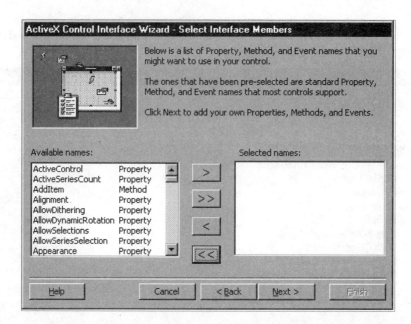

6. The "Create Custom Members" dialog allows you to create custom public interface from scratch. Click the New... button to add new properties, methods and events, as shown:

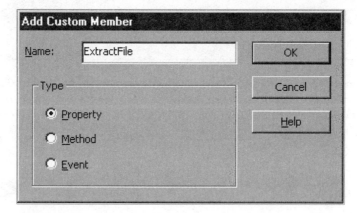

We need to add the two properties and two events that were mentioned above: the `ExtractFile` and `ChartType` properties, and the `FileStatus` and `PointSelected` events. The dialog box should look like the screenshot below when you are complete:

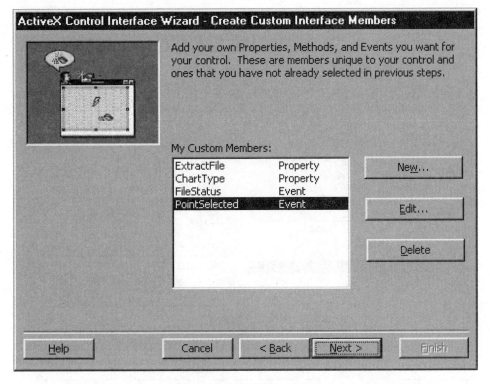

7. The next dialog box called "Set Mapping" allows you to map public interface members to the private interface members of constituent controls. We'll map the public `PointSelected` event to the private `PointSelected` event of `MSChart1`, and the public `FileStatus` event to the private `Click` event of `cmdExtract`:

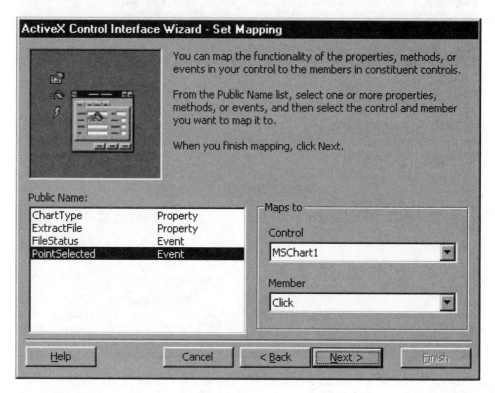

8. The "Set Attributes" dialog box lets us set the attributes of the remaining unmapped public members. If a public member is already mapped to a private member from a previous dialog, then it will not be available now. Here we are also able to set whether an attribute may be set at runtime, design-time, both, or even neither. Design-time only properties are intended solely for the developer, while runtime properties are intended for both developer and user. In our case, we will set the ChartType property to be available in design time only, for read and write operations. The ExtractFile property will be available for read and write operations in design-time, but only for read operations at runtime.

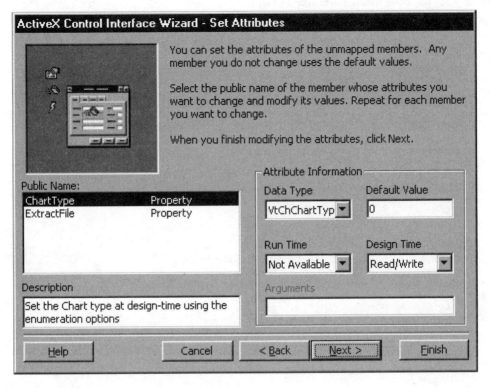

9. At the final dialog of the wizard, simply hit the Finish button to start generating code.

Step 4: Working from the Auto-Generated Code

As you might expect, the auto-generated code needs to be changed and enhanced. Sometimes you will need to modify the arguments that are passed to methods and functions and you will almost always need to implement custom business logic. The wizard does a good job of creating useful code without requiring many cleanups. In order to create a customized public interface we have to add some features that the wizard is not capable of generating, for example, enumerated constants and custom event arguments. The additions and changes that we need to for Analyzer.vbp are as follows:

> Add a UserControl_Initialize event

> Chang the arguments of the custom events, FileStatus and PointSelected

> Add enumerated constants for the ChartType property

> Add enumerated constants for the StatusCode argument of the FileStatus event

> Modify the InitProperties, ReadProperties and WriteProperties events, so that they no longer use default values or constants.

> Delete default property settings generated by the wizard.

Here is what the code listing looks like so far:

```
Option Explicit

'Property Variables:
Dim m_ExtractFile As String
Dim m_ChartType As ChartFormat

'Enumerations:
Public Enum Status
 FileOK
 FileEmpty
 FileNotFound
End Enum

Public Enum ChartFormat
 Bar3D
 Bar2D
End Enum

'Event Declarations:
Event FileStatus(ByVal StatusCode As Status)
Event PointSelected(evtCompanyName As Variant, evtOrderID As Variant, _
 evtSalesAmount As Variant, evtShippedDate As Variant)

Private Sub UserControl_Initialize()
'This event fires first at both design-time and runtime
 With MSChart1
   .ColumnCount = 1
   .RowCount = 1
   .RowLabel = ""
   .Data = 0
 End With
 lblTitle.Visible = False
End Sub


'Initialize Properties for User Control
Private Sub UserControl_InitProperties()
 m_ExtractFile = ""
 m_ChartType = Bar2D
End Sub

'Load property values from storage
Private Sub UserControl_ReadProperties(PropBag As PropertyBag)
 m_ExtractFile = PropBag.ReadProperty("ExtractFile", "")
 m_ChartType = PropBag.ReadProperty("ChartType", "")
End Sub

'Write property values to storage
Private Sub UserControl_WriteProperties(PropBag As PropertyBag)
 Call PropBag.WriteProperty("ExtractFile", m_ExtractFile, "")
 Call PropBag.WriteProperty("ChartType", m_ChartType, "")
End Sub

'Properties:
Public Property Get ChartType() As ChartFormat
 If Ambient.UserMode Then Err.Raise 393
 ChartType = m_ChartType
End Property
```

```
Public Property Let ChartType(ByVal New_ChartType As ChartFormat)
 If Ambient.UserMode Then Err.Raise 382
 m_ChartType = New_ChartType
 PropertyChanged "ChartType"
End Property

Public Property Get ExtractFile() As String
 ExtractFile = m_ExtractFile
End Property

Public Property Let ExtractFile(ByVal New_ExtractFile As String)
 m_ExtractFile = New_ExtractFile
 PropertyChanged "ExtractFile"
End Property
```

```
'Events (not coded yet):
Private Sub cmdExtract_Click()
 'RaiseEvent FileStatus() 'Not coded yet
End Sub
```

```
Private Sub MSChart1_PointSelected(Series As Integer, DataPoint As Integer,
MouseFlags As Integer, Cancel As Integer)
 'RaiseEvent PointSelected() 'Not coded yet
End Sub
```

The highlighted code shows the changes we've made from the original code produced by the wizard.

Step 5: Coding the Business Logic

Now that the public interface is in place we can move on to implementing business logic. The interface definition is just a framework of methods, properties and events, and so far there is very little that these interface members are actually doing. Business logic must be implemented behind each interface member in order to process the requests that the members are expected to handle. For example, when the user wishes to view sales data, she selects a customer from the combo box then clicks the control's single command button labeled Run Extract. When the user clicks this button, the control must gather sales data for the selected customer from the database. The Click event of the command button in turn calls a private procedure called GetData, which actually performs the database operation.

Coding the Data Loading Procedures

The sample data set for the Sales Analyzer control comes from the "Order Details" query of the Northwinds database. The query provides customer orders by sales amount, and is ordered by shipping date, not customer, so that repeat customers are scattered throughout the data file. I created a comma-delimited extract file by exporting the query results to a text file called Sales.txt. The file contains four fields: OrderID, SaleAmount, CompanyName and ShippedDate. Here are the first few records of the file:

```
SaleAmount,OrderID,CompanyName,ShippedDate
"$7,390.20",10360,Blondel père et fils,34701
"$9,210.90",10372,Queen Cozinha,34708
"$2,900.00",10382,Ernst Handel,34715
```

The ActiveX control assumes that the data will only be in this format, and is not currently equipped to handle exceptions. Switch over to `Sales.ctl` in code view, and start a new code listing by dimensioning 3 variant arrays in the Declarations section of the form. These will hold data that has been retrieved from the text file:

```
Private vSales() As Variant
Private vCustomers() As Variant
Private vBookmarks() As Variant
```

When the user clicks **Run Extract**, which, to our code, is the `cmdExtract` button, the control checks if the `ExtractFile` property of the ActiveX control was set, and whether the file exists. This property may be set directly at run time by direct assignment, or it may be set at design time using a property page which we will be developing later in the chapter. Regardless of the outcome, the public `FileStatus` event is always raised to communicate back to the user at runtime, using the enumerated type `Status` as an argument. As you may recall:

```
Public Enum Status
 FileOK
 FileEmpty
 FileNotFound
End Enum

Event FileStatus(ByVal StatusCode As Status)
```

This listing should look familiar because we added it immediately after running the wizard. There is no need to add it to your code pane again.

The code behind the `cmdExtract_Click` event should now read:

```
Private Sub cmdExtract_Click()
'Purpose: Load the extract file

Dim nI As Integer

'Test the Extract File
   If m_ExtractFile = "" Then
      RaiseEvent FileStatus(Status.FileEmpty) 'ExtractFile property is empty
      Exit Sub
   ElseIf Dir(m_ExtractFile) = "" Then
      RaiseEvent FileStatus(Status.FileNotFound) 'Extract File was not found
      Exit Sub
   Else
      RaiseEvent FileStatus(Status.FileOK) 'Extract File OK
   End If

Call GetData
```

```
'Populate combo
For nI = 1 To UBound(vCustomers)
   Call cboCustomers.AddItem(vCustomers(nI))
Next nI

cboCustomers.ListIndex = 0
Call cboCustomers_Click

End Sub
```

If the Extract file is valid, then the cmdExtract_Click procedure calls the private GetData procedure, shown below. GetData opens the sales data file and reads it into a private variant array called vSales. This array is ordered by column then row, to accommodate the MSChart control, which expects data in this order. Next, the GetData procedure examines vSales for unique customer names, and populates them into the vCustomers array:

```
Private Sub GetData()
'Purpose:
'1. Read contents of 'Sales.txt' into vSales()
'2. Add the customers to vCustomers()
'Note: Header row is assigned index of zero

    Dim nI As Integer
    Dim nJ As Integer
    Dim blnFound As Boolean
    Dim nCustomers As Integer

'Read the extract file into vSales()
nI = 0
Open m_ExtractFile For Input As #1
    Do While Not EOF(1)
    ReDim Preserve vSales(4, nI) As Variant
        Input #1, vSales(0, nI), vSales(1, nI), _
            vSales(2, nI), vSales(3, nI)
        nI = nI + 1
    Loop
Close #1

'Initialize
nCustomers = 1
ReDim vCustomers(nCustomers) As Variant
vCustomers(nCustomers) = vSales(2, 1)

'Assemble array of customers
For nI = 1 To UBound(vSales, 2)
   For nJ = 1 To UBound(vCustomers)
       If vCustomers(nJ) = vSales(2, nI) Then
       blnFound = True
           Exit For
       End If
   Next nJ
       If Not blnFound Then
           nCustomers = nCustomers + 1
           ReDim Preserve vCustomers(nCustomers)
           vCustomers(UBound(vCustomers)) = vSales(2, nI)
       Else
```

```
            blnFound = False
        End If
    Next nI
End Sub
```

Coding the Charting Procedure

Once vCustomers has been filled, it can populate the control's drop-down combo box, cboCustomers. If you refer back to the cmdExtract_Click event, you will see where this is done immediately following the call to GetData. Once the combo box is populated, the user can click around in it to select different customers. The cboCustomers_Click event implements code to automatically chart the selected customer's sales data. Specifically, when the user clicks on a customer, code executes to retrieve the customer's sales data from vSales, and to add it to the chart.

Because the customer sales data is scattered throughout the vSales array, the procedure must search through the entire array to locate all the order entries for the selected customer. When the procedure locates a relevant record, it checks the row number of the entry in vSales, and adds this row number to the vBookmarks array. So the vBookmarks array simply points to the customer's sales data in vSales:

```
Private Sub cboCustomers_Click()
'Chart selected Customer
'Note: vSales() must have (column, row) order to work with MSChart control

    Dim nI As Integer
    Dim nJ As Integer

Erase vBookmarks

With MSChart1
    nJ = 1
    .ColumnCount = nJ 'Update
    .Column = 1

    For nI = 1 To UBound(vSales, 2)

    If vSales(2, nI) = cboCustomers.Text Then
        'Store position in vBookmarks()
        ReDim Preserve vBookmarks(nJ) As Variant
        vBookmarks(nJ) = nI
        'Add to chart
        .RowCount = nJ
        .Row = nJ
        .RowLabel = vSales(1, nI)
        .Data = vSales(0, nI)
        nJ = nJ + 1
    End If

    Next nI
```

```
End With

lblTitle.Visible = True

End Sub
```

Step 6: Coding the Public Events

Once the chart displays, the user can select a point and display summary sales information. The `PointSelected` event of the `MSChart` control maps to the custom `PointSelected` event of the Sales Analyzer control. The custom event's arguments are elements of the sales data records. Recall:

```
Event PointSelected(evtCompanyName As Variant, evtOrderID As Variant, _
  evtSalesAmount As Variant, evtShippedDate As Variant)
```

The event is called from:

```
Private Sub MSChart1_PointSelected(Series As Integer, DataPoint As Integer, _
              MouseFlags As Integer, Cancel As Integer)

'Raise an event with summary information on the selected data point
nK = vBookmarks(DataPoint) 'Get current position in vSales()
RaiseEvent PointSelected(vSales(2, nK), vSales(1, nK), vSales(0, nK), vSales(3,
nK))

End Sub
```

The control needs property pages before it is completely ready for shipping, but we'll pause for a moment to deploy our control on a form and see what a splash it makes.

Step 7: Testing the Sales Analyzer Control on a Form

Testing our new Sales Analyzer control is a simple process:

1. Close the Sales UserControl Designer by clicking on the X button in the Control-menu box. This enables the UserControl icon in the ToolBox, essentially putting it into runtime mode, although the Test project remains in design time mode.

2. Switch to the Test project and add the Sales Analyzer control to Form1. If the UserControl icon is still grayed out, then you need to close the UserControl Designer again. Form1 should now look like this:

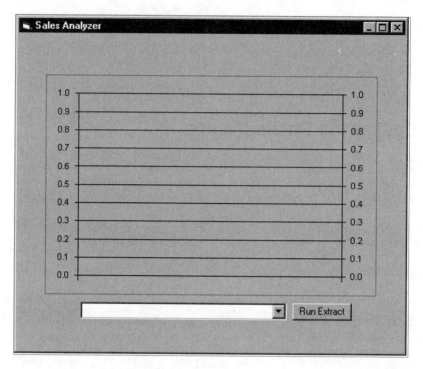

3. Right-click on the embedded control to open its property page, and set the ExtractFile and ChartType properties using the browse button and option buttons, respectively. The property page is the only way that you can set these (Test project) design time properties.

4. Implement code behind the control's public events. Try adding the following simple code listing behind Form1:

```
Private Sub Sales1_FileStatus(ByVal StatusCode As Analyzer.Status)
'Purpose: Trap event that shows Extract File status

Select Case StatusCode
   Case Analyzer.FileOK
      'File is valid: no action
   Case Else
      Sales1.ExtractFile = InputBox("The ExtractFile property was not set or" & _
      "is invalid." & vbCrLf & "Please enter a valid path, then click the " & _
      "extract button:", "Extract File Invalid")
End Select

End Sub
```

```
Private Sub Sales1_PointSelected(evtCompanyName As Variant, _
                                 evtOrderID As Variant, _
                                 evtSalesAmount As Variant, _
                                 evtShippedDate As Variant)

MsgBox "Order #" & evtOrderID & " for " & Format(evtSalesAmount, "Currency") & _
    vbCrLf & "Shipped on " & Format(CDate(evtShippedDate), "mm/dd/yyyy"), _
    vbInformation, evtCompanyName

End Sub
```

5. Start the Test project, and click the **Run Extract** button. The control should populate with data. If the filename property happens to be invalid, you will be prompted with an input box to provide a valid file.

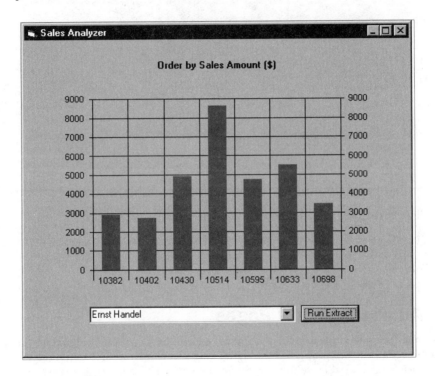

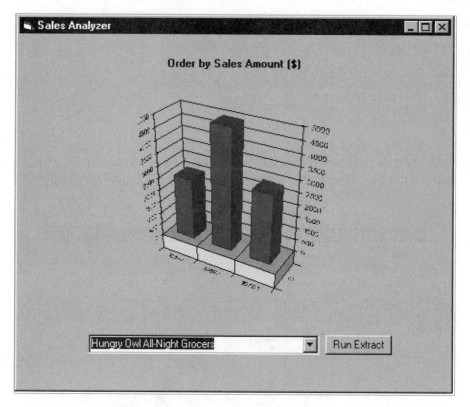

6. Click on any data point to see a summary of the sales data.

7. When you are satisfied that the control works, select File | Make Analyzer.ocx to compile the control and register it to your system.

Step 8: Adding Property Pages

Property pages provide a user-friendly way to set control properties at design-time. They allow a developer to set a control's properties through dialog sheets instead of through the Properties window in Visual Basic's Integrated Development Environment (IDE). Property pages are opened by right-clicking on a control and selecting "Properties" from the pop-up menu. If the control does not support property pages, then in design-time this action will activate the standard Properties window that we're used to seeing in the Visual Basic Integrated Development Environment (IDE).

The next figure shows the property pages for the MSChart control as they appear at design-time. These pages are shown for illustration purposes only, and it is important to point out that you will only see these pages if you open the MSChart control independently. As soon as you aggregate the MSChart control into a User control, its property pages are no longer available, since its role now is to contribute to the User control, not to act as an independent control. Property pages in a User control are entirely the responsibility of the developer to create.

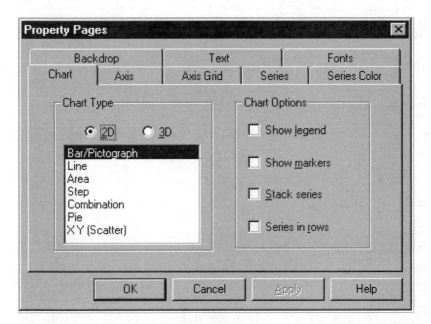

Property pages completely customize how properties can be set, in contrast to the standard Properties window, which has limited display options. Property pages provide a code pane for Visual Basic code, which allows you to validate user input and make the experience more interactive than the standard Properties window.

As an exercise we will create a property page for the Sales Analyzer control, focusing on the ChartType and ExtractFile properties, both of which can be set at design-time. The property page limits the ChartType property to one of two types, and lets the developer select the ExtractFile using a browse button. The final view of the compiled property page is shown below

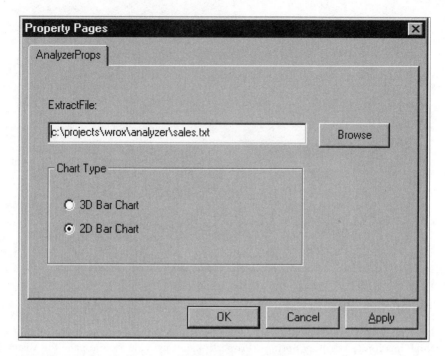

Create a property page for the Sales Analyzer control as follows:

1. Open a new property page in Analyzer.vbp using Project | Add Property Page. You should see a new folder called Property Pages open within the Analyzer project window, and a property page icon appear.

2. Change the (Name) property of the page to `AnalyzerProps`.

3. Add the controls as shown in the above figure, and as shown in the table below. You will notice that the compiled view has 3 additional buttons at the bottom of the page (OK, Cancel and Apply) as well as a Tab control with 'AnalyzerProps' as the caption. These are added automatically, but will not appear in design view.

Control (Name)	Property	Value
Label (`LblExtractFile`)	Width, Height	2700, 240
	Top, Left	240, 240
	Caption	Extract File:
TextBox (`TxtExtractFile`)	Width, Height	3780, 330
	Top, Left	600, 240

Control (Name)	Property	Value
Frame (Frame1)	Width, Height	3855, 1335
	Top, Left	1200, 240
	Caption	Chart Type
OptionButton (OptChart)	Width, Height	1815, 375
	Top, Left	360, 240
	Caption	3D Bar Chart
OptionButton (OptChart)	Width, Height	1815, 375
	Top, Left	1920, 480
	Caption	2D Bar Chart
CommandButton (cmdBrowse)	Width, Height	1095, 375
	Top, Left	600, 4200
	Caption	&Browse
CommonDialog (CommonDialog1)	Top, Left	1680, 4560

4. Add the following code listing to the property page, in order to associate the Sales Analyzer control attributes with the textbox and option button controls on the property page:

```
Private Sub txtExtractFile_Change()
 Changed = True
End Sub
Private Sub optChart_Click(Index As Integer)
 Changed = True
End Sub
Private Sub PropertyPage_ApplyChanges()
    SelectedControls(0).ExtractFile = txtExtractFile.Text
    If optChart(0).Value = True Then
       SelectedControls(0).ChartType = 0
    Else
       SelectedControls(0).ChartType = 1
    End If
End Sub
Private Sub PropertyPage_SelectionChanged()
    txtExtractFile.Text = SelectedControls(0).ExtractFile
    If SelectedControls(0).ChartType = 0 Then
       optChart(0).Value = True
    Else
       optChart(1).Value = True
    End If
End Sub
```

```
Private Sub cmdBrowse_Click()
'Purpose: Browse for sales data text files

Dim CancelError As Boolean

    On Error GoTo ErrHandler
    CancelError = True    ' Set filters.
    CommonDialog1.Filter = "Text Files (*.txt)|*.txt"    ' Specify default filter.
    CommonDialog1.FilterIndex = 2    ' Display the Open dialog box.
    CommonDialog1.ShowOpen    ' Call the open file procedure.

    'Open new Extract File
    txtExtractFile.Text = CommonDialog1.FileName

    Exit Sub
ErrHandler:
    'User pressed Cancel button.
    Exit Sub
End Sub
```

The simple code listing manages the association between `Sales` control properties and the property page controls. When the user first opens the property page, the `SelectionChanged` event fires, which assigns the current `Sales` property settings to the property page controls. When the user types in the textbox, or clicks one of the option buttons, the `Changed` property of the Property Page object is set to `True`. Once the **Apply** button is clicked, the `ApplyChanges` event fires, and the property page controls are used to set the `Sales` control properties. If the user clicks the **OK** button to close the property page, then the `ApplyChanges` event only fires if the `Changed` property equals `True`.

This wraps up our discussion of property pages and almost wraps up our development tasks for the Sales Analyzer control. As a finishing touch we should add descriptions of each public interface member using the dialog box in **Tools | Procedure Attributes**. These descriptions will show up in Visual Basic's Object Browser. For example, for the `ChartType` property:

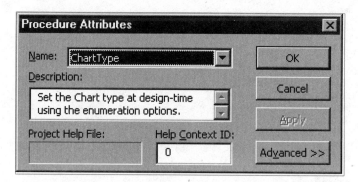

This is a good time to compile the control again, to incorporate the property pages into the OCX file. If you've been following the steps outlined here, then you already compiled the control once, at the end of Step 7. Before recompiling you should confirm that Binary Compatibility is set, in order to maintain a single Global Unique Identifier (GUID), which uniquely identifies the component in the client computer's registry. It is especially important to maintain a consistent GUID if the ActiveX control will be deployed on a web page (see Step 9).

To set Binary Compatibility:

> Copy the current OCX file to a new directory called \Compatibility. I usually place this directory as a subfolder of the directory where the VB source files reside.

> Open Project | Properties and switch to the Component tab.

> Select the radio button for Binary Compatibility

> Type or browse to the location of the compatibility OCX file.

> Hit Apply or OK to commit the new settings.

> Finally, select File | Make Analyzer.ocx to compile the control and register it to your system.

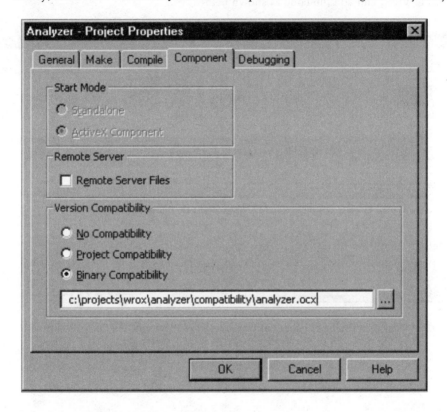

Step 9: Testing the Sales Analyzer Control on a Web Page

We can easily add the Sales Analyzer Control to a Web page using the ActiveX Control Pad, which was introduced in Chapter 4. Using the Script Wizard we can quickly add VBScript code to the FileStatus and PointSelected events. Use the following steps:

1. Open the ActiveX Control Pad and select **Edit I Insert ActiveX Control**.

2. Select **Analyzer.Sales** from the list of available, registered ActiveX controls. If it does not show up, browse to the location of the `Analyzer.ocx` file, and select it there.

3. The control will appear in design mode. Right-click on the control to open the property page and set the `ExtractFile` and `ChartType` properties. You can also set these properties in the floating Properties window. Click the close button on the designer when you are finished.

4. Next, open the Script Wizard from **Tools I Script Wizard**. You will see the interface members of the **Sales1** control displayed in an Explorer-type view. Select the `FileStatus` event in Code View, and add the code as shown below:

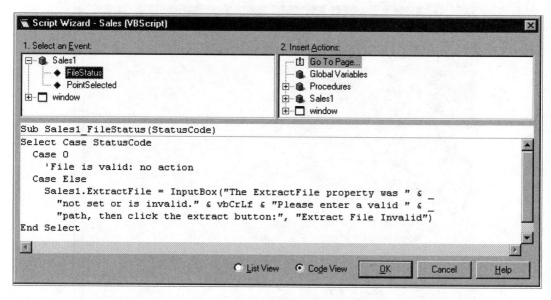

5. Select the `PointSelected` event in Code View, and add the code as shown here:

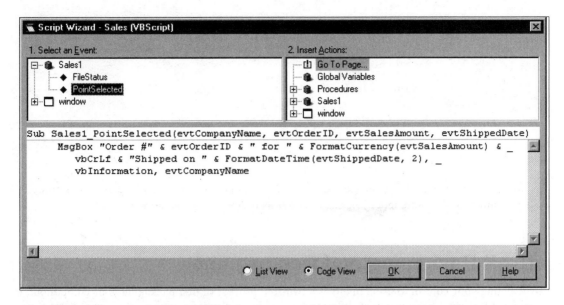

Click **OK**, and you should see the following listing in the code pane (except for the CODEBASE attribute, which I added):

```html
<HTML>

<HEAD>
<TITLE>Sales Analyzer</TITLE>
</HEAD>

<BODY>
<H2>Sales Analysis </H2>
<H4>View the latest sales data using the Sales Analyzer Control</H4>

<OBJECT ID="Sales1" WIDTH=436 HEIGHT=343
   CLASSID="CLSID:9C352639-DA4C-11D2-BB19-000000000000"
    CODEBASE="Analyzer.ocx#version=1,2,0,0">
   <PARAM NAME="_ExtentX" VALUE="11536">
   <PARAM NAME="_ExtentY" VALUE="9049">
   <PARAM NAME="ExtractFile" VALUE="c:\projects\wrox\analyzer\sales.txt">
   <PARAM NAME="ChartType" VALUE="1">
 </OBJECT>

<SCRIPT LANGUAGE="VBScript">
<!--

Sub Sales1_FileStatus(StatusCode)
Select Case StatusCode
   Case 0
   'File is valid: no action
   Case Else
      Sales1.ExtractFile = InputBox("The ExtractFile property was " & _
     "not set or is invalid." & vbCrLf & "Please enter a valid " & _
     "path, then click the extract button:", "Extract File Invalid")
   End Select
end sub
```

```
Sub Sales1_PointSelected(evtCompanyName, evtOrderID, evtSalesAmount,_
  evtShippedDate)
MsgBox "Order #" & evtOrderID & " for " & FormatCurrency(evtSalesAmount) & _
      vbCrLf & "Shipped on " & FormatDateTime(evtShippedDate, 2), _
      vbInformation, evtCompanyName
end sub

-->
</SCRIPT>
</BODY>

</HTML>
```

6. Finally, save the Web page as `Sales.htm`, and open it in Internet Explorer. The control functions the same in a browser container as it does in a form container.

ActiveX Packaging and Deployment

Distributing your control to users involves a two-step process of first packaging your component, then deploying it. Visual Basic provides different options for packaging components. Visual Basic 6 provides a wizard for packaging your control into a compressed **cabinet file** (`.cab`) that users can download directly from the Web. You can include all of the support files in the cabinet file, or you can specify that some or all of the support files be downloaded from another URL. For example, an ActiveX control always requires the Visual Basic runtime DLL, which is well over 1 MB in size. You can specify that the runtime file should be downloaded from Microsoft's Web site, thereby dramatically decreasing the size of the cabinet file.

You have different options for deploying your control. You can make it available on your Web page for download. Alternatively, you could go commercial, and sell your control in a shrink-wrapped box. Either way, you need to consider adding a **license key**, to ensure that only registered developers use your control. Visual Basic makes it very easy to add a license key.

As a professional developer, you are responsible for distributing software that does not contain any potentially harmful content that could disrupt a user's Registry or interfere with their system files. **Code signing** or **Digital Signing**, is a technology that certifies to the control's user that you are a trusted software provider. Although digital signing does not guarantee per se that your content is safe to run, it does identify you as a known, trusted developer who is registered with a **Certificate Authority**. Many developers poorly understand Digital signing, but its popularity is on the rise in response to the proliferation of ActiveX content on the Internet.

Packaging your ActiveX Control

Visual Basic 6 provides a Packaging and Deployment Wizard for creating a cabinet file for your ActiveX control that bundles the OCX and all support files into a single compressed file. Run the Wizard as follows:

1. In Visual Basic 6, select **Add-Ins I Add-In Manager** and load the Package and Deployment Wizard.

2. Open the ActiveX control project then run the wizard from **Add-Ins I Package and Deployment Wizard**.

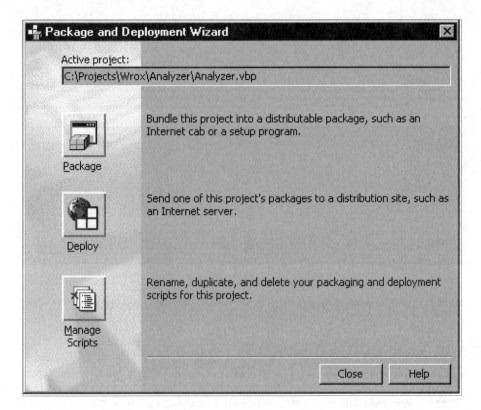

3. Click the **Package** button to create a new cabinet file.

4. Select "**Internet Package**" as the Package Type.

5. Choose a location for the package files.

6. Include all of the check-marked files in the package.

7. Mark the component as safe for initialization and scripting from the drop-down items. "**Safe for scripting**" means that the component can be safely accessed using an ActiveX scripting language, such as VBScript. "**Safe for initialization**" means that the component can be instanced with no potential harm to the user's system. You should only mark the component as "**Safe for initialization**" if it does not interact with the user's file system.

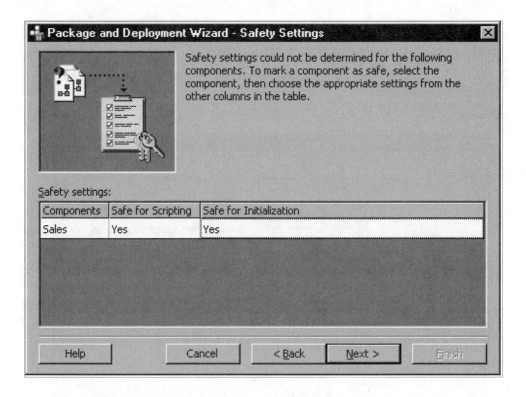

8. Finally, give the package a name, such as "Analyzer CAB", and click Finish.

Deploying your ActiveX Control

Once you have packaged your control, you'll want to make it available for others to install and use. The deployment wizard in Visual Basic 6 simplifies the process of uploading your production-ready control files to a storage location on a Web server. If you are using Visual Basic 5 you will need to upload your files manually. The deployment wizard lets you specify a storage location on a remote server and an upload method, including FTP and HTTP Post. If you created a server-side install package, then you can request that the deployment wizard unpack and install the files after they have been uploaded to the Web server.

The steps for deploying an ActiveX control package to a Web server are:

1. Open the ActiveX control project then run the wizard from Add-Ins | Package and Deployment Wizard.

2. Click the Deploy button.

3. Select a Package to deploy.

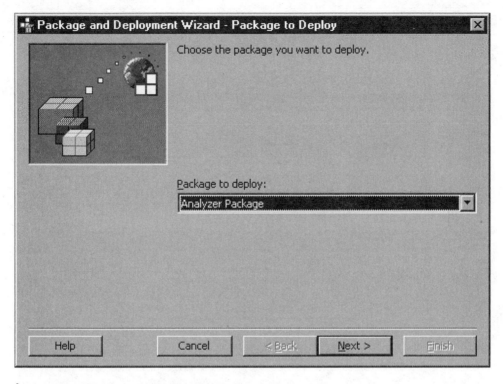

4. Select Web Publishing as the Deployment Method.

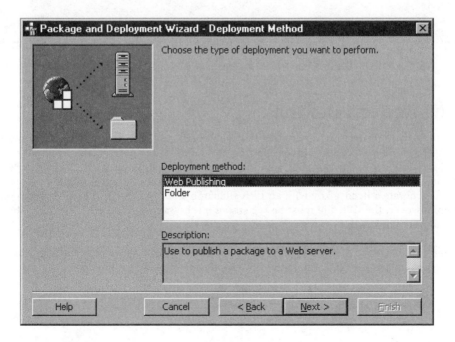

5. Select the Items to Deploy. Note that the Package wizard automatically created a basic HTML page to host your control. The page inserts your control using an <OBJECT> tag.

6. Choose a destination URL and a Web publishing protocol.

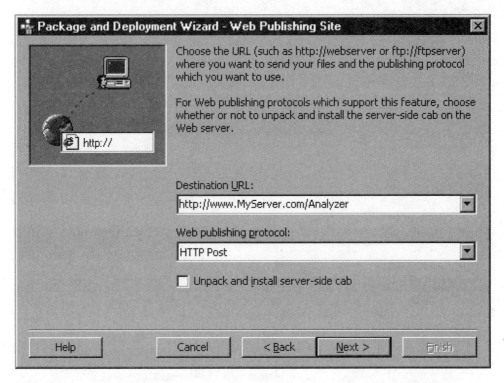

7. Click the Finish button to save a script for future Web server deployments.

Licensing ActiveX Controls

Licensing helps you protect the investment of time, money and research that you have put into developing your ActiveX control. Licensing prevents another developer from using your control in their project without your permission. To add a license key, simply put a check against Require License Key in the Project | Project Properties dialog box. When you compile the project, the wizard will generate a license key with an LPK filename extension. The LPK file is separate from the OCX file; however, the LPK file must be registered on the same machine as the OCX file in order for someone to use your control.

If someone simply copies a licensed OCX file over to their machine without the LPK file then they will not be able to use the OCX file, either in design-time or run-time modes

Container applications such as Visual Basic and Microsoft InterDev will not load a licensed control in design time unless they can match a local, registered license key with the control. If you wish to provide design-time licensing rights to a developer, then you should provide them with a setup program for your control that includes the license file. Keep in mind that the Packaging and Deployment wizard will not automatically add license files to a setup program or cabinet file, so you must add these yourself in the Included Files wizard dialog

Licensed ActiveX controls that are deployed on a Web page have a further requirement. Microsoft's Internet Explorer requires that all components on a single Web page be covered under a **license package** that contains runtime-licensing information on all the components. You can think of it as an array of CLSID and license key pairs. To create a license package, you need to use the utility LPK_TOOL.exe, which can be found in the Tools directory on the Visual Basic CD. Once you've created this file, place it in the same directory where the HTML page resides. You also need to include a reference in the HTML page to the Internet Explorer Licensing Manager ActiveX object. The following code listing shows a sample Web page that uses the Sales Analyzer control:

```
<! Reference to the IE Licensing Manager !>
<OBJECT CLASSID="clsid:5220cb21-c88d-11cf-b347-00aa00a28331">
    <PARAM NAME="LPKPath" VALUE="AnalyzerPkg.lpk">
</OBJECT>

<! Reference to the Sales Analyzer Control !>
<OBJECT CLASSID="CLSID:9C352639-DA4C-11D2-BB19-000000000000" WIDTH=100 HEIGHT=25>
 CODEBASE="Analyzer.cab#version=1,2,0,0">
    <PARAM NAME="_ExtentX" VALUE="11536">
    <PARAM NAME="_ExtentY" VALUE="9049">
    <PARAM NAME="ExtractFile" VALUE="c:\projects\wrox\analyzer\sales.txt">
    <PARAM NAME="ChartType" VALUE="1">
</OBJECT>
```

If your licensed control is deployed on a web site in this manner then there is nothing stopping an unauthorized user from downloading the control, using it, and even redistributing it. If you need to prevent an unauthorized user from downloading your control then you will need to implement security to restrict access to the web page where the control resides. Another alternative is to distribute just the control over the web site, and to distribute the licensing package independently, either from a secure web site, or else directly to the user. So while anyone can download the control binary source code, Internet Explorer will not create an instance of control unless it can match the license key.

Other developers who use your licensed control in developing their own need to make special distribution arrangements to accommodate licensing restrictions. The options are:

➤ Require that all users of the new control have a licensed version of your control on their machine.

➤ Distribute your license key with the new control, with your permission and a shared revenue agreement.

➤ None of the above if you give the developer unlimited run-time distribution rights.

Digital Signing and Authenticode

Digital Signing is a confusing topic for many developers, but with the proliferation of ActiveX controls on the Internet, it's a critical one to understand. This section provides you with an overview of the technology and an introduction to the buzzwords. However, since information changes rapidly, I will also include online references that you should consult for the most up-to-date information on Digital signing.

What is Certification?

As we will discuss in Chapter 6, before using a control, you need to ensure that the control is **authentic** and has **integrity**. Enter the Certificate Authority (CA), which is an organization that issues **Digital Certificates** to developers who have gone through an application process and are now certified as trusted sources. There are several CAs to choose from, but Microsoft currently recommends VeriSign:

```
http://www.verisign.com
```

There are two types of certification you can receive. Each is valid for one year before it must be renewed:

1. Class 2 Certification is for "Individual Developers", and costs $20 per year. The application process is relatively simple and it takes about 5 business days to receive your certificate.

2. Class 3 Certification is for commercial developers and costs $400 per year. The lengthy application process requires the developer to:

   ➢ Prove their employment status

   ➢ Make "The Pledge" that their software is not potentially harmful

   ➢ Submit a Dun & Bradstreet Rating that certifies that their company is solvent.

Once you have been approved for certification, the CA will provide you with two files:

   ➢ The Software Publisher Certificate (SPC), which identifies the software publisher and provides their public key. The SPC provides an X.509 certificate that is distributed with the published software.

   ➢ The private encryption key that the publisher uses to generate a digital signature for their software.

How Does Digital Signing Work?

As we discussed in Chapter 2, when a developer is ready to publish their software to the Web, they use the Authenticode utilities (available from `http://msdn.microsoft.com/downloads/tools/ActiveXSDK/axsdk.asp`, and currently in version 2.0) their private encryption key and their SPC to digitally sign their software. You aren't limited to just signing ActiveX controls. In addition to OCX files, you can sign EXE, DLL and CAB files. The signing process works as follows:

1. Compile the software component.

2. Locate your private key and SPC files. (Microsoft recommends that you store the files on a removable medium, such as a floppy disk, in a secure location).

3. Open an MS-DOS Window and navigate to the directory where the SignCode utility is located.

4. The `SignCode` utility uses the following syntax, which you type at the command line:

```
signcode -spc SPC -v PVK -n ControlName -i URL -$ commercial -t
http://timestamp.verisign.com/scripts/timestamp.dll -x ControlName
```

SPC is the SPC filename, PVK is the private key filename, ControlName is the name of the software component, and URL is the home page of your company. The -t switch adds a **timestamp** to the component. This feature ensures that once your component has been signed, it will continue to be stamped as secure, even if you let your certificate expire after one year. The -x switch indicates that the component has already been signed once, and that you are re-signing it in order to add a timestamp. A component must also be resigned if it is recompiled. Here's a more specific example of using the SignCode utility:

```
signcode -spc a:\MySpc.spc -v MyPvk.pvk -n "Sales1" -i http://www.mycompany.com -$
commercial -t http://timestamp.verisign.com/scripts/timestamp.dll -x
"Analyzer.ocx"
```

Authenticode provides utilities that generate test certificates, including a test SPC. So before you rush out to get a real certificate from a CA, be sure to take advantage of test certificates to learn more about how the signing process works.

Reading a Digital Signature

To get the full protection of digital signing, you need to set the security level in Internet Explorer to at least medium. This level ensures that Internet Explorer will follow up the information provided by the digital signature to verify that the software is from a trusted source and has not been altered. In fact, the medium security setting, by default, will not allow you to download unsigned components (but the low setting will). The high setting will not allow you to download an untrusted component at all.

When a user downloads a component that has been digitally signed, they receive a Security Warning prompt that contains the following information:

> ➢ The name of the Certificate Authority
> ➢ The identity of the publisher
> ➢ A prompt asking if they want to continue downloading the software component.

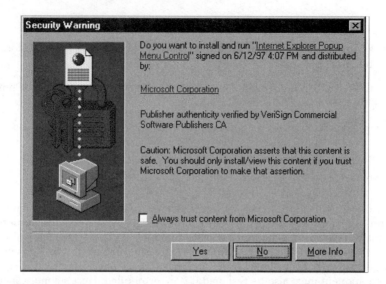

If the security setting is at least medium, Internet Explorer uses the digital signature to confirm the identity of the publisher, and uses the public key to verify that the software has not been altered. If any problems are found, or if the component is not signed, Internet Explorer will not permit the component to be downloaded.

Clicking the More Info button on the Security Warning prompt gives you access to all the certificate information.

Remember, no control is guaranteed to be safe, even one that comes from a trusted source, so use your judgement about whether to deploy it. If there is any doubt, just say no, then research the control. On the brighter side, if you find a publisher whom you are comfortable with, then you can add them to your list of trusted publishers, and Internet Explorer will not prompt you for that publisher again, *unless* it finds that the software was tampered with. Remember, if you have *any* doubt at all about the authenticity or integrity of a software component then *always* avoid downloading it. You should also *never* use less than a medium security level in Internet Explorer.

Code Signing Resources

Your best source for information on Authenticode and Digital signing is Microsoft's Web site. For an excellent introduction to code signing see the article:

`http://www.microsoft.com/workshop/security/authcode/intro_authenticode.asp`

Another good resource on these security topics is *ASP/MTS/ADSI Web Security* by R.Harrison, *ISBN: 0130844659*

The Site Builder Network section on Security and Cryptography is a must-visit, at:

`http://www.microsoft.com/workshop/c-frame.htm#/workshop/security/default.asp`

For a high-level Authenticode FAQ, visit VeriSign at:

```
http://www.verisign.com/developers/authenticodefaq.html
```

Summary

This chapter provided you with a hands-on look at how to create ActiveX controls and how to package and deploy them for the Web. The example Sales Analyzer control illustrates how ActiveX controls can provide a level of functionality that would be difficult to provide on the Web with other technologies. It is relatively easy to leverage your existing understanding of desktop development in Visual Basic to the Web because the coding methodology does not change for different containers (e.g., the browser versus a Visual Basic form). However, you should not get lulled into a false sense of complacency, because distribution over the Web has more complications than distribution for the desktop.

Topics such as licensing and digital signing are complicated and always changing, so your best source of information will be the Internet. This chapter attempted to provide you with an overview of these complex technologies, and hopefully a starting point from which to learn more. Whether you are a small, home-grown development firm or a major software development company, every developer needs to think through Web deployment issues and how to roll your components out in a way that protects the security of your customers and the legal rights of developers like yourself.

In summary, this chapter introduced you to the following topics:

> ➢ ActiveX Control Creation using Visual Basic
> ➢ Distributing Controls to the Web
> ➢ Utilities that help you create, test and deploy your Control, including the ActiveX Control Pad and the Package and Deployment Wizard
> ➢ Licensing and Digital Signing Issues

Component development is a changing topic, and I encourage you to keep up to date by visiting the Component Development section of the Site Builder Network at:

```
http://www.microsoft.com/workshop/c-
frame.htm#/workshop/components/default.asp
```

In the next chapter, we're going to explore the advantages of the new Visual Basic DHTML Application, which offers you a whole new range of flexible and powerful programming tools to take your applications on to the web.

6

Dynamic HTML Applications

What is a Dynamic HTML Application?

A Dynamic HTML (DHTML) Application is a type of Visual Basic 6 project that you can use to build "smart" Web pages. It works in a similar way to the traditional Visual Basic Standard.EXE project, but in DHTML Applications you distribute the applications by giving users access to a Web page, rather than giving them an executable file.

The General Idea

When you start a DHTML Application project in Visual Basic, you're presented with a form that you can use to build up your page. This works in a similar way to Microsoft FrontPage or your favorite HTML editing tool. All you do is enter the text into the page and when you want something special like a form or a picture, you grab the appropriate tool from a palette and draw it directly on to a page.

In fact, this is exactly how DHTML Applications are created, but the word 'dynamic' should be tipping you off that there's something special going on. Simply, what VB lets you do is add some intelligence to your page, and that intelligence is able to change the content on your page *dynamically*. Consequently, a web page will interact with the user as if it was an application, rather than simply being passive like the pages of a book.

The Document Object Model

Internet Explorer's Document Object Model (DOM) is a set of objects that lets you control all of the elements on your HTML page.

Before Internet Explorer 3, Internet Explorer did have an object model, but no one outside of Redmond knew about it. All the Microsoft developers wanted to do was get a page from a Web site and display it on the screen. To do this, they had to build a whole number of internal structures and gizmos that'd let them take the HTML and interpret (or 'parse') it into a format they could use to draw it on the screen.

But, when Netscape decided that Java was the way to go and brought out Navigator 3, Netscape had to make their counterpart object model available to page designers. Both Java and JavaScript needed to be able to interact with elements on the page. The object model makes it possible to identify any of the elements on a page and change their properties - for example, to alter the source of an image.

When Internet Explorer 3 was released, Microsoft's browser now had support for Java, JavaScript and their own cut down version of Visual Basic called VBScript. They also turned their own object model inside out so that developers could see it, just like Netscape did. They modeled their object model so it was mostly compatible with Netscape's.

The only way script code can communicate with what's already on the page and add new things to the page is by manipulating the DOM programmatically. Although the DOM has been around for a while now, DHTML has only been around since Internet Explorer 4. The impact that IE4 has on the DOM is that it is now extremely feature rich.

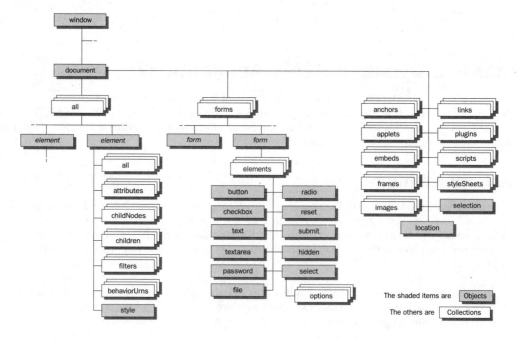

What does all this have to do with us today? Well, Microsoft have long touted the significance of ActiveX technology and, along with it, their Component Object Model (COM) technology. Simply, these technologies let applications and components cooperate by sharing functionality and data. Much of what you read in this book is only possible because of ActiveX. In fact, as we shall see in Chapter 7, Internet Explorer itself is just a window frame and an ActiveX control that functions as a Web browser! ActiveX controls allow us to do one important thing – *they let us access Internet Explorer's Document Object Model from any application we like*. And what this chapter is all about is how we can manipulate the DOM using a Visual Basic component hosted inside a Web page.

A 30,000-foot view of the Document Object Model

As you can see from the figure on the previous page, the Document Object Model is laid out as a tree, much like most object models that you're familiar with.

At the base of this tree is the Document object. This object provides programmatic access to the rest of the tree, and is the object we'll be using a lot of throughout this chapter. For example, you can ask the Document object for the object that contains stuff inside the BODY tag of your HTML document (the Body object, no less), or for the frames that make up the page. In fact, when you ask for a specific frame, you can access that frame's Document object too so you can effectively walk through and around anything that Internet Explorer can see.

What's important about the DOM is that it is not read-only. You can manipulate it by changing methods and properties on the DOM objects just like you would with, say, the Form or Button objects inside Visual Basic itself. This means that not only can you ask IE to load a document and then query the elements that appear on that page, but you can either make a page completely from scratch (not entirely recommended, but do-able), or you can locate and modify elements already on that page to get the desired effect.

One important point – in order to access an element on the page, it must have an ID attribute (also known as an ID property). A neat thing that IE does that Netscape doesn't, is say you define a button as having an ID of ClickMe, IE will define an object called ClickMe as part of the global scope of your script. This means that you can refer to that object directly from code, like this:

```
MsgBox ClickMe.innerHTML
```

An alternate way of accessing the same object is to use the "All" property of the Document object:

```
MsgBox Document.All("ClickMe").innerHTML
```

Those of you interested in performance should note that the latter example is less efficient, basically because IE has to walk a list of objects to find the one you wanted.

To show you how to modify the document, later in this chapter we'll see how we can add rows and columns to a table. We do this by finding the table we want to manipulate (and in our case, we give it an ID, like MyTable) and then calling methods on it to modify it. Like this:

```
Set NewRow = MyTable.insertRow
```

We'll be laboring this point later, but pretty much everything you get back from the DOM is an object in its own right, with its own set of methods and properties. In the `insertRow` example, we get back an HTMLTableRow object. Once we have that, we can call the "insertCell" method and then we get back another object, and so on.

One of the neat things about the DOM is that there's literally nothing you can't do with it. You can change any part of any element on your pages.

Here's some examples:

> You can create new elements. For example, you can actually add OPTION elements to a SELECT element after the page is loaded.

> You can remove elements. For example, removing sentences from a paragraph as the user changes other elements on the page.

> You can hide elements, or control any part of an element's style. For example, hiding an INPUT element when the user clicks off a check box, or changing the color of a table.

> You can dynamically build a table then take the HTML that's used to build up that table and save it to a file. (That's the example we'll be working on next.)

The DOM is a pretty large object model, but it's thoughtfully and logically laid out. One of the good parts about API's like this is once you get the hang of how a little bit works, you can usually take that same paradigm and 'guestimate' how parts your not so familiar with works.

You can find a whole load of raw reference materials at `http://msdn.microsoft.com/` in the Web Workshop. (Look for DHTML References.) Naturally, Wrox publishes a number of books on the subject, and you can find more information on those at `http://www.wrox.com/`.

Introducing DHTML Applications

To start the DHTML Application project, open Visual Basic and choose DHTML Application from the New Project dialog as shown in the screenshot.

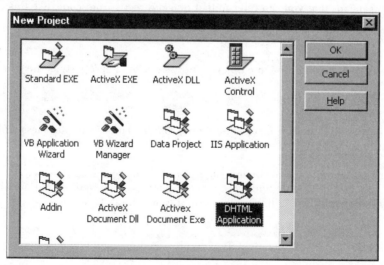

When VB opens the new project, you need to kick start it into giving you something to work with, so using the Project tree in the top right, expand Designers and double-click DHTMLPage1. You will end up with something that looks like Figure 6.2.

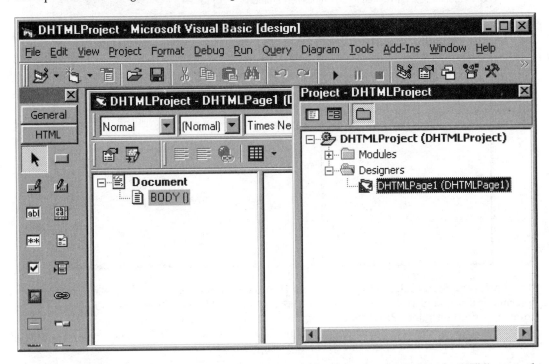

An important thing to note here is that VB has automatically suggested we use the HTML control palette, rather than the General control palette that we're used to using. It's suggesting that we use this because it's better to use HTML specific controls on a Web page, rather than using the general purpose Visual Basic ones, which may not be installed on the client machine.

The DHTML Designer

The DHTML Designer that VB presents us with is similar to the one you might find in Microsoft FrontPage or another popular page editor. Simply, it lets you create an HTML file using a WYSIWYG editor. Try it now and you'll see it's natural to use. Below is a simple example of what can be done. It's a fairly crude editor, but you can input text and images in the right-hand pane of the window, and the elements you add are mirrored on the left.

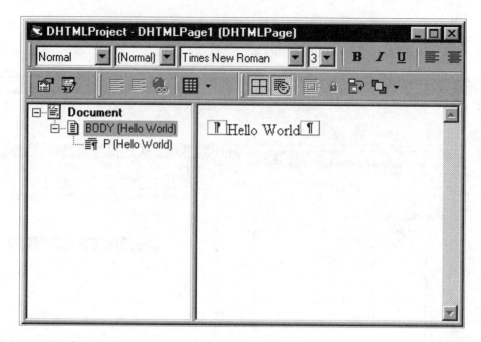

If you press the Start toolbar button, or select Run|Start from the menu, Visual Basic will open Internet Explorer and you'll be able to see your new page. (The very first time you do this, VB will come up with the Project Properties dialog box with the Debugging tag selected. Select the Start Component radio button and click OK.) When you return to VB you'll have to press the End toolbar button, or select Run-End to get the DHTML Designer back.

Nothing special's happened so far, so let's try building a simple application. Using the HTML control palette, select the Button control and draw a new button on your page. Once it's in place, double-click the button and enter this code:

```
Private Function Button1_onclick() As Boolean
    Document.Location = "http://www.wrox.com/"
End Function
```

Now try running your application again. When the button appears, click on it and you should be taken to Wrox's home page.

What is VB doing?

What's happening here is very straightforward. We're using the DOM to control the Document object and we're telling it to navigate to a new page. VB is taking over the job of understanding the technical part of telling Internet Explorer that when the button is pressed it should go ahead and change the Location property of the Document object to the new Web page.

With Internet Explorer open, go ahead and select View|Source from the menu. VB doesn't do a very good job of formatting the original source code and for this example I've added some white space to aid reading. Normally, the source will open in Notepad. What you get will look similar to this:

```
<!DOCTYPE HTML PUBLIC "-//W3C//DTD HTML 4.0 Transitional//EN">
<HTML>
    <HEAD>
        <META content="text/html; " http-equiv=Content-Type>
        <META content="MSHTML 5.00.2314.1000" name=GENERATOR>
    </HEAD>
    <BODY class=(Normal)>
        <!--METADATA TYPE="MsHtmlPageDesigner" startspan-->
        <object id="DHTMLPage1" classid="clsid:D60D7F1C-0E4F-11D3-AFAE-00A0CC40290A"
width=0 height=0>
        </object>
        <!--METADATA TYPE="MsHtmlPageDesigner" endspan-->

        <P>Hello World.
        <INPUT id=Button1 name=Button1 style="HEIGHT: 45px; LEFT: 40px; POSITION:
absolute; TOP: 94px; WIDTH: 196px" type=button value=Button1>
        </P>
    </BODY>
</HTML>
```

The highlighted code tells Internet Explorer to load an ActiveX object. As part of the DHTML Application project, Visual Basic is responsible for generating that ActiveX control.

The ActiveX component encapsulates all of the logic we build into the page. This is a different approach to the majority of DHTML editing tools. Macromedia Dreamweaver, for example, generates JavaScript code and inserts it directly into the page. That's not what's happening here, and the VB approach has two distinct advantages and one disadvantage. Firstly, people viewing your page can't see your source code, which is important if you want to protect your intellectual property, or stop people from playing with the code and breaking it. Secondly, compiled Visual Basic code runs faster than interpreted JavaScript code. The balancing disadvantage is that our pages can only be used on Windows machines that have Internet Explorer 4 or later installed as the web client.

When our ActiveX component is initialized, it hooks itself into Internet Explorer and starts listening for any events that occur. When it detects an OnClick event, it searches for the source element (the button) and looks to see if there's anything it should do in response. By virtue of the fact that the component has been linked into the Internet Explorer environment, the VB code you write now has the same access to the Document Object Model as IE itself does. Therefore, you are able to find and control the Document object.

A Practical Example

Let's imagine that Barb is the manager of a sales team of three people: Edward, Amir and Stephanie. Each week, she wants her salespeople to send her a report on how much they sold and to whom. Presently, each member of the team has to enter the values into a Microsoft Word document and then send it to her over e-mail.

What she'd like is to give her people access to a Web page that they can use to fill in their figures. When the form is complete, she'd like to have the report saved to a server so she can access it at her leisure the following week.

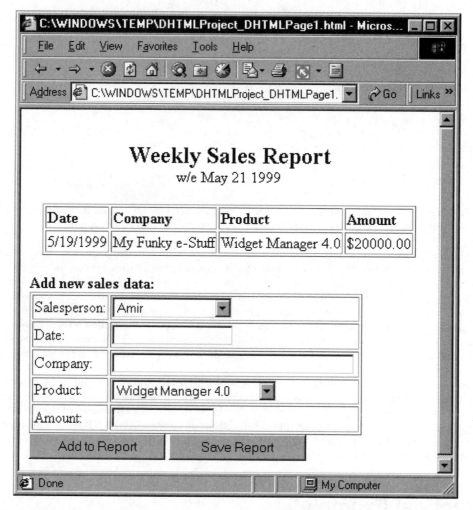

We can make this happen for Barb by building her a DHTML Application. Just so you know where we're headed, the screenshot above shows the page we're going to build.

Getting Started

Looking at the page we want to build, it's obvious what we need to do. The page is divided into two sections: an area where the report data will appear and an area containing the form that the salesperson can use to enter the data.

Let's start off by building the page in Visual Basic. I'll assume you're familiar with how to build up a VB form, and creating a DHTML page is a similar process. So, start a new project, open the DHTML Designer and try to duplicate what you can see in the screenshot above. (Don't enter the sample report data row, in the top section, because we'll do this dynamically later).

By default, the text on the page works how you'd expect but the form elements float on top, leading to a tricky situation where you're fighting the designer to keep the layout stable. The answer is to check off the **Absolute Position** *toolbar button immediately after you've dropped on a new element. This'll stop the elements from floating around on top of the text and the whole thing will behave more logically.*

When you want to add values to the product list, you'll need to use the SELECT element's property sheet. To do this, right-click on the element and choose **Properties**. The screenshot below shows an example of a property sheet with two products.

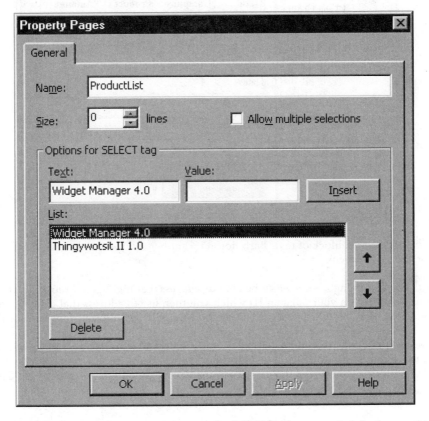

OK, so we've gone through the process of using the DHTML Designer, let's look at making the page responsive.

Dynamically Changing Text

You should now have something that looks like the screenshot below. By default, VB does not show the symbols showing the paragraph and line breaks. Click the "Show Details" toolbar button so you can see this hidden stuff.

Look at the highlighted block of text. Barb doesn't want her salespeople having to fill out the date, so our app will do it for them.

In order to do that, though, we need to be able to *address* that highlighted block. In DHTML, you can give any element on your page an ID which you then use to address that element from your code. Once you know what the ID is, you can run methods on and get and set properties for that element.

Firstly, we need to define that block of text as being addressable in its own right. As it stands, the text is part of the whole paragraph which includes the 'Weekly Sales Report' text, so right now we can't just alter the little bit concerning the date. With the date highlighted, press the Wrap Selection in <SPAN>...</SPAN> toolbar button.

It's time to start looking at the DOM tree that takes up the left-hand side of the DHTML Designer:

The DOM is represented *hierarchically*, just like the way Windows Explorer represents the folders on your computer's hard disk. In the Figure, we can see that Document is at the root of the tree. Body appears as the only child of document, so we know that BODY is parented by Document and, by association, Document *contains* BODY. The highlighted portion shows our new SPAN element which is parented by the Paragraph element.

To make the current date appear in the top section of the page, the SPAN has to be programmable, and to be programmable it has to have an ID. With the SPAN selected in the DOM Tree, go over to the **Property Palette** and set the (Id) property to read: CurrentDate.

> *Although Visual Basic refers to this property as (Id), the parenthesis is just there so VB will display it at the top of the property list. In the Document Object Model itself, the ID property doesn't have parenthesis, it's simply called ID.*

Double-clicking on CurrentDate in the DOM Tree will bring up the Code Editor. (Careful here, because you can't just click on the selected text, you have do to it from the tree.) What we need to do now is hook into the load event so as soon as the SPAN is loaded we can change the text. If, however, you look in the Event drop down on the Code Editor, you'll notice there is no event that looks like it'll get called when the page loads. This is by design. Our component has to hook into IE somehow, and it can't do that until it's loaded and it may only load after the SPAN element does – which means it can't properly capture the event. Instead, you have to drop down the **Object** list, select **DHTMLPage** and then select the Load event. The screenshot below shows the correct object and event to choose.

Enter the code for DHTMLPage_Load as you see it here:

```
Private Sub DHTMLPage_Load()
    CurrentDate.innerHTML = "w/e " & MonthName(Month(Now)) _
        & " " & Day(Now) & " " & Year(Now)
End Sub
```

You'll be glad to know that the full Visual Basic debugger works when you're building DHTML Applications. You can set breakpoints, move the execution pointer and watch variables as usual.

This is similar to the trick we saw before with navigating to a new page when a button was pressed. When the page gets initialized, it fires its own Load event. That event requests that the innerHTML property of a control called CurrentDate is changed to reflect a string we construct dynamically. In this case CurrentDate points to our SPAN element. The innerHTML property is a DHTML property that the majority of elements have. InnerHTML contains the HTML that the control is required to display. When we change that value, Internet Explorer is prompted to re-render the part of the page that accommodates that control and so our new text is seen!

Building up the Report

Our next job is a little more complicated. What we want is whenever one of our salespeople presses the "Add to Report" button, we want to take the information in the form and add a new row to the table to reflect the sales data.

Let's start by making sure the table that is going to contain the report data is addressable, so set the ID value of the table, in the Property Window, to ReportTable. If you prefer, you can select elements directly from the DHTML tree..

If you find it tricky to select elements on the WYSIWYG part of the DHTML Designer, remember you can select elements directly from the DHTML Tree.

Now we need to make every element in the form addressable. Assign IDs to your elements like this:

> Sales person list – PersonList
> Date field – DateBox
> Company field – CompanyBox
> Product list – ProductList
> Amount field – AmountBox
> Add To Report Button – AddToReport
> Save Report Button – SaveReport

Now let's get down to business and start adding the data to the report. In this example, we're going to simplify things by not worrying about validating the input.

So where do we start? Well, we know we need to create a row on the table, so let's start there. The HTMLTable element has a method called insertRow. The method returns an HTMLTableRow object, so let's do that first.

> **Bear in mind that the Document Object Model has the word "Object" in it because every single part of a document is represented with an *object*. That may seem obvious, but you'll get a clearer understanding of what's happening when you remember the majority of properties and methods you will use will return objects.**

```
Private Function AddToReport_onclick () As Boolean
    Set NewRow = ReportTable.insertRow
End Function
```

You can try running the application, but not a great deal will happen. Next, we need to add some columns to our new row:

```
Private Function AddToReport_onclick() As Boolean
    Set NewRow = ReportTable.insertRow
    Set DateCell = NewRow.insertCell
    DateCell.innerHTML = DateBox.Value
End Function
```

Inserting a new cell into the row returns an object just like inserting a new row into the table did. (Just so you know, the kind of object that represents individual cells is called HTMLTableCell and, in fact, DateCell will contain one of these objects after the call to insertCell.) Once we've created the cell, we can go ahead and set the HTML text for that cell to be equal to the value our user entered into the date box.

After adding the code to create the other three columns, our code looks like this:

```
Private Function AddToReport_onclick() As Boolean

    ' Create a new row in the report...
    Set NewRow = ReportTable.insertRow

    ' Insert a new cell to contain the date value
    Set DateCell = NewRow.insertCell
    DateCell.innerHTML = DateBox.Value

    ' Do the same with the company name
    Set CompanyCell = NewRow.insertCell
    CompanyCell.innerHTML = CompanyBox.Value

    ' Add a cell and set the product name (see notes)
    Set ProductCell = NewRow.insertCell
    ProductCell.innerHTML = ProductList.children(ProductList.selectedIndex).Text

    ' Add a cell and set the amount
    Set amountcell = NewRow.insertCell
    amountcell.innerHTML = AmountBox.Value

End Function
```

The statement "ProductList.children(ProductList.selectedIndex).Text" is used because by default when we ask a SELECT box for it's Value and there's no value set, it returns an empty string. This can happen when you use the property sheet and specify Text values, but not a corresponding Value entry.

> You can get a better understanding of what I mean by going back and looking at the figure showing the **Property Pages** for the ProductList select box. Notice how the Value edit box is blank, where the Text one isn't.

The code that's been added returns the text value instead. It does this by getting the index of the selected item and asking ProductList for its corresponding OPTION element. Once we have the OPTION element, we ask it for its Text value and we then add this to the report.

The screen shot below shows what we have so far.

We can improve the formatting by changing the code:

```
ProductCell.innerHTML = ProductList.children(ProductList.selectedIndex).Text
```

```
        ' Add a cell and set the amount (nicely formatted)
        Set amountcell = NewRow.insertCell
        amountcell.Style.TextAlign = "right"
        amountcell.innerHTML = "$" & FormatNumber(AmountBox.Value, 2)

End Function
```

The new line we've added there uses **Cascading Style Sheets** (CSS) to alter the formatting of the cell. CSS was introduced along with DHTML. It has two functions. Firstly, it lets page designers lay out their pages with far greater control than was previously possible. Secondly, it has mechanisms that reduce the need to constantly repeat yourself when using styling tags in HTML. When you're sending data over a network of any sort, you don't want to ever repeat yourself because it's a waste of bandwidth. One of the many things CSS lets us do is generate a "class" which we can configure with the appropriate font settings. When we add elements to our page, we can assign that class to those elements and eliminate the repetition. Here's an example of what we can do:

```
<HTML>
   <HEAD>
      <STYLE>
         .myclass { font-family:"arial,geneva"; font-size:10pt; }
      </STYLE>
   </HEAD>
   <BODY>
      <TABLE CLASS=myclass>
         <TR>
            <TD>Value</TD>
            <TD>Another</TD>
            <TD>Value 3</TD>
            <TD>And so on</TD>
         </TR>
      </TABLE>
   </BODY>
</HTML>
```

The STYLE tag is used to define a style-sheet. We've created a class inside this style-sheet called myclass. We've then assigned that class to the TABLE element so now everything inside the table will be nicely formatted. Since this is a small styling element for only one page, we've included it on the page itself. That said, one of the biggest advantages of stylesheets is that you can include them as a separate .css file, and then call it from your HTML page using @import

```
<style>
    @import URL("http://mywebsite/mystyles.css")
<style>
```

Obviously, this will allow you to use a single stylesheet across several pages – guaranteeing lower file sizes (because you can skip the formatting in HTML) and a consistent style across your website (because all your pages use the same styling information).

In our VB example the line amountcell.Style.TextAlign = "right" is accessing the style definition for the cell (through the Style property), and then altering that definitions TextAlign property to right-align the cell. We could, if we wanted, assign a class to the cell with a line like:

```
amountcell.className = "myclass"
```

Although the adoption of CSS isn't as widespread as it could be because not every browser on the everyday desktop implements it, CSS makes life much easier for Web designers. As a DHTML Application designer, you can take as much advantage of it as you like because these applications are only supported by Internet Explorer 4.0 onward- in other words, only those which support DHTML applications anyway!

CSS is an involved technology so we won't cover it in too much detail here, but you can find a lot of information about CSS on any of the popular Web building sites, the MSDN Library or Wrox's Professional Style Sheets for HTML and XML (ISBN 1861001657).

Saving the Report on the Server

Recall that in the pre-DHTML Application scenario, our salespeople are e-mailing Barb with their reports once a week. Ideally, Barb would like the reports put in the correct place on her departmental server so she knows that they are getting filed and backed up properly.

The following code snippet will create the appropriate folder on the server and configure the name of a file that we can use to store the report data in. To give this a context, we know the path of a shared folder on a server where we want to store the reports and we'll create a subfolder inside that folder based on the current date. Then, we'll create an HTML file based on the name of the salesperson.

```
Private Function SaveReport_onclick() As Boolean

    ' Create the FileSystemObject...
    Set fso = CreateObject("Scripting.FileSystemObject")

    ' Where do we want to save all reports?
    ' (Change this path when you're debugging to make it save
    ' somewhere on your local computer!)
    ' The trailing slash is important!
    basepath = "\Sales\Reports\Weekly\"

    ' Each week has it's own folder...
    basepath = basepath & Month(Now) & "-" & Day(Now) & "-" & Year(Now)

    ' Now create the folder...
    ' BUT, as any of our salespeople can do this, the folder may
    ' already be in place. Ignore any errors that occur, and
    ' then reset the error handler back to normal operation.
    On Error Resume Next
    fso.CreateFolder basepath
    On Error GoTo 0

    ' Make up a filename based on the name of the salesperson...
    FileName = basepath & "\" & PersonList.children _
                (PersonList.selectedIndex).Text & ".htm"

    ' Create our new file...
    Set file = fso.CreateTextFile(FileName)

    ' ...and this is where we'll draw our report!

    ' Close the file
    file.Close
    Set file = Nothing

    ' Cleanup
    Set fso = Nothing
End Function
```

That code should be self explanatory, but remember you will need to reference the Windows Scripting Library from your project. Note that `PersonList.Value` cannot be used, as the value could be empty.

In order to make that snippet useful we need to write some VB code that'll generate the HTML of the report. Active Server Pages developers should already be familiar with the concept of writing VB code that generates HTML pages.

We'll start by adding the framework of the document. The HTML to do that looks like this:

```
<HTML>
    <HEAD>
        <TITLE>Weekly Sales Report</TITLE>
    </HEAD>
    <BODY>
        ...report goes here...
    </BODY>
</HTML>
```

And we can add this to the report with these lines:

```
' ...and this is where we'll draw our report!
file.WriteLine "<HTML><HEAD><TITLE>Weekly Sales Report</TITLE><BODY>"
file.WriteLine "</BODY></HTML>"
```

When we're building reports up by directly writing to a file, we want to keep the number of `WriteLine` commands to a minimum. The `File` object will add a carriage-return/line-feed pair to the end of each line written with `WriteLine` and frequent use of carriage-return/line-feeds can break the parsing code of Internet Explorer leading to horrible looking results. As a rule of thumb, don't worry about nicely formatted HTML on simple, dynamically generated pages– optimize for speed and size by not adding white-space characters.

Adding the report information to the HTML file is possibly the easiest part of the whole procedure. We can simply ask Internet Explorer for the actual HTML that was built up using our code:

```
' ...and this is where we'll draw our report!
file.WriteLine "<HTML><HEAD><TITLE>Weekly Sales Report</TITLE><BODY>"
file.WriteLine ReportTable.outerHTML
file.WriteLine "</BODY></HTML>"
```

Notice that we were using the `innerHTML` property of our elements and now we're using `outerHTML`. We've had to take this approach because `innerHTML` returns the HTML that makes up the children inside of the element. `OuterHTML` gives us the HTML of the actual element as well as the HTML of the children. (To get a good understanding of this, try running the sample using `innerHTML` instead. You'll notice the report data will be displayed in a single line because there won't be a table to frame the data.)

We can now finish our example by adding some code to add the salesperson's name to the report and place the report in the center of the page:

```
' ...and this is where we'll draw our report!
file.WriteLine "<HTML><HEAD><TITLE>Weekly Sales Report</TITLE><BODY>"
file.WriteLine "<CENTER><FONT SIZE=5><B>" & PersonList.Value & "</FONT>"
file.WriteLine "<BR><FONT SIZE=3>Weekly Sales Report for " _
    & MonthName(Month(Now)) & " " & Day(Now) & " " & Year(Now) & "</FONT>"
file.WriteLine "<BR><BR>"
file.WriteLine ReportTable.outerHTML
file.WriteLine "</CENTER></BODY></HTML>"
```

When you run the code, clicking the Save Report button will add an HTML file to the folder created by the code. This page should look like this:

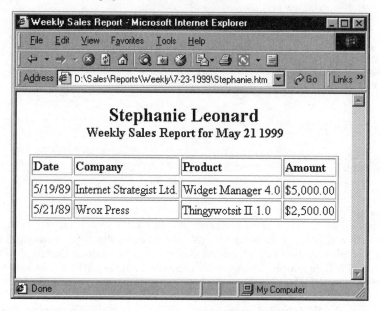

In order to keep this example simple, I refrained from adding a "Total" line to the report. If you want to put one in, you can and I would suggest two approaches. The simplest one is keep a global variable that you increment each time you add a line to the report. Then, when you come to render the report to the file, tack on another row, as shown below. (Don't forget, `innerHTML` won't give us the table framing that we need, so we have to write the frame ourselves and then use `innerHTML`.)

```
file.WriteLine "<TABLE BORDER=1>"
file.WriteLine ReportTable.innerHTML
file.WriteLine "<TR><TD COLSPAN=3></TD><TD>TOTAL: " & total & "</TD></TR>"
file.WriteLine "</TABLE>"
```

The more complex approach involves keeping the preview up-to-date as the report is being built. You could either define a separate <SPAN> element on your document that you change as you add rows, or you could add a permanent row to `ReportTable` and make sure that when you insert new rows, you always insert above the permanent one. Either way, it's possible.

Deploying DHTML Applications

Now that you're going great guns building DHTML Applications for everyone who wants one, you need to find an effective way to deploy them. This is where the trade-off between fast, secure code balances itself out against deployment issues. Whereas a server-side application requires no specialized deployment code, our DHTML Application has some client-side stuff and that has to be automatically installed when our application is first used.

The principle behind what we're going to do is build a "cabinet" file containing all the stuff that the client computer needs to have installed so that we can run our application.

Cabinet files (which have the extension ".CAB") are used a lot by Microsoft for installing their software. In fact, cabinet files were developed specifically for Windows 95 Setup, and have since found their way into all Microsoft Setup programs.

> *Microsoft have developed a utility called CabView which can be used to examine the contents of cabinet files. You can find this on the Microsoft Web site by searching for 'CabView'. The popular shareware package WinZip 7.0 can also read .CAB files.*

When you visit a page that uses an ActiveX control or component, Internet Explorer is informed of the control through an OBJECT tag. (You may recall that we saw an OBJECT tag when we first viewed the source code of our test HTML page.) Every single ActiveX object in existence is identified by a Globally Unique Identifier (or GUID). This is in fact a huge, 128-bit number and is generated from a combination of a unique number burned into the originator's network card and the current time on the originator's computer. No two GUIDs are alike, so any developer can be certain that when he or she allocated a GUID to a control, there will never be a conflict.

When IE finds an OBJECT tag, it uses the GUID to see if the appropriate object is installed on the local computer. If it is then it just goes ahead and initializes the object. If it isn't, the OBJECT tag contains an attribute called CODEBASE which directs IE to a URL where it can download the object. Usually this URL points to a .CAB file.

As we discussed in Chapter 5, there is one more point about ActiveX controls that's important, and it bears repeating. ActiveX controls have full access to the system they are running on. There is nothing stopping any ActiveX control from harvesting all the Word documents off of your hard disk and e-mailing them to everyone in your address book. ActiveX's counterpart, Java applets, have no such problem. Java applets run in a conceptual device called the "sandbox", which is a collection of functions and operations that the Java architects have deemed safe. It's not physically possible for a Java applet to start scanning your hard disk for Word documents.

Because ActiveX is supposed to compete with Java applets, Microsoft decided to develop an authentication scheme where you have to go to a third-party called a "certificate authority" and pay them to for a digital signature which you then use to sign your code. (This technology is called Microsoft Authenticode.) By signing their code, developers know that when you visit their Web sites, you're either warned about using code that hasn't been marked as safe or prevented from doing so completely. We'll cover signing code and security in the next section.

Packaging Our Application

Now that we've tested and debugged our example, compile it by selecting Make YourProject.dll from VB's File menu. You'll be asked to save the DLL (save it to the project folder), and you'll then be asked to save the HTML file that we built using the DHTML Designer. Save this into the project folder as well, and call it `ReportForm.htm`.

By default, the **Package and Deployment Wizard** is not loaded into Visual Basic. Select **Add-In Manager** from the **Add-Ins** menu. Select **Package and Deployment Wizard**, and check **Loaded/Unloaded**. Confirm that the **Load Behavior** column says **Loaded** and click **OK**, resulting in a screen that should look like the screenshot below.

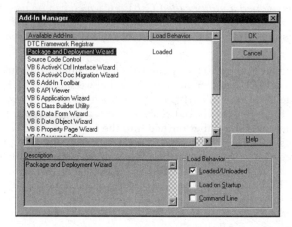

Now, return to the **Add-Ins** menu and select **Package and Deployment Wizard**. When asked, say that you do want to save the project.

The Package and Deployment Wizard, shown in the screenshot below, works by building scripts that contain instructions on where to find the constituent parts of your project. This is an expansion on the simpler form of deployment we covered in Chapter 5. These scripts stay with the project so you can reuse them later. Microsoft designed it that way because some developers could have multiple scripts for the same project that do slightly different jobs. For this example we're only going to create and use one script.

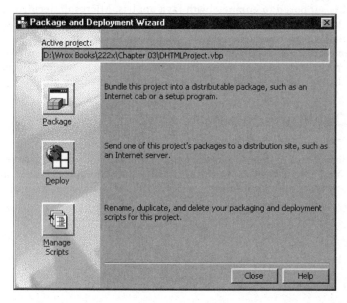

To start with, we need to package the code, so using the Package and Deployment Wizard, select Package.

The Package Type dialog below lets us choose from three different packages. Standard Setup Package is used when we want to wrap our project up in an executable file that we physically give to someone, Internet Package is used to create a .CAB file (which is what we want to do) and Dependency File is used to create a list of what other DLLs and packages the components in the project have access to in order to work. Dependency files are particularly useful for debugging installations because you can use them to quickly find what's missing.

Make sure Internet Package is selected and click Next.

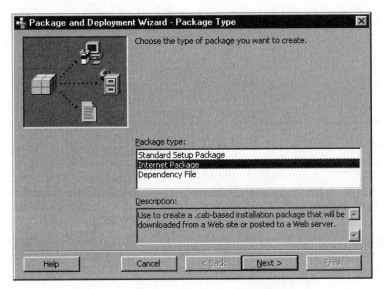

The next dialog, Package Folder, simply wants to know where we want the put the files on our local computer before we move them over to the Web server. Choose a folder and click Next.

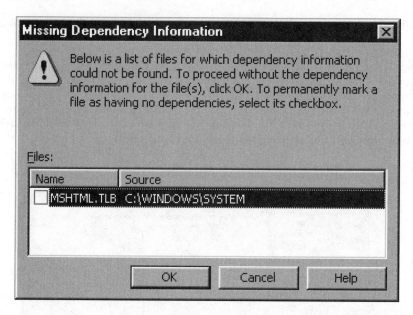

The screenshot above shows a dialog that appears when the dependency information for one of the DLLs we're using cannot be found. For some reason, Microsoft chose not to put dependency information on MSHTML.TLB which is used in all DHTML Application projects. This file is a **Type Library** (hence the extension .TLB) and contains support information for the controls that appear on the HTML control palette. Make sure the checkbox is unchecked and click OK.

The screenshot below shows the "Included Files" dialog which is where we're told what files will be included in the package by default. We are also given the opportunity to add files to the package. You may, for example, wish to include other executable files or documentation in the package.

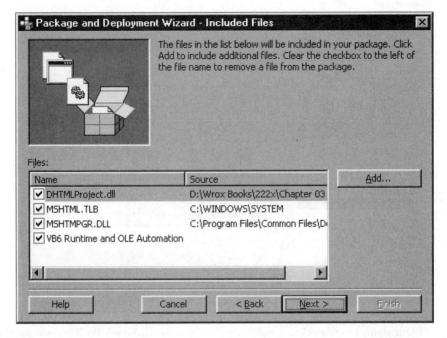

DHTMLProject.dll is, obviously, our project DLL. MSHTML.TLB we covered above and MSHTMPGR.DLL is the DHTML Designer run-time support file. **VB6 Runtime and OLE Automation** is actually another package that's supplied with VB for deployment with your applications. It is used to make sure the computer you're installing onto has all of the files VB needs to run your application properly on the client machine.

Click **Next** to proceed.

The **File Source** dialog shown below lets us decide if we want all of the bits of our project included in our package. If you select **VB6 Runtime and OLE Automation** you'll notice that rather than **Include in this cab** being checked, **Download from the Microsoft Web Site** is instead. The theory behind this is that because this package is pretty large, you may not want to include it in your package. If the package is needed (because the VB runtimes aren't installed on the computer you're installing your application onto) IE can go download it from the Microsoft website.

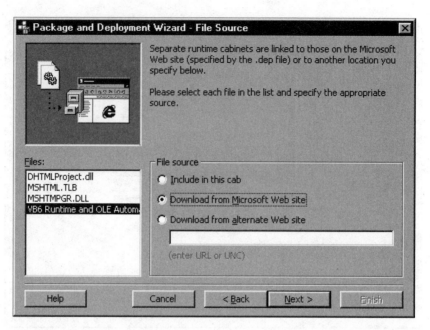

In the list of four items in the package, only MSHTMPGR.DLL and the VB6 Runtime packages can be downloaded from the Microsoft Web site. DHTMLProject.dll is our own DLL, and MSHTML.TLB has to be available for our DLL to load. Naturally, as it is our own DLL, it can't be downloaded from the Microsoft site! Make sure than when you select MSHTMPGR.DLL and the VB6 Runtime that Download from Microsoft Web site is selected.

If you're trying to deploy your applications in an environment where it's not reasonable to have your applications downloading stuff from Microsoft's site, you can choose to put these other DLLs and packages on another server in your building. Use the Download from alternate Web site option to direct IE to the other resources. Including the run-time components in your package will increase the size by 1.1MB.

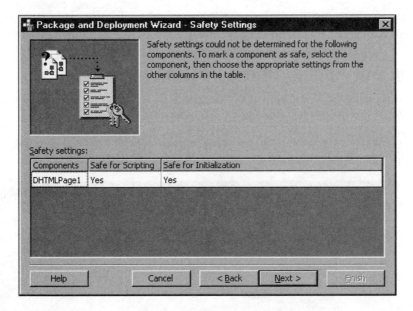

The screenshot above shows the Safety Settings dialog which prompts us to revisit the signing discussion we started earlier

Because Microsoft respect the fact that not everyone is in a position to pay for certificates, VB can mark your DLLs as safe for certain functions. This is dependent on the honor system – *there is no mechanism for guaranteeing the promise you're making here!*

By setting "Safe for Scripting" to "Yes" you are saying that the code in your component will not create, change or delete arbitrary files, including temporary files when the code is running. "Safe for Initialization" means the component won't do anything like that when it's starting up.

> **Some of you have probably noticed that although we've checked these options, our example project does create files. We're doing this for demonstration purposes, and because you've seen all the code that goes into the application. Normally you should always leave unsafe components marked as Unsafe, and leave the user or customer to make the final decision- for a clean demonstration of what can go wrong with ActiveX, check out** `http://mclain.wa.com/ActiveX/welcome.html`

The Microsoft documentation has these words to say on this issue:

"By marking a component as safe for scripting or safe for initialization, you are guaranteeing that your component can never corrupt or cause undesirable behavior on an end user's machine, even if used in a Web page that you yourself did not author. Marking a component as either safe for scripting or safe for initialization implies that you are accepting liability for this guarantee."

Set the security settings and click Next. When the Finish dialog appears, leave the package name as it is and press Finish.

If you open Explorer and navigate to the folder you specified in the "Package Folder" dialog you'll find the .CAB file and an HTML file. Try opening the HTML file and running your application!

Publishing our Application's Package

Now we have to make the application available on a Web server. From the start page of the "Package and Deployment Wizard" (as seen in Figure 6.12), select `Deploy`.

When the new Wizard starts, select the package you wish to deploy. You should only have one possible option, and that'll be the name you set in the "Finish" dialog before.

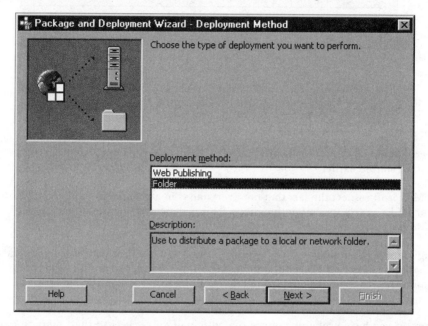

There are three ways you can publish your application. You can either publish through HTTP Post or FTP (denoted by "Web Publishing" above, or by supplying the path to a folder on your network.

Whichever method you chose, you'll be asked for the files you wish to deploy in the Items to Deploy dialog. You should make sure both the CAB file and the HTML file are both checked on and press Next.

You'll then be prompted by the "Additional Items to Deploy" dialog to supply the names of other files or folders you wish to deploy. You could here, for example, supply the names of documentation files you also wanted to upload.

Publishing Directly to a Web Site.

The alternate Web publishing method is to use FTP, and this is the method illustrated in the screenshot below

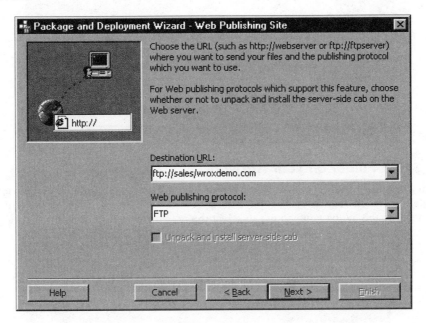

Whichever you choose, you'll need to supply the location of the server. When you've done this, click "Next". If the site you've chosen has never been used before, the Wizard will ask you if you want to save the configuration information on your computer for use in other projects.

The server you want to publish to will usually require some form of proof of identity before it'll allow you to transfer the data. The commonest method is simply to use the inbuilt NT challenge/response dialog:

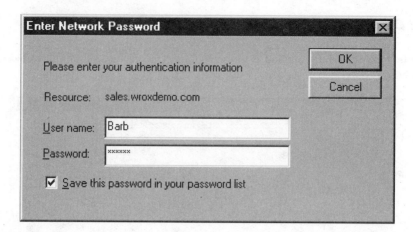

Publishing to a Folder on your Network

If you're posting applications to a departmental server, you may well find that you have direct access to the folders on that server. If you do, publishing becomes a little more straightforward. The next screenshot shows the dialog you can use to select the network folder to save the package and Web pages to.

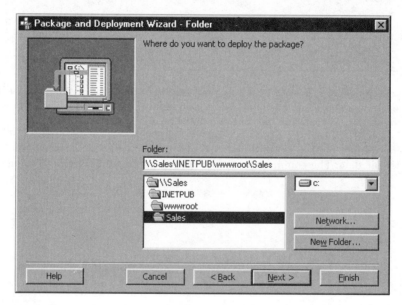

Summary

After reading this chapter you should be able to...

> Explain to your peers what a DHTML Application is.

> Create a new DTHML Application.

> Design DHTML pages using the DHTML Designer.

> Add code to elements on the pages that can react to events and manipulate the data on the page.

> Package your application so it can be deployed.

> Deploy your new application so people can use it.

Our example raises a number of questions. For one thing, we're not using ASP, which is the typical way of providing dynamic applications to users on a network. In fact, our example does not even use a database, which is pretty unusual in its own right. If you were to ASP-enable this application, the only advantage you're going to get is that it can store the reports on the server in a more "purist" manner, and we could also rig our application to e-mail the reports.

What the DHTML Application does give us is the ability to quickly build interactive Web pages that don't have to keep calling back to the server. Just as ADO's Remote Data Service can retrieve queries directly from a database server without having to re-execute an ASP page, DHTML Applications can modify the page content without having to make repeated calls to a Web server. A big advantage for using VB's DHTML Applications as opposed to manipulating the DOM using raw VBScript is that VB's editing and debugging environment is much stronger. The disadvantage is the deployment and signing of your ActiveX component.

Integrating Web Browsing Using the WebBrowser Objects

In this chapter, we will introduce the concept of the `WebBrowser` and `InternetExplorer` objects. We will investigate the current architecture of the Internet Explorer application, and look into how Microsoft has modified the design of the browser to allow developers, like yourself, to leverage this free, encapsulated functionality. We will investigate all the major properties, methods, and events of the controls. The abilities that these controls provide us open the door for incredible flexibility in application development.

While many options exist for developing web solutions for your company's application needs, in many cases, web-enabling existing applications may prove to be a more desirable option. Sometimes, it is not feasible to completely rewrite an existing application into a web-based equivalent. In other scenarios, developing a completely non-Win32 solution may also carry with it limitations that are unacceptable to the development needs of the company.

In this chapter, we will cover:

➤ Creating a basic web browser

➤ The differences between the `WebBrowser` and `InternetExplorer` control

➤ Scenarios and uses of the controls

➤ Properties of the controls

➤ Methods of the controls

➤ Events of the controls

Let's start by investigating the heart and soul of Internet Explorer.

The Heart and Soul of Internet Explorer

Starting with the introduction of Internet Explorer 3.x, Microsoft extracted the technology for accessing the Internet and exposed it to the Windows desktop and any Win32-based application. In order to provide improved access and documentation to the internet functionality exposed and supported by the core elements of Internet Explorer, Microsoft supplied the **Internet Client SDK**. The Internet Client SDK provides examples, demos, and valuable references for the full range of functionality available through the Internet Explorer **core files**.

> *The Internet Client SDK can be downloaded from*
> `http://www.microsoft.com/ie/ie50`

When they released Internet Explorer 4.x, Microsoft separated the core functions such as issuing HTTP requests and rendering HTML into a separate dynamic-link library which registers as the Microsoft Internet Controls on any system that has Internet Explorer 4.x or better installed.

The DLL encapsulating this functionality, `shdocvw.dll`, not only provides all the necessary logic to request and render HTML pages, but also exposes this functionality through a series of programmable controls and OLE automation objects. Registering this DLL on your system, usually accomplished through installation of Internet Explorer itself, will provide several newly registered controls whose `ProgId` will begin with `SHDocVwCtl`.

> You can obtain and register the `Shdocvw.dll` file independently of a Microsoft IE installation. Doing so may result in less functionality, as other, newer functions of the browser such as scripting and DHTML support are not directly handled by this DLL. Also, you should check with Microsoft accounting and licensing requirements for using portions of Internet Explorer without a standard installation preceding use.

The primary control on which we will be focusing is the `WebBrowser` object. This object exposes the key functionality of Internet Explorer in a generic object arrangement. While the WebBrowser is provided as an ActiveX control for use directly on a Visual Basic form, another important object, called `InternetExplorer`, is available within the DLL.

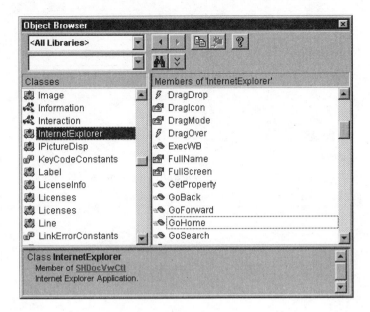

The `InternetExplorer` automation object allows Internet Explorer itself to be programmatically controlled. This can be quite useful at times when you would prefer to make small changes to Internet Explorer rather than building a browser-like application from the ground-level up.

> `SHDocVwCtl`, *is rumored to stand for Simple HTML Document Viewer Control. Whether or not this is actually true, this is a good method for remembering the* `ProgID` *and DLL name. Don't forget, though, that the DLL name is actually shortened to* `Shdocvw.dll` *to conform to the 8.3 naming conventions.*

IE-based Browsing Objects

Internet Explorer exposes two objects that can be used for browsing the web. These objects, `WebBrowser` and `InternetExplorer`, are encapsulated within the `Shdocvw.dll`. Both objects share the same programmatic COM interface, `IWebBrowser2`, although not all methods, events, and properties exposed through this interface apply to both objects. From version 4, onward the `WebBrowser` control container was modified so it could be hosted directly by the Windows shell, thereby exposing its use by other Windows-based applications.

Properties

InternetExplorer	WebBrowser Control
AddressBar	AddressBar
Application	Application
Busy	Busy
Container	Container
Document	Document
FullName	*Partially implemented*
FullScreen	FullScreen
Height	Height
HWND	
Left	Left
LocationName	LocationName
LocationURL	LocationURL
MenuBar	MenuBar
Name	Name
Offline	Offline
Parent	Parent
Path	*Partially implemented*
ReadyState	ReadyState
RegisterAsBrowser	RegisterAsBrowser
RegisterAsDropTarget	RegisterAsDropTarget
Resizable	Resizable
Silent	Silent
StatusBar	StatusBar
StatusText	StatusText
	Tag
TheaterMode	TheaterMode
ToolBar	ToolBar
	ToolTipText
Top	Top
TopLevelContainer	TopLevelContainer
Type	Type
Visible	Visible
Width	Width

According to the MSDN documentation, the properties available to the WebBrowser object are a proper subset of those available for the InternetExplorer object. As you can see from our table this isn't strictly true, since the WebBrowser object has access to two properties from Visual Basic-Tag and ToolTipText. The main difference in available properties, however, focuses mostly on added visual elements available in Internet Explorer, such as ToolBar, StatusBar, and MenuBar, that go beyond the core browsing window provide by the basic WebBrowser object. The two properties described as partially implemented, FullName and Path are special cases; refer to the relevant sections for a fuller description.

Methods

InternetExplorer	WebBrowser Control
ClientToWindow	
ExecWB	ExecWB
GetProperty	
GoBack	GoBack
GoForward	GoForward
GoHome	GoHome
GoSearch	GoSearch
Navigate	Navigate
Navigate2	Navigate2
PutProperty	
QueryStatusWB	QueryStatusWB
Quit	Quit
Refresh	Refresh
Refresh2	Refresh2
ShowBrowserBar	ShowBrowserBar
Stop	Stop

The collection of methods for the WebBrowser object is actually a proper subset of those available to the InternetExplorer object. The differences, though small, focus on additional cookie support and the ability to query OLE command status.

Events

InternetExplorer	WebBrowser Control
BeforeNavigate2	BeforeNavigate2
CommandStateChange	CommandStateChange
DocumentComplete	DocumentComplete
DownloadBegin	DownloadBegin
DownloadComplete	DownloadComplete
NavigateComplete2	NavigateComplete2
NewWindow2	NewWindow2
OnFullScreen	OnFullScreen
OnMenuBar	OnMenuBar
OnQuit	
OnStatusBar	OnStatusBar
OnTheaterMode	OnTheaterMode
OnToolBar	OnToolBar
OnVisible	OnVisible
ProgressChange	ProgressChange
PropertyChange	
StatusTextChange	StatusTextChange
TitleChange	TitleChange

The collection of events for the `WebBrowser` object is a proper subset of those available for the `InternetExplorer` object.

The 60-Second Browser

We have a browsing object to work with now... so what, you may ask. This method of encapsulating and exposing the ability to navigate to and render HTML-based pages opens the door to unique applications. These options are far more flexible than we have ever had before. A few simple lines of code and a couple of quickly placed objects are all that are needed to create hybrid applications that are exposed to the new web-based functionality. The developer can look at it from two angles. You can either add web browsing functionality to existing applications, which can include access to databases anywhere in the world using Active Server Pages, Remote Data Services and the Internet, or you can add extended functionality to your web browser without being limited by the customization options afforded to the developer through the Internet Explorer Administration Kit.

The flexibility which this type of application provides is absolutely tremendous. A fraction of these opportunities includes:

- ➤ Kiosk-based applications which use a dial-up line to access the Internet
- ➤ Hyper-customized web browsers.
- ➤ POS systems using a centralized credit card processing system on the web server
- ➤ Web-based applications with Win32-based front-ends sold out of the box.
- ➤ Applications with world-wide database connectivity direct to the source
- ➤ Browser-based navigation filters which send the browse history back to a central database
- ➤ Applications comprised entirely of web pages, replacing Form objects with embedded ActiveX controls

One of the obvious places to start down this journey of merging web-browsing into existing applications is to create a basic web browser. The ability to create a functional browser in 60 seconds should be a testament to the flexibility the web truly provides. To start this process, let's take a look at the recipe for the 60-second browser.

The Recipe

The browser we will create will be extremely simple in nature. We will include the following items in the user interface:

- ➤ Form object for the basic visual structure of the browser
- ➤ TextBox for the rudimentary method of URL input
- ➤ Command button to initiate browsing
- ➤ WebBrowser control for the rendering of the web page.

To begin the process, we need to start Visual Basic with a Standard Exe project.

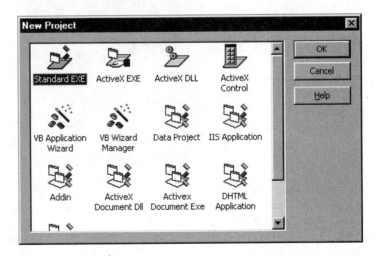

Once we have opened our Standard Exe project and resized the default Form object to be of a sufficient size for a browser (400 pixels by 360 pixels should work) we must include a reference to the WebBrowser component. Perform this by selecting Project | Components (or using *Ctrl-T*) and then select the checkbox next to Microsoft Internet Controls.

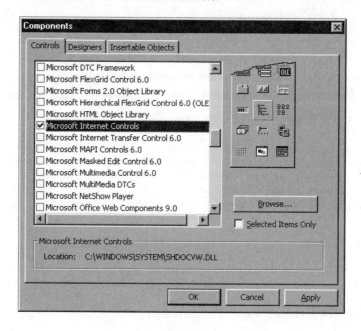

At this point, your toolbox should now contain a couple of additional controls ready for placement. The globe is the WebBrowser control.

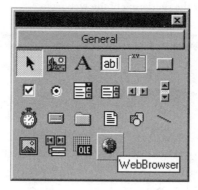

Add the following controls to your form:

> WebBrowser
> Textbox
> CommandButton

Position the WebBrowser component to take up most of the Form, but leave a vertical strip along the left-hand side of the Form object. We will use this to add assorted buttons later in the chapter. Your browser might now look a little like the following.

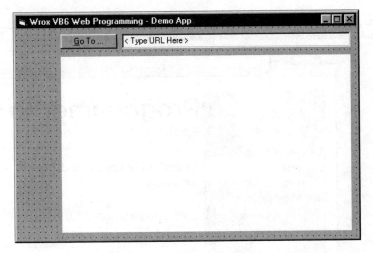

Of course, we've spiced up the browser a little. I could not perform this whole process in 60 seconds with these visual enhancements, but the objects and code can be written in around 60 seconds.

Surfing the Web

Now that we have the visual elements in place, it's time to add a little functionality to the Form. Let's add one line of code to the Click event of the CommandButton. Double-click on the CommandButton and add the following lines of code:

```
Private Sub Command1_Click()
    WebBrowser1.Navigate Text1.Text
End Sub
```

Once this code has been added, clicking the command button will cause the WebBrowser control to issue an HTTP request for the URL provided in the `TextBox` named `Text1`. Running this application, and providing the URL of a prebuilt HTML page may result in something similar to the following:

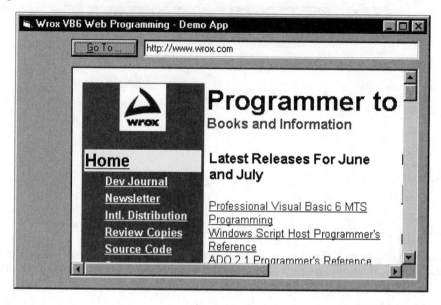

At this point we now have a fully functionally web browser. What? You disagree! OK, I understand that companies like Microsoft and Netscape have radically changed what web browsers are capable of performing, hence raising the bar on the expectations of a fully-functional browser. Keep in mind though, that simply requesting and rendering web pages alone, with support for hyperlinking, is a tremendous functionality enhancement to provide with such little effort. An entirely new breed of applications can be developed that leverage portions of UI being housed, maintained, and developed remotely on a web server. Application enhancements can be obtained every time a web page is requested.

Beyond Browsing

Certainly, this newly found ability to request and render web pages is not enough. Not even close! If you remember earlier when I described that starting with Internet Explorer 4.0, the WebBrowser object is now hosted by the Windows shell. This simple fact allows not just HTML pages to be loaded and rendered, but anything that can be loaded by Windows Explorer itself. This can be used to extend the functionality provided by the use of the `WebBrowser` in multiple, unique ways.

Browsing your system

If we load up our little demo application, and attempt to navigate to `C:\`, we will find that our application now appears to behave suspiciously similar to Windows Explorer.

This similarity is borne out by the screenshot below, which shows the right click context menu available in Explorer. When browsing a folder through the `WebBrowser` object, this gives you access to the View mode, Arrange mode, and other assorted options.

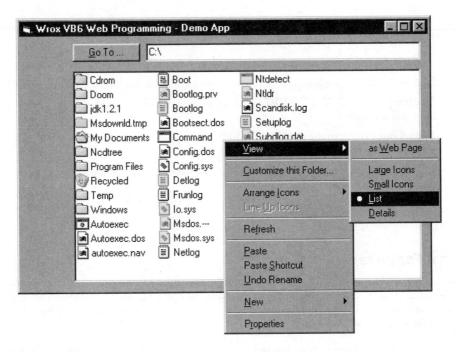

Loading Office Documents

To go even beyond the simplistic local browsing functionality derived from the Windows shell, through the WebBrowser object, additional technologies are supported. As we discussed in Chapter 3, Microsoft created a member of the ActiveX technology family known as ActiveX Documents (formerly OLE documents). The WebBrowser object is able to act as an ActiveX Document container, just as Internet Explorer itself can, thus allowing Office documents to be loaded and edited directly from our demo application.

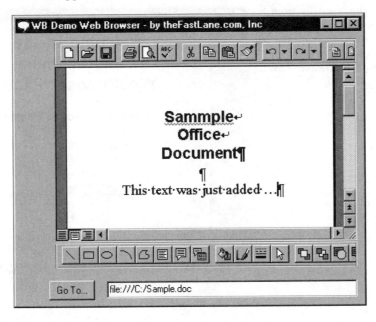

You'll notice that even Word's spell checking function is working! Of course, there are some limitations to the functionality you can get:

> The appropriate Office application must be legally installed to support the document.

> The last used environment configuration (toolbars, etc) for the Office application will be used.

> The full path (UNC, local, or URL) must be provided. Prefixing with the "file://" protocol indicator is optional.

> Limitations exist as to the extent of the full Office application functionality (menu items, etc) that will be exposed to the WebBrowser object.

> Editing the document is allowed. Keep in mind that when you use the original is edited, as opposed to a temporary copy stored in storage.

These limitations notwithstanding, the WebBrowser object is an incredibly powerful control that allows numerous functions from within a single control.

Additional Features

It stands to reason that some of the goodies would have to be reserved for Internet Explorer's use of the underlying control. Sure enough, this is the case. Not all of Internet Explorers functions are available from the WebBrowser, although some functionality can be obtained through a special method of the WebBrowser control.

Covered in some detail later in the chapter, the ExecWB method opens up the door to several common actions performed within Internet Explorer. We will take a brief look at three of the functions:

> Opening a file/URL

> Page Setup

> Printing

To provide this functionality from our application, we will add a ComboBox to provide a mechanism for choosing these options. Not too complicated, but just enough to get the job done.

Once this `ComboBox` has been added, we need to add a little code behind one of its events to initiate the functionality when requested. We will be adding a `Select Case` statement to account for the three options we included within our `ComboBox` list. The code is placed within the `Click` event of the `ComboBox` and for our example looks like this:

```
Private Sub Combo1_Click()
    If Len(WebBrowser1.LocationURL) > 0 Then
        Select Case Combo1
            Case "Print"
                WebBrowser1.ExecWB OLECMDID_PRINT, 0, Null, Null
            Case "Page Setup"
                WebBrowser1.ExecWB OLECMDID_PAGESETUP, 0, Null, Null
            Case "Open Location"
                WebBrowser1.ExecWB OLECMDID_OPEN, 0, Null, Null
        End Select
    End If
End Sub
```

Now that we have set things up with the UI and code, let's test each element to see what it looks like.

Opening a file/URL

The standard Internet Explorer Open dialog box for opening a folder or file according to its "Internet address" or URL, is normally invoked from the File | Open drop-down menu, and when choosing the "Open Location" item we have added to our `ComboBox` list, we are presented with the following, familiar scene:

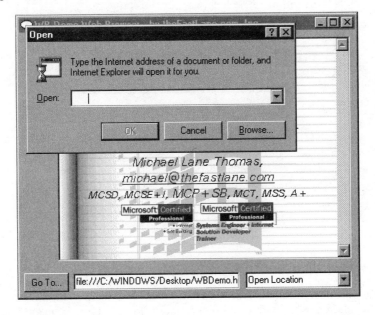

The ability to navigate to a URL can be performed programmatically, without the use of an input box, standard or custom, with other, more direct methods then shown here. If the standard Internet Explorer Open dialog box is desired, this is the best method.

Page Setup

The Page Setup dialog is a useful functionality of Internet Explorer. It provides the ability to modify the orientation of the web pages, which affects printing, as well as other features such as dictating the header and footer information to be included with every web page printed. This dialog is normally invoked from the File | Page Setup... menu item on the Internet Explorer menus.

After choosing our Page Setup option from the ComboBox, the standard Internet Explorer setup dialog will appear:

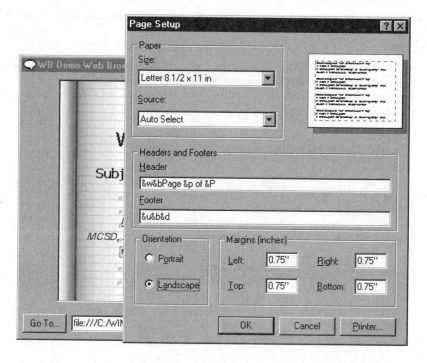

Printing

The standard Internet Explorer printing dialog box is a powerful tool. Printing a web page loaded into a WebBrowser control on a form can certainly be performed in numerous ways, but the IE print dialog provides a great deal of functionality and several choices that pertain directly to the printing of web pages. The standard method within Internet Explorer for invoking the print dialog is to select File|Print... from the drop-down menus.

The dialog itself, when invoking through our `ComboBox`, would normally look very similar to the following:

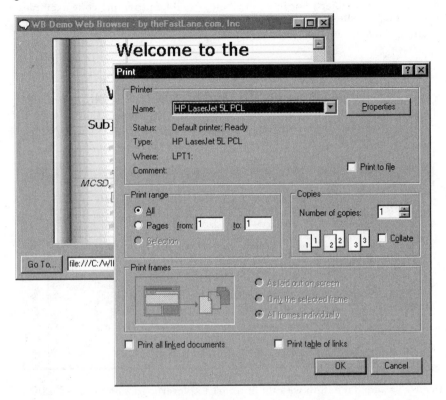

Control Properties, Methods and Events

Now we've set up a simple browser, and shown how you can add some basic functionality, we'll look at extending our application. In order to fully embrace the functionality of the `WebBrowser` and `InternetExplorer` objects, including their strengths and weaknesses, you should be aware of the available properties, methods, and events that are exposed by these objects. We have already taken a look at some of these object attributes in creating our 60-second browser. We are going to continue to expand and enhance the `WBDemoApp` web browser to provide a strong foundation for you, the developer, to experience the process of expanding the `WebBrowser` and `InternetExplorer` objects in many different ways. As you read through the remainder of the chapter, you should be thinking about the unique and creative ways in which you can leverage this packaged web accessibility to provide unique solutions to your application development needs.

> Keep in mind that the properties, events, and methods available with a given version of `Shwdocvw.dll` may differ, at the discretion of Microsoft. Applications written with a particular version of the `WebBrowser` may function differently with another..

For the attributes that apply to both the `WebBrowser` and `InternetExplorer` objects, we will focus on implementing the attribute for the `WebBrowser` object. Many of the attributes only apply to the `InternetExplorer` object. For those attributes, we'll be providing code examples to demonstrate the functionality by controlling Internet Explorer. Consequently, we'll need to provide some foundational code to support those examples.

Calling and Controlling Internet Explorer

With the `InternetExplorer` object automation server object exposed by `ShDocVw.dll`, an instance of Internet Explorer can be easily called and controlled from within a Visual Basic application. To provide this functionality to `WBDemoApp`, we need to modify the user interface a little.

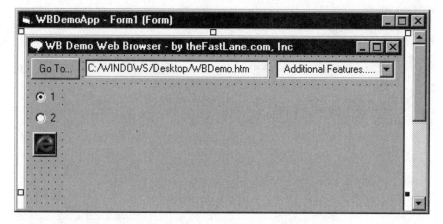

You'll notice we've added a button with the Internet Explorer logo, and assigned it the name `cmdIELaunch_Click`. We've also added a couple of radio buttons, which we'll be using later. Once this UI change has been completed, we need to add some code to create an instance of `InternetExplorer`. We will add the necessary code to load an instance of Internet Explorer and set an object reference to it that may be used later. This code involves three steps:

1. Dim an object variable to hold the `InternetExplorer` reference

2. Create an instance of the `InternetExplorer` object in the `Form_Load` event

3. Set some of Internet Explorer's properties, before revealing it.

```
' Prepare Global Reference for loading IE
Dim IE As Object
Private Sub Form_Load()

    ' Start instance of IE
    ' Note: IE is not visible at this time

    Set IE = CreateObject("InternetExplorer.Application")

End Sub
Private Sub cmdIELaunch_Click()
```

```
' Navigate IE to location provided in TextBox
' Note: Setting the Visible property last will decrease perceived
' response time for the navigation.

With IE
    .Navigate Text1.Text
    .Width = 420
    .Height = 360
    .Visible = True
End With

End Sub
```

Note that we've added code to modify the height and width of Internet Explorer by setting the appropriate properties of the `InternetExplorer` object reference. We've also used the `Navigate` property to set Internet Explorer's target to the URL in the text box. Finally, we set the `Visible` property to true so that the document can be seen.

When the application is run, clicking on the Go To... button and then the new IE button will result in similar pages being loaded, side-by-side, rendered within the `WebBrowser` object and a programmatically controlled instance of Internet Explorer. Note the width and height of Internet Explorer is appropriate for the settings made.

Control Properties

We will start our investigation of the `WebBrowser` control by looking at the available properties. Many of the properties listed are standard for visual COM controls in general, therefore many of the properties will be grouped into scenarios and used together to obtain the desired effect.

General Properties

The `WebBrowser` control provides some of the same basic properties as any other ActiveX control. Some of these standard properties include the basic size properties, and the visible property.

Height, Left, Top, and Width

Imagine that you want to adjust our original `WebBrowser` object whenever the parent `Form` object is resized. This can be accomplished, as expected, by using the `Height`, `Left`, `Top`, and `Width` properties from within the form's `Resize` event. This brings up a good point about the benefits of the `WebBrowser` control and the combination of application functionality plus user interface advantages that can be obtained by using rendered web pages. As the page is resized, the visual elements on the web pages will generally adjust to fit the modified browser window size, and scroll bars will appear as needed. This allows the user to exercise the ability to adjust the application as necessary without losing any information being presented by the web page.

```
Private Sub Form_Resize()

    With WebBrowser1
        .Width = Form1.Width - .Left - 225
        .Height = Form1.Height - .Top - 525
    End With

End Sub
```

If you notice, the width and height of the browsing window is adjusted based on the form's `Width` and `Height` properties, plus the necessary offset to account for the border and other controls on the form. The resulting `WBDemoApp`, once resized, will highlight the effect of the resize. Note the automatic appearance of the scroll bars.

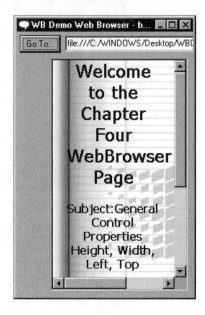

Visible

Use of the Visible property for the WebBrowser control would generally be no different than for any other ActiveX control. The nature of web browsing though, generally involves switching between multiple pages, to reduce the effect of longer download times. This is especially so for power surfers performing research. You, as developer, may prefer to hide windows when they're not in use. Using the Visible property, combined with the radio buttons we added earlier, will allow you to do this.

To implement this scenario, let's modify the design of the Form object.

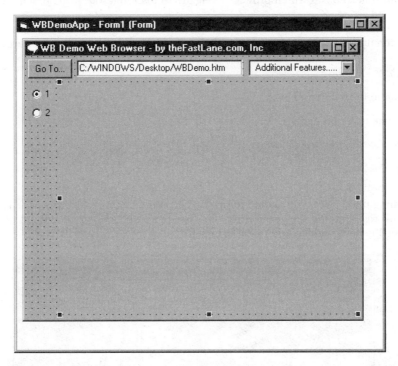

After modifying the Form appropriately, we need to add code for two different events. We need to alter the behavior of the **Go To...** button to switch which WebBrowser object is set to navigate. We also need to modify the Visible property of the first WebBrowser object to allow viewing of the second "browser", which we add in the same way we added the first. We attach this procedure to the radio button array, Option1 in our code.

```
Private Sub Command1_Click()
    If Option1.Item(0) Then
        WebBrowser1.Navigate Text1.Text
    Else
        WebBrowser2.Navigate Text1.Text
    End If
End Sub
```

```
Private Sub Option1_Click(Index As Integer)
    Select Case Index
        Case 0
            WebBrowser1.Visible = True
        Case 1
            WebBrowser2.Visible = False
    End Select
End Sub
```

Notice that the code chooses which browser navigates to the requested page, based on which radio option is selected.

To highlight the functionality we have just added, we will perform the following steps:

1. Run WBDemoApp.

2. Switch to browser number 2.

3. Navigate to a web page.

4. Switch back to browser number 1.

5. Resize WBDemoApp.

After performing these tasks, you should notice that a skinny band of WebBrowser2 is visible along the bottom and right sides of the application. This is due to the fact that we did not enter the same resize code for the newly added additional browser.

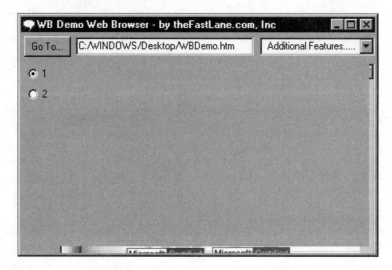

Visual UI Elements

A number of properties are exposed by the `InternetExplorer` objects to allow manipulation of some of the commonly recognized graphical UI elements. By modifying these properties, a running instance of Internet Explorer can be controlled by your application. This opens the door to numerous avenues of customization.

> *The `WebBrowser` control ignores any attempts to set these properties for it. Attempting to set, for example, the `StatusBar` property of a `WebBrowser` control will not generate an error, but will not produce any functional result.*

AddressBar

In order to support the ability to programmatically reveal or hide the address bar, independent of Internet Explorer, the `AddressBar` property will need to be modified. We can use the Menu Editor in VB, accessible from the Tools drop-down menu, to provide a convenient method to toggle the value of the `AddressBar` property.

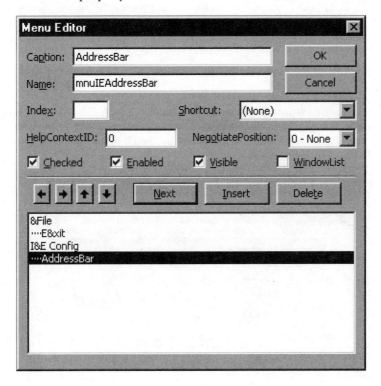

Once we have added the menu item as shown, we must add the necessary code to keep the menu's Checked property in sync with the actual InternetExplorer AddressBar property.

```
Private Sub mnuIEAddressBar_Click()

    MnuIEAddressBar.Checked = Not mnuIEAddressBar.Checked
    IE.AddressBar = mnuIEAddressBar.Checked

End Sub


Private Sub cmdIELaunch_Click()

    ' Navigate IE to location provided in TextBox
    ' Note: Setting the Visible property last will decrease perceived
    ' response time for the navigation.

    With IE
        .Navigate Text1.Text
        .Width = 420
        .Height = 360
        .Visible = True
        .AddressBar = mnuIEAddressBar.Checked
    End With

End Sub
```

Notice how the AddressBar property is merely kept in sync with the Checked property whenever the instance of Internet Explorer is launched. If we attempt to run WBDemoApp at this point, we will see that the instance of Internet Explorer referenced by the IE object variable is visually in sync with the menu item Checked property.

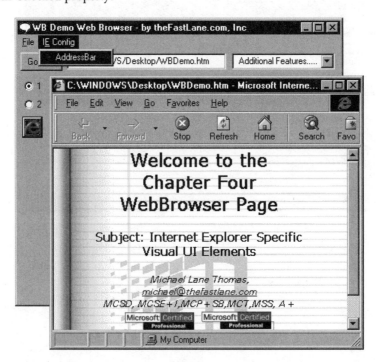

MenuBar, StatusBar, and ToolBar

The MenuBar, StatusBar, and ToolBar properties perform in much the same fashion as the AddressBar we looked at earlier.

If we perform the same modifications through the Menu Editor, we can produce similar results for the other "Bar" properties exposed by the InternetExplorer object. Of course we will have to add the appropriate functions to the appropriate events for the newly created menu items, as well as modify the event in which the Internet Explorer instance is launched, to ensure the properties are kept in synch.

```
Private Sub cmdIELaunch_Click()

    ' Navigate IE to location provided in TextBox
    ' Note: Setting the Visible property last will decrease perceived
    ' response time for the navigation.

    With IE
        .Navigate Text1.Text
        .Width = 420
        .Height = 360
        .Visible = True
        .AddressBar = mnuIEAddressBar.Checked
        .MenuBar = mnuIEMenuBar.Checked
        .StatusBar = mnuIEStatusBar.Checked
        .ToolBar = mnuIEToolBar.Checked
    End With

End Sub

Private Sub mnuIEMenuBar_Click()
    MnuIEMenuBar.Checked = Not mnuIEMenuBar.Checked
    IE.MenuBar = mnuIEMenuBar.Checked
End Sub

Private Sub mnuIEStatusBar_Click()
    MnuIEStatusBar.Checked = Not mnuIEStatusBar.Checked
    IE. StatusBar = mnuIEStatusBar.Checked
End Sub

Private Sub mnuIEToolBar_Click()
    MnuIEToolBar.Checked = Not mnuIEToolBar.Checked
    IE. ToolBar = mnuIEToolBar.Checked
End Sub
```

Upon successfully modifying the code, running our `WBDemoApp` application will now allow all four Bar attributes to be modified by our customized application.

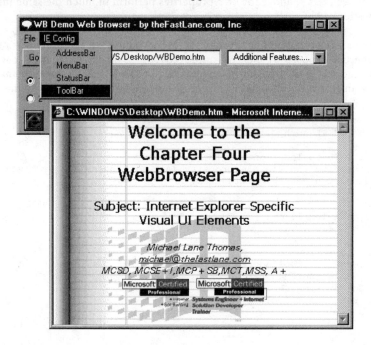

FullScreen and TheaterMode

The `FullScreen` and `TheaterMode` properties of the `InternetExplorer` object are somewhat confusing. Both properties effectively result in an Internet Explorer instance being enlarged to take over the entire screen. In fact, you may have used that property in the `FullScreen` toolbar button that is available on the Internet Explorer toolbar.

The strange thing is that the FullScreen button on the Internet Explorer toolbar actually toggles the `TheaterMode` property and there is no method to actually set the `FullScreen` property in Internet Explorer. The difference between these two properties is very simple. The `FullScreen` property causes Internet Explorer to maximize to the full size of the desktop, without any "bars". The `TheaterMode` causes Internet Explorer to maximize to the size of the desktop, also without borders, while providing the following:

> Minimized version of the toolbar

> AddressBar

> MenuBar

> Integration of the bars on one line (no stacking bars)

> Modified Minimize, Maximized, and Close buttons in upper-right corner of Internet Explorer

In other words, the `FullScreen` goes completely full screen, while `TheaterMode` maintains application UI elements, as seen here:

Its important to note that mixing the settings for FullScreen and TheaterMode has been known to confuse Internet Explorer and result in weird combinations, such as:

> `FullScreen` with no borders, but a title bar;

> `TheaterMode` with full-sized toolbars and stacked bars!

Because of the difference in these properties from the "Bar" properties, we've chosen to put a separator between the two groups of menu items on our IE Config dropdown. We should also default the `Checked` property of these two menu items to not selected.

We now need to add the code necessary to synch the menu items and Internet Explorer:

```
Private Sub cmdIELaunch_Click()
    With IE
        .Navigate Text1.Text
        .Width = 420
        .Height = 360
        .Visible = True
        .AddressBar = mnuIEAddressBar.Checked
        .MenuBar = mnuIEMenuBar.Checked
        .StatusBar = mnuIEStatusBar.Checked
        .ToolBar = mnuIEToolBar.Checked
        .FullScreen = mnuIEFullScreen.Checked
        .TheaterMode = mnuIETheaterMode.Checked
    End With
End Sub

Private Sub mnuIEFullScreen_Click()
    mnuIEFullScreen.Checked = Not mnuIEFullScreen.Checked
    IE.FullScreen = mnuIEFullScreen.Checked
End Sub

Private Sub mnuIETheaterMode_Click()
    mnuIETheaterMode.Checked = Not mnuIETheaterMode.Checked
    IE.TheaterMode = mnuIETheaterMode.Checked
End Sub
```

Once this code is added, we can run the WBDemoApp application. If we choose the **FullScreen** menu item and then resize and move WBDemoApp, we can obtain a unique functionality that is unobtainable with Internet Explorer alone.

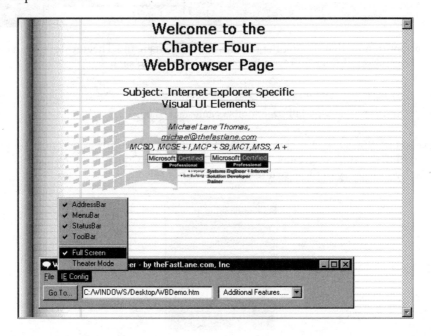

StatusText

The StatusText property provides a mechanism for assigning a text string to the lower left-hand section of the StatusBar previously modified. This property performs the same action as commonly performed via scripting within a web page. If the code

```
IE.StatusText = "Launched by WBDemoApp"
```

is executed at some point, then the StatusText will be displayed as seen here.

This text will only remain until overwritten by page scripting, another property set, or a normal Internet Explorer event.

Web Page Specific

Several properties are exposed by the WebBrowser control that provide direct information about the document or web page being loaded itself. Two of these properties, `LocationName` and `LocationURL` are very simple. The third property, `Document`, is possibly the most powerful property exposed by the control. It seems like an innocent, and obvious property to provide, but the ramifications on potential functionality this exposes is incredible.

LocationName and LocationURL Properties

The `LocationName` and `LocationURL` properties are related to each other in the information that they provide regarding the currently rendered document, file, or location. The value returned by these properties varies based on whether the File or HTTP protocol is used to access the target.

Let's add the following code to the `DocumentComplete` event of `WebBrowser1`:

```
Private Sub WebBrowser1_DocumentComplete(ByVal pDisp As Object, URL As Variant)

    MsgBox WebBrowser1.LocationName
    MsgBox WebBrowser1.LocationURL

End Sub
```

The first line of code, upon navigating to a file local to the development system may result in the following:

The purpose of the `LocationName` property is to return the Title of the Web page which has been loaded and rendered. Should the `<TITLE>` tag within the HTML page contain the value of "Demo Page", then this value is returned by the `LocationName` property only if the file is loaded from the Web, or more specifically, only if delivered via the HTTP protocol and served up by a web server. If the file is loaded locally, using the File protocol, then `LocationName` property will returned the name of the file being loaded, even if its an HTML with a `<TITLE>` tag.

The `LocationURL` property performs the same no matter where the file is found, or what protocol is used to load the file.

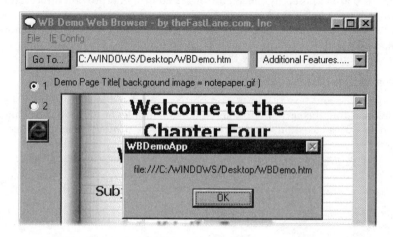

Note that the URL includes the protocol type used, even if the file path provided did not explicitly include the protocol.

The behavior shown in the figure for the `LocationName` *property differs from the behavior dictated within Microsoft documentation in the MSDN Library. Testing should be performed to confirm the behavior when using this property.*

Document Property

The `Document` property is an incredibly powerful attribute to be exposed by the `WebBrowser` control. The `Document` property is an object reference to the very **Document Object Model** generated for a web page loaded by Internet Explorer. In other words, the entire collection of elements, or objects within a web page are directly and immediately accessible to the Visual Basic code through the `Document` property – exactly as for the DHTML application we saw in the previous chapter. Any HTML tag within a web page can be accessed directly and its properties read or modified.

Let me repeat that! ANY element within a web page can be dynamically modified by the Visual Basic code. Furthermore, this feature can be used to send commands to an application via the attributes of non-visual or hidden HTML tags. Essentially, the full functionality of DHTML is completely and totally exposed to the Visual Basic application through the Document property. The ramifications and uses of this feature could fill an entire book completely by itself. Fortunately, I will give but a simple example.

We are going to use the web page title, and the value of the background attribute of the web page's <BODY> tag to change the caption of a label added just above the WebBrowser control, as shown here:

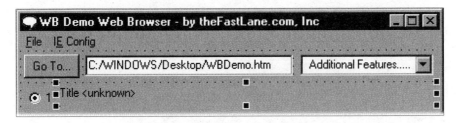

To modify the Caption property of the Label, we will use the DocumentComplete event of the WebBrowser control (described in more detail later) to set the Caption. We will set the Caption to the combination of the title of the Document and the background property of the <BODY> tag.

```
Private Sub WebBrowser1_DocumentComplete(ByVal pDisp As Object, URL As Variant)

      Label1.Caption = WebBrowser.Document.Title _
                     & "( background image = " _
                     & WebBrowser.Document.All("BodyID").background & " )"

End Sub
```

Note that the Title property and the background property of the BodyID item of the All collection are used in the assignment of Label1's Caption property. The Document property is an object reference to the top-level object in the Document Object Model for a web page. The value of the standard <TITLE> tag in a web page is automatically assigned to the Title property of the Document object. The "BodyID" member of the All collection is a little bit trickier. To explain, let's look at the starting HTML in the WBDemo.htm web page being loaded.

```
<HTML>
<HEAD>
   <META NAME="GENERATOR" CONTENT="Microsoft Visual Studio 6.0">
   <TITLE> Demo Page Title </TITLE>
</HEAD>
<BODY id="BodyID" background="notepaper.gif" leftmargin=10>
```

The <BODY> tag has been given an id of "BodyID". By providing an id attribute for an HTML tag within the web page, an element (or tag) can be more easily accessed through the Document object property. The All collection is a collection within the Document Object Model which contains all HTML tags within the web page, therefore the HTML code listed above would create a "BodyID" member of the All collection upon the page being rendered.

If we go ahead and run the `WBDemoApp` application, we should get the following error:

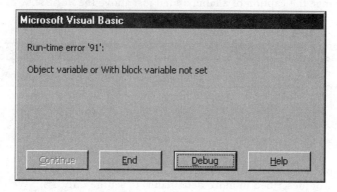

If we choose debug, it should lead up right back to the line assigning the new `Caption` property of the `Label` object.

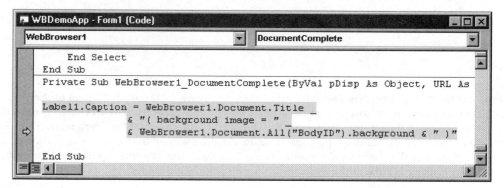

What is wrong you ask? One little step was overlooked. Remember that the actual Document Object Model and `Document` property are not provided by the `Shdocvw.dll` file. The actual HTML Object Library is provided by another Internet Explorer provided file, `MSHTML.dll`. Therefore, we need to provide a Visual Basic project Reference to the Microsoft HTML Object Library.

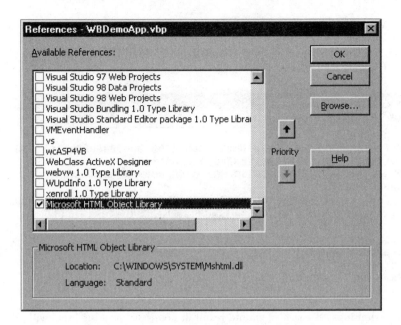

Some of you might not find this item in the Reference list. If this is the case, one of four things has happened:

> Internet Explorer is not installed on the system.

> Internet Explorer is installed but MSHTML.dll is not registered properly.

> MSHTML.dll has been registered and referenced, but a bug in VB6 removes it from the list at that time. In this option, just open your Visual Basic VBP file in Notepad and confirm the Reference line..

> MSHTML.dll is registered, but shows up as the Internet Explorer Scripting Object Model.

> **MSHTML is the true parsing and rendering engine behind Internet Explorer. It provides the framework for creating the object model and the type library for the HTML Object Model**

While the HTML Object Library is provided by the `MSHTML.dll` file, the registered name, depending on the version of `MSHTML.dll` used, will probably be the Internet Explorer Scripting Object Model. Once this reference is made, viewing the Visual Basic Project file (`.vbp`) will reveal the Microsoft HTML Object Library reference

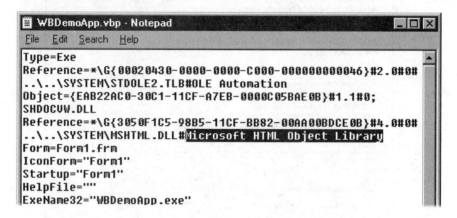

```
Type=Exe
Reference=*\G{00020430-0000-0000-C000-000000000046}#2.0#0#
..\..\SYSTEM\STDOLE2.TLB#OLE Automation
Object={EAB22AC0-30C1-11CF-A7EB-0000C05BAE0B}#1.1#0;
SHDOCVW.DLL
Reference=*\G{3050F1C5-98B5-11CF-BB82-00AA00BDCE0B}#4.0#0#
..\..\SYSTEM\MSHTML.DLL#Microsoft HTML Object Library
Form=Form1.frm
IconForm="Form1"
Startup="Form1"
HelpFile=""
ExeName32="WBDemoApp.exe"
```

At this time, re-running `WBDemoApp` should result in no errors, and the label will now reflect the appropriate value.

> **It is HIGHLY recommended that the Visual Basic developer become familiar with DHTML and the Document Object Model. A strong understanding of the DOM, DHTML, and the WebBrowser control can lead to incredibly powerful applications.**

Navigation-Related

A number of properties exposed by both the `WebBrowser` and `InternetExplorer` objects deal with the process of navigating, or modifying the process of navigating. These properties include `Busy`, `Offline`, and `Status`

Busy

The `Busy` property is a Boolean value which indicates whether or not the control is currently in the middle of browsing to a document or in the middle of a download operation. This property is often used in conditional statements to determine whether or not code, which would be dependent upon the free state of the control, can be safely executed.

Silent

The `Silent` property is used to modify the behavior of the `WebBrowser` control when faced with a dialog box. Normally, the dialog boxes are presented to the user for confirmation or evaluation, such as when a web site cannot be navigated. By setting the `Silent` property to TRUE, dialog boxes are completely suppressed. Keep in mind that setting this property may cause vital information normally conveyed through dialog boxes to be lost.

To add this functionality to our `WBDemoApp`, we can add a menu item similar to the previous IE Config.

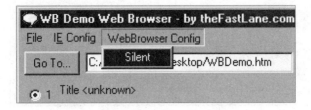

Offline

The `Offline` property is used to force either the `InternetExplorer` or `WebBrowser` control to read the necessary data about the target file or URL from the local cache. Even if the information is available over the network to be refreshed, the file will be loaded from the local data cache maintained for the web browser. This property can be useful so that the application can degrade gracefully when a network connection becomes temporarily unavailable.

Miscellaneous Properties

Of course, a very large number of properties remain to be discussed. We will endeavor to cover most of those properties within this section. These properties can help to ascertain almost any information necessary about the `WebBrowser` or `InternetExplorer` objects.

Name, Path, and FullName

The `Name`, `Path`, and `FullName` properties are closely related to each other. The order these properties are listed above might seem somewhat out of the expected order, but the relationship between these values is not completely intuitive.

A series of `Msgbox` commands will be used to emphasize the differences between these values. I will use the `WBDemoApp` application as the example. To bring things into context, the copy of Visual Basic 6 used to produce this demo was installed in the default location, and the `WBDemoApp` folder for the project file was my local drive location of `C:\Windows\Desktop\writing\demoapp\`.

First of all, let's start with the `WebBrowser` control. As one might expect, using a `Msgbox` command with the Name property for WebBrowser2 will give a value of **WebBrowser2**.

This value was probably fairly predictable. Now the `Path` property value, on the other hand, is not very intuitive in its returned value:

For those developers familiar with the default installation folder for Visual Studio, this is the folder where Visual Basic 6 is installed by default. That would seem a little strange to some, since the Visual Basic project is in another directory. The path to the application would seem to be more appropriately set to the Visual Basic project directory. A little explanation is revealed if we produce a message box with the `FullName` property value for WebBrowser2:

As you can see, the `FullName` and `Path` properties are referring to the location of Visual Basic 6. This certainly seems a little strange and definitely not intuitive. The description of the `FullName` property, for example, states that it "Returns a string that evaluates to the fully qualified path of the executable file that contains the Internet Explorer application." But wait a minute! First of all, what about the executable file that contains the `WebBrowser` control? Second, wouldn't the executable file be the `WBDemoApp`?

If you check out the `Path` and `FullName` properties in MSDN Library, you will see that those properties only apply to `InternetExplorer`. In reality, these properties obviously apply to the `WebBrowser` control. Furthermore, the executable file containing the `WebBrowser` control is actual Visual Basic when in the Design environment; hence the returned values reference the appropriate information for `VB6.exe`. This should lead to the obvious question of what value is returned when `WBDemoApp` is compiled. If the executable is compiled into the project directory, the value of `Path` changes, when `WBDemoApp.exe` is run, from the Visual Basic installation directory to C::

The value of the `FullName`, likewise, produces the expected full name and path of the container executable, or `C:\WINDOWS\DESKTOP\writing\demoapp\wbdemoapp.WBDemoApp.exe`.

If we explore the value of these properties for an instance of the `InternetExplorer` automation object, we will find a similarly unintuitive result. The results of the properties are obtained by using a message box command on the IE object reference that we have used thus far in our `WBDemoApp` demonstration application. The `Name` property, as might be expected, is predictable, returning the value Internet Explorer.

The `Path` and `FullName` properties of the InternetExplorer do not, as one might expect, return a value that is equivalent to the location or full name of `iexplore.exe`. The actual results returned point to a different container executable, `C:\WINDOWS\`

The value of `C:\WINDOWS\` might seem surprising, but keep in mind that starting with Internet Explorer 4.x, the `WebBrowser` and `InternetExplorer` objects are now hosted by the Windows Shell, which is `Explorer.exe`. Therefore, the results of `IE.FullName` is much more sensible, giving `C:\Windows\Explorer.exe` This indicates that the "container" executable for the `InternetExplorer` object is, in fact, `Explorer.exe`, otherwise known as the Windows Shell.

One last thing to keep in mind, is that these message box dialogs were returned either prior to the instance of Internet Explorer being launched and assigned as an object reference to IE, or after launching, but without the instance of Internet Explorer having been closed. Closing the launched instance of Internet Explorer will result in an error dialog box indicating that the remote server component cannot be found, thus halting the `WBDemoApp` application.

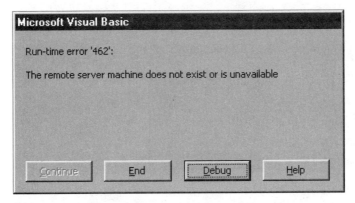

This error dialog will be the same for attempting to access numerous properties of the `InternetExplorer` object whenever an instance has been launched and closed manually, as long as the appropriate error handling code has not been provided.

Parent

The `Parent` property, as might be expected, returns an object reference to the Parent of the `WebBrowser` or `InternetExplorer` objects. In order to obtain the following dialogs, the `Name` property of the `Parent` property was used to return a functionality reference to the identity of the object returned. The `Parent` property of the `WebBrowser` control returns `Form1`

This result should seem very predictable, as we have yet to modify the name of the Form object on which we had placed the WebBrowser control instance. The results of the Parent property on InternetExplorer object is a little different, in that it returns a named reference to itself, giving Microsoft Internet Explorer.

HWND

The hWnd property provides the same functionality for the InternetExplorer object as for other objects. The hWnd property returns the window handle for the main window of the Internet Explorer instance being controlled by the InternetExplorer object reference.

ReadyState

The ReadyState property is useful for programmatically checking on the status of the WebBrowser and InternetExplorer objects while navigating to a target prior to running additional code which could result in a run-time error if ran at an improper time. The ReadyState property returns a value of the type tagReadyState.

The ReadyState property can return the status of the browsing controls to determine if there are currently involved in a process. For example, if the Form_Load event were to be modified to include the following code:

```
Private Sub Form_Load()
    ' Start instance of IE
    ' Note: IE is not visible at this time
    Set IE = CreateObject("InternetExplorer.Application")
    MsgBox IE.ReadyState
End Sub
```

then the application would generate a message box dialog like this

A quick look at the type definition of the tagReadyState type:

```
typedef enum tagREADYSTATE{
    READYSTATE_UNINITIALIZED = 0,
    READYSTATE_LOADING = 1,
    READYSTATE_LOADED = 2,
    READYSTATE_INTERACTIVE = 3,
    READYSTATE_COMPLETE = 4
} READYSTATE;
```

shows us that the value of "0" indicates IE (InternetExplorer object) is currently un-initialized, although it does exist as an object reference.

The primary use of this property could be to determine if the WebBrowser or InternetExplorer objects are in an **interactive state**, or a **complete** state – in other words, whether they will accept user input. The earlier states are intermediary states that internet Explorer tracks and can be hooked to other methods (such as triggering a pop-up sponsors window on READYSTATE_LOADED). Browsing a web page with WBDemoApp, but checking the ReadyState property prior to the DocumentComplete event firing would result in a value of 3 for the StatusReady property.

RegisterAsDropTarget

The RegisterAsDropTarget property, despite its long name, is very simple to set. Since Internet Explorer has the ability to read and render many different types of targets, such as image files, text files and, of course, HTML files, sometimes it is advantageous to use an instance of the WebBrowser control, or even the InternetExplorer object as a target for dragging and dropping files into them. This allows these objects to behave as simple viewers. Even if a WebBrowser control does not have a file currently loaded and rendered, it can still act as a drop target if the RegisterAsDropTarget property is set.

Other times, a WebBrowser control may be meant to only load those targets programmatically chosen or navigated. In these cases, the RegisterAsDropTarget should be set to false. Although this property can be modified programmatically, certain behaviors are noticed. For example, if the RegisterAsDropTarget property for an instance of the InternetExplorer object is set to false after the Visible property is set to true, then Internet Explorer will still allow a graphic image to be dropped onto it and displayed, but subsequent attempts to drop a file onto the browser will be greeted with the standard **Deny** icon. In order to ensure the instance is setup to not allow dropping operations from the beginning, the RegisterAsDropTarget property should be set prior to the Visible property being set to true.

Resizable

The Resizable property is a valuable property for use in conjunction with dynamically rendered web pages. Sometimes, no matter how hard a developer tries, an HTML page may not degrade gracefully as an instance of Internet Explorer is resized to a smaller size. Although an event sink – where elements pass their events on to their parents – can be set up for the events firing within an instance of the InternetExplorer object, sometimes this is not a very flexible option. Other times, the desired events are just not publicly exposed. In cases where the size of the browsing window must not be modified or otherwise resized, and the InternetExplorer object must be used over the WebBrowser control, setting the Resizable property can force the instance of Internet Explorer to remain at the same size as originally set.

When using this property, keep in mind these characteristics of its use.

> The double arrows indicating resizability will show no matter the value set for the Resizable property

> The Height and Width of the InternetExplorer object can still be set anytime programmatically

> The Resizable property, if changed for a visible Internet Explorer instance, will take effect immediately

Keep in mind that the WebBrowser object ignores the Resizable property if used.

Tag

The Tag property is a simple little property that allows a single string to be associated with a WebBrowser control. The description provided through the Object Browser indicates that this property is used to "store any extra data needed for your program". This property serves as a form of custom property, allowing a single text string to be stored. Note that this property is one of the few that is not available for use with the InternetExplorer object.

ToolTipText

The ToolTipText property is used for exactly the same purpose with other controls, hence setting a little description at design-time through the Properties window will result in a nice little description when the mouse is paused over the control. Note that this takes effect even when the WebBrowser control has not actually navigated to a target item. We've set it to This control is a fully functional Web Browser.

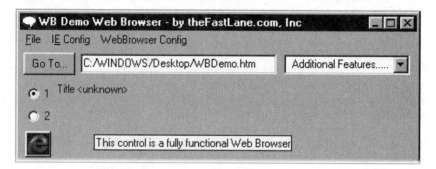

It should be noted that this property is one of the few that is not available for use with the InternetExplorer object.

TopLevelContainer

The TopLevelContainer property is used to indicate whether or not the object is a top level container. In most uses, the WebBrowser object would return a value of false for the TopLevelContainer property, while the InternetExplorer object would return a value of true.

Type

The Type property, applying to both the WebBrowser and InternetExplorer objects, provides a string value which indicates the type or type name of the contained document. In the case of anything that the browser renders, such as web pages, text files, or graphic images, the result of the Type property returns Microsoft HTML Document.

For most office documents, since Internet Explorer can perform the function of an ActiveX Document container, the value returned will depend on the type of office document loaded.

Standard Control Properties

Just like any other control, the WebBrowser has a series of properties which directly map to the standard properties that many other controls expose. For these properties, I have simply included the Properties window description for quick reference.

> ➤ `CausesValidation` – Returns/sets whether validation occurs on the control which lost focus.

> ➤ `HelpContextID` – Specifies the default HELP File context ID for an object.

> ➤ `Index` – Returns/sets the number identifying a control in a control array.

> ➤ `TabIndex` – Returns/sets the tab order of an object within its parent form.

> ➤ `TabStop` – Returns/sets a value indicating whether a user can use the TAB key to give the focus to an object.

> ➤ `WhatThisHelpID` – Returns/sets an associated context number for an object

> ➤ `DragIcon` – Returns/sets the icon to be displayed as the pointer in a drag-and-drop operation.

> ➤ `DragMode` – Returns/sets a value that determines whether manual or automatic drag mode is used.

Control Methods

Now that we have finally finished talking about the numerous properties that either a `WebBrowser` or `InternetExplorer` object exposes, its time to take a look at the myriad of methods that are exposed to the developer. We have already seen uses of the `ExecWB` method, and numerous uses of the `Navigate` method, but now we will look closer at these and other methods.

Navigating HTML Pages

We will start our discussion of the `WebBrowser` and `InternetExplorer` objects by taking a look at the collection of methods that focus on the process of navigating to a target. The main method, `Navigate`, was used heavily during our discussion of the available properties. Fortunately, many more methods exist to complement, enhance, and extend the functionality of the browsing controls beyond the simple `Navigate` method.

Navigate and Navigate2

`Navigate` is the heart and soul of the `WebBrowser` control. It is the core method which turns the browsing control into a full-featured browser. The `Navigate` method opens the door to the world of nearly unlimited potential for hybrid applications.

The `Navigate` method allows for two primary optional parameters, `Flags` and `TargetFramename`, as in the following syntax;

```
object.Navigate URL [Flags,] [TargetFrameName,]
```

The `Flags` parameter has four constants or values that can be used in any combination to modify the behavior of the Navigate method. These four options can be summarized in the following list.

Constant	Value	Description
navOpenInNewWindow	1	Opens the target file or page in a new window
navNoHistory	2	Do not add the target resource to the history list
navNoReadFromCache	4	Do not read the target file from the local cache
navNoWriteToCache	8	Do not add the target file to the local cache

The `TargetFrameName` parameter accepts five possible values, equating to the common target attributes values used by the `<A>` tag;

> ➤ _blank
> ➤ _parent
> ➤ _self
> ➤ _top
> ➤ <window_name>

Note that use of the `navOpenInNewWindow` constant for the `Flag` parameter, when used in conjunction with the `WebBrowser` control, will still result in a new Internet Explorer instance being loaded.

The `Navigate2` method is worth noting. It is an extension of the `Navigate`, which allows navigation to special folders like **My Computer** and **Desktop**. These folders require item identifier list pointers (PIDL) to refer to them. Unfortunately, this is not applicable to the Visual Basic language, and should only be used with Visual C++.

Refresh and Refresh2

The `Refresh` method is a commonly used activity within a Web browser, not just Internet Explorer. This type of functionality allows a web page to simply be re-requested or reload a web page that is currently being viewed. Although you may think a page is requested and reloaded when a URL is manually or programmatically navigated to, in many cases, the page is loaded from a local disk-based cache.

Internet Explorer stores recently navigated pages on the user hard drive by default, in temporary Internet files folder. The rationale, of course, is that this saves time in loading due to the ability to pull from a fast local media rather than getting the file from a remote HTTP server across the Internet. In Internet Explorer, this option is found in the **Internet Properties** dialog on the **General** tab.

The method to modify this setting, and the look-and-feel of the dialogs used to alter the setting may vary, but the concept is the same. Three basic options exist to indicate the caching behavior of Internet Explorer, hence the `InternetExplorer` and `WebBrowser` objects:

The default setting is **Every time you start Internet Explorer**. Many individuals modify this value to **Every visit to the page**. Doing so would effectively eliminate the need to use the `Refresh` method. For many web-based applications, it is almost required to refresh on every visit to the page in question, although since the default is to refresh only the first time a page is loaded after Internet Explorer is started, using the `InternetExplorer` object may not yield the desired results. This is where the `Refresh` method comes into play.

From the Internet Explorer toolbar, the `Refresh` method is invoked through one of four methods:

> ➤ clicking the **Refresh** button on the standard Internet Explorer toolbar
>
> ➤ selecting **View | Refresh** from the drop-down menus
>
> ➤ pressing F5 on the keyboard
>
> ➤ or right-clicking in the window and choosing **Refresh** from the pop-up menu.

Remember, files navigated to using the `Navigate` method can also use the `navNoReadFromCache` or the `navNoWriteToCache` flags, which could provide the same net effect as desired when using the `Refresh` method.

The `Refresh2` method provides an enhancement feature that is absent in the generic `Refresh` method. `Refresh2` includes a required parameter which is used to indicate the degree of refreshing to perform. This parameter, syntactically referred to as `Level`, has three possible values from which to choose.

The options deal with the sending of an HTTP header known as "pragma:nocache". This header is typically sent as part of a refresh option by a browser. When a web server receives this HTTP header as part of the HTTP request, it is being instructed not to return a cached copy of the request file. This is a little different than returning a locally cached copy of a requested file. The cache referred to in the "pragma:nocache" header is the server-based cache that all modern web servers maintain. Thus, a normal Refresh would instruct the web server to return the freshest possible copy of the requested file. In some cases, though, it might be permissible, or even desired to allow this possibility to occur. In steps the Refresh2 method.

The Level parameter of Refresh2 can be passed the following three constant values;

Constant	Value	Description
REFRESH_NORMAL	0	Performs the equivalent of a "lightweight" refresh. The "pragma:nocache" header is not sent, resulting in the option of the file being pulled from the server-based cache
REFRESH_IFEXPIRED	1	Performs a "lightweight" refresh, explained above, only if the page has expired
REFRESH_COMPLETELY	2	Performs a full refresh, including sending the "pragma:nocache" header

Additional Navigation Control Methods

In addition to the core Navigate, Navigate2, Refresh, and Refresh2 methods, a number of methods exist to support the features that are consider absolutely mandatory for a browser to be considered complete. All modern browsers support the concept of a history list. This internal list is maintained as pages or targets are navigated to, allowing a quick and automatic method of recognizing and referring to previously loaded pages.

This list is often stored on the hard drive or made available in a visual manner, but the primary usage is internal, and exposed through the concepts of navigation control buttons such as moving forward or moving backward. In this section, we will take a look at the methods, GoForward and GoBack, which support this functionality for the WebBrowser and InternetExplorer objects. We will also look at the related methods of GoHome, Stop, and GoSearch.

GoBack and GoForward

For long-time users of Internet Explorer, the buttons on the toolbar that provide the functionality to move forward or backward through the history should be very familiar. The GoBack method is invoked through the toolbar **Back** button and the GoForward method through the "**Forward**" button

In order to support these functionalities within our WBDemoApp, we will provide a number of command buttons along the reserved strip of space on the left hand side of the Form1 object. With apologies to Microsoft, we will also borrow the icons used in Internet Explorer itself to provide a similar look and feel, for demonstration purposes.

Furthermore, to provide a convenient centralization of the code for these methods, we'll create a control array of five buttons, called `cmdNavigate`, and centralize the method invocations within this array.

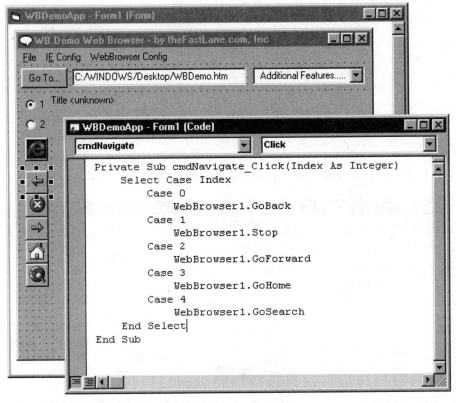

```
Private Sub cmdNavigate_Click(Index As Integer)
    Select Case Index
        Case 0
            WebBrowser1.GoBack
        Case 1
            WebBrowser1.Stop
        Case 2
            WebBrowser1.GoForward
        Case 3
            WebBrowser1.GoHome
        Case 4
            WebBrowser1.GoSearch
    End Select
End Sub
```

If you notice, the icons used on the buttons are in normal color. On Internet Explorer itself, the **Back**, **Forward**, and **Stop** buttons are initially gray. This color/grayscale relationship provides a visual indicator of when invoking the methods would provide a functional change in the current activity or document loaded with the browser. The `GoBack` and `GoForward` methods rely on the `CommandStateChange` event that will be discussed later.

GoHome

The GoHome method provides, as if you couldn't guess, the feature of automatic navigation to a URL defined as the "Home" page. Only one URL can be associated with the concept of Home. This method functions identical with both the WebBrowser and InternetExplorer objects. The GoHome method is normally invoked through the toolbar **Home** button.

The real question is where is this value set for the WebBrowser control. There does not exist a Home property, which could be consider a major oversight on the part of Microsoft, as this functionality being separated on a per browsing object instance would be immensely useful. Nevertheless, the Home URL is defined within the same Internet **Properties** dialog used to configure Internet Explorer.

This should bring up the obvious question of "How do you programmatically change the Home page from within your Visual Basic code"? Fortunately, all the information modified within the Internet Properties is stored within the registry in HKEY_CURRENT_USER\Software\Microsoft\Internet Explorer. The information for the Home Page is stored in the **Main** subkey, and is named **StartPage**, as seen here:

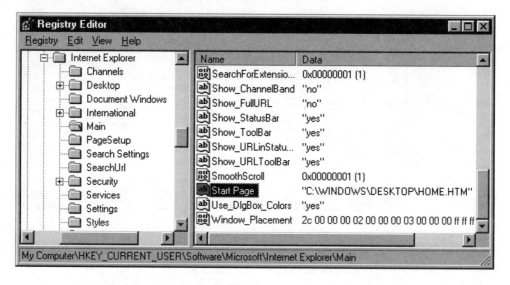

Once we have set this value for the Home/Start page, either manually through Internet Properties or programmatically through modifying the registry, running our WBDemoApp demonstration application and clicking on the Home button will result in the following completed navigation.

GoSearch

The GoSearch method provides the ability to automatically invoke the front end to a web-based search engine. Many customized versions of Internet Explorer modify this value to provide a branded search engine interface to provide a target look and feel.

This value is stored in the registry and set doing installation of the browser, and is rarely changed after that time. This does not mean that this value cannot be modified; it is just usually not altered, as very few pages would qualify as acceptable search engines, while almost any page can be used as a Home page. This value is stored in the registry in HKEY_CURRENT_USER\Software\Microsoft\Internet Explorer. The information for the Search Page is stored in the Main subkey, and is named Search Page, as seen here.

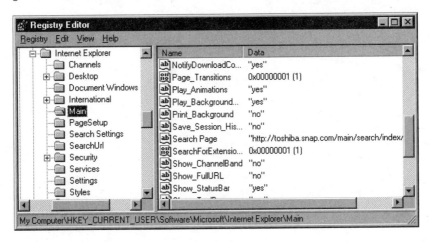

You are probably wondering about the Search button found in direct sight on the standard toolbar. This button does invoke a search page, but it performs this in a different manner. A "Search Bar" is loaded in the left-hand side of the browser, and this value is controlled by a different setting found within the registry. The `GoSearch` method invokes the equivalent of the "Search" function.

Stop

The `Stop` method and `Busy` property work hand in hand to provide an option for interrupting a download or navigation operation in progress. Sometimes, a navigation process is hung by excessive network traffic or other reasons. In some instances, a process is simply taking longer than desired and the operation might want to be stopped prior to completion. In this case the `Stop` method can be invoked to terminate any currently running download operation or navigation. The Stop method will also terminate currently executing dynamic page elements such as DHTML animations or background sounds.`Stop` can also be invoked from the View|Stop menu item.

The `Busy` property can be used to check if the `WebBrowser` or `InternetExplorer` objects are currently in the process of a download or navigation. If so, the `Stop` method can then be used if desired. Checking the `Busy` property is not required, as using the `Stop` method when a browsing control is not busy will not result in a run-time error.

Miscellaneous Methods

At this point, we will continue to look at the remaining list of miscellaneous methods that are exposed and available for invocation against the `WebBrowser` control, `InternetExplorer` object, or both.

ClientToWindow

The `ClientToWindow` method is a convenient method for re-orientating the location of elements within a web page to its relative location within the application or window. This method can be used in conjunction with the `Document` property previously described to convert dynamic page elements within a rendered web page into a window-based coordinate system.

For example, if we focus on the Windows flag watermark on the default page for the `WBDemoApp` application, we can convert its coordinates into windows-based value. To perform this function, we can add the following code to the event that is used to launch the `InternetExplorer` object

```
Private Sub cmdIELaunch_Click()

    ' Navigate IE to location provided in TextBox
    ' Note: Setting the Visible property last will decrease perceived
    ' response time for the navigation.

    With IE
        .Navigate Text1.Text
        .Width = 420
        .Height = 360
        .Visible = True
        .AddressBar = mnuIEAddressBar.Checked
        .MenuBar = mnuIEMenuBar.Checked
        .StatusBar = mnuIEStatusBar.Checked
        .ToolBar = mnuIEToolBar.Checked
        .FullScreen = mnuIEFullScreen.Checked
        .TheaterMode = mnuIETheaterMode.Checked
    End With
```

```
        ' Link up to the Document object and grab the
        ' left and top properties from the Style attribute
        ' of the img tag.
        strFlagLeft = IE.Document.All("Flag").Style.Left
        strFlagTop = IE.Document.All("Flag").Style.Top

        ' Drop off the default unit indicator "px"
        strFlagLeft = Left(strFlagLeft, Len(strFlagLeft) - 2)
        strFlagTop = Left(strFlagTop, Len(strFlagTop) - 2)

        ' Convert to window coordinates
        IE.ClientToWindow CLng(strFlagLeft), CLng(strFlagTop)
    End Sub
```

Some portions of this code might need a little explaining. The All collection was previously explained when we discussed the Document object property. As a part of the Microsoft Document object model, any values assigned to the style attribute of an HTML tag are assigned as the value of an equivalently named property of a Style object. The Style object is a property of the All collection. Through this hierarchy, we are able to obtain style attribute values assigned.

The HTML code being referenced by this Visual Basic is listed here:

```
<HTML>

<HEAD>
<META NAME="GENERATOR" Content="Microsoft Visual Studio 6.0">
<TITLE>Demo Page Title</TITLE>
</HEAD>

<BODY id="BodyID" background=notepaper.gif leftmargin=10>
<IMG id=Flag SRC="FLAG.GIF"
     style="LEFT: 62px; POSITION: absolute; TOP: 124px">
```

The structure of the style attribute string, even to the apprentice DHTML developer, should be fairly obvious in this simple case. In the above Visual Basic code example, the Left property of the Style object will be assigned the string value of "62px". Even if the unit (pixels) was not explicitly set, the px would still have been assigned. Therefore, in order to obtain the raw numerical value for Left and Top, we need to strip out the last two characters in the strings, as seen in the next two lines. Finally, upon passing the values into the method, we convert the values to Long, to accommodate the definition of the method parameters.

It should be noted that the ClientToWindow only applies to the InternetExplorer object. Unlike other properties and methods which have been ignored, the ClientToWindow will generate an error if used on a WebBrowser control. Even though the ClientToWindow method is part of the IWebBrowser2 interface which the WebBrowser object implements,

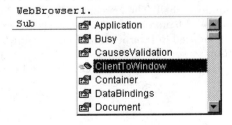

attempting to use the `ClientToWindow` method on a WebBrowser control will generate a run-time failure of the method.

GetProperty and PutProperty

The `GetProperty` and `PutProperty` methods allow the creation of dynamic property definitions and assignment, associating a piece of information, or value, with a property name of the programmer's choice. The syntax of the two methods

```
object.GetProperty szProperty, vtValue
object.PutProperty szProperty, vtValue
```

is identical. The `szProperty` parameter is a normal string value that represents the value for retrieval purposes. The official definition of the method from the Object Browser states "Associates `vtValue` with the name `szProperty` in the context of the object".

Let's examine the following code:

```
Private Sub Command2_Click()
    WebBrowser1.PutProperty "TestProp", "Hello"
End Sub
```

```
Private Sub Command3_Click()
    MsgBox WebBrowser1.GetProperty("TestProp")
End Sub
```

We have temporarily added a couple of command buttons to demonstrate these methods, and the code added for the Command buttons is listed here. In `Command2_Click`, we are going to assign a value of "Hello" to the newly defined "property" of "TestProp". The context of this property is the run-time instance of this object. Until this code is executed, the "TestProp" property does not exist. Fortunately, though, attempting to retrieve the value of a property not yet generated will not result in a run-time error. It will merely return a blank value. The code example provided here will result in the standard message box stating a pleasant "Hello".

> The properties generated at run-time using the `PutProperty` method are not equivalent to the design time properties described within this chapter for the **WebBrowser** control itself. The `GetProperty` method cannot be used to return the value of a literal property.

ShowBrowserBar

The `ShowBrowserBar` method works together with a brand-new feature of not only Internet Explorer 4.x, but also of the Windows shell. The concept of Explorer Bars, Desktop Bars, or Browser Bars all deal with the same concept of **band objects**. Band objects are a special category of COM objects which are designed to be housed in Internet Explorer, Window's Task Bar, or other container. Band objects are OLE automation servers that can show HTML pages, house other controls, accept user input, and other interactive activities, but they are designed to be movable and dockable.

The band objects used by Internet Explorer are called Explorer Bars. The standard Explorer Bars that come with Internet Explorer are vertically oriented, docked on the left side of Internet Explorer, and accessed through the Explorer Bars option off the View menu item.

Internet Explorer installs the following four standard Band objects onto a Windows system:

- ➢ Search
- ➢ Favorites
- ➢ History
- ➢ Folders

These Explorer Bars provide a vertical frame within the Internet Explorer window, docked to the left-hand side, which provides a centralized location to enter search criteria, access previous URLs, favorite URLs, or installed Channels. The Explorer Bars are designed to only show one at a time. Using back-to-back calls to the ShowBrowserBar method will result in the last invocation taking precedence. When in normal mode, Internet Explorer displays the standard Explorer Bars. When Internet Explorer is in TheaterMode, the Explorer Bars take on a slightly different look-and-feel. The Explorer Bars are designed to auto-hide when the mouse moves away. Clicking the image of a pin, to signify pinning open the bar, turns off this behavior:

The ShowBrowserBar method takes two required parameters. The first parameter, pvaClsid, represents the class id or GUID of the browser bar to be loaded. The second parameter, pvarShow, is a Boolean value used to either hide or show the bar. Remember, it is not necessary to hide an Explorer bar before displaying a different bar. As I mentioned above, Internet Explorer registers four Explorer Bars. The class ids of these four bars are:

- ➢ Search – {30D02401-6A81-11D0-8274-00C04FD5AE38}
- ➢ Favorites – {EFA24E61-B078-11D0-89E4-00C04FC9E26E}
- ➢ History – {EFA24E62-B078-11D0-89E4-00C04FC9E26E}

So, for example, to cause the Favorites bar to display, the following code should be used:

```
IE.ShowBrowserBar "{EFA24E61-B078-11D0-89E4-00C04FC9E26E}", True
```

Note that the MSDN library indicates that the second parameter is optional, when in fact it is not optional. The default value for the second parameter is true, although failure to provide an explicit true as a second parameter will generate an error. The error, unfortunately, is not the standard message expected, thus I will show it here. Normally, failure to provide a required parameter usually results in an error dialog about the required parameter missing. The ShowBrowserBar method, on the other hand, generates a seemingly unrelated message about a mismatched type.

Standard Control Methods

The WebBrowser and InternetExplorer objects have their share of fairly standard methods that are exposed. Their use is consistent with the same methods when used on other controls. I will give a simpler explanation of these methods, without going into too much detail.

Drag

The `Drag` method is consistent with its equivalent for other controls. It takes an action parameter which indicates what visual and event state should be entered regarding a dragging operation under way.

```
object.Drag action
```

For the `WebBrowser` control, beginning a drag operation by using the `Drag` method will result in a thin gray outline of the control appearing and moving in synch with the mouse pointer, as is considered normal behavior. For the `InternetExplorer` object, the method, although available as a part of `IWebBrowser2` interface, results in a run-time error.

Quit

The `Quit` method, which only applies to the `InternetExplorer` object, forces the application to close down. The official Object Browser definition for the `Quit` method states "Exits application and closes the open document".

SetFocus

The `SetFocus` method cause the `WebBrowser` control to obtain the current focus of user input, as with other controls. The official Object Browser definition to the `SetFocus` method states "Moves the focus to the specified object".

ZOrder

The `Zorder` method can be used just like with any other control. With the `WebBrowser` control and DHTML pages, the `Zorder` method can be used to increase the perception of interaction between standard form controls and DHTML page elements. A standard command button placed in front of a `WebBrowser` control:

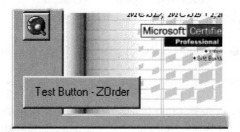

can be place behind the web page using the `Zorder` method.

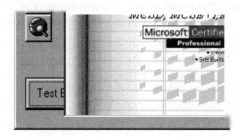

QueryStatusWB

The `QueryStatusWB` method provided by the `IWebBrowser2` interface, as of Internet Explorer 4.x, provides a cleanly packaged ability to query an OLE object (such as the `WebBrowser` control) and determine the relative support of an OLE Command. This method uses the `IOLECommandTarget` interface, and relays the results of the `IOLECommandTarget::QueryStatus` method. This method takes one parameter, nCmdID, and is explained in more detail in the `ExecWB` section. The results of the method are from the `OLECMDF` enumeration. Possible values include:

- ➤ `OLECMDF_SUPPORTED` – Command is supported by this object.
- ➤ `OLECMDF_ENABLED` – Command is available and enabled.
- ➤ `OLECMDF_LATCHED` – Command is an on-off toggle and is currently on.
- ➤ `OLECMDF_NINCHED` – Reserved for future use.

Generally, a `QueryStatusWB` return value of `OLECMDF_ENABLED` is required to indicate that a command is supported by the OLE object.

The next section of `ExecWB` provides more detail on related concepts.

ExecWB

As we mentioned a few times so far in this chapter, the `WebBrowser` and `InternetExplorer` controls both implement the `IWebBrowser2` interface. Starting with Internet Explorer 4.x, the `WebBrowser` control added the `IWebBrowser2::ExecWB` method, or simply `ExecWB`. This method encapsulates the process of obtaining an interface pointer to the `IOleCommandTarget` interface and passing in an OLE Command to the underlying `Exec` method. The `Exec` method would execute the command, such as initiating printing or pasting information from the clipboard. The `ExecWB` method can be used to perform numerous advance features of the `WebBrowser` control that are not exposed as explicit methods. We have already seen a preliminary example of this functionality at the beginning of the chapter when we briefly investigated adding the ability to invoke the `Open`, `Page Setup`, and `Print` dialog screens.

The syntax of the `ExecWB` command is a smidge more complicated than most of the methods of the `WebBrowser` control, and unfortunately, it will take some trial and error to iron the proper usage of all the possible commands, but a few more are shown here to help you initiate your use of this powerful method. The reason for this trial and error approach on some commands is that Microsoft's documentation in MSDN Library has a number of inaccuracies in what commands are supported.

The ExecWB syntax is as follows:

```
object.ExecWB nCmdID, nCmdExecOpt, [pvaIn], [pvaOut]
```

The `ExecWB` method requires an OLE Command ID (`OLECMDID`) to be passed in to identify the command to execute. This value is of type `long`, and is represented by the nCmdID parameter in the `ExecWB` method definition. The nCmdExecOpt method parameter represents the value for the command execution option (`OLECMDEXECOPT`). Together, these values instruct the control as to what supported command to execute and what degree of user prompting should occur. We will take a look at the possible values for these two types of parameters, in addition to showing some examples of command executions.

The last two parameters, pvaIn and paOut, are optional, are will be set to either NULL or an empty string for the production of results and the figures you will see.

OLE Commands

The OLECMDID parameter can take on a number of possible assignments. The standard list, seen below, of assignments represents the official list of commands as defined by Microsoft Office 95. Not all of these commands are supported, in part or in whole, by the WebBrowser and/or InternetExplorer controls. The following chart lists the commands, and the status of support for each by these controls:

Name (Value)	Notes
OLECMDID_OPEN (1)	
OLECMDID_NEW	Not supported
OLECMDID_SAVE (3)	No dialog
OLECMDID_SAVEAS (4)	
OLECMDID_SAVECOPYAS	Not supported
OLECMDID_PRINT (6)	
OLECMDID_PRINTPREVIEW	Not supported
OLECMDID_PAGESETUP (8)	
OLECMDID_SPELL	Not supported
OLECMDID_PROPERTIES	Not supported
OLECMDID_CUT (11)*	
OLECMDID_COPY (12)*	
OLECMDID_PASTE (13)*	
OLECMDID_PASTESPECIAL	Not supported
OLECMDID_UNDO	Not supported
OLECMDID_REDO	Not supported
OLECMDID_SELECTALL	Not supported
OLECMDID_CLEARSELECTION	Not supported
OLECMDID_ZOOM	Not supported
OLECMDID_GETZOOMRANGE	Not supported
OLECMDID_UPDATECOMMANDS (21)	
OLECMDID_REFRESH (22)	
OLECMDID_STOP (23)	
OLECMDID_HIDETOOLBARS	Not supported
OLECMDID_SETPROGRESSMAX (25)	
OLECMDID_SETPROGRESSPOS (26)	
OLECMDID_SETPROGRESSTEXT (27)	
OLECMDID_SETTITLE (28)	
OLECMDID_SETDOWNLOADSTATE (29)	
OLECMDID_STOPDOWNLOAD	Not supported
OLECMDID_ONTOOLBARACTIVATED	Not supported
OLECMDID_FIND	Not supported
OLECMDID_DELETE	Not supported
OLECMDID_HTTPEQUIV	Not supported
OLECMDID_HTTPEQUIV_DONE	Not supported
OLECMDID_ENABLE_INTERACTION	Not supported
OLECMDID_ONUNLOAD	Not supported

* QueryStatusWB returns not supported/enabled, but tests confirm functionality is supported.

After looking at this list, one of the first questions to come to mind should be the "Not supported" status listed on the last block of 8 commands. These commands seem to be directly related to browsing the web. `HTTPEQUIV` and `HTTPEQUIV_DONE`, in particular, seem tailor-made for these controls. The determination of whether or not the command is supported or not came from the results of the `QueryStatusWB`. Those listed as supported returned a value of `OLECMDF_ENABLED`. The following code could be used to help query the status of a command supported by the `WebBrowser` control, using the `QueryStatusWB` method:

```
Private Sub Command2_Click()

' Value type returned by QueryStatusWB
Dim equerry As OLECMDF

    On Error Resume Next

    ' Get command query status - intCommand represents the
    ' numerical value of the command to test
    eQSWBResult = WebBrowser1.QueryStatusWB(intCommand)

    If Err.Number = 0 Then

    If eQSWBResult And OLECMDF_SUPPORTED Then
        MsgBox "The command tested is supported."
    Else
        MsgBox "The command is currently disabled."
    End If

    Else
        MsgBox "Print command Error: " & Err.Description
    End If

End Sub
```

Apparently not all OLE Commands returned by `QueryStatusWB` are unsupported or unavailable. The `Cut`, `Copy`, and `Paste` OLE commands all indicated as not enabled or not supported, yet attempted usage of those commands results in expected functionality. In fact, these commands provide functionality that is both unique and unavailable through the standard Internet Explorer UI.

The following examples highlight the results of using `ExecWB` with selected OLE Commands.

Open Dialog

The Open dialog window is produced by executing the `OLECMDID_OPEN` command. This window was highlighted in the earlier section entitle "The 60-second Browser". This command produces the standard Open input box that is invoked through the File | Open menu option.

Save Command

The Save command, `OLECMDID_SAVE`, produces the same effect as choosing the Save option on the File drop-down menu.

Because this command won't give any visual dialog box or other indication that it has succeeded, hence an error handler should be used to help ascertain the success.

SaveAs Dialog

The OLE command OLECMDID_SAVEAS is responsible for the standard Save As dialog box. For the saving of files from the browser, the Save As dialog will naturally attempt to save the currently loaded HTML or web page into the default project directory. As seen in the next image, the initial directory selected in the Save dialog window is the Visual Basic installation folder. This holds true when the command is executed by request from the application during testing within the Visual Basic IDE.

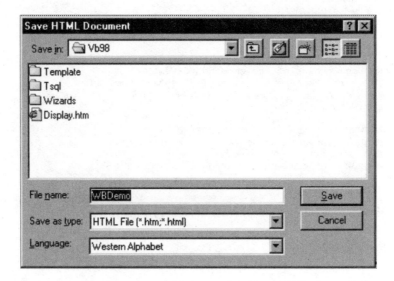

You should be aware that if the OLECMDID_SAVEAS command is executed via ExecWB after the application has been compiled and run from a different directory, the application will default to the application's directory.

Print Dialog

The OLECMDID_PRINT command was revealed much earlier in this chapter in the section entitled "The 60-Second Browser" section. The OLECMDID_PRINT command opens up the print dialog screen customized by Internet Explorer. This is an enhanced version of the standard Windows Print dialog box, with an additional section. A standard print dialog box contains three sections; Printer, Print range, and Copies. The Internet Explorer enhanced print dialog screen adds a "Print frames" section, with print options tailored for web pages, a a couple of additional web page-related print checkboxes.

Page Setup

The OLECMDID_PAGESETUP command invokes the standard Page Setup dialog as seen earlier in the "60-second Browser" section.

Cut, Copy, and Paste Commands

The Cut, Copy, and Paste commands represent the exact same functionality that you see in almost all applications. These commands are normally invoked by using an Edit menu or by using the shortcut keys of *Ctrl-C* and *Ctrl-V*. In Internet Explorer, you may notice that when an HTML page is loaded, the Cut and Paste options are disabled or grayed out.

The Cut, Copy, and Paste commands are represented by OLECMDID_CUT, OLECMDID_COPY, and OLECMDID_PASTE commands. After adding a menu item to accommodate these new choices, double-clicking on a word in the web page to highlight the word, and then choosing Copy will actually copy the text included to the clipboard buffer. This functionality is absolutely identical to that achieved by using the Copy option on the Edit drop-down menu seen in the standard Internet Explorer toolbar. The Cut and Paste option seen in the same menu option are not usually available when items within a web page have been selected.

That said, the use of the ExecWB method, specifically in conjunction with the OLECMDID_CUT and OLECMDID_PASTE commands, allows the WebBrowser or InternetExplorer controls to go beyond that functionality provided by the Internet Explorer application itself. For example, if we highlight a new piece of text displayed in our web page, and choose the Cut option in our WBDemoApp browser, the net result of the command is the removal of the highlighted section of the web page, just as if we had accessed the element through the previously discussed Document object property, and literally removed the HTML code!

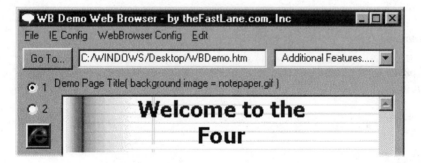

This may not seem like an amazing fact at first, but it does provide the foundation for an intriguing feature set. It is important to note that the underlying HTML code having produced the visual rendered effect is not actually deleted from the file. In fact, no changes have been made or registered in the underlying HTML file, either on the hard drive or even in memory.

To provide an example of the Paste command, let's quickly highlight the text currently in the WBDemoApp's "Go To..." box.

With this text now safely in the clipboard buffer, let's position the mouse pointer on your screen anywhere over the running `WBDemoApp`, and choose the Paste option on our previously added Edit menu.

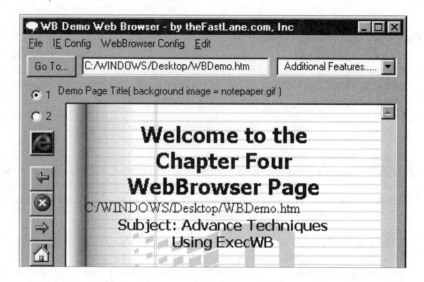

As you can see, the net effect is that the elements in the clipboard buffer are "added" to the rendered web page, but only in the visual representation. Once again, the HTML code that would be necessary to add the elements to the actual page are not dynamically generated and added to the page. This functionality also works for graphical images, such as the MCP logos seen previously in our start-up `WBDemo.htm` page.

Refresh Command

The `OLECMDID_REFRESH` provides the same type of document refresh functionality that the Refresh option exposed by the standard Internet Explorer toolbar provides. Therefore, there is no effective functional difference between the following lines of code:

```
WebBrowser1.ExecWB OLECMDID_REFRESH, OLECMDEXECOPT_PROMPTUSER, "", ""
```

and

```
WebBrowser1.Refresh
```

Stop Command

The `OLECMDID_STOP` provides the same functionality of stopping a download or navigation operation as the functionality that the Stop option provided by the standard Internet Explorer toolbar. Therefore, there is no effective functional difference between the following lines of code:

```
WebBrowser1.ExecWB OLECMDID_STOP, OLECMDEXECOPT_PROMPTUSER, "", ""
```

and

```
WebBrowser1.Stop
```

Progress Indicators Commands

The Progress Indicator commands provide a mechanism to relaying information to the viewer through the Progress Indicator Bar, which is on the Status Bar. Three commands are supported to allow modification to the look-and-feel of the Status Bar. The commands are OLECMDID_SETPROGRESSMAX, OLECMDID_SETPROGRESSPOS, and OLECMDID_SETPROGRESSTEXT. These commands apply only to the InternetExplorer object and not to the WebBrowser control.

The OLECMDID_SETPROGRESSMAX command provides a mechanism for setting the maximum value of the progress indicator, if one is currently owned (in use) by the recipient of this command, which in this case would be the instance of Internet Explorer under control by the InternetExplorer object being referenced.

The OLECMDID_SETPROGRESSTEXT command provides a means for placing your own custom messages in the progress indicator area, similar to the StatusText property. This command is applicable only when a progress indicator is owned by the recipient, meaning a download of some type is probably under way. With our WBDemoApp application the Status Bar was populated with a string by the StatusText property.

If we use the ExecWB method to issue the OLECMDID_SETPROGRESSTEXT command, with an input string of some non-empty character string, the code might look like

```
IE.ExecWB OLECMDID_SETPROGRESSTEXT, OLECMDEXECOPT_PROMPTUSER, _
    "Set Using ExecWB", ""
```

The result of this command would be the modification of the text in the status bar area:

Notice that the icon is different. This is the result of actually modifying the Progress Indicator when it was present, as opposed to modifying the Status Bar area. The functional difference is the icon left showing. The information appears in the same panel of the Status Bar, but the text just has a different lifespan depending on whether the text was set using StatusText, ExecWB while a progress indicator exists, or whether one does not at the time the ExecWB is invoked. As far as you should be concerned, use testing to determine which method you want to leverage.

The very same command, invoked while absolutely no downloads were occurring, maintained the same icon as the StatusText property being set, and the text remained, whereas if it was set using ExecWB, it would have been removed after the download was complete

The `OLECMDID_SETPROGRESSPOS` command allows the value currently sitting in the progress bar to be set to whatever value is desired. Of course, anything past the max will not carry on into the other Status Bar panels. For example, using:

```
IE.ExecWB OLECMDID_SETPROGRESSPOS, OLECMDEXECOPT_PROMPTUSER, 85, ""
```

would result in a blue progress bar being stretched to cover 85%.

Set Title Command

The `OLECMDID_SETTITLE` command provides the ability to set the title bar of Internet Explorer. The title bar still contains the phrase "- Microsoft Internet Explorer", but is preceded by the text passed as input for the `OLECMDID_SETTITLE` command. Keep in mind that the title bar of Internet Explorer is also set by the title attribute of an HTML page, therefore using this command to set the title bar text prior to the navigation completing will rewrite the title bar:

Control Events

We have finally made it through two-thirds of our discussion on the `WebBrowser` and `InternetExplorer` objects. We have covered the properties and methods of the objects, so the only thing left is to explore the events that are raised and exposed by the controls. When possible, I will provide images to emphasize certain events, but for the most part, I will show the syntax, describe the primary parameters, and provide an explanation of the timing and purpose of the events, along with an occasional suggestion for the events' use.

With that having been said, let's first take a look at some events related to page navigation.

Page Navigation

Events related to page navigation could be said to comprise the life of a web page. All the major events in the process of navigating to a page are covered by these events. Of course, the first event should fire immediately after the navigation request has been issued, but before navigation has begun.

BeforeNavigate2

`BeforeNavigate2` event is raised by both the `WebBrowser` and `InternetExplorer` objects after a navigation request has been issued, but before being initiated. This event provides the option to cancel a navigation request based on your code placed within this event. This navigation request can be initiated by several different sources, including;

> External automation, such as using the `Navigate` method.
> Internal automation, such as client-side script executed within the web page itself
> Default behavior of a hyperlink being initiated by a user interaction with the page
> Manual typing of a URL within an address bar

Two things should be pointed out with these sources. External and internal automation is described in reference to the web page itself. Client-side script is internal, while Visual Basic code within an application using the controls is external to the web page. Second, the fourth option would only pertain semantically to the `InternetExplorer` object, as the equivalent source created in conjunction with the `WebBrowser` control would explicitly require us to code the use of the `Navigate` method, which would technically be the first possibility listed.

The syntax of the event procedure is as follows;

```
Private Sub object_BeforeNavigate2(ByVal pDisp As Object, ByVal URL As String,
                ByVal Flags As Long, ByVal TargetFrameName As String,
                PostData As Variant, ByVal Headers As String, Cancel As Boolean)
```

> `pDisp` – Evalutes to the object that will handle the navigation, such as `WebBrowser1`
> `URL` – Evalutes to the URL being requested
> `Flags` – Currently not used.
> `TargetFrameName` – Either the name of the frame being targeted, or `NULL`
> `PostData` – Evalutes to the data being sent as a part of a `POST HTTP` transaction, such as a form submittal
> `Headers` – Used to supply additional HTTP headers to sent to the browsing control
> `Cancel` – A Boolean flag providing the option to cancel the operation.

Use of these events would primary fall into the following categories:

> Modify the URL parameter dynamically
> Modify properties of objects based on the frame being targeted
> Capture the `PostData` information and recording it locally, rather than caching such information on a server or via cookies. This allows greater flexibility when connections to the server are down.
> Canceling the navigation using the `Cancel` parameter.

The naming of this event may seem unusual as there is no `BeforeNavigate` event. In truth, previous versions of these controls supported the raising of both a `BeforeNavigate` and a `FrameBeforeNavigate` event. These two events have now been replaced with the `BeforeNavigate2` event, hence its numerical naming. The use of the `FrameBeforeNavigate` is handled through passing of the frame target as a parameter of the `BeforeNavigate2` event.

DownloadBegin

The DownloadBegin event is raised by both controls immediately after the BeforeNavigate2 event procedure has completed processing. This is true given two assumptions having been made:

➢ The Cancel parameter of the BeforeNavigate2 was not set to TRUE
➢ The object being targeted is accessible

This event is generally used where busy indicators should be configured or set up. Also, the firing of this event ensures that a corresponding DownloadComplete event will fire.

The syntax of the event procedure is as follows:

```
Private Sub object_DownloadBegin()
```

NavigateComplete2

The NavigateComplete2 event, supported by both controls, occurs as soon as a portion of the target has been received or downloaded, indicating a completed navigation process. Additional elements will generally still need to be downloaded for the document to become fully rendered, but the act of navigation to the beginning of the document has successfully completed, and the document viewer has been generated. This event differentiates the act of navigating from downloading.

Examples of elements not yet downloaded as of the firing of the NavigateComplete2 event might include:

➢ Images used in an HTML page
➢ Data downloaded by data source objects
➢ Embedded ActiveX controls
➢ Web pages being downloaded by embedded floating frames

The syntax of the event procedure is as follows;

```
Private Sub object_NavigateComplete2(ByVal pDisp As Object, URL As Variant)
```

➢ pDisp – Evalutes to the object that will handle the navigation, such as WebBrowser1
➢ URL – Evalutes to the URL being requested

You can easily use a different URL to that received through the BeforeNavigate2 URL parameter. Any of the following operations or activities would result in a modified URL value:

➢ Explicit modification of the URL within the BeforeNavigate2 event
➢ Redirection by the web server
➢ Qualification of the URL to add the required protocol prefixes

The naming of this event has the same history as the `BeforeNavigate2` *event. Previous versions of these controls supported the raising of both a* `NavigateComplete` *and a* `FrameNavigateComplete` *event. These two events have now been replaced with the* `NavigateComplete2` *event.*

DownloadComplete

The `DownComplete` event, supported by both controls, always fires after a navigation starts, and can either finish, be halted, or fail. Any busy indicator previously set within the `DownloadBegin` event should be reset within this event to indicate that the operation has terminated.

The syntax of the event procedure is as follows;

```
Private Sub object_DownloadComplete()
```

DocumentComplete

The `DocumentComplete`, supported by both controls, differs from the `DownComplete` event in one subtle manner. The `DocumentComplete` event provides a mechanism for differentiating between the entire download of a requested document, and the individual completed downloads of constituent documents within frames. In a single frame web page, the `DocumentComplete` event is fired once, and it fires after the `DownloadComplete` event, as evidenced by the placing of message box statements into the individual events.

When a document is comprised of multiple frames, the `DocumentComplete` event fires once for each frame document upon completing its download, and then once again for the top-level, or parent, document.

The syntax of the event procedure is as follows;

```
Private Sub object_DocumentComplete(ByVal pDisp As Object, URL As Variant)
```

> ➤ `pDisp` – Evalutes to the object that will handle the navigation, such as `WebBrowser1`
> ➤ `URL` – Evalutes to the URL being requested

> ➤ The URL can differ from the URL parameter received during the `BeforeNavigate2` event in the same fashion as indicated in the `NavigateComplete2` event description.

> **To capture the firing of the last** `DocumentComplete` **event representing the top-level browser, check the value of** `pDisp`**. If** `pDisp` **is equal to the** **WebBrowser** **control, then that instance of the firing of the event represents the final** `DocumentComplete` **event for the requested URL.**

NewWindows2

The `NewWindows2` event is a powerful event for controlling the flow of page navigation. This event is fired for both controls whenever a new window is to be created to hold the navigated page. This can provide some very useful features for an application using the WebBrowser control in particular. A new window might be created in one of several ways, such as;

> ➤ Right-clicking on a hyperlink and choosing "**Open in New Window**"
> ➤ Shift-clicking on a hyperlink.
> ➤ Choosing "**Create New Window**" from the Internet Explorer Menu Bar
> ➤ Pressing the short-cut keys *Ctrl-N*
> ➤ Targeting a non-existent frame for a page
> ➤ Using the `navOpenInNewWindow` flag for the `Navigate2` method

The syntax of the event procedure is as follows;

```
Private object_NewWindow2 (ByVal ppDisp As Object, ByVal Cancel As Boolean)
```

> ➤ `ppDisp` – Evalutes to the object that will handle the navigation, such as `WebBrowser1`
> ➤ `Cancel` – Provide a mechanism for canceling the navigation in the New Window

This event syntax may look very similar to other events, but the two parameters, upon modification within the event procedure, will result in different action than typically though. For example, setting `Cancel` to `TRUE` does not cancel the navigation, but will only cancel the use of the new window for the navigation. Furthermore, `ppDisp` can be reset to another object, thus shifting the container of the navigated page.

With this modified behavior in mind, the application initiating the new window can typically provide three responses to the request for a new window:

> ➤ Create a new `WebBrowser` or `InternetExplorer` object, and set `ppDisp` to reference the new object.
> ➤ Force the original browser control to handle the navigation by setting cancel to `TRUE`.
> ➤ Do nothing

The first option is common for the `WebBrowser` control. The default behavior for the `WebBrowser` control is to load up an instance of Internet Explorer to act as the new window. This poses two problems. First, the look-and-feel of the new window will no longer be consistent with your browsing application. Second, and potentially bigger issue is that no immediate or convenient programmatic control is maintained over this instance of Internet Explorer.

Therefore, a nice solution is to simply create another instance of a child MDI window to act as the new browser, and return a reference to the new child window through `ppDisp`. Of course, this is not an ideal solution for application not leveraging a multiple document interface format. In that case, the second option becomes ideal. Control can be still maintained by setting `Cancel` to `TRUE`, which effectively disables the open in a new window functionality.

The naming of this event has the same history as the `BeforeNavigate2` *and* `NavigateComplete2` *events. Previous versions of these controls supported the raising of both a* `NewWindow` *and a* `FrameNewWindow` *event. These two events have now been replaced with the* `NewWindow` *event. Either though no frame target parameter is supplied with this event, setting* `Cancel` *to* `TRUE` *will still cause the correct frame to load the desired document.*

"On" Events

Now that we have covered the primary page navigation related events, let's switch over to covering briefly the events which correlate to the modification of assorted visible properties of the `InternetExplorer` object. Although these events also apply to the `WebBrowser` control, this is very misleading.

Effectively, these events do not have the same use as with the `InternetExplorer` object. The properties that correspond to these events can be set for the `WebBrowser` control, but they are ignored when set. The corresponding events do fire, but no visual modification to the `WebBrowser` controls appearance occurs. Therefore, in regards to the `WebBrowser` control, these events would predominantly be used to provide a feedback mechanism to inform the application to perform whatever code would be necessary to provide this functionality, if possible.

OnFullScreen

The `OnFullScreen` event is fired when the `FullScreen` property is changed.

The syntax of the event procedure is as follows;

```
Private Sub object_OnFullScreen(ByVal FullScreen As Boolean)
```

If client-side HTML code executes a `window.open` command, and supplies the size properties, then this event will fire.

OnMenuBar

The `OnMenuBar` event is fired when the `MenuBar` property is changed.

The syntax of the event procedure is as follows:

```
Private Sub object_OnMenuBar(ByVal MenuBar As Boolean)
```

If client-side HTML code executes a `window.open` command, then this event will correspond to the value of the menu bar property having been sent.

OnQuit

This event is fired only by Internet Explorer prior to the instance of the browser closing. This event generally corresponds to the invocation of the `Quit` method.

OnStatusBar

The `OnStatusBar` event is fired when the `StatusBar` property is changed.

The syntax of the event procedure is as follows:

```
Private Sub object_OnStatusBar(ByVal StatusBar As Boolean)
```

OnTheaterMode

The `OnTheaterMode` event is fired when the `TheaterMode` property is changed.

The syntax of the event procedure is as follows:

```
Private Sub object_OnTheaterMode(ByVal TheaterMode As Boolean)
```

OnToolBar

The `OnToolBar` event is fired when the `ToolBar` property is changed.

The syntax of the event procedure is as follows:

```
Private Sub object_OnToolBar(ByVal ToolBar As Boolean)
```

If client-side HTML code executes a `window.open` command, then this event will correspond to the value of the toolbar property having been sent.

OnVisible

The `OnVisible` event is fired when the `Visible` property has changed.

The "Change" Events

At this point, we will take a look at three events that are only related by the proximity of their names to each other. These "change" events fire in response to the changing of state of three different aspects of the controls; `CommandState` support, progress state, and property state.

CommandStateChange

The `CommandStateChange` event corresponds to the changing of enabled status of one of the buttons on the Internet Explorer standard toolbar. This `Command` parameter, described below, is used to determine which command status changed. This event is predominantly used to determine when Forward and Back toolbar buttons should be enabled.

The syntax of the event procedure is as follows:

```
Private Sub object_CommandStateChange (ByVal Command As Long,
                ByVal Enable As Boolean)
```

The Command parameter can provide one of three possible values:

- CSC_UPDATECOMMANDS (-1)
- CSC_NAVIGATEFORWARD (1)
- CSC_NAVIGATEBACK (2)

A value of -1, for the Command parameter would indicate that at least one of the toolbar buttons may have changed. When using the WebBrowser control, this might correlate to the Stop button now being enabled. When -1 is returned for Command, the Enabled parameter should be ignored. For values of 1 and 2, the Enable parameter will accurately indicate the status of the **Forward** and **Back** toolbar buttons. This event can be used for the WebBrowser control to provide the same look and feel with the navigation buttons. For example, let's consider placing some code in the CommandStateChange event to keep our WebBrowser **Forward** and **Back** command buttons in synch with the status of the standard toolbar equivalents:

```
Private Sub WebBrowser1_CommandStateChange(ByVal Command As Long, _
                                           ByVal Enable As Boolean)
    If Command = 2 Then
        CmdNavigate(0).Enabled = Enable
    End If

    If Command = 1 Then
        CmdNavigate(2).Enabled = Enable
    End If

End Sub
```

Code such as this is necessary to allow the WebBrowser control, which can not view the standard bars of the Internet Explorer, to keep an equivalent set of visual elements in synch through this notification mechanism. Since the initial loading of the application and navigation to an initial page will fire the CommandStateChange event at least three times, covering the initial disabled status of the **Forward** and **Back** buttons, the buttons will be disabled.

Keep in mind that if your application does not initially navigate to a page, the command buttons used for navigating forward and backward will need to be defaulted to not enabled. Once the browser navigates to a brand new page, the toolbars should stay in synch, initially leaving only the go backward button enabled. On our WebBrowser, the go back arrow will be colored, with all the others grayed out.

> **Microsoft's MSDN Library indicates, in at least one location, that the value of the CSC_NAVIGATEBACK constant is 3. In fact, this is incorrect. The correct value is 2, therefore checking for a value of 3 as notification of the ability to now move back in the history list would not provide the desired functionality.**

ProgressChange

The `ProgressChange` event is used to notify the container of the browsing control when the status of a download operation has shifted. This allows visual notifications to be produced, informing the user of the application as to the state of the download operations under way.

The syntax of the event procedure is as follows;

```
Private Sub object_ProgressChange(ByVal Progress As Long,
                                  ByVal ProgressMax As Long)
```

➤ Progress – Indicates the current progress value of the current download operation
➤ ProgressMax – Indicates the maximum value with which the Progress value is associated.

To fully demonstrate the use of this event, consider the following code;

```
' Prepare Global Reference for loading IE
Dim IE As Object
Dim strProgress As String
```

```
Private Sub WebBrowser_ProgressChange(ByVal Progress As Long, _
                                      ByVal ProgressMax As Long)

    StrProgress = strProgress & Chr(13) & Chr(10) & _
                  CStr(Progress) & " out of max of " & _
                  CStr(ProgressMax)

End Sub
```

```
Private Sub WebBrowser1_DownloadComplete()
    MsgBox "Progress recorded at:" & _
        Chr(13) & Chr(10) & strProgress

End Sub
```

I have placed in the `ProgressChange` event of the `WebBrowser` control code to concatenate the results of each successive firing of the event into a string variable, and the generated a message box at the conclusion of the download. Note that the message box statement was placed in the `DownloadComplete` event in order to guarantee that it will fire and produce the results for us. To invoke this little demonstration, I will navigate to a URL inaccessible from the development system.

Notice that the default max value is `10000`, and the increments are in units of 50, equating to 1/2 of a percent implied progress. At this point, the determination was made that the target could not be reached and the attempt was aborted.

PropertyChange

The `PropertyChange` event fires whenever the `PutProperty` method of the `InternetExplorer` object is invoked.

The syntax of the event procedure is as follows;

```
Private Sub object_PropertyChange(ByVal szProperty As String)
```

> `szProperty` – Identifies the name of the property having been modified by the `PutProperty` method.

StatusTextChange

The `StatusTextChange` event is used to notify the container of the control when the text information within the Status Bar has been modified. This could happen through several methods:

> - Client-side code explicitly modifying the Status
> - The browser control implicitly modifying the status text
> - The `StatusText` method of the control having been invoked
> - The `OLECMDID_SETPROGRESSTEXT` command fired through the `ExecWB` method of the control

The syntax of the event procedure is as follows:

```
Private Sub object_StatusTextChange(ByVal Text As String)
```

> - `Text` – Identifies the body of the status text.

This event provides a mechanism for the container of a `WebBrowser` control to provide the desired notification of the information that is automatically shown in the Status Bar of Internet Explorer, when shown.

TitleChange

The `TitleChange` event is fired when the title of a document is available or changes. There is a distinction, in that during the download of a typical HTML page by one of the browsing controls, the title of a page is initially set to the URL of the page. As soon as the Title tag of an HTML page is parsed, the title is change to reflect the explicitly defined page title.

The syntax of the event procedure is as follows;

```
Private Sub object_TitleChange(ByVal Text As String)
```

> - `Text` – Identifies the body of the title text.

Standard Control Events

Just like any other control, the `WebBrowser` has a series of events which directly map to the standard events that many other controls expose. For these events, I have simply included the Object Browser standard description of the events.

> - `DragDrop` – Occurs when a drag-and-drop operation is completed.
> - `DragOver` – Occurs when a drag-and-drop operation is in progress.
> - `GotFocus` – Occurs when an object receives the focus.
> - `LostFocus` – Occurs when an object loses the focus.
> - `Validate` – Occurs when a control loses focus to a control that causes validation.

Summary

In this chapter, we have taken a very in-depth look at the WebBrowser and InternetExplorer objects that are exposed by the core DLL components of the Internet Explorer application. We have taken a look at samples and demonstration of many of the properties, methods, and events that these controls support. We started from scratch and created a web browser, WBDemoApp, using the WebBrowser control. We slowly built this application up to include numerous functionalities exposed by the control, and to provide demonstrations of numerous functions supported by the controls.

Many of the pros and cons of using the WebBrowser object, versus the InternetExplorer object were addressed, as well as the differences in functionalities supported by each. We even managed to address a number of issues for which standard Microsoft documentation and reference material currently provide inaccurate or misleading statements. Finally, we were able to throw in a number of mini-scenarios, suggestions, and ideas for leveraging this incredibly flexible and useful pair of web browsing controls.

The main points of this chapter are:

> - The WebBrowser control has existed since Internet Explorer 3.x

> - Numerous enhancements have been provided in the IE4 version.

> - The controls are now hosted by the Windows shell, as opposed to previous versions of the controls being hosted within the actual Internet Explorer application.

> - Almost all standard functions of Internet Explorer are supported by the WebBrowser control

> - A couple of functions supported by the WebBrowser control are not accessible by the Internet Explorer application.

> - Internet Explorer can be controlled and automated through the InternetExplorer object

> - Both controls support DHTML.

> - The DHTML object model is accessible through the Document property.

> - The parsing of the HTML tags is handled by the MSHTML.dll file.

> - The HTML Object Library is found in the MSHTML.dll file.

> - Specialized Explorer bars can be programmed and controlled through these objects.

Now that we've taken a look at adding web browsing functionality to standard Visual Basic applications, we've completed our tour of the client-side potential of Visual Basic and can move on to looking at the server side aspects of web programming.

8

Getting Started By Understanding ASP

Up until this chapter, we've been focusing mainly on client-side programming and applications. Now it's time to take a look at the server side. Creating web sites with only client-side scripting is all well and good, but your functionality is severely limited. By adding server-side scripting, you gain a huge advantage. You are able to draw upon the wealth of data available to you on the server and across the enterprise in various databases. You are able to customize pages to the needs of each different user that comes to your web site. In addition, by keeping your code on the server-side you can build a library of functionality. This library can be drawn from again and again to further enhance other web sites. Best of all, using server-side script libraries will allow your web sites to scale to multi-tier, or distributed, web applications.

To do this, you'll need a good understanding of the HTTP protocol, and how an HTTP server interacts with a browser. This model is important to understand when developing web applications that exist on the client and server side.

Next, we'll introduce you to Active Server Pages, or ASP. ASP is Microsoft's server-side scripting environment. It can be used to create everything from simple, static web pages, to database-aware dynamic sites, using HTML and scripting. It's other important use is as a programming "glue". Through the use of ASP, you can create and manipulate server-side components. These components can perhaps provide data to your application such as graphic image generation, or maybe link to a mainframe database. The important thing is that the ASP code does nothing more than facilitate the use of these components on the Web.

ASP comes with some built-in objects that are important to understand before their full potential can be unleashed. We will cover these objects in depth.

Finally, we'll look at some real-world examples of using ASP on a web site. These should give you some idea of the power and beauty of server-side scripting with ASP.

The Anatomy of the HTTP Protocol

As you know, surfing the web is as simple as clicking a link on your browser. But do you know what really goes on beneath the hood of your web browser? It can be quite complex, but isn't too difficult to understand. More importantly, it will help you to understand the intricacies of client and server side scripting.

Overview

The **Hypertext Transfer Protocol**, or **HTTP**, is an *application level* TCP/IP protocol. An application level protocol is one that travels on top of another protocol. In this instance, HTTP travels on top of TCP, which is also a protocol. When two computers communicate over a TCP/IP connection, the data is formatted and processed in such a manner that it is guaranteed to arrive at its destination. This elaborate mechanism is the TCP/IP protocol.

HTTP takes for granted, and largely ignores, the entire TCP/IP protocol. It relies instead on text commands like GET and PUT. Application level protocols are implemented, usually, within an application (as opposed to at the driver level), hence the name. Some other examples of application level protocols are the **File Transfer Protocol** (FTP) and the mail protocols, **Standard Mail Transfer Protocol** (SMTP) and the **Post Office Protocol**, POP3. Pure binary data is rarely sent via these protocols, but when it is, it is encoded into an ASCII format. This is inefficient at best, and future versions of the HTTP protocol will rectify this problem. The most up-to-date version of HTTP is version 1.1, and almost all web servers available today support this version.

There is also a new HTTP protocol in the works called HTTP-NG, or HTTP-Next Generation. This newer, robust protocol will utilize bandwidth more efficiently and improve on many of the original HTTP's shortcomings. The biggest improvement in the new protocol is that data will be transferred in binary as opposed to text, thus making transactions quicker. More technical information about HTTP-NG is available from the W3C at http://www.w3.org/Protocols/HTTP-NG.

The HTTP Server

To carry out an HTTP request, there must be an HTTP or web server running on the target machine. This server is an application that listens for and responds to HTTP requests on a certain TCP port (by default, port 80). An HTTP request is for a single item from the web server. The item may be anything from a web page to a sound file. The server, upon receipt of the request, attempts to retrieve the data asked for. If the server finds the correct information, it formats and returns the data to the client. If the requested information could not be found, the server will return an error message.

Pulling up a single web page in your browser may cause dozens of HTTP transactions to occur. Each element on a web page that is not text needs to be requested from the HTTP server individually. The main point of all this is that each HTTP transaction consists of a request and a response:

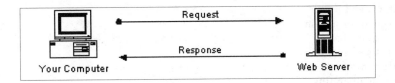

And it is in this transaction model that you must place yourself when you are programming web applications.

Protocol Basics

There are four basic states that make up a single HTTP transaction. They are:

> The Connection
> The Request
> The Response
> The Disconnection

A client connects to a server and issues the request. It waits for a response, then disconnects. A connection typically lasts only for a few seconds. On web sites like Yahoo where the data is not laden with graphics, and the information is fairly static, requests last less than one second.

The Connection

The client software, a web browser in this case, creates a TCP/IP connection to an HTTP server on a specific TCP/IP port. Port 80 is used if one is not specified. This is considered the default port for an HTTP server. A web server may, however, reside on any port allowed. It is completely up to the operator of the web server, and port numbers are often deliberately changed as a first line of defense against unauthorized users.

The Request

Once connected, the client sends a request to the server. This request is in ASCII, and must be terminated by a carriage-return/line-feed pair. Every request must specify a method which tells the server what the client wants. In HTTP 1.1, there are eight methods: OPTIONS, GET, HEAD, POST, PUT, DELETE, TRACE, and CONNECT. For more information about the different methods and their use, please check out the HTTP specification on the W3C web site. For the purpose of this chapter, we are going to focus on the GET method.

The GET method asks the web server to return the specified page. The format of this request is as follows:

```
GET <URL> <HTTP Version>
```

You can make HTTP requests yourself with the telnet program. Telnet is a program that is available on most computer systems and it was originally designed for use on UNIX systems. Since basic UNIX is character-based, one could log in from a remote site and work with the operating system. Telnet is the program that allows you to connect to a remote machine and all versions of Windows come with a telnet program. The following picture to the right shows what it looks like.

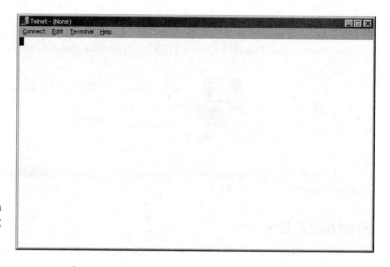

Microsoft's telnet leaves much to be desired. Thankfully, a company called Van Dyke Technologies (`www.vandyke.com`) created an excellent telnet program called CRT. In fact, figure 5 is a screen shot of CRT.

Telnet defaults to TCP/IP port 23. On UNIX systems, in order to telnet into a machine, that machine must be running a telnet server. This server listens for incoming telnet connections on port 23. However, almost all telnet programs allow you to specify the port on which to connect. It is this feature that we can utilize to examine HTTP running under the hood.

If you choose not to download the Van Dyke telnet client, you can test this by running Window's own telnet. Windows has no predefined menu item for this program, but on NT it can usually be found at `C:\WINNT\system32\Telnet.exe`. To run it, press the Start button and select Run. Type in telnet and press ENTER. You should see a telnet window similar to the one above above.

Select Remote System from the Connect menu and you'll be presented with the following dialog:

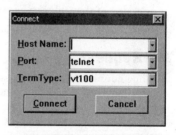

Type in the name of any web server; we chose `http://www.mindbuilder.com`. Then enter the web server's port. This is almost always 80.

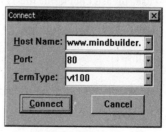

Once you are connected, the title bar will change to contain the name of the server to which you are connected. There is no other indication of connection. It is at this point that you need to type in your HTTP command. Type in the following, all in upper case:

```
GET / HTTP/1.0
```

Please note that unless you have turned on Local Echo in the Preferences, you will not see what you type. After you've entered the command you must send a carriage return (*Ctrl-M*) followed by a line feed (*Ctrl-J*). What is returned is shown as follows, and is the response to your HTTP request.

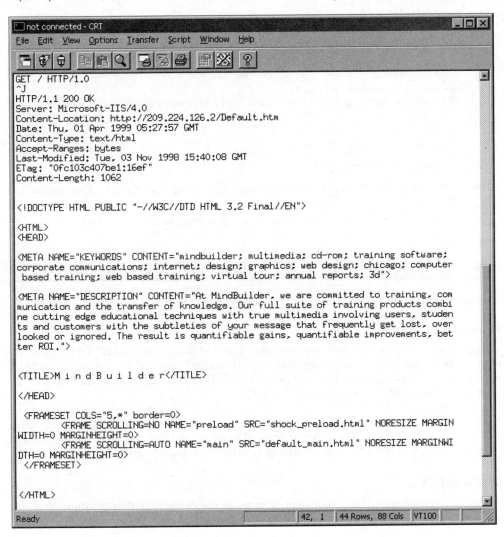

The Response

Upon receipt of the request, the web server will answer. This will most likely result in some sort of HTML data as shown previously. However, you may get an error as in the following example:

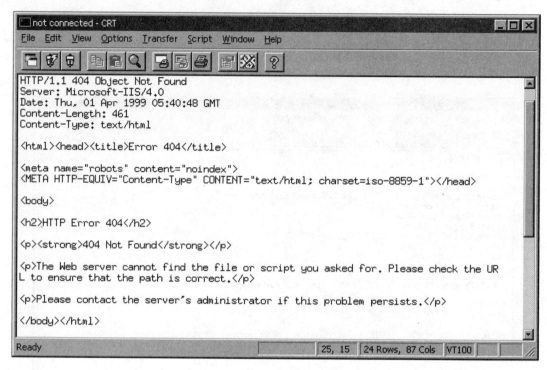

Again, the response is in HTML, but the code returned is an error code (404) instead of an OK (200).

HTTP Headers

What was actually returned is a two-part response. The first part consists of HTTP headers. These headers provide information about the actual response to the request, the most important header being the `status` header. In the listing above, it reads **HTTP/1.1 404 Object Not Found**. This indicates the actual status of the request.

The other headers that were returned with this request are `Server`, `Date`, `Content-Length`, and `Content-Type`. There are many different types of headers, and they are all designed to aid the browser in easily identifying the type of information that is being returned.

The Disconnect

After the server has responded to your request, it closes the connection thus disconnecting you. Subsequent requests require you to re-establish your connection with the server.

Introducing Active Server Pages

With the HTTP architecture laid out in the last section, you can clearly see that the real heart of the HTTP protocol lies in the request and the response. The client makes a request to the server, and the server provides the response to the client. What we're looking at here is really the foundations of client/server computing. A client makes a request from a server and the server fulfills that request. We see this pattern of behavior throughout the programming world today, not only in Web programming.

Microsoft recognized this pattern and developed a new technology that rendered web programming a much more accessible technique. This technology is Active Server Pages or ASP for short. ASP is a server-side scripting environment that comes with Microsoft's Internet Information Services. ASP allows you to embed scripting commands inside your HTML documents. The scripting commands are interpreted by the server and translated into the corresponding HTML and sent back to the server. This enables the web developer to create content that is dynamic and fresh. The beauty of this is that it does not matter which browser your web visitor is using, because the server returns only pure HTML. Sure you can extend your returned HTML with browser specific programming, but that is your prerogative. By no means is this all that ASP can do, but we'll cover more of its capabilities like form validation and data manipulation later on in this chapter.

By default, the ASP scripting language is VBScript. You can choose other languages such as JavaScript or even Perl, but as a Visual Basic programmer, it is to your advantage to leverage your knowledge of VB and be creating dynamic web pages in less than 20 minutes!

How the Server recognizes ASPs

ASP pages do not have an `html` or `htm` extension; they have an `.asp` extension instead. The reason for this is twofold. First, in order for the web server to know to process the scripting in your web page, it needs to know that there is some in there. Well, by setting the extension of your web page to `.asp`, the server can assume that there are scripts in your page.

A nice side effect of naming your ASP pages with the `asp` *extension is that the ASP processor knows that it does not need to process your HTML files. It used to be the case, as in ASP 2.0, that any page with the* `.asp` *extension, no matter whether it contained any server side scripting code or not, was automatically sent to the server, and would thereby take longer to process. With the introduction of ASP 3.0 in Windows 2000, the server is able to determine the presence of any server side code and process or not process the page accordingly. This increases the speed of your HTML file retrieval and makes your web server run more efficiently.*

Secondly, using an `asp` extension (forcing interpretation by the ASP processor every time your page is requested) hides your ASP scripts. If someone requests your `.asp` file from the web server, all he is going to get back is the resultant processed HTML. If you put your ASP code in a file called `mycode.scr` and requested it from the web server, you'll see all of the code inside.

ASP Basics

ASP files are really just HTML files with scripting embedded within them. When a browser requests an ASP file from the server, it is passed on to the ASP processing DLL for execution. After processing, the resulting file is then sent on to the requesting browser. Any scripting commands embedded from the original HTML file are executed and then removed from the results. This is excellent in that all of your scripting code is hidden from the person viewing your web pages. That is why it is so important that files that contain ASP scripts have an `asp` extension.

The Tags of ASP

To distinguish the ASP code from the HTML inside your files, ASP code is placed between <% and %> tags. This convention should be familiar to you if you have ever worked with any kind of server-side commands before in HTML. The tag combination implies to the ASP processor that the code within should be executed by the server and removed from the results. Depending on the default scripting language of your web site, this code may be VBScript, JScript, or any other language you've installed. Since this book is for the Visual Basic programmer, all of our ASP scripts will be in VBScript.

In the following snippet of HTML, you'll see an example of some ASP code between the `<%` and `%>` tags:

```
<TABLE>
<TR>
<TD>
<%
    x = x + 1
    y = y - 1
%>
</TD>
</TR>
</TABLE>
```

<SCRIPT> Blocks

You may also place your ASP code between `<SCRIPT></SCRIPT>` blocks. However, unless you direct the script to run at the server level, code placed between these tags will be executed at the client as normal client-side scripts. To direct your script block to execute on the server, use the `RUNAT` command within your `<SCRIPT>` block as follows:

```
<SCRIPT Language="VBScript" RUNAT="Server">
… Your Script …
</SCRIPT>
```

The Default Scripting Language

As stated previously, the default scripting language used by ASP is VBScript. However, you may change it for your entire site, or just a single web page. Placing a special scripting tag at the beginning of your web page does this. This tag specifies the scripting language to use for this page only.

```
<%@ LANGUAGE=ScriptingLanguage %>
```

"ScriptingLanguage" can be any language for which you have the scripting engine installed. ASP comes with VBScript and JScript.

You can set the default scripting language for the entire application by changing the **Default ASP Language** field in the Internet Service Manager on the **App Options** tab. This is shown in the following screenshot.

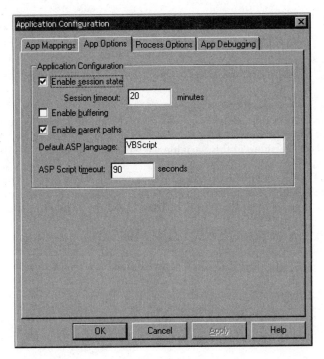

Mixing HTML and ASP

You've probably guessed by now that you can easily mix HTML code with ASP scripts. The power of this feature is phenomenal! VBScript has all of the control flow mechanisms like `If Then`, `For Next`, and `Do While` loops. But with ASP you can selectively include HTML code based on the results of these operators. Let's look at an example.

Suppose you are creating a web page that greets the viewer with a "Good Morning", "Good Afternoon", or "Good Evening" depending on the time of day. This can be done as follows:

```
<HTML>
<BODY>
<P>The time is now <%=Time()%></P>
<%
  Dim iHour

  iHour = Hour(Time())

  If (iHour >= 0 And iHour < 12 ) Then
```

```
%>
Good Morning!
<%
   ElseIf (iHour > 11 And iHour < 5 ) Then
%>
Good Afternoon!
<%
   Else
%>
Good Evening!
<%
End If
%>
</BODY>
</HTML>
```

First we print out the current time. The `<%=` notation is shorthand to print out the value of an ASP variable or the result of a function call. We then move the hour of the current time into a variable called `iHour`. Based on the value of this variable we write our normal HTML text.

Notice how the HTML code is outside of the ASP script tags. When the ASP processor executes this page, the HTML that lies between control flow blocks that aren't executed is discarded, leaving you with only the correct code. Here is the source of what is returned from our web server after processing this page:

```
<HTML>
<BODY>
<P>The time is now 7:48:37 PM</P>

Good Evening!

</BODY>
</HTML>
```

As you can see, the scripting is completely removed leaving only the HTML and text.

The other way to output data to your web page viewer is using one of ASP's built-in objects called `Response`. We'll cover this approach in the next section as you learn about the ASP object model.

Commenting Your ASP Code

As with any programming language, it is of the utmost importance to comment your ASP code as much as possible. However, how many times have you come across a piece of code and said "eh?" Someone once told me that the only purpose comments served were to amuse the compiler. In some instances, he may have been correct. However, unclear comments are not worth putting in your code.

Comments in ASP are identical to comments in VB. When ASP comes across the single quote character it will graciously ignore the rest of the line:

```
<%
Dim iLumberJack

'I'm a comment and I'm O.K.
iLumberJack = iLumberJack + 1
%>
```

The Active Server Pages Object Model

ASP, like most Microsoft technologies, utilizes the Component Object Model, or COM, to expose functionality to consumer applications. ASP is actually an extension to your web server that allows server-side scripting. At the same it also provides a compendium of objects and components, which manage interaction between the web server and the browser. These objects form the **Active Server Pages Object Model**. These 'objects' can be manipulated by scripting languages. Take a look at the following diagram:

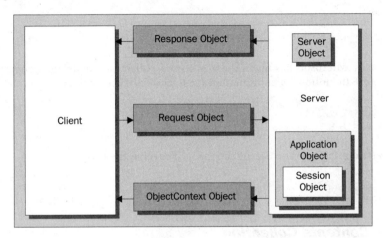

ASP neatly divides up into six objects, which manage their own part of the interaction between client and server. As you can see in the diagram, at the heart of the interaction between client and server are the Request and Response objects, which deal with the HTTP request and response; but we will be taking a quick tour through all of the different objects and components that are part of ASP.

The object model consists of six core objects, each one with distinct properties and methods. The objects are:

> ➢ Request
> ➢ Response
> ➢ Application
> ➢ Session
> ➢ Server
> ➢ ObjectContext

Each of the objects, barring the Server and ObjectContext object, can use collections to store data. Before we look at each object in turn we need to take a quick overview of collections.

Collections

Collections in ASP are very similar to their VB namesakes. They act as data containers that store their data in a manner close to that of an array. The information is stored in the form of name/value pairs.

The `Application` and the `Session` object have a collection property called `Contents`. This collection of variants can hold any information you wish to place in it. Using these collections allow you to share information between web pages.

To place a value into the collection, simply assign it a key and then assign the value:

```
Application.Contents("Name") = "Evil Knievil"
```

Or

```
Session.Contents("Age") = 25
```

Fortunately for us, Microsoft has made the `Contents` collection the default property for these two objects. Therefore the following shorthand usage is perfectly acceptable:

```
Application("Name") = "Evil Knievil"
Session("Age") = 25
```

To read values from the `Contents` collections, just reverse the call:

```
sName = Application("Name")
sAge = Session("Age")
```

Iterating the Contents Collection

Because the `Contents` collections work like regular Visual Basic collections, they are easily iterated. You can use the collection's `Count` property, or use the `For Each` iteration method:

```
for x = 1 to Application.Contents.Count
    ...
next

for each item in Application.Contents
    ...
next
```

> Please note that the Contents collections are 1 based. That is to say that the first element in the collection is at position 1, not 0.

To illustrate this, the following ASP script will dump the current contents of the `Application` and `Session` objects' `Contents` collections:

```
<HTML>
<BODY>
<P>The Application.Contents</P>
<%
    Dim Item

    For Each Item In Application.Contents
      Response.Write Item & " = [" & Application(Item) & "]<BR>"
    Next
```

```
%>
<P>The Session.Contents</P>
<%
   For Each Item In Session.Contents
    Response.Write Item & " = [" & Session(Item) & "]<BR>"
   Next
%>
</BODY>
</HTML>
```

Removing an Item from the Contents Collection

The `Application` Object's `Contents` collection contains two methods, and these are `Remove` and `RemoveAll`. These allow you to remove one or all of the items stored in the `Application`'s `Contents` collection. At the time of this writing, there is no method to remove an item from the `Session`'s `Contents` collection.

Let's add an item to the `Application Contents` collection, and then remove it.

```
<%
   Application("MySign") = "Pisces"
   Application.Contents.Remove("MySign")
%>
```

Or we can just get rid of everything...

```
<%
   Application.Contents.RemoveAll
%>
```

Not all of the collections of each object work in this way, but the principles remain the same and we will explain how each differs when we discuss each object.

The Request Object

When your web page is requested, much information is passed along with the HTTP request, such as the URL of the web page request and format of the data being passed. It can also contain feedback from the user such as the input from a text box or drop down list box. The `Request` object allows you to get at information passed along as part of the HTTP request. The corresponding output from the server is returned as part of the `Response`. The `Request` object has several collections to store information that warrant discussion.

The Request Object's Collections

The `Request` object has five collections. Interestingly, they all act as the default property for the object. That is to say, you may retrieve information from any of the five collections by using the abbreviated syntax:

```
ClientIPAddress = Request("REMOTE_ADDR")
```

The `REMOTE_ADDR` value lies in the `ServerVariables` collection. However, through the use of the collection cascade, it can be retrieved with the above notation. Please note that for ASP to dig through each collection, especially if they have many values, to retrieve a value from the last collection is inefficient. It is always recommended to use the fully qualified collection name in your code. Not only is this faster, but it improves your code in that it is more specific, and less cryptic.

ASP searches through the collections in the following order:

- QueryString
- Form
- Cookies
- ClientCertificate
- ServerVariables

If there are variables with the same name, only the first is returned when you allow ASP to search. This is another good reason for you to fully qualify your collection.

QueryString

Contains a collection of all the information attached to the end of an URL. When you make an URL request, the additional information is passed along with the URL to the web page appended with a question mark. This information takes the following form: URL?item=data[&item=data][…]

The clue to the server is the question mark. When the server sees this, it knows that the URL has ended, and variables are starting. So an example of a URL with a query string might look like this: http://www.buythisbook.com/book.asp?bookname=ProfessionalWebProgramming

We stated earlier that the collections store information in name/value pairs. Despite this slightly unusual method of creating the name/value pair, the principle remains the same. Bookname is the name and ProfessionalWebProgramming is the value. When ASP gets hold of this URL request, it breaks apart all of the name/value pairs and places them into this collection for easy access. This is another excellent feature of ASP. Query strings are built up using ampersands to delimit each name/value pair so if you wished to pass the user information along with the book information, you could pass the following:
http://www.buythisbook.com/book.asp?bookname=ProfessionalWebProgramming&buyer=JerryAblan

Query strings can be generated in one of three ways. The first is, as discussed, by a user typed URL. The second is as part of a URL specified in an Anchor tag.

```
<A HREF="book.asp?bookname=ProfessionalWebProgramming">Go to book buying page</A>
```

So when you click on the link, the name/value pair is passed along with the URL. The third and final method is via a form sent to the server with the GET method.

```
<FORM ACTION="book.asp" METHOD="GET">
Type your name: <INPUT TYPE="TEXT" NAME="buyer"><BR>
Type your requested book:  <INPUT TYPE="TEXT" NAME="bookname" SIZE=40><BR>
<INPUT TYPE=SUBMIT VALUE=Submit>
</FORM>
```

You input the information onto the text boxes on the form and the text is submitted when you click on Submit and two query strings are generated.

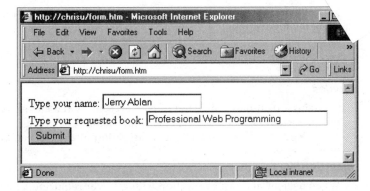

Next you need to be able to retrieve information, and you use this technique to retrieve from each of the three methods used to generate a query string.

```
Request.QueryString("buyer")
Request.QueryString("bookname")
```

> *Please note that these lines won't display anything by themselves, you need to add either the shorthand notation (equality operator) to display functions in front of a single statement, or when a number of values need displaying then use Response.Write to separately display each value in the collection.*
>
> *e.g.* `<%=Request.QueryString("buyer")%>` *or*
> `Response.Write(Request.QueryString("bookname") )`

The first of the two `Request` object calls should return the name of Jerry Ablan on the page and the second of the two should return Professional Web Programming. Of course you could always store this information in a variable for later access.

```
sBookName = Request.QueryString("bookname")
```

Form

Contains a collection of all the form variables posted to the HTTP request by an HTML form. Query strings aren't very private as they transmit information via a very visible method, the URL. If you want to transmit information from the form more privately then you can use the form collection to do so which sends its information as part of the HTTP Request body. The easy access to form variables is one of ASP's best features.

If we go back to our previous example, the only alteration we need to make to our HTML form code is to change the `METHOD` attribute. Forms using this collection must be sent with the `POST` method and not the `GET` method. It is actually this attribute that determines how the information is sent by the form. So if we change the method of the form as follows:

```
<FORM ACTION="book.asp" METHOD="POST">
Type your name: <INPUT TYPE="TEXT" NAME="buyer"><BR>
Type your requested book:  <INPUT TYPE="TEXT" NAME="bookname" SIZE=40><BR>
<INPUT TYPE=SUBMIT VALUE=Submit>
</FORM>
```

Once the form has been submitted in this style, then we can retrieve and display the information using the following:

```
=Request.Form("buyer")
```

Cookies

Contains a read-only collection of cookies sent by the client browser along with the request. Because the cookies were sent from the client, they cannot be changed here. You must change them using the `Response.Cookies` collection. A discussion of cookies can be found in the next topic.

ClientCertificate

When a client makes a connection with a server requiring a high degree of security, either party can confirm who the sender/receiver is by inspecting their digital certificate. A digital certificate contains a number of items of information about the sender, such as the holder's name, address and length of time the certificate is valid for. A third party, known as the Certificate Authority or CA, will have previously verified these details.

The `ClientCertificate` Collection is used access details held in a client side digital certificate sent by the browser. This collection is only populated if you are running a secure server, and the request was via an `https://` call instead of an `http://` call. This is the preferred method to invoke a secure connection.

ServerVariables

When the client sends a request and information is passed across to the server, it's not just the page that is passed across, but information such as who created the page, the server name, and the port that the request was sent to. The HTTP header that is sent across together with the HTTP request also contains information of this nature such as the type of browser, and type of connection. This information is combined into a list of variables that are predefined by the server as environment variables. Most of them are static and never really change unless you change the configuration of your web server. The rest are based on the client browser.

These server variables can be accessed in the normal method. For instance, the server variable `HTTP_USER_AGENT`, which returns information about the type of browser being used to view the page, can be displayed as follows:

```
<%=Request.ServerVariables("HTTP_USER_AGENT")%>
```

Alternatively you can print out the whole list of Server Variables and their values with the following code:

```
For Each key in Request.ServerVariables
    Response.Write "<B>" & (Key) &"</B> "
    Response.Write (Request.ServerVariables(key)) & "<BR>"
Next
```

This displays each of the `ServerVariables` collection in bold, and the contents of the key (if any) after it. The final product looks like this:

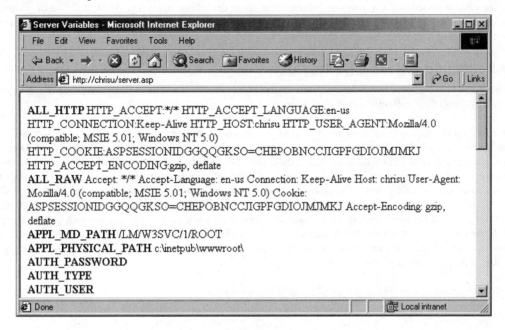

Server variables are merely informative, but they do give you the ability to customize page content for specific browsers, or to avoid script errors that might be generated.

Request Object Properties and Methods

The Request object contains a single property and a single method. They are used together to transfer files from the client to the server. Uploading is accomplished using HTML forms.

TotalBytes Property

When the request is processed, this property will hold the total number of bytes in the client browser request. Most likely you'd use it to return the number of bytes in the file you wish to transfer. This information is important to the `BinaryRead` method.

BinaryRead Method

This method retrieves the information sent to the web server by the client browser in a `POST` operation. When the browser issues a `POST`, the data is encoded and sent to the server. When the browser issues a `GET`, there is no data other than the URL. The `BinaryRead` method takes one parameter, the number of bytes to read. So if you want it to read a whole file, you pass it the total number of bytes in the file, generated by the `TotalBytes` property.

It's very rarely applied because `Request.QueryString` and `Request.Form` are much easier to use. That's because `BinaryRead` wraps its answer in a safe array of bytes. For a scripting language that essentially only handles variants, that makes life a little complicated. However this format is essential for file uploading. You can find full details on how to upload files and then decode a safe array of bytes in this excellent article at 15seconds.com
`http://www.15seconds.com/Issue/981121.htm`

287

The Response Object

After you've processed the request information from the client browser, you'll need to be able to send information back. The `Response` object is just the ticket. It provides you with the tools necessary to send anything you need back to the client.

The Response Object's Collections

The `Response` object contains only one collection: `Cookies`. This is the version of the `Request` object's `Cookies` collection that can be written to.

If you've not come across them before, cookies are small (limited to 4kb of data) text files stored on the hard drive of the client that contain information about the user, such as whether they have visited the site before and what date they last visited the site on. There are lots of misapprehensions about cookies being intrusive as they allow servers to store information on the user's drive. However you need to remember that firstly the user has to voluntarily accept cookies or activate an Accept Cookies mechanism on the browser for them to work, secondly this information is completely benign and cannot be used to determine the user's email address or such like. They are used to personalize pages that the user might have visited before. Examples of things to store in cookies are unique user ids, or user names; then, when the user returns to your web site, a quick check of his cookies will let you know if he is a return visitor or not.

You can create a cookie on the user's machine as follows:

```
Response.Cookies("BookBought") = "Professional Web Programming"
```

You can also store multiple values in one cookie using an index value key. The cookie effectively contains a VBScript `Dictionary` object and using the key can retrieve individual items. Its functioning is very close to that of an array.

```
Response.Cookies("BookBought")("1") = "Professional Web Programming"
Response.Cookies("BookBought")("2") = "Instant HTML"
```

A cookie will automatically expire (i.e. disappear from the user's machine) the moment a user ends their session. To extend the cookie beyond this natural lifetime, you can specify a date with the `Expires` property. The date takes the following format *WEEKDAY DD-MON-YY HH:MM:SS*

```
Response.Cookies("BookBought").Expires = #31-Dec-99#
```

The # sign can be used to delimit dates in VBScript or ASP.

Other properties that can be used in conjunction with this collection are:

- ➢ `Domain`: A Cookie is only sent to page requested within the domain from which it was created
- ➢ `Path`: A Cookie is only sent to pages requested within this path
- ➢ `HasKeys`: specifies whether the Cookie uses an index/Dictionary object or not
- ➢ `Secure`: specifies whether the cookie is secure. A cookie is only deemed secure if sent via the HTTPS protocol.

You can retrieve the cookies information using the Request object cookies collection, mentioned earlier. To do this you could do the following:

```
You purchased <%=Request.Cookies("BookBought")%> last time you visited the site.
```

If there were several cookies in the collection you could iterate through each cookie and display the contents as follows:

```
For Each cookie in Request.Cookies
    Response.Write (Request.Cookies(cookie))
Next
```

The Response Object's Methods

To understand what the Response Object's methods and properties do, we need to examine the workings of how ASP sends a response in more detail. When an ASP script is run, an **HTML output stream** is created. This stream is a receptacle for the web server to store details and create the dynamic/interactive web page in. As mentioned before, the page has to be created entirely in HTML for the browser to understand it (excluding client-side scripting, which is ignored by the server).

The stream is initially empty when created. New information is added to the end. If any custom HTML headers are required then they have to be added at the beginning. Then the HTML contained in the ASP page is added next to the script, so anything not encompassed by <% %> tags is added. The Response object provides two ways of writing directly to the output stream, either using the Write method or it's shorthand technique.

Write

Probably the most used method of all the built-in objects, Write allows you to send information back to the client browser. You can write text directly to a web page by encasing the text in quotation marks:

```
Response.Write "Hello World!"
```

Or to display the contents of a variant you just drop the quotation marks:

```
sText = "Hello World!"
Response.Write sText
```

For single portions of dynamic information that only require adding into large portions of HTML, you can use the equality sign as a shorthand for this method, as specified earlier, e.g.

```
My message is <% =sText %>
```

This technique reduces the amount of code needed, but at the expense of readability. There is nothing to choose between the techniques in terms of performance.

AddHeader

This method allows you to add custom headers to the HTTP response. For example, if you were to write a custom browser application that examined the headers of your HTTP requests for a certain value, you'd use this method to set that value. Usage is as follows:

```
Response.AddHeader "CustomServerApp", "BogiePicker/1.0"
```

This would add the header `CustomServerApp` to the response with the value of `BogiePicker/1.0`. There are no restrictions regarding headers and header value.

AppendToLog

Calling this method allows you to append a string to the web server log file entry for this particular request. This allows you to add custom log messages to the log file.

BinaryWrite

This method allows you to bypass the normal character conversion that takes place when data is sent back to the client. Usually, only text is returned, so the web server cleans it up. By calling `BinaryWrite` to send your data, the actual binary data is sent back, bypassing that cleaning process.

Clear

This method allows you to delete any data that has been buffered for this page so far. See discussion of the `Buffer` property for more details.

End

This method stops processing the ASP file and returns any currently buffered data to the client browser.

Flush

This method returns any currently buffered data to the client browser and then clears the buffer. See discussion of the Buffer Property for more details.

Redirect

This method allows you to relinquish control of the current page to another web page entirely. For example, you can use this method to redirect users to a login page if they have not yet logged on to your web site:

```
<%
If (Not Session("LoggedOn") ) Then
    Response.Redirect "login.asp"
End If
%>
```

The Response Object's Properties

Buffer

You may optionally have ASP buffer your output for you. This property tells ASP whether or not to buffer output. Usually, output is sent to the client as it is generated. If you turn buffering on (by setting this property to `True`), output will not be sent until all scripts have been executed for the current page, or the `Flush` or `End` methods are called.

`Response.Buffer` has to be inserted after the language declaration, but before any HTML is used. If you insert it outside this scope you will most likely generate an error. A correct use of this method would look like:

```
<@ LANGUAGE = "VBSCRIPT">
<% Response.Buffer = True %>
<HTML>
...
```

The `Flush` method is used in conjunction with the `Buffer` property. To use it correctly you must set the `Buffer` property first and then at places within the script you can flush the buffer to the output stream, while continuing processing. This is useful for long queries, which might otherwise worry the user that nothing was being returned.

The `Clear` method erases everything in the buffer that has been added since the last `Response.Flush` call. It erases only the response body however and leaves intact the response header.

CacheControl

Generally when a proxy server retrieves an ASP web page, it does not place a copy of it into its cache. That is because by its very nature, an ASP page is dynamic and most likely will be stale the next time it is requested. You may override this feature by changing the value of this property to `Public`.

Charset

This property will append its contents to the HTTP content-type header that is sent back to the browser. Every HTTP response has a content-type header that defines the content of the response. Usually the content-type is "text/html". Setting this property will modify the type sent back to the browser.

ContentType

This property allows you to set the value of the content-type that is sent back to the client browser.

Expires

Most web browsers keep web pages in a local cache. The cache is usually as good as long as you keep your browser running. Setting this property allows you to limit the time the page stays in the local cache. The value of the `Expires` property specifies the length of time in minutes before the page will expire from the local cache. If you set this to zero, the page will not be cached.

ExpiresAbsolute

Just like the `Expires` property, this property allows you to specify the exact time and date on which the page will expire.

IsClientConnected

This read-only property indicates whether or not the client is still connected to the server. Remember that the client browser makes a request then waits for a response? Well, imagine you're running a lengthy script and during the middle of processing, the client disconnects because he was waiting too long. Reading this property will tell you if the client is still connected or not.

Status

This property allows you to set the value returned on the status header with the HTTP response.

The Application and Session Objects

The `Application` and `Session` objects like `Request` and `Response` work very closely together. `Application` is used to tie all of the pages together into one consistent application, while the `Session` object is used to track and present a user's series of requests to the web site as a continuous action, rather than an arbitrary set of requests.

Scope Springs Eternal

Normally, you will declare a variable for use within your web page. You'll use it, manipulate it, then perhaps print out its value, or whatever. But when your page is reloaded, or the viewer moves to another page, the variable, with its value, is gone forever. By placing your variable within the Contents collection of the `Application` or `Session` objects, you can extend the life span of your variable!

Any variable or object that you declare has two potential scopes: procedure and page. When you declare a variable within a procedure, its life span is limited to that procedure. Once the procedure has executed, your variable is gone. You may also declare a variable at the web page level but like the procedure-defined variable, once the page is reloaded, the value is reset.

Enter the `Application` and `Session` objects. The Contents collections of these two objects allow you to extend the scope of your variables to session-wide, and application-wide. If you place a value in the Session object, it will be available to all web pages in your site for the life span of the current session (more on sessions later). Good session scope variables are user ids, user names, login time, etc, things that pertain only to the session. Likewise, if you place your value into the `Application` object, it will exist until the web site is restarted. This allows you to place application-wide settings into a conveniently accessible place. Good application scope variables are font names and sizes, table colors, system constants, etc, things that pertain to the application as a whole.

The global.asa File

Every ASP application may utilize a special script file. This file is named `global.asa` and it must reside in the root directory of your web application. It can contain script code that pertains to the application as a whole, or each session. You may also create ActiveX objects for later use in this scripting file.

The Application Object

ASP works on the concept that an entire web site is a single web application. Therefore, there is only one instance of the Application object available for your use in your scripting at all times. Please note that it is possible to divide up your web site into separate application, but for the purposes of this discussion we'll assume there is only one application per web site.

Collections

The Application object contains two collections: `Contents` and `StaticObjects`. The `Contents` collection we discussed a few pages earlier. The `StaticObjects` collection is similar to `Contents`, but only contains the objects that were created with the `<OBJECT>` tag in the scope of your application. This collection can be iterated just like the Contents collection.

> *You cannot store references to ASP's built-in objects in* `Application`*'s collections.*

Methods

The `Application` object contains two methods as detailed below.

`Lock`	The `Lock` method is used to "lock-down" the `Contents` collection so that it cannot be modified by other clients. This is useful if you are updating a counter, or perhaps grabbing a transaction number stored in the `Application`'s `Contents` collection.
`Unlock`	The `Unlock` method "unlocks" the `Application` object thus allowing others to modify the Contents collection.

Events

The `Application` object generates two events: `Application_OnStart` and `Application_OnEnd`. The `Application_OnStart` event is fired when the first view of your web page occurs. The `Application_OnEnd` event is fired when the web server is shut down. If you choose to write scripts for these events they must be placed in your `global.asa` file.

The most common use of these events is to initialize application-wide variables. Items such as font names, table colors, database connection strings, perhaps even writing information to a system log file. The following is an example `global.asa` file with script for these events:

```
<SCRIPT LANGUAGE=VBScript RUNAT=Server>
Sub Application_OnStart
    'Globals...
    Application("ErrorPage") = "handleError.asp"
    Application("SiteBanAttemptLimit") = 10
    Application("AccessErrorPage") = "handleError.asp"
    Application("RestrictAccess") = False
```

```
        'Keep track of visitors…
        Application("NumVisits") = Application("NumVisits") + 1
    End Sub
    </SCRIPT>
```

The Session Object

Each time a visitor comes to your web site, a `Session` object is created for him if he does not already have one. Therefore there is an instance of the `Session` object available to you in your scripting as well. The `Session` object is similar to the `Application` object in that it can contain values. However, the `Session` object's values are lost when your visitor leaves the site. The Session object is most useful for transferring information from web page to web page. Using the Session object, there is no need to pass information in the URL.

The most common use of the `Session` object is to store information in its `Contents` collection. This information would be session-specific in that it would pertain only to the current user.

Many web sites today offer a "user personalization" service. That is to customize a web page to their preference. This is easily done with ASP and the `Session` object. The user variables are stored in the client browser for retrieval by the server later. Simply load the user's preferences at the start of the session and then, as he browses your site, utilize the information regarding his preferences to display information.

Suppose your web site displays stock quotes for users. You could allow a user to customize the start page to display his favorite stock quotes when he visits the site. By storing the stock symbols in your Session object, you can easily display the correct quotes when you render your web page.

This session management system relies on the use of browser cookies. The cookies allow the user information to be persisted even after a client leaves the site. Unfortunately, if a visitor to your web site does not allow cookies to be stored, you will be unable to pass information between web pages within the Session object.

Collections

The Session object contains two collections: `Contents` and `StaticObjects`. The `Contents` collection we discussed above. The `StaticObjects` collection is similar to `Contents`, but only contains the objects that were created with the `<OBJECT>` tag in your HTML page. This collection can be iterated just like the `Contents` collection.

Properties

Below are the properties that the `Session` object exposes for your use:

Property	Description
CodePage	Setting this property will allow you to change the character set used by ASP when it is creating output. This property could be used if you were creating a multinational web site.
LCID	This property sets the internal locale value for the entire web application. By default, your application's locale is your server's locale. If your server is in the U.S., then your application will default to the U.S. Much of the formatting functionality of ASP utilizes this locale setting to display information correctly for the country in question. For example, the date is displayed differently in Europe versus the U.S. So based on the locale setting, the date formatting functions will output the date in the correct format.
	You can also change this property temporarily to output data in a different format. A good example is currency. Let's say your web site had a shopping cart and you wanted to display totals in U.S. dollars for U.S. customers, and Pounds Sterling for U.K. customers. To do this you'd change the LCID property to the British locale setting, and then call the currency formatting routine.
SessionID	Every session created by ASP has a unique identifier. This identifier is called the `SessionID` and is accessible through this property. It can be used for debugging ASP scripts.
Timeout	By default, an ASP session will timeout after 20 minutes of inactivity. Every time a web page is requested or refreshed by a user, his internal ASP time clock starts ticking. When the time clock reaches the value set in this property, his session is automatically destroyed. You can set this property to reduce the timeout period if you wish.

Methods

The Session object contains a single method, Abandon. This instructs ASP to destroy the current Session object for this user. This method is what you would call when a user logs off your web site.

Events

The Session object generates two events: Session_OnStart and Session_OnEnd. The Session_OnStart event is fired when the first view of your web page occurs. The Session_OnEnd event is fired when the web server is shut down. If you choose to write scripts for these events they must be placed in your global.asa file.

The most common use of these events is to initialize session-wide variables. Items like usage counts, login names, real names, user preferences, etc. The following is an example global.asa file with script for these events:

```
<SCRIPT LANGUAGE=VBScript RUNAT=Server>
Sub Session_OnStart
      Session("LoginAttempts") = 0
      Session("LoggedOn") = False
End Sub

Sub Session_OnEnd
      Session("LoggedOn") = False
End Sub
</SCRIPT>
```

The Server Object

The next object in the ASP object model is the Server object. The Server object enables you to create and work with ActiveX controls in your web pages. In addition, the Server object exposes methods that help in the encoding of URLs and HTML text.

Properties

ScriptTimeout

This property sets the time in seconds that a script will be allowed to run. The default value for all scripts on the system is 90 seconds. That is to say that if a script has run for longer than 90 seconds, the web server will intervene and let the client browser know something is wrong. If you expect your scripts to run for a long time, you will want to use this property.

Methods

CreateObject

This method is the equivalent to Visual Basic's CreateObject, or using the New keyword - it instantiates a new instance of an object. The result can be placed into the Application or Session Contents collection to lengthen its life span.

Generally you'll create an object at the time the session is created and place it into the Session Contents collection. For example, let's say you've created a killer ActiveX DLL with a really cool class that converts Fahrenheit to Celsius and vice versa. You could create an instance of this class with the `CreateObject` method and store it in the Session Contents collection like this:

```
Set Session("MyConverter") = Server.CreateObject("KillerDLL.CDegreeConverter")
```

This object would be around as long as the session is and will be available for you to call. As you'll see in later chapters, this method is invaluable when working with database connections.

ASP comes with its own built in set of components that you can create instances of using the `CreateObject` method. These are:

> **Ad Rotator** – used to display a random graphic and link every time a user connects to the page.

> **Browser Capabilities** – manipulates a file browscap.ini contained on the server computer to determine the capabilities of a particular client's browser.

> **Content Linker** – provides a central repository file from where you manage a series of links and their URLs, and provide appropriate descriptions about them.

> **Content Rotator** – a cut down version of the Ad Rotator that provides the same function but without optional redirection.

> **Page Counter** – Counts the number of times a page has been hit.

> **Permission Checker** – checks to see if a user has permissions before allowing them to access a given page.

> **Counters** – counts any value on an ASP page from anywhere within an ASP application

> **MyInfo** – can be used to store personal information about a user within an XML file.

> **Status** – used to collect server profile information.

> **Tools** – a set of miscellaneous methods that are grouped under the generic heading of Tools

> **IIS Log** - allows you to create an object that allows your applications to write to and otherwise access the IIS log.

Execute

This method executes an ASP file and inserts the results into the response. You can use this call to include snippets of ASP code, like subroutines.

GetLastError

This method returns an `ASPError` object that contains all of the information about the last error that has occurred.

HTMLEncode

This method encodes a string for proper HTML usage. This is useful if you want to actually display HTML code on your web pages.

MapPath

This method returns a string that contains the actual physical path to the file in question. Subdirectories of your web site can be virtual. That is to say that they don't physically exist in the hierarchy of your web site. To find out the true whereabouts of a file, you can call this method.

Transfer

The `Transfer` method allows you to immediately transfer control of the executing page to another page. This is similar to the `Response.Redirect` method except for the fact that the `Transfer` method makes all variables and the Request collections available to the called page.

URLEncode

This method, as the title says, encodes a URL for transmission. This encoding includes replacing spaces with a plus sign (+) and replacing unprintable characters with hexadecimal values. You should always run your URLs through this method when redirecting.

The ObjectContext Object

The final object we shall consider is the `ObjectContext` object, which comes into play when you use transactions in your web page. When an ASP script has initiated a transaction, it can either be committed or aborted by this object. It has two methods to do this with.

SetAbort

`SetAbort` is called when the transaction has not been completed and you don't want resources updated.

SetComplete

`SetComplete` is called when there is no reason for the transaction to fail. If all of the components that form part of the transaction call `SetComplete`, then the transaction will complete.

Using Active Server Pages Effectively

Is it true that a little bit of knowledge is a bad thing? In the realm of ASP, I think not. A little bit of knowledge is probably just piquing your interest. For the final part of this chapter we're going to build a web site to demonstrate some of the features of ASP. This sample site will demonstrate many of the ASP features and principles described earlier in this chapter.

Designing the Site

Before we start creating our new web site, we should discuss the design. For your first ASP application, we'll keep it quite simple. What we want to create is an HTML form that accepts for input the following information: first name, last name, and email address. After the user submits the form, our ASP page will reformat the first and last name, and check the email address for proper syntax.

The user will be given three attempts to enter the information correctly or else a warning message will display at the bottom of the screen. The following illustrates what the screen should look like.

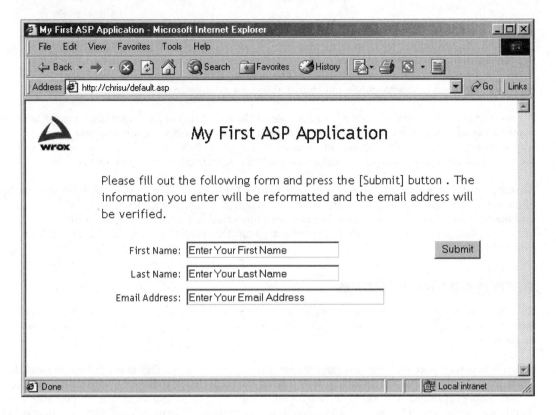

Creating the global.asa file

The first step in creating a new ASP application is to create your global.asa file. This is the file that houses your event handlers for the Application and Session objects. In addition, in this file you may set application, and session-wide variables to their default values. To create this file, in the root of your web server directory create a file called global.asa with the text editor of your choice.

Here is the content of our sample global.asa:

```
<SCRIPT LANGUAGE=VBScript RUNAT=Server>
Sub Application_OnStart
    Application("AllowedErrorsBeforeWarning") = 3
End Sub

Sub Session_OnStart
    Session("ErrorCount") = 0
End Sub

Sub Session_OnEnd
    'Nothing to do here...
End Sub
```

```
Sub Application_OnEnd
    'Nothing to do here...
End Sub
</SCRIPT>
```

Our file has handlers defined for `Application_OnStart`, `Application_OnEnd`, `Session_OnStart`, and `Session_OnEnd`. The `Application_OnEnd` and `Session_OnEnd` events are not used in this example, but shown above for completeness.

We want to set a limit on the number of submissions the user gets before a warning message is shown. Since this is a feature of the application and affects all users, we will store this constant in the Application's `Contents` collection. This is done in the `Application_OnStart` event. We add to the collection an item named `AllowedErrorsBeforeWarning` and set its value to 3.

Now that we know how many times a user can *try* to get it right, we need a place to store the number of times the user has *tried* to get it right. Since this counter is different for each user, we'll place this into the Session's Contents collection. We initialize our variable to 0. This is done in the `Session_OnStart` event. We add to the collection an item named, appropriately, `ErrorCount`, with a value of 0.

Creating our Main Page

Now that we've got the groundwork lain for our ASP application, it's time to build the main page. Since this is a simple example, we will only utilize a single web page. Let's begin by creating this single page.

Create a new web page on your site and rename it to `default.asp`. This is the file name used by IIS as the default web page. The default web page is the page that is returned by a web server when no web page is specified. For example, when you call up `http://www.wrox.com/`, you aren't specifying a web page. The server looks through its list of default file names and finds the first match in the web site's root directory.

The following shows the contents of your `default.asp` page.

```
<%@ Language=VBScript %>
<%
Dim txtFirstName, txtLastName, txtEmailAddr
Dim sMessage

'*****************************************************************
'* Main
'*
'* The main subroutine for this page...
'*****************************************************************

Sub Main()
    'Was this page submitted?
    if ( Request("cmdSubmit") = "Submit" ) Then
        'Reformat the data into a more readable format...
        txtFirstName = InitCap(Request("txtFirstName"))
        txtLastName = InitCap(Request("txtLastName"))
```

```
      txtEmailAddr = LCase(Request("txtEmailAddr"))

      'Check the email address for the correct components...
      If (Instr(1, txtEmailAddr, "@") = 0 or Instr(1, txtEmailAddr, ".") = 0 ) & _
      Then
        sMessage = "The email address you entered does not appear to be valid."
      Else
        'Make sure there is something after the period..
        If (Instr(1, txtEmailAddr, ".") = Len(txtEmailAddr) _
         or Instr(1, txtEmailAddr, "@") = 1 or _
         (Instr(1, txtEmailAddr, ".") = Instr(1, txtEmailAddr, "@") + 1) ) Then
          sMessage = "You must enter a complete email address."
        End If
      End If

      'We passed our validation, show that all is good...
      If (sMessage = "" ) Then
        sMessage = "Thank you for your input. All data has passed verification."
      Else
        Session("ErrorCount") = Session("ErrorCount") + 1

        If (Session("ErrorCount") > & _
           Application("AllowedErrorsBeforeWarning") ) Then
          sMessage = sMessage & "<P><Font Size=1>You have exceeded the normal
                     number of times it takes to get this right!</Font>"
        End If
      End If
    Else
      'First time in here? Set some default values...
      txtFirstName = "Enter Your First Name"
      txtLastName = "Enter Your Last Name"
      txtEmailAddr = "Enter Your Email Address"
    End If
End Sub

'*********************************************************************
'* InitCap
'*
'* Capitalizes the first letter of the string
'*********************************************************************

Function InitCap(sStr)
    InitCap = UCase(Left(sStr, 1)) & LCase(Right(sStr, Len(sStr) - 1))
End Function

'*********************************************************************
'* Call our main subroutine
'*********************************************************************

Call Main()
%>

<HTML>
<HEAD>
   <META NAME="GENERATOR" Content="Microsoft FrontPage 3.0">
   <TITLE>My First ASP Application</TITLE>
</HEAD>
```

301

```
<BODY>

<TABLE border="0" cellPadding="0" cellSpacing="0" width="600">
<TBODY>
   <TR>
      <TD width="100"><A href="http://www.wrox.com" target="_blank" border=0>
      <IMG border=0 title="Check out the Wrox Press Web Site!"
          src="images/wroxlogo.gif" WIDTH="56" HEIGHT="56"></a></td>
      <TD width="500"><CENTER><FONT size="5" face="Trebuchet MS">
         My First ASP Application</FONT></CENTER></TD>
   </TR>

   <TR>
      <TD width="100"> </TD>
      <TD width="500" align="left"><FONT face="Trebuchet MS"><BR>
      Please fill out the following form and press the [Submit] button. The
      information you enter will be reformatted and the email address will be
      verified.</FONT>
   <FORM action="default.asp" id="FORM1" method="post" name="frmMain">
      <TABLE border="0" cellPadding="1" cellSpacing="5" width="100%">
      <TR>
         <TD width="100" nowrap align="right">
         <FONT size="2" face="Trebuchet MS">First Name:</FONT></TD>
         <TD width="350"><FONT size="2" face="Trebuchet MS">
           <INPUT title="Enter your first name here" name="txtFirstName" size="30"
               value="<%=txtFirstName%>" tabindex="1"></FONT></TD>
           <TD width="50"><DIV align="right"><FONT size="2" face="Trebuchet MS">
              <INPUT type="submit" title="Submit this data for processing..."
                 value="Submit" name="cmdSubmit" tabindex="4"></FONT></TD>
      </TR>

      <TR>
         <TD width="100" nowrap align="right">
           <FONT size="2" face="Trebuchet MS">Last Name:</FONT></TD>
         <TD width="400" colspan="2">
           <FONT size="2" face="Trebuchet MS">
           <INPUT title="Enter your last name here" name="txtLastName" size="30"
               value="<%=txtLastName%>" tabindex="2"></FONT></TD>
      </TR>

      <TR>
         <TD width="100" nowrap align="right">
         <FONT size="2" face="Trebuchet MS">Email Address:</FONT></TD>
         <TD width="400" colspan="2"><FONT size="2" face="Trebuchet MS">
         <INPUT title="Enter your valid email address here" name="txtEmailAddr"
             size="40" value="<%=txtEmailAddr%>" tabindex="3"></FONT></TD>
      </TR>
      <TR>
         <TD nowrap width=500 colspan="3" align="center">
         <FONT face="Trebuchet MS"><BR>
         <STRONG><%=sMessage%></STRONG> </FONT></TD>
      </TR>
      </TABLE>
   </FORM>
   <P> </TD>
   </TR>
</TBODY>
</TABLE>
</BODY>
</HTML>
```

As you can see, the page is quite long. But it breaks logically into two distinct sections: the ASP/VBScript portion, and the HTML portion. Let's examine each section individually.

The ASP/VBScript Section

The top half of our file is where the ASP code lives. This is the code that is executed by the server before the page is returned to the browser that requested it. Any code, as you've seen, that is to be executed on the server before returning is enclosed in the special `<%` and `%>` tags.

For clarity (and sanity!), the ASP code has been divided into subroutines. This not only makes the code more readable, but also will aid in its reuse. Our code has two routines: Main, and InitCap.

Before we do anything however, we declare some variables:

```
Dim txtFirstName, txtLastName, txtEmailAddr
Dim sMessage
```

When variables are declared outside of a subroutine in an ASP page, the variables retain their data until the page is completely processed. This allows you to pass information from your ASP code to your HTML code as you'll see.

After our variables have been declared, we have our `Main` routine. This is what is called by our ASP code every time a browser retrieves the page. Please note that unlike Visual Basic, the Main subroutine is not called automatically. We must explicitly call it ourselves.

```
'********************************************************************
'* Main
'*
'* The main subroutine for this page...
'********************************************************************

Sub Main()
  '  Was this page submitted?
  if ( Request("cmdSubmit") = "Submit" ) Then
    '  Reformat the data into a more readable format...
    txtFirstName = InitCap(Request("txtFirstName"))
    txtLastName = InitCap(Request("txtLastName"))
    txtEmailAddr = LCase(Request("txtEmailAddr"))

    '  Check the email address for the correct components...
    if ( Instr(1, txtEmailAddr, "@") = 0 or Instr(1, txtEmailAddr, ".") = 0 ) Then
      sMessage = "The email address you entered does not appear to be valid."
    Else
      '  Make sure there is something after the period..
      if ( Instr(1, txtEmailAddr, ".") = Len(txtEmailAddr) & _
          or Instr(1, txtEmailAddr, "@") = 1 or & _
          (Instr(1, txtEmailAddr, ".") = Instr(1, txtEmailAddr, "@") + 1) ) Then
        sMessage = "You must enter a complete email address."
      end if
    End If

    'We passed our validation, show that all is good...
    if ( sMessage = "" ) Then
```

```
            sMessage = "Thank you for your input. All data has passed verification."
         Else
            Session("ErrorCount") = Session("ErrorCount") + 1

            If ( Session("ErrorCount") > Application("AllowedErrorsBeforeWarning") ) _
            Then
               sMessage = sMessage & "<P><Font Size=1>You have exceeded the normal" & _
                          " number of times it takes to get this right!</Font>"
               End If
            End If
         Else
            ' First time in here? Set some default values...
            txtFirstName = "Enter Your First Name"
            txtLastName = "Enter Your Last Name"
            txtEmailAddr = "Enter Your Email Address"
         End If
      End Sub
```

First we see if the form was actually submitted by the user, otherwise we initialize our variables. To determine if the page has been submitted, we check the value of the cmdSubmit Request variable. This is the button on our form. When pressed, the form calls this page and sets the value of the cmdSubmit button to "Submit". If a user just loads the page without pressing the button, the value of cmdSubmit is blank (""). There are other ways to determine if a web page was submitted, but this method is the simplest.

After we have determined that the page was in fact submitted, run the names through the second function on this page: InitCap. InitCap is a quick little function that will format a word to proper case. That is to say that the first letter will be capitalized, and the rest of the word will be lowercased. Here is the function:

```
'**********************************************************************
'* InitCap
'*
'* Capitalizes the first letter of the string
'**********************************************************************

Function InitCap(sStr)
    InitCap = UCase(Left(sStr, 1)) & LCase(Right(sStr, Len(sStr) - 1))
End Function
```

Now that we've cleaned up the names, we need to check the email address for validity. To do this we ensure that it contains an "@" sign and a period (.). Once past this check, we make sure that there is data after the period and that there is data before the "@" sign. This is 'quick and dirty' email validity checking.

If either of these checks fail, we place a failure message into the string sMessage. This will be displayed in our HTML section after the page processing is complete.

Now, if our email address has passed the test, we set the message (sMessage) to display a thank you note. If we failed our test, we increment our error counter that we set up in the global.asa file. Here we also check to see if we have exceeded our limit on errors. If we have, a sterner message is set for display.

Finally, the last thing in our ASP section is our call to Main. This is what is called when the page is loaded:

```
'*****************************************************************
'* Call our main subroutine
'*****************************************************************

Call Main()
```

The HTML Section

This section is a regular HTML form with a smattering of ASP thrown in for good measure. The ASP that we've embedded in the HTML sets default values for the input fields, and displays any messages that our server side code has generated.

The most important part of the HTML is where the ASP code is embedded. The following snippet illustrates this:

```
<input title="Enter your first name here" name="txtFirstName" size="30"
 value="<%=txtFirstName%>" tabindex="1">
```

Here we see a normal text input box. However, to set the value of the text box we use the `Response.Write` shortcut (`<%=`) to insert the value of the variable `txtFirstName`. Remember that we dimensioned this outside of our ASP functions so that it would have page scope. Now we utilize its value by inserting it into our HTML.

We do exactly the same thing with the Last Name and Email Address text boxes:

```
<input title="Enter your last name here" name="txtLastName" size="30"
 value="<%=txtLastName%>" tabindex="2">
<input title="Enter your valid email address here" name="txtEmailAddr"
 size="40" value="<%=txtEmailAddr%>" tabindex="3">
</tr>
```

The last trick in the HTML section is the display of our failure or success message. This message is stored in the variable called `sMessage`. At the bottom of the form, we display the contents of this variable like so:

```
<td nowrap width=500 colspan="3" align="center">
  <font face="Trebuchet MS">
  <br>
  <strong>
  <%=sMessage%>
  </strong>
  </font>
</td>
```

The beauty of this code is that if `sMessage` is blank then nothing is shown, otherwise the message is displayed.

Summary

You should have learned much in this chapter. We first learned how HTTP is the transaction system that sends web pages to requesting clients. It is a very important piece of the puzzle. We then discussed Active Server Pages, or ASP. You learned how ASP pages are created, and what special HTML tags you need to include in your files to use ASP. We looked through the ASP object model and saw that the `Request` and `Response` objects are used to manage details of the HTTP request and responses. We saw that the `Application` object is used to group pages together into one application and we saw that the Session is used to create the illusion that the interaction between user and site is one continuous action. Finally we created a small application that demonstrates two uses for ASP: form validation and data manipulation.

To aid you when creating your Active Server Pages in the future, we have included many appendices at the end of this book to use for reference. One in particular is on ASP commands, and another is on HTML tags. Good Luck!

Building Server Components in Visual Basic

By now you have learned how Active Server Pages (ASP) use components. In the next two chapters we will focus our attention on creating our own ActiveX DLL components. This chapter focuses on creating server side ActiveX DLLs that can be called by your Active Server Pages. To duplicate the examples listed in this chapter you will need Visual Basic version 5 or 6, FrontPage or Visual InterDev and SQL Server version 5,6 or 7. You will also need an understanding of ASP and a familiarity of creating stored procedures.

Server components can be in many forms (DLL, EXE and OCX):

> **ActiveX DLL** – an in-process component that can be shared simultaneously by multiple programs. This type of component runs in the same address space of the calling program.

> **ActiveX OCX** (also known as an ActiveX Control – a control component that usually includes a single control or a collection of controls that perform specialized functions. This type of component can be used in application programs as well as Web pages.

> **ActiveX EXE** – an out-of-process server component that can perform its own processes as well as expose objects for use with other programs. This type of component usually runs as a DCOM server component, which communicates with other programs across the network on other machines.

We will focus our attention on creating our own server components as ActiveX DLLs. Incorporating the use of server side ActiveX DLLs in your web page can solve a number of business problems and make your ASP more functional and dynamic.

In this chapter we will cover:

- An introduction to building ActiveX components
- Using the ASP `ScriptingContext` object in our components
- Web page Provider and Consumer components

Introduction to Building ActiveX DLL Components

Visual Basic 5.0 really introduced us to the rapid development of ActiveX DLLs. This has been carried forward and expanded in Visual Basic 6.0. We can now create ActiveX DLLs that can be accessed by a number of other programming and scripting languages, specifically by the VB Scripting language in Active Server Pages. The ActiveX DLLs that we will be creating can be run on Windows 95, Windows 98, and Windows NT Workstation and Server without any modifications.

Component Types

ActiveX DLLs can be broken down into many categories such as Web page components, business components and data access components. We will focus on Web page server components in this chapter, which can be broken down even further into two more categories, which we will call Web page consumers and Web page providers.

A **Web page consumer** component will read and process data from the Web page. This can significantly increase the performance of your Web page when there is a large amount of data to be read and processed. An ActiveX DLL can process information and execute stored procedures on your database, processing the data from your ASP faster than your ASP can. An ASP uses the VB scripting language and the page is interpreted not compiled. For this reason it makes sense to use an ActiveX DLL to process information from Web pages that contain large amounts of data that need to be processed and stored in a database. It also helps to separate the business and presentation layers of your application.

On the other hand a **Web page provider** component provides data to your ASP. This can be as simple as creating custom data elements to pass back to your Web page, or creating the actual content of the Web page from the ActiveX DLL by implementing the `ScriptingContext` object.

Sometimes the functionality of these two types of components are combined into one component that we will call a Web server component.

You might wonder why we would want to build a Web page using an ActiveX DLL. Suppose you have information to display to the user that requires several stored procedures to be run and you need to combine this information using selective criteria. You then want to present this information to the user in a table with a field that allows them to selectively update rows in the table, and this table has several hundred rows of data. This is where the power of an ActiveX DLL can come to the rescue. We can gather this information and build the Web page table in less than half the time it would take the ASP to do it.

Before we dive into the specifics of creating our Web page provider component let's briefly touch on the business component. The business component can provide server side processing of data or encapsulate the business rules for you application. Let's assume your application is an online warehouse that sells books to retailers. One of your options might be to provide a detailed inventory to the retailer. You could display this information on a Web page but the retailer might want to download this information so they could load it into their system. You can write a business component to provide XML data for the retailer. We will cover more on business server components in the next chapter.

ASP Objects

ASP exposes two object models to Visual Basic for our use, the `ObjectContext` and `ScriptingContext` objects. The `ObjectContext` object is mainly used with transactional ASP that interacts with Microsoft Transaction Server (MTS) which is covered in depth in Chapter 11. The `ScriptingContext` object exposes the entire ASP functionality contained in the five intrinsic ASP objects to our Web page server components. Refer to the relevant appendix for further information on the ASP object model.

ObjectContext

The `ObjectContext` object is used to commit and abort transactions in MTS that were initiated from an ASP. MTS can handle transactions from our ASP and update multiple databases at the same time. This eliminates a lot of worry about coordinating all of this processing from our ASP. The `ObjectContext` object exposes two methods for handling these transactions, `SetComplete()` and `SetAbort()`. Calling `SetAbort()` will abort the transaction and MTS will roll everything back so no updates are applied. Calling `SetComplete()` will complete the transaction and all updates are applied. Chapter 11 will cover MTS in detail and will discuss all of the intricacies of transaction termination. The following code fragment shows how a transaction is initiated in an ASP and how it is either aborted or committed.

```
<%
  'Start the transaction
  @Transaction = Required

  'Create the Server Component
  Set objUpdate = Server.CreateObject("Authors.Books")
  'Call the component
  lngRC = objUpdate.Titles

  If lngRc <> 0 Then
    'Abort the Transaction
    ObjectContext.SetAbort
  Else
    'Complete the Transaction
    ObjectContext.SetComplete
  End If

    'De-reference the component
    Set objUpdate = Nothing
%>
```

ScriptingContext

The ScriptingContext object exposes many individual ASP objects for use in Visual Basic. You are probably familiar with these objects by now so we'll just briefly cover them before we move on. To get a better look at these objects and their methods, you can set a reference to the Microsoft Active Server Pages Object Library in the **References** dialog in Visual Basic. Once this is done, you can open the object browser to take a closer look at these objects.

Application Object

The application object is a persistent collection of all users of an application and provides two main methods, Lock() and UnLock(), as well as several properties. Since application variables are shared among all users of the application, it would be very easy and very likely that an application variable could become corrupt due to two or more users trying to update the same application variable at the same time. This is where these methods come into play. Before a Web page updates an application variable, it should lock updates to the application, update the variable, and then unlock the application. This next code fragment demonstrates how to use the Lock() and UnLock() methods.

```
<%
    Application.Lock
    Application("ConnectString") = "dsn=Pubs Connection; uid=sa; pwd=;"
    Application.UnLock
%>
```

Request Object

The Request object provides information from a client request and is one of the most used objects in ASP. We can request information from a Form submission, QueryString submission, Cookies, ClientCertificates and ServerVariables.

Response Object

The Response object provides a means of sending information back to the client. With it we can write data to the Web page, send cookies to the client, redirect the browser, buffer a page and set various properties of an ASP.

Server Object

The Server object provides server side processing functions to our ASPs and is at the core of what we do with ASPs. It helps control how our pages operate and function and helps us handle encoding HTML and URL information. The MapPath() method provides a means of mapping virtual paths in our Web pages to physical paths on the server. One of the most important functions the Server object provides is the ability to create and load server side components.

```
<%
    'Create the Web Provider Component
    Set objDisplay = Server.CreateObject("Authors.Display")

    'Call the Component
    objDisplay.AllAuthors
%>
```

Session Object

The `Session` object provides information for a single user across all Web pages for a single session. You can set `Session` variables to store information for a user that needs to be carried through the entire Web application. `Session` variables are usually set in the `Session_OnStart` procedure in the `Global.asa` file. These variables are available for use on any Web page for that `Session`. The `Abandon()` method can be used to destroy all `Session` objects that have been set. This will automatically happen when a session times out but can also be forced using this method.

Designing for IIS 3 versus IIS 4/5

While you probably know what version of Internet Information Server you are using when writing your application, there might come a time when you want to write a Web application that can be marketed. In this case you probably would not know what version of IIS the purchaser would be running and you don't want to limit them to a specific version.

You can use the Browser Capabilities component to determine what type of browser the user is using and likewise you can perform the same type of test to determine which version of IIS your Web application is running on. The `Request` object provides a collection called `ServerVariables`. This collection can provide you with not only the name of the server on which the script page is running but also the name and version of the software that answers that request.

An example of this request running on a Windows NT workstation running Personal Web Server would look like this.

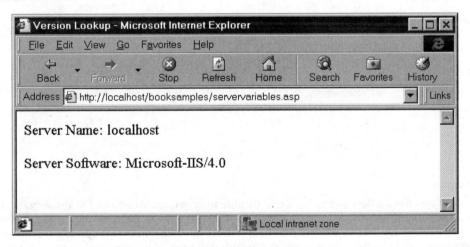

Now let's take a look at the two lines of code that produced this.

```
Response.Write "Server Name: " & Request.ServerVariables("SERVER_NAME") & "<P>"
Response.Write "Server Software: " & Request.ServerVariables("SERVER_SOFTWARE")
Response.Write "<P>"
```

As you can see, the server software version is displayed as software/version. You can use this information to code for multiple versions and take advantage of the newer features of IIS 4/5 while still providing support for IIS 3.0.

The Authors Sample Web Provider Component

The sample component that we are going to build will provide the `DisplayAuthors` ASP with a table of authors and related information read from SQL Server. You will need a copy of SQL Server 6.5 or SQL Server 7.0 installed on your machine. If you cannot get either one of these you can use a SQL Server database on your network. You will be accessing the Pubs sample database and if you do not have select permission to the tables in Pubs contact your Database Administrator.

SQL Server 6.5 Developers Edition is included with Visual Basic Enterprise Edition. If you do not have the Enterprise Edition of Visual Basic you can download an evaluation edition of SQL Server 7.0 from the Microsoft Web site.

Global.asa File

You will need to add the following lines to your `global.asa` file for this project to work correctly. The `ConnectionTimeout` and `CommandTimeout` Session variables will be used when we make our connection to SQL Server. The Application variable `ConnectString` provides the string we will use to connect to the database. Ensure you use the correct user ID and password provided by your database administrator.

```
Sub Session_OnStart
    Session("ConnectionTimeout") = 30
    Session("CommandTimeout") = 30
End Sub

Sub Session_OnEnd
    Session("ConnectionTimeout") = ""
    Session("CommandTimeout") = ""
End Sub

Sub Application_OnStart
    Application("ConnectString") = "dsn=Pubs Connection;uid=sa;pwd=;"
End Sub

Sub Application_OnEnd
    Application("ConnectString") = ""
End Sub
```

Data Source

You will also need a data source set up to be able to access the database. For those readers that are not already familiar with setting up a data source please refer to the relevant appendix. For those readers that are familiar with setting up data sources go ahead and set it up with a name of "Pubs Connection" and the Pubs database as the default database.

To set up the data source double click on **ODBC Data Sources** in the **Control Panel** to invoke the ODBC Data Source Administrator. Click on the **System** tab and click **A̲dd** to begin adding a new data source.

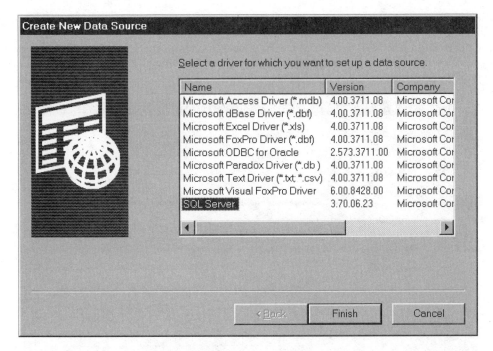

Select the SQL Server driver and click Finish.

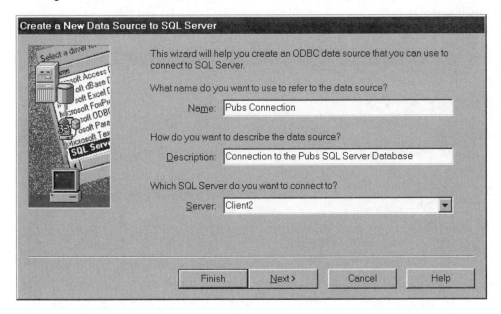

Fill in the name of the connection as "Pubs Connection", add any relative description you might want and choose the server where your database is installed. If you installed the SQL Server 6.5 Developers Edition or SQL Server 7.0 Desktop Edition on your machine, then the server name will be you computer name. If you are using SQL Server off the network, then enter the Server Name where SQL Server is running. Click Next to continue.

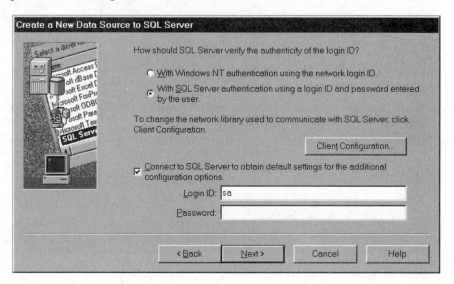

Be sure to use SQL Server authentication and enter the Login ID and Password that you have been assigned or that you set up. Click Next to continue.

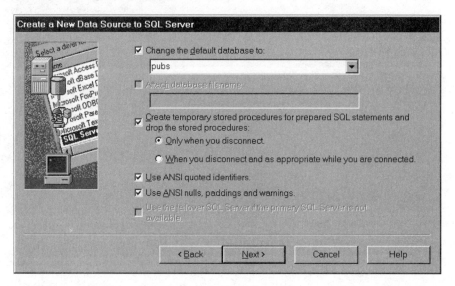

Make sure that the default database is set to Pubs and leave all other options as they are. Click Next to continue. Choose the default options on the next dialog and click Finish. You can test your data source or Click OK to finish. Click OK to close the ODBC Data Source Administrator.

RequestAuthors Page

Before we can create our component we need to set up a page that will request the authors to be displayed. This is going to be a simple page with one form. Use the code below to create your page and save it as `RequestAuthors.htm`.

```html
<HTML>
<HEAD>
<TITLE>Request Authors</TITLE>
<META NAME="GENERATOR" Content="Microsoft Visual Studio 6.0">
</HEAD>
<BODY>
<p><big><big>Request Authors </big></big></p>
<form method="POST" action="DisplayAuthors.asp" name="form1">
    <table border="0">
        <tr><td><input type=radio name=AuthorOption value=0 checked>Display
Authors by Last Name</td></tr>
        <tr><td><input type=radio name=AuthorOption value=1>Display Authors by
First Name</td></tr>
        <tr><td><input type=radio name=AuthorOption value=2>Display Authors by
Book Title</td></tr>
        <tr><td>  </td></tr>
        <tr><td><input type=submit value=Submit name=B1><input type=reset
value=Reset name=B2></td></tr>
    </table>
</form>
</BODY>
</HTML>
```

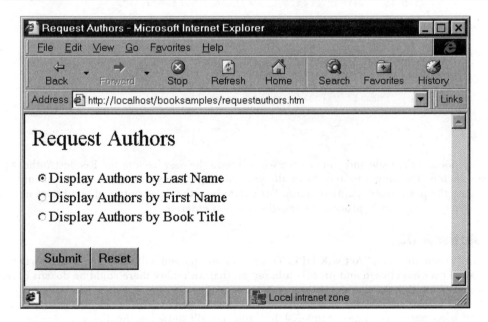

We are setting up three option buttons that will allow the user to select how the output will be displayed.

When the user clicks on the Submit button the page will post the form variable `AuthorOption` to the requested form, in this case `DisplayAuthors.asp`.

An option button, also referred to as a radio button, exists as a group of buttons. The buttons presented in a group allows only one button to be turned on at any one time.

DisplayAuthors ASP

Since this is going to be a simple component with minimal input from the requesting ASP we can go ahead and set up our `DisplayAuthor` ASP. This page will simply call our component and let it build the page data for us. The only thing we will do is build a skeleton form and call our new component from within the middle of the form to build the table of data.

Create a new page and add the following code and save it as `DisplayAuthors.asp`.

```
<HTML>
<HEAD>
<TITLE>Display Authors</TITLE>
<META NAME="GENERATOR" Content="Microsoft Visual Studio 6.0">
</HEAD>
<BODY>
<p><big><big>Display Authors</big></big></p>

<form method="POST" action="RequestAuthors.asp" name="form1">
<%
     'Create the Web Provider Component
     Set objDisplay = Server.CreateObject("Authors.Display")

     'Call the component
     objDisplay.AllAuthors

     'Dereference the component
     Set objDisplay = Nothing
%>
     <input type="submit" value="Submit" name="B1">
</form>
</BODY>
</HTML>
```

Take a close look at the code and you can see we will send the user back to the RequestAuthors page when they click on the submit button. Normally you would probably want to do some type of processing on the page we are going to build. For example, if the data contained text boxes next to each entry you would want to process the text the user has entered.

Authors ActiveX DLL

Now we will create the actual ActiveX DLL. This server component will read the request form to get the option the user has chosen and process it based on that. In reality there could be dozens of fields on the request form that we would want to use for processing.

Start Visual Basic and select a new ActiveX DLL project as illustrated in the dialog.

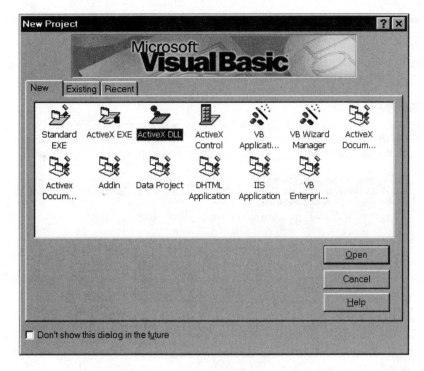

By default the project is created with a project name of Project1 with a class name of Class1. Let's start here and change the defaults. From our code sample in the ASP we were going to set our ActiveX DLL project name to Authors and the class name to Display.

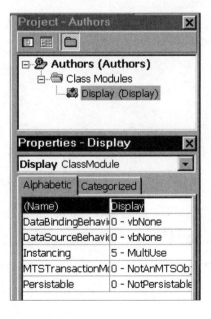

The project name will, by default, become the actual compiled component name. We will however have the opportunity to override this when we compile our project.

Normally I prefix all my class names with 'cls' but since this class is going to be exposed as an interface, I like to use names that make sense and are clear.

Project Properties

The next thing that we want to do is set all of the project's properties. We can do this by selecting Project from the menu and then selecting Authors Properties or by right-clicking on the project name in the Project Explorer and selecting Authors Properties on the popup menu.

The Project Description text that you enter here will be the description that is displayed in the References dialog once you compile your project. The next tab (Make) is where we will provide most of our information. We need to pay special attention in what we put here.

The first thing we need to do is check the Auto Increment checkbox. This will automatically increment the Revision number every time we recompile our project. Only change the Major and Minor number when you make major and minor revisions to the project. This is explained in detail in the section titled 'Key Items to Remember' at the end of this chapter.

The Title text box is populated with the project name by default. Here we have changed this to something a little more descriptive. Since this is a Web page provider component and does not have a user interface there are no icons to display. The system will assign a default icon to it for us that is used for all DLLs.

Normally, all forms in your project are displayed in the Icon combo box. If you select a form the associated form icon is then displayed. Since this is a server component there are no forms in this project and we can ignore this field.

The Version Information section should be filled in with the appropriate information. There's just one special note that I would like to point out here. When you scroll down the Type list you will see an entry for File Description. The value that you enter here is displayed on the Version tab of the Properties dialog next to Description and the amount of text that is displayed is very limited. Use a one liner here to describe the DLL at a high level. Use the Comments value to describe in detail what functions this DLL performs.

The **Compile** tab is where we want to change our **DLL Base Address** to avoid conflicts with other DLLs, and to avoid having the system rebase our DLL when it is first loaded. For our example today we are going to use a base address of &H11140000.

A random base address between &H11000000 and &H80000000 should be chosen. These addresses are on 64K boundaries and should not conflict with other DLLs or OCXs. You need to keep track of the addresses you use to avoid conflicts. This is also explained in detail in the section titled 'Key Items to Remember' at the end of this chapter.

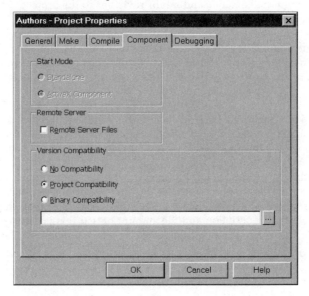

The Component tab is automatically set to Project Compatibility for us. This allows us to retain any references we set to other objects in the References dialog. We will accept this for now. After we compile our component the first time, we will come back to this dialog and set the Version Compatibility to Binary Compatibility. Compatibility is explained in depth in the section titled "Key Items to Remember".

Click OK to save the information we have entered and to close this dialog.

References

The References dialog allows us to set a reference to other objects for use in our project. To open the dialog, select Project on the menu and then select References. Scroll down the list until you see Microsoft Active Server Pages Object Library and click the check box next to this item. We will also need a reference to the **Microsoft ActiveX Data Objects Library** (ADO) to provide an access method to the database. Click on the latest version that you have available in your Reference dialog. Click OK to close this dialog.

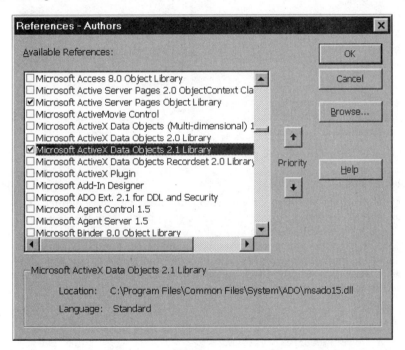

Object Browser

To open the Object Browser, select the View menu and then select Object Browser. The Object Browser will display the Properties, Methods, Events and Constants for objects that you have set a reference to, as well as for your own classes and modules. Select the ASPTypeLibrary and click on the Response class to view all the available methods and properties associated with this class. You can refer to the object browser to reference what methods might be available for use and the parameters they accept, if any.

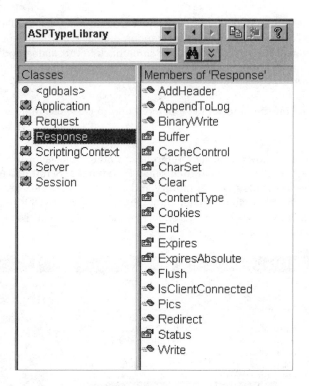

Close the Object Browser, save the project and let's start writing some code.

Variable Declarations

We know right from the start that we will need some basic variables defined. These variables will allow us to access the different `ScriptingContext` objects from the `RequestAuthors` ASP and the `DisplayAuthors` ASP. We also know that we need some basic variables to provide access to the database. To keep the code at a minimum, detailed error handling will be omitted. Do not omit the error handling functions in your code. It is very important that you handle all possible errors in your ActiveX DLLs. The variables that we need to define are shown in the code fragment below and are declared in the General Declarations section of the class module.

```
Option Explicit

'Declare ScriptingContext variables
Private m_Application As Application
Private m_Request As Request
Private m_Response As Response
Private m_Session As Session

'Declare Database variables
Private m_objConn As New ADODB.Connection
Private m_objRs As New ADODB.Recordset

'Declare Class variables
Private m_blnProceed As Boolean
```

We are going to use the `Application, Request, Response,` and `Session` objects in our ActiveX DLL and need to declare variables for them. We are also going to use ADO as our data access method and need to declare variables for the database connection and recordset. One Boolean variable is going to be accessible to all functions and procedures in our class and is also defined here.

OnStartPage and OnEndPage

Before an ASP processes any script it calls the `OnStartPage()` method for all objects except those with application scope. We use the `OnStartPage()` with the `ScriptingContext` object to retrieve pointers to the built-in ASP objects. This allows our component to access these objects just like we do in VB script.

When an ASP has finished processing the script it calls the `OnEndPage()` method. This is where we need to release and free up our pointers to the built-in ASP objects.

With that being said, we need to define a procedure for the `OnStartPage()` and `OnEndPage()` methods which allows us access to the `ScriptingContext` object. Create your `OnStartPage()` and `OnEndPage()` procedures and set your `ScriptingContext` variables as shown in the code sample.

```
Public Sub OnStartPage(objScriptingContext As ScriptingContext)

    'Set references to the Web's ScriptingContext objects
    Set m_Application = objScriptingContext.Application
    Set m_Request = objScriptingContext.Request
    Set m_Response = objScriptingContext.Response
    Set m_Session = objScriptingContext.Session

End Sub


Public Sub OnEndPage()

    'Dereference all ScriptingContext objects
    Set m_Application = Nothing
    Set m_Request = Nothing
    Set m_Response = Nothing
    Set m_Session = Nothing

End Sub
```

Database Connection and Disconnection

We know that we need to establish a connection to the database and open it so let's create that code next. We are going to create a function to open the database. The `OpenDatabase()` function will return a `Boolean` value indicating success or failure. This allows us to handle connection failure gracefully and return to the calling function or procedure and exit our code from there. There are two procedures to close and de-reference our recordset and database connection. Use the code sample below to create your code.

```
Private Function OpenDatabase() As Boolean
    'Connect to SQL Server and open the database
    On Error GoTo SQLErr
    With m_objConn
        .ConnectionTimeout = CInt(m_Session("ConnectionTimeout"))
        .CommandTimeout = CInt(m_Session("CommandTimeout"))
        .Open m_Application("ConnectString")
    End With
```

```
   On Error GoTo 0
   OpenDatabase = True
   Exit Function
SQLErr:
   OpenDatabase = False
End Function

Private Sub CloseRecordset()
   'Close recordset objects and dereference them
   m_objRs.Close
   Set m_objRs = Nothing
End Sub

Private Sub CloseDatabase()
   'Close database objects and dereference them
   m_objConn.Close
   Set m_objConn = Nothing
End Sub
```

If you take a close look at the code in the OpenDatabase() function you will see we are getting the timeout values from Session variables defined on the Web site in the Global.asa file. We are getting the ConnectString from the Application variable, also defined in the Global.asa file. Using these variables makes our component more flexible. Suppose if you will that you are having some network problems and access to your database is really slow. All of your scripts and database connections and query operations start timing out. By increasing the value in the Global.asa file you can prevent the timeouts and this is carried forward in your Web components without any code modifications or recompilations.

Also note that all of these procedures and functions are coded as private. There is no need to expose them to the rest of the world as they are only needed in your component and should not be accessed from other code.

AllAuthors Procedure

Now we are ready to start working on the main procedure, AllAuthors(). Since this is our interface for this DLL that is called from the ASP, we need to declare the procedure as public so that it is exposed to other objects. We do not need to accept any parameters or return any values from our interface, as we will be writing directly to the ASP.

We can start by declaring the variables that are local to this procedure and calling the OpenDatabase() function. If this function returns false, this is an indication to us that it failed and we want to handle this failure and quit. We will use the Response object to write a message to the DisplayAuthors ASP indicating there was an error opening the database.

```
Public Sub AllAuthors()
   'Declare local variables
   Dim strSQL, strOrderBy As String
   Dim intCount As Integer

   'Open the database and check for errors
   If Not OpenDatabase Then
     m_Response.Write "<P><strong><font color=""#FF0000"">" & _
       "Error Opening Database</font></strong><P>"
     Exit Sub
   End If
```

If you recall, we set up the `RequestAuthors` ASP to provide a display of authors by last name, first name or by book title. When the user clicked on an option, the value corresponding to the user's choice was placed in the variable `AuthorOption`. We need to retrieve that variable from the request form and process based on it as demonstrated in the following code.

```
'Build the order by clause based on request.form("AuthorOption")
  Select Case CInt(m_Request.Form("AuthorOption"))
    Case 0
      strOrderBy = "order by au_lname"
    Case 1
      strOrderBy = "order by au_fname"
    Case 2
      strOrderBy = "order by title"
    Case Else
      strOrderBy = ""
  End Select
```

Remember that all variables in VB script are Variants and while Visual Basic will automatically determine and convert the variant value to the correct data type, it is more efficient for us to tell Visual Basic what data type to convert this value to. Based on the option selected by the user we want to build part of the query string that sorts our data by setting a string value to the correct order by clause for SQL Server. Once this is done we can build the SQL string that we want to execute.

```
'Set the SQL string
  strSQL = "select au_lname, au_fname, pubdate, title " & _
    "From Authors " & _
    "join titleauthor on authors.au_id = titleauthor.au_id " & _
    "join titles on titleauthor.title_id = titles.title_id " & _
    strOrderBy
```

While our ActiveX DLL will process data faster that an ASP we are still developing a Web application. Keeping this in mind, we don't want to hold onto a database connection any longer than necessary, especially when we are only reading data. For this reason, it makes sense to use a disconnected recordset for our processing. We will open the recordset and disconnect from the database immediately using the code illustrated below. The next chapter will go into ADO in more depth and you can also refer to the relevant appendix for more information.

```
On Error GoTo SQLErr

  'Set the cursorlocation
  m_objRs.CursorLocation = adUseClient
  'Open the recordset
  m_objRs.Open strSQL, m_objConn, adOpenForwardOnly, , adCmdText
  'Set the recordset to no active connection
  Set m_objRs.ActiveConnection = Nothing

  On Error GoTo 0

  'Close the database to free the connection
  Call CloseDatabase
```

The first thing that we need to do is set the cursor location and we are specifying that we want to use a client side cursor. Next we open the recordset that executes the SQL string we specified. Since we only want to read forward, we specify the `adReadForwardOnly` parameter. We then have to set the recordset object's active connection to `Nothing` to disconnect it, and then we are able to close the database and de-reference the database object.

Now that we have a disconnected recordset we want to start processing the records. Before we can do that we need to start building the table where we are going to place the data. Here we will build the header row of the table as shown in this code.

```
'Build the first part of the table containing all header information
   m_Response.Write "<TABLE BORDER=""1""><TR>"
   m_Response.Write "<TH NOWRAP BGCOLOR=""#800000""><FONT COLOR=""#FFFFFF"">" & _
      "Last Name</FONT></TH>"
   m_Response.Write "<TH NOWRAP BGCOLOR=""#800000""><FONT COLOR=""#FFFFFF"">" & _
      "First Name</FONT></TH>"
   m_Response.Write "<TH NOWRAP BGCOLOR=""#800000""><FONT COLOR=""#FFFFFF"">" & _
      "Dated Published</FONT></TH>"
   m_Response.Write "<TH NOWRAP BGCOLOR=""#800000""><FONT COLOR=""#FFFFFF"">" & _
      "Book Title</FONT></TH>"
   m_Response.Write "</TR>"
```

Now that the header row of the table is built we can loop through the recordset building each row of the table. We format the published date because we only want to display the date and the published date is a datetime field in SQL Server.

```
'Loop through the recordset building each row of the table
   Do While Not m_objRs.EOF
      m_Response.Write "<TR>"
      m_Response.Write "<TD BGCOLOR=""#C0C0C0"">" & m_objRs!au_lname & _
         "</TD>"
      m_Response.Write "<TD BGCOLOR=""#C0C0C0"">" & m_objRs!au_fname & _
         "</TD>"
      m_Response.Write "<TD BGCOLOR=""#C0C0C0"">" & _
         Format(m_objRs!pubdate, "mm/dd/yyyy") & "</TD>"
      m_Response.Write "<TD BGCOLOR=""#C0C0C0"">" & m_objRs!title & _
         "</TD>"
      m_Response.Write "</TR>"
      m_objRs.MoveNext
   Loop
```

The last part of the code includes writing the `</TABLE>` tag, closing the recordset and exiting the procedure. You will notice that the error label, `SQLErr`, is at the end of our procedure. You will want to add some meaningful error handling here as I have only included a brief statement to report an error.

```
   'Build the last part of the table
   m_Response.Write "</TABLE>"

   'Close the recordset
   Call CloseRecordset

   Exit Sub

SQLErr:
```

```
m_Response.Write "<P><STRONG><FONT COLOR=""#FF0000"">" & _
    "SQL Error Occurred Reading From The Database</FONT></STRONG><P>"

End Sub
```

Testing Our Component

With script debugging we are able to interactively test our in-process components and our ASP with the browser. Start by setting a break point in your code where you would like to start stepping through, perhaps at the `OnStartPage()` procedure, and then start your Web server component. The first time you run your component, a dialog will appear for the debugging options; accept all defaults and click on OK to continue. Next, start Internet Explorer and navigate to the `RequestAuthors` page, select an option and click on **Submit** and wait for Visual Basic to be activated to the foreground window. You can now step through your code checking for errors.

Your `DisplayAuthors` page should look like this.

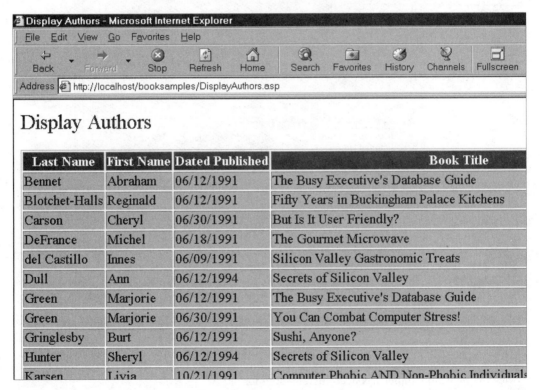

Compiling the ActiveX DLL

We are now ready to compile our ActiveX DLL. Select **File** on the menu and then **Make Authors.dll**. At this point you can override the default DLL name of **Authors**, but for our purposes this is fine. Click on **OK** and your DLL will be compiled and registered in the system registry.

The very next thing that we want to do is set binary compatibility. Activate the **Project Properties** dialog and click on the **Component** tab and click on the **Binary Compatibility** radio button. You will notice that `Authors.dll` is already in the text box for binary compatibility. Click **OK** to close the dialog. Compile your code once more to set binary compatibility and then save your project again. Refer to the section titled 'Key Items to Remember' for further information on compatibility.

File Properties Dialog

Let's take a look at the **File Properties** dialog for our newly created DLL. In Windows Explorer, navigate to your project folder and right click on the `Authors.dll` and choose **Properties** in the popup menu.

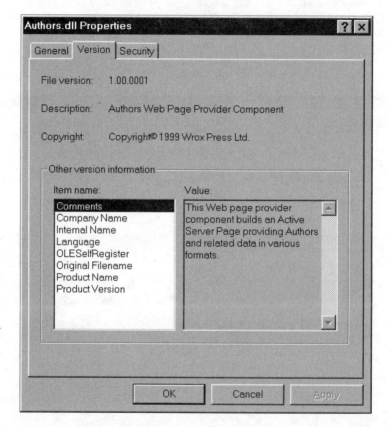

Click on the **Version** tab and the first thing that comes to our attention is the version number. Because we chose to have the version number auto incremented and we compiled our component twice the revision number has been incremented for us.

Remember the information you enter for **File Description**? Well it's displayed on the dialog next to the word **Description**. As you can see there is not a lot of room on the dialog and the text will not be wrapped; it will just be cut off. This is why it's important to just enter a simple one-liner here.

The **Product Name** displays the data you entered for **Application Title** if you did not enter any information for **Product Name** in the **Project Properties** dialog.

Packaging Our Component for Distribution

We are now ready to package our component for distribution to our test Web server before implementing it on our production Web server. Start the Package & Deployment Wizard from the program group folder or using the add-ins menu and select the `Authors` project we just created.

We want to package this component for distribution to our test Web server for complete testing so we need to click on the **Package** button. If you see a dialog asking if you want to recompile, answer **No**.

We want to choose the **Standard Setup Package** in the next step so just click **Next** to move to the next step. The next step prompts us for a directory to create the package in. Choose a directory that's appropriate for you. For our purposes here we'll take the default folder of **Package** under our project directory. If you choose a folder that does not exist the wizard will prompt you and ask if it should create it, choose **Yes**.

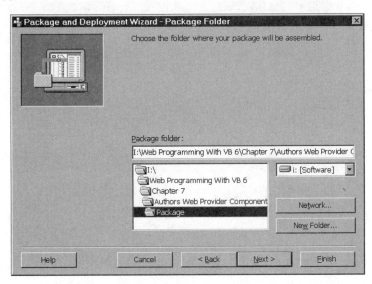

The next step will list all of the components that will be distributed with your package. You can add and remove components here. If you created a help file that you want distributed with your component you would include it here.

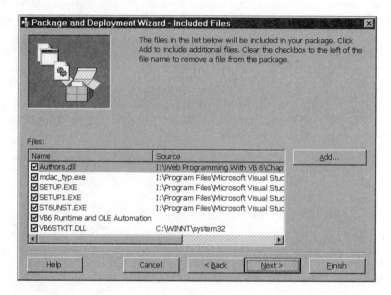

Unless you are distributing your package on diskettes, click the Next button to move to the next step. The next step is very important. This is the title that will be displayed on the setup screen as your component is being installed and this is also the title that will be displayed in the Add/Remove Programs dialog. By default the dialog displays the application title that you entered in your project. If you entered a simple application title and do not want that displayed in the setup program and the Add/Remove Programs dialog, then change it here. Click the Next button when you are ready to proceed.

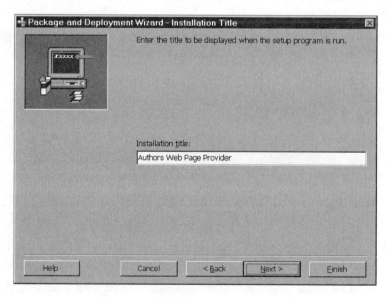

Since this is an ActiveX DLL the wizard knows not to create a group or item for this project. But since this is also an important step I'll cover it briefly.

If this were an executable program, a program group and program item would automatically be created for you. If this program is being installed on a Windows NT Workstation or Server, you have the option of installing it as a Private or Common group. If multiple users can share the program then click on the group name and click the Properties button and change the Windows NT Group Option to Common. This will cause the installation of the group to be accessible to all users of the workstation. If you want to install a help file that is accessible from the menu you could set it up here as a new item under the group.

Since we don't need a group or item to be set up in the Programs folder just click next to continue.

Microsoft wants us to install our components in our own program folder under Program Files versus being installed in the System/System32 folder so the default is set to AppPath (application path). You should note that you have the option to override this if for some reason you need to install your component in the Windows/WinNT folder or the System/System32 folder, or other folders.

For our purposes, here the default application path will be fine. Remember that the installation program will take care of the registration of your component for you so it really does not matter for this project where it is installed. Click Next to move to the next step.

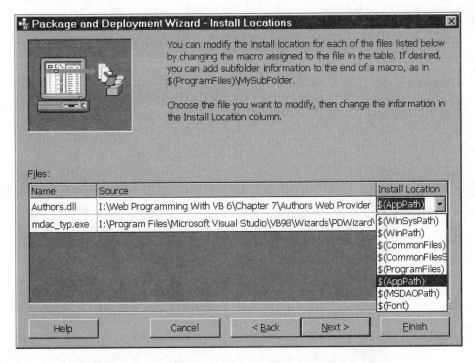

The next step talks about shared files. This does not apply to our project this time as our component can only be accessed from our Web application; no other programs can use it. Just click the Next button to move to the next step. You should enter a meaningful name for the script name if you plan to run multiple scripts for different file distributions. Click Finish to have the wizard create the setup program.

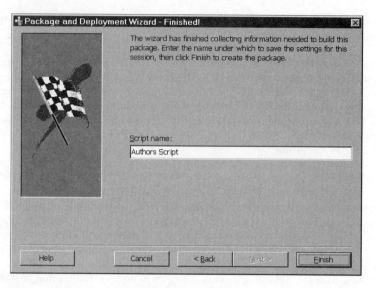

A report is produced as the last step in the process. Pay close attention to this report when you plan to distribute components that are using COM and DCOM and you plan to install on a Windows 95/98 system. Click Close to close the report and Close again to close the wizard.

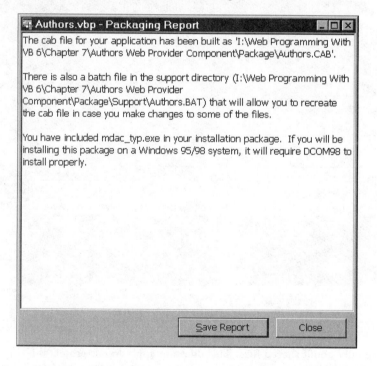

Package Directory

Under your package directory is a directory named Support. You do not have to distribute this directory with your package. This directory is used to rebuild you .cab file if you make changes to any of your files. A .cab (cabinet) file contains all the files needed to install and support your component and is used by the setup program when installing your component.

You are now ready to install your component on your web server by using the setup.exe program that was created for you in the directory you specified when creating your package.

Interesting Observations

When you install your component on Windows NT and then navigate to the DisplayAuthors page you will notice a slight delay before your page is displayed. This is because the system has to locate and load your ActiveX DLL into memory.

Now click on the button at the bottom of the screen to display another author, choose another option and click Submit. You will notice an instantaneous display of your DisplayAuthors page. Now shut down your browser and then start it back up again. Now navigate to the RequestAuthors page again, and choose an option followed by clicking on Submit. Your DisplayAuthors page is instantaneously displayed once again.

Why does this happen? Once a DLL is loaded and then unloaded, the memory pages of that DLL are moved to what is called a standby list in memory. Subsequent calls to that DLL by any application are then loaded from this standby list. As you can see from our little experiment, this has a significant performance increase on subsequent loads.

Examples to Try

This next section will suggest some examples to try to help reinforce what we have covered in this chapter. It will also help to show you some of the other possibilities that can be achieved with your Web server component.

Text Boxes

In a real world Web application you would probably want to add a text box to the table of authors, so that a user could order a specific number of books for a given title. The code fragment to do this is illustrated below in two segments. We will cover how to read the information the user entered later on.

```
'Declare local variables
   Dim strSQL, strOrderBy As String
   Dim intCount As Integer
```

The intCount variable is used to assign a unique number to each textbox name that you build. This will allow you to access the textboxes by name. You could also access the textboxes in an array if they all had the same name.

The second code fragment shows the addition of an extra column header and the text box being built on each row. Notice that the name of each textbox gets sets to a value of 'txtOrder' plus the number contained in the variable intLoop. The first time in the loop the textbox gets a name of txtOrder1 and the second time txtOrder2 and so on.

```
'Build the first part of the table containing all header information
 m_Response.Write "<TABLE border=""1""><TR>"
 m_Response.Write "<TH nowrap bgcolor=""#800000""><FONT color=""#FFFFFF"">" & _
   "Last Name</FONT></TH>"
 m_Response.Write "<TH nowrap bgcolor=""#800000""><FONT color=""#FFFFFF"">" & _
   "First Name</FONT></TH>"
 m_Response.Write "<TH nowrap bgcolor=""#800000""><FONT color=""#FFFFFF"">" & _
   "Dated Published</FONT></TH>"
 m_Response.Write "<TH nowrap bgcolor=""#800000""><FONT color=""#FFFFFF"">" & _
   "Book Title</FONT></TH>"
 m_Response.Write "<TH nowrap bgcolor=""#800000""><FONT color=""#FFFFFF"">" & _
   "Order</FONT></TH>"
 m_Response.Write "</TR>"

'Loop through the recordset building each row of the table
 Do While Not m_objRs.EOF
   intCount = intCount + 1
   m_Response.Write "<TR>"
   m_Response.Write "<TD bgcolor=""#C0C0C0"">" & m_objRs!au_lname & _
     "</TD>"
   m_Response.Write "<TD bgcolor=""#C0C0C0"">" & m_objRs!au_fname & _
     "</TD>"
   m_Response.Write "<TD bgcolor=""#C0C0C0"">" & _
     Format(m_objRs!pubdate, "mm/dd/yy") & "</TD>"
   m_Response.Write "<TD bgcolor=""#C0C0C0"">" & m_objRs!Title & _
     "</TD>"
   m_Response.Write "<TD bgcolor=""#C0C0C0"">" & _
     "<input type=""text"" size=""5"" name=""" & "txtOrder" & _
     intCount & """ value></TD>"
   m_Response.Write "</TR>"
   m_objRs.MoveNext
 Loop
```

Stored Procedures

Stored Procedures should be used in your program instead of SQL statements whenever possible. A Stored Procedure is a set of compiled SQL statements on a database and is optimized for use. When a Stored Procedure is used for the first time, SQL Server loads the Stored Procedure into memory and subsequent calls to the Stored Procedure are executed from memory in SQL Server.

When you send SQL statements in your code for execution, SQL Server must first optimize your SQL statements before executing them. Another consideration is the amount of network traffic involved. It is much more efficient to send one line of code to call a Stored Procedure than to send a dozen lines of SQL code.

Maintenance of Stored Procedures does not involve recompiling your program and can be quickly performed in SQL Server.

To create the Stored Procedures in the Pubs database you will need write permission to the database. The following code shows the three Stored Procedures to display authors by last name, authors by first name, and the authors by their book titles.

```
CREATE PROCEDURE up_select_authors_by_last_name AS

 SELECT au_lname, au_fname, pubdate, title
   FROM authors
```

```
JOIN titleauthor ON authors.au_id = titleauthor.au_id
JOIN titles ON titleauthor.title_id = titles.title_id
ORDER BY au_lname
```

> **Note: If you are using SQL Server 6.5, there is a limitation of 30 characters for a Stored Procedure name and you will have to shorten the Stored Procedure name `up_select_authors_by_first_name` by one character.**

```
CREATE PROCEDURE up_select_authors_by_first_name AS

SELECT au_lname, au_fname, pubdate, title
    FROM authors
    JOIN titleauthor ON authors.au_id = titleauthor.au_id
    JOIN titles ON titleauthor.title_id = titles.title_id
    ORDER BY au_fname
```

```
CREATE PROCEDURE up_select_authors_by_title as

SELECT au_lname, au_fname, pubdate, title
    FROM authors
    JOIN titleauthor ON authors.au_id = titleauthor.au_id
    JOIN titles ON titleauthor.title_id = titles.title_id
    ORDER BY title
```

Now that we have created our Stored Procedures, we need to change our code to call the correct Stored Procedure based on user input. We can drop the section of code that builds the SQL query string and modify the selection of the user input to set the variable strSQL to the correct Stored Procedure instead of an order by clause.

```
'Build the SQL string based on request.form("AuthorOption")
  Select Case CInt(m_Request.Form("AuthorOption"))
    Case 0
      strSQL = "dbo.up_select_authors_by_last_name"
    Case 1
      strSQL = "dbo.up_select_authors_by_first_name"
    Case 2
      strSQL = "dbo.up_select_authors_by_title"
    Case Else
      strSQL = "dbo.up_select_authors_by_last_name"
  End Select

  On Error GoTo SQLErr
  'Set the cursorlocation
  m_objRs.CursorLocation = adUseClient
  'Open the recordset
  m_objRs.Open strSQL, m_objConn, adOpenForwardOnly, , adCmdText
```

Web Page Consumer Component

Now that we have built a Web page provider component and added the text boxes to the form that allows for user input, it would only make sense to be able to read the information back from the web page using a Web page consumer component. This is easier than you might think as you already have the foundation for building this component.

Let's start by modifying the `DisplayAuthors` ASP. We will add some server side logic to this page to break it up into two sections. The first section will display the authors and the second section will process the user's selection.

```
<%
If Len(Request.Form("FormAction")) = 0 Then
%>

<FORM METHOD="POST" ACTION="DisplayAuthors.asp" NAME="form1">
  <INPUT TYPE="hidden" NAME="FormAction" VALUE="Step2">
  <INPUT TYPE="hidden" NAME="AuthorOption"
VALUE="<%=Request.Form("AuthorOption")%>">

<%
  'Create the Web Provider Component
  Set objDisplay = Server.CreateObject("Authors.Display")

  'Call the component
  objDisplay.AllAuthors

  'De-reference the component
  Set objDisplay = Nothing
%>

<P><INPUT TYPE="submit" VALUE="Process Selections" NAME="B1"> </P>

</FORM>
```

As you can see in this code fragment, we are processing a server side script to check the length of the variable `FormAction`. A zero length variable will indicate to us if this is the first time this page has executed. We also need to change the form action to have the form post back to itself. The last modification to `form1` in the ASP is to change the value on the **Submit** button from `Submit` to `Process Selections`, which makes more sense as to what this button actual does.

The next modification to `form1` in the ASP is to add two hidden fields to hold the variables that will be posted to the next step. The first field, `FormAction`, will tell us what step to process in this ASP. While it is not necessary for this example, it does show you how you can set up an ASP to contain and process multiple steps. The next field is the `AuthorOption` value from the `RequestAuthors` ASP and we will need that variable in the next step.

```
<%
ElseIf Request.Form("FormAction") = "Step2" Then

  'Create the Web Consumer Component
  Set objProcess = Server.CreateObject("Authors.Process")

  'Call the component
  objProcess.UserSelections

  'Dereference the component
  Set objProcess = Nothing

End If
%>
```

In this section of the code we are checking the Request Form variable `FormAction` for a value of `Step2`. Processing of this section will indicate that this is the second time this page has been executed by the user and we want to process their selections. Again we call a Web component to process the results of the previous Web page but this time the Web component is a consumer component.

Now let's create the Visual Basic code to process the user's selections. We will use the `Authors` ActiveX DLL again and add a new class called `Process`. We need to add the same variables in the **General Declarations** section as we did in the `Display` class, so just copy them.

Now copy the `CloseDatabase()`, `CloseRecordset()`, `OnEndPage()`, `OnStartPage()` and `OpenDatabase()` procedures and functions from the `Display` class and paste them into the `Process` class. These procedures and functions are going to perform the same processing as they did in the `Display` class.

We want to create a public procedure called `UserSelections()` as a method to perform the processing of the user's selections. You will notice that this procedure starts the same way as the `AllAuthors()` procedure did.

```
Public Sub UserSelections()
  'Declare local variables
  Dim strSQL As String
  Dim intCount As Integer

  'Open the database and check for errors
  If Not OpenDatabase Then
    m_Response.Write "<P><STRONG><FONT COLOR=""#FF0000"">" & _
      "Error Opening Database</FONT></STRONG><P>"
    Exit Sub
  End If

  'Build the order by clause based on request.form("AuthorOption")
  Select Case CInt(m_Request.Form("AuthorOption"))
    Case 0
      strSQL = "dbo.up_select_authors_by_last_name"
    Case 1
      strSQL = "dbo.up_select_authors_by_first_name"
    Case 2
      strSQL = "dbo.up_select_authors_by_title"
    Case Else
      strSQL = "dbo.up_select_authors_by_last_name"
  End Select

  On Error GoTo SQLErr
  'Set the cursorlocation
  m_objRs.CursorLocation = adUseClient
  'Open the recordset
  m_objRs.Open strSQL, m_objConn, adOpenForwardOnly, , adCmdText
  'Set the recordset to no active connection
  Set m_objRs.ActiveConnection = Nothing
  On Error GoTo 0

  'Close the database to free the connection
  Call CloseDatabase
```

The difference in the code actually comes were we are processing the user's selections rather than building a table.

```
'Loop through the recordset matching the record to the user's selections

Do While Not m_objRs.EOF

    intCount = intCount + 1

    'If the length of the field is > 0 the user entered something so process their
    'selection
    If Len(m_Request.Form("txtOrder" & intCount)) > 0 Then
        'You could validate the users input to make sure they entered
        'the correct value as in:

        If UCase(m_Request.Form("txtOrder" & intCount)) = "S" Then
            'Do the valid processing here
        Else
            'Handle invalid options here

        End If

    End If

    m_objRs.MoveNext

Loop
```

We need the same recordset as the first part of the ASP so we can make the correct match to the user's selection. We process each record, incrementing the counter (intCount) and check the length of the input field. If the length is greater than zero, we know the user has entered something. We then validate the user's input to make sure it is valid and do some processing with that information.

```
'Close the recordset
Call CloseRecordset

'Display a message indicating all processing is complete
m_Response.Write "<P><STRONG>Your selections have been processed." & _
    "</STRONG><P>"

Exit Sub

SQLErr:
m_Response.Write "<P><STRONG><FONT COLOR=""#FF0000"">" & _
    "SQL Error Occurred Reading from the Database</FONT></STRONG><P>"
```

When all processing is complete we close the recordset, write a message for the user, letting them know that the processing of their selections is complete, and end the program.

Points to Ponder

We provided a Web component that was specific to Authors. This component was a Web page consumer and a Web page provider component, and different classes separated the two functions. These examples were presented in the clearest way possible and as such there was a lot of duplicate code. The next chapter will take this into consideration and show you how to share the common procedures and functions among all classes in your components.

Another item to consider is the input text boxes that we added to the table. In a real-world database table, you would probably have unique keys in the database that could be used as the text box names instead of `txtOrder1`. This makes it safer to process as you can perform validations against the database to make sure the actual row still exists in the table before processing the data from the Web page.

Key items to remember

This section covers some important details that you should be aware of when developing ActiveX DLLs. These items are personal observations that I have run across in developing ActiveX DLLs and by no means is a complete list. More information is available on the MSDN library CDs or at the MSDN online library at `http://msdn.microsoft.com/library/default.htm`.

Choosing Names

The names you choose will affect your interface calls, application title, installation title and the display name in the Add/Remove Programs dialog. The following table outlines the various names and their implications.

Name	Implications
Project Name	Can affect you interface call and should be something meaningful. By default your ActiveX DLL executable name will be the same as the project name but you can override this when compiling your DLL.
Class Name	Affects your interface call. A class name of `Class1` would be called as: `Set objTest = CreateObject("Project1.Class1")`
Function / Procedure Name	Affects your interface call. A function/procedure name of `MyInterface` would be called as: `lngRC = objTest.MyInterface(interface parameters)`
Application Title	Affects the `App` object and can affect your installation title and the application title displayed in the Add/Remove Programs dialog.
File Description	Affects the `App` object and also the properties dialog of your ActiveX DLL.
Comments	Affects the `App` object and also the properties dialog of your ActiveX DLL.
Copyright	Affects the `App` object and also the properties dialog of your ActiveX DLL.
Company Name	Affects the `App` object and also the properties dialog of your ActiveX DLL.
Legal Trademarks	Affects the `App` object and also the properties dialog of your ActiveX DLL.
Product Name	Affects the `App` object and also the properties dialog of your ActiveX DLL.

Auto Increment the Version Number

Auto incrementing the version number will help you to maintain version control. The revision number is automatically incremented with each compile when the auto increment checkbox is checked. The major and minor version numbers should be manually set to the next highest number on major and minor program changes, so do not change these numbers for bug fixes. When changing the major and minor version numbers, always set the revision number to 0.

Version Compatibility

A whole chapter could be written on version compatibility in Visual Basic. However, to keep this section brief we'll discuss the three levels of compatibility that are available in the Project Properties dialog at a high level. Further research should be done on your part to determine the best level of compatibility for your project. You can find valuable information on the MSDN library.

No Compatibility, which as its name implies maintains no compatibility. New type library information, including new class IDs and new interface IDs are generated each time you compile your project.

Project Compatibility maintains the type library identifier and class IDs from previous versions when you recompile your project. Interface IDs are only changed for classes that are no longer binary compatible with their counterparts.

Binary Compatibility is a bit more complicated, but overall is probably the best choice. This does, however, impose several restrictions on changes. You cannot change the interface (public methods) of your component in any way, but you can add new interfaces to your project. If you break binary compatibility, Visual Basic will warn you when you recompile your project, heed this warning! The major benefit that binary compatibility provides, is the ability to add new or enhanced functionality to your component without having to recompile the programs or other ActiveX DLLs that use this component. This functionality cannot be achieved if you use No Compatibility or Project Compatibility.

ActiveX DLL Base Addresses

You should change the base address of your ActiveX DLL to avoid conflicts with other ActiveX DLLs and to enhance performance. If two ActiveX DLLs have the same base address and the first ActiveX DLL is loaded, the system will have to rebase the second ActiveX DLL in memory (known as *fixups*) and this slows down load time as well as performance of the ActiveX DLL.

Memory addresses at and beyond &H11000000 are typically used for Visual Basic ActiveX DLLs and OCXs. The maximum address that should be used is &H80000000 and the addresses are on 64K boundaries. Even if an ActiveX DLL is less than 64K in size, it reserves the entire 64K-address space for its use. This means that an ActiveX DLL that is 34K in size could be loaded at &H11080000, an ActiveX DLL that is 84K is loaded at &H11090000 and a 15K ActiveX DLL is loaded at &H110B0000 and there are no conflicts. Keep in mind that the ActiveX DLL that was 84K was larger than 64K and therefore automatically crossed over into the next address space and therefore reserved that address space for its use also. Also keep in mind when using the last address, &H80000000, that the ActiveX DLL should be no larger than 64K.

Interfaces

Any functions or procedures that you want to expose as an interface in your ActiveX DLL must be defined as public. Any functions or procedures that you don't want exposed should be defined as private.

Your interface does not have to accept parameters or return any values unless needed.

Unattended Execution

Remember that your ActiveX DLL is running unattended, that is, it has no graphical user interface. With this in mind, you need to place extra error handlers in your code to handle all possible errors and to prevent run time error message boxes.

NT Event Log

Log all errors to the NT Event log if running on Windows NT. If running on Windows 95 or Windows 98 you need to set the `App.LogPath` property before logging events when using the `App.LogEvent()` method. If no file is specified on Windows 95 or Windows 98, the events are logged to a file called `vbevents.log`. If you choose to log errors to the NT Event log or to a file you should following the guidelines for logging described in the Win32 SDK. You can choose to log your errors directly to your database using a standard interface that you develop. However keep in mind that a database error could be the cause of the error and would prevent logging to it. Don't overuse the NT Event log. This log should only be used to log informational messages of importance, warning messages and error messages.

Component Registration

When you compile an ActiveX DLL, Visual Basic automatically registers the component for you in the system registry. After a component is compiled you can see your component in the list of available components in the **Reference** dialog. For this reason, you should never manually move a component on a computer and you should always un-register the components that you compile for test and production releases unless you want to reference these components in other programs.

To un-register a component, open a Command Prompt window and either navigate to the folder where the component is located and enter `Regsvr32 /u Authors.DLL` to un-register the `Authors.DLL` component or enter the path name and DLL name. If your path name contains spaces put the string in quotes. When the ActiveX DLL has been successfully unregistered you will see a dialog like this:

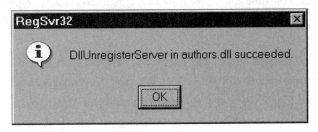

To manually register an ActiveX DLL at a Command prompt, enter Regsvr32 Project.DLL. Once successfully registered, your will see a similar dialog like the one above stating that the component has been registered. You should never have to register an ActiveX DLL manually if you install the setup package you built, but this information is nice to know just in case.

Key items to avoid

The following items are personal observations that I have noted while working with ActiveX DLLs. You will no doubt come across more items as you begin to explore the world of creating ActiveX components. These are provided here to help you avoid some common mistakes.

Interface Changes

Do not change the interface of your components once they have been built and implemented, especially if you have specified binary compatibility. If you do, you must recompile all programs and ActiveX DLLs that use these components. This does not affect ASPs as they are interpreted and not compiled.

Remember, Visual Basic will warn you if you try to break binary compatibility.

Bulky Components

Avoid bulky components; keep them lightweight and designed for a specific purpose. There is an exception to this, and that is when a component performs similar functionality that can be shared by multiple ASP's. In this case you could set up the interface with optional parameters that would allow your component to be called by these multiple ASPs.

Dialogs

Avoid any use of dialogs and message boxes in your components.

NT Event Log

Do not overwrite to the NT Event log.

Summary

In this chapter you have learned the basics of creating a Web page provider component using Visual Basic ActiveX DLLs. You should also see how easy it is to create a Web page consumer component using the foundation of the Web page provider component. To summarize, here are the key items to remember:

> Plan ahead and choose meaningful names that will be used in your Visual Basic project.

> Set your project options so your ActiveX DLL will not conflict with other DLLs on the system.

> Set version compatibility and auto increment version numbers.

> Set your references to access other components (ASP and ADO).

> Use disconnected recordsets where possible.

> Use Stored Procedures where possible.

> Create a deployment package to distribute your Web component.

10

Advanced Visual Basic Server Components

In the previous chapter you were introduced to server components, specifically Web server components. This chapter will help you to expand on that knowledge by showing you when and how to use business server components and how to develop them. The business server components that will be discussed in this chapter will not interact with your Active Server Pages the way that the Web server components did. That is, the business server components will not read data from or write data to your web page using the `ScriptingContext` object. They will be designed to handle specific business functions independent of your ASP. Your ASP will pass parameters to your business component and your business component will process the parameters passed according to the business logic contained in the component.

This chapter will cover:

- ➢ Components that provide business rules
- ➢ Interfacing with other services
- ➢ ActiveX Data Objects
- ➢ Building a business server component

Components That Provide Business Rules

When we talk about business server components in this chapter, we are referring to ActiveX DLLs that implement business rules and perform specific business tasks.

Business server components allow us to encapsulate business rules and data and provide services to many types of clients simultaneously, not just Web clients. They also help us to build component-based applications that can be distributed across the enterprise. Keeping the business rules centralized and encapsulated in server components helps to reduce the need to redistribute front-end programs when business rules change.

When we talk about business rules most people traditionally think about data retrieval and storage. However, business rules go far beyond data access, in that they describe a business's preferred method of handling and manipulating data. Business rules also define how a business performs various functions and operations, such as calculations.

Business components expose interfaces to other applications and objects. These interfaces normally accept a standard set of parameters, do the required processing based on the business rules and return a return code to the requesting application or object. These components can be shared with other applications in the enterprise that need to expose similar functionality. Other programs don't need to know the details of a component, only the required interface to get the desired results.

The Role of a Business Component

Business server components implement the business rules that drive your business. By encapsulating these business rules into server components the rules are available enterprise wide in individual components. The maintenance associated with the changes in your business rules are minimal because of the implementation of these components. There is only one component to be changed but this component immediately affects all applications using it.

A business component enforces the way data is handled, how processing decisions are made and how calculations are handled. In light of this, a business component should be designed to perform a very specific task or set of related tasks.

Keep in mind that these business components can be used by the various Web applications running on your intranet. Other front-end programs can also use them also. Basically any application, Web or otherwise, that needs to implement the business rules defined by you component can use your server component.

Typical Uses of Business Server Components

We mentioned that we could use business rules to define how we handle the retrieval and storage of data. Let's take a look back out our Authors Web server component. That component retrieved a list of authors and their published titles. If you take a look at the SQL statements that we used, you will discover that we joined two addition tables using specific criteria to select the required data. This could be defined as a business rule, a standard way to retrieve the authors and their published titles.

In this chapter we will create a business server component that will encapsulate the rules behind how we add, update and delete authors on the authors table in the Pubs database. Creating this component and sharing it with other applications that use the Pubs database will help ensure there is one standard method in performing these tasks and help to ensure data integrity.

If we take a look at the `Discounts` table in the `Pubs` database we will notice that there are several types of discounts available. A standard business rule could be defined to handle the calculation of these discounts and how they are applied.

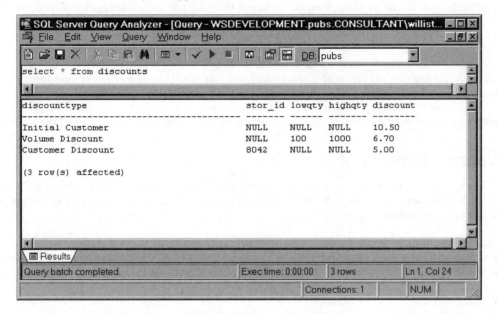

Let's assume that every Monday morning we create a sales report for management that details our top-selling book titles and gross sales for the past week. This process is to be performed the same way every week and is considered a business rule that we could incorporate into a business server component.

Types of Business Components

There are two types of ActiveX components that we can use to encapsulate our business rules and data, an **executable** (EXE) and a **dynamic link library** (DLL). Let's take a moment to examine each of these components and how they differ from one another.

An ActiveX EXE is an out-of-process component that runs in its own address space. Because this component runs in its own address space, it can run as a stand-alone server component and still expose objects to other applications. This component can process requests on an independent thread of execution and notify clients when their process is done, using asynchronous notification events or callbacks. This allows the client to continue with other work while the ActiveX EXE performs that client's requested task.

There is extra overhead associated with ActiveX EXEs because they run as out-of-process component and must communicate across process boundaries. The overhead of crossing over machine boundaries is even higher. You might wonder why you would use an ActiveX EXE server component. As an ActiveX component, the ActiveX EXE component implements COM. When used as a remote server, the ActiveX EXE implements DCOM and allows the server component to communicate with other applications and processes on other machines across the enterprise, running different operating systems.

An ActiveX DLL is an in-process component that runs in the same address space with the application that is using it. Because it runs in the same address space, an ActiveX DLL does not suffer the performance degradation of an ActiveX EXE because it does not have to cross process boundaries. An ActiveX DLL allows us to use apartment-model threading to provide synchronous access to objects. This means a multithreaded application can access the DLLs objects on multiple threads at the same time without the worry of cross-thread marshaling.

Cross-thread marshaling is when a multi-threaded client accesses multiple objects in a single threaded DLL. Let's assume that the client app accesses object-1 in the DLL. The client creates thread one to initialize the interface to the DLL and access obect-1. The client now needs to access object-2 in the DLL while object-1 is still processing. It creates thread two to access object-2. However, thread two must access object-2 in the DLL through thread one in the client, hence cross-thread marshaling.

In-Process Threading

Our discussion here today will be limited to threading of in-process components since that is what this chapter focuses on. See the MSDN library for further information on threading in general and out-of-process threading.

Basically when you create an ActiveX DLL in VB, you have two threading choices, Apartment-Model threading and Single threading. The options are listed in the General tab of the Project Properties dialog and by default the project is set to Apartment-Model threading. So what is Apartment-Model threading?

Apartment-Model threading means that all objects in the DLL created on a single thread from the client has it's own apartment. Objects in one apartment don't know about objects in another apartment. Each apartment has it's own copy of global data (public variables) and can not share them with other apartments. Using this type of threading in a component is considered thread-safe. This means that multi-threaded clients can safely access your component as shown in the diagram below.

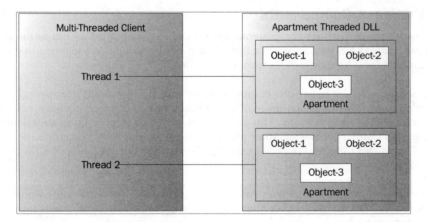

Single threaded components also use the apartment model, however a single threaded component has only one apartment. Thus calls to objects in this DLL from a multi-threaded client will use cross-thread marshaling which as we discussed above is not very efficient. The illustration below shows how cross-thread marshaling works with a single threaded DLL.

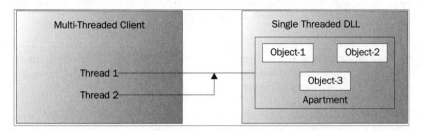

In-Process and Out-of-Process Components

If your component is implemented as a programmable object then it will run as an in-process component. A programmable object means that that component cannot run on it's own. It has methods and events that have to be invoked from other programs or components. Examples of this would be ActiveX Server Components (DLLs) and ActiveX Controls (OCX). These types of components need a host if you will, to be able to implement and execute any of their objects because they can not run in their own address space. In our case the Active Server Page becomes the host when we create a reference to the business server component using the `Server.CreateObject` method.

An ActiveX EXE is an out-of-process component because it can run as a stand-alone server. It implements it own logic and can also expose objects to other applications. Because this component runs in it's own address space and is independent it can create threads on which to expose objects. We discussed above that this type of component could process requests on an independent thread of execution and notify clients when their process is complete. Microsoft Word and Excel are good analogies to use when talking about out-of-process server components. This is because Word and Excel run as stand-alone applications but can also expose objects for use in other applications such as a Visual Basic application.

Interfacing with Other Services

There are a number of other services that are available for use by your business components on the web. These services come as part of Windows NT Server and will help to make your business components more functional and robust. We already know something about Internet Information Server (IIS) as that is the main focus of this book, but we will talk briefly about Microsoft Message Queuing (MSMQ) and Microsoft Transaction Server (MTS).

Because these services are integrated into the Windows NT Server operating system, you have the technology and leverage available to build feature rich business components. Visual Basic and Active Server Pages support these services through the COM interfaces of these services, which makes it even easier to integrate the functionality of these services into your business components.

Microsoft Message Queuing (MSMQ) allows applications across the enterprise to communicate with one another through the use of messages. These messages are delivered to queues, which the receiving application must retrieve. MSMQ guarantees delivery of messages in the order that they were sent which provides the security of knowing that once a message has been sent it will be received. This is especially important in networks that are less than reliable or slow in response time. This service is also integrated closely with MTS, IIS and ASP.

MSMQ implements asynchronous communications that allow your application to send messages and continue to process other tasks while waiting for an answer. The receiving application does not have to be running for your application to send a message. Once a message has been sent, it waits in a message queue for the receiving application to retrieve it.

If you think about the possibilities of MSMQ you can probably think of dozens of uses for it. But let's think about this for a minute. Supposed you have a Web site that sells books and a user wants to order a book. You only process orders once or twice a day so where is that order going to be placed? You could implement a business server component that is called from your Web page that will send the users' order to a message queue on your network. When you are ready to process the orders you log onto your Web site and pull all of the messages from the queue and process the orders.

Microsoft Transaction Server (MTS) is a component-based transaction processing system. MTS is ideal for three-tiered architecture because it can process individual transactions from ASP, or component based transactions from a Visual Basic ActiveX DLL business component. MTS provides the middle layer to help ensure data integrity from the front-end application to the backend database by managing the transactional business components.

Among the many features provided by MTS is the ability to manage a pool of database connections. SQL Server and Oracle are supported through the use of ODBC compliant drivers. MTS can manage the data integrity of a transaction that performs updates to both types of databases at the same time.

Using the previous discussion about the book order, we could build a business server component that will place the orders you request from your Web page into the database. Using MTS transactions in our business server component will insure all orders are placed on the database without having the worry about something going wrong and having corrupt data in the database.

Chapter 11 will cover these and other services in more detail. It is important to know about these services so that you are aware of the features that you are able to incorporate into your business components.

ActiveX Data Objects

ActiveX Data Objects (ADO) is part of the Microsoft Data Access Components (MDAC), which also includes Remote Data Services (RDS), OLE DB and Open Database Connectivity (ODBC). These components together make up Microsoft's Universal Data Access (**UDA**) strategy that allows access to relational and non-relational data across the enterprise.

ADO provides a lightweight object with high-performance access to data. Designed to provide access to any type of data store, ADO has replaced Data Access Objects (DAO) and Remote Data Objects (RDO) as the preferred data access method. ADO was designed to be easy to learn and use as evidenced by its programming model.

ADO Programming Model

The ADO programming object model is very simple and you can see from the diagram why it outperforms DAO and RDO.

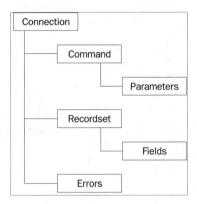

The `Connection` object is at the very heart of the model and allows you to connect to the data store. All other objects in this model are derived from the `Connection` object. Once a connection is made, it is used to execute commands and transactions.

The `Command` object defines SQL strings, stored procedures and action queries. The `Command` object is an optional object in the model as not all data sources support command execution. Associated with the `Command` object is the `Parameters` collection, which allows you to create parameters for execution with a command.

The `Recordset` object should be familiar to everyone who has done database programming before. Also known as a cursor, the `Recordset` object now supports a number of new parameters that make programming with the `Recordset` object easier. The `Fields` collection contains all the information about a field in the recordset such as the field name in the database, the data type, attributes and the actual value of the field.

The `Error` object is also an optional object. The `Error` object is used to hold all the details pertaining to a single error from an OLEDB provider. It is used in conjunction with the **Errors** collection which can hold any number of `Error` objects.

Common Techniques

This section will demonstrate the most common techniques of ADO. All of the examples presented here use SQL Server as the database. You can find plenty of examples using ADO with SQL strings but finding examples of using ADO with stored procedures is difficult, so they are covered here in detail.

All of these examples are taken from real projects so you can use the code samples where they apply to you and provide your own stored procedures. These samples are only provided as a guide and to demonstrate the common techniques that you might run across. The Microsoft online documentation provides plenty of examples of using ADO with SQL strings.

Variable Declarations

The first thing that must be done is to define your variable declarations for accessing ADO. Normally these declarations are defined in the General Declarations section of your form, module or class. This example shows the common declarations. You must also set a reference to ADO in the References dialog.

```
Private m_objConn As New ADODB.Connection
Private m_objCmd As New ADODB.Command
Private m_objRS As New ADODB.Recordset
Private m_objErrors As ADODB.Errors
Private m_objErr As Error
```

Notice that the variables are declared as `Private`. This will indicate that the variables are only accessible to the form, module, or class in which they are defined. Declare the variables as `Public` to share them with all forms, modules, and classes in your project.

Establishing a Connection

There are two ways to establish a connection. The most popular method is to use a Data Source Name (DSN) as we did in the last chapter. Let's take a look at it again.

```
m_objConn.ConnectionTimeout = 30
m_objConn.CommandTimeout = 30
m_objConn.Open "Pubs Connection", "your ID here", "your password here"
```

There are other defaults that can be set at connection time and you should look at the `Connection` object in the Object Browser in Visual Basic to see a list of all available options.

If your program needs to provide a dynamic connection to multiple databases then you can create a dynamic DSN on the fly. Your program needs to provide the user with some options such as which server the database resides on, the available databases on that server, and a place to enter a User ID and Password. Once you have all of this information you can create a dynamic connection as show in this example.

```
m_objConn.ConnectionTimeout = 30
m_objConn.CommandTimeout = 30
m_objConn.Open "driver={sql server}; server=" & _
    cboServer.List(cboServer.ListIndex) & _
    "; uid=" & txtUserID.Text & _
    "; pwd=" & txtPassword.Text & _
    "; database=" & cboDB.List(cboDB.ListIndex)
```

We are getting the server name and database names from a combo box in which the user has selected their choices and the User ID and Password are coming from text boxes.

Using the Errors Collection

The first thing that we want to do is set up a generic error handler in our code to handle all the errors. The error handler demonstrated here is very simplistic in design and you will need to write one that meets your standards and requirements. I wrote a generic Errors ActiveX DLL that handles the logging of all errors from the ActiveX Data Objects to be used as a common error handler for all programs. This is something that might be worth doing so all error handling is performed in a consistent manner.

The code below will first set the error object to the database errors collection and then we are able to loop through the errors collection logging all errors.

```
SQLErr:
  Set m_objErrors = m_objConn.Errors
  For Each m_objErr In m_objErrors
    strError = m_objErr.Description & "," & CStr(m_objErr.NativeError) _
        & "," & CStr(m_objErr.Number) & "," & m_objErr.Source _
        & "," & CStr(m_objErr.SQLState)
    App.LogEvent strError, vbLogEventTypeError
  Next
```

Using the Command Object

The Command object is most useful in receiving a return value from a stored procedure that does not return any records but only a return value. This type of stored procedure can perform processing based on the parameters you passed it and perform inserts, updates and deletes on the database and return a value indicating its success or failure. The stored procedure could also just return a value for a numeric key so that you can process records based on that key.

This example shows you how to use the Command object to call a stored procedure passing it values and then processing based on the return value.

```
Set m_objCmd.ActiveConnection = m_objConn

m_objCmd.CommandText = "{? = call dbo.myprocedure ('" & strParameter1 & _
                    "', " & lngParameter2 & ")}"
m_objCmd(0).Direction = adParamReturnValue
m_objCmd.Execute

If m_objCmd(0) <> 0 Then
  'An error occurred
Else
  'Everthing is good

End If
```

The first thing that we did was to set the Command object that we declared in the General Declarations section to the active Connection object.

Next, we set the text of the CommandText to the stored procedure that we want to call and passed it the appropriate parameters. The first parameter is a string parameter that we declared as a string variable and the second parameter is a long parameter that we declared as a long variable.

Remember that this stored procedure will pass back a return value, which is a long data type that we want to check for success or failure and process based on the value. The `CommandText` is set up with a question mark `?` indicating a placeholder for the return value. We then had to tell the `Command` object which direction the parameter was going; in this case it was a return value.

Using the Recordset Object

Most of our processing will be with the recordset object since we want to get a set of records and process them based on the values of those records. There are several common techniques that we will use here. These may vary depending on your circumstances, but these examples will give you a solid foundation to build on. The examples are broken down into different sections based upon the type of processing to be performed with the recordsets.

Read-Only, Forward-Only

This first example builds a string value using a stored procedure and input parameters. Once we have built the string we can then open the recordset by passing the string as a parameter. This example is a read-only, one directional recordset. This means that you cannot apply updates to the records and you can only move forward in the recordset.

```
strSQL = "dbo.up_parmsel_top_selling_books ('" & strAuthor & "')"
m_objRS.Open strSQL, m_objConn, adOpenForwardOnly, , adCmdStoredProc
```

Notice that there is one parameter missing in our open statement. This is the record locking method to be used on this recordset. Since we are only going to read this recordset and not process any updates on it we can omit the default `adLockReadOnly` parameter.

The other parameters, listed in order, are the SQL string to be executed, the active `Connection` object, the cursor type (in this case we are only reading forward) and the options. The `adCmdStoredProc` parameter tells SQL Server that we are executing a stored procedure.

If we want to be able to navigate this recordset using `Move`, `MoveFirst`, `MoveLast`, `MovePrevious` and `MoveNext` then we would need to specify the `adOpenDynamic` parameter for the cursor type.

Another alternative method to executing the above stored procedure is to use this syntax.

```
Set m_objRS = m_objConn.Execute("dbo.up_parmsel_top_selling_books ('" & _
              strAuthor & "')", lngRecords, adCmdStoredProc)
```

When you use this method, the recordset returned is always read only and is always forward only. The extra parameter (`lngRecords`) that you see in this new statement is used by the data provider to return the number of records affected.

Multiple Recordsets in One Recordset Object

There may be a time when you want to generate multiple read-only, forward-only recordsets in one recordset object. This would come in handy in a disconnected recordset, which will be demonstrated after this example. The first thing we want to look at is the stored procedure that we will be calling. This stored procedure was created on SQL Server with the following code. You will notice that the stored procedure is actually executing two separate stored procedures. This is where we get multiple recordsets. The stored procedure will return a recordset for each of the stored procedures it executes here.

```
create procedure up_select_muliple_recordsets as

exec up_select_authors_by_title
exec up_select_authors_by_first_name
```

In order to process multiple recordsets that are returned from SQL Server, we need to set up our code like this.

```
Set m_objRS = m_objConn.Execute("dbo.up_select_muliple_recordsets", , _
            adCmdStoredProc)

Do While Not m_objRS.EOF
  List1.AddItem m_objRS!Title
  m_objRS.MoveNext
Loop

Set m_objRS = m_objRS.NextRecordset()

Do While Not m_objRS.EOF
  List2.AddItem m_objRS!au_fname
  m_objRS.MoveNext
Loop
```

We execute our stored procedure as usual and process the first recordset also as usual. Once we have reached an end of file condition on the first recordset we need to get the next recordset for processing. Using the NextRecordset method of the Recordset object, the next recordset will be set as the current recordset for processing.

Disconnected Recordsets

This next example demonstrates the use of disconnected recordsets.

```
strSQL = "dbo.up_select_authors_by_title"
m_objRs.CursorLocation = adUseClient
m_objRs.Open strSQL, m_objConn, adOpenDynamic, , adCmdStoredProc
Set m_objRs.ActiveConnection = Nothing
Call CloseDatabase
```

Notice that we have to set the recordsets cursor to adUseClient in order to be able to use a disconnected recordset. After we open the Recordset, we need to set its active connection to nothing and then close the database. We can then process the recordset in any fashion needed.

Using Batch Recordset Updating

When you need to process all records in a Recordset and make changes you can update the records on the database one at a time or use the batch update method. There are some special notes to observe when using this method. First, you must use the `adOpenKeyset` or `adOpenStatic` cursor. Next you must set the lock method to `adLockBatchOptimistic`.

```
m_objRS.Open "dbo.up_select_authors_by_title", objConn, adOpenKeyset, _
  adLockBatchOptimistic, adCmdStoredProc

Do While Not m_objRS.EOF
  'Update your recordset fields
  m_objRS.MoveNext
Loop

m_objRS.UpdateBatch
m_objRS.Close
```

Once you have finished applying your updates to the recordset, you need to call the `UpdateBatch` method of the `Recordset` to apply the changes to the database. If only some of the records are updated then a warning is returned. If all updates fail an error is returned. You can use the `Errors` collection to enumerate the warnings or errors.

Using Single Recordset Updates

You might want to update a single record at a time especially when writing a front-end program that allows the user to navigate and update records. In this case you would want to call the `Update()` method of the `Recordset` when the user clicks on the **Update** button. The code below illustrates the use of a single update.

```
m_objRS.Open "dbo.up_select_authors_by_last_name", m_objConn, _
  adOpenKeyset, adLockPessimistic, adCmdStoredProc
m_objRS!au_fname = txtFirstName.Text
m_objRS.Update
```

You could use the locking parameter `adLockOptimistic` instead of `adLockPessimistic`. The difference between the two is that when you use `adLockOptimistic` the record is only locked when you call `Update()` on the recordset. When you use `adLockPessimistic` the record is locked immediately upon editing the record in your recordset. You must determine which is best for your particular situation.

Updating Using a Stored Procedure

Sometimes you need to open a read-only recordset and process the records calling a stored procedure to process some type of update as you are working on the data in the recordset. To perform this type of update use the code illustrated below.

```
strSQL = "dbo.up_parmupd_author_address ('" & strAuthorKey & "', '" & _
  strNewAddress & "')"
m_objConn.Execute strSQL
```

This type of update could perform updates to multiple tables depending on what is coded in the stored procedure you are calling.

Using the Fields Collection

At some point in your coding you will come across a situation where you will need to access the Fields collection of a Recordset. This collection can tell you everything about a field in the Recordset. This information is very useful if you find yourself having to build dynamic SQL on the fly. Below is a listing of some of the more common elements of the Fields collection.

```
m_objRS.Open "dbo.up_select_authors_by_last_name", m_objConn, _
    adOpenForwardOnly, adLockReadOnly, adCmdStoredProc

intIndex = 0

'Display the number of fields in the recordset
Debug.Print m_objRS.Fields.Count                   'Displays 4

'Display the field name
Debug.Print m_objRS.Fields(intIndex).Name          'Displays au_lname

'Display the data type
Debug.Print m_objRS.Fields(intIndex).Type          'Displays 200

'Display the data in this field
Debug.Print m_objRS.Fields(intIndex).Value         'Displays Bennet

'Display the actual size of the field
Debug.Print m_objRS.Fields(intIndex).ActualSize    'Displays 6

m_objRS.Close
```

To see a list of all the data type properties associated with the Fields collection open the object browser in Visual Basic and click on DataTypeEnum in the Classes column of the display. If you scroll down the list on the right and click on adVarChar you will see the constant value at the bottom of the display.

ADO Summary

We have demonstrated the most common techniques for using ADO. As you can see by the examples, ADO is very easy to use and you can now understand why ADO is fast becoming the preferred data access method to use. ADO is also very powerful and easy to implement in Visual Basic as well as in ASP. If you are hungry for more details then you can read more in the appendix or purchase one of the good books that Wrox publishes on this subject. Now let's move on to actually building our component since you should have a good grasp of the capabilities of ADO.

The AuthorData Business Component

Before we start coding our business component we need to define the business rules surrounding our component. That is, what tasks do we want to perform in our component and what are the business rules to perform these tasks?

Let's start with what we want to accomplish. We want our business component to handle the inserting, updating and deleting of authors, their addresses and phone numbers. Our component will expose three interfaces, one for Add(), one for Update() and one for Delete().

Next, we need to determine the business rules surrounding these tasks. These business rules are the preferred and standard method of inserting, updating and deleting authors.

Insert Business Rules

The authors' table has a key, which consists of the authors' social security number. Before we can insert a new author, we need to validate the required fields. In this case the following fields will be required:

Field Description	Data Type	Valid Format
Social Security Number	varchar(11)	format(999-99-9999)
First Name	varchar(20)	
Last Name	varchar(40)	
Phone Number	char(12)	format(999-999-9999)
State	char(2)	valid state abbreviation
Contract	bit	valid number (1,0)

As you can see in the fields above, the Social Security Number and the Phone Number have special formatting that must be adhered to; this is a business rule. We will validate that all of the required fields are present and validate the fields that must be formatted or contain valid data.

The Contract field must be supplied with an integer value of 0 or 1. Since this is meaningless to the user updating the fields on a form, we will accept the values of either 1, 0, True or False. If the values of True or False are passed they will be converted to 1 and 0 respectively.

The Address is a varchar(40) field and is not required so no validation is necessary, other than to truncate any extra length. You could check the length and if over 40 characters reject the insert but this really isn't necessary.

The City is a varchar(20) field and the same rules apply to the City field as they do for the Address field.

The State field must contain the two-character abbreviation for state so we need to validate that two characters being passed are valid state abbreviations.

The Zip field is a char(5) field and must contain all five digits of the zip code. Since validating actual zip codes is not practical for this example, we will only validate that all five characters are present.

Update Business Rules

In order to update a record, we require that the `Author` key be present. Only the fields that should be updated should be passed. In other words, all fields will be optional parameters except for the Social Security Number.

All validation of the data will be performed as described above.

Delete Business Rules

The author's key (`Social Security Number`) along with the author's `First Name` and `Last Name` will be required before a delete can take place. We will validate that this data matches the table before we perform the delete.

Stored Procedures

Let's go ahead and build our stored procedures. We will be using the `Pubs` database that we used in the last chapter. We will be creating three stored procedures, one for each of the functions that we want to perform. The first stored procedure we want to create will be to insert authors. Use the code below to create your stored procedure.

We are keeping the stored procedures simple for our examples. You might want to add more error handling and checking in your stored procedures. These stored procedures do not take into account for foreign key relationships and as such will not delete the existing authors; you can only delete the authors you insert. You can however, update all existing authors.

```
CREATE PROCEDURE up_parmins_authors (@ssn varchar(11), @last_name varchar(40),
    @first_name varchar(20), @phone char(12), @address varchar(40),
    @city varchar(20), @state char(2), @zip char(5), @contract bit) as

-- ****************************************************************************
-- * Insert a new author
-- ****************************************************************************

INSERT INTO authors
    (au_id, au_lname, au_fname, phone, address, city, state, zip, contract)
    VALUES(@ssn, @last_name, @first_name, @phone, @address, @city, @state, @zip,
        @contract)
```

Notice how we specify the actual column names in the insert statement, followed by the actual values that we are inserting. This is a good practice to follow and allows for expansion of the table without affecting your code. We can now safely add a new column to the table, and we do not have to worry about our stored procedure returning an error specifying that not enough input parameters are present.

We have already explored a method to update rows in the database using `Update()` and `BatchUpdate()` so now we are going to explore a different approach. This method of updating rows will involve the use of a stored procedure.

This next stored procedure to update authors might look intimidating at first glance but is really quite simple. Since we do not know what parameters will contain data we need to check the length of the parameters and build the SQL string to execute, updating only the columns that have updates to be applied. Let's step through this code one line at a time.

```
CREATE procedure up_parmupd_authors (@ssn varchar(11), @last_name varchar(40),
   @first_name varchar(20), @phone char(12), @address varchar(40),
   @city varchar(20), @state char(2), @zip char(5), @contract varchar(1)) as

-- *********************************************************************
-- * Update an existing author
-- * Declare variables
-- *********************************************************************

declare @buf varchar(500)

-- *********************************************************************
-- * Start building the SQL string
-- *********************************************************************

select @buf = 'update authors set '

-- *********************************************************************
-- * Check the length of each parameter passed and append it to the SQL
-- * string if the length is > 0
-- *********************************************************************

if datalength(@last_name) > 0
   select @buf = @buf + 'au_lname = ''' + @last_name + ''', '

if datalength(@first_name) > 0
   select @buf = @buf + 'au_fname = ''' + @first_name + ''', '

if datalength(rtrim(convert(varchar(12),@phone))) > 0
   select @buf = @buf + 'phone = ''' + @phone + ''', '

if datalength(@address) > 0
   select @buf = @buf + 'address = ''' + @address + ''', '

if datalength(@city) > 0
   select @buf = @buf + 'city = ''' + @city + ''', '

if datalength(rtrim(convert(varchar(2),@state))) > 0
   select @buf = @buf + 'state = ''' + @state + ''', '

if datalength(rtrim(convert(varchar(5),@zip))) > 0
   select @buf = @buf + 'zip = ''' + @zip + ''', '

if datalength(@contract) > 0
   select @buf = @buf + 'contract = ' + cast(@contract as char(1))

-- *********************************************************************
-- * Finish building the SQL string
-- *********************************************************************

if rtrim(right(@buf,2)) = ', '
   select @buf = substring(@buf,1,datalength(@buf)-2)
   select @buf = @buf + ' where au_id = ''' + @ssn + ''''

-- *********************************************************************
-- * Execute the SQL string
-- *********************************************************************
exec(@buf)
```

The first thing we want to do is declare a variable for the SQL string we are going to be building. We are defining this variable as a `varchar` field that will contain 500 characters.

If you are using SQL Server 6.5 you are limited to 255 characters for this variable which would be plenty. I wanted to make this variable larger so readers would know that the limits in SQL Server 7.0 have been increased. The actual limit for a varchar field in SQL Server 7.0 is 8,000 characters.

The next thing we want to do in our stored procedure is to start building the SQL string. Next, we start checking the length of each field and if it is greater than zero we append the correct statement to the SQL string. Each field is passed as parameters to this stored procedure. If a field is not to be updated then the field will contain no data.

Checking the `datalength` for the `varchar` fields poses no problems. The problem arises when we come to a `char` field. Here even if no data is present we have a space representing each character. The solution to this problem is to convert the `char` field to a `varchar` field with the same number of characters and then trim the spaces from it. This must only be done in the evaluation statement, which does not alter the actual data field.

There is one other little snag that we run into here. In order to have the `@contract` variable as an optional variable we need to pass it as a `varchar(1)` field. This variable must be a bit when it is updated in SQL Server so we must `cast` this variable to a `char(1)` data type.

> **Note to SQL Server 6.5 users: the `cast` command is new to SQL Server 7.0 so you must use the `convert` command. The syntax is:** convert(char(1),@contract)

The reason that we convert it to a `char(1)` data type instead of a bit data type is because we are using the plus sign + to concatenate our string. If we used a bit data type, SQL Server would try to add this field to our string instead of concatenating it to a string.

In order to finish building our SQL string we must check the second to the last character for a comma. If it is a comma we need to get rid of it using the `substring()` function. Once this is done we set our `where` clause of the SQL string and then execute the string.

The last stored procedure we need to create is one to delete authors. Remember that our business rule states that the author's first and last name must be passed to the stored procedure along with the social security number. We will validate the first and last name against the data on the table before deleting the author. Doing this will leave no doubt that this is the correct row that the caller wanted to delete.

```
CREATE PROCEDURE up_parmdel_authors (@ssn varchar(11), @last_name varchar(40),
    @first_name varchar(20)) as

-- ************************************************************************
-- * Delete an existing author
-- * Declare variables
-- ************************************************************************
```

```
DECLARE @au_last_name  varchar(40),
  @au_first_name varchar(20),
  @return_status int

SELECT @return_status = 0

-- *****************************************************************
-- * Select the authors first and last name
-- *****************************************************************

SELECT @au_last_name = au_lname, @au_first_name = au_fname
  FROM authors
  WHERE au_id = @ssn

-- *****************************************************************
-- * Compare the authors first and last name and set the @return_status if
-- * they are not equal
-- *****************************************************************

if @au_last_name <> @last_name
  SELECT @return_status = 1

if @au_first_name <> @first_name
  SELECT @return_status = 2

-- *****************************************************************
-- * Only delete the author if the @return_status = 0
-- *****************************************************************

if @return_status = 0
  DELETE authors
    WHERE au_id = @ssn

-- *****************************************************************
-- * Return to the caller
-- *****************************************************************

RETURN @return_status
```

If you take a close look at this stored procedure, you can see we are selecting the authors' last and first name into some variables that will be used for the comparison. The next step is the comparison of the last and first names. If neither names match, then a return status is set accordingly.

The next step checks the @return_status variable for a zero value. If it is zero, then the author is deleted and a zero return status is returned to the caller. If the @return_status variable is not equal to zero, then the delete is bypassed and the return status is returned to the caller with the appropriate value.

AuthorData Project

Now that we know what tasks to perform and the business rules we need to perform those tasks, and we have the stored procedures built, we need to start building our business component.

In the last chapter we had duplicated some variable declarations and some code to keep the project simple while you got your feet wet building an ActiveX DLL. This chapter will show you how to share those declarations and the common code.

Start a new Visual Basic ActiveX DLL project. Set the project name to **AuthorData** and the class name to **Authors**. Leave the Instancing property set to **MultiUse**. We are going to use `Authors` for the class name to `Add`, `Update` and `Delete` authors. If we want to come back later and add some additional functionality to `Add`, `Update` and `Delete` author titles then we could add a class called `Titles` at that point.

We are going to read and write from the system registry so we need to add a class called `clsRegistry`. Make sure to set the Instancing property to `Private`, as we will not expose any interfaces to other programs in this class. Notice that we prefixed the class name with `cls`. This is preferred since we are not going to expose this class as an interface. Add a new module with the name `modDBAccess`. This module will provide global access to the database objects to all classes in this project.

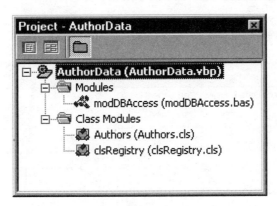

Project Properties

Let's go ahead and set all of the project properties as we did in the last chapter. Set the project description as shown in this dialog:

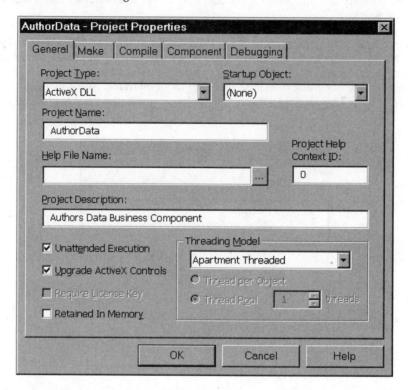

Fill in the descriptions of your choice on the **Make** tab as you did in the previous chapter. Make sure you check the box to auto increment the version number. Set the base address to &H11180000 on the **Compile** tab. Once done, click **OK** to save the changes you have made.

References

We need to set a reference to ADO in the References dialog. Click on the latest version of ADO that you have available. If you recall in the last chapter we also set a reference to the Active Server Pages Object Library. While this business server component will also be called from our Web page, it does not interact with our Web page in the same manner as our Web server component did and thus we do not need this reference.

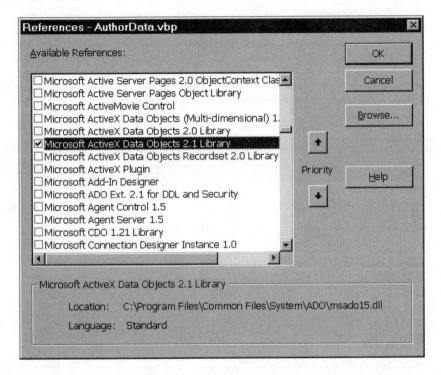

Registry Class

In our last component we read the database connect string and timeout values from the Session and Application ScriptingContext objects. These objects are not available to us in this project so we need to get those values from somewhere else. We could read the global.asa file where those values are stored but that's not very efficient. We could hard code the values but that is definitely not the way to go. We need to be able to dynamically change the values and have them effective immediately. The best place to get those values is from the system registry.

We need to read and write all the values from the HKEY_LOCAL_MACHINE hive of the registry as this business component will be running on a server where no user is logged on. The HKEY_CURRENT_USER hive is only accessible if a user is logged on to the server whereas the HKEY_LOCAL_MACHINE hive is accessible to all programs, even if no user is logged on.

We need to define a set of private variables that will be used to store the values read from the registry. We also need to declare some public enumerations and private constants in the clsRegistry class.

This is a good time to introduce you to the VB Class Builder Utility if you are not already familiar with it. Have you ever used the object browser to browse the objects in your projects such as the VB library? Ever notice that when you click on a method, event, or property that the bottom pane of the display gives you the format of the method, event, or property and also gives you a description of what it performs? Well, we can do all of these things in our ActiveX DLL with the **VB Class Builder Utility**.

To ensure the VB 6 Class Builder Utility loads on startup and is loaded, click on the **Add-Ins** menu and click on **Add-In Manager**. Find the **VB 6 Class Builder Utility** from the list of available add-ins and click on that entry. Click on the **Loaded/Unloaded** and **Load on Startup** check boxes. This will load the VB 6 Class Builder Utility and ensure it loads the next time you start Visual Basic.

While we are here we also need to make sure the API Viewer entry is loaded and loads at startup. Find the VB 6 API Viewer in the list and perform the same steps as above. Click **OK** to close the Add-In Manager dialog.

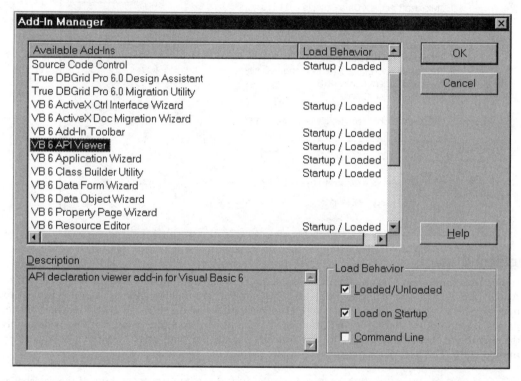

Start the VB Class Builder Utility by going to the **Add-Ins** menu and clicking on Class Builder Utility. No class is active until you click on the class name but notice how our classes in the project are listed here. Click on the `clsRegistry` class so we can add our public enumerations and then click on the **Enumeration** toolbar button. We want to add a public enumeration for **RegDataTypes** as illustrated in the dialog below.

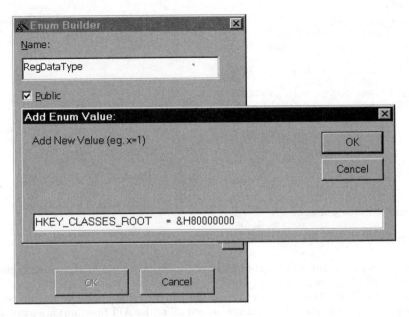

Add all of the following constants to the enumeration.

```
HKEY_CLASSES_ROOT        =   &H80000000
HKEY_CURRENT_USER        =   &H80000001
HKEY_LOCAL_MACHINE       =   &H80000002
HKEY_USERS               =   &H80000003
HKEY_PERFORMANCE_DATA    =   &H80000004
HKEY_CURRENT_CONFIG      =   &H80000005
HKEY_DYN_DATA            =   &H80000006
```

Click **OK** to save the enumeration. These constants came from Win32API constants declarations in the API Viewer. These constants are used by the registry APIs to access the different hives of the registry. We put these constants in an enumeration so we do not have to remember which constants to use. They are automatically displayed for us in a drop down list when we are typing the parameters for a function that uses this enumeration.

We need to add one other public enumeration for **KeyTypes** with the following constants.

```
REG_SZ                   =   1
REG_DWORD                =   4
```

To add the enumerations to your class, click on the **File** menu and then click on **Update Project**. Exit the VB Class Builder Utility.

You see the following enumerations in the `clsRegistry` class minus the comments. Add the two private constants shown in this code fragment.

```
'Declare enumerations
Public Enum RegDataType
    HKEY_CLASSES_ROOT = &H80000000
    HKEY_CURRENT_USER = &H80000001
    HKEY_LOCAL_MACHINE = &H80000002
    HKEY_USERS = &H80000003
    HKEY_PERFORMANCE_DATA = &H80000004
    HKEY_CURRENT_CONFIG = &H80000005
    HKEY_DYN_DATA = &H80000006
End Enum

Public Enum KeyTypes
    REG_SZ = 1
    REG_DWORD = 4
End Enum

'Declare private constants
Private Const KEY_ALL_ACCESS = &H3F
Private Const REG_OPTION_NON_VOLATILE = 0
```

We need to declare all of the API functions that we are going to use to access the registry. Instead of trying to key in all of this code from the book, it would be safer to use the API viewer from the Add-Ins menu of Visual Basic. However, if you have the patience it might be preferable typing all of this in, or downloading it from the Wrox website, as not all of the API functions are available to the viewer.

While this is not the complete list of registry APIs, this is a list of the APIs we need to read and write our keys.

```
'Declare registry APIs
Private Declare Function RegCloseKey Lib "advapi32.dll" (ByVal hKey As Long) _
    As Long

Private Declare Function RegCreateKeyEx Lib "advapi32.dll" Alias _
    "RegCreateKeyExA" (ByVal hKey As Long, ByVal lpSubKey As String, _
    ByVal Reserved As Long, ByVal lpClass As String, ByVal dwOptions _
    As Long, ByVal samDesired As Long, ByVal lpSecurityAttributes As _
    Long, phkResult As Long, lpdwDisposition As Long) As Long

Private Declare Function RegOpenKeyEx Lib "advapi32.dll" Alias _
    "RegOpenKeyExA" (ByVal hKey As Long, ByVal lpSubKey As String, _
    ByVal ulOptions As Long, ByVal samDesired As Long, phkResult _
    As Long) As Long

Private Declare Function RegQueryValueExString Lib "advapi32.dll" Alias _
    "RegQueryValueExA" (ByVal hKey As Long, ByVal lpValueName As _
    String, ByVal lpReserved As Long, lpType As Long, ByVal lpData _
    As String, lpcbData As Long) As Long

Private Declare Function RegQueryValueExLong Lib "advapi32.dll" Alias _
    "RegQueryValueExA" (ByVal hKey As Long, ByVal lpValueName As _
    String, ByVal lpReserved As Long, lpType As Long, lpData As _
    Long, lpcbData As Long) As Long
```

```
Private Declare Function RegQueryValueExNULL Lib "advapi32.dll" Alias _
   "RegQueryValueExA" (ByVal hKey As Long, ByVal lpValueName As _
   String, ByVal lpReserved As Long, lpType As Long, ByVal lpData _
   As Long, lpcbData As Long) As Long

Private Declare Function RegSetValueExString Lib "advapi32.dll" Alias _
   "RegSetValueExA" (ByVal hKey As Long, ByVal lpValueName As _
   String, ByVal Reserved As Long, ByVal dwType As Long, ByVal _
   lpValue As String, ByVal cbData As Long) As Long

Private Declare Function RegSetValueExLong Lib "advapi32.dll" Alias _
   "RegSetValueExA" (ByVal hKey As Long, ByVal lpValueName As _
   String, ByVal Reserved As Long, ByVal dwType As Long, lpValue _
   As Long, ByVal cbData As Long) As Long
```

The first method we need to create is one that will create new keys. This function will accept a string parameter for the section name and a string parameter for the key name to create and a long value specifying the hive of the registry to use.

Start up the VB Class Builder Utility again and click on the `clsRegistry` class. Click on the **Add New Method** toolbar button and give the method a name of `CreateKey` and add the following arguments:

```
ByVal strSectionName As String
ByVal strKey As String
Optional ByVal lngRegDataType As RegDataType = HKEY_LOCAL_MACHINE
```

The easiest way that I could illustrate how to do this is by stepping through the third argument.

- ➢ Press the + key
- ➢ Enter `lngRegDataType` as the name of the argument
- ➢ Click the **ByVal** and **Optional** check boxes
- ➢ Set the **Data Type** as **RegDataType**
- ➢ Enter **HKEY_LOCAL_MACHINE** as the default argument
- ➢ Click on **OK**

The return data type is a long value. While its not important here, take notice of the **Attributes** tab of this dialog. Here we can specify any comments about this method and also specify a `Help Context ID` number that corresponds to a `Help ID` number that maps to a help topic in the help file that you write.

The parameter `lngRegDataType` is defined as `RegDataType`. This is our enumeration of registry datatypes. We also define this parameter as optional and gave it a default value. Using the enumeration will automatically give you a dropdown list of the available constants for `lngRegDataType` when you are typing the parameters for this function. The return value returns zero on success or the error code if it failed.

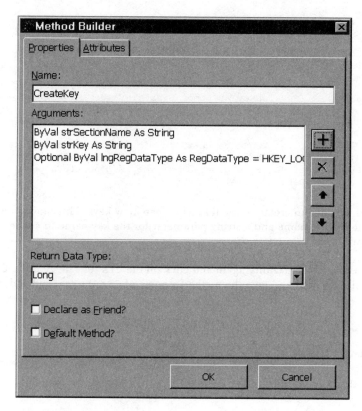

Add the following two methods using the same procedures as above.

QueryKeyValue:

```
ByVal strSectionName As String
ByVal strKeyName As String
Optional ByVal lngRegDataType As RegDataType = HKEY_LOCAL_MACHINE

Return value as Long
```

SetKeyValue:

```
ByVal strSectionName As String
ByVal strKeyName As String
ByVal varKeyData As Variant
ByVal lngKeyType As KeyTypes
Optional ByVal lngRegDataType As RegDataType = HKEY_LOCAL_MACHINE

Return value as Long
```

We need to add two properties to retrieve the values returned from the QueryKeyValue() method. These properties will return a long value and a string value.

To add the properties, click on the **Add New Property** toolbar button, enter a name of
`LongKeyValue` and set the data type to a `Long`.

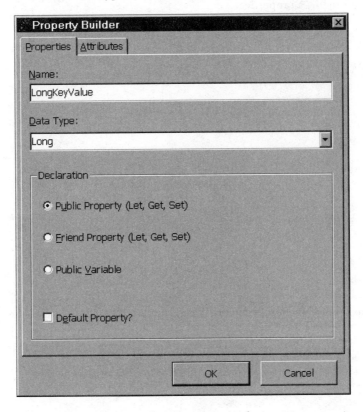

Add another property for `StringKeyValue()` and set its data type to a `String`.

Click on the **File** menu and then click on **Update Project** to add the code you have just created to the
class.

Go to the **General Declarations** section of the `clsRegistry` class and modify the two variables as
shown.

```
'local variable(s) to hold property value(s)
Private mvarLongKeyValue As Long 'local copy

'local variable(s) to hold property value(s)
Private mvarStringKeyValue As String 'local copy

'becomes...

'Declare private variables
Private m_lngKeyValue As Long
Private m_strKeyValue As String
```

The VB Class Builder Utility creates two public properties for us, one to let the user retrieve a value (Get) and one to let the user set a value (Let). Since both of these properties need to be read-only delete the code for the Let properties.

Modify the code for the two Get properties as shown in the code below.

```
Public Property Get LongKeyValue() As Long
    LongKeyValue = m_lngKeyValue
End Property

Public Property Get StringKeyValue() As String
    StringKeyValue = m_strKeyValue
End Property
```

Add the following code to the CreateKey function.

```
Public Function CreateKey(ByVal strSectionName As String, ByVal strKey As _
    String, Optional ByVal lngRegDataType As RegDataType = _
    HKEY_LOCAL_MACHINE) As Long

    'Create a new key
    CreateKey = CreateKeyEx(strSectionName & strKey, lngRegDataType)

End Function
```

This next function is the function that actually calls the Registry API to create the key. We want to keep this function private so no other part of the code can call it. The only steps that are performed by these two functions are to create the section name and the key. No key values are set here.

```
Private Function CreateKeyEx(strSectionName As String, Optional _
    lngRegDataType As Long = HKEY_LOCAL_MACHINE) As Long

    'Declare variables
    Dim lngHwd As Long
    Dim lngRC As Long

    'Create the key and close it
    lngRC = RegCreateKeyEx(lngRegDataType, strSectionName, 0&, _
        vbNullString, REG_OPTION_NON_VOLATILE, KEY_ALL_ACCESS, 0&, lngHwd, _
        lngRC)

    RegCloseKey (lngHwd)

    'Return with the return code
    CreateKeyEx = lngRC

End Function
```

Now that we have our key created, we need a method to set the values for that key. This next function was created using the VB Class Builder Utility and serves as the top-level access to our code that we call to create the key values. The section name and key name are passed as strings. The actual key data is passed as a variant so that we can use this function to pass string and long key data. The KeyTypes enumeration is set here to display a list of valid key types for the programmer.

```
Public Function SetKeyValue(ByVal strSectionName As String, ByVal _
    strKeyName As String, ByVal varKeyData As Variant, ByVal lngKeyType _
    As KeyTypes, Optional ByVal lngRegDataType As RegDataType = _
    HKEY_LOCAL_MACHINE) As Long

    'Declare variables
    Dim lngRC As Long
    Dim lngHwd As Long

    'Open the key, set the value and close the key
    lngRC = RegOpenKeyEx(lngRegDataType, strSectionName, 0, _
        KEY_ALL_ACCESS, lngHwd)
    lngRC = SetValueEx(lngHwd, strKeyName, lngKeyType, varKeyData)

    RegCloseKey (lngHwd)

    'Return with the return code
    SetKeyValue = lngRC

End Function
```

Before we can read or write a key we must first open it. If it does not exist, the registry API will create it for us. When we are done reading or writing the key value we must close the key.

This next function is the actual function to set the value of the new or existing key. Notice that we are passing the key value as a variant data type. This function will determine the correct data type and must be coded as a Private.

```
Private Function SetValueEx(ByVal lngHwdKey As Long, ByVal strValueName _
    As String, ByVal lngType As Long, ByVal varValueData As Variant) _
    As Long

    'Declare variables
    Dim lngValue As Long
    Dim strValue As String

    'Determine the size and type of data to be written
    Select Case lngType

        'Strings
        Case REG_SZ
            strValue = varValueData & Chr$(0)
            SetValueEx = RegSetValueExString(lngHwdKey, strValueName, _
                0&, lngType, strValue, Len(strValue))

        'DWORDs
        Case REG_DWORD
            lngValue = varValueData
            SetValueEx = RegSetValueExLong(lngHwdKey, strValueName, _
                0&, lngType, lngValue, 4)

    End Select

End Function
```

Now that we are able to set the key values, we need a method to read the data back from the registry. This next function was also created using the VB Class Builder Utility and will read the key value for the key that you specify. It opens the key, calls the function to actually read the key value and then closes the key.

```
Public Function QueryKeyValue(ByVal strSectionName As String, ByVal _
    strKeyName As String, Optional ByVal lngRegDataType As RegDataType _
    = HKEY_LOCAL_MACHINE) As Long

    'Declare variables
    Dim lngRC As Long
    Dim lngHwd As Long
    Dim varValue As Variant

    'Get the value currently in the key and close it
    lngRC = RegOpenKeyEx(lngRegDataType, strSectionName, 0, _
        KEY_ALL_ACCESS, lngHwd)
    lngRC = QueryValueEx(lngHwd, strKeyName, varValue)

    RegCloseKey (lngHwd)

    'Return with the return code
    QueryKeyValue = lngRC

End Function
```

This next function reads the actual key value, determines what type of key it is and returns the key value in the appropriate variable for the key type that it read. You need to code this function as `Private` so it is not exposed as an interface.

```
Private Function QueryValueEx(ByVal lngHwdKey As Long, ByVal strKeyName _
    As String, ByVal varValue As Variant) As Long

    'Declare variables
    Dim lngDataLen As Long
    Dim lngRC As Long
    Dim lngType As Long
    Dim lngTemp As Long
    Dim strTemp As String

    On Error GoTo QueryErr

    'Determine the size and type of data to be read
    lngRC = RegQueryValueExNULL(lngHwdKey, strKeyName, 0&, lngType, _
        0&, lngDataLen)
    If lngRC <> 0 Then Error 5
        Select Case lngType

        'Strings
          Case REG_SZ:
            strTemp = String(lngDataLen, 0)
            lngRC = RegQueryValueExString(lngHwdKey, strKeyName, 0&, _
                lngType, strTemp, lngDataLen)
```

```
            If lngRC = 0 Then
                m_strKeyValue = Left$(strTemp, lngDataLen - 1)
            Else
                m_strKeyValue = Empty
            End If

        'DWORDs
        Case REG_DWORD:
            lngRC = RegQueryValueExLong(lngHwdKey, strKeyName, 0&, _
                lngType, lngTemp, lngDataLen)

            If lngRC = 0 Then
                m_lngKeyValue = lngTemp
            Else
                m_lngKeyValue = -1
            End If

        'All other data types
        Case Else
            lngRC = -1

    End Select

    On Error GoTo 0
    QueryValueEx = lngRC

    Exit Function

QueryErr:
    lngRC = -1
    QueryValueEx = lngRC

End Function
```

Now that we have our `clsRegistry` class complete with all of the functionality that we need for this project, we need to move on the to the next part of our code. You can go back later and add more functionality to the `clsRegistry` class at your convenience and as your needs dictate.

Database Module

The `modDBAccess` module will provide all of our database routines and will be accessible to all classes in our project. Let's start by declaring some basic variables in the General Declarations section of the module.

```
'Declare public Database variables
Public g_objConn As New ADODB.Connection
Public g_objCmd As New ADODB.Command
Public g_objErrors As ADODB.Errors
Public g_objErr As Error

'Declare private variables
Private m_lngRC As Long
Private m_lngConnectionTimeout As Long
Private m_lngCommandTimeout As Long
Private m_strDSN As String
Private m_strUID As String
Private m_strPWD As String
```

```
Private m_strStandardKeyName As String

'Declare private objects
Private m_objReg As clsRegistry
```

The public variables are prefixed with a g_ to indicate that they are global to the project. These include all of our database objects. The private variables are prefixed with a m_ to indicate that they are module level variables and only accessible within the modDBAccess module. The last private declaration is for an object to represent the clsRegistry class. We will declare an instance of this class for our use in this module.

The first code we want to write is the code to open the database. This function is the same as in the last chapter with one change. Instead of getting the database values from the ScriptingContext objects, we will be reading them from the registry. We need to call a procedure to read the values from the system registry.

```
Public Function OpenDatabase() As Boolean
  'Get the connection settings from the registry
  Call ReadRegistry

  'Connect to SQL Server and open the database
  On Error GoTo SQLErr

  With g_objConn
    .ConnectionTimeout = m_lngConnectionTimeout
    .CommandTimeout = m_lngCommandTimeout
    .Open m_strDSN, m_strUID, m_strPWD
  End With

  On Error GoTo 0

  OpenDatabase = True

  Exit Function

SQLErr:
  OpenDatabase = False

End Function
```

```
  'Get the connection timeout value
  m_lngRC = m_objReg.QueryKeyValue(m_strStandardKeyName & "Database", _
    "Connection Timeout", HKEY_LOCAL_MACHINE)

  If m_lngRC <> 0 Then
    'No key was found, set the default
    m_lngConnectionTimeout = 30
    'No key was found, create the key
    m_lngRC = m_objReg.CreateKey(m_strStandardKeyName, "Database", _
      HKEY_LOCAL_MACHINE)

    If m_lngRC <> 0 Then
      App.LogEvent "Error creating registry key", _
        vbLogEventTypeError
    End If
```

```
    'No key was found, write the default keys
    Call WriteRegistry

Else
    m_lngConnectionTimeout = m_objReg.LongKeyValue

End If
```

This first section of the code is just a little different that the rest of the procedure. The first thing we need to do is declare a new instance of the clsRegistry class. Then we set the standard section name where we are going to be reading and writing our registry keys.

Next, we query the first key to get the value. The first time the code is executed the value does not exist; so we set the default value for the key we just queried and then create the new key. Next we need to write all the default values in the registry. We do this by calling the WriteRegistry() procedure.

The rest of the code is pretty much repetitive, just querying the various key values that we need.

```
'Get the command timeout value
    m_lngRC = m_objReg.QueryKeyValue(m_strStandardKeyName & "Database", _
      "Command Timeout", HKEY_LOCAL_MACHINE)

    If m_lngRC <> 0 Then
      'No key was found, set the default
      m_lngCommandTimeout = 30
    Else
      m_lngCommandTimeout = m_objReg.LongKeyValue
    End If

    'Get the dsn string
    m_lngRC = m_objReg.QueryKeyValue(m_strStandardKeyName & "Database", _
      "DSN", HKEY_LOCAL_MACHINE)

    If m_lngRC <> 0 Then
      'No key was found, set the default
      m_strDSN = "Pubs Connection"
    Else
      m_strDSN = m_objReg.StringKeyValue
    End If

'Get the userid string
    m_lngRC = m_objReg.QueryKeyValue(m_strStandardKeyName & "Database", _
      "UID", HKEY_LOCAL_MACHINE)

    If m_lngRC <> 0 Then
      'No key was found, set the default
      m_strUID = "sa"
    Else
      m_strUID = m_objReg.StringKeyValue
    End If
```

```
        'Get the password string
        m_lngRC = m_objReg.QueryKeyValue(m_strStandardKeyName & "Database", _
          "PWD", HKEY_LOCAL_MACHINE)

        If m_lngRC <> 0 Then
          'No key was found, set the default
          m_strPWD = ""
        Else
          m_strPWD = m_objReg.StringKeyValue
        End If

        'Dereference the registry object
        Set m_objReg = Nothing

    End Sub
```

Notice that if a value was not found we need to set the default value for that key.

This next section of code writes the default values in the system registry and is called by the ReadRegistry() procedure if the first key queried was not found. We use the SetKeyValue() method to write the keys.

```
Private Sub WriteRegistry()
    'Write the connection timeout value
    m_lngRC = m_objReg.SetKeyValue(m_strStandardKeyName & "Database", _
      "Connection Timeout", 30, REG_DWORD, HKEY_LOCAL_MACHINE)

    If m_lngRC <> 0 Then
      App.LogEvent "Write Key Failed for Key: Connection Timeout", _
        vbLogEventTypeError
    End If

    'Write the command timeout value
    m_lngRC = m_objReg.SetKeyValue(m_strStandardKeyName & "Database", _
      "Command Timeout", 30, REG_DWORD, HKEY_LOCAL_MACHINE)

    If m_lngRC <> 0 Then
      App.LogEvent "Write Key Failed for Key: Command Timeout", _
        vbLogEventTypeError
    End If

    'Write the dsn string value
    m_lngRC = m_objReg.SetKeyValue(m_strStandardKeyName & "Database", _
      "DSN", "Pubs Connection", REG_SZ, HKEY_LOCAL_MACHINE)

    If m_lngRC <> 0 Then
      App.LogEvent "Write Key Failed for Key: Connect String", _
        vbLogEventTypeError
    End If

    'Write the user id string value
    m_lngRC = m_objReg.SetKeyValue(m_strStandardKeyName & "Database", _
      "UID", "sa", REG_SZ, HKEY_LOCAL_MACHINE)
```

```
      If m_lngRC <> 0 Then
        App.LogEvent "Write Key Failed for Key: Connect String", _
          vbLogEventTypeError
      End If

      'Write the password string value
      m_lngRC = m_objReg.SetKeyValue(m_strStandardKeyName & "Database", _
        "PWD", "", REG_SZ, HKEY_LOCAL_MACHINE)

      If m_lngRC <> 0 Then
        App.LogEvent "Write Key Failed for Key: Connect String", _
          vbLogEventTypeError
      End If

    End Sub
```

After you write the default values to the HKEY_LOCAL_MACHINE hive of the registry, when you run your component your entries should look like the screenshot below. While the password is shown here is in plain text for demonstration purposes, in the real world you would want to provide some type of encryption of the password. This can be in the form of third party encryption routines or by using Microsoft's Crypto API.

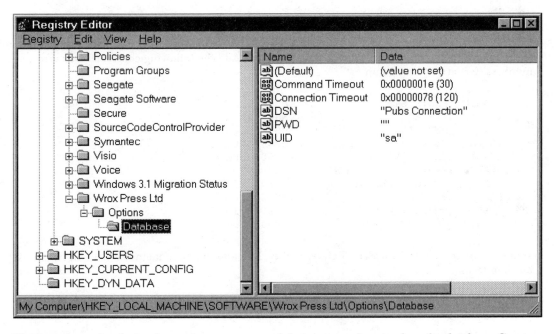

The last piece of code for the modDBAccess module is a procedure to close the database. Create your code as follows.

```
Public Sub CloseDatabase()

    'Close database objects and dereference them
    Set g_objcmd = Nothing
    Set g_objerrors = Nothing
    Set g_objerr = Nothing
    g_objConn.Close
    Set g_objConn = Nothing

End Sub
```

That wraps up our code for our supporting classes and modules. Now it's time to start on the main class, Authors. Remember that this class will implement the methods to Add, Update, and Delete authors, and also implement all the business rules to support these operations.

Authors Class

The variables that are needed in this class are fairly simple. We will define an enumeration of custom errors that will be raised when an error occurs. When defining your own errors, you have a large range of available error numbers in which to work, 513 - 65535. When you define your own error numbers, you must add the error number to the vbObjectError constant, which has a value of &H80040000.

Lets start by building the enumeration for the custom errors we are going to define. Start the VB Class Builder Utility and select the Authors class. Click on the **Add New Enum** toolbar button and enter a name of CustomErrors for the enumeration. Add the following constants. Our error numbers start at 520 and go up.

```
INVALID_LENGTH_STRING        =   &H80040208
MISSING_HYPHEN               =   &H80040209
DATA_NOT_NUMERIC             =   &H8004020A
MISSING_SPACE                =   &H8004020B
INVALID_NUMERIC_RANGE        =   &H8004020C
INVALID_STATE_ABBREVIATION   =   &H8004020D
INVALID_ZIP_CODE_LENGTH      =   &H8004020E
OPEN_DATABASE_ERROR          =   &H8004020F
NO_MATCH_ON_LAST_NAME        =   &H80040210
NO_MATCH_ON_FIRST_NAME       =   &H80040211
```

While we are here in the VB Class Builder Utility, let's add the three methods that will be exposed as our interfaces.

Click on the **Add New Methods** toolbar button and enter Add for the method name. Add the following arguments.

```
ByVal strSSN As String
ByVal strFirstName As String
ByVal strLastName As String
ByVal strPhone As String
ByVal bytContract As Byte
Optional ByVal varAddress As Variant
Optional ByVal varCity As Variant
Optional ByVal varState As Variant
Optional ByVal varZip As Variant
```

Set the return data type to a `Long` value. Click on the **Attributes** tab and enter a description describing this method. If you want to provide a help file with your component, you can enter a number for the **Help Context ID**. This number would be mapped to a help topic in your help file. We will not be demonstrating how to create help files in this book but you should be aware that you can provide help files with your components that provide context sensitive help.

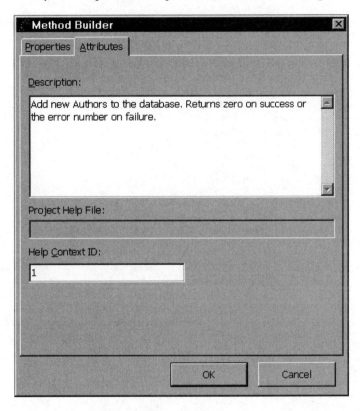

Click on **OK** to close the dialog. Add another method for `Update` and add the following arguments.

```
ByVal strSSN As String
Optional ByVal varFirstName As Variant
Optional ByVal varLastName As Variant
Optional ByVal varPhone As Variant
Optional ByVal varAddress As Variant
Optional ByVal varCity As Variant
Optional ByVal varState As Variant
Optional ByVal varZip As Variant
Optional ByVal varContract As Variant
```

Set the return data type to a long value. Click on the **Attributes** tab and enter a description.

Add the final method with a name of `Delete` and add the following arguments.

```
ByVal strSSN As String
ByVal strFirstName As String
ByVal strLastName As String
```

Set the return data type to a long value. Click on the **Attributes** tab and enter a description. Update the project and close the VB Class Builder Utility.

We should add a comment to our enumeration and we need to add one module level variable to handle our return code. Code your General Declarations section like this.

```
'Enum Custom Errors
Public Enum CustomErrors
    INVALID_LENGTH_STRING = &H80040208
    MISSING_HYPHEN = &H80040209
    DATA_NOT_NUMERIC = &H8004020A
    MISSING_SPACE = &H8004020B
    INVALID_NUMERIC_RANGE = &H8004020C
    INVALID_STATE_ABBREVIATION = &H8004020D
    INVALID_ZIP_CODE_LENGTH = &H8004020E
    OPEN_DATABASE_ERROR = &H8004020F
    NO_MATCH_ON_LAST_NAME = &H80040210
    NO_MATCH_ON_FIRST_NAME = &H80040211
End Enum

'Declare private variables
Private m_lngError As Long

Private Function SSN_Validation(ByVal strSSN As String) As Boolean
    'Validate the Social Security Number passed is in the following
    'format: nnn-nn-nnnn
    Dim intIndex As Integer
    On Error GoTo ValidateErr

    'First validate the length of the string
    If Len(strSSN) <> 11 Then
        Err.Raise INVALID_LENGTH_STRING, "SSN_Validation", _
            "Invalid Length String"
    End If

    'Next validate the hyphens
    If Mid$(strSSN, 4, 1) <> "-" Or Mid$(strSSN, 7, 1) <> "-" Then
        Err.Raise MISSING_HYPHEN, "SSN_Validation", _
            "Missing or Misplaced Hyphen"
    End If
```

Remember our business rules? They stated that we should perform certain validations and verify certain fields are present. Let's code the validation routine for SSN, which is the authors' key in the database to validate the SSN is in a valid format.

We accept the SSN string as input and will return a Boolean value indicating success or failure. Notice that this function is coded as `Private`. There is no need to expose the validation routines as interfaces so we can code all our validation routines as `Private`.

The first validation check is to ensure we have the correct length string to validate. There's no reason to go any further in the validation process if we don't have the correct length string.

The next validation is to ensure we have all the hyphens and they are in the correct positions within the string.

```
'Next validate the numeric data
  For intIndex = 1 To 3

    If Not IsNumeric(Mid$(strSSN, intIndex, 1)) Then
      Err.Raise DATA_NOT_NUMERIC, "SSN_Validation", _
       "Data not Numeric"
    End If

  Next
  For intIndex = 5 To 6

    If Not IsNumeric(Mid$(strSSN, intIndex, 1)) Then
      Err.Raise DATA_NOT_NUMERIC, "SSN_Validation", _
        "Data not Numeric"
    End If

  Next
  For intIndex = 8 To 11

    If Not IsNumeric(Mid$(strSSN, intIndex, 1)) Then
      Err.Raise DATA_NOT_NUMERIC, "SSN_Validation", _
        "Data not Numeric"
    End If

  Next
```

The last validation is to ensure the rest of the data is numeric data. Here we are validating the correct positions in the string to ensure they are numeric.

Notice that if any validation fails we are raising an error. The first part of our code was to handle an error by telling our procedure to go to the error handler if an error occurred. As soon as we raise an error, the next line of code to be executed is the error handler code.

```
  SSN_Validation = True

  Exit Function

ValidateErr:
  'Your error handling code here
  m_lngError = Err.Number
  SSN_Validation = False

End Function
```

If all the tests were passed, we set the function to `True` to indicate the success of the validation and exit the function, bypassing the error handler.

If an error was raised, we come to the error handler where we set the class level variable, m_lngError, to the error number that we raised and set the function to False. When we raise an error, the error number is only valid in the procedure or function in which it was raised. As soon as control is passed to another procedure or function the error is cleared.

Instead of using a Boolean value for the return data type we could use a long value and set the error number there.

The next validation routine we need is one to validate phone numbers. The phone numbers also need to be in a certain format.

```
Private Function Phone_Validation(ByVal strPhone As String) As Boolean
    'Validate the Phone Number passed is in the following
    'format: nnn nnn-nnnn
    Dim intIndex As Integer
    On Error GoTo ValidateErr

    'First validate the length of the string
    If Len(strPhone) <> 12 Then
      Err.Raise INVALID_LENGTH_STRING, "Phone_Validation", _
        "Invalid Length String"
    End If

    'Next validate the hyphens
    If Mid$(strPhone, 8, 1) <> "-" Then
      Err.Raise MISSING_HYPHEN, "Phone_Validation", _
        "Missing or Misplaced Hyphen"
    End If

    'Next validate the spaces (Chr$(32)= Space)
    If Mid$(strPhone, 4, 1) <> Chr$(32) Then
      Err.Raise MISSING_SPACE, "Phone_Validation", _
        "Missing or Misplaced Space"
    End If
```

The first part of this code looks like the last validation routine. We add code to handle the errors, check the length of the string and validate the hyphens are present and in the correct positions.

The phone number has a space separating the area code from the rest of the phone number. We have added the appropriate code to check for a space in the correct position. Instead of using two quotes with a space to check for a space we use the actual ASCII value. This makes the code easier to read and understand.

```
    'Next validate the numeric data
    For intIndex = 1 To 3
      If Not IsNumeric(Mid$(strPhone, intIndex, 1)) Then
        Err.Raise DATA_NOT_NUMERIC, "Phone_Validation", _
          "Data not Numeric"
      End If

    Next
```

```
    For intIndex = 5 To 7
      If Not IsNumeric(Mid$(strPhone, intIndex, 1)) Then
        Err.Raise DATA_NOT_NUMERIC, "Phone_Validation", _
          "Data not Numeric"
      End If

    Next

    For intIndex = 9 To 12
      If Not IsNumeric(Mid$(strPhone, intIndex, 1)) Then
        Err.Raise DATA_NOT_NUMERIC, "Phone_Validation", _
          "Data not Numeric"
      End If

    Next
```

As in the last validation routine, we check the rest of the data to ensure it is numeric.

```
    Phone_Validation = True

    Exit Function

ValidateErr:
    'Your error handling code here
    m_lngError = Err.Number
    Phone_Validation = False

End Function
```

We end this validation routine the same way we ended the last one. You may need to add more error handling code in these routines, depending on your standards and needs.

The next validation routine is one that validates state abbreviations.

```
Private Function State_Validation(ByVal strStateIn As String) As Boolean
    'Validate the State Abbreviation passed matches one of the values
    'in the array
    Dim varState As Variant
    Dim intIndex As Integer
    On Error GoTo ValidateErr

    'Set the state array with a list of all state abbreviations
    varState = Array("AL", "AK", "AZ", "AR", "CA", "CO", "CT", _
      "DE", "FL", "GA", "HI", "ID", "IL", "IN", "IA", "KS", "KY", _
      "LA", "ME", "MD", "MA", "MI", "MN", "MS", "MO", "MT", "NE", _
      "NV", "NH", "NJ", "NM", "NY", "NC", "ND", "OH", "OK", "OR", _
      "PA", "RI", "SC", "SD", "TN", "TX", "UT", "VT", "VA", "WA", _
      "WV", "WI", "WY")
```

We added an extra variable to this function to hold the array of state abbreviations. Ideally these state abbreviations would be in a database table somewhere so that even the caller could validate and select the correct state abbreviation to pass. We set the array variable, varState, to the array of state abbreviations.

```
'Loop through the array looking for a match
  For intIndex = LBound(varState) To UBound(varState)
    If UCase(strStateIn) = CStr(varState(intIndex)) Then
      State_Validation = True
      Exit Function
    End If

  Next

  Err.Raise INVALID_STATE_ABBREVIATION, "State_Validation", _
    "Invalid State Abbreviation"

ValidateErr:
  'Your error handling code here
  m_lngError = Err.Number
  State_Validation = False

End Function
```

We loop through the array looking for a match. If a match is found, we set the validation function to true and exit. If we search through the entire array and come out of the loop, we know we did not find a match and we raise the appropriate error.

The last validation routine that we need is a routine to validate the Contract. The Contract field on the database is a bit data type, which means it can be a 1, 0 or NULL. The smallest data type available in Visual Basic is the byte data type and its value range is 0 – 255. We need to validate that the correct value is passed and is within the acceptable range.

```
Private Function Contract_Validation(ByVal bytContract As Byte) As Boolean

  'Validate the Contract Flag passed contains the following
  'data: 0 or 1
  On Error GoTo ValidateErr

   'First validate the numeric data
  If Not IsNumeric(bytContract) Then
    Err.Raise DATA_NOT_NUMERIC, "Contract_Validation", _
            "Data not Numeric"
  End If

  'Next validate the numeric range
  If bytContract > 1 Then
    Err.Raise INVALID_NUMERIC_RANGE, "Contract_Validation", _
            "Invalid Numeric Range"
  End If

  'Next convert True value (-1) to 1
  If bytContract = True Then
    bytContract = 1
  End If

  Contract_Validation = True

  Exit Function
```

```
ValidateErr:
  'Your error handling code here
  m_lngError = Err.Number
  Contract_Validation = False

End Function
```

We first validate the data type to ensure it is numeric and then validate the range to ensure the value is not greater than 1. Next we check to see if the parameter was passed as a Boolean value in which case we convert it. That's all there is to this validation.

Now we need to add the code to our methods that we exposed as interfaces. Let's start with the Add method.

```
Public Function Add(ByVal strSSN As String, ByVal strFirstName As _
    String, ByVal strLastName As String, ByVal strPhone As String, _
    ByVal bytContract As Byte, Optional ByVal varAddress As Variant, _
    Optional ByVal varCity As Variant, Optional ByVal varState As _
    Variant, Optional ByVal varZip As Variant) As Long

    'Delcare variables
    Dim strAddress, strCity, strState, strZip, strSQL As String
    On Error GoTo AddErr

    '****************************************************************
    'Perform data validations
    '****************************************************************

    'Perform SSN validation
    If Not (SSN_Validation(strSSN)) Then
      GoTo AddErr
    End If

    'Verify the first name is not > 20 characters
    If Len(strFirstName) > 20 Then
      strFirstName = Left$(strFirstName, 20)
    End If

    'Verify the last name is not > 40 characters
    If Len(strLastName) > 40 Then
      strLastName = Left$(strLastName, 40)
    End If

    'Perform Phone validation
    If Not Phone_Validation(strPhone) Then
      GoTo AddErr
    End If
```

The first thing we need to do is declare some variables for the variant data that is being passed. We will convert the variant data types to string data types before we pass them to SQL Server.

Next we perform the validation routines on the required fields which are the SSN and Phone fields. We do not need to check to ensure the First and Last names are present because they are required fields in the interface. If the caller tried to leave them out they would get an error before their code even reached us. All we need to do is validate the length is not greater than what can be accepted by SQL Server. If it is, we trim the spaces on the right side of the string.

```
'Convert to string if present
  If Not IsMissing(varAddress) Then
    strAddress = CStr(varAddress)
    'Verify the address is not > 40 characters

    If Len(strAddress) > 40 Then
      strAddress = Left$(strAddress, 40)
    End If

  End If
```

Because we declared the optional parameters as variants we can use the `IsMissing` keyword to check if a parameter was passed. If the optional parameters were declared as strings we would have to check the length of the strings because the `IsMissing` keyword would always return `True`.

```
'Convert to string if present
If Not IsMissing(varCity) Then
  strCity = CStr(varCity)
  'Verify the city is not > 20 characters

  If Len(strCity) > 20 Then
    strCity = Left$(strCity, 20)
  End If

End If

If Not IsMissing(varState) Then
  'Convert state to a string and perform State validation
  strState = CStr(varState)

  If Not State_Validation(strState) Then
    GoTo AddErr
  End If

End If

'Convert to string if present and validate length
If Not IsMissing(varZip) Then
  strZip = CStr(varZip)

  If Len(strZip) <> 5 Then
    m_lngError = INVALID_ZIP_CODE_LENGTH
    Err.Raise INVALID_ZIP_CODE_LENGTH, "Add", "Invalid Zip Code Length"
  End If

End If

'Perform Contract validation
If Not Contract_Validation(bytContract) Then
  GoTo AddErr
End If
```

The Address and City parameters do not require validation only conversion to a string data type and ensuring the length is not greater than allowed. If the State field is present, we convert it to a string and then validate the string.

We need to convert the Zip Code parameter to a string also, if present, and check the length to ensure it contains five digits.

The Contract field is a required field and validation is performed to ensure it contains the correct data.

Now that all of the validations have been performed we are ready to build our SQL string that will be executed to add the new author.

```
'*******************************************************************
'Add the data to the database
'*******************************************************************

'Connect to the database
If Not OpenDatabase Then
  m_lngError = OPEN_DATABASE_ERROR
  Err.Raise OPEN_DATABASE_ERROR, "Add", _
    "Open Database Error"
End If

'Build the SQL string
strSQL = "dbo.up_parmins_authors ('" & strSSN & "','" & _
  strLastName & "','" & strFirstName & "','" & strPhone _
  & "'," & _
  IIf(IsMissing(varAddress), "Null", "'" & strAddress & "'") _
  & "," & _
  IIf(IsMissing(varCity), "Null", "'" & strCity & "'") _
  & "," & _
  IIf(IsMissing(varState), "Null", "'" & strState & "'") _
  & "," & _
  IIf(IsMissing(varZip), "Null", "'" & strZip & "'") _
  & "," & bytContract & ")"
```

We establish a connection to the database and then build the SQL string. Notice that we use the IsMissing keyword again in the Immediate If (IIf()) function. The IIF() function expects three parameters. The first parameter is an expression that can be evaluated to either True or False. The second parameter is the value or expression that is returned if the evaluated expression is True and the third parameter is the value or expression returned if the evaluated expression is False. IIf() will always return the True part of the statement or the False part of the statement. The evaluation statement must be as such as to always evaluate to True or False. If the optional parameter is missing then we want to pass Null to SQL server so those fields that do not contain data will have a Null value inserted into them.

Once the SQL String is built we then want to execute the string to add the new author.

```
'Add the Author to the database
On Error GoTo SQLErr
g_objConn.Execute strSQL
On Error GoTo 0

'Close the database
Call CloseDatabase
```

```
     'Return to caller
     Add = 0

     Exit Function

SQLErr:
   'Your error handling code here
   'Loop through the ADO errors collection
   Add = 1
   'Close the database
   Call CloseDatabase

   Exit Function

AddErr:
   'Your error handling code here
   Add = m_lngError  'The error raised by the validation routines

End Function
```

Before executing the SQL string, we set up the code to handle any database errors that might occur. Once the SQL String has been executed we turn off the error handling and then close the database connection and return to the caller.

The SQLErr error handling code is coded with minimal error handling code. You need to add your own code here and return with the appropriate database error that occurred.

The AddErr error handling code is set up to return with the actual error that occurred while validating data. The caller can use the public enumeration, CustomErrors, to determine which error occurred.

Now that we have a method of adding authors lets switch to the method to update the existing Authors table. We need to start by validating the only required field, which is the SSN, the key to the Authors table.

```
Public Function Update(ByVal strSSN As String, Optional ByVal _
   varFirstName As Variant, Optional ByVal varLastName As Variant, _
   Optional ByVal varPhone As Variant, Optional ByVal varAddress _
   As Variant, Optional ByVal varCity As Variant, Optional ByVal _
   varState As Variant, Optional ByVal varZip As Variant, Optional _
   ByVal varContract As Variant) As Long

   'Delcare variables
   Dim strFirstName, strLastName, strPhone, strAddress, strCity, _
      strState, strZip, strSQL As String
   Dim bytContract As Byte

   On Error GoTo UpdateErr

   '**************************************************************
   'Perform data validations
   '**************************************************************

   'Perform SSN validation
   If Not SSN_Validation(strSSN) Then
      GoTo UpdateErr
   End If
```

As with the Add() method, we need to declare the string variables that will hold the optional data we receive.

```
'Convert to string if present
If Not IsMissing(varFirstName) Then
  strFirstName = CStr(varFirstName)
  'Verify the first name is not > 20 characters

  If Len(strFirstName) > 20 Then
    strFirstName = Left$(strFirstName, 20)
  End If

End If

'Convert to string if present
If Not IsMissing(varLastName) Then
  strLastName = CStr(varLastName)
  'Verify the last name is not > 40 characters

  If Len(strLastName) > 40 Then
    strLastName = Left$(strLastName, 40)
  End If

End If

If Not IsMissing(varPhone) Then
  'Convert phone to a string and perform Phone validation
  strPhone = CStr(varPhone)

  If Not Phone_Validation(strPhone) Then
    GoTo UpdateErr
    End If

End If
```

If the First and Last Names are not missing, we coerce them to their string equivalents and verify the length is not greater than allowed. If the Phone number is present we coerce it to a string and then validate the string.

```
'Convert to string if present
If Not IsMissing(varAddress) Then
  strAddress = CStr(varAddress)
  'Verify the address is not > 40 characters

  If Len(strAddress) > 40 Then
    strAddress = Left$(strAddress, 40)
  End If

End If

'Convert to string if present
If Not IsMissing(varCity) Then
  strCity = CStr(varCity)
  'Verify the city is not > 20 characters
```

```
      If Len(strCity) > 20 Then
        strCity = Left$(strCity, 20)
      End If

  End If
```

If the Address and City parameters are passed we need to convert them to their string equivalents and validate the length is not greater than allowed.

```
  If Not IsMissing(varState) Then
    'Convert state to a string and perform State validation
    strState = CStr(varState)

    If Not State_Validation(strState) Then
      GoTo UpdateErr
    End If

  End If

  'Convert to string if present and validate length
  If Not IsMissing(varZip) Then
    strZip = CStr(varZip)

    If Len(strZip) <> 5 Then
      Err.Raise INVALID_ZIP_CODE_LENGTH, "Add", _
                "Invalid Zip Code Length"
    End If

  End If

  If Not IsMissing(varContract) Then
    'Convert contract to a byte and perform Contract validation
    bytContract = CByte(varContract)

    If Not Contract_Validation(bytContract) Then
      GoTo UpdateErr
    End If

  End If
```

The last three parameters we need to check and validate are the State, Zip and Contract fields. We convert the State field to a string and call the validation routine for States. The Zip code gets converted to a string and then we validate the length. The Contract field gets converted to a byte and then we call the Contract validation routine.

```
  '*****************************************************************
  'Update the Author on the database
  '*****************************************************************

  'Connect to the database
  If Not OpenDatabase Then
    m_lngError = OPEN_DATABASE_ERROR
    Err.Raise OPEN_DATABASE_ERROR, "Update", _
      "Open Database Error"
  End If
```

```
'Build the SQL string
strSQL = "dbo.up_parmupd_authors ('" & strSSN & "','" & _
   IIf(IsMissing(varLastName), "", strLastName) & "','" & _
   IIf(IsMissing(varFirstName), "", strFirstName) & "','" & _
   IIf(IsMissing(varPhone), "", strPhone) & "','" & _
   IIf(IsMissing(varAddress), "", strAddress) & "','" & _
   IIf(IsMissing(varCity), "", strCity) & "','" & _
   IIf(IsMissing(varState), "", strState) & "','" & _
   IIf(IsMissing(varZip), "", strZip) & "','" & _
   IIf(IsMissing(varContract), "", bytContract) & "')"
```

After all validations have been performed we need to connect to the database. Next we build the SQL string that we are going to execute. If you remember when we built the Update stored procedure that we check each field passed for a zero length. This time when we build our SQL string we do not want to set the missing fields to Null, we want to pass empty strings.

```
'Update the Author on the database
   On Error GoTo SQLErr
   g_objConn.Execute strSQL
   On Error GoTo 0

   'Close the database
   Call CloseDatabase

   'Return to caller
   Update = 0

   Exit Function

SQLErr:
   'Your error handling code here
   'Loop through the ADO errors collection
   Update = 1
   'Close the database
   Call CloseDatabase

   Exit Function

UpdateErr:
   'Your error handling code here
   Update = m_lngError   'The error raised by the validation routines

End Function
```

The last part of the Update method looks like the Add method. We add error handlers to handle any database errors that we might receive and then we execute the update.

After that, we close the database and return to the caller.

The last method we need to code is the Delete method. This method is pretty straight forward as we only have three required parameters and no optional parameters.

```
Public Function Delete(ByVal strSSN As String, ByVal strFirstName _
   As String, ByVal strLastName As String) As Long

   'Delcare variables
   Dim strSQL As String

   On Error GoTo DeleteErr

   '*****************************************************************
   'Perform data validations
   '*****************************************************************

   'Perform SSN validation
   If Not SSN_Validation(strSSN) Then
     GoTo DeleteErr
   End If

   'Verify the first name is not > 20 characters
   If Len(strFirstName) > 20 Then
     strFirstName = Left$(strFirstName, 20)
   End If

   'Verify the last name is not > 40 characters
   If Len(strLastName) > 40 Then
     strLastName = Left$(strLastName, 40)
   End If
```

As in the last two methods, we need to validate the SSN to ensure it is in the valid format expected. We only validate the First and Last Name parameters to ensure they are not greater than the allowed length.

```
   '*****************************************************************
   'Delete the Author from the database
   '*****************************************************************

   'Connect to the database
   If Not OpenDatabase Then
     m_lngError = OPEN_DATABASE_ERROR
     Err.Raise OPEN_DATABASE_ERROR, "Delete", _
       "Open Database Error"
   End If

   'Delete the Author from the database

   On Error GoTo SQLErr

   Set g_objCmd.ActiveConnection = g_objConn
   g_objCmd.CommandText = "{? = call dbo.up_parmdel_authors ('" & _
     strSSN & "','" & strLastName & "','" & strFirstName & "')}"
   g_objCmd(0).Direction = adParamReturnValue
   g_objCmd.Execute

   On Error GoTo 0
```

After we connect to the database we need to set the ADO command object to the stored procedure we are calling and pass it the required parameters. The Delete stored procedure will return a long value indicating the success or failure of our request.

Again, we set up the error handlers before we execute the command and then turn it off after our command has been executed.

```
On Error GoTo DeleteErr
  Select Case g_objCmd(0)

    Case 0
      'Normal return code

    Case 1
      'Last name does not match
      m_lngError = NO_MATCH_ON_LAST_NAME
      Err.Raise NO_MATCH_ON_LAST_NAME, "Delete", _
        "Last Name Passed Does Not Last Name On Database"

    Case 2
      'First name does not match
      m_lngError = NO_MATCH_ON_FIRST_NAME
      Err.Raise NO_MATCH_ON_FIRST_NAME, "Delete", _
        "First Name Passed Does Not First Name On Database"

  End Select
```

We turn on the `DeleteErr` error handler to handle any non-database related errors. We check the return value from the ADO command object and raise the appropriate error if it is not zero.

```
'Close the database
  Call CloseDatabase

  'Return to caller
  Delete = 0

  Exit Function

SQLErr:
  'Your error handling code here
  'Loop through the ADO errors collection
  Delete = 1
  'Close the database
  Call CloseDatabase

  Exit Function

DeleteErr:
  'Your error handling code here
  Delete = m_lngError   'The error raised by the validation routines
  'Close the database
  Call CloseDatabase

End Function
```

The last part of this code is the same as the Add and Update methods.

Now that we have all of our code written it is time to save the project and compile it. Once that it is done, open the **Project Properties** dialog and click on the **Component** tab and set **Binary Compatibility**. Notice that the `AuthorData.dll` is already set in the **Compatibility** text box. Click OK to close the dialog and compile your project again and then save your project.

Browsing the Business Component

Open a new project as a standard executable and set a reference to the Authors Data Business Component. Click OK to close the References dialog.

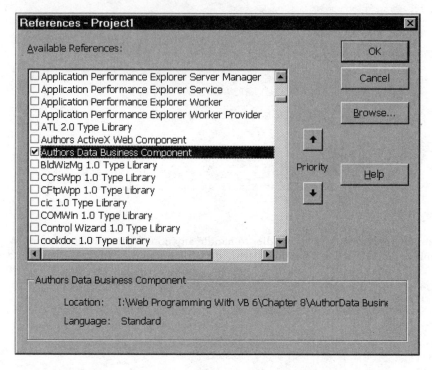

Next open the object browser and click on the **AuthorData** library. Click on the Authors class and then click on the Add method. Notice that at the bottom of the object browser you can see all of the parameters the Add method expects. Also notice your comments that you entered when you built this method using the VB Class Builder Utility.

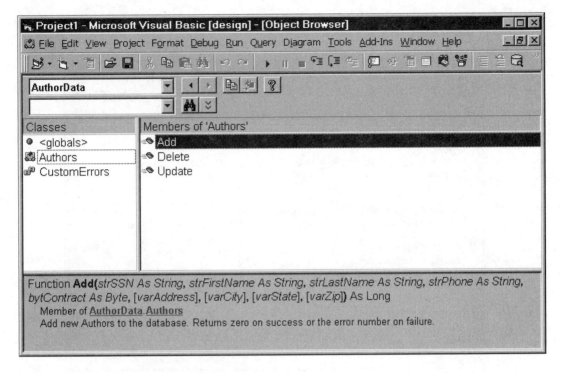

Calling the Business Component

We call our new business component in an Active Server Page in a similar manner as we called the Web Page Components. The only difference is that this time our component accepts parameters and will only return a return code to our Web page that we would need to evaluate; it does not read or write data to the ASP.

```
'Create the Business Component
Set objAuthor = Server.CreateObject("AuthorData.Authors")

'Call the component
lngRC = objAuthor.Update(CStr(Request.Form("txtSSN")),, _
CStr(Request.Form("txtPhone"))

'Check the return code
If lngRC <> 0 Then
   'Add your error handling here
End If

'Dereference the component
Set objDisplay = Nothing
```

If you build your ASP using Visual InterDev, the methods, properties, and parameters are displayed, just like in Visual Basic, with dropdown lists.

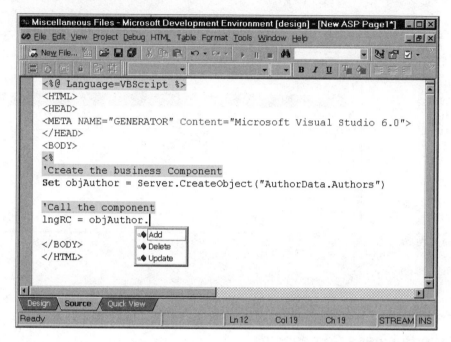

Help Files

You should build help files for your business components. This will allow other developers to use your components and get context sensitive help on the methods and events that you build. Remember when we added the Description and Help Context ID to the methods that we built using the VB Class Builder Utility? If you map that Help Context ID to a specific topic dealing with the method, the developer using your component can press the *F1* key while the cursor is on the method and get help for that method.

It would be a good idea to display the format of the method and the parameters it accepts. You should also describe the parameters in detail. Giving the developer a sample call of the method is always a good idea and can be very useful to the developer using your component.

Writing help files for your business component is very important especially if they are distributed across the enterprise for use in other applications.

Below is a screen shot from the help file of the Registry DLL that I wrote. You can see that it provides the developer using the component with the required syntax of the method as well as a description of all of the parameters. There is also a jump to an example of how this call should be made.

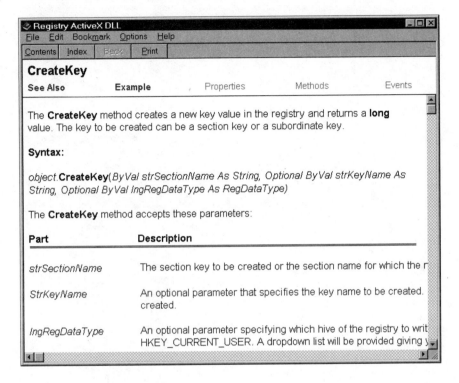

Summary

In this chapter you have learned what a business component is and how to implement your business rules in a component. We demonstrated how to build a server business component and all of the pieces that make it such a powerful tool. Not only can we use this business component from our Active Server Pages but we can also call this component from other programs as well.

The ADO object model was covered in detail and the most common uses were demonstrated. You can see now why ADO is the preferred method of database access. Not only is it simple to use, but also it provides great flexibility to your components.

When building your business server components remember the following items:

> Determine what tasks you are trying to accomplish.
> Determine the business rules surrounding those tasks.
> Separate related tasks into separate classes.
> Use the registry for values that are prone to change.
> Add descriptive comments to your methods and Context Help IDs.

11

Interfacing With Server Services in Visual Basic

In the previous chapter you learned how to create a business server component that can be used by Active Server Pages as well as other programs. This chapter will introduce you to the server-side services available to your component. These services come as part of the Windows NT Server operating system and as such allow you to leverage the existing technology at your disposal to build robust enterprise components.

These services provide a wide array of functionality that enables your components to update databases without the worry of backing-out failed transactions, send queued messages, send mail, and access directory information on any type of server using a common interface. All of this functionality is made available through the services built in to the Windows NT Server operating system. This chapter will cover these topics:

> Microsoft Transaction Server
> Microsoft Message Queuing
> Collaboration Data Objects
> Active Directory Service Interfaces

Before you can complete any of the examples in this chapter you will need to ensure that you have installed the software mentioned above. Microsoft Transaction Server (MTS) and Microsoft Message Queuing (MSMQ) can be installed from the NT 4.0 Option Pack which is included as part of Visual Studio Enterprise Edition. You can also download this option pack from the Microsoft Web site. Collaboration Data Objects (CDO) gets installed along with Microsoft Outlook or you can download it from the Microsoft Web site. Active Directory Service Interfaces (ADSI) gets installed with NT service pack 4 or 5.

Microsoft Transaction Server

MTS is a component-based transaction server that processes transactions for compiled and interpreted components. This means that you can create a business server component and incorporate MTS within your component. You can also create transactional Active Server Pages, written with interpreted script, that incorporate MTS to leverage the same functionality that is available to compiled components.

With remote components, executing on the behalf of clients, which are modifying data stored in different data sources, many pieces of complex software and hardware must work together seamlessly. If an error was to occur, data cannot be left in an inconsistent state. An entire set of operations or changes performed on one or more data sources must *all* succeed (**commit**) or *all* fail (**roll back**).

To accomplish this all-or-nothing work management that ensures data consistency and integrity, we use transactions. A transaction is an operation, or series of operations that change data from one consistent state to another. In other words, a transaction simply treats multiple operations as one unit of work. MTS considers creating a component, letting it execute its functionality and releasing the component and all of its resources as a transaction.

MTS provides the middle-tier in an n-tier programming model by allowing you to execute components that are located anywhere on your network. MTS provides security and transactional processing of your components while ensuring the integrity of your backend data stores.

> *For a comprehensive guide to the features of MTS, please refer to* Professional Visual Basic 6 MTS Programming *from Wrox, ISBN 1-861002-44-0*

Benefits of Using MTS

Possibly the greatest benefit of MTS from a developer's standpoint is the fact that you can develop your components and stored procedures for a single user environment. MTS takes care of server issues such as concurrency, connection pooling and security. All you have to do is begin an MTS transaction and end or abort the MTS transaction at completion. This allows you, the developer, to concentrate on implementing the business rules, letting MTS handle the complex server issues like committing or backing out the transaction.

Using MTS in your Active Server Pages and your Web server components helps to add scalability to your Web site by letting you access multiple tiers. You also gain transaction support in your ASP, which can help ensure the integrity of your data when dealing with the database directly from your Web pages.

MTS handles distributed transactions across multiple databases by using Microsoft Distributed Transaction Coordinator (MS DTC). This means that a transaction can update a SQL Server database on one server and at the same time update an Oracle database on another server. MS DTC ensures all parts of the transaction are either committed or aborted.

Managing MTS packages is easy when using the MTS Explorer, which is simply a snap-in to the Microsoft Management Console (MMC). Developers can create packages that contain one or more components, test the components and then distribute the packages. To start the MTS Explorer, from the Start button, navigate to the Windows NT 4.0 Option Pack folder under Programs, and then to Microsoft Transaction Server and click on Transaction Server Explorer.

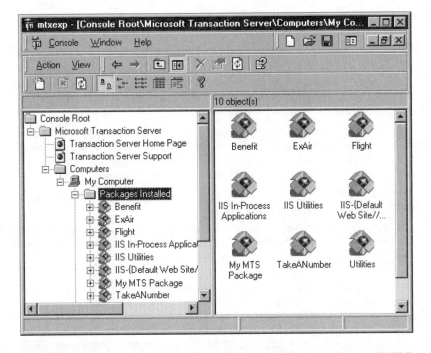

Setting up new packages is very straightforward and you can add any ActiveX DLL component to your packages. If your components have not been coded using MTS support, you can add MTS support to these new components through the Properties dialog.

The right-hand pane displays a complete view of your packages and components. You can get a detailed list of information related to each package installed on a computer or a detailed list of information related to each component in a package:

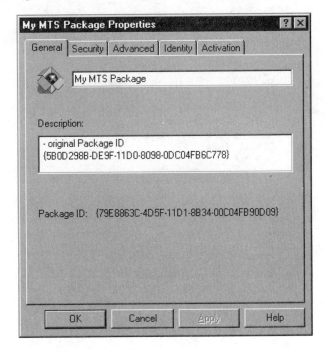

The Properties dialog has five tabs that allow you to set various attributes for your components:

> the General tab – shows the PackageID and allows the developer to define a description for their package.

> the Security tab – enables security for the selected package. The check box for Enable authorization checking is selected by default. When package security is enabled, security credentials of all client calls to the package are verified.

> the Advanced tab – displays shutdown options for the server process. You can either choose to have the server process that is associated with the selected package constantly running, or you can specify a time before a selected package automatically shuts down after being inactive. This tab can also be used to safeguard against accidental changes to the package.

> the Identity tab – provides a security feature that allows the administrator to decide under which account the components in the selected package will run.

> the Activation tab – you can set the package activation type to either Library Package (that runs in the same process as the client that called it) or Server Package (that runs in its own dedicated process on the local machine).

The MTS Explorer also lets you trace messages related to transaction processing, monitor the state of active transactions, and view transaction statistics for all transactions that are executing and have already been executed.

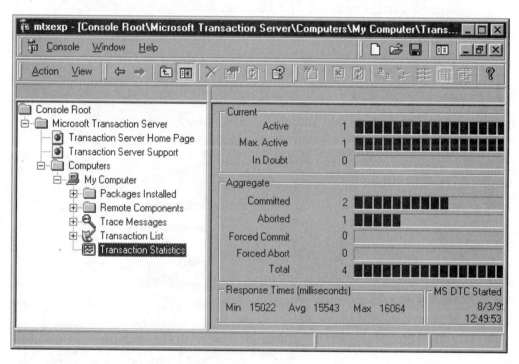

Because MTS runs on the Microsoft desktop operating systems, you can deploy standalone business solutions that include MTS support to the desktop. This is very beneficial for smaller one-client systems that also need the transactional support that larger systems usually benefit from. You can install and run an MTS component on a desktop operating system as long as MTS is also installed on that system. MTS has limited functionality running on a stand-alone system like this does provide the security features that are available on Windows NT Server.

Adding MTS to a Visual Basic Server Component

When building a server component that supports MTS and runs in the MTS run-time environment, the server component must be an ActiveX DLL. This is fine in our case since we are dealing with server components that are Visual Basic ActiveX DLLs. Remember that these server components can also be called from our Web pages as the business server component was in the last chapter.

The first thing we need to do in VB is set a reference to MTS using the Reference dialog.

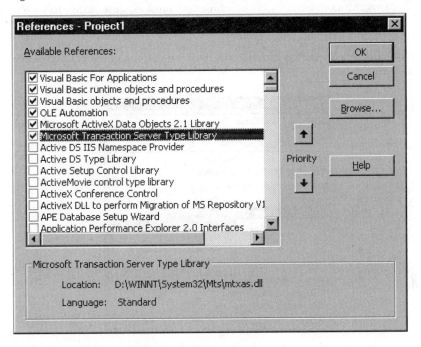

The next thing we need to do is determine the type of transaction processing our component should support. Every class in our project has an MTSTransactionMode property except for private classes. By default this property is set to NotAnMTSObject. The other MTS options available are:

Property value	Description
NotAnMTSObject	This default value indicates that this component does not support MTS.
NoTransactions	This component will run outside of any transactions created by the client.
RequiresTransactions	This component will run with the transaction created by the client. If the client did not create a transaction then MTS will create one for this component.
UsesTransactions	This component will inherent the transaction created by the client. If the client did not create a transaction then this component will run without one also.
RequiresNewTransaction	This component must execute within its own transaction. MTS will always create a new transaction for this component.

These options can be set in our class or we can set these options in the package when we install our component in MTS.

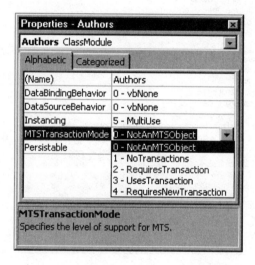

For our purposes, we will instruct MTS to create a transaction for us even if the client does not use one. This will ensure that any database changes will be backed out if our component fails.

Starting and Ending an MTS Transaction

MTS exposes an `ObjectContext` class that we need to declare. Once we declare an instance of this class we need to get a reference to this COM interface using the `GetObjectContext()` method of MTS.

```
'Declare and set MTS Object
Dim objMTS As ObjectContext
Set objMTS = GetObjectContext
```

> As a side note, we can use the `ObjectContext` to commit our transaction, disable a transaction from being committed, commit a portion of a transaction before the entire transaction is complete, and determine if security is enabled.

Once a transaction is complete, we can commit the changes to the database by calling the `SetComplete()` method.

```
'Tell MTS to commit the transaction
objMTS.SetComplete
```

If the transaction or any part of the transaction has failed, we need to tell MTS to abort the transaction by calling the `SetAbort()` method. Place this code in your error handler.

```
'Tell MTS to abort the transaction
objMTS.SetAbort
```

Once our transaction code has completed and we either committed or aborted the transaction, we need to de-reference the MTS object.

```
'De-reference the MTS object
Set objMTS = Nothing
```

Installing a Component in MTS

Start the MTS console and expand the navigation tree to select Packages installed under My Computer. You can either click on the Action menu and select New and then Package, or right click on Packages Installed and select New and then Package. An MTS package contains one or more components and is used by MTS to manage the components and their roles.

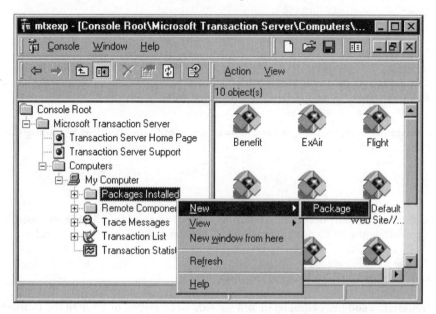

Click on Create an empty package and then enter a name for your package. Once you click on the Next button the option for Interactive user is turned on. Click the Finish button to create the package. The other option on this screen is to install pre-built packages. Once a package has been built or copied on another machine you can use this option to install the package.

Once you have created a package you need to install some components in the package. These components do not have to implement MTS to benefit from MTS. Adding them to your package and setting some options will provide the same basic benefits as coding MTS in your component.

To add a new component, expand the newly created package and click on Components. You can either click on the Action menu, select New and then Component or right click on Components and then select New and then Component.

Click on the Install new component(s) button to install the component you have created. Click on the Add Files button to find and open the ActiveX DLL you have created or want to add. Click on the Finish button to install the component in the package.

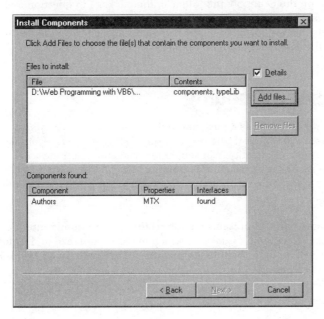

To check and set the transactional support of the component you have just added, select the component, bring up the **Properties** window for that component and click on the **Transaction** tab. A component that does not implement MTS will have the **Does not support transactions** option turned on. You can change this to the appropriate option for your situation.

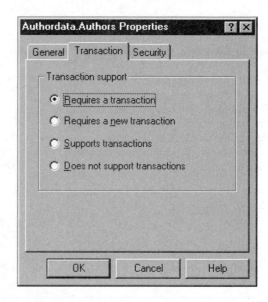

A component that implements MTS will have the appropriate Transactional support option set and in our case it is set to **Requires a transaction**.

Whenever you recompile an MTS component you will have to refresh that component in the Transaction Server Explorer. This is because Visual Basic rewrites all the registry entries and depending on the compatibility option set may write new GUIDs. After this happens the component is no longer properly registered in MTS.

To fix this problem, click on the **Components** folder in the package in question and use the **Refresh** button on the toolbar in the Transaction Server Explorer to refresh all components in the package. To refresh all components that are installed under **My Computer**, click on the **Packages Installed** folder and then click on the **Refresh** button on the toolbar.

Microsoft Message Queuing

Microsoft Message Queuing (MSMQ) is a push and pull messaging service. Messages are stored in queues while in transit from the sender to the receiver, protecting messages from network and hardware failures. The sending application can send a message and continue with other work regardless of whether the receiving application is running or not. The sending and receiving applications do not communicate directly with each other providing a more resilient interface between components.

Providing full COM support, MSMQ presents an application programming interface for languages such as Visual Basic, Visual C++, and Visual J++ which makes it a breeze to develop messaging applications. Five simple API methods handle the majority of the requests to MSMQ making the programming interface easy to use.

Benefits of Using MSMQ

There are numerous benefits to using MSMQ, the first of which is its integration with MTS. This allows you to bundle the power of transactional components with the messaging services of MSMQ. You can perform database updates and send messages and either commit or abort the entire transaction.

Both the database transactions and the message sent will be rolled back if we abort the transaction, otherwise all is committed and the message is guaranteed to be sent. Referring back to our discussion of MSMQ in the last chapter, we talked about using MSMQ to post our orders from our fictitious Web site when the user ordered a book. What if we bundled this functionality into a Web server component and ran it under MTS control? Here, we could rest assured that the order is going to make it to the message queue.

MSMQ uses some sophisticated techniques to ensure message delivery, such as **dynamic routing** around failed servers and **recoverable storage**. Messages are delivered only once and the messages are delivered in the order they are sent providing the receiving application with the correct messages in the correct order. The sending application can receive notifications that the messages sent were received and processed. This allows the sending application to commit a transaction if necessary or perform other required processing.

A third party software vendor provides integration of MSMQ with IBM's MQSeries. This allows new applications to be coded using MSMQ and access legacy systems on any platform that use IBM's MQSeries preserving your investment in legacy systems and technology.

The MSMQ Explorer lets you view the message queues across the network and provides a GUI interface that you are already familiar with. You can manage one or more queues locally or across the network using the MSMQ Explorer.

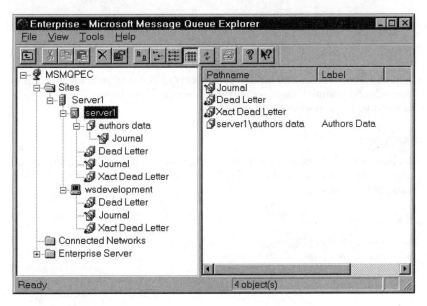

413

Listed under Sites are a list of servers that contain message queues and a list of workstations that contain message queues. Each computer has three basic queues. The Dead Letter queue is where undeliverable messages are stored and the Xact Dead Letter queue is where undeliverable transactional messages are stored. The Journal queue is where a copy of messages that are sent or received can be stored.

Adding MSMQ to a Visual Basic Server Component

The first thing that should be done when adding MSMQ to your business server component is to set a reference to the MSMQ DLL. The References dialog below shows MSMQ added to a component.

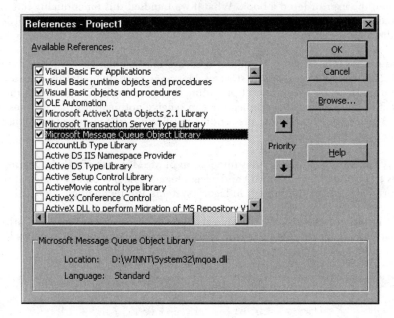

Next ensure a queue has been created on a network server. The one used for this demonstration was set up on a domain server named 'Server1' and the queue name is 'Authors Data'. You can create a queue on your local machine for testing.

Sending Messages

We need to declare some MQ objects and in this case, in the General Declarations section of the class. These objects are used to set and retrieve the queue information, identify the receiving queue and an object to hold the message.

```
'Declare MQ objects
Private m_objQueueInfo As New MSMQQueueInfo
Private m_objReceiveQueue As New MSMQQueue
Private m_objQueueMessage As New MSMQMessage
```

Now we need to set the path name for the receiving queue.

```
Private Sub SendMessage()
    'Set the pathname for the receiving queue
    m_objQueueInfo.PathName = "server1\authors data"
```

Now that we have set the `QueueInfo` object to a valid path name for the receiving queue we need to open the receiving queue using the information supplied from the `QueueInfo` object. The `QueueInfo` object accepts two parameters, one for the access mode and another for share mode.

```
    'Open the receiving queue
    Set m_objReceiveQueue = m_objQueueInfo.Open(MQ_SEND_ACCESS, MQ_DENY_NONE)
```

Notice that we are opening the queue for send access. We will only be able to send messages to this queue.

Before sending a message we need to set the message object's label and body. The message label and message body is set from class level variables that have been previously populated The message label relates to a subject field in an email and the body relates to the body of your email (the actual message).

```
    'Set the message header and body
    m_objQueueMessage.Label = m_strMsgLabel
    m_objQueueMessage.Body = m_strMsgBody
```

We now have the receiving queue open and the message has been constructed. All that is left to do is to actually send the message and then close the queue. The `MQ_NO_TRANSACTION` parameter specifies that this message is not part of a transaction.

```
    'Send the message
    m_objQueueMessage.Send m_objReceiveQueue, MQ_NO_TRANSACTION
    'Close the receiving queue
    m_objReceiveQueue.Close

End Sub
```

In the class terminate event we need to de-reference our MQ objects by setting them to nothing.

```
    'De-reference the objects
    Set m_objQueueInfo = Nothing
    Set m_objReceiveQueue = Nothing
    Set m_objQueueMessage = Nothing
```

Receiving Messages

Now that we have sent a message to MSMQ and it is sitting in the queue, we need a way to retrieve the message that we have sent. This next section of code will demonstrate just one method of receiving messages from a queue and can be fired at regular intervals or when needed. You can set up your code to receive notification events from MSMQ when messages arrive in the queue.

First we need to declare our MQ objects in the general declarations section of our class.

```
'Declare MQ objects
Private m_objQueueInfo As New MSMQQueueInfo
Private m_objReceiveQueue As New MSMQQueue
Private m_objQueueMessage As New MSMQMessage
```

Now we can set the path name of the receiving queue. This is the queue that we will be reading from.

```
Private Sub ReceiveMessage
  'Set the pathname for the receiving queue
  m_objQueueInfo.PathName = "server1\authors data"
```

We need to open the receiving queue before we can receive messages. The open method uses the information from the `QueueInfo` object.

```
'Open the receiving queue
Set m_objReceiveQueue = m_objQueueInfo.Open(MQ_RECEIVE_ACCESS, _
  MQ_DENY_NONE)
```

Now we want to retrieve the first message in the message queue.

```
'Receive the first message
Set m_objQueueMessage = m_objReceiveQueue.Receive(ReceiveTimeout:=0)
```

We are going to call a procedure to process all the messages that we receive, passing the label and body information from the message. We will perform the loop until the message queue object is equal to nothing indicating that there are no more messages.

```
'Add the message to the list
Do Until m_objQueueMessage Is Nothing

  'Process the message
  Call ProcessMessage(m_objQueueMessage.Label, m_objQueueMessage.Body)
    'Get the next message
    Set m_objQueueMessage = m_objReceiveQueue.Receive(ReceiveTimeout:=0)

Loop
```

Once we fall out of the loop, indicating there are no more messages to receive, we need to close the sending queue.

```
'Close the sending queue
m_objReceiveQueue.Close

End Sub
```

In the class terminate event we need to de-reference the MQ objects.

```
'De-reference the MQ objects
Set m_objQueueInfo = Nothing
Set m_objReceiveQueue = Nothing
Set m_objQueueMessage = Nothing
```

Security Issues

If you are testing your components from your workstation, sending and receiving to a network queue, you will need to ensure your login id has the appropriate permissions to send and receive from the network queue. If your component is running unattended on a server, it should have the appropriate permissions to access the message queue.

Collaboration Data Objects

Active Messaging Objects (AMO) came into existence with Microsoft Exchange 5.0 to provide developers with an object library that could be used in server-side components that provided messaging functionality. ADO provides a COM wrapper around the older MAPI object that most developers are familiar with. Microsoft Exchange and Microsoft Outlook provide functionality for developers to create collaborative applications using the existing messaging infrastructure.

Recognizing that developers needed the same functionality in an object library as provided by Exchange and Outlook, Microsoft introduced Collaboration Data Objects (CDO) and shipped it with Microsoft Exchange 5.5. This new object library, which replaced AMO, allows developers to build server-side components that provide collaboration, workflow and calendaring functionality.

Benefits of Using Collaboration Data Objects

One of the greatest benefits of using CDO is its ease of use. It runs as an in-process, self-registered COM server. Like its predecessor AMO, CDO provides the same familiar interface with more features and enhancements.

CDO supports caching of data which helps to make it run faster. CDO also uses the existing user interfaces of Microsoft Exchange 5.5. This means that CDO does not have the extra overhead or bulk to display its own dialog boxes or logon screens and this makes the object library more efficient.

The calendaring features of CDO support both Microsoft Schedule+ and Microsoft Outlook, so your component can access both data stores from a single API. This allows you to schedule meetings and appointments from your component. The `GetDefaultFolder()` method allows you to directly access a user's calendar folder as well as other folders.

Because CDO replaced AMO, the former is backward compatible with the latter, so you can leverage your existing code written using AMO with simply a recompile, referencing the CDO object library.

Adding CDO to a Visual Basic Server Component

The first thing we need to do is set a reference to the CDO object library in the References dialog. The dialog below shows CDO added to our component.

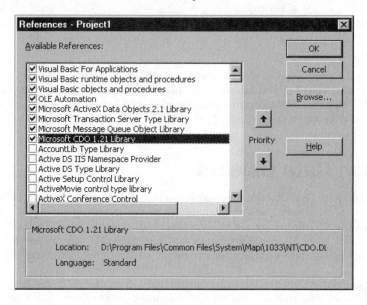

Now that we have a reference set we need to decide what type of access to use. CDO supports both anonymous and authenticated logins. Because anonymous logins are usually restricted to a certain set of public folders only, we are going to use an authenticated login. A special Exchange email user profile has been set up for our server component to use, called 'Business Component'.

Sending Mail Messages

There are three basic objects we need to declare in our procedure to send mail. The first is an object that will contain our active session connection to the Exchange Server. The second is an object for the message that we will be creating and the third is an object to contain the recipient list.

```
Private Sub SendMail()
    'Declare mail objects
    Dim objSession As Object
    Dim objMessage As Object
    Dim objRecipient As Object
```

The next step we need to perform is to create an active mail session using the code illustrated below.

```
'Create the Session Object
Set objSession = CreateObject("mapi.session")
```

Once our session object contains an active mail session we need to log on to the Exchange Server using a profile, which is the name by which you log on to the Exchange Server to access your mail account. It is critical to make sure the profile you are specifying is a valid profile. Otherwise the Exchange Server will prompt you for a valid one and, since our business component will be running unattended, there will be no one there to logon.

```
'Logon using the session object
objSession.Logon profileName:="Business Component"
```

Now that we have successfully logged on we need to create a new message. We do this by adding a message to the outbox. Using the `Session` object, we specify that we want to access the `Outbox` folder and add a message to it.

```
'Add a new message object to the outbox
Set objMessage = objSession.Outbox.Messages.Add
```

We have to set the properties of the message object to contain our subject and message text. We do this as illustrated below using class level variables that have already been set with the appropriate values.

```
'Set the message object properties
objMessage.Subject = m_strMsgSubject
objMessage.Text = m_strMsgText
```

Now that we have our message created we need to add our recipient object to the `Recipients` collection.

```
'Add a recipient object to the recipients collection
Set objRecipient = objMessage.Recipients.Add
```

We now need to set the `Recipient` object properties. This can be an individual or a public or private distribution list. The distribution list we are using today is an entry in our personal address book.

```
'Set the properties of the recipient object
objRecipient.Name = "New Authors"
```

In order to complete the recipient object and have our recipient added to the message we must have CDO resolve the reference in the address book contained in Exchange. We do this by adding the following code.

```
'Resolve the recipient name
objRecipient.Type = CdoTo
objRecipient.Resolve
```

This code adds the recipient on the 'To' line of our message. In order to carbon copy a recipient and have them added to the 'Cc' line, we would use the `CdoCc` type property. To blind carbon copy a recipient and have them added to the 'Bcc' line, we would use the `CdoBcc` type property.

For each recipient that we want to add to a message, we must add the recipient object to the `Recipients` collection, set the recipients name and resolve the reference.

After adding all the recipients we can then send our message and logoff using the code as illustrated below. As this is a server component, we want to ensure no dialogs are displayed, hence we specify `showDialog:=False` in our code.

```
'Send the message
objMessage.Send showDialog:=False

'Logoff using the session object
objSession.Logoff

End Sub
```

Sending Meeting Appointments

This section will demonstrate how to send a meeting appointment using the CDO object library. Not all message store providers support all folder types. If your profile specifies a personal message store (**PST**) and you call `GetDefaultFolder` specifying `CdoDefaultFolderCalendar`, you may get a return code of `Cdo_E_NO_SUPPORT`.

To start, we need to declare the mail objects that we will need when sending a meeting appointment. This code introduces two new objects, the `Folder` object, which we use to access the various folders in Exchange, and the `AppointmentItem` object, which is used to set the appointment details. We will go over the `AppointmentItem` object in just a little bit.

```
Private Sub ScheduleMeeting()
    'Declare mail objects
    Dim objSession As Session
    Dim objCalendarFolder As Folder
    Dim objMessage As Messages
    Dim objNewAppointment As AppointmentItem
    Dim objRecipients As Recipients
```

The next thing we need to do is create an active mail session and logon. Here again we are using the special profile that was set up for our business components.

```
'Create the Session Object
Set objSession = CreateObject("mapi.session")

'Logon using the session object
objSession.Logon profileName:="Business Component"
```

We now need to set our calendar folder object to the default calendar folder on Exchange Server.

```
'Get the default calendar folder
Set objCalendarFolder = objSession.GetDefaultFolder(CdoDefaultFolderCalendar)
```

Now that we have our calendar folder object active, we need to set our message object to a calendar folder message.

```
'Set the message object to a calendar message
Set objMessage = objCalendarFolder.Messages
```

Next we add a new appointment message to the message collection and set the appointment properties. The `AppointmentItem` object describes all of the details of the appointment. As you can see, we are setting the importance of the appointment, the subject, text, start time and the end time of the appointment. The last item added to the appointment is the recipients.

```
'Add a new appointment message to the message collection
Set objNewAppointment = objMessage.Add

'Set the appointment properties
With objNewAppointment
   .Importance = CdoNormal
   .Subject = m_strMsgSubject
   .Text = m_strMsgText
   .StartTime = m_dteStartTime
   .EndTime = m_dteEndTime
   Set objRecipients = .Recipients
End With
```

Once we have all of the appointment properties set we need to add the recipients to the appointment message. We do this by adding the user name and their email address. The email addresses used are the users email address as they appear in MS Exchange.

```
'Add recipients to the recipients collection
With objRecipients
   .Add "John Doe", "Doe, John"
   .Add "Mary Smith", "Smith, Mary"
   .Resolve
End With
```

Everything is complete at this point and all we need to do is send the appointment message and logoff.

```
'Send the meeting item
objNewAppointment.Send

'Logoff using the session object
objSession.Logoff

End Sub
```

Active Directory Service Interfaces

The Active Directory Service Interfaces (ADSI) is a set of COM programming interfaces that allow applications to access any type of network operating system, mail system folders or GroupWare directory structures through a single set of APIs. Like Open Data Base Connectivity (ODBC), Microsoft is providing ADSI as an open set of interfaces so third party vendors like Novell and Lotus can provide interfaces for their products to ADSI thus allowing developers to use a standard set of APIs to access directory structures.

Active Directory Service provides users and applications a means of accessing and naming information on the network. This can be user accounts, computers, printers, mail folders and the like. ADSI provides an easy to use interface to the Active Directory Service.

Active Directory Service provides this interface that allows developers to code applications and components that can access and manipulate directory services and objects such as user profiles, printers and system objects. It also makes finding these objects on the network easier by going through a set of standard interfaces.

Benefits of Using ADSI

ADSI is really geared toward Windows 2000 and as such has been tightly integrated in the new operating system. There is however a small subset of functionality that is available today. By starting to use ADSI now you will be better prepared to fully use ADSI when you migrate to Windows 2000.

Windows 2000 MSMQ will use ADSI to store information about message queues in the Active Directory. This makes the developers' job easier when trying to locate a message queue on the network. Microsoft Exchange will also use ADSI to store such information as address books and certificates.

ADSI uses DNS naming which allows for simplified naming of objects and easy location of these objects by using standard Internet protocols. Suppose you have a computer on your network named `mycomputer.mycompany.com`. ADSI will translate this address into a standard IP (Internet Protocol) address.

One of the key benefits beyond a single interface to manage all objects is the fact that Active Directory provides a single point of management using the global catalog. This high performance catalog stores information about the entire network which makes it easy to find any object no matter where on the network it is located.

Adding ADSI to a Visual Basic Server Component

Before we can add any code to use ADSI we must set a reference to it. Open the References dialog and select the Active DS Type Library as shown below.

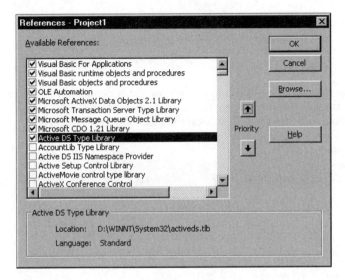

Given the limited set of functionality currently available in ADSI for the operating systems we use today, the examples demonstrated here will be simple. These examples should however give you a good idea of how to use ADSI and what can be accomplished using this new directory interface.

Schema Information

The following example will display schema information for a specific computer connected to a network. This example uses a form for informational and display purposes only. Your actual component would not use a form but would process the information retrieved.

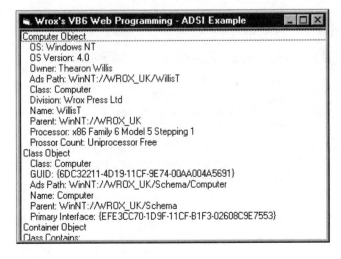

To reproduce this example start by adding a **ListBox** element to your VB form, and then add the ADSI declarations as illustrated below. The IADsComputer object allows us to access various computers on the network. The IADsClass object allows us to access the class schema information about the computer that we have queried.

```
'Declare ADSI objects
Dim objComputer As IADsComputer
Dim objClass As IADsClass
Dim varItem As Variant
```

Next we want to set the computer object to a valid computer connected to the network. The first parameter of the path is the domain name in which the computer resides. The next parameter is the actual computer name to be queried. In this case the domain name is Consultant and the computer workstation name is WSDevelopment.

```
'Set the computer object to a valid computer
Set objComputer = GetObject("WinNT://Consultant/WSDevelopment,computer")
```

Once our computer object has been set we can list the properties for this object.

```
'List the computer object properties
List1.AddItem "Computer Object"
List1.AddItem "OS: " & objComputer.OperatingSystem
List1.AddItem "OS Version: " & objComputer.OperatingSystemVersion
List1.AddItem "Owner: " & objComputer.Owner
List1.AddItem "Ads Path: " & objComputer.ADsPath
List1.AddItem "Class: " & objComputer.Class
List1.AddItem "Division: " & objComputer.Division
List1.AddItem "Name: " & objComputer.Name
List1.AddItem "Parent: " & objComputer.Parent
List1.AddItem "Processor: " & objComputer.Processor
List1.AddItem "Prossor Count: " & objComputer.ProcessorCount
```

Next we want to set the class object to the computers schema.

```
'Set the class object to the computer object's schema
Set objClass = GetObject(objComputer.Schema)
```

Now we can list the class object properties associated with this computer.

```
'List the class object properties
List1.AddItem "Class Object"
List1.AddItem "Class: " & objClass.Name
List1.AddItem "GUID: " & objClass.Guid
List1.AddItem "Ads Path: " & objClass.ADsPath
List1.AddItem "Name: " & objClass.Name
List1.AddItem "Parent: " & objClass.Parent
List1.AddItem "Primary Interface: " & objClass.PrimaryInterface
```

To list the container objects for this class add the following code.

```
'List the container items in the class object
If objClass.Container Then
  List1.AddItem "Container Object"
  List1.AddItem "Class Contains:"

  For Each varItem In objClass.Containment
    List1.AddItem " " & varItem
  Next varItem

Else
  List1.AddItem "Leaf Object"

End If
```

To list all of the mandatory and optional properties for this class we add the code illustrated below.

```
'List the manadatory and optional items in the class object
List1.AddItem "Properties in this Class: "

For Each varItem In objClass.MandatoryProperties
  List1.AddItem " " & varItem
Next varItem

For Each varItem In objClass.OptionalProperties
  List1.AddItem " " & varItem
Next varItem
```

This example provides many properties of a computer and class object that could prove to be very useful for server side components.

Enumerating User Groups

This example shows you how to enumerate a user group. The group can be any valid group name such as Administrators or Domain Users. Like the previous example we are going to use a form for informational and display purposes only. Computer names in the list end with a dollar sign.

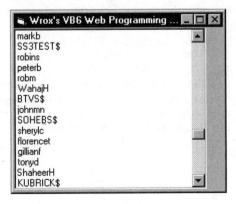

To start, declare your ADSI objects.

```
'Declare ADSI objects
Dim objGroup As IADsGroup
Dim objMember As IADs
```

We need to set the group object next to a valid domain and group name.

```
'Set the group object to a valid user group
Set objGroup = GetObject("WinNT://Consultant/Domain Users")
```

Now that you have a valid object that points to a valid user group we can enumerate all of the users in that group.

```
'List each user in the group
For Each objMember In objGroup.Members
   List1.AddItem objMember.Name
Next objMember
```

That's really all there is to this example. It is pretty straightforward.

Creating and Adding Users

This example will demonstrate how to create a new user and add the user to a specific group. We need to declare our ADSI objects first as illustrated below. The IADsContainer object will represent a valid domain name in which to add the user. The IADsUser object will contain the user information to add to the domain.

```
'Declare ADSI objects
Dim objContainer As IADsContainer
Dim objGroup As IADsGroup
Dim objUser As IADsUser
```

The next thing we need to do is set the container object to a valid domain. All information in the container object gets cached. That is to say that the information is written in memory and does not actually get written to disk until we call the SetInfo method, which we will be describing shortly.

```
'Set the container object to a valid domain (all information is cached)
Set objContainer = GetObject("WinNT://Consultant")
```

Now we set the user object to the valid container object setting the appropriate parameters, in this case the parameter that specifies we are creating a user and the actual user id. The information contained in the IADsContainer object is created in cache. Only the information that is changed is written to disk. You can explicitly update the information by calling the SetInfo() method or the changed data will be written once the program ends.

```
'Create the new user in cache
Set objUser = objContainer.Create("User", "Doe3811")
objUser.FullName = "John Doe"
```

We use the `SetInfo()` method to actually write the cached data back to the domain that was specified in the `IADsContainer` object. We have to add the user before we can set their password, in other words the user information in cache must be written to disk before we can set their password.

```
'Write the cache back to the domain (only changed items are written)
objUser.SetInfo
```

Now that the user is added we have to set their password using the following code. We don't have to call the `SetInfo` method again because when the program ends any information that has changed in cache will be automatically written.

```
'Set the users password
objUser.SetPassword ("123456")
```

After we have created the user, we need to add the user to the group or groups of our choice. In this case we are going to add the new user to two separate groups.

```
'Set the group object to a valid group name
Set objGroup = GetObject("WinNT://Consultant/Users")

'Add the new user to this group
objGroup.Add ("WinNT://Consultant/Doe3811")

'Set the group object to a valid group name
Set objGroup = GetObject("WinNT://Consultant/Print Operators")

'Add the new user to this group
objGroup.Add ("WinNT://Consultant/Doe3811")
```

Before running this example you need to ensure that your logon has permissions to create and add new users.

Practical Examples

This section will show you how to implement the server services we have discussed into the `AuthorData` business server component. This should help you build upon what you have just read and give you a solid working component to study later when you add these new features to your own components.

Most of the examples given previously will be added to our `AuthorData` component. We will step through adding each of these components individually. After each service is added, we will compile our component. You can then test the new functionality just added before continuing on.

Utilizing the new `AuthorData` business component in your Active Server Pages will add increased functionality to your Web site by allowing you to leverage the new found technology in this chapter. What functionality can you add to your Web site by incorporating a component that can send messages and send mail? What about dynamically adding users to your domain? What about running your components in MTS? This should open up a whole new world for your Web site and give you lots of ideas to build on.

Adding Transactions

The first server service we will add is MTS. We will implement transactions for the Add(), Update() and Delete() methods in the Authors class. If the method completes successfully we will commit the transaction, else we will abort the transaction.

The first thing we need to do is set a reference to the Microsoft Transaction Server Type Library in the References dialog. Next we need to set the MTSTransactionMode property in the Authors class to 2 -Requires Transaction.

Add Method

We will start with the Add() method in the Authors class. Insert the code to declare and set the MTS object right after we declare the variables and before any data validations. This will tell MTS to start a transaction and MTS will monitor all activities from this point on.

```
'Delcare variables
Dim strAddress, strCity, strState, strZip, strSQL As String
On Error GoTo AddErr

'Declare and set MTS Object
Dim objMTS As ObjectContext
Set objMTS = GetObjectContext

'*****************************************************************
'Perform data validations
'*****************************************************************
```

If all goes well and we are able to reach the code to close the database then we want to commit the transaction. Place the code to commit the MTS transaction following the code that closes the database.

```
'Close the database
Call CloseDatabase

'Tell MTS to commit the transaction
objMTS.SetComplete
```

If we get a SQL error we definitely want to abort the MTS transaction. We place the MTS abort method in the SQLErr error handling code right after we close the database.

```
SQLErr:
  'Your error handling code here

  'Loop through the ADO errors collection
  Add = 1

  'Close the database
  Call CloseDatabase

  'Tell MTS to abort the transaction
  objMTS.SetAbort

  Exit Function
```

Likewise if we get a general error from the validations we also need to abort the transaction. Place the abort method right before we exit the `Add()` method.

```
AddErr:
     'Your error handling code here
     Add = m_lngError  'The error raised by the validation routines
     'Tell MTS to abort the transaction
     objMTS.SetAbort
End Function
```

Delete Method

Adding MTS to the `Delete()` method is very similar to adding it to the `Add()` method. We start by adding the code declarations and setting the MTS object, which begins a transaction.

```
'Delcare variables
Dim strSQL As String
On Error GoTo DeleteErr

'Declare and set MTS Object
Dim objMTS As ObjectContext
Set objMTS = GetObjectContext

'*****************************************************************
'Perform data validations
'*****************************************************************
```

Next, we add the code to commit the transaction right after we call the procedure to close the database and right before we exit the `Delete` method.

```
'Close the database
Call CloseDatabase

'Tell MTS to commit the transaction
objMTS.SetComplete
```

As in the `Add` method if we get any type of SQL error we want to abort the transaction. We add code to abort the MTS transaction in the `SQLErr` error handler.

```
SQLErr:
     'Your error handling code here
     'Loop through the ADO errors collection
     Delete = 1
     'Close the database
     Call CloseDatabase
     'Tell MTS to abort the transaction
     objMTS.SetAbort
     Exit Function
```

If there is any kind of validation or general error before actually trying to delete the author we will fall into the `DeleteErr` error handling code. We also want to abort the MTS transaction at this point.

```
DeleteErr:
   'Your error handling code here
   Delete = m_lngError  'The error raised by the validation routines
   'Close the database
   Call CloseDatabase
   'Tell MTS to abort the transaction
   objMTS.SetAbort

End Function
```

Update Method

Adding MTS to the `Update` method is just like adding it to the `Add` and `Delete` methods. Add the code to declare and set the MTS object right after you declare your variables.

```
'Delcare variables
   Dim strFirstName, strLastName, strPhone, strAddress, strCity, _
      strState, strZip, strSQL As String
   Dim bytContract As Byte
   On Error GoTo UpdateErr

   'Declare and set MTS Object
   Dim objMTS As ObjectContext
   Set objMTS = GetObjectContext

   '*****************************************************************
   'Perform data validations
   '*****************************************************************
```

We want to commit the transaction right after we close the database so add the following code right after we close the database.

```
'Close the database
   Call CloseDatabase

   'Tell MTS to commit the transaction
   objMTS.SetComplete
```

If we get a SQL error we need to abort the transaction. Add the code to abort the MTS transaction in the `SQLErr` error handling code.

```
SQLErr:
   'Your error handling code here

   'Loop through the ADO errors collection
   Update = 1

   'Close the database
   Call CloseDatabase

   'Tell MTS to abort the transaction
   objMTS.SetAbort

   Exit Function
```

If a general error occurs we need to abort the transaction. Add the code to abort the transaction as shown below.

```
UpdateErr:
   'Your error handling code here
   Update = m_lngError   'The error raised by the validation routines

   'Tell MTS to abort the transaction
   objMTS.SetAbort

End Function
```

Compiling the Component

Now that we have added all of the code to begin, commit and abort MTS transactions we need to compile our component. Before we compile our component we should increment the Minor version number in the Project Properties dialog and reset the Revision number.

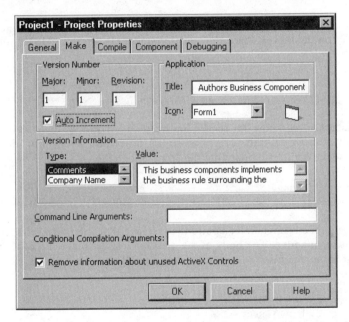

Click OK to save the changes and close the dialog and then compile your component. To install your component in MTS following the steps outlined earlier in this chapter.

Adding Message Queuing

When we add a new author to our database, we want to inform a fictitious Welcome application so that it can automatically send out a fictitious welcome package to the new author. The Welcome application only processes at night in a batch run. It reads a message queue to determine if there are any new authors to generate a welcome package for. Given this scenario, we only want to send a message to a message queue instead of trying to communicate directly with another application.

In order for your code to work correctly you will need to ensure that you have a transactional message queue set up on your workstation or network called 'Authors Data'.

The first step we need to perform is to set a reference to the **Microsoft Message Queue Object Library** in the **References** dialog.

Next, we need to declare our MSMQ objects. We'll place these declarations right after the declaration for the MTS object in the Add() method.

```
'Declare and set MTS Object
Dim objMTS As ObjectContext
Set objMTS = GetObjectContext

'Declare MQ objects
Dim objQueueInfo As New MSMQQueueInfo
Dim objReceiveQueue As New MSMQQueue
Dim objQueueMessage As New MSMQMessage
```

We need to set the QueueInfo object's pathname to our queue on the workstation or server. In this case the queue resides on the server. Place this code immediately after the MSMQ object declarations.

```
'Set the pathname for the receiving queue
objQueueInfo.PathName = "server1\authors data"
```

After we close the database, we know our record has been added and we then want to send a message. Immediately after we call the CloseDatabase procedure we want to add our code to send the message to the queue. We start by opening the receiving queue.

```
'Open the receiving queue
Set objReceiveQueue = objQueueInfo.Open(MQ_SEND_ACCESS, MQ_DENY_NONE)
```

Now that the message queue is opened let's build the message. For the message label we simply state that a new author has been added. The body of the message lets the receiving application know the author's first and last name and also the key to the new record so it can retrieve addition information.

```
'Set the message header and body
objQueueMessage.Label = "New Author Added"
objQueueMessage.Body = "Author " & strFirstName & " " & _
   strLastName & " has been added. The key is " & strSSN
```

Next we need to actually send the message. Note that this MSMQ transaction is running under the control of MTS and we are specifying that this message transaction should also be under MTS control. Hence, if for some reason we fail to complete the entire transaction, adding the author and sending a message, MTS will back out both the inserted record on the database and the message sent to the message queue. In actuality the message is never sent to the queue until you commit the transaction.

```
'Send the message
objQueueMessage.Send objReceiveQueue, MQ_MTS_TRANSACTION
```

After we have sent the message, we have to close the message queue and then commit the entire transaction.

```
'Close the receiving queue
objReceiveQueue.Close

'Tell MTS to commit the transaction
objMTS.SetComplete
```

Before we compile our component, let's once again change the minor revision number as show here. Don't forget to add `objMTS.SetAbort` in your error handling code to tell MTS to abort the transaction if something goes wrong.

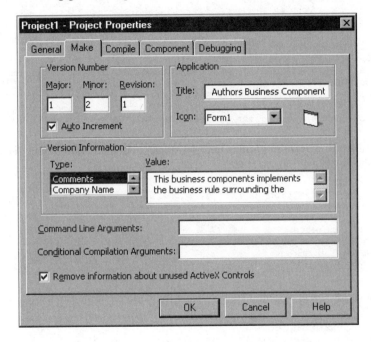

Click **OK** to save the changes and close the dialog and then compile your component. Remember that you must refresh your component in the MTS console.

Adding Mail

After adding a new author to the database we want to send a mail message to a distribution list that contains administrators for various departments such as Sales, Accounting and Payroll. This will notify the appropriate personnel that a new author has joined our fictitious company and needs to be set up in their systems.

To start we need to set a reference to the Microsoft CDO 1.21 Library in the **References** dialog.

Next we need to come up with a standard mail message format that contains the pertinent information to be sent. We can start by using the MSMQ body text that we sent to the message queue and expand on that. To keep things simple we will just add a statement that specifies whether or not we have received a signed contract by using the contract field being passed to the Add() method. All code being added here will be contained in a private method called SendMail() and will be called from the Add() method.

Let's define some constant strings in the General Declarations section of our class module that we will use to build the message. As you can see the message is pretty straightforward and we will fill in the blanks with the actual variable data being passed from the Add method.

```
'Declare mail message constants
Private Const MSG_PART1 As String = "A new author, "
Private Const MSG_PART2 As String = ", has joined our company " & _
                                     "and has been added to the database."
Private Const MSG_PART3 As String = "We have "
Private Const MSG_PART3A As String = "not "
Private Const MSG_PART4 As String = "received a signed contract from "
Private Const MSG_PART5 As String = "Please setup "
Private Const MSG_PART6 As String = " in your systems. If you need " & _
             "additional information regarding this author, please access the " & _
             "Pubs database using the author's key of "
```

We need to create a new private method called SendMail. Add the mail object declarations in our new method as shown below.

```
Private Sub SendMail(strSSN As String, strFirstName As String, _
   strLastName As String, bytContract As Byte)

   'Declare Mail objects
   Dim objSession As Object
   Dim objMessage As Object
   Dim objRecipient As Object
```

Next, we want to create the active mail session using the code illustrated below.

```
   'Create the Session Object
   Set objSession = CreateObject("mapi.session")
```

Once we have a valid session object we need to log on to the Exchange Server using the special logon id and password that has been setup for our component.

```
   'Logon using the session object
   objSession.Logon profileName:="Business Component"
```

Now that we have successfully logged on we need to create a new message. We do this by adding a message to the Outbox.

```
   'Add a new message object to the outbox
   Set objMessage = objSession.Outbox.Messages.Add
```

We have to set the properties of the message object to contain our subject and message text. We will use a string constant for the subject and build the message text by putting together the message part constants.

```
'Set the message subject
objMessage.Subject = "A New Author Has Joined Our Company"

'Set the message text
objMessage.Text = MSG_PART1 & strFirstName & " " & strLastName & _
    MSG_PART2 & vbCrLf & vbCrLf & MSG_PART3 & _
    IIf(bytContract = 0, MSG_PART3A, "") & MSG_PART4 & _
    strFirstName & "." & vbCrLf & vbCrLf & MSG_PART5 & _
    strFirstName & MSG_PART6 & strSSN & "."
```

Once the message has been created, we need to add the recipient object to the recipients collection and set the recipient name. This time we are using a public distribution list called New Authors as the recipient.

```
'Add a recipient object to the recipients collection
Set objRecipient = objMessage.Recipients.Add
'Set the properties of the recipient object
objRecipient.Name = "New Authors"
```

In order to complete the recipient object and have our recipient added to the message we must have CDO resolve the reference. We do this by adding the following code.

```
'Resolve the recipient name
objRecipient.Type = CdoTo
objRecipient.Resolve
```

We are now ready to send the message and log off.

```
'Send the message
objMessage.Send showDialog:=False

'Logoff using the session object
objSession.Logoff

End Sub
```

Since sending mail is not covered under MTS as a transaction that can be backed out, we will send our mail message after we commit the MTS transaction. Add your code to call the SendMail method as shown below. Again, don't forget to add objMTS.SetAbort to your error handling code.

```
'Tell MTS to commit the transaction
objMTS.SetComplete

'Send the mail message
Call SendMail(strSSN, strFirstName, strLastName, bytContract)
```

Before compiling your component, let's once again change the revision number to reflect the additional code features.

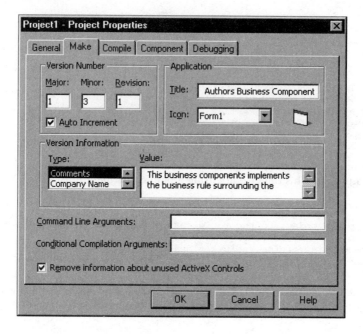

Adding New Users

The final part of our practical demonstration is to add new users to the domain using ADSI. Once we have added a new author to the database, sent a message to the `Welcome` application and sent mail to the responsible administrators to have the new author added to their systems, we want to add the new author to our domain so they will be able to log onto our system.

We start by creating a new private method in the Authors class called `AddDomainUser()`. We will pass the SSN, First Name and Last Name to this method. Next, we add the ADSI object declarations that we need and the private variables that we need.

```
Private Sub AddDomainUser(strSSN As String, strFirstName As String, _
                          strLastName As String)

'Declare ADSI objects
Dim objContainer As IADsContainer
Dim objGroup As IADsGroup
Dim objUser As IADsUser

'Declare local variables
Dim strUserID As String
```

Now we can set the container object to a valid domain name.

```
'Set the container object to a valid domain (all information is cached)
Set objContainer = GetObject("WinNT://Consultant")
```

The user ID will consist of the user's last name and the last four digits of their social security number. We set a string value using this information to be used later in our code.

```
'Create the user id
strUserID = strLastName & Right$(strSSN, 4)
```

We create the new user by setting the user object using the container object's Create() method. Remember that all information is cached and no updates are applied until you call the SetInfo() method.

```
'Create the new user in cache
Set objUser = objContainer.Create("User", strUserID)
objUser.FullName = strFirstName & " " & strLastName
```

Once we have the user id and the user's name set we want to apply these updates to the domain.

```
'Write the cache back to the domain (only changed items are written)
objUser.SetInfo
```

Next, we want to set the user's password using the code illustrated below.

```
'Set the users password
objUser.SetPassword ("123456")
```

The new user ID is added to the group Domain Users by default. We want to add the new user to two other groups. The first group is called Users which is a group for normal users. The second group is called Authors and is a special group just for authors.

```
'Set the group object to a valid group name
Set objGroup = GetObject("WinNT://Consultant/Users")

'Add the new user to this group
objGroup.Add ("WinNT://Consultant/" & strUserID)

'Set the group object to a valid group name
Set objGroup = GetObject("WinNT://Consultant/Authors")

'Add the new user to this group
objGroup.Add ("WinNT://Consultant/" & strUserID)

End Sub
```

We want to place the code to call this new method after we send the mail message in the Add() method. Add your code as shown below.

```
'Send the mail message
Call SendMail(strSSN, strFirstName, strLastName, bytContract)

'Add domain user
Call AddDomainUser(strSSN, strFirstName, strLastName)
```

Once again, before compiling your code, change the revision number in the Project Properties dialog to reflect the new code addition.

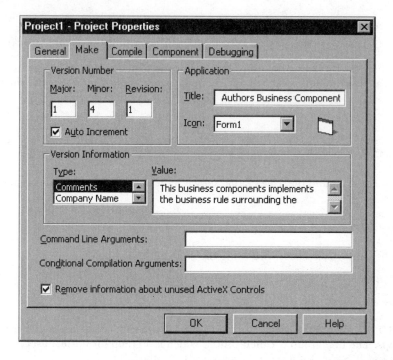

Summary

This chapter has covered only a small portion of the server side services that are available for your Visual Basic business components. Likewise the services we did cover, we covered briefly just to give you an idea of what is available and how your components could benefit from using them.

Additional reading should be done to explore these components in depth. You can find valuable information in the Platform SDK on the Microsoft Developer Network Library CDs that ship with both the Professional and Enterprise editions of Visual Studio 6.0. If you don't have the MSDN Library CDs you can find the same information online at
`http://msdn.microsoft.com/library/default.htm`

Visit the Wrox Web site at `http://www.wrox.com/` *to order books on ADSI, ASP, MTS, MSMQ and CDO.*

To summarize this chapter, we have learned:

- ➤ How Microsoft Transaction Server can help us to manage our transactions and database connections
- ➤ How Microsoft Message Queuing can help us to send information to other applications across poor network connections, or to applications that are not running at the same time as we are
- ➤ How Collaboration Data Objects can help us to mail-enable our components
- ➤ How we can benefit from Active Directory Service Interfaces now, and when Windows 2000 is released
- ➤ How ADSI plays a significant role in the Windows 2000 architecture

Introducing Webclasses and IIS Applications

So far, we have explored many different options through which Visual Basic developers can produce solutions for the web. We have talked about the infrastructures of web technologies like Internet Information Server, Microsoft Transaction Server, and Active Server Pages. We have spent time discussing superstructure elements such as ADO, CDO, MMC, ADSI, ActiveX components, and so on. After a discussion of design methodology we spent time discussing the requirements for developing web-based applications and issues such as scalability, security, transactions, and threading models. The discussion of the current crop of technologies available for web development could go on and on, and it takes a lot of experience and knowledge to master these technologies. Fortunately however, as VB developers we have another option, one that directly leverages our Visual Basic experience.

In this chapter, we will introduce Visual Basic webclasses and IIS Applications. We will take a look at the basic advantages that IIS Applications can provide over other web technologies. IIS Applications provide an alternative to the very popular Active Server Pages platform for web application development. IIS Applications seek to address numerous requests and concerns that Visual basic developers have had in attempting to find the best platform for the Visual Basic programmer to use for developing web solutions.

In Chapter 6 we looked at DHTML Applications, which are a version 6.0 addition to the repertoire of available Visual Basic projects. DHTML applications are designed for client-side solutions. Now we will explore the server-side equivalent, IIS Applications.

In this chapter, we will focus on the introduction of the IIS Application project type. In the next two chapters, we will go into more detail about the specifics of webclass events, techniques and examples.

In this chapter, we will cover:

> ➤ The basics of IIS Application

> ➤ A roadmap for developing IIS Applications

> ➤ Preparations and requirements for creating IIS Applications with webclasses.

Let's start by introducing Microsoft's new type of web application...

A New Type of Web Application

Of all the improvements, enhancements, and new features that Visual Basic 6.0 has brought to the Visual Basic developer community, Visual Basic IIS Applications are the most interesting and useful for the development of server-side web-based applications. While the technology is new, it provides a combination of features that are extremely useful to the Visual Basic programmer seeking to develop server-side applications for use on Intranets, the Internet, or any IP-based networks over which HTTP messages may be transmitted. Microsoft Visual Basic IIS Applications are server-side applications hosted on Microsoft's Internet Information Server (for a detailed discussion of how to set IIS up, see the discussion in Appendix F). The output of the IIS Application comprises the user interface for the application, and can be viewed within a client web browser, or browsing control such as the Microsoft WebBrowser control discussed in Chapter 7. This closely parallels previous solutions and technologies, while providing a wealth of features geared specifically for the Visual Basic programmers.

With Visual Basic IIS Applications, Microsoft have added a brand new twist to the concept of an IIS-based application. Prior to Visual Basic 6.0, the phrase IIS application was used in Microsoft Official Curriculum course material to refer to what was basically an ASP-based web application. ASP pages that collectively acted as a functional application, through unified design, interaction, and configuration within Internet Information Server, was described was a web application. The term IIS application now has a more specific meaning within Visual Basic.

IIS Applications owe their existence to the growing need for an application development framework to facilitate the creation of web applications. Although many web application development platforms have cropped up with the rise of the Internet and intranets, none have allowed the use of a particular popular set of development tools, namely Visual Basic. As discussed in Chapters 9 and 10, component development - using Microsoft transactions within Visual Basic has been an option for sometime, going back as far as Visual Basic 5. Unfortunately, the pace of change demands ever more options.

Since application development is rapidly reaching a stage of evolution where most applications will require some degree of web-enabling or exposure, Visual Basic is striving to make the development of these applications as straightforward as coding standard Visual Basic Form behavior. In order to accomplish this, and allow the huge Visual Basic developer base to leverage their skills onto the web, the concept of the Visual Basic IIS Application was born. Although the web development paradigm has fostered the creation of wonderfully appropriate development tools such as Visual Interdev, the traditional benefit leveraging existing development skills cannot be, and with Visual Basic IIS Applications, is not, ignored.

IIS Application Basics

Visual Basic IIS Applications are a variation of the standard Visual Basic ActiveX DLL project. ActiveX DLL projects, also known as COM DLLs, have been available since Visual Basic 5. IIS Applications projects include a project reference to the Microsoft WebClass Library, which brings up the core of an IIS Application, a **WebClass object**. This is specifically what makes an IIS Application unique – it leverages a brand new type of COM component called the Webclass object. A Webclass object is a COM component that functions in conjunction with a Webclass Run-time Manager COM object provided by Visual Basic.

The WebClass Run-time Manager COM component is provided by the dynamic link library files utilized by a compiled Visual Basic IIS Application. The WebClass Run-time Manager object provides the necessary run-time communication channels to Internet Information Server, to allow the WebClass object to become the new recipient of HTTP requests. This means a WebClass object is the core component in a Visual Basic IIS Application.

A Webclass object is therefore a specialized COM component used by an IIS Application to generate responses to client HTTP requests. By handling the responses, the WebClass object is designed to process Visual Basic code that has been associated with assorted application events, such as submitting data in a form, or requesting a particular page. These events are initiated by user interaction with HTTP request generating elements – such as the ubiquitous submit button – within an HTML page sent to the client.

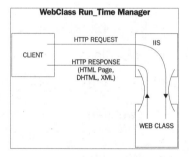

In most cases, the response sent back to a client is a traditional HTML web page. IIS Applications still rely very much on the web browser as client: the source of the application has merely changed. Since the user's interface still consists of HTML pages rendered within a browser on the client, and the code to process requests received by the web server is now on the server-side, some aspect of the interface must be designated as entry points to the server-side code. These entry points to executing code within the server-based application are the HTML elements which generate HTTP requests. These are the same elements which have always been the source of web server requests within traditional web pages. Requests of this nature are traditionally serviced by the web server, just as if they were normal requests originating within web pages, images, or other MIME file types returnable as an HTTP response. Fortunately, webclasses are not limited to returning only HTML to the client. DHTML, XML, or any other valid MIME type can be returned by the webclass.

A webclass is encapsulated within an ActiveX DLL, and resides on the web server. By residing on the web server, the webclass COM component can be easily instantiated in response to a request by multiple clients. The actual instantiation of the webclass object is performed within a host Active Server Page generated automatically by Visual Basic, and we'll look again at this relationship in a later section. Upon instantiation, an instance of the COM component, now more correctly referred to as a WebClass object, resides in the memory of the web server. By default, the WebClass object will only remain instantiated for the duration of the HTTP request that resulted in its instantiation, although this behavior can be altered by setting the appropriate properties of the WebClass object.

Upon successful processing of the HTTP request – that is, once any Visual Basic code associated with the request has been run – the instance of the WebClass is typically destroyed. The WebClass object can be configured to remain instantiated for the entire duration of the user session with the application, although such modified behavior should be analyzed to determine the net effects on the scalability of the IIS Application. When we talk in terms of a session governing the life of the webclass object, we are talking about an Active Server Page user session, as was discussed in Chapter 8. Specifically, the applicable session is defined by the standard Active Server Page user session that was established in response to a client's request for the base Active Server Page that Visual Basic created to serve as the host or gateway to the IIS Application. Since a one-to-one mapping exists between webclasses and the Active Server Pages created by Visual Basic to host the webclasses, and multiple webclasses may be added to a single IIS Application, multiple Active Server Pages may actually be associated with a single IIS Application.

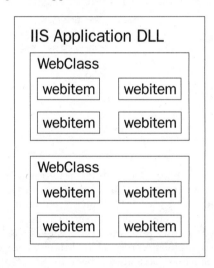

Webclasses contain a series of resources which are used to send responses back to the client making the HTTP request. These resources are referred to as **webitems**. Webitems are child objects within the webclass component that are typically associated with external resources. The external resources, such as an HTML template file, can be packaged up and sent out as HTTP packets in response to a client HTTP request. Typically, webitems are HTML templates that are used as the foundation for the user interface which is presented to the client. External HTML templates, which could be built by User Interface specialists, can be imported into the Visual Basic 6 IDE, and the origin of the templates will not impact the ability to use them.

By existing as an in-process, binary dynamic link library, the IIS application is able to encapsulate various advanced abilities, such as:

- Streamlining database access into a single installable binary application file (although this has drawbacks, because webclasses can't take advantage of MTS)
- Providing ASP-like dynamic content generation, taking advantage of Visual Basic's superior capabilities compared to scripting languages
- Creating HTML elements within page responses dynamically, without requiring a DHTML-capable browser
- Combining scripting and application processing into a single, unified platform running on the server

By encapsulating application logic in a single binary DLL running on a Microsoft Internet Information Server, IIS Applications also provide a strong degree of built-in security for protecting proprietary code, since the executable runs entirely within the memory space of the web server.

General Advantages

Using Visual Basic IIS applications provides several distinct advantages over existing methods for developing web or client/server applications. These advantages involve:

- Cost of Deployment
- Development Environment
- Programming Model
- Object Model
- Audience Scope
- Reusability
- Code Separation
- State Management

Cost of Deployment

You don't need any client-side software other than the basic browser for IIS applications. Using the terminology from Chapter 2, we use a thin client for accessing the presentation tier of an application. By using a thinner, more universally available piece of client software for rendering and presenting the user portion of an application, application-specific software requirements are significantly reduced. In fact, upon successful deployment of a functional IIS application, the client-side software requirements for further IIS applications is effectively reduced to zero, since most users already have access to a reasonable browser.

Development Environment

Developing IIS applications within Visual Basic allows you to use a familiar design environment and programming model. You can use your own familiarity with the layout of the VB IDE to speed up your development time. Furthermore, you have all the debugging tools of VB at your fingertips, and the inclusion of additional Visual Basic elements such as standard class modules and ActiveX components allows much greater flexibility in developing advance application features.

Object Model

You can use the core Active Server Page object model to make accessing Internet Information Server resources easier. Direct manipulation of the core objects and capabilities of Internet Information Server allows you to include a great deal of functionality in your web pages with little extra coding. This functionality includes information retrieval and communication with the client web browser, as well as complex manipulation of content within the web pages themselves.

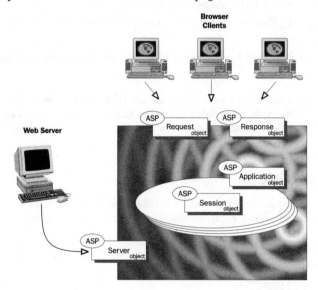

Audience Scope

The scope of the intended audience of an IIS application is broadened by the elimination of restrictions imposed by inherent client limitations. This allows an IIS application to interact with clients working on any platform. Gone are the concerns for the viability of a given vendor's operating system. Should a major shift occur in the browser base or operating systems in use, then you would need only a minimal degree of recoding.

Reusability

Reusable webclass COM components maintain one of the primary tenets of distributed application development and design. The concept of reusability is supported by encapsulating a collection of HTML page HTTP responses within a single, reusable piece of component code. As a result, webclasses can be saved and imported into other IIS applications, with a consequent decrease in the development time of future applications. Furthermore, many other types of Visual Basic applications can leverage the webclass objects to expose a portion of an application's functionality to the web. This addresses the forecoming need for almost all applications to expose some degree of functionality via the web.

Code Separation

Separating the code used to respond to HTTP requests from the actual HTML allows you to separate out the design processes. Writing, testing and debugging application logic is independent of the development of the user interface exposed through the client-side HTML. This allows a clean separation of roles within a standard application development process.

State Management

State information management is a concept often taken for granted in traditional vertical applications, as use of the proper variable scope guarantees accessibility of state information from form to form. When developing web applications, the separation of user interface elements into distinct HTML pages blocks the easiest way for you to maintain state information. By using the Active Server Page object model in the WebClass object, state information can be easily maintained and managed within the webclass State information can therefore be maintained either through traditional binary application mechanisms of database storage or member variables, as well as through the traditional Active Server Page mechanisms of Session object variables, Application object variables, or Cookies.

Previous Visual Basic Options

Prior to VB 6.0 webclasses, assorted Visual Basic options existed for providing application functionality through the web. In VB 4, CGI/WIN interface solutions were developed to create executable files whose functionality could be reached through the web. Starting with Visual Basic 4, the ability to create Visual Basic OLE DLLs, which became in Visual Basic 5 the ActiveX DLLs we discussed in Chapters 9 and 10. This opened the door to accessing selected pieces of code from Active Server Pages. While much of the functionality provided by webclasses could be manually constructed with custom COM components, the advantages of webclasses revolve mostly around the enhanced functionality, productivity, and simplified development that they provide.

Comparison to DHTML Applications

When first examining the new features of Visual Basic, a programmer might initially be confused as to the relationship that DHTML Applications, mentioned in Chapter 4, have with IIS Applications. Both are new Visual Basic additions that address developing web-based applications, but they are aimed at different environments. In order to gain a better understanding of the relationship between the two, let's take a look at the similarities:

> ➢ Designed for creating applications that are web-enabled to some degree.
> ➢ Allow the processing of events initiated by user interaction within an HTML page.
> ➢ Compiled into a DLL component for encapsulation of the processing code

Differences

While these basic similarities do exist, the differences in the functionality and implementation of an IIS Application versus a DHTML Application clearly differentiate the use and purpose of the two types of Visual Basic applications. The differences in the two application types include:

> ➢ Object Model
> ➢ Processing location
> ➢ Browser dependency
> ➢ Network profile
> ➢ Degree of web-enabling
> ➢ HTML events processed
> ➢ Processing Scope

Object Model

The object model that is leveraged within the two application types is significantly different. DHTML applications use the Dynamic HTML object model, otherwise known as the Document Object Model (DOM). Since DHTML Applications are designed to leverage the benefits of a richer DHTML-based user interface, access to the Document Object Model is required to expose the objects for which the application will be providing application logic. User interaction which affects the objects within a page will only be programmable if the object themselves are accessible. On the other hand, IIS Applications utilize the Active Server Pages object model. These objects are passed into the WebClass object, allowing the information which governs interaction among multiple HTTP requests to be accessible and maintainable by the webclass. Since IIS Applications run on the web server itself, a webclass object within an IIS Application is more concerned with information at the server level, or information which spans multiple HTTP requests issued to the web server.

Processing location

When an IIS Application is created, the resulting ActiveX DLL runs on the web server. This server-side component is thereby stationed at the receiving point where the HTML page will ultimately access the web server, thereby seeking to initiate code within the application. While the IIS Application is designed to perform most, if not all of its processing on the server, a DHTML Application performs its processing on the client side. The browser machine will download the application code, which will exist within the memory of the client machine, handling requests for all manner of user events within the page.

Browser dependency

IIS Applications, by running on the web server, are not inherently designed for using Internet Explorer as the client-side client portion of the application. The limitations of the client piece of the application puzzle are determined by the nature of the HTML tags and scripting placed within the HTML template files used by the webclass. This allows the IIS Application to be designed for heterogeneous browser environments and still leverage Microsoft Visual Basic for the application logic. DHTML Applications, on the other hand, are clearly dependent on Internet Explorer 4.0 or later, to guarantee the existence of Dynamic HTML support.

Network profile

In many ways, the browser requirements the application must support works hand in hand with the profile of the typical network for which the application is designed. IIS Applications, due to their ability to support the use of multiple browser varieties on the client-side, are designed for use on the Internet, or on larger WANs or LANs. These network environments either involve many different browsers, or are apt to involve more variety or flexible in browser choices. DHTML Applications, due to their reliance on guarantees of DHTML support, are designed more for intranets, where the official browser platform can be controlled or enforced, providing a reasonable guarantee of a homogenous browser environment.

Degree of web-enabling

IIS Applications are designed for applications which are expected to, or may ultimately have some form of their functionality exposed through the web. An IIS Application may still contain COM components, or other, non-HTTP based server mechanism. IIS Applications are not inherently limited to providing server-side webclass components for processing HTTP requests, and conversely the use of webclasses is not limited to IIS Applications. DHTML Applications, on the other hand, are for use in developing applications that are designed entirely as web-based applications. Rather than simply having the option of some, or all functionality exposed to the web through inclusion of webclasses, DHTML Applications primarily expose functionality that works in conjunction with a DHTML-enhanced web-based application.

448

HTML events processed

IIS Applications are designed to provide application code behind the entry points that an HTML page makes to the web server. For each potential tag attribute which could initiate an HTTP request, and thus serve as an entry point into the functionality of the web server, the IIS Application provides application logic. For events that occur solely within the confines of the client memory space, the IIS Application does not expose functionality or application logic. DHTML Applications are designed to allow responses to many different events within an HTML page. These events include a much greater degree of user interaction, rather than being limited to only those HTML events resulting in communication with the web server.

Processing Scope

IIS Applications are designed to function within a broader scope than DHTML Applications. Because they're hosted on the web server, IIS Applications work within a larger, server-oriented scope. They also focus on interaction that spans multiple web pages, including maintenance of information across these pages. This requires that issues of scalability be addressed when designing and developing the application. DHTML Applications focus more on a page by page scope, dealing more with user events and interactions that concentrate on single pages.

IIS Apps vs Visual Interdev

While the development of IIS Applications within Visual Basic may seem to be a useful addition to the capabilities of one of the world's most popular languages, we should ask one important question: Why duplicate the functionality which already exists in development tools such as Visual Interdev in Visual Basic? Visual Interdev is the newest premium member of the Visual Studio application development suite of tools. Its primary purpose is to integrate elements, components, and controls developed in the Visual Studio languages. The resulting integration of elements, combined with visual development tools and debugging support provides an excellent environment for creating IIS-based applications, using Active Server Page technology. While this may seem like the perfect development tool for some web application developers, we can get a couple of design time benefits from using IIS Applications:

➢ retain the familiar Visual Basic programming model, rather than migrating to the different programming model incorporated into Visual Interdev

➢ Use a single integrated design environment for your web application and the custom VB COM components utilized by the application

Project Differences

The specific differences with the new Visual Basic 6 IIS Application and the relatively new Visual Interdev web applications hinge on several aspects of the project design:

➢ Type of developers creating the physical implement of the application

➢ Degree of importance placed on the separation of presentation from content

➢ Production Web server to be implemented

Based on the answers provided to these application design concerns, Visual Basic IIS Applications can provide a more appropriate or efficient application framework within which to work.

Application Developers

For obvious reasons, pure Visual Basic developers will prefer the new IIS Application project type for development of web applications. Fresh from a homogenous Visual Basic environment, the use of newer web technologies such as Active Server Pages, remote scripting, and Internet Information Server is rather unfamiliar. Having to design web applications within the constraints imposed on application logic by the limitations inherent in scripting languages is a drag for the seasoned Visual Basic programmer. On the other hand, web developers who have learned to master the skills used in developing web applications based on the flexibility of Active Server Pages, HTML, and the primary features of scripting languages will probably prefer using Visual Interdev to create Active Server Page application.

Separating Content From Presentation

Ever since the emergence of the web, people have insisted that the coding and development of the actual content of a website or web application should be separate from the coding representing the presentation of that content. Early on, this debate took the form of arguing whether proprietary HTML tags, such as Microsoft's proprietary <MARQUEE> tag should be allowed. In essence, the <MARQUEE> tag both identified the text to be used within the marquee (the content) and told the browser that the text was a rotating string of text (the presentation) all within a single defined tag. As a result the World Wide Web Consortium (W3C), which has the job of drafting and forming any new HTML recommendation, decided not to integrate this particular tag into any official HTML recommendation.

The debate has continued, and taken a very decisive turn with the establishment of Cascading Style Sheets as an official W3C recommendation. Both Microsoft and Netscape, whose various browser versions account for well over 90% of the browser traffic on the Internet, have independently announced that they recommend and support the separation of presentation markup into Cascading Style Sheets. With this latest development, it seems quite reasonable that a prime design directive in the future will include the separation of content from presentation.

IIS Applications help to support this by cleanly separating the application and presentation logic from the actual source of the HTML. While a complete separation of presentation from content would mean presentation design dealt solely with the development of the HTML template files themselves, a portion of presentation design deals with the application logic that is applied to the elements themselves. With IIS you can keep the functionality of any HTML elements which deal with the generation of HTTP requests for subsequent presentation elements – like images and additional web pages – on the server within the webclass.

Web Server Implementation

For obvious reasons, the type of production web server to be implemented would impact whether or not an IIS Application would be chosen over Active Server Page applications. Since IIS Applications are designed to run on Internet Information Server, Personal Web Services, or Personal Web Server, if a different type of web server is used in production, then IIS Applications would not be an option. Visual Interdev can be used to develop web applications that will ultimately run on non-Microsoft web servers, while an IIS Application specifically requires a Microsoft web server, and ideally, IIS.

Chaining Visual Interdev and Visual Basic

Developing IIS Applications may primarily be an alternative to developing Active Server Page web applications in Visual Interdev, but you might find combining the two to be a powerful option. While there are benefits of IIS Applications which aren't provided by Visual Interdev web applications, most of those benefits do not apply to the development of the actual HTML templates. Microsoft did not turn Visual Basic into a potential HTML editor. They clearly expect you to use external HTML designers and editors to create or modify the actual templates, and then use Visual Basic webclass objects to provide code behind the actual web server entry points. You might find that designing, developing and coding HTML template files is best done with Visual Interdev. Visual Interdev can be set up as the default HTML editor within an IIS Application project. In many cases, though, the initial HTML template files may simply be created within Visual Interdev, and then imported into an IIS Application.

Windows DNA Participation

As we discussed in Chapter One, Windows Distributed interNet Architecture (DNA) is a roadmap for building modern distributed applications. The applications are designed in a multi-tier architecture, with the middle tier commonly being referred to as the business tier. Visual Basic COM components are already common within this middle tier, especially when written to work in conjunction with Microsoft's primary middle tier server product, Microsoft Transaction Server, which we discussed briefly in Chapter 11. WebClass objects within an IIS Application are meant to function within this middle tier. Webclasses are intended to provide an integrated development mechanism for providing application logic which can be accessed from HTTP.

Prior to webclasses and IIS Applications, middle tier business components written in Visual Basic were commonly accessed from within Active Server Pages by instantiating instances of the components, installed on the web server. This process is very much the server-side equivalent of embedding ActiveX controls within an HTML page. Just as ActiveX controls are binary components of Win32 functionality embedded within a text-based file of client-side HTML, server-side Visual Basic COM components are binary components of Win32 functionality executed within text-based file of server-side script commands. If the same comparison were attempted for IIS Applications, what would be the equivalent? IIS Applications would essentially be the server equivalent of the traditional Visual Basic standard application. With the use of an Active Server Page to instantiate the webclass notwithstanding, IIS Applications completely encapsulate the application logic of a web application within a single binary file just like a standard Visual Basic application encapsulates the forms, images, and standard windows controls into a single binary executable.

IIS Application RoadMap

The roadmap for creating an IIS Application is a well-defined series of steps. While you'll recognize some obvious similarities to the steps you take to create many other types of Visual Basic applications, there are some obvious differences you should be aware of. We'll present an overview of these steps before moving on to examine each in more depth.

In general, the steps to be followed are:

1. Start Visual Basic and open a new IIS Application project. As we said earlier, an IIS Application could also be created manually by starting a new ActiveX DLL project, removing the default class module and replacing it with a Webclass ActiveX Designer, and then making a project reference to Microsoft WebClass Library v1.0. When you compile, the DLL will include the WebClass object and the appropriate host Active Server Page will be created for the webclass.

> **The Active Server Page host file is produced by the WebClass object, not the project type. Simply adding an instance of a Webclass Designer to a Visual Basic project will ensure that the necessary ASP file is generated.**

2. Save the project. A distinct difference between standard Visual Basic applications and IIS Applications is that you need to save the project before you can add HTML templates. Within an IIS Application, HTML Templates act as the equivalent of Forms in a standard Visual Basic application. You need to save the IIS application because Visual Basic copies the HTML template file to the project, and needs to know the project location to do so. If you try to add a template without first saving the project, you'll see the dialogue box below.

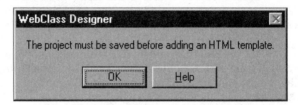

3. Add HTML template to the project to provide a core set of HTML pages to be sent back to the client as HTTP responses. These template files are developed outside of Visual Basic and provide the presentation layer for the application.

4. Add custom webitems to the project for processing events and supplying the code to be associated with HTTP request-generating elements within the HTML pages. You use Webitems when HTTP response sent to the client will not involve HTML, or when the HTML sent to the client as a response will be generated on-the-fly by Visual Basic code.

5. Add custom events to the application to allow you to code application processes outside of a standard Webitem event.

6. Add code to the events contained within the application. The most important part of this step is coding the `Start` event for the WebClass object itself. Without any initialization code to provide a default response for the application when the WebClass object is instantiated, no response will be generated or sent to the client.

It is possible to manually construct URLs in such a way as to instruct the WebClass object to fire specific events within the object. In fact, the standard method for instructing a WebClass object to fire a given event is performed through syntactically correct construction of the proper URL. These values, appended to the URL for the host Active Server Page, are passed to the webclass through the appropriate method of the Webclass Manager object and analyzed by the webclass.

7. Add any additional code modules or Webclass objects you want to the project by repeating steps 3 through 6 as required.

8. Test and debug the application. Since the presentation tier of the application is viewed through a web browser, you should test the application according to the expected mix of browsers to be used by the users of the application.

9. Compile the application. The host Active Server Page is created at this stage, along with the binary DLL that houses the webclass components added to the application.

10. Deploy the application. You should use the Package and Deployment Wizard provided with Visual Basic to create a setup executable that registers the webclass components on the production web server and sets up the application for use with a web server.

IIS Application Preparations

Creating a Visual Basic IIS Application begins, of course, by starting Visual Basic 6 and choosing a new IIS Application project.

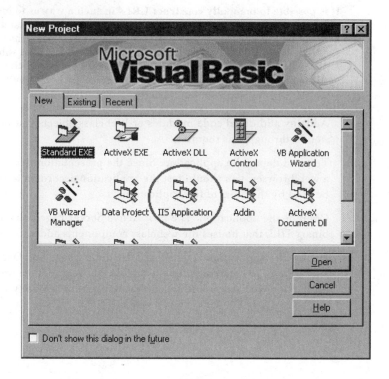

Web Server Required

IIS Applications are designed to run as in-process DLLs, cooperating with HTTP services provided by Internet Information Server. You'll therefore need a web server available even during the design stages.

Server Unavailable

If you don't have a web server available, you'll get a number of error messages when you try to start up a new IIS application. The first error that Visual Basic will produce will indicate a failed attempt to locate a web server installed on the developer's system.

> Note that the web server must be installed on your development machine. This is not like Visual Interdev 6.0, which merely needs access to a web server with FrontPage Extensions installed, anywhere on the LAN.

Visual Basic, initially, will merely attempt to confirm that web server software is installed on the development system on which the project will be built. This Web server would be either Internet Information Server on a Windows NT Server, Peer Web Services on a Window NT Workstation, or Personal Web Server on a Windows 95/98 developer system. The Web server does not have to be running, but you must have it installed in order to start a new IIS Application project. Although the initial error message only lists Internet Information Server and Peer Web Services version 3.0 or later has not been found, you can start a new IIS Application project on a Windows 95/98 system running Personal Web Server.

The dialogue will then tell you that, in the absence of an installed web server, the errors have been logged to a `Webclass.log` file.

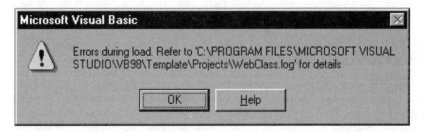

Finally, the default Webclass Designer file, `WebClass.Dsr`, won't load into the project. Furthermore, Visual Basic will fail to open a project of any nature.

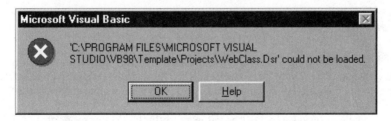

Server Available

If you have a web server available on your development machine, the project will load, giving you an initial instance of a Webclass object in the Project Explorer.

Although an IIS Application is provided as an independent project type, it is not an entirely unique project type. Creating a new IIS Application project basically creates a variation of the ActiveX DLL projects that are also available within Visual Basic. The IIS Application ActiveX DLL will physically live on the web server.

Webclass Hosting Requirement

The WebClass object is a COM component that, by virtue of its housing within an in-process DLL, functions as a server-side component. Upon instantiation, a WebClass object provides custom HTTP processing of incoming HTTP requests made by a client of the IIS Application. In this manner, the WebClass object is acting as a base for a web-based application. Since a webclass is a COM component, without its own binary client application to instantiate the component, you need some form of gateway or host to provide a starting point for an IIS Application, and its webclass components.

Active Server Page Host

An IIS Application goes through the same standard compilation process as any other Visual Basic project, with a unique twist. Upon compiling the IIS Application into an ActiveX DLL, each Webclass object added to the IIS Application is provided with a separate Active Server Page (ASP).

This Active Server Page serves as a host or gateway to the COM component. If a default IIS Application, containing a Webclass object with the default name of WebClass1, is compiled into a Project1.dll file, then an Active Server Page of the same name (WebClass1.ASP) is created in the project directory. VB automatically generates the following code for the .ASP:

```
<%
Response.Buffer=True
Response.Expires=0

If (VarType(Application("~WC~WebClassManager")) = 0) Then
    Application.Lock
    If (VarType(Application("~WC~WebClassManager")) = 0) Then
        Set Application("~WC~WebClassManager") = _
```

```
            Server.CreateObject("WebClassRuntime.WebClassManager")
        End If
        Application.UnLock
    End If

    Application("~WC~WebClassManager").ProcessNoStateWebClass "Project1.WebClass1", _
        Server, _
        Application, _
        Session, _
        Request, _
        Response
    %>
```

The Active Server Page acts as the starting point for the application. The URL (Uniform Resource Locator) for the Active Server Page serves the same function as the path name of a standard .exe file. An HTTP request for the URL of the host Active Server Page loads the Active Server Page into the web server, thereby allowing the web server to begin processing the application.

Active Server Page Functionality

When the Active Server Page is requested by a client, two purposes are fulfilled. The Active Server Page checks for the presence of an instance of the WebClassRuntime.WebClassManager COM component. This is performed by checking whether or not the Application variable Application("~WC~WebClassManager") is empty, which would be indicated by a value of 0 for the VarType function:

```
    If (VarType(Application("~WC~WebClassManager"))) = 0) Then
        ...
    End If
```

Remember that this code is contained within an Active Server Page, and that, as we discussed in Chapter 8, the Application object is part of the core Active Server Page object Model. If an instance of the WebClassRuntime.WebClassManager object is not already stored within the Application object variable, the code on the page locks the Application object (preventing changes while the code is run), and an instance is created by using the CreateObject method of the built-in Active Server Page Server object:

```
    If (VarType(Application("~WC~WebClassManager"))) = 0) Then
        Application.Lock
        If (VarType(Application("~WC~WebClassManager"))) = 0) Then
            Set Application("~WC~WebClassManager") = _
                Server.CreateObject("WebClassRuntime.WebClassManager")
        End If
        Application.UnLock
    End If
```

Note that the code checks that a WebClassManager hasn't been created while the code was locking the Application object, and that it unlocks the Application at the end of the process.

The WebClassRuntime.WebClassManager object, found within MSWCRUN.DLL, provides the processing directives and management services to redirect HTTP requests to the appropriate component during run-time. This DLL is installed onto the developer system with Visual Basic and is known as the Microsoft WebClass Library v1.0. A reference to this library is automatically made for IIS Application projects.

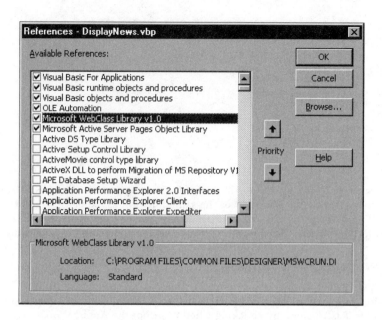

After the Webclass run-time manager is confirmed, instantiated and ready for use, one of two different methods of the `WebClassManager` is invoked:

➤ `ProcessRetainInstanceWebClass`

➤ `ProcessNoStateWebClass`

```
Application("~WC~WebClassManager").ProcessNoStateWebClass "Project1.WebClass1", _
        Server, _
        Application, _
        Session, _
        Request, _
        Response ·
```

By default, a WebClass object is created when an HTTP request is received, and exists for the duration of the processing of the HTTP request. After the HTTP request of completed, the WebClass object is destroyed. This behavior corresponds with setting the WebClass object `StateManagement` property to `wcNoState`. With this setting, the `ProcessNoStateWebClass` method is used, instructing the Webclass Manager to be instantiated only for the duration of the HTTP request.

If the `StateManagement` property is set to `wcRetainInstance`, then the Active Server Page is altered slightly, to run the `ProcessRetainInstanceWebClass` method. The `ProcessRetainInstanceWebClass` method allows the WebClass object to be created upon receiving the first HTTP request and to remain instantiated until one of the following things happen:

➤ The `ReleaseInstance` method is called by the `WebClass` object

➤ The user's session automatically times out

➤ The `Abandon` method of the `Session` object is called

The purpose of these two Webclass Manager methods is twofold. First, you should notice that the ProgID of the Webclass object created within your IIS Application is passed as a parameter of the method invoked. This allows the Webclass run-time Manager to be notified of the correct component to instantiate for each HTTP request.

```
Application("~WC~WebClassManager").ProcessNoStateWebClass "Project1.WebClass1", …
```

Secondly, the methods accept as arguments the five primary members of the Active Server Page object model. The Server, Application, Session, Request, and Response objects are passed into the methods. This provides the specified webclass object with a reference to HTTP request information, Session information, and Application information, as well as a mechanism for sending information back to the client through the Response object.

```
Application("~WC~WebClassManager").ProcessNoStateWebClass "Project1.WebClass1", _
     Server, _
     Application, _
     Session, _
     Request, _
     Response
```

Active Server Page Syntax

While acting as the host file or gateway for the webclass, the Active Server Page is requested repetitively by the client, to invoke each individual event and resource provided by the webclass. The syntax of the URL requesting the webclass resources contains the information necessary to invoke the events. The syntax of the URL contains three main pieces of information appended to the end of the URL. This information is appended in the syntax used by the QueryString collection of the Active Server Page Request object.

This information is therefore passed into the webclass object and retrieved automatically by the webclass in order to determine which events to fire. The three pieces of information include:

> Webitem

> Event

> URL Data

By default, this information is not inherently required to launch the IIS Application. If fact, in most cases, only the base URL is used to launch the application. A sample base URL might look like:

```
http://localhost/WC1.asp
```

Webitem

A specific webitem can be requested through the URL syntax by utilizing the WCI (abbreviated from Web Class Item) variable. This variable is appended to the end of the URL:

```
http://localhost/WC1.asp?WCI=Template1
```

This syntax would result in an Active Server Page QueryString collection being created containing an entry with an index name of "WCI". On instantiation, the webclass will search the Request object, and on finding a WCI member variable will automatically attempt to return a webitem with the same name – in this case Template1 – as the value passed into this variable. If found, the Respond event of the webitem would be fired. If not found, then an error would be generated.

Event

Along with specifying a webitem, a specific event can be invoked through a WCE (Web Class Event) `querystring` variable. Invoking an event called `Event1` would modify the URL as follows:

```
http://localhost/WC1.asp?WCI=Template1&WCE=Event1
```

If there is no event of this name, then the `UserEvent` will be fired instead, passing the desired event in as a parameter of the `UserEvent` event.

URL Data

Probably the least used appendage to the URL involves the specifying of what is called URL data. Webitems have a property called `URLData` which can be used to provide information to be directly appended to the URL as the value associated with the `WCU` variable. Any string assigned to the `URLData` property will be placed in the `WCU` variable, giving a URL that might look a little like this:

```
http://localhost/WC1.asp?WCI=Template1&WCU=MLThomas
```

This simply provides a mechanism for automatically appending information to the URL, and retrieving it through the `URLData` property. The same can be performed by manually appending custom `querystring` variables to the end of the URL and manually retrieving them through the Request object's `QueryString` collection.

Controlling the Web Server from within Visual Basic

Since IIS Applications require the use of a web server to run and debug the application, you should be aware of how to start and stop the web server software. Because you need a functional web server present on the development system, Visual Basic provide a mechanism for controlling a Microsoft web server from within the Visual Basic environment, as well as using the usual Internet Server Manager.

Internet Information Server is the primary web server Microsoft expect you to use. This web server is designed as a Windows NT operating system service which can be stopped and restarted without affecting any other aspect of the core operating system functionality. Internet Information Server variations such as Personal Web Server running on Windows 98 are designed to run in the same way. By mimicking the architectural design of Internet Information Server on versions of the Windows operating system other than Windows NT Server, your web servers will all behave consistently.

From within the Visual Basic environment itself, the ability to start or stop the existing web server software is provided as a context menu option within a Webclass Designer. By right-clicking on the webclass object within the Treeview panel of its Webclass Designer, the programmer is provided with the option to Start Peer Web Services, or conversely to stop the web service currently available and running.

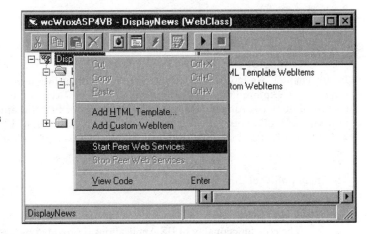

If a Microsoft web server is started in this manner, or an IIS Application is run from within the Visual Basic design environment with the web server currently stopped, then you'll see the following notification.

Stopping a Microsoft web server from within Visual Basic will result in a similar notice telling you that the WebClass Designer is stopping Peer Web Services.

Summary

In this chapter, we have taken an introductory look at the new Visual Basic IIS Application project type. We've explored the needs that brought this new type of application project to life. We briefly discussed the basic roadmap that is followed in order to build and develop an IIS Application. The new type of COM component that serves as the foundation of IIS Applications was introduced. Finally, we discussed some of the basic requirements for developing and instantiating webclass objects.

The main points of this chapter are:

> The user interface provided by IIS Applications is still HTML

> The core functionality of IIS Applications is provided by the Webclass object

> Management functions are provided by the Microsoft Webclass Library

> IIS Applications only provide code for responding to HTTP requests

> IIS Applications are ActiveX DLLs.

> IIS Applications leverage the Active Server Page object model

> webclasses are hosted by an automatically-generated Active Server Page

> Developing IIS Applications requires a web server on the developer system

Now that we've taken an introductory look at webclasses and IIS Applications, in the next chapter we will take a closer look at IIS Applications, including exploring events, connecting events to code, and webclass properties.

13

The Fundamentals of IIS Applications

What good would a new component such as a webclass be without a plethora of events, methods, and properties to control the functionality and behavior of the object? Working knowledge of the primary events, methods, and properties is critical for leveraging the full power of IIS Applications. We will take a look at the attributes of both webclasses and webitems. Webclasses have a series of events that define the life cycle of the webclass, which we will explore. Webitems also have a number of events that can be categorized into three groups, which we will cover in detail.

In Chapter 12, we took an introductory look at the new Microsoft Visual Basic IIS Application project type, including a look at the basic requirements of IIS Applications. A roadmap of the steps to be taken in developing an IIS Application was presented. In this chapter, we will go into more detail concerning the specifics of creating IIS Applications. The process of connecting HTTP requests with code to process the requests will also be presented.

During our discussion within this chapter, we will focus on the life cycle of webclasses and webitems. This chapter will present the necessary topics to round out the body of webclass code needed to provide a functional framework for an IIS Application.

In this chapter, we will cover:

> ➤ IIS Application events, properties, and methods
> ➤ Connecting HTTP requests to code

To begin, let's take a look at some webclass characteristics.

IIS Applications – The Basics

Any new IIS Application will start with a single `WebClass` object. Double-clicking on the `WebClass` object in the Project Explorer will open up the Webclass Designer associated with the object. A one-to-one mapping exists between webclasses and Webclass Designers. A Webclass Designer is a graphical representation of the information stored about a webclass and only exists within the Visual Basic IDE. Unlike Visual Basic Forms that exist both within the IDE and represent the actual graphical interface of a standard Visual Basic application, Webclass Designers only assume a graphical form during design-time.

Representing non-visual COM components, webclasses do not have a run-time visual representation. In order to facilitate development, webclass objects are given a visual development existence as a form of ActiveX designer. This allows an easier method of writing and assigning code to the HTML presentation elements that are created and designed in external HTML editors.

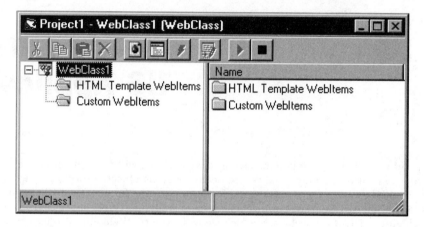

A webclass Designer can be used for many purposes, including:

> Defining the contents of the webclass (known as webitems)

> Adding procedural events to the webitems in a webclass

> Writing event code for the webitem events

Events, Properties, and Methods

Webclass objects, just like your standard form objects, have a series of events that determine their life cycle. These events fire during the course of instantiation of the object. From initialization to termination, a webclass object experiences five main events. Although somewhat different than the events marking the stages in the life of a form object, webclass events are still used to provide the opportunity to initialize values, provide validation code, and execute code needed for the proper function of the webclass and webitems associated with the webclass. Specifically, these events are used to indicate when the client browser will display the first webitem, usually an HTML template resource, as well as when HTTP requests are received and processed.

In addition to the webclass events, a number of properties and methods exist for use by the Visual Basic programmer. Properties such as `NextItem` are primarily for controlling the flow of the IIS Application, while methods such as `ReleaseInstance` are used to programmatically terminate an instance of the webclass object and force the `Terminate` event to fire.

For starters, let's take a look at the core webclass events that define the life cycle of the webclass object itself.

Webclass Events

It's important to be familiar with the primary life cycle events of the webclass object. Since the webclass serves as a funnel or conduit for all HTTP requests generated through the client HTML interface, and webclass objects themselves can be configured to exist either per request or span HTTP requests, different events will fire at different times. The rules determining which events will fire for a given request are more complex than for the simpler form objects used in standard Visual Basic applications. For this reason, understanding the differences can play a role in designing for scalability and efficiency. The set of primary events for a webclass are:

Event	Description
Initialize()	Creates the webclass as an object when an end user accesses the `.asp` (Active Server Pages) file that acts as the host for your IIS application.
BeginRequest()	Fired each time the webclass receives a subsequent request from the browser, this event marks the beginning of processing for an HTTP request.
Start()	Occurs the first time `BeginRequest` is fired in the application, but not fired on subsequent requests. This event is generally used to send an initial response to the browser, launching the `Respond` event for the specified webitem
EndRequest()	Occurs when the webclass has finished processing an HTTP request and has returned a response to the client.
Terminate()	Tells the run-time DLL to destroy the instance of the webclass object.
FatalErrorResponse()	Occurs when the processing of a webclass object is terminated due to an error.

Let's take a look at each of these events one by one.

Initialize Event

The `Initialize` event is the first event within the life cycle of the webclass object. This event is fired when a client makes an HTTP request for the Active Server Page that is acting as a host for the webclass. Since an IIS Application may have several different webclasses within it, a particular `Initialize` event for a given webclass only fires when the exact Active Server Page associated with that webclass is requested.

As we saw in Chapter 12, the second function of the Active Server Page host file is to invoke one of two methods of the webclass run-time Manager object. Both of these methods are passed the `ProgID` of the webclass object to be instantiated. These methods, upon instantiating the desired webclass, cause the `Initialize` event to fire. This event is always the first event in the life of the webclass object. It is within the `Initialize` event that the webclass actually becomes an object.

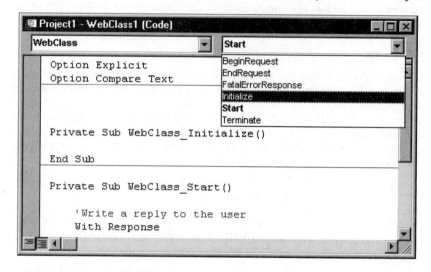

You should note that the relationship between the firing of the `Initialize` event and the receipt of HTTP request to be processed by the webclass varies depending on the value of the `StateManagement` property. This is a webclass-specific property and, if you remember from Chapter 12, has an effect on the duration of instantiation of the webclass object.

If the `StateManagement` property is set to `wcNoState`, then the webclass object will be destroyed at the conclusion of processing of each HTTP request. Therefore the `Initialize` event will fire for each HTTP request processed by the webclass, due to the re-instantiation of the webclass for each request.

If the `StateManagement` property is set to `wcRetainInstance`, then the webclass will remain instantiated for the life of the applicable Active Server Pages user session. This will cause any subsequent HTTP request, after the initial request, to fail.

BeginRequest Event

The `BeginRequest` event typically marks the second event in the life of the webclass object, and is fired for each HTTP request received. The `BeginRequest` event is always fired after the `Initialize` event, if it occurs, and is considered the official start of processing of an HTTP request. Since this event marks the beginning of processing of any HTTP request received by the webclass, this would be the appropriate event in which to place any code needed universally for each HTTP request the webclass will execute. Examples of code to be placed within the `BeginRequest` event might include:

> Storing state information within a database
> Logging HTTP request processing
> Retrieving state information from a database
> Validate user information

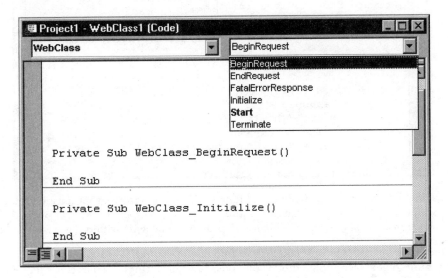

Start Event

The Start event is the primary event in which code is inherently required to be added. This event is typically fired the first time that the BeginRequest event is fired for a webclass. This is primarily equated to the first time a client accesses the IIS Application. This access occurs by navigating to the Active Server Page host file. In order for the Start event to fire, rather than some custom event, the base URL for the Active Server Page must be requested.

For example, the base URL for a webclass named WebClass1, within a project named Project1, on a web server called www.stockcarreport.com, would be:

    http://www.stockcarreport.com/Project1_WebClass1.asp

Once the Start event has fired, it does not re-fire after subsequent occurrences of the BeginRequest event. The primary purpose of the Start event is to provide or send the initial HTTP response to the client regarding the webclass.

> **If the NameInURL property is set to WC1, then the file name portion of a base URL would be WC1.asp**

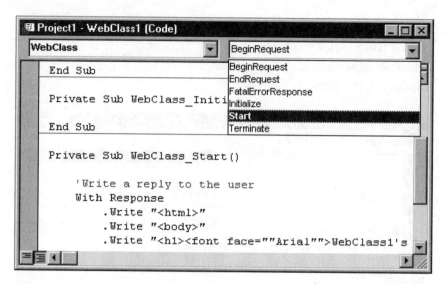

Before an IIS Application can provide useful functionality, the Start event must be set, or be supplied with code. While the Initialize and BeginRequest events may easily be left empty for many applications, it is almost impossible not to provide some code within the Start event.

Within the Start event, it is very common to find one of two primary types of Visual Basic code. The Response object's Write method is often used to send strings of character data representing HTML code. For any developer accustomed to using Active Server Pages, this would be one of the most common methods of programmatically sending HTML to the browser while scripting.

```
Private Sub WebClass_Start()

    'Write a reply to the user
    With Response
        .Write "<html>"
        .Write "<body>"
        .Write "<h1><font face=""Arial"">WebClass1's Starting Page</font></h1>"
        .Write "<p>This response was created in the Start event of WebClass1.</p>"
        .Write "</body>"
        .Write "</html>"
    End With

End Sub
```

If the initial intended HTML response to be sent back to the browser for the webclass is to originate from an HTML template, then the Start event would typically utilize, at some stage, the NextItem property of the webclass object. As we will see later in this chapter, this property is used to notify the webclass which webitem to send next. This will typically cause the Respond event (described later) of that webitem to fire, thereby sending some manner of HTML response to the browser.

```
Private Sub WebClass_Start()

    Set NextItem = tplNewsList

End Sub
```

One very important aspect of the firing of the `Start` event should be pointed out. You may have noticed by now that the webitem and event to fire is specified within the URL for the host Active Server Page being requested. In many of the graphics appearing in Chapter 12, the changes made to the HTML template files included the addition of a URL that comprised of the base URL for the Active Server Page host file, including information appended to the URL. We'll discuss the syntax of the URL in Chapter 14, but it should be noted that if the client of the IIS Application indicates, within the URL, a specific webitem and event to fire, then the `Start` event will not fire.

> Using a manually constructed URL that indicates a specific webitem and event to fire within an IIS Application, launching the application will effectively replace the `Start` event. Subsequent generic requests sent to the webclass, assuming a `StateManagement` value of `wcRetainInstance`, will effectively prevent the `Start` event from ever firing for the webclass, during the same user session.

EndRequest Event

The `EndRequest` event is fired only upon the error-free conclusion of all template and custom webitem processing that comprises the HTTP response being sent to the browser. Since the processing of an HTTP request could involve the chaining of several HTML templates, by using the `NextItem` property or requiring the processing of multiple custom webitems, the `EndRequest` event is used to signify the end of the full response processing. This event is typically considered the final event in the processing of an HTTP response.

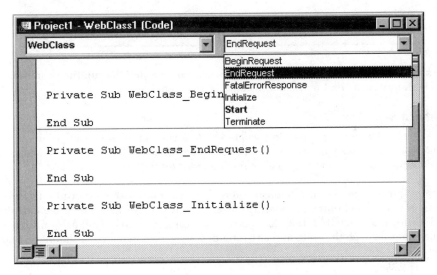

While the `EndRequest` event is typically the last event in the processing of an HTTP response, there are circumstances where this will not be the case. If an error should occur within the Visual Basic code during the processing of an HTTP response, then the `EndRequest` event may not actually fire.

If the error occurs prior to the `EndRequest` actually firing, then it will be skipped, and processing will go directly to the `FatalErrorResponse` event. If the error occurs during the `EndRequest` event, then the event will finish processing, and then the `FatalErrorResponse` event will be fired.

Terminate Event

The `Terminate` event is the flip side of the `Initialize` event. It fires in the same circumstance as the `Initialize` event. If the `StateManagement` property of the webclass is set to `wcNoState`, then the `Terminate` event is fired at the conclusion of each response sent to the browser. If the `StateManagement` property is set to `wcRetainInstance`, then the `Terminate` will only be fired when the `ReleaseInstance` method of the webclass object is invoked. This happens automatically when the user session either timeouts, is abandoned, or the web server is restarted. The `ReleaseInstance` method can also be manually invoked from code.

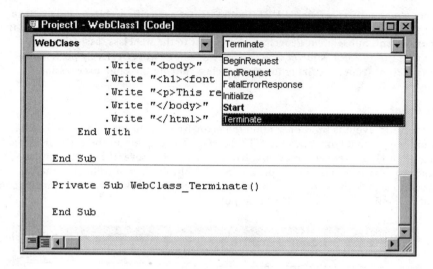

The `Terminate` event is the flag which the webclass raises to tell the run-time component of the webclass DLL to destroy that particular instance of the webclass.

In The Event of a Real Error....

The `FatalErrorResponse` event fires whenever an error causes processing of the webclass object to terminate prematurely. This error could be the result of Visual Basic code or a system error. The `FatalErrorResponse` event passes a single argument through the event.

The `SendDefault` argument is a Boolean value that determines whether or not the default ASP error message is returned to the browser. If this argument is set to `TRUE`, then the default processing will continue for the error. By setting `SendDefault` to `FALSE`, no default error processing will be sent to the client through the ASP, and any intended error messaging code should be placed within this event.

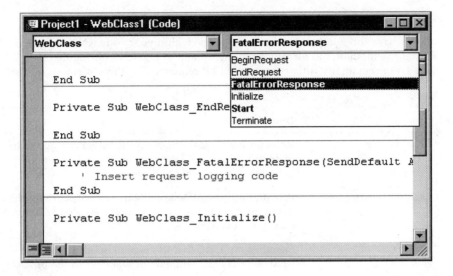

Life Cycle Dimensions

The behavior of webclasses varies based on the StateManagement property and the URL used to launch the application. This variation in behavior decides under what conditions the Initialize, Start, and Terminate events will fire.

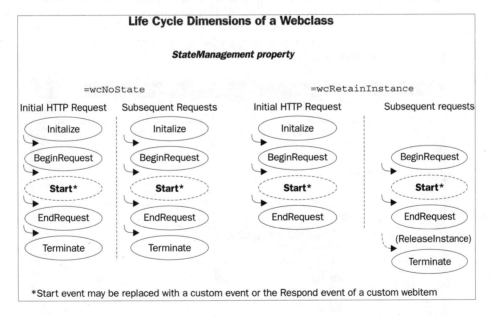

Webclass Methods

Webclass objects have three important methods for use within your code. One of these methods, the `ReleaseInstance` method, has already been mentioned in regards to firing the `Terminate` event for webclasses set to remain instantiated across HTTP requests. The three methods to be aware of are:

Event	Description
ReleaseInstance()	Releases a webclass object and is called during the processing of an HTTP request when the webclass has completed its processing and should be terminated.
Trace(*traceoutput* As String)	Provides advanced debugging information, where the trace string might contain error messages, as well as performance and statistical data.
URLFor(*WebItemObject* As WebItem, [eventname])	Specifies the URL that the system needs to reference a webclass's HTML template or webitem in the browser.

ReleaseInstance

The `ReleaseInstance` method, as discussed briefly earlier, is used to release a webclass object. This method instructs the webclass run-time component to destroy the instance of the webclass object in which the `ReleaseInstance` method was called. This method is primarily used in conjunction with setting the `StateManagement` property to `wcRetainInstance`. The `ReleaseInstance` method can be used even in a webclass object with a `StateManagement` property of `wcNoState`, although its use is not inherently required.

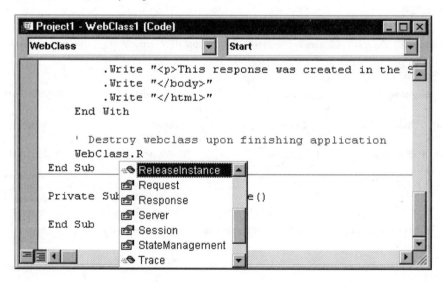

Prior to invoking this method, some manner of UI element should be sent to the client browser to provide the final results of the process. Since the `ReleaseInstance` method guarantees that the webclass object instance will be destroyed, this method should only be used when the webclass has concluded all processing and no additional interaction between the client and the IIS Application is required.

This generally requires that some manner of hyperlink be returned to the client browser to provide navigation ability to a resource outside that provided by the IIS Application itself, such as a different website. Should the hyperlink involve a URL to another webitem within the webclass, another instance of the webclass will be instantiated.

Trace

The `Trace` method is used to provide advanced debugging information. This method allows debugging on a production server by passing a specified string to the Win32 `OutputDebugString` API. This string can then be captured and analyzed through suitable debugging tools, such as DBMon.

URLFor

The `URLFor` method is used to provide a Uniform Resource Locator (URL) for a webitem or event. This event is able to provide the correctly formed URL in order to instruct a webclass to return a specified webitem or to run a particular custom event.

The `URLFor` method is typically used in conjunction with sending the results to the client as the source for a hyperlink. This method returns a URL that incorporates a URL to the host Active Server Page for the webclass, and the necessary information appended to the URL. This method is used during run-time to programmatically generate the desired URL to be embedded in the response sent back to the client.

```
Private Sub Template1_Respond()

    Response.Write "<A HREF="
    Response.Write URLFor(Template2)
    Response.Write ">Go to Page 2</A>"

End Sub
```

The correct syntax for this method looks like the following:

```
object.URLFor(WebItemobject As WebItem, [eventname])
```

> There are two uses of the URLFor method you should note. In order to include a double-quotation mark, as is common with HREF or SRC attributes, two double-quotation marks in a row should be used. Also, while the use of double-quotation marks are optional for the non-optional `WebitemObject` parameter, quotes are non-optional with the optional `eventname` argument. If quotes are not used with the `eventname` parameter you provide, Visual Basic will interpret the value as a variable name, often resulting in a run-time error.

This method requires a `WebItemObject` argument that is used to identify the webitem whose URL is to be generated. An optional argument, `eventname`, can be used to identify a specific event to be fired within the webitem in place of the default `Respond` event (described below).

If the `eventname` argument is not set, then the `Respond` event will be fired. If `eventname` is set to the name of an event which does not exist within the webitem (was not defined at deign-time) then the `UserEvent` event is fired, passing the name of this "run-time" defined event as an argument of the `UserEvent` event.

Webclass Properties

Before beginning the process of coding and developing the application logic to be found within the webclass object, it's important to be familiar with the primary webclass properties and configuration settings available for adjustment. The properties include:

- ➢ `NameInURL`
- ➢ `Public`
- ➢ `StateManagement`
- ➢ `NextItem`
- ➢ `BrowserType`
- ➢ `Unattended Execution`

NameInURL

The `NameInURL` property of webclass objects identifies the name given to the Active Server Page automatically created for the webclass when the IIS Application is created. By default, this assumes the same value as the `Name` property of the webclass object.

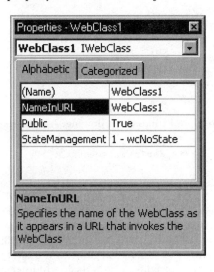

Public

The `Public` property is a standard property for use with ActiveX controls, yet its existence with webclass object is something of a strange occurrence. A webclass object must be set to `Public` in order for the IIS Application to be able use it. If only one webclass object exists within an IIS Application, then the application will not even run if the webclass object `Public` property is set to `FALSE`.

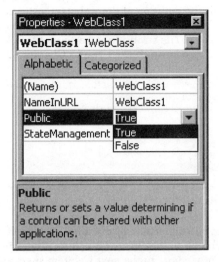

The default value for the `Public` property is `TRUE` and any attempts to change it will result in an error message that webclass designers cannot be set to private.

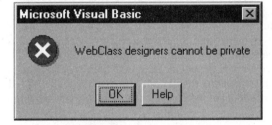

To take the unusual a bit further, choosing Help on the error box will reveal that no help topic exists for this particular Visual Basic 6 error condition.

StateManagement

We first saw the `stateManagement` property when we discussed webclass hosting requirements. The `StateManagement` property defaults to `wcNoState`, and controls the lifetime of the webclass object after instantiation for purposes of responding to an HTTP request.

The two possible values for this property affect the Active Server Page host file by affecting which method of the webclass run-time Manager is used to instantiate the webclass object. The method, in turn, controls the duration of the webclass instantiation. If the `StateManagement` property is set to `wcRetainInstance`, then the Active Server Page is altered slightly, to run the `ProcessRetainInstanceWebClass` method. You can compare this to the automatically pre-generated ASP code we showed you in Chapter 12:

```
Application("~WC~WebClassManager").ProcessRetainInstanceWebClass _
    "Project1.WebClass1", _
    "~WC~Project1.WebClass1", _
    Server, _
    Application, _
    Session, _
    Request, _
    Response
%>
```

NextItem

The `NextItem` property is used within the webclass code. This valuable property is set to send a separate webitem to the client. This shifts processing from the current webitem, at the conclusion of the current procedure, to the next webitem specified. The setting of this property, and the resulting modification in webclass processing behavior differs from what one might expect.

Before any webclass events have been fired, the `NextItem` property has a value of `Nothing`. Once an event is fired for a webitem, if this property has been set to reference another webitem, then the webclass will fire the `Respond` event of the newly specified webitem. The primary purpose of this property is to specify the initial webitem to process and send to the client. The code provided earlier, which showed the default Visual Basic code added to a webclass using the `Response.Write` method, can be replaced with a single line setting the `NextItem` property:

```
Private Sub webclass_Start()

    Set NextItem = WebItem1

End Sub
```

Setting the `NextItem` property does not initiate immediate action or code execution in the same as a direct procedure call. A webclass only checks the value of the `NextItem` property at the conclusion of webitem or webclass events. Certain exceptions exist, however. The value of the `NextItem` is ignored during, or at the conclusion of, the following events:

- ProcessTag
- EndRequest
- FatalErrorResponse

The `NextItem` property is ignored within the `ProcessTag` event to allow HTML template tag processing, described in Chapter 14, to continue uninterrupted. This property is ignored in the `EndRequest` because this event signifies that the processing of the current HTTP request has already concluded, and can't be continued by setting the `NextItem` property. Finally, the `FatalErrorResponse` event indicates that a serious fatal error has occurred, and therefore the webclass would be unable to process the new webitem.

BrowserType

The `BrowserType` property of the webclass object is used to return the Active Server Pages `BrowserType` object. This allows the Visual Basic webclass code to establish the capabilities of the browser which is communicating with the IIS Application. This can provide a convenient mechanism for coding based on the functionality supported by the client browser.

Unattended Execution

The Unattended Execution option, on the project Properties dialog, is an important project configuration setting for IIS Applications. This setting allows instances of the components to be allocated on different threads. Within IIS Applications, it's important to avoid having the different instances of a given webclass object being placed on the same thread. This setting helps to increase the scalability of the IIS Application.

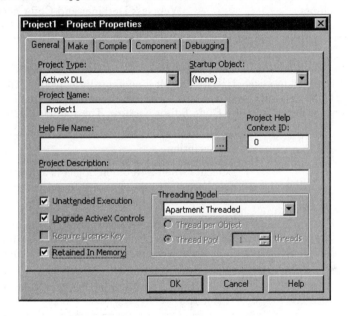

Webitems

In addition to the webclass events, every webitem added to a webclass has its own series of events used to define the life and functionality of the webitems. The events pertaining to webitems can generally be divided into three main classifications:

> Standard
> Template
> Custom

The following table can provide a better understanding of the similarities and differences between these categories.

Category	Event Definition Origins	Location Seen in IDE	Applies to
Standard	Predefined	Code Editor Window only	templates and custom webitems
Template	Generated by Visual Basic upon parsing an HTML template file	Treeview panel of the Webclass Designer and Code Editor Window after connect	templates
Custom	Added and defined by the developer	Treeview panel of the Webclass Designer and Code Editor Window	templates and custom webitems

Standard Events

Whenever a webitem is added to a webclass, by default it contains three events. These standard events exist for both HTML template webitems and custom webitems (described below). These standard events are only visible within the Code Editor window. The standard webitem events are:

Event	Description
Respond()	Occurs when a webitem object is activated by a user request, if no other event is found that directly corresponds to the selected element.
ProcessTag(TagName As String, TagContents As String, SendTag As Boolean)	When a token-prefixed tag is found in an HTML template during WriteTemplate processing, this event is fired to allow the webclass to replace the contents of that tag.
UserEvent(eventname As String)	Occurs in response to the firing of a run-time defined event.

Respond

The Respond event is the most commonly used event of the three standard events. This event is considered the default event for a webitem. In the absence of a specific event being requested or invoked, the Respond event will be chosen for invocation. The Respond event is fired either when the webitem is first activated, or when a request is received that doesn't correspond to a template event described below.

Furthermore, the Respond event can be invoked through either a server-side or client-side activation. As we discussed above, a server-side activation occurs through setting the NextItem property. A client-side activation occurs through the HTTP request itself including a reference to the webitem to invoke, which will fire its Respond event.

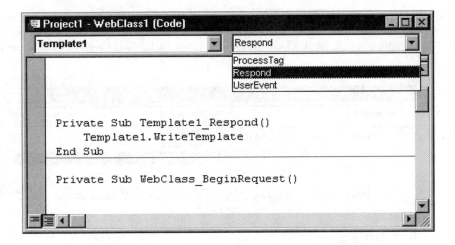

ProcessTag

The `ProcessTag` event is used when processing XML tokens placed within HTML template files. These XML tokens, called **indicator tags**, are used to identify areas of an HTML template file that are to be targeted for replacement during processing. Special tag syntax is used to identify these areas. These tags are inserted into the template files and upon locating them during processing the `ProcessTag` event is fired, passing the `tagname` into the `ProcessTag` event.

The `ProcessTag` event is generally populated with either `Select Case` or `If..Then` syntax for conditional processing of the tags.

```
Sub DisplayNews_ProcessTag(ByVal TagName as String, _
                           TagContents as String, SendTags as Boolean)
   ' Insert Select Case or If..Then code here
   SendTags = False
End Sub
```

More information concerning the `ProcessTag` event can be found in Chapter 14 in the section entitled "Processing HTML Template Files".

UserEvent

The `UserEvent` event is quite interesting. It is passed a single argument, called `eventname`, and is fired whenever a client makes an HTTP request that instructs the webclass to fire an event which was not defined at design-time. What this means is that `UserEvent` is a catch-all event to provide processing for events requested, but not yet defined.

```
Private Sub object_UserEvent(eventname As String)
```

For example, consider the following URL:

```
http://localhost/WC1.asp?WCI=Template1&WCE=Event2
```

If you remember the section in Chapter 12 concerning URL syntax, this URL is requesting that an event called `Event2` be fired in a webitem called `Template1`. If this event does not actually exist, then the `UserEvent` event is fired. Code should be placed within this event to handle the processing of this "event".

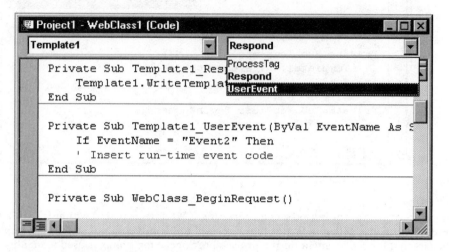

The unusual aspect of this event is that even though the user events are raised during run-time, only their explicit event handler procedure is not defined during design-time. Code to be executed in response to the raising of an event in this way must still be defined during design-time, otherwise no processing will be invoked by the raising of a run-time defined event. The code is centralized for all such events within the `UserEvent` event. The description of an event of this kind, as a "run-time" defined event, is very much of a misnomer.

Template Events

Template events are a unique type of event that are derived from HTML template files being added to a webclass. These events correspond to HTML elements within the template files that hold the potential for generating HTTP requests. Every such element within an HTML template file may result in a template event once a process known as **connecting** is completed. All such events added to the code editor window after connecting comprise the category referred to as template events. Since the source of templates resides in the template being used, and depends on which of those elements are actually connected, every template can have its own unique set of template events. We'll discuss this in more depth in the section entitled *Connecting HTTP Requests to Events*.

Custom Events

An additional type of event can be added to webitems to provide additional programmatic resources and event handling for the webitems. This category of event handlers is known as custom events. These are merely additional procedures added or associated with webitems. Custom events can then be called from hyperlinks added to the HTML response sent to the browser. Adding custom events is as simple as right-clicking on an HTML template webitem or custom webitem.

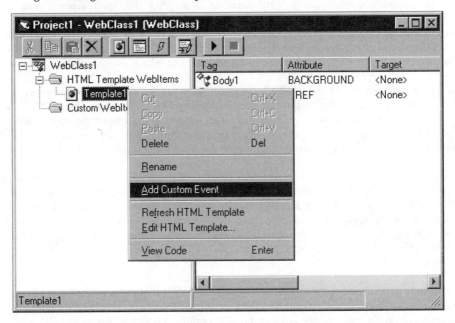

Once a custom event has been added to a webclass by association with a webitem, this event can be called or invoked through an HTTP request for the appropriately constructed URL. Calling a custom event utilizes the WCE variable appended to the URL for the host page.

This URL can be either constructed manually within the Visual Basic code, or more likely by leveraging the URLFor method of the webclass object. This hides the complexity of manually creating the URL. For example, the following code would provide a hyperlink in the browser that would cause the Event1 to be invoked within the CustomWI custom webitem:

```
Response.Write "<A HREF=""" & URLFor(CustomWI,"Event1") & """></A>"
```

If a user chooses the hyperlink, this will pass the information into the webclass object through the gateway Active Server Page and result in the desired event being raised and processed.

> Custom Events within a webitem are different from Template events. Template events correspond to and start with specific HTML elements within an HTML template file. Custom events are generally the reverse. Custom events do not map to elements within an HTML template file initially. After being added to a webitem, a custom event generally requires that an HTML element be sent at run-time to the browser in order to provide an entry point to the custom event.

483

Connecting HTTP Requests to Events

Once HTML templates have been added, edited, or modified as desired, it is important to establish a connection between elements within the templates and events coded within the webclass object. This is the connecting process we looked at in the *Template Events* section of this chapter.

Initially, no interactive relationships exist between elements within the templates and code within the webclass. Since no initial connection exists between elements generating HTTP requests and code within the webclass object, a process known as **connecting** must be performed. Connecting involves mapping elemental attributes responsible for generating HTTP requests to events within the webclass, or more specifically, to events within the exact webitem to which the template is attached.

Normal processing of an HTML file by a client browser involves parsing and rendering all of the HTML markup tags according to the standard established for each tag by the W3C HTML recommendation. For many of the HTML tags, this merely involves recognizing whether an individual tag has a visible graphical meaning, or a structural connotation. For many HTML tags, additional data about the configured meaning of the markup is stored as attributes of the markup tag.

For example, a <TABLE> tag has an optional border attribute which can be applied to identify the thickness of border, if any, to paint around a table and its cells. While this HTML element attribute is not responsible for generating an HTTP request, other elemental attributes do generate HTTP requests. For example, the SRC attribute of an <IMG> tag supplies a URL and generates an HTTP request in order to retrieve the appropriate graphic file from the web server. Any such HTML element attribute which does, or can, generate an HTTP request is a candidate for generating an event within a webclass.

The attributes that can result in the generation of an HTTP request are candidates for event invocation because initially no event handlers exist for the events. The HTTP request-generating element attributes do not initially possess a direct connection to any event handler within a webclass object. This leaves the default behavior of these attributes unaffected, until you choose to implement code within the webclass to process the incoming HTTP request.

For example, if the SRC attribute of an <IMG> tag is assigned a value, such as "mygraphics/FaxNotFound.gif", then the tag can still request and receive the graphic file. However, once an event has been connected to the attribute, the original value of the attribute is completely replaced with a webclass URL constructed to call the connected event within the webclass.

Typical Event Candidates

Connecting an attribute to an event requires that all the eligible event candidates be available within the webclass Designer. When an HTML template is first added to a webclass, Visual Basic parses the template file and determines which element attribute might generate HTTP requests. It then adds them to the Details panel of the webclass Designer.

For example the following HTML template:

```
<HTML>

<HEAD>
<TITLE>Wrox's Web programming With VB6</TITLE>

<STYLE>
BODY {FONT-FAMILY: Arial; BACKGROUND-COLOR: white;}
</STYLE>

</HEAD>

<BODY>

<H2>WebClasses ... in action</H2>
<IMG SRC="Image1.gif">
<P><WC@GREETING>Greeting</WC@GREETING>
<A href=""><H4>Enter</H4></A>
</BODY>

</HTML>
```

would generate this list in the Details panel of the webclass Designer:

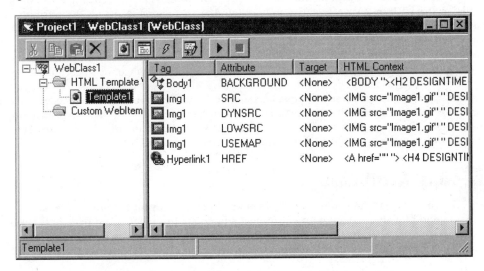

Examples of attributes that would be listed include:

> ➢ BACKGROUND attribute of the BODY tag
>
> ➢ SRC attribute of an IMG tag
>
> ➢ ACTION attribute of a FORM tag
>
> ➢ HREF attribute of an A tag

Name Assignment

The name given to the elements added to the Details panel of the webclass Designer is determined by the ID property of the HTML tags. Should an ID property not be set, a default value is assigned based on the type of markup tag involved and the relative location of the tag within the page. For example, the second instance of an <A> tag without an explicit ID property would be given the name HyperLink2 within the webclass Designer.

This name property is generated dynamically by Visual Basic when it opens the webclass, although the name is not stored permanently within the HTML page or within the webclass Designer file. Once an attribute of the element is associated with Visual Basic code, the name value is permanently stored within the webclass Designer file.

Multiple Attributes

There's not a one-to-one mapping between tag attributes and the elements added to the Details panel. This is because some HTML tags have more than one attribute that may generate different HTTP requests. For example, the <IMG> tag has four defined attributes which could result in HTTP requests, and consequently four entries in the Details panel, as seen in the previous screenshot.

The SRC attribute is the most common attribute set for an <IMG> tag, but an <IMG> tag can also have a DYNSRC, LOWSRC, or USEMAP attributes. A DYNSRC attribute is used to specify a video, such as an AVI file, or the URL to a VRML source to load into the IMG element. A LOWSRC attribute is used to identify a lower resolution version of the graphic file to load first. This attribute is used to provide a graphic file with minimal detail, and size, thereby decreasing load time for an initial image but giving an indication of what the final image will look like. A USEMAP attribute is used to load a server-side image map file for the image, one that specifies 'hot spots' on the image for hyperlinks.

If any of these attributes are unused, you can safely leave these attributes unconnected. Keep in mind that every <IMG> tag that exists within an HTML template file will have these four attributes added to the webclass Designer. This can result in significant increases in the number of attributes available for connecting to events, occasionally resulting in minor confusion.

Connecting Attributes

There are two main ways to connect an element attribute to an event for processing on the server. The first method involves a context menu. Select a template in the left-hand pane of the webclass Designer. In the right-hand pane, the available tag/attribute pairs will be listed. Right-click on a tag and a context menu will provide the option to connect either to a custom event or a webitem.

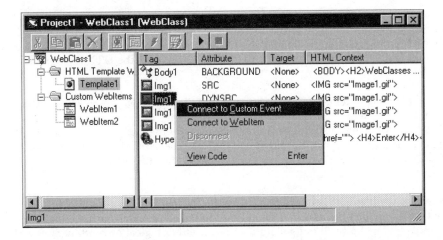

The second method of connecting an attribute to an event is to simply double-click on the tag name. This will cause the attribute to be connected to a custom event. Double-clicking can't be used to connect an attribute to either Custom WebItems or HTML Template Resources. Should an attribute need to be disconnected from either a webitem or a custom event, right-clicking on the tag/attribute pair will allow the Disconnect option to be chosen from the context menu.

Connecting to WebItem

The primary difference between connecting to a custom event or a webitem has to do with the source of the initial event fired to process the HTTP request. Typically, tags that result in HTTP requests for entire web pages will be connected to webitems. The webitem to which the attribute is connected can be either an HTML Template Resource, or a Custom Webitem.

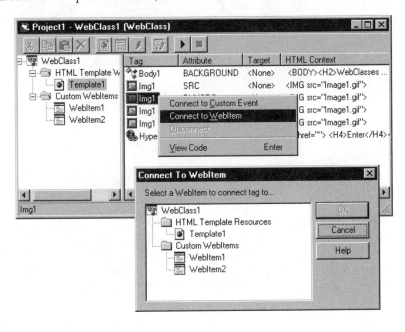

After connecting an attribute to a webitem, the connection will be stored within the webclass Designer file, although no visible indication of the connection will show in the code editor window. The only visible indication of the connection of the attribute to the webitem can be found in the Target column of the webclass Designer's right-hand pane when the HTML template file is selected in the left-hand pane.

A Custom Webitem could be referred to as an HTML Template Resource without the template. Although this is a rather simplistic look at the difference, it's essentially accurate. When connecting an attribute to a webitem, the request will be processed by the `Respond` event of the Webitem. If the Webitem is an HTML Template Resource, the typical expectation is that the `WriteTemplate` method will be invoked within the `Respond` event, thereby utilizing the associated HTML template file.

If an associated template file is not to be processed and sent back in response to the processing of a connected attribute, then the attribute should be connected to a Custom Webitem. Failure to call the `WriteTemplate` method will not generate an error, either logical or run-time, but will reduce the effective functionality of the HTML Template Resource to nothing more than a Custom Webitem.

Connecting to Custom Event

Connecting an attribute to a Custom Event will result in a new event being added to the webclass. The name of this event will initially take on the form *Tag + Attribute*. Therefore connecting the `DYNSRC` attribute of an `IMG` tag named `Img1` will generate a new event named `Img1DynSrc`. Although the initial naming scheme of Custom Events will follow this pattern, the names can be changed simply by right-clicking and choosing **Rename**.

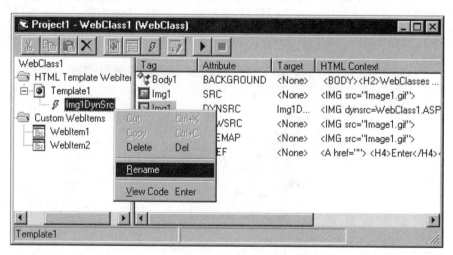

Once an attribute has been connected to a Custom Event, not only will the new event show up in the left-hand pane of the webclass Designer under the applicable template file, but also within the code editor window for the webclass. The true name of the routine, within code, will be of the typical format *ObjectName_ProcedureName,* where `ObjectName` is the name of the HTML Template Resource webitem and `ProcedureName` is the name given to the Custom Event as previously described.

Within the code editor window, the Custom Event can now be found in the Procedure drop-down, once the `Template` object is chosen in the Object drop-down.

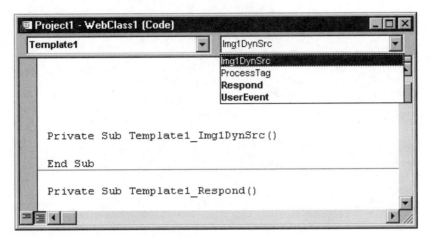

Initially, the Private Sub code will not actually be added. The Custom Event will only be added to the appropriate Procedure drop-down, and therefore registered for use. Also, simply typing in the properly constructed public subroutine within the webclass code editor window according to the default naming scheme for Custom Events will not connect that event to an attribute as a HTTP request processing event handler. While this type of automatic event handler attachment is typical in other environments, such as writing VBScript event handlers within an Active Server Page, it's important to note that this doesn't happen for webclasses.

Updating Changes in the Webclass Designer

It's helpful to understand the general procedure followed when changes to HTML template files are actually recorded or enforced within a Visual Basic IIS Application, primarily with the webclass Designer. When an HTML template is added to the HTML Template Resources folder in the tree view Panel of a webclass Designer, we have seen that Visual Basic goes through a process of parsing the template file to ascertain the existence of HTTP request-generating HTML element attributes. If any are found, they are initially added to the Details panel of the webclass Designer.

At this point, you're free to connect the tag/attribute pairs to either webitems or Custom Events within the webclass Designer. When a connection of this nature is established, changes are made to the physical template file. Since an HTML template file is essentially a text file that is retained as an external resource for use by the webclass object when compiled and installed onto the web server, changes made within a webclass Designer that involve an HTML template file must be saved within the file itself during run-times.

Let's assume that we have just loaded a brand new HTML template file previously created within the ever-popular editor, Notepad.

```
<!DOCTYPE HTML PUBLIC "-//W3C//DTD W3 HTML//EN">
<HTML>

<HEAD>
  <META content="text/html; charset=iso-8859-1" http-equiv=Content-Type>
  <META content='"MSHTML 4.72.3110.1"' name=GENERATOR>
</HEAD>

<BODY>
<CENTER>
  <H1><FONT face=Arial>WebClass1 Starting Page</FONT></H1>
  <P>Welcome to our Website <WC@USER>John Doe</WC@USER></P>
  <P><IMG src="Image1.gif"></IMG></P>
</CENTER>
</BODY>

</HTML>
```

Containing only a single <IMG> tag without an explicit ID attribute set, in addition to the standard HTML tags, the Detail Panel of the webclass Designer would contain only four items:

➤ Body1/BACKGROUND pair

➤ Img1/SRC pair

➤ Img1/DYNSRC pair

➤ Img/LOWSRC pair

➤ Img1/USEMAP pair

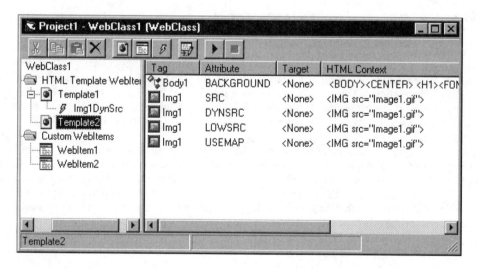

Within the **Details** Panel of the webclass Designer, you will notice that the HTML Context column shows exactly the same HTML code for the `<IMG>` tag as seen in the HTML template file. At this point, if you were to either right-click the `Img1/SRC` pair and connect to a custom event, or simply double-click, then the altered `<IMG>` tag code would only be displayed in the HTML Context column of that single pair. Notice that at this time, the new custom event does show up in the tree view panel with the default name and the all-inspiring yellow lightning bolt icon.

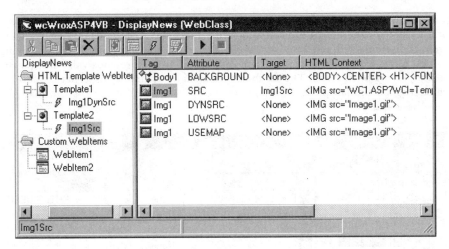

While this webclass Designer's behavior may seem confusing, it actually enforces the fact that changes are only considered durable or implemented once the changes are saved to the underlying HTML template file saved within the Visual Basic project directory. Until the project is actually saved, or run from within the Visual Basic IDE, the changes made to the HTML template file by connecting an attribute to an event or webitem exist only within the copy of the webclass Designer in memory.

The changes to be made to the template file will only show up in the related tag/attribute pairs once the information makes a round-trip through storage within the physical template file and reloading back into the webclass Designer.

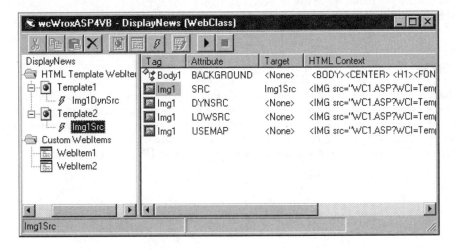

After changes have been made, saved, and refreshed back into the Details panel of the webclass Designer, you may want to disconnect an attribute from an event. Fortunately, doing so will not leave any residual active code within the webclass. If code has been added to the custom event, the procedure will be left within the code editor window, but will not be attached to any event as an active event handler. The event will also remain listed in the Details panel. Should the connection be re-established, the code will be reconnected to the attribute just as before.

Although no residual error-inducing conditions would exist, a quick glance at the HTML Context column of the Details panel might indicate otherwise. Once an attribute having been attached to a custom event is disconnected, the value of the affected <IMG> tag attribute will not be completely cleared, as you might expect. In fact, it will not revert back to the previous value in existence prior to the connection having been made. The attribute will actually assume an Internet Explorer shell processing instruction similar to the ever-familiar about:NavigationCanceled loaded when a URL can not be found.

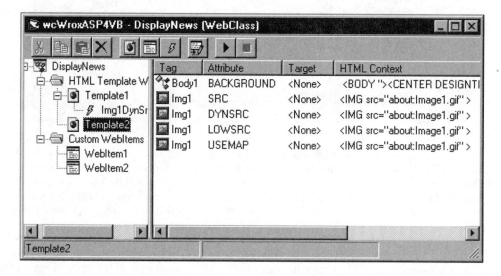

Because of the unique behavior of the webclass Designer when disconnecting attributes from events, you must be careful to reassign the attribute values properly.

Summary

In this chapter, we have explored the events which make up the life cycle of a webclass. We have discussed the properties and methods available for use with webclasses and webitems. The different categories of webitem events have been presented, and their use described. Furthermore, the important process of connecting HTML attributes to event code within a webclass has been presented and discussed. This process is central to the very function of an IIS Application.

From this chapter you should have learnt:

- Webclass Designers appear only in the VB IDE
- The webclass life cycle consists of `Initialize`, `BeginRequest`, `Start`, `EndRequest`, and `Terminate` events
- `Initialize` is the first event in a webclass's life
- `BeginRequest` is used to provide code universally for all HTTP requests processed
- The `Start` event is the primary webclass event and is considered the default event for sending an HTTP response
- The `ReleaseInstance` method is needed to destroy a webclass instance when the `StateManagement` property is set to `wcRetainInstance`
- `URLFor` is used to generate URLs for webitems and events
- The `StateManagement` property is used to control webclass instantiation
- The `NextItem` property is used to shift processing from webitem to webitem
- The default event for a webitem is its `Respond` event
- Template events must be connected before they show up in the Code Editor window

Now that we've finished taking a tour of the primary events, methods, and properties, we will finish our look at IIS Applications in the next chapter by exploring some advanced webclass and IIS Application concepts. We will explore specific uses and examples of webclasses, including talking to a database and HTML template tag replacements.

14

Advanced Webclass Techniques

In Chapters 12 and 13, we introduced and detailed the fundamentals of IIS Applications. The requirements and concepts needed to understand the basic aspects of an IIS Application and its functionality have been presented. With this foundation, we can now delve into the advanced techniques available with webclass development. We can explore sending HTTP responses to the client with template files and the `Response` object. We can investigate how to process template files, and most importantly, we can take a look at numerous examples for implementing activities such as form submittals, sending binary HTTP responses, using the `URLFor` method, and more.

In this chapter, we will cover:

> Sending HTTP responses
> Processing template files
> Building an IIS Application
> Implementing advanced techniques

We will also build a functional IIS Application To begin, let's take a look at sending HTTP responses.

Sending HTTP Responses

Since the whole purpose of webclasses within an IIS Application is to handle the processing of incoming HTTP requests from a user of the application, the methods of sending HTTP responses back to the client are important skills to master. With the exception of potentially sending binary streams of data representing images, the data stream consists of HTML, or even XML, code originating from one of two possible sources:

> ➤ HTML template files
> ➤ Dynamic, Visual Basic code-generated output

The method chosen for sending HTTP to the client depends on the nature of the code being sent. For simple web pages or responses, an HTML template file is usually best. For minor responses, using Visual Basic code in conjunction with the ASP `Response` object is a convenient method.

For example, generating an HTTP response to a form submittal where insufficient information has been provided with the form would generally be short in nature. Such a response could easily be completely encapsulated within the Visual Basic code and generated dynamically. In most cases though, a combination of the two is needed to provide the most convenient response mechanism for the Visual Basic Developer.

HTML Template files

HTML templates files must be created before they can be used as a resource within a webclass. The development of HTML template files is the same as for any other HTML page. Since Visual Basic is not meant to provide another HTML editor to choose from, you must use other tools to develop the pages. The primary structure of the HTML template file is generally designed, developed, coded, and otherwise 'set' prior to being introduced as a resource, known as a webitem, within the webclass. This allows the programmer to either choose the HTML editor of their choice, or completely offload the production of the template files to a team member specializing in HTML development.

Tools to use

When choosing a tool for developing the HTML template files, you might want to pick a tool that provides the most convenient set of features for developing the initial HTML code needed. Keep in mind that initially, the tool you use should be both familiar and able to conveniently generate the necessary base set of HTML tags needed for the template file. Typical tools include Visual Interdev, FrontPage, and Notepad.

Visual Interdev

One of the best tools for developing the initial HTML pages to be used as template files is Microsoft's Visual Interdev. Although this tool is designed to produce entire web sites or Active Server Page applications, the features in this tool can just as easily be used to produce single HTML pages for purposes of adding to IIS Applications.

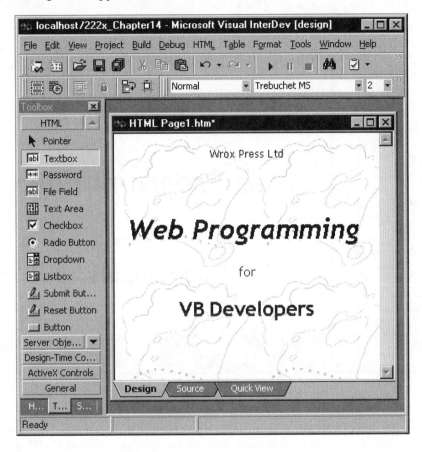

FrontPage

One of the more common tools for lower-end HTML development is Microsoft's FrontPage. FrontPage comes in a number of versions and varieties, including FrontPage Express that comes free with Internet Explorer. FrontPage Express provides tools for quickly producing a base set of HTML tags for a web page, although it is much more restrictive than both FrontPage and Visual Interdev.

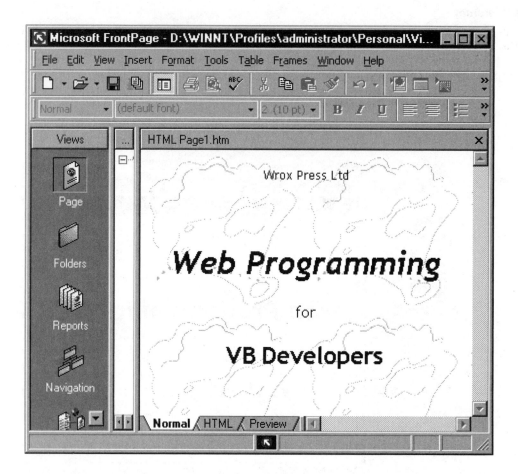

Notepad

Without a doubt, since an HTML page is simply a text file, the most common HTML editor is Notepad. Although we wouldn't recommend Notepad for creating the initial HTML page, it is almost always guaranteed to be available, and is useful for editing pre-existing HTML pages.

DHTML Designer

This is one of the least considered forms of HTML template file creation, although it has some considerable advantages over the use of Notepad. DHTML Designers provide several graphical and logistical advantages over other HTML development tools that make discussion of their usage within IIS Applications a worthwhile activity.

As a refresher, a DHTML Designer is used most commonly in conjunction with DHTML Applications, as detailed in Chapter 4. As a form of ActiveX Designer available within Visual Basic, they are used as a means of graphically designing DHTML pages within the Visual Basic environment. Typically, DHTML Designers are compiled with a Visual Basic project, resulting in the production of a Visual Basic DLL containing the code used to respond to user events within the context of the DHTML Page.

DHTML Designers can be used within an IIS Application in a unique way to provide an integrated method of designing HTML template files. Doing so, though, tends to violate a few assumptions generally made when using DHTML Designers:

> The DHTML Designer will remain in the compiled project
> The HTML page produced will use explicit elements of Dynamic HTML
> The HTML page produced will only be viewed within Internet Explorer
> DHTML Designers will only be used in DHTML Applications

These assumptions may be safe to make when using DHTML Designers within the traditional DHTML Application, but not when using them as a pure development tool within an IIS Application. Leaving the Designer in an IIS Application would not be desired, as that portion of the resulting application would only be useful given a need to drop out of the processing framework of the IIS Application and return to a traditional form of HTTP request for HTML web pages. For this reason, prior to final compiling, the DHTML Designer should be removed from the IIS Application project.

When using a DHTML Designer as a pure design tool, no inherent requirement exists for the explicit use of DHTML tags or syntax. DHTML Designers can simply be used for the numerous graphical design features provided. Along these same lines, using a DHTML Designer within an IIS Application as a pure design tool does not force the requirement that Internet Explorer be used as the client browser.

Taking care to avoid use of explicit DHTML syntax or elements, supported by shelling out to the system's registered HTML editor for manual tweaking of the HTML code, can help ensure that the resulting HTML template file will be viewable in browsers other than Internet Explorer.

When using a DHTML Designer as the source of an HTML template certain steps must be performed in order to set up proper use. Since Webclass Designers do not modify the original version of an HTML file chosen for use as an HTML template resource, a copy is either made or added to the IIS Application project directory. This means that any file created originally from a DHTML Designer added to an IIS Application will become disassociated from any Webclass Designer upon adding the HTML file as a template to the Webclass Designer. The DHTML Designer will continue to modify the original, while the Webclass will only represent the copy. To overcome this, take the following steps:

1. Create the initial HTML file in your choice of HTML development tool:

> Visual Interdev – Good for creating base HTML tags, but requires ownership of tool
> Notepad – Not recommended, since the goal is to simply create the base set of tags efficiently
> DHTML Designer – Use the designer to create a new HTML file, save the file, and then remove the designer
> Webclass Designer – While in the Add HTML Template dialog, add a text file and rename the file to have an HTM extension

> Using the Webclass Designer to add a new HTML page is generally not recommended. Several logistical issues arise that make the process somewhat inconvenient. Even though the **Add HTML Template** dialog has the standard hooks into the Window context menu system, adding a new text file by right-clicking and choosing **New | Text Document** will result in a file with a `.TXT` extension. The file will also not be visible unless the dialog is set to show all files. Renaming the file will be necessary. Upon selecting this new file, the Webclass Designer will make a copy of the file. At this point, a quirk in the Webclass Designer will add only the `<BODY></BODY></HTML>` tags to the file, but fail to add the initial `<HTML>` tag. Since these steps are not considered very convenient, it is best to use one of the other tools for generating the initial HTML file.

2. Add the HTML file to the Webclass Designer as an HTML template resource.

3. Add an instance of a DHTML Designer to your project, and choose to save the file to an external file, rather than saving with the project. Make sure to choose open an existing file and select the copy of the HTML file creating by Step 2.

4. As changes are made to the DHTML page within the DHTML Designer, save the project, or at least the designer.

5. Upon switching to the Webclass Designer, you will be presented with a message that the template file has been changed outside of the Designer. Select Yes to refresh and the changes made within the DHTML Designer will be represented in the HTML template file.

6. Repeat steps 4 and 5 whenever changes are desired in the HTML template file.

Using a DHTML Designer can provide several benefits to the Visual Basic developer. These benefits include the best of several HTML editor options merged into a simplified, integrated development arrangement:

> ➤ Integration of a mini-HTML editor within the Visual Basic IDE. No need to shell into a separate HTML editor

> ➤ Graphical design features such as WYSIWYG text editing within the HTML page, including a standard text toolbar

> ➤ Property sheets for setting properties of HTML elements graphically

The use of DHTML Designers is a unique alternative to the traditional method of using HTML editors for creating and modifying HTML pages. Despite the minor idiosyncrasies of using DHTML Designers in this manner, you may find the convenience of using an integrated design solution a significant advantage.

3rd Party

Numerous third party HTML editors are available in today's market. If you already have significant skills in the use of a third-party HTML development tool, then you should utilize that existing strength. However, the HTML editor should be capable of embedding non-standard HTML tags (such as <WC@*xxx*>) and it would be an advantage if it can be invoked directly from within VB (by means of the tool button) as you can with FrontPage and Visual InterDev.

Manipulating HTML Template Files

Once HTML template files have been created, manipulation of these files is required to incorporate the files with an IIS Application. In order to use HTML template files, they must be first added to a Webclass object. After having been added, the template files can still be edited by shelling out to an HTML editor. The changes made to HTML templates can be revealed within the Webclass Designer through refreshing the template, although in many cases, changes made to an HTML file used within an open Webclass Designer will be recognized and a notification will be made.

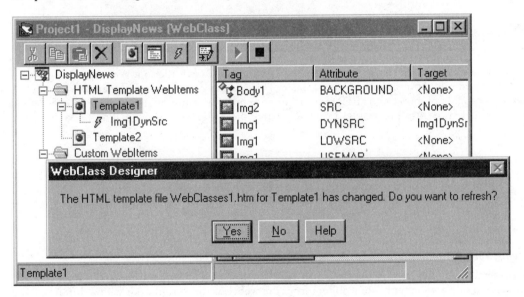

Adding Template Files

Once an HTML file has been created initially, it must be added to a Webclass object in order to be available to serve as a resource. Within a Webclass Designer, the tree view panel includes an HTML Template WebItems folder. Right-clicking on this folder provides a context-menu. Choosing Add HTML Template will allow an existing HTML file to be added to the webclass as a webitem.

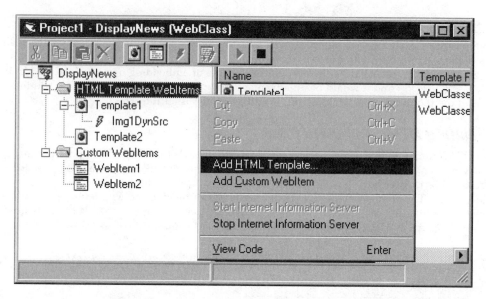

Recall from the previous chapter, the process of adding an HTML file to a Webclass Designer initiates a scanning process within Visual Basic. This scanning process is designed to locate HTML elements capable of initiating HTTP requests upon rendering within a browser on the client. Once elements such as <IMG> or <FORM> tags are located, these elements are added to the Webclass Designer.

> A one-to-one mapping exists between template webitems and HTML pages. For each HTML page to be made available through the webclass, a separate template webitem must be added to the Webclass object.

Removing Template Files

Occasionally, you might need to remove an HTML template file from a webclass. Rather than permanently delete the template webitem from the webclass, or to replace it with a different template, you can delete a template from a webclass is performed simply by right-clicking a template webitem and choosing Delete. Upon deleting a template webitem, any event procedures or code written for the previous template will remain within the webclass code editor window. If a new template is added to the webclass and given the same name as a previously existing template, then any code previously associated with the first template will be attached and used by the new template of the same name.

Editing HTML Template Files

Of course, once template files are loaded into a webclass, the need to tweak the HTML code is near impossible to avoid. Minor changes here and there are bound to become a necessity. Even if the changes are limited to the addition of XML token indicator tags (described later in the section titled *Processing HTML Template Files*), editing the template files will be a common activity.

Prior to editing a template file for the first time, it is recommended to configure the default HTML editor to be used when editing HTML template files. You can do this by choosing the Advance tab of the Project Options dialog box. This tab contains a field for setting the External HTML Editor. It is recommended for simple editing of existing template files that this field be set to Notepad.

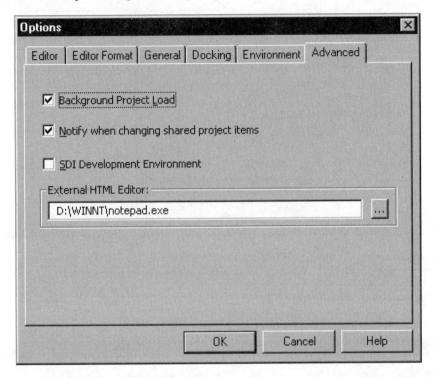

It's required that you save an IIS Application project after making any changes in the External HTML Editor in order for the change to take effect.

Once the External HTML Editor has been set to the desired application, then editing can be initiated by one of two primary means. Right-clicking on a template webitem will provide the option for Edit HTML Template, while the same option is provided through a toolbar button.

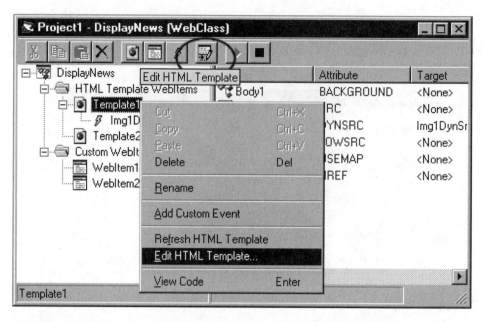

When HTML template files are modified by choosing the Edit HTML Template option, Visual Basic notifies the programmer of the change whenever the Webclass Designer receives the focus again. At this point, the programmer is given the option of refreshing the template file within the Webclass Designer. If the template file is refreshed, Visual Basic rescans the file to synchronize the Details panel with any changes that may have occurred.

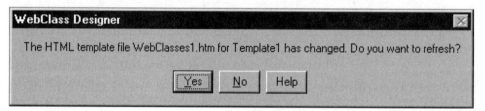

The Webclass Designer can be used to make changes such as renaming webclasses or templates, but modifications to internal HTML elements such as ID properties of HTML tags can not be made from within the Webclass Designer. In general, any HTML specific modifications can not be manually performed from within a Webclass Designer. Making internal changes such as this requires shelling out to the configured HTML editor.

Changes Made to HTML Templates

When an HTML page is added as a template webitem, Visual Basic follows a few basic rules regarding the copying of the template files. These rules are designed to ensure that changes made to the template file are made only to a copy used by the IIS application project. The rules regarding making a copy of the HTML template file are as follows:

> ➤ If the project has not been saved, the template will not be added to the project and no copy will be made.

> ➤ If the HTML file originated outside the project directory, then a copy is made with the same name in the project directory

> ➤ If the HTML file originated within the project directory, then a copy is made in the project directory, appending a sequentially incrementing number to the end of the name

These rules are followed the first time that either the project is saved or debugged, or the HTML template file is edited for the first time. If the HTML file uses any external files such as graphics, then those files will have to be manually copied to the project directory in order for any relative references to the files to be functional. Also, from this point forwards, any changes made to the template file must be made to this new copy in order to be reflected within the Webclass Designer.

Response Object

In addition to using HTML template files, the ASP `Response` object can be used to send HTTP responses to the client from within Visual Basic code. This object has two primary methods which can be used to insert data into the client data stream: `Write` and `BinaryWrite`.

Write

The `Write` method is the most common means for sending small portions of text back to the client as an HTTP response. The `Response` object is passed into the `WebClass` object through the webclass run-time `Manager` object. The `Response` object is available throughout the webclass code, allowing a very convenient method of sending HTTP responses programmatically. For example, every new `webclass` object starts with Visual Basic code within its `Start` event. This code uses the `Write` method of the `Response` object to provide a default HTTP response to the webclass's client.

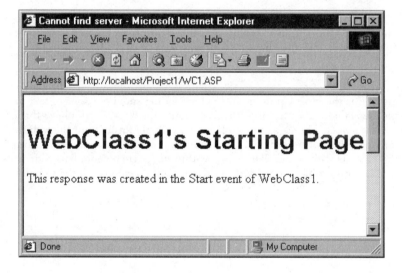

Looking carefully at this code, you will see a basic web page being constructed and sent to the client one segment at a time. By the conclusion of this code's execution, the resulting page will look like the following:

BinaryWrite

The BinaryWrite method of the Response object provides the ability to send binary information to the client as an HTTP response. This method is used in conjunction with the processing of HTTP requests normally resulting in the return of binary data, such as images.

Let's imagine a basic web page where the only HTTP generating element is the background attribute of the <BODY> tag:

```
<HTML>
<HEAD>
    <META NAME="GENERATOR" Content="Microsoft Visual Studio 6.0">
    <TITLE>Web for VB Developer Webclass Demo</TITLE>
</HEAD>

<BODY leftmargin=60  background="notepaper.gif">
```

Note that the background attribute is currently set to use a file by the name of notepaper.gif.

```
<WC@NEWSLIST>No news was found</WC@NEWSLIST>

</BODY>
</HTML>
```

If this HTML page is added as an HTML template to a webclass, and the background attribute of the <BODY> tag is connected to a custom event, then code can be placed into that event to respond to the request for the source of the background for the <BODY> tag. This would be a perfect opportunity to use the BinaryWrite method of the Response object.

Custom Event Code

Several options exist for using the BinaryWrite method. The Visual Basic code could either load the file from the local hard drive, or retrieve the binary data from a database table. Since loading the binary file directly from a local hard disk provides very few benefits over the standard HTTP request for the same file, let's consider using a database lookup to retrieve the binary data representing the image file previously having been loaded into the database table.

If the HTML template file has been given the name of tplNewsList, and the <BODY> tag is without an explicit ID attribute, then the customer event might begin with:

```
Private Sub tplNewsList_Body1()
```

Retrieving data from a database requires the standard project references to the Microsoft ActiveX Data Objects Library 2.0. Once this is performed, the necessary ADO objects can be added to the custom event:

```
        Dim Conn As ADODB.Connection
        Dim rs As ADODB.Recordset
        Dim sqlCommand As String

        ' Create the ADO objects needed
        Set Conn = New ADODB.Connection
        Set rs = New ADODB.Recordset
```

First, open the connection, using variables previously assigned in the webclass Initialization event, and executing the necessary SQL command:

```
Conn.Open strConn, strUser, strPassword
sqlCommand = "Select GifFile From Images"

Set rs = Conn.Execute(sqlCommand)
```

Then, the `BinaryWrite` method can be used to send the binary contents retrieved from the database table to the client:

```
If Not (rs.EOF And rs.BOF) Then
    Response.BinaryWrite rs("GifFile")
End If
Set rs = Nothing
Set Conn = Nothing
End Sub
```

HTML Template Changes

Once the connection is made between the background attribute and the custom event, changes are made to the HTML template file in order to instruct the webclass to fire the necessary event:

```
<HTML>
<HEAD>
    <META NAME="GENERATOR" Content="Microsoft Visual Studio 6.0">
    <TITLE>Web for VB Developer Webclass Demo</TITLE>
</HEAD>

<BODY leftmargin=60  background="WC1.ASP?WCI=tplNewsList&amp;WCE=Body1&amp;WCU">

<WC@NEWSLIST>No news was found</WC@NEWSLIST>

</BODY>
</HTML>
```

Note that the `background` attribute now represents the URL of the host Active Server Page for the Webclass object, along with the necessary information so that the webclass invokes the appropriate event code. The non-standard HTML tags `<WC@NEWSLIST>...</WC@NEWSLIST>`, which we'll come across later, are indicator tags used by webclasses to signify possible areas of the page that will change.

Processing HTML Template Files

The ability to dynamically alter the HTML code contained within a physical HTML file stored on the web server is one of the primary advantages of a server-side scripting platform like Active Server Pages. Since IIS Applications replace the scripting platform with a binary compiled platform, lack of the equivalent ability would actually be a step backwards in the evolution of web application technology. Therefore, IIS Applications provide the ability to parse or process HTML template files by providing a mechanism for processing specially constructed XML tokens inserted into the HTML template.

This replacement mechanism is implemented as an event automatically fired upon locating an instance of this token. The process occurs prior to sending the HTML template webitems to a client as an HTTP response. This activity is very similar to the functionality and advantages provided by Active Server Pages, while also maintaining the separation of code from the HTML source.

Active Server Pages – Dynamic, but Limited

One of the main advantages of Active Server Pages is the ability to dynamically generate HTML pages based on scripting logic directly inserted or embedded with the Active Server Page itself. The provision of an additional, server-side scripting platform allows an entirely separate level of decision making to be inserted into the interaction between application and user. Not to be confused with Dynamic HTML, which allows for dynamic manipulation on the client side, Active Server Pages originally opened the door to programmatically scripting the building or development of HTML pages, hence responses to the client, in a real-time manner.

The dynamic capability provided by ASP is integrally tied into using various different scripting platforms. The scripting platforms available for use in applying logic to the real-time HTTP responses that ASPs produce is limited only by the available scripting engines installed on the web server. While this sounds like a very flexible and open solution, it has several drawbacks:

> Inherent limitations of scripting languages

> Insecure nature of text-based scripting

> Performance of interpreted scripting

> Limited transactional participation

Scripting Language Limitations

The very fact that the application logic applied is based upon scripting languages limits their ultimate power. Scripting languages, themselves, are usually designed as limited subsets of the functionality provided by their full-featured cousins. VBScript, for example, provides a much smaller subset of features and support for advanced capabilities than Visual Basic for Applications (VBA), let alone the full range of functionality allowed by full Visual Basic.

Active Server Pages, which is an additional scripting platform preceding client-side scripting, is designed to leverage scripting languages as their source of logical execution. Due to this fact, a solution that allows for the use of a fuller-featured programming environment or language would yield significantly more power.

Code Security

Active Server Pages are essentially standard text-based files, which does raise the issue of security. While the fact that Active Server Pages exist as text files leads to significantly more flexible development options, this strength of flexibility and development exposes a potential weakness. Theoretically, the more standard the form that information takes on, the more avenues through which the information can be deciphered, analyzed, or compromised.

As text files, the only roadblock between processing and unfettered transmission to the client browser is the processing routines initiated by the ASP filters. As has been revealed in the past, numerous bugs have been uncovered which circumvent the ASP script processing. A major bug of this nature that comes to mind is the rather famous "::$DATA" bug. This bug, which has been all but eliminated (provided you use the latest fixes in the service packs), resulted in the text-based Active Server Page to be passed unprocessed to the client, with an obvious security risk.

With the growing demand for web-based applications in today's business environment, n-tier application design methodology is starting to take on increasing levels of importance in new application development projects. Microsoft's Services Model for application development places heavy emphasis on separating distinct layers of application functionality into concrete layers. With this emphasis, placement of application logic within Active Server Pages serves to exaggerate the potential impact of a security violation.

With the existence of such minimal roadblocks between the processing of Active Server Page scripting as application logic, and the erroneous transmission of the same ASCII characters as unfiltered text, the provision of any additional roadblocks, such as binary compiling of application logic, can provide significant benefits.

Scripting Performance

Active Server Pages, existing as text files, must go through an interpretation process to convert the scripting commands and keywords into native functions and commands. While Visual Basic can be used to compile directly to native code, scripting languages inherently incur additional overhead at run time as the scripting commands are converted or interpreted into native commands by the scripting engine. This additional overhead is the cost exacted by any scripting or interpreted language in return for increased development flexibility or various degrees of platform independence.

Limited Transactional Participation

One of the less well publicized limitations of Active Server Pages involve their ability to participate in transactions. Transactions, which we discussed in Chapter 11, are a relatively new concern for application developers, especially for developers concentrating on Internet or web-based applications. The reason why transactional participation by Active Server Pages is usually not promoted as a limiting factor, is that the very ability for Active Server Pages to be transacted is considered an advantage. Allowing Active Server Pages to initiate a transaction using Microsoft Transaction Server (MTS) provides a management framework for web-based applications to gain much greater scalability, reliability, and consistency.

```
<% @TRANSACTION = REQUIRED %>

<HTML>
    <HEAD>
        <TITLE>Display News Form</TITLE>
    </HEAD>...
```

> **Active Server Pages could be transacted, or initiate an MTS-managed transaction by including the ASP processing directive @TRANSACTION = REQUIRED.**

Unfortunately, Active Server Pages can initiate transactions, but their "lifetime" is limited to the duration of a single Active Server Page. While this may not initially seem to be a significant disadvantage, when attempting to combine multiple sources of HTML and application logic into a single transaction, the use of Active Server Pages can become a disadvantage.

Webclass Tag Processing

If HTML template files inserted into webclass objects, as webitems, could not be dynamically altered based on code processing, then the ultimate usefulness of the static HTML templates would be somewhat dubious. Fortunately, webclasses provide an automatic mechanism for parsing HTML templates to create a search and replace routine that adds some of the functionality considered core to Active Server Pages.

While ASP combines the script and HTML code destined for the client into a single, seamless Active Server Page, a webclass utilizes a split processing mechanism. HTML template files are separate external resources that are programmatically added to webclass objects within the Visual Basic IDE, but remain separate.

While this allows the development of the actual HTML template files, or webitems, to be separate from the development of the application code that ultimately resides within the webclass object, this also removes the ability to integrate the application logic code with the actual client HTML.

To obtain the same degree of dynamic, inline processing of HTML template files that Active Server Pages inherently provides by integrating server-side script and client-side HTML, webclasses utilize a split-processing mechanism that incorporates special indicator tags into the HTML template file. These special tags indicate to the webclass object where replacement might occur. While simple text replacements do not initially appear to rank up there with the power that ASP script processing provides, the same power is not only obtained, but surpassed by using Visual Basic as the processing language.

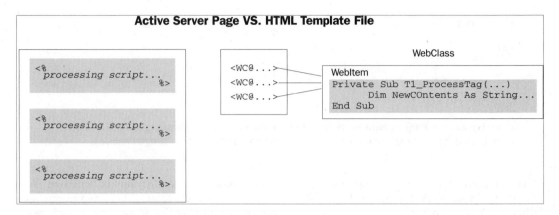

In a nutshell, the entire mechanism used by webclasses to provide Active Server Page-like processing of HTML template files involves four main elements:

> Method for template initialization
> Event for tag processing
> Indicators for targeting replacement areas
> Arguments for controlling tag processing

Template Initialization

The entire process of dynamically replacing portions of an HTML template file with programmatically derived content begins with an initialization method. Since webclasses may, and usually do involve many different HTML templates as potential HTTP response resources, a defined method exists to initiate the process of processing an HTML template file. The `WriteTemplate` method of a webitem is available for use when an HTML template file is associated with a webitem.

If a webitem by the name of `DisplayNews` has been added to a webclass object, and `DisplayNews` has an HTML template file associated with it, then the `WriteTemplate` method could be used to invoke

```
Private Sub OrderSearch_Respond()
    OrderSearch.WriteTemplate
End Sub
```

The `WriteTemplate` method of a webitem instructs the webclass object to begin processing an HTML template either associated with a webitem, or one specified. The `WriteTemplate` method is generally invoked from a webitem's `Respond` event, as seen in the procedure above.

HTML Template Tag Indicators

During the processing of an HTML template, the webclass object seeks special indicator tags and code associated with the processing is invoked. In order to specify areas of the HTML template that are to be parsed, analyzed and potentially replaced with other content, special markup tags must be added to the HTML template. These tags are added within an HTML editor, and then imported into the webclass Designer by refreshing the HTML template.

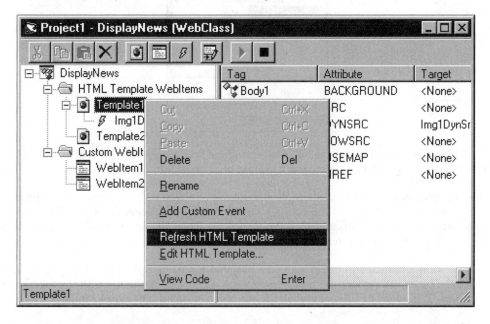

> Note: Webclass designers do not provide any tools for applying changes or inserting code into HTML template files. The DHTML Designer could be used to add tags, alter tag attributes, and so on, but no avenue exists for inserting the non-standard HTML Template tag indicators.

HTML indicator tags are really just a specialized form of HTML markup that is not part of any W3C HTML recommendation. The HTML markup is recognized by a webclass designer as an HTML indicator tag only if the tag prefix portion of the indicator tag matches the TagPrefix property set within the Properties windows in the Visual Basic IDE.

Now that I have let the cat out of the bag concerning the first of the three parts of the HTML template indicator tag syntax, let's look at a sample of an indicator tag.

Let's pretend you want to dynamically replace a portion of a web page with the correct graphic file for a faxed press release that is stored within your Microsoft SQL Server database. The client has been presented with a list of links on a page representing the available press releases. Each hyperlink is in fact a call to the same webitem, DisplayNews.

DisplayNews is a standard webitem with an associated HTML template file. This page is designed to process the page, and replace the generic FaxNotFound.gif image file with the specific image file requested. Within the HTML Template file, an indicator tag might exist as follows:

```
<WC@NewsGifName><IMG src=FaxNotFound.gif></WC@NewsGifName>
```

The indicator tag itself consists of separately defined elements:

- ➤ tag prefix
- ➤ tag name
- ➤ tag contents

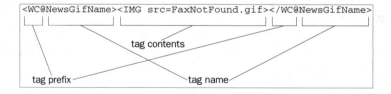

The tag prefix is the series of characters used to uniquely identify an area to be targeted for evaluation and possible modification. The default tag prefix for an HTML Template file is the WC@ combination. Any instance of a piece of HTML markup is evaluated and if the initial characters in the markup tag correspond to the TagPrefix property, the webclass will fire the necessary event to process the indicator tag. When a tag prefix is defined and used within an HTML Template, it must adhere to the following restrictions:

> ➤ Be consistent within a given HTML Template file being parsed
>
> ➤ Begin with a standard alphabetic character
>
> ➤ Should contain a unique character, such as @, to improve indicator tag recognition

Once an indicator has been found, the second portion of the indicator is the tag name. The tag name is generally a descriptive phrase used to both visually and programmatically identify the specific area targeted for replacement. Tag names are usually unique, existing only once per template, although this is not a specific restriction.

The combination of the tag prefix, tag name, and surrounding delimiters (<>) together allow the indicator tag to take on the format of a standard HTML markup.

Editors like FrontPage will ignore these tags in the WYSIWYG mode, but allow editing of the HTML Template in HTML mode. In this way, an HTML template file can maintain the look of a standard HTML file, although the meaning of the markup corresponding to the indicator tags will only have meaning in the webitem itself, assuming the tag prefix used matches that defined and set for the TagPrefix property.

The final portion of the indicator tag is the content itself. No real restrictions exist on the nature of the initial tag content. In many cases, the value originally found within the HTML template file is used to provide a descriptive indication of its use, and would correspond to the concept of a default value being set for the indicator tag. When the indicator tag is replaced, either the content and the indicator tag, or just the content can be replaced.

Tag Processing

When the WriteTemplate method of a webitem is invoked, the HTML template file is loaded and parsed by the webclass object. Each time an indicator tag is found, the ProcessTag event is fired and used to evaluate the indicator tag located. This event is used to provide the necessary conditional logic to independently evaluate and process each of the unique indicator tags found within the HTML template file. The steps leading up to, and followed during processing an HTML Template file with tags involves a loose series of steps:

1. Visual Basic code is executed that invokes the WriteTemplate method. This is usually called within a webitem's default Respond event.

2. The template file is loaded and evaluated to locate any instances of HTML markup adhering to the defined indicator tag format.

3. The ProcessTag event is fired for each instance of an indicator found, and the content of these tags is modified as designed.

4. After all indicator tags are processed, the webclass object writes the modified template to the built-in ASP `Response` object

5. The `Response` object packages the content of the template file into an HTTP response and sends it to the client.

It should be noted that the `ProcessTag` event is not, or more accurately, cannot be fired explicitly from within the Visual Basic code. The `ProcessTag` event is fired only in response to the successful location of a defined indicator tag within an HTML template file. Therefore, if no indicator tags are found in the HTML template file, then the `ProcessTag` event will not be fired.

Tag Processing Arguments

The `ProcessTag` event provides three arguments for use in ascertaining exactly which indicator tag initiated the firing of the `ProcessTag` event for any particular instance. Two of the arguments are used to pass in the specific information identifying the indicator tag, while the third is merely a processing directive to instruct the webitem whether to behave inclusively, that is retaining the original markup, or exclusively. These arguments are:

- ➢ `TagName`
- ➢ `TagContents`
- ➢ `SendTags`

TagName

The `TagName` argument value is not exactly intuitive. While the indicator tag format separates the actual markup into two elements, the value of the `TagName` argument passed into the `ProcessTag` event contains the combination of the defined tag prefix (`TagPrefix` property) and the tag name. `TagName` is used as the primary source of identification of the specific indicator tag being processed. The `TagName` value is used as the pivotal variable in any `Select` or `If...Then` statements coded within the `ProcessTag` event, as seen in the following example:

```
Sub DisplayNews_ProcessTag(ByVal TagName as String, _
    TagContents as String, SendTags as Boolean)

Select Case TagName
    Case "WC@NewsGifName"
        TagContents = Request("NewsGifName")
    Case "WC@FaxTitle"
        TagContents = Request("FaxTitle")
End Select

SendTags = False

End Sub
```

TagContents

The TagContents value contains the actual text found between the beginning and ending tags that make up the actual indicator tag markup. The developer should view the TagName and TagContents arguments as a standard name/value pair. In the following example, during processing of the ProcessTag event, the TagContents value would equal "<IMG src=FaxNotFound.gif>".

```
<WC@NewsGifName><IMG src=FaxNotFound.gif></WC@NewsGifName>
```

In the above code example, it should be noted that the source of the modified tag content is the value currently assigned to a variable in the built-in ASP Request object. This works, of course, because for either of the possible methods of the Webclass run-time Manager component used to instantiate the webclass object to which the current webitem belongs, all of the primary built-in ASP objects were passed in as arguments. Through this method, and several others, new tag content can be assigned to the TagContents argument during the processing of the ProcessTag event. Several of the possible methods for obtaining new tag contents can be summarized as follows:

➢ Request.Form collection for webitems connected to a form submittal

➢ Request.QueryString collection for explicit values attached to the URL

➢ Session object variables assigned with a previous template or standard event

➢ Application object variables assigned with a previous template or standard event

➢ Standard variables

➢ Static, hard-coded variable strings

➢ Database table lookups

➢ Cookie values stored on the client and accessed through the Request.Cookies collection

➢ COM and MTS business logic components

SendTags

The SendTags argument is used to identify whether or not the ProcessTag event should include the original indicator tag information or markup with the tag contents just modified. The default value for this argument is FALSE, which will instruct the ProcessTag event to behave exclusively, that is to exclude the tag markup itself from the modified tag contents being used. This has the effect of simply tossing the original indicator tag markup into the trash, after fulfilling its primary job of identifying the areas to be processed. If Sendtags is set to TRUE, then the original markup will be retained.

Setting SendTags might not initially seem to be very useful, or even desired. Since the format of indicator tags does not adhere to any standard HTML markup syntax, retention of the original markup would simply be passed onto the client as a part of the client HTML data stream. The result would either be to display the markup as basic text, or ignore it as non-standard HTML markup, depending on the browser being used by the client. As neither of these results are entirely useful, Visual Basic provides a property of webitems used to instruct the webclass to rescan the HTML template file for additional indicator tags.

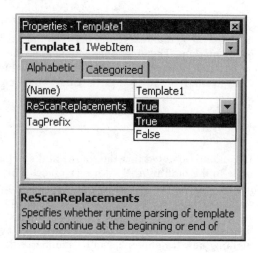

The ReScanReplacements property instructs the webclass to recursively scan the template file during the ProcessTag event. This will allow remaining tags to be processed. This property is only relevant during the ProcessTag event, therefore setting the ReScanReplacements property to TRUE in other events will not result in the template being scanned.

It should also be noted that improper use of the SendTags argument, combined with the ReScanReplacements property could result in a recursive loop being induced as the webclass object attempts to continually retain the indicator tags while rescanning the template file.

Building an IIS Application

Now that we have taken a look at many of the foundational aspects of IIS Applications, it's time to combine many of these techniques, methods, properties, events, and concepts into a working IIS Application. We will start by creating a basic IIS Application, followed by adding successively more complex elements to the sample application. The steps we will take a look at can be duplicated and combined in many ways to produce a functional IIS Application.

Basic IIS Application

Let's assume that your developer system already has a functional web server installed, with Internet Explorer 4.0 or later. Let's begin by running Visual Basic and choosing a new IIS Application project. Upon starting an IIS Application, only a single Webclass object will exist:

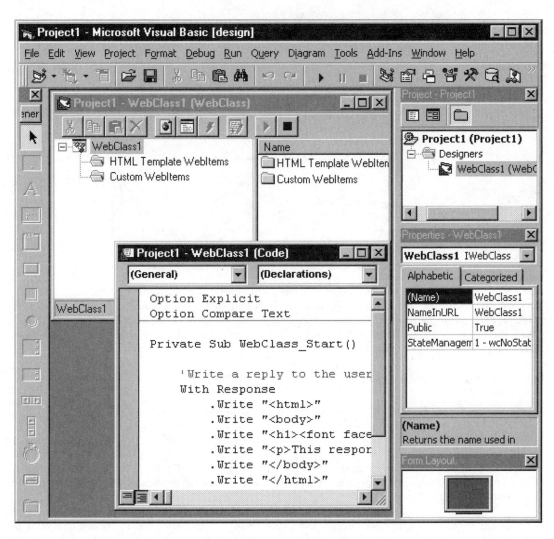

Just for fun, and to point out several default behaviors of an IIS Application, let's immediately run the new IIS Application. Keep in mind that we have yet to add any Visual Basic code, HTML templates, webitems, or resources of any kind. Being the first time that the application has been run, we will be presented with a single Debugging tab from the Project1 properties dialog.

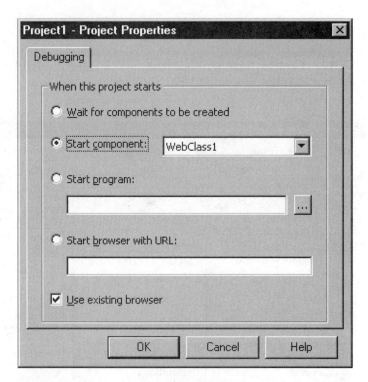

By default, the debugging tab will be set to Start **C**omponent, with the default `WebClass1` set to start. With this setting, Visual Basic will actually start by loading the default browser on the developer system, assumed to be Internet Explorer 4.0 or later, and navigate to the host Active Server Page. Two other settings should be noted on this tab. Start **b**rowser with URL could be set to the default URL for the host Active Server Page, such as:

```
http://localhost/Temp/WebClass1.asp
```

Navigating to this URL with your browser is effectively the same as starting the component `WebClass1`, including the same ability to automatically enter into debugging mode. Several advantages still exist in maintaining the default settings for starting the application. If the `NameInURL` property, project name, or default webclass object should change, then the value in the Start **b**rowser with URL field would have to be changed. If the default value of the Start **c**omponent field is used, any changes in this information will not affect the ability of the IIS application to be started properly from within the Visual Basic IDE.

The second setting of which to take note is the **U**se existing browser checkbox. If this checkbox is deselected, then running the application from Visual Basic will create a new instance of the browser each time the application is run from Visual Basic. The implications of this include a loss in speed of the application, and by using a new browser you will get a new ASP `Session` object each time.

At this point, upon choosing OK, a dialog box will be presented regarding the establishment of a virtual directory.

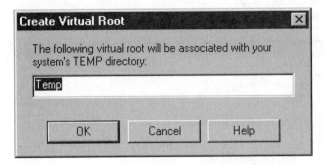

A little explanation is in order. A virtual directory for a web server is a directory that is associated with the directory hierarchy of the web server as if it existed within the hierarchy. In other words, any hard drive folder can be associated with the web server such that it appears as if it actually existed under the web server's root directory. In this way, an external folder can be accessed by the web server to act as another source of HTTP resources.

In order to allow IIS Applications to be invoked from Visual Basic, the Active Server Page host file must be accessible through the web server. This is only possible if the project directory is configured as a virtual directory off the web server. Since the project has yet to be saved, the Active Server Page host file will be temporarily saved to the system's temp directory, therefore the dialog box for creating a web server virtual root called Temp, and associated with the system temp directory, is provided. Once the project is saved, a similar dialog box will be presented on order to establish a new virtual root with the actual project directory, and will take the project name as the default name.

At this point, the initial HTTP response and web page will look like:

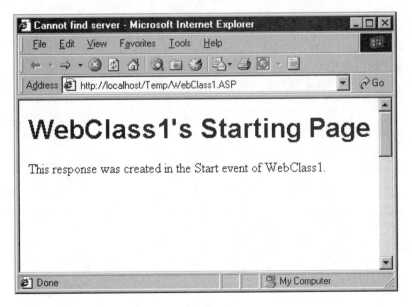

Notice that the URL contains a virtual directory of `Temp`, and an Active Server Page host file name of `WebClass1.asp`. Also notice that a full-fledged web page is presented to the browser, even though no code was written, nor an HTML template file added. If you remember from Chapter 13, the code for this initial HTML page is generated programmatically, as seen in the `WebClass_Start` event:

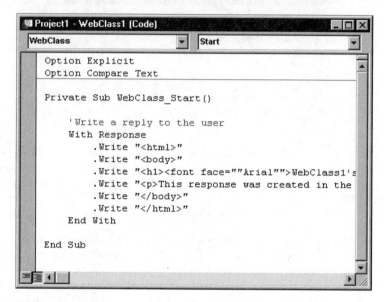

Let's start by altering the code in the `Start` event to better reflect the meaning of our IIS Application demo, by modifying the code to appear as follows:

```
Private Sub WebClass_Start()

    'Write a reply to the user
    With Response
        .Write "<html>"
        .Write "<body bgcolor=""cornsilk"">"
        .Write "<h1><font size=4 face=""Arial"">WEB4VB Demo "
        .Write "<BR>IIS Application</font></h1>"
        .Write "Please click here to go to "
        .Write "the <A href=""http://www.wrox.com"">"
        .Write "Wrox website</A>"
        .Write "</body>"
        .Write "</html>"
    End With

End Sub
```

Once these changes have been made, the resulting default HTML page sent to the browser should look like this:

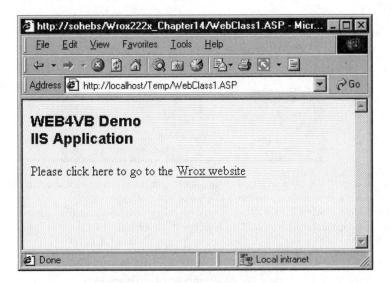

Once this has been accomplished, it is about time to go ahead and save the project to a permanent directory. Doing so will provide a permanent location to copy any additional files needed by the HTML template. Prior to doing so, let's make a few change to the project and webclass properties. Let's start by changing the project name to something like IISappDemo.

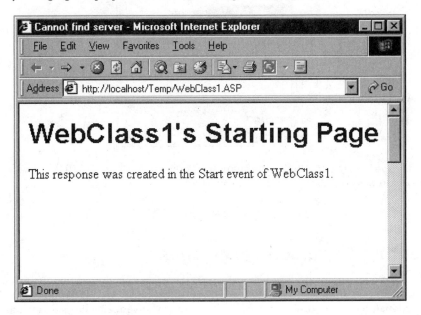

Remember, this will result in an additional virtual root being created on the local web server, on saving the project. This new virtual root will be given the same name as the project name, in this case IISappDemo.

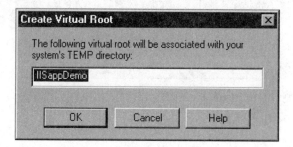

In addition to changing the project name, and consequently the name of the virtual root appearing in the URL, let's make a few changes to both the webclass name and NameInURL properties. If we shorten the name to something like WC1, it will be more accessible in our Visual Basic code. Along the same lines, changing the NameInURL property to something like wcHost will ensure a shorter base URL and give a little meaning to the Active Server Page's URL.

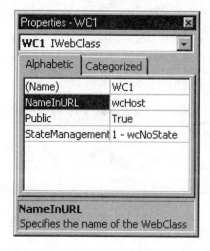

At this point, upon saving and then re-running the application, the base URL will now represent the changes made to the project and webclass properties:

```
http://localhost/IISappDemo/wcHost.ASP
```

Implementing Advanced Techniques

Now that we have set up our IIS Application, saved the project, and modified the primary properties for the project and webclass, we have succeed in creating a functional IIS Application. This project is indeed functional, but very boring. We have yet to use any advance techniques such as using templates, processing templates, retrieving data from a database, using the Request object's BinaryWrite method, or coding Form submittals. Let's take this basic IIS Application and begin to add some of the advance features or functions that we have described so far.

Let's begin with shifting the HTTP responses to HTML template files...

Adding Templates

The most logical candidate, in our example thus far for adding a template is the HTML code being sent to the browser in the Webclass's `Start` event. This HTML is generated by using the `Write` method of the `Response` object.

```
With Response
    .Write "<html>"
    .Write "<body bgcolor=""cornsilk"">"
    .Write "<h1><font size=4 face=""Arial"">WEB4VB Demo "
    .Write "<BR>IIS Application</font></h1>"
    .Write "Please click here to go to "
    .Write "the <A href=""http://www.wrox.com"">"
    .Write "Wrox website</A>"
    .Write "</body>"
    .Write "</html>"
End With
```

Since this code produces a full HTML page, with all the necessary markup, it would be better to shift this HTML code into a template file and then send the entire template to the browser. This would require a small amount of modification to the code itself, but can easily be accomplished by opening Notepad. After cutting and pasting, and then removing the Visual Basic code, the resulting HTML file might look like:

```
<HTML>

<BODY bgcolor="cornsilk">
    <H1>
        <FONT size=4 face="Arial">
        WEB4VB Demo<BR>IIS Application
        </FONT>
    </H1>
Please click here to go to the
<A id=A1 href="http://www.wrox.com">Wrox website</A>
</BODY>

</HTML>
```

More importantly, notice that an `ID` attribute of `A1` has been added to the `<A>` tag to provide a shorter `Name` value when adding the template to the webclass object. After saving the file as `Welcome.htm`, the template file must be added to the webclass. Just as we described earlier in this chapter, a template can be added by right-clicking on the webclass and choosing **Add Template** file. Upon adding the template file, and renaming it to `tplWelcome`, the Visual Basic project will look a little like this:

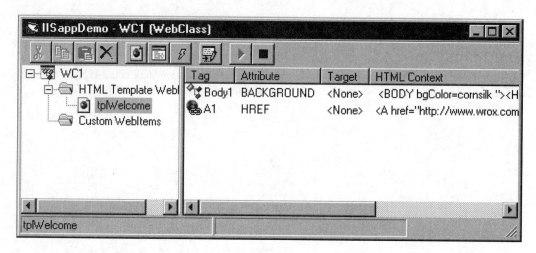

Notice that the ID of the `<A>` tag has been used as the `Name` value for the `HREF` attribute of the `<A>` element. Also notice that the HTML Context column of the Details panel shows the HTML code for the tags added to the HTML template file while building the file in Notepad.

In order to utilize this newly added template file in place of the code that still exists in the Start event for the Webclass object, the following code modifications need to be made to the Start event:

```
Private Sub WebClass_Start()

    'Write a reply to the user
    Set NextItem = tplWelcome

End Sub
```

These modifications to the `Start` event alone will not cause the template to be sent to the browser. So far, only the `Respond` event of the `tplWelcome` template webitem will fire. Since this event has no code within it by default, the result of running the application at this time would be an empty browser. Not very useful. The `WriteTemplate` method must be used within the `Respond` event to instruct the webclass object to send the template file.

```
Private Sub tplWelcome_Respond()

    tplWelcome.WriteTemplate

End Sub
```

At this point, the Code Editor for the Webclass object should appear as follows,

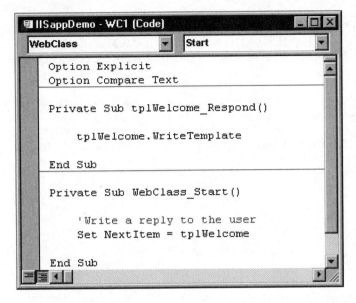

```
Option Explicit
Option Compare Text

Private Sub tplWelcome_Respond()

    tplWelcome.WriteTemplate

End Sub

Private Sub WebClass_Start()

    'Write a reply to the user
    Set NextItem = tplWelcome

End Sub
```

Running the application should result in a web page identical to the one created programmatically. The difference in the pages is that one is the result of a template webitem, while the first version had the HTML hard-coded within the programming logic.

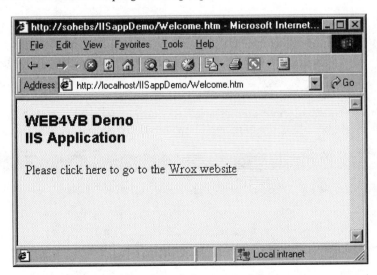

Connecting WebItems

At this point, let's consider adding another template file and connecting an attribute to a webitem to shift processing from one webitem to another. It is almost impossible to generate much functionality without using multiple HTML template files. This will almost certainly involve sequencing the functionality of the application into stages, where each stage correlates to a separate HTML template file.

For starters, we need to make a modification to the `tplWelcome` template webitem file. We will add an additional hyperlink to the template file to be used for navigating to a different page. This page will be served up as a template webitem. We can choose to edit the template file, which will open the `Welcome1.htm` file in the default external HTML editor. Consider the following HTML, which represents the new template file:

```
<HTML>

<BODY bgcolor="cornsilk">

    <H1><FONT face="Arial">
        WEB4VB Demo <BR> IIS Application</FONT>
    </H1>

    Please click here to go to the<BR>
    <A ID=A1 href="http://www.wrox.com">Wrox website</A><BR>
    <A ID=A2 href="">Racing Press Releases</A>

</BODY>
</HTML>
```

> Notice that the file being changed is `Welcome1.htm`. The "1" was appended to the original `Welcome.htm` file name when the project was first saved after adding the template file.

Once these changes are made, and the file is saved, returning focus back to Visual Basic will generate a message box about refreshing the template file within the Webclass Designer.

Once these changes have been made to the template file, the Webclass Designer will reflect the new changes:

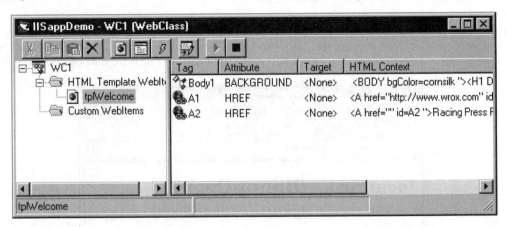

Notice, at this time, that the Target for the newly added A2 hyperlink is set to "<NONE>". This is the same value assigned to the first hyperlink. Once we connect the hyperlink to a custom event, this value will change to the name of the custom event.

Before this step is taken, let's take a look at what running the application will produce in this stage of development. The resulting default HTTP response will look like the following:

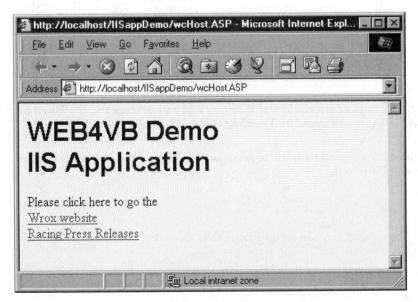

If you take a good look at the modifications to the template file, you will notice that the HREF attribute was left blank. At this point, clicking on the new hyperlink will produce a directory of the project directory.

You may need to switch on directory browsing in the IIS Manager, which is a snap-in
for the Microsoft Management Console (MMC).

This occurs because the blank HREF corresponds to loading nothing into the browser. The link is considered relative; therefore the directory itself is loaded up as the only portion of the base URL still left. Since the directory is a virtual root associated with the project directory, its contents are shown:

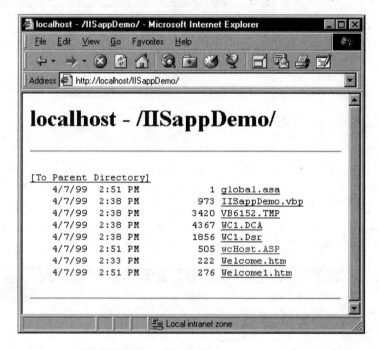

Directory browsing is a configurable setting with web servers and is allowed by default
on the virtual roots created by Visual Basic for IIS Applications.

Now let's produce a second template to serve as the source of the additional webitem. Let's consider the following HTML code:

```
<HTML>

<HEAD>
    <TITLE>Web for VB Developer Webclass Demo</TITLE>
</HEAD>

<BODY leftmargin=60  background="notepaper.gif">

<WC@NEWSLIST></WC@NEWSLIST>

</BODY>

</HTML>
```

Notice the non-standard HTML tags `<WC@NEWSLIST></WC@NEWSLIST>` – these indicator tags will be explained alittle later. Let's take the following steps at this point:

1. Open Notepad and type in the above HTML code

2. Save the file as `DisplayList.htm` in the project directory

3. Add a new template to the webclass, using `DisplayList.htm` as the source, and rename it to `tplDisplayList`

Once these steps are taken, the Webclass Designer will look a little different.

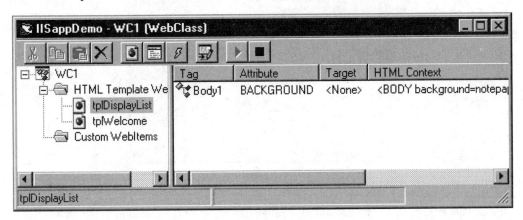

Now that we have a source for the recently added hyperlink named A2, we can connect this attribute to the brand new `tplDisplayList` template webitem. Once again, we use the same context menu found by right-clicking on an attribute:

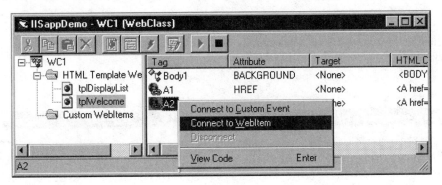

Of course, we have many different webitems from which to choose. Okay, not really, but we do have at least two from which to choose. In complex IIS Applications, we might reasonable expect to have dozens, if not a hundred or more from which to choose. For this reason, a small select dialog box appears:

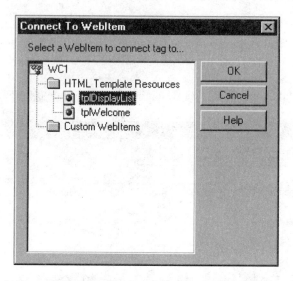

Once the webitem is chosen, which is tplDisplayList in our case, several changes can be found within the webclass Designer. The first change involves the value of the A2 tag in the **Target** column of the **Details** panel. This value should now reflect the name of the webitem to which it was connected, that is tplDisplayList. The second change involves the value of the **HTML Context** column. This should now show that the HREF attribute takes on the URL value necessary to call the Active Server Page host file, appending the necessary information through the WC1 QueryString variable.

> **Changes to underlying HTML template files are not actually recorded or saved in the physical file until the project is saved.**

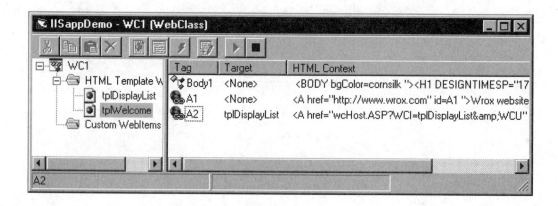

Let's go ahead and run the application to check on the resulting output. We will still receive the same initial response in the browser as before. The difference will become evident once we click on the newest hyperlink added to the page. This will send an HTTP request to the IIS Application, which will fire the `tplDisplayList_Respond` event, resulting in a blank page. Note, however, the extension to the URL, which matches the HREF attribute in the **HTML Context** column for A2.

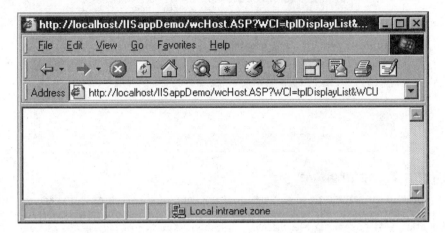

Of course, this is quite unsatisfactory as far as the user experience is concerned. To correct this, the same change must be made to the `Respond` event of the `tplDisplayList` template as was earlier made to the same event for the `tplWelcome` webitem. This involves using the `WriteTemplate` method.

```
Private Sub tplDisplayList_Respond()

    tplDisplayList.WriteTemplate

End Sub
```

Keep in mind that this newest template involves a background image file used by the template file, by the name of `notepaper.gif`. In order to obtain the desired look, this image file will need to be placed either into the project directory, or a subdirectory. Assuming the relative path for the `bgcolor` attribute of the `<BODY>` tag matches the location of the image file, the HTTP response will look like this:

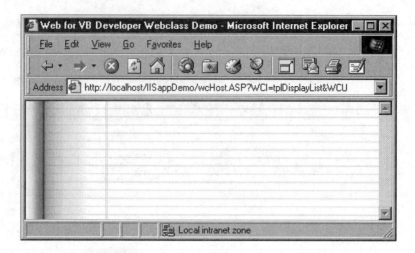

Processing a Template File

In order to obtain the same type of server-side processing of HTML files that is accomplished by using Active Server Pages, we will have to provide code to the `ProcessTag` event to handle the replacement of XML tokens. These tokens, also known as indicator tags, act as placeholders for Visual Basic code, identifying not the location of the code, but rather the location affected by the code.

If you noticed earlier, the HTML template used for the `tplDisplayList` template webitem contained an indicator tag by the name of `NEWSLIST`. This indicator tag is using the default tag prefix of `WC@`. Our desire is to provide a default value to be assigned as the contents of this indicator tag. We could just as easily modify the HTML template file to provide default tag content.

```
<HTML>

<HEAD>
    <TITLE>Web for VB Developer Webclass Demo</TITLE>
</HEAD>

<BODY leftmargin=60  background="notepaper.gif">

<WC@NEWSLIST> No news was found </WC@NEWSLIST>

</BODY>

</HTML>
```

Rather than place the default tag content directly into the template file, we will provide this value through the `ProcessTag` event. This will increase reusability of this template file. To handle the processing of this indicator tag, we need to modify the `ProcessTag` event.

```
Private Sub tplDisplayList_ProcessTag(ByVal TagName As String,
                                 TagContents As String, SendTags As Boolean)

    Select Case TagName
        Case "WC@NEWSLIST"
            TagContents = " No news was found "
    End Select

End Sub
```

The `Select Case` statement is used to prepare for future indicator tags being added to the template file at a later time during development. When the template file is processed during run-time, the tag contents of the indicator tag, initially blank, will be replaced with "No news was found". Assuming the `SendTags` parameter is not modified or otherwise set to `TRUE`, the resulting HTTP response generated by selecting the second hyperlink of the initial HTTP `Response` will now look somewhat different, due to the processing of the indicator tag.

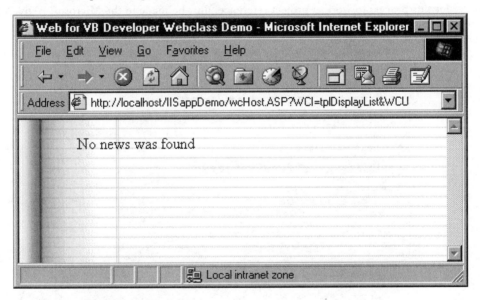

Advanced Tag Processing

In many cases, significantly more advanced tag processing will need to be performed to provide functionality similar to that of Active Server Pages. To account for this, we're going to modify the steps taken in the previous section to provide an example of advanced tag processing. This processing will pull the data to serve as the new tag contents from a database and build up a string representing HTML code. The string will be a series of links representing hyperlink resources outside the IIS Applications.

To start, we will dimension a couple of variables. For simplicity, we will simply add the following code to the General Declarations section of the webclass Code Editor.

```
Dim strConn As String
Dim strUser As String
Dim strPassword As String
```

After this, we will modify the `Initialize` event to assign values to these variables. They will serve to provide a globally available source for the arguments of the ADO Connection object `Open` method, whenever it may be invoked.

```
Private Sub WebClass_Initialize()

    strConn = "DRIVER=SQL Server;UID=SA;DATABASE=WEB4VBDemo..."
    strUser = "sa"
    strPassword = "goofyrules"

End Sub
```

In order for this process to work, a project reference must be made to the Microsoft ActiveX Data Objects 2.0 Library.

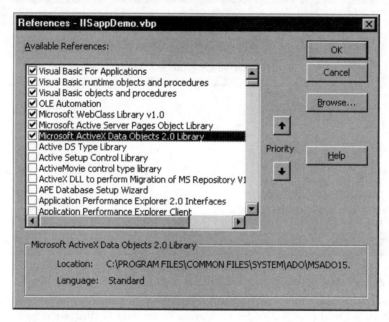

Once we add this code, we need to significantly modify the `ProcessTag` event to provide a complex series of concatenations to produce the desired tag contents.

```
Private Sub tplDisplayList_ProcessTag(ByVal TagName As String,
                                      TagContents As String, SendTags As Boolean)

Dim strTemp As String

    Select Case TagName
        Case "WC@NEWSLIST"
            Dim Conn As ADODB.Connection
            Dim rs As ADODB.Recordset
            Dim sqlCommand As String

            ' Create the ADO objects needed
            Set Conn = New ADODB.Connection
            Set rs = New ADODB.Recordset

            Conn.Open strConn, strUser, strPassword
            sqlCommand = "Select Title,GifName From PressReleases"

            Set rs = Conn.Execute(sqlCommand)

            If Not (rs.EOF And rs.BOF) Then

                Do While Not rs.EOF
                    strTemp = strTemp + "<A href=PRs.asp?GifName="
                    strTemp = strTemp + rs("GifName")
                    strTemp = strTemp + ">" + rs("Title") + "</A><BR>"
                    rs.MoveNext
                Loop
            End If

            Set rs = Nothing
            Set Conn = Nothing

            TagContents = strTemp
    End Select
```

Notice that the section of code modified inside the `Select Case` statement connects to a database, retrieves a list of records, and then integrates the information with the necessary HTML code to produce a hyperlink dynamically in the same fashion as performed by scripting within an Active Server Page. The resulting HTTP response generated by select the second hyperlink will now include a series of hyperlinks itself.

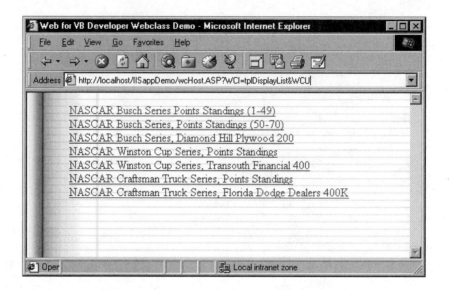

Processing Form Submittals

One of the common advanced techniques incorporated within an IIS Application is processing a form submitted to the web server. This is a common process with Active Server Pages, and is equally simple to perform with webclasses. Let's start by adding some form of code to the HTML template file. Click on the `tplWelcome` template webitem, and then choose the Edit button on the toolbar, or simply right-click and choose Edit Template.

```
<HTML>

<BODY bgcolor="cornsilk">

    <H1><FONT face="Arial">
        WEB4VB Demo <BR> IIS Application</FONT>
    </H1>

    Please click here to go the<BR>
    <A ID=A1 href="http://www.wrox.com">Wrox website</A><BR>
    <A ID=A2 href="">Racing Press Releases</A>

    <FORM METHOD=POST ACTION="">
       <INPUT TYPE=TEXT Name=User size=20>
       <INPUT TYPE=SUBMIT VALUE=Login>
    </FORM>

</BODY>
</HTML>
```

The resulting page will now be modified to show the form elements.

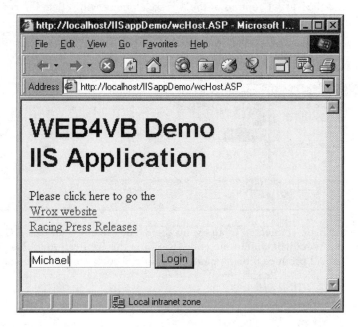

After saving the edited template file, and returning focus back to VB, the webclass Designer will generate a request to refresh. Upon refreshing the template webitem within the webclass Designer, right-clicking on the newly added `Form1` element found in the Details panel will provide an option to connect to a Custom Event.

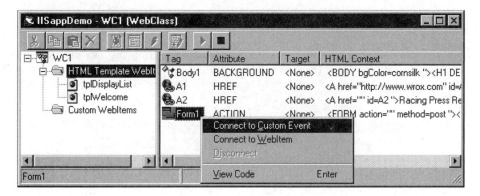

After connecting to the custom event, the Treeview panel of the webclass Designer will now show the new event added, and the Target column of the Form1 element will reflect the connection.

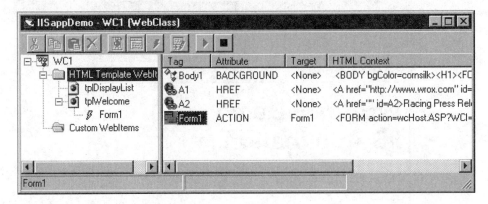

Once an attribute has been connected to an event, the event will show up in the Code Editor window. Although present, the event will contain no code. Running the application at this point, and clicking on the submit button will produce a blank page. To produce some functional behavior, code should be added to the tplWelcome_Form1 event:

```
Private Sub tplWelcome_Form1()

    With Response
        .Write "<HTML><BODY><BR><FONT size=4 face=arial><CENTER>"
        .Write "Thank-you for logging in " & Request.Form("User") & _
               "</FONT></CENTER>"
        .Write ""</BODY></HTML>"
    End With

End Sub
```

As you can see, this code will produce an HTTP Response that thanks the user for logging in to the application. Notice that the use of the Active Server Page Request.Form collection allows the information provided in the submitted form to be accessed and used by the webclass. Clicking on the submit button will produce the following HTTP response:

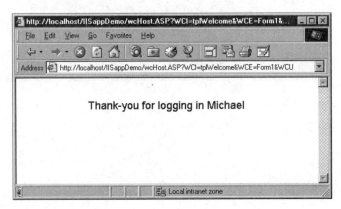

Using the URLFor Method

In many cases, webitems will need to be introduced into the HTTP response as the target for HTTP requests. In these cases, the URLFor method becomes very helpful. This method, as described in Chapter 13, is used to produce the necessary URL for accessing or invoking webclass resources. In the previous section, the custom event generated for the form submittal processing produced an HTTP response that provide no link for navigating to any other page, or webclass resource. This would be a perfect opportunity to use the URLFor method. A little modification to this code, using the URLFor method, can provide a navigation method for the application.

```
Private Sub tplWelcome_Form1()

With Response
    .Write "<HTML><BODY><BR><FONT size=4 face=arial><CENTER>"
    .Write "Thank you for logging in " & Request.Form("User")
    .Write "<BR>Click <A href=""" & URLFor(tplWelcome) & """>"
    .Write "Here</A> to return to previous screen</FONT><BR>"
    .Write "<P>URLFor output = <B>" & URLFor(tplWelcome) & "</P></CENTER>"
    .Write ""</BODY></HTML>"
End With

End Sub
```

Notice that the added code uses the URLFor method to generate the URL for the tplWelcome template webitem. Clicking on this link will return the browser back to the Welcome page of the IIS Application.

With the modifications made above, the HTTP response for the form submittal is now slightly changed.

Notice the code included a line to produce the results of the URLFor method within the HTTP response. In real life, this would not be performed, but it conveniently shows us the syntax of the URL, using the WCI querystring variable.

A second location to add a link generated with the `URLFor` method would be in the `tplDisplayList` template webitem. This template also provides no return link. To correct this, the code added above would need to be modified somewhat. Since this template only has a single indicator tag, and the entire HTTP response is generated through the template and its `ProcessTag` event, we need to add the code to the appropriate section of the Select Case within that event.

```
        Private Sub tplDisplayList_ProcessTag(ByVal TagName As String,
                                    TagContents As String, SendTags As Boolean)

    Dim strTemp As String

        Select Case TagName
            Case "WC@NEWSLIST"
                strTemp = "<BR>Click <A href=""" & URLFor(tplWelcome) & """>"
                strTemp = strTemp & "Here</A> to return to previous screen<BR>"

                Dim Conn As ADODB.Connection
                Dim rs As ADODB.Recordset
                Dim sqlCommand As String

                ' Create the ADO objects needed
                Set Conn = New ADODB.Connection
                Set rs = New ADODB.Recordset

                Conn.Open strConn, strUser, strPassword
                sqlCommand = "Select Title,GifName From PressReleases"

                Set rs = Conn.Execute(sqlCommand)

                If Not (rs.EOF And rs.BOF) Then

                    Do While Not rs.EOF
                        strTemp = strTemp + "<A href=PRs.asp?GifName="
                        strTemp = strTemp + rs("GifName")
                        strTemp = strTemp + ">" + rs("Title") + "</A><BR>"
                        rs.MoveNext
                    Loop
                End If

                Set rs = Nothing
                Set Conn = Nothing

                TagContents = strTemp
        End Select
```

The resulting modified HTTP response, after template processing, will reflect the addition of the return link.

Using BinaryWrite

So far, the `tplDisplayList` template webitem has used a background image file. This link has been controlled outside of the IIS Application. If desired, the `Response` object's `BinaryWrite` can be used to provide the binary graphic, in a similar fashion to the `Write` method. Visual Basic code can be used to load the file directly from a hard drive, or from a database. Since loading from the hard drive would be very similar to serving up an image file from the hard drive through the web server, we will take a look at loading from a database.

To start this process, we need to connect the BODY1 element of the tplDisplayList template webitem to a Custom Event.

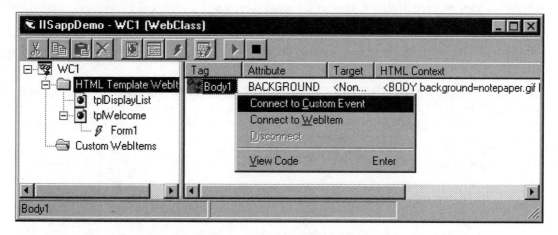

Once the connection has been complete, code will need to be added to the custom event to provide a binary-based HTTP response to the request for the binary image file.

```
Private Sub tplDisplayList_Body1()
        Dim Conn As ADODB.Connection
        Dim rs As ADODB.Recordset
        Dim sqlCommand As String

        ' Create the ADO objects needed
        Set Conn = New ADODB.Connection
        Set rs = New ADODB.Recordset

        Conn.Open strConn, strUser, strPassword
        sqlCommand = "Select GifFile From Images"

        Set rs = Conn.Execute(sqlCommand)

        If Not (rs.EOF And rs.BOF) Then
            Response.BinaryWrite rs("GifFile")
        End If

        Set rs = Nothing
        Set Conn = Nothing

    End Sub
```

For this process to work, the binary image file will need to be available in the database table being queried.

Summary

In this chapter, we have explored some of the more complex and advanced concepts associated with IIS Applications. We took a look at processing HTML template files. We looked at the options for sending HTTP responses to the browser. The most important element we explored was the building of a basic IIS Application. We then expanded the functionality of the application by exploring more complex elements.

We took a look at handling form submittals, using the `URLFor` method to create return links, and sending a binary HTTP response. The process of parsing a template file was shown, including retrieving data from a database to create a very complex replacement for the tag contents of an indicator tag.

The main points of this chapter are:

> ➢ HTTP responses can be sent primarily with the `Write` method or HTML template files
>
> ➢ Template file processing is similar to ASP processing, but geared for using Visual Basic code
>
> ➢ Numerous tools can be used to edit template files
>
> ➢ Template files are generally developed and edited externally
>
> ➢ The DHTML Designer can be used as a HTML editor, provided precautions are taken

15

Meet RDS

Remote Data Services (RDS) is a powerful technology from Microsoft that adds a new type of arrow to our application development quiver. We can use RDS to retrieve recordsets from remote databases and manipulate these databases in client-side script – in a way that also succeeds in reducing network traffic (compared to other methods) and gives us a great set of functionality.

In this chapter we will discuss ways that RDS can benefit your applications and we will begin the discussion of how to bring RDS into your applications. RDS consists of a set of objects: we'll be looking at the `DataControl`, `DataFactory` and `DataSpace` objects of the RDS object model. We will cover the following topics:

- An introduction to RDS – what can RDS do for me?
- The structure of RDS
- Business Object Proxies
- RDS objects and their properties and methods

Using RDS – an Introduction

So, this chapter is essentially an overview of RDS and how it can help you build high-performance data-aware application. By 'data-aware application', I mean an application that can retrieve and/or modify data in a data store. The data store could take many forms, but for this chapter we will assume that it is a traditional RDBMS.

We'll also look at the RDS objects – so that by the end of the chapter you'll know enough to be able to work effectively with them in your applications. But before you find out how to implement RDS, you should know why you might want to, and what RDS can do for you.

Why Use RDS? An Example

Let's consider an example that will give us a feel for the power of RDS. Suppose that you must write a web application that will allow users to retrieve and display information about cars. A typical user might be a potential car-buyer, using browsing information in their purchase decisions. This web application should allow the user to select from a list of automobile makers – BMW, Nissan, Ford etc. They might then choose a specific model about which they want information.

Alternatively, the application should be able to group vehicles by price range, by type of vehicle, by horsepower, or by a number of other attributes. In addition, it should have a feature that allows customers to compare an attribute – e.g. estimated fuel economy – from several cars, perhaps by multiple manufacturers, in an appropriate visual form like a bar chart. Obviously, an application like this would need to manage a tremendous amount of information. There are plenty of car manufacturers out there, even more models of cars, and lots of attributes to consider before we buy one of them.

On the web, this type of application might involve a series of listboxes – each one narrowing the user's selection and each one initiating a round trip to the server. Using a very fast Internet connection, each round trip might take about three seconds to complete. Functionally, this design works fine, and in fact, the vast majority of web applications that are currently in use today provide this type of functionality and employ this method for bringing data back to the user.

However, there may be a better choice. We could use RDS to build this application – because it would dramatically increase the performance of the application. For example, if our customer selects Audi cars, he should be able to immediately see every single Audi model – without waiting for a page to reload with new information. We can achieve this with RDS – while using ASP or CGI script alone would require that the browser request new data, wait for a response from the server, receive the new data and then reload the page. RDS can help eliminate the pause that occurs each time the web browser displays different information. Using RDS, the speed of web applications approaches that of more traditional desktop applications.

The following two screenshots demonstrate this difference. Without RDS, viewing data in multiple ways usually means many trips to and from the server:

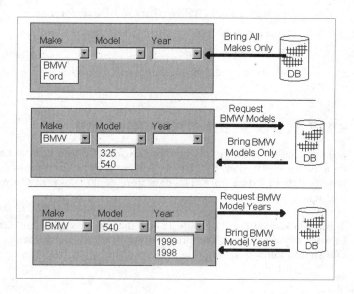

However, using RDS, an entire set of data can be returned to the client. This enables client code to filter and manage the recordset without the server:

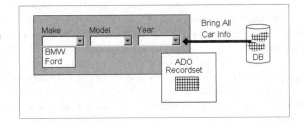

RDS Eases the Network Burden

Using RDS, we can create applications that can receive an entire recordset from a remote database and manipulate this database in client-side script. This can happen over the HTTP protocol. Note that this is not just an HTML page that has data embedded in it – rather, it's an actual ADO recordset that exists in the client's PC memory and provides sorting, filtering and other features. In addition, once the data has been retrieved it exists physically on the client – so there's no need for additional trips over a network to the web server. Fewer trips to the server means less network traffic.

We can also combine the client-side functionality with another client-side feature – Dynamic HTML – to display the data. The end result can be a web application that provides an abundance of information in a visually appealing manner, and that can provide this information with virtually zero wait time between views of the data (except of course for the initial data fetch).

Using HTTP

Delivering Web pages via HTTP means that those pages – text, images and all – are physically copied from the server to the client machine. If a Web application requires round trips to the server in order to display new information, it's a potential headache to network administrators who want to minimize network traffic (especially with increasing numbers of users). RDS can help to minimize the impact the application has on the company LAN. So how can we build an application that will run across HTTP, if we want to limit the amount of network traffic the application generates? Simple – that feature is built right in! Because RDS applications store the application data on the client-side, there is no need to request the server for more data. Fewer requests translate into less traffic on the network. This fact becomes more significant as the number of users of the application increases.

We still use a browser to receive and display information – whether we use RDS to retrieve a recordset, or we download ASP to pages with this information embedded. The difference is that we manage to keep the number of network transmissions down, in two ways:

> ➢ RDS enables us to retrieve *all* of the information at once, rather than piece-by-piece
> ➢ RDS gives us the functionality to query and manipulate the data on the client, not the server

Each network transmission requires a certain amount of overhead – using RDS to keep the number of transmissions down translates to lower overhead, which translates into an overall lighter network load. For the client, it also translates to faster response time! Of course if the user only wants to examine a few records, downloading all of them to the client would be wasteful of bandwidth. In this case, you can use a query on the server to select a subset of all the records and then send just this subset via RDS. Moreover, if the data in your database doesn't change frequently, your application can save the recordset to the local hard drive of the client machine. Each time the client starts the application, it can check with the server to find out whether there's any new information to download. If not, the previously saved local recordset can be used – further reducing the load on the network.

Data on the Client

The `Expires` property of the ASP `Response` object also allows your application to save information on the client-side. The `Expires` property determines how long a particular page should be cached on the client-side. As long as the page has not expired, the locally saved copy of the page (rather than the actual page from the web site) will be viewed in the browser when the user browses to it. The difference between the two approaches is that the `Expires` property allows saving only HTML pages, whereas RDS allows an actual recordset to be saved on the client. Saving the actual recordset on the client allows for much more functionality and flexibility than just pure HTML.

Web Clients don't Need a Constant Data Connection

RDS allows you to build web applications that can display and update information derived from a data store. This data will be held in an ADOR `Recordset` object. This object is a smaller, lightweight version of the full ADO `Recordset` object (it doesn't have the explicit `Command` or `Connection` objects). The ADOR `Recordset` object is designed for transmission over the relatively low-bandwidth connections of the Internet and, thus, has a smaller memory footprint. Your application won't require a constant data connection, because the connection that brought the data to the client can be severed without affecting the data. This is because RDS is very closely associated with ADO, which provides disconnected recordsets.

The fact that the web client does not consume a data connection benefits your application because no resources are required to maintain a data connection. The client can then use the stand-alone recordset object and all of the methods and properties that come with it. This means that you can sort, filter, update, insert and delete records without a live connection to the source database. Your application can later reconnect and send data changes back to the source server.

Data Can Be Accessed From Virtually Anywhere

RDS enables your applications to retrieve ADO recordsets across HTTP. HTTP is the protocol of the Internet, so your applications can retrieve recordsets across the Internet. This is possible because the recordset can be broken down into a text-like format on the server, sent over HTTP, and reassembled into an ADO recordset object on the client. We will talk more about this later in this chapter.

Since HTTP is running on the Internet, and it is probably also running on your organization's LAN, you have the pathways by which you can retrieve data. This functionality enables applications running in Web browsers to retrieve and update data from nearly anywhere in the world! Of course, there are other factors (such as security permissions) that will determine whether or not your application can actually retrieve the recordset, but assuming those are configured properly, RDS makes it work.

RDS Improves the User's Experience

Because RDS can bring a recordset to the client, web pages do not make round trips to the server when new information needs to be displayed. Instead, the new data is simply loaded from the recordset locally. This makes for a very smooth transition. In fact, the page on which the data is displayed does not change at all. It is not reloaded. The only changes are to the data being displayed by intrinsic HTML controls or objects such as applets and ActiveX controls. This enables the user-perceived speed of web applications to rival that of standard Windows applications.

What's more, because the recordset is accessible to client-side script, dynamic HTML can present information. The data does not have to be confined to controls like text boxes or listboxes. Data can be presented in a very rich and interactive manner. For instance, if you like data to smoothly fade in, in response to a "mouseover" event or after a specified amount of time: no problem. Would you like to enable drag-and-drop on information that has been loaded from a database? That can be done as well. In fact there are innumerable presentation options provided by Dynamic HTML. By combining that functionality with data from a data store, you can build applications that are information-rich, interactive and highly satisfying for users of your application.

The Structure of RDS

Although primarily used to retrieve data over HTTP, the more generic purpose of RDS is to allow the creation and use of COM objects over HTTP. When retrieving data, the ADOR Recordset is the vehicle by which the data travels from server to client. Other objects could also be involved, depending on how the application is built.

RDS can be used from within a web client, such as IE 4.0, or from within a more traditional LAN-based client, such as one built with Visual Basic. There are many ways to write code to provide the benefits of RDS to an application.

> *We can write to the RDS data control.* The `RDS.DataControl` uses other RDS objects without requiring you, the programmer, to interact with those other components. It is a quick and easy way to bring a disconnected recordset to the client, but is less flexible than other techniques.
> *We can write directly to the* `RDS.DataSpace` *and* `RDS.DataFactory` *objects.* These objects also enable us to retrieve data but provide us with more flexibility in terms of what we can do in our applications.
> *We can write to ADO only.* RDS functionality has been rolled into ADO and so that I can retrieve a disconnected recordset from a remote server by writing to ADO objects only. I do not have to write directly to any RDS object.

Any of these approaches could bring a recordset from a server to a client and each has it's own set of benefits and drawbacks. We'll move on to looking at the RDS objects a little further on in this chapter.

ADO and RDS are very flexible in terms of exactly how their services can be included in our applications. There are many different ways to write code to implement their functionality. The purpose of this section is to provide you with enough information to get you started using RDS – but not so much detail that you feel overwhelmed. So we won't cover *every* way of writing RDS code, but we will enable you to use RDS to bring data from a data store to a web client (and we'll show you easy ways to do so).

As stated earlier, the purpose of RDS is to provide access to remote data sources from client applications and COM components. RDS is used to transport ADO recordsets from a server to a client computer. However, to appreciate the principle behind RDS we need to have an understanding of n-tier applications – so let's revisit that first.

RDS and n-tier Applications

Applications built with RDS fit very nicely with the n-tier application model, as do all Internet applications. The great thing about n-tier application design is that it can greatly enhance scalability– the application's ability to support more and more users. It can do this by relieving the server from maintaining recordsets and from executing supporting code, such as cursors. In addition, the n-tier approach encourages simplified application management (if implemented correctly) – so when the time comes to update the application, the job should be easier.

N-tier Applications in General

RDS applications are built as n-tier applications. Let's have a quick revision of n-tier applications. An n-tier application separates the various components of a client/server system into three layers: client, middle (or business-level) and data source.

These tiers are logical tiers that do not necessarily map to physical machines. For example, the Web Server and the components it uses (middle tier) can often be on the same machine as the data store (data tier). The tiers do not necessarily map to specific types of software, either. Code that defines the reason the application was created usually runs in the middle tier(s), such as code that processes orders in a shopping cart application. These are the business rules and are often associated with COM objects running on an application server, although you can find these business rules in other places. This diagram shows a traditional three-tier model:

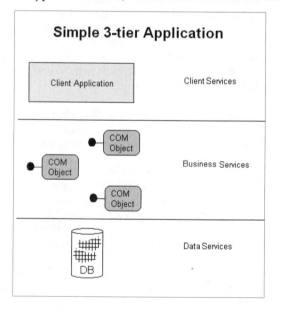

The three tiers can be described as follows:

- User services typically run on the client computer. This tier handles displaying data and implements code that supports displaying data. Also, code in the client tier will, usually, manage the client application itself, in such ways as opening and closing windows and showing visual cues to the end-user. In the case of a web application, it is where the browser is running, with RDS stored data and DHTML. In the case of a standard client-server Window application, it is where that client is running.

- The middle tier typically relates to a server that is running COM components. This server might be a dedicated application server, or it might be a web server, or many other types of servers. These COM server components will handle managing, processing, and passing data from a data store to the client and vice-versa. These components sit between the user and the data, transforming the raw data from the data store into usable information for display on the client. These are the business rules that are implemented as code running in the middle (business) layer. A business object is an ActiveX component that can retrieve and processes data or can perform just about any other work that the code can support. Business objects are usually on the middle tier. The middle tier, also known as the application server tier is the logical layer between a user interface or Web client and the database. This is typically where the Web server resides, and where business objects are instantiated.

- The data tier (or data layer) usually maps to where the data store is located, together with all of the associated processes that support management of the raw data. Insert, update and delete operations are in the data tier. Do not be mislead: those operations can be initiated from within the business layer, but the actual functionality is controlled in the data layer.

Although these three tiers are generally implemented as a user computer, an application server, and a database server (with the appropriate software at each level), there is no rule that requires it. Business rules can appear on any computer involved in the application and can take forms other than COM components. For example, if you have added code to your client application that ensures only numbers will be keyed into a "Product ID" text box, you have added a business rule that will be executed by the client computer. If you create a SQL Server stored procedure that aggregates financial data before sending the results to the caller of the stored procedure, you have created a business rule that will be executed by the database server. Remember that the N-tier application model defines logical layers for your application, not physical ones.

The Place of RDS in n-tier Applications

RDS is the set of components that allows your applications to access data across HTTP. When you create an RDS application (an application that uses RDS functionality), you can partition your application into two or three logical tiers. In fact, RDS itself is partitioned into client-side and server-side components.

In order to accomplish its work, RDS uses some components that run on the client and some that run on the web server (we'll see a diagram of this a little further on). In addition, the data that RDS delivers is derived from a back-end data store. This short description roughly follows the n-tier application development model described above. Thus, you could say that all RDS applications are n-tier applications. However, the server-side component is somewhat limited in what it can do and there are some drawbacks to using it, as we will see. In addition, there is no custom business logic running in the default server-side business component. This default server-side business component is known as the `RDSServer.DataFactory` object.

It is possible to build your own server-side component. You can build a COM server and install it on the server-side to access a data store and return the results to the client. You can implement your own functionality, but even when writing such a custom server-side business object, you can create an instance of an `RDSServer.DataFactory` object (we'll meet this formally in a moment) and use some of its methods to accomplish your own tasks.

RDS Architecture

So, RDS consists of client-side components and server-side components. Typically, the client-side components are hosted in an IE browser, using HTTP to communicate with the server components. Alternatively, they could be used in an application built using Visual Basic. The client-side RDS components are installed with IE 4.01, thus simplifying your custom application deployment. In other words, if you build an application using IE 4.01 and RDS, you can expect that the application will work on other systems with IE 4.01 or higher. There is usually no need to distribute additional software.

The diagram below shows how RDS works from a very high-level perspective. The idea is that client-side scripting code can use ADO to access a database through an IIS server. The client could be the actual web browser client or it could be a middle tier component acting as the client to the database. The code provides the name of the IIS server and information about the database. If the information is correct, a recordset can then be retrieved from the database and sent over the HTTP connection back to the client. Note that it's the recordset object that is sent to the client, not the database connection.

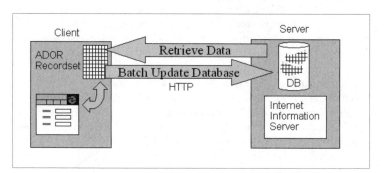

This is a high-level overview of an RDS application. It can be broken down into more detailed pieces, some of which we will discuss below.

Note that the client will receive an ADOR `Recordset` object, not just a web page with information derived from a database. This will enable the web page to display data from the recordset and to use client-side script to execute the `Move` methods, such as `MoveNext` and `MovePrevious`, as well as other features of the `Recordset` object. As previously mentioned, one of the best and most visible effects of this design is that the web page is not re-loaded when new data is displayed. Only the contents of the control that is displaying the data changes. The actual page does not. There are other ways to implement RDS in enterprise applications, but this is one of the simplest.

The RDS Information Flow

Let's look at the flow of information with an RDS application. The following diagram shows the flow of data from a web client, across HTTP to the web server, into the database, and back to the client. Glance briefly at this diagram. We will discuss each step in more detail later in this chapter.

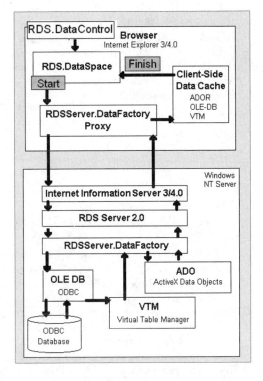

An RDS application accepts input from a user. The `RDS.DataControl` will make requests on behalf of the user for various sets of data. When the user enters the request, the client-side RDS components send the query to the Web server. The server-side RDS components process the request and send it to the DBMS.

The DBMS responds to the request, sending back the data. The RDS components on the web server transform that data into an **ADOR** `Recordset` object. The data is converted into MIME format for transport to the client and sent back across the network to the client computer. Among other things, it may be bound and displayed in a data-aware or data-bound control, such as a text box or grid control. The control can then be bound to the data using the `RDS.DataControl` object. The `RDS.DataControl` object can provide fields of data to controls on the page. In fact, one `RDS.DataControl` can channel data to many data-aware controls.

The resulting data is cached on the client computer – this reduces the number of connections to the Web and makes it easier for a user to manipulate the data. The only calls requiring a trip to the server are those to the default RDS business object (the `DataFactory`) or a custom object of your own creation. Those calls might include those that perform updates to the data server, or requests for new data.

The RDS Object Model

When using RDS, objects running on multiple computers will interact with one another to bring data to your client. In this section, we will discuss the RDS object model and we will talk about which objects run where and when. The object model itself looks like this:

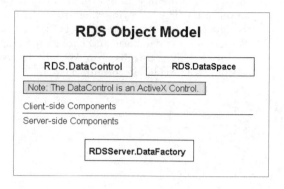

For a complete listing of the RDS object model, see the RDS Appendix.

The RDS objects that you will work with include the RDS.DataSpace, and the RDS.DataControl. In addition, the RDSServer.DataFactory object always provides services, but your code will not interact with it directly. The RDS.DataSpace and the RDS.DataControl are installed on the client and are the objects that your code will manipulate to bring data down from a server. The difference between the two is that RDS.DataSpace is an object, in the sense that it must be instantiated, and provides methods and properties. The RDS.DataControl is also an object but it acts more like an ActiveX control than a COM server object. Although the most obvious difference between an ActiveX control and a COM server is that the ActiveX control provides a graphical user interface while the COM server does not, the RDS.DataControl is an ActiveX control and yet it does not provide a graphical user interface (similar to the VB Timer control). It can get confusing, so continue reading.

First we'll discuss the RDS.DataSpace object, and the related subject of business object proxies. Next we'll cover the RDSServer.DataFactory object and four of its most commonly used methods. Finally we look at the methods and properties of the RDS.DataControl. In all our syntax examples we'll use objDF, objDC and objDS to represent instances of RDSServer.DataFactory, RDS.DataControl and RDS.DataSpace objects respectively.

The RDS.DataSpace Object

The RDS.DataSpace object runs on the web client. The job of the RDS.DataSpace object is to create COM objects on an IIS server, and return an object reference from the server to the web client application. These references are called proxies and are a bit like your television remote control. In a similar manner that you can press a button on your remote control to make something happen on your television, your client application can call a method provided by the proxy to make something happen on the server object. This client-side proxy object is the remote control that can be used to control a server-side object across the Internet. When the client uses the business object proxy, it can manipulate that object as if it were there on the client.

`RDS.DataSpace` is the object that is used to instantiate COM servers that are located on remote IIS servers. In addition, the `RDS.DataSpace` object can instantiate objects on the same computer, the same local area network, or from across the Internet, assuming security allows this. Under the hood, the location of the object does matter in that the reference that is returned is different. Let's look at business object proxies in detail before we move on to the `RDS.DataSpace` object's `CreateObject` method.

Business Object Proxies

What are business object proxies, and why do we need them? To answer this let us start this section with some information related to COM objects.

> In general, a process is a space in memory that has been allocated to a COM object for it's use
> More than one COM object can run in a single process space simultaneously
> COM objects can communicate directly only if they are running in the same process space
> COM objects cannot communicate directly if they are not running in the same process space

The third and fourth bullet points are different ways to say the same thing. I repeated it because this is important and is the reason that business object proxies exist.

Because objects cannot communicate with one another unless they are running in the same process, there needs to be a mechanism by which they can communicate when they are running in different processes. The proxy serves this purpose. A proxy is itself an object that provides a pointer to another object in another process. The other object that is in the other process is known as a stub. The proxy and the stub point to each other across processes. This is an exception to the rule about objects not being able to communicate across processes.

This idea of a business object proxy is similar to the idea of a vote-by-proxy in an election. When an individual can not be present at an election, a proxy vote can be cast for that individual. A business object proxy works in a similar manner. When an object cannot be present in the same process space as the caller, a proxy object can be created to represent the business object in its absence. When a caller needs to communicate with a business object running in another process space, the following sequence of steps occur:

1. The caller communicates with the business object proxy that is running in the same process as the caller.

2. This proxy will, in turn, communicate with another object that is running in the other process. That object is called a stub.

3. The stub receives the message from the proxy and passes the message on to the destination business object.

As you can tell, the caller cannot talk to the business object from separate processes, but the caller can talk to a business object proxy. The business object proxy will assume the functionality of the business object and will appear to the caller that it actually IS the business object. The caller never knows that it is not communicating with actual object, but is actually communicating with a proxy object that is emulating that actual business object.

Similarly the stub object runs in the same process space as the business object and assumes the place of the caller. The business object never knows that it is not talking to the actual caller. The proxy sends the message to the stub, the stub sends the message to the business object. This means that when a client instantiates an object that is running in another process, the client receives a reference to the proxy rather than to the actual object. Talking to the business object proxy will enable the client to communicate with the business object.

Let's look at a diagram that will make this all a little clearer:

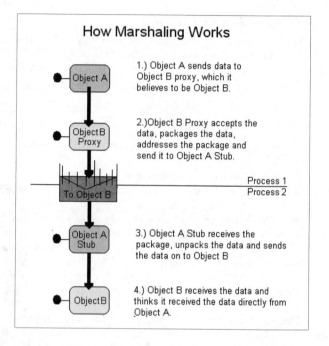

As you may notice, this diagram shows not only how proxies and stubs bridge the process gap, but also provides an illustration of marshalling. Marshalling is the process that must occur when a proxy communicates with a stub. When they communicate with one another, the message must be packaged for transport across process boundaries. After the message is packaged, it is sent (copied) from the proxy to the stub. When the stub receives the message, it must be unpackaged and sent on to the business object. This practice of packaging and unpackaging messages and copying them across processes is known as marshalling. Marshalling does not include the instantiation or destruction of objects, but is the activity of passing data across process boundaries.

Proxies and Stubs – an Analogy

The idea is a bit like a telephone. If you want to communicate with a friend, but that friend is in his own house, you might use the phone to call that friend and have a conversation. Assume that you and your friend are both objects. You cannot communicate directly because you are in different houses. Let us call each house a process. You need a mechanism by which to communicate. Your telephone at your house will be the proxy. Your friend's telephone at his house will be the stub. Your proxy is in your process and his stub is in his process. When you pick up and dial, you enter in the number that will connect you to the other object, your friend.

The phone number is like the class ID that uniquely identifies an object. Each person has a unique phone number and each object has a unique class ID. You, as a caller, are not concerned with exactly where the other object (your friend) is but the unique number will ensure that you get connected properly. When you begin to have a conversation with your friend over the phone, you have connected. However, you are not actually talking to your friend, you are actually talking to the telephone (the proxy). When your friend talks, he too, is talking to a telephone (the stub), not you. The telephones and underlying switched network take care of sending your speech, your message, to the other telephone, where your friend the COM object can hear it and respond to it.

The DataSpace.CreateObject Method

The `RDS.DataSpace`'s `CreateObject` method creates a proxy for the business object and returns a reference to it, as we discussed above. The proxy marshals data to the server-side stub when it needs to communicate with the business object. This happens when the client needs to send requests and data over the Internet.

RDS supports the following protocols:

> HTTP – the standard Web protocol

> HTTPS – a secure Web protocol (HTTP over Secure Socket Layer)

> DCOM (Distributed COM) – Microsoft's technology that enables COM components to communicate with each other across a network. DCOM is language neutral. This means that so any language that can produce COM components can have those components run over DCOM. Use DCOM when running COM components on a local-area network without HTTP.

> In-process – a local dynamic-link library (DLL); it runs as a local process and it does not use a network.

The syntax to use the `CreateObject` method across HTTP is:

```
Set MyObj = DataSpace.CreateObject("ProgramID", "http://MyWebServer")
```

HTTPS and DCOM are both similar to HTTP; for HTTPS the second parameter is an `https://` URL, and for DCOM it is a machine name. The syntax for in-process is slightly different:

```
Set MyObj = DataSpace.CreateObject("ProgramID ", "")
```

> For in-process, `MyObj` is an object variable holding a reference to the `ProgramID` object. For the other three protocols, `MyObj` holds a reference to a client-side proxy object that has been created on the named server.

> `DataSpace` is an object variable that represents an `RDS.DataSpace` object, used to create an instance of the new object. The `RDS.DataSpace` object runs on the client.

> `ProgramID` represents a string that is the programmatic ID identifying a server-side business object, which implements your application's business rules, eg "`MyComponent.Class`".

> `MyWebServer` is a string that name a URL (if the machine is across the Internet), or UNC machine name (if on the same LAN), identifying the IIS web server where an instance of the server business object is created.

The DataSpace.InternetTimeout Property

The `InternetTimeout` property indicates the number of milliseconds to wait before a request times out. Requests in a three-tier environment can take several minutes to execute. Use this property to specify additional time for long-running requests. This property sets or returns a Long value and applies only to requests sent with the HTTP or HTTPS protocols.

The RDSServer.DataFactory Object

`RDSServer.DataFactory` is the RDS server-based object that talks to the data source. When you use RDS, this is the object that does the bulk of the work. It can do either of the following:

> ➢ Perform a SQL query against the data source and return a `Recordset` object
> ➢ Take a `Recordset` object and update the data source

In addition, this object has a method for creating an empty `Recordset` object that you can fill programmatically, and another method for converting a `Recordset` object into a text string to build a web page.

The server program is sometimes called a business object. You can write your own custom business object that can perform complicated data access, validity checks, and so on. Let's look at some of the methods of the `RDSServer.DataFactory` object: `ConvertToString`, `Query`, `SubmitChanges` and `CreateRecordset`.

The ConvertToString Method

The `ConvertToString` method converts a recordset to a MIME string.

> *MIME is a standard that allows binary data to be published and read on the Internet. The header of a file with binary data contains the MIME type of the data; this informs client programs (Web browsers and mail packages, for instance) that they will need to handle the data in a different way than they handle straight text. For example, the header of a JPEG graphic file is image/jpeg. This allows a browser to display the file in the web page or in its JPEG viewer, if one is present.*

The syntax of the method is:

`objDF.ConvertToString(MyRecordset)`

In this syntax `MyRecordset` represents the recordset we want to convert.

`ConvertToString` can be used to send a recordset generated on the server to a client. It converts the recordset by generating a stream that represents the recordset in MIME format. When the MIME data reaches the client, RDS can convert the MIME string back into an ADO recordset.

When a recordset is passed from a server to a client, that recordset is passed in MIME format. The browser receives the MIME-format data and rebuilds the recordset from the MIME data. The recordset that will be created on the client side, from the MIME data is the ADOR `Recordset` object. In this scenario, there are functional size restrictions, due to the way the MIME handler works. If data exceeds these limits, poor performance will result. They are:

- Less than 400 rows of data
- 1024 max bytes per row.

The Query Method

The `Query` method, as you might guess, executes a query against a data source, and returns a recordset. The query should be a valid SQL string, appropriate for the specific data source, as this method does not check the SQL syntax. The syntax of the method is:

```
Set objRS = objDF.Query(txtConn, txtMyQuery)
```

Here,

- `objRS` is an object variable which will contain our recordset.
- `txtConn` is a string containing the server connection information. This is similar to the `Connect` property.
- `txtMyQuery` is a string containing the SQL query that defines the recordset to be returned.

Let's look at an example using `ConvertToString` and `Query` methods:

```
Sub MyRDSConvert()
    Dim objRS
    strMyServer = "http://<%=Request.ServerVariables("SERVER_NAME")%>"
    set DS = CreateObject("RDS.DataSpace")
    Set objDF = DS.CreateObject("RDSServer.DataFactory", strMyServer)
    ' objRS WILL BE AN ADOR RECORDSET
    Set objRS = objDF.Query (txtConn.Value, txtQueryRS.Value)
    strRsAsMIME = objDF.ConvertToString(objRS)
End Sub
```

The sample code above is running in ASP. The `SERVER_NAME` value is passed into the `ServerVariables` method of the ASP `Request` object, to retrieve the name of the web server on which this code is running. Next, the VBScript version of `CreateObject` is used to instantiate an `RDS.DataSpace` object. There are actually multiple versions of `CreateObject`. Usually, the `CreateObject` method of the `Server` object should be used when creating objects in ASP. However, I have seen occurrences where that version did not correctly create an object and the VBScript version did. If one of these versions does not work, use the other.

Next, the `CreateObject` method of the `DataSpace` object is used to create an instance of the `RDSServer.DataFactory` object. After that, the `Query` method of the `RDSServer.DataFactory` is called to return an ADO recordset. Finally, the `ConvertToString` method of the `RDSServer.DataFactory` object will convert the recordset to text in MIME format. In other words, the recordset is converted to text just before it is sent over HTTP. The text is used to create a recordset on the client as the text is received.

The CreateRecordset Method

The `CreateRecordset` method creates an empty, disconnected recordset. The syntax for using the method is:

```
MyObject.CreateRecordset(ColumnInformation)
```

Here,

> ➤ `MyObject` can represent either a `RDSServer.DataFactory` or an `RDS.DataControl` object – we call this method with either.

> ➤ `ColumnInformation` is a variant array of arrays, defining each column in the recordset being created. Each column definition contains an array of four required attributes: the column header name, the data type of the column, the width of the field and a boolean value indicating whether the field can be NULL.

The set of column arrays is then grouped into an array, which defines the recordset. This recordset can then be populated with data by the business or `RDSServer.DataFactory` object on the server.

Remember, there are two types of ADO recordsets, the ADODB recordset and the ADOR recordset. We can explicitly create either type. (the R signifies reduced and is more lightweight). The full ADODB recordset cannot be used to transfer data over HTTP, but the ADOR recordset can. Even if your code creates an ADODB recordset on the server-side, the client will not receive it. The client will receive an ADOR recordset.

The `RDSServer.DataFactory` object's `CreateRecordset` method supports a number of data types, which can be fixed length or variable length. Fixed-length types are defined with a size of –1. Variable-length data types sizes can range from 1 to 32767.

> **For a complete list of the data type constants (and their values) supported by the `CreateRecordset` method, see the `DataTypeEnum` class in Appendix G, *ADO 2.0 and RDS 2.0 Enumerators*.**

Here's a code example that creates an `ADODB.Recordset` on the server side. The recordset is then assigned to an RDS control. The recordset has two columns. The `CreateRecordset` method will automatically create the ADODB type.

```
Sub CreateRecSet
    Dim ColInfo(1),
    Dim ColDef0(3)
    Dim ColDef1(3)

    ' Define Column 1.
    ColDef0(0) = "CustomerID"       ' Column name.
    ColDef0(1) = CInt(3)            ' Column type (3 = adInteger)
    ColDef0(2) = CInt(-1)           ' Column size.
    ColDef0(3) = True               ' Is the column nullable?
```

```
' Define Column 2.
ColDef1 (0) = "Customer"          ' Column name.
ColDef1 (1) = CInt(129)           ' Column type (129 = adChar).
ColDef1 (2) = CInt(40)            ' Column size.
ColDef1 (3) = False               ' Is the column nullable?

' Add the columns to the recordset definition.
ColInfo (0) = ColDef0
ColInfo (1) = ColDef1

' Set the recordset definition to a DataControl Object Variable.
MyDC.SourceRecordset = MyDF.CreateRecordset(ColInfo)
End Sub
```

The RDS.DataControl Object

The RDS.DataControl is used to bind query results with HTML controls, such as textboxes. It uses the functionality of the RDS.DataSpace and RDSServer.DataFactory objects. It also enables visual controls to easily use the Recordset object returned by a query from a data source. RDS attempts, for the most common case, to do as much as possible to automatically gain access to information on a server and display it in a visual control. The RDS.DataControl has two aspects.

One aspect pertains to the data source. If you set the Command and Connection properties of the RDS.DataControl, it will automatically use the RDS.DataSpace object to create a reference to the default RDSServer.DataFactory object. Then the RDSServer.DataFactory will use the Connection property value to connect to the data source, use the Command property value to obtain a Recordset from the data source, and then return the Recordset object to the RDS.DataControl.

The second aspect pertains to the display of returned recordset information in a visual control. You can associate a visual control with the RDS.DataControl (in a process called binding) and gain access to the information in the associated ADOR Recordset object, displaying query results on a web page in Internet Explorer. Each RDS.DataControl object binds one Recordset object, representing the results of a single query, to one or more visual controls (for example, a text box, combo box, grid control, and so forth). There may be more than one RDS.DataControl object on each page. Each RDS.DataControl object can be connected to a different data source and contain the results of a separate query.

The RDS.DataControl object also has its own methods for navigating, sorting, and filtering the rows of the associated Recordset object. These methods are similar, but not the same as the methods on the ADO Recordset object. The required syntax for instantiating the RDS.DataControl is:

```
<OBJECT CLASSID="clsid:BD96C556-65A3-11D0-983A-00C04FC29E33" ID="MyDC">
<PARAM NAME="Connect" VALUE="DSN=MyDSN;UID=Admin;PWD=password;">
<PARAM NAME="Server" VALUE="http://MyWebServer">
<PARAM NAME="SQL" VALUE="Select * from Customers">
</OBJECT>
```

563

For a basic scenario, you need to set only the SQL, Connect, and Server properties of the RDS.DataControl object, which will automatically call the default business object, RDSServer.DataFactory. All the properties in the RDS.DataControl are optional because custom business objects can replace their functionality.

Using the RDS.DataControl object

The RDS.DataControl is used only in Web-based applications – a Visual Basic client application has no need for it. You can use one RDS.DataControl object to link the results of a single query to one or more visual controls. For example, suppose you code a query that requests customer data such as Name, Residence, Place of Birth, Age, and Priority Customer Status. You can use a single RDS.DataControl object to display a customer's Name, Age, and Region in three separate text boxes, Priority Customer Status in a check box, and all the data in a grid control.

Use different RDS.DataControl objects to link the results of multiple queries to different visual controls. For example, suppose you use one query to obtain information about a customer, and a second query to obtain information about employees. You want to display the results of the first query in three text boxes and one check box, and the results of the second query in a grid control. If you use the default business object (RDSServer.DataFactory), you need to do the following:

4. Add two RDS.DataControl objects to your Web page.

5. Write two queries, one for the SQL property of each of the two RDS.DataControl objects. One RDS.DataControl object will contain a SQL query requesting customer information; the second will contain a query requesting a list of employees.

6. In each of the bound controls' <OBJECT> tags, specify the DATAFLD, DATASRC and optionally the DATAFORMATAS parameter values in each visual control. There is no count restriction on the number of RDS.DataControl objects that you can embed via <OBJECT> tags on a single web page.

When you define the RDS.DataControl object on a web page, use non-zero height and width values such as 1 (to avoid the inclusion of extra space). RDS client components are already included as part of the Internet Explorer 4.0 installation; therefore, you don't need to include a CODEBASE parameter in your RDS.DataControl object tag.

It is possible to use data-aware controls with the RDS.DataControl, to provide an interface for working with the data. A data-aware control is a control that is able to use data from a database. Once you bind the control to a database via the RDS.DataControl object, the control is referred to as a bound control. The term data-aware is used interchangeably with data-bound.

> *The Sheridan data-aware grid control has been tested to work with the*
> RDS.DataControl *object and associated client-side components. Other controls may also work with RDS, but they have not been tested. The file name of the grid control is* SSDATB32.ocx *and the class id is* AC05DC80-7DF1-11d0-839E-00A024A94B3A.

With Internet Explorer 4.0 and higher, you can bind to data by using HTML controls and ActiveX controls only if they are apartment-threaded controls. The apartment-threading model enables each thread of a process to be created and run in it's own "apartment" that is isolated from other threads. This makes the control thread-safe and more fault-tolerant. The Sheridan data-aware grid control is not distributed with RDS, but ships as part of Microsoft Visual Basic 6, Enterprise Edition.

DataControl Methods and Properties

For the rest of this section we'll cover some of the methods, properties and events belonging to the RDS.DataControl object. Among other things, we'll see how to use the Refresh method to run a query (contained in the SQL property) against a data source (specified in the Connect property). We can also can update the data source (using the SubmitChanges method), or cancel changes made to the recordset (using the CancelUpdate method). In addition, the RDS.DataControl object provides mechanisms to specify synchronous or asynchronous execution and fetching (the ExecuteOptions and FetchOptions properties), or to cancel asynchronous operations (the Cancel method). We'll also look at using the Reset method to execute a filter specified by the various Filter properties.

Methods of the RDS.DataControl object

The methods of the RDS.DataControl object include Cancel, CancelUpdate, CreateRecordset, MoveFirst, MoveLast, MoveNext, MovePrevious, Refresh, Reset, SubmitChanges. Some of these methods apply to the RDSServer.DataFactory as well as to the RDS.DataControl. I won't repeat the explanation of those methods that we've already seen in the section above.

The SubmitChanges and CancelUpdate Methods

When you have made changes to a recordset, you can choose to either save these changes, or to discard them. With the SubmitChanges method, any data changes that are pending will be sent back to the back to the datasource. With the CancelUpdate method all pending changes will be discarded, and the data in the recordset will revert to the last values that were retrieved from the data source.

You can use the syntax:

objDC.SubmitChanges or objDC.CancelUpdate

With the SubmitChanges method you can also specify:

objDF.SubmitChanges strConn, objRS

strConn is a string value that represents the connection created with the RDS.DataControl object's Connect property. objRS represents the Recordset object containing the changed data. As you can see above, you can call SubmitChanges with an instance of either an RDS.DataControl object (objDC) or an RDSServer.DataFactory object (objDF), although this may only be the default RDSServer.DataFactory object. Custom business objects can't use the SubmitChanges method.

To call the `SubmitChanges` method with the `RDS.DataControl` object there are three properties that must first be set: `Connect`, `Server`, and `SQL`. We'll see these in the *Properties* section a little further on. When you call `SubmitChanges`, only the changed records are sent for modification, and either all of the changes succeed, or all of them fail together. If you call the `CancelUpdate` method after you have called `SubmitChanges` for the same `Recordset` object, the `CancelUpdate` call fails because the changes have already been committed. The Client Cursor Engine keeps both a copy of the original recordset values, and a cache of the changes. When you call `CancelUpdate`, the cache of changes is reset to empty, and the bound controls are refreshed with the original data.

The Move Methods

The `MoveFirst`, `MoveLast`, `MoveNext`, `MovePrevious` methods move the cursor to the first, last, next, or previous record in a recordset. The syntax for using the methods is:

```
objDC.Recordset.MoveFirst
objDC.Recordset.MoveLast
objDC.Recordset.MoveNext
objDC.Recordset.MovePrevious
```

You can use the `Move` methods with the `RDS.DataControl` object to navigate through the data records in the data-bound controls on a Web page. For example, suppose you display a recordset in a grid by binding to an `RDS.DataControl` object. You can then include First, Last, Next, and Previous buttons that users can click to move to the first, last, next, or previous record in the displayed recordset. You do this by calling the `MoveFirst`, `MoveLast`, `MoveNext`, and `MovePrevious` methods of the `RDS.DataControl` object in the `onClick` procedure of each button. Once these are called, the data-bound controls automatically refresh themselves to show the current record..

The Refresh Method

You can execute the SQL query defined in the `SQL` property, by issuing the `Refresh` method. This will run the query against the data source specified by the `Connect` property. The syntax for using the `Refresh` method is

```
objDC.Refresh
```

As with the `SubmitChanges` method, you must set the `Connect`, `Server`, and `SQL` properties of the `RDS.DataControl` before you use `Refresh`. All data-bound controls on the form associated with an `RDS.DataControl` object will reflect the new set of records. Any pre-existing `Recordset` object is released, and any unsaved changes are discarded. The `Refresh` method automatically makes the first record the current record.

It's a good idea to call the `Refresh` method periodically when you work with data. If you retrieve data, and then leave it on your client machine for a while, it is likely to become out of date with respect to the server.

The Reset Method

You use the `Reset` method to execute a sort or a filter on a recordset held on the client. The actual sort or filter performed will depend on the value of the `Sort` or `Filter` properties. The syntax for using the `Reset` method is:

```
objDC.Reset([blnValue])
```

`blnValue` is an optional Boolean value that is `True` if you want to filter on the current "filtered" rowset. `False` indicates that you filter on the original rowset, removing any previous filter options. If you do not set the value of `blnValue`, it will be set to `True` by default.

We'll see how to use the `Reset` method in the section *A Filtering Example* further on in the chapter.

Properties of the RDS.DataControl object

The properties of the `RDS.DataControl` object include `Connect`, `ExecuteOptions`, `FetchOptions`, `FilterColumn`, `FilterCriterion`, `FilterValue`, `InternetTimeout`, `Recordset` and `SourceRecordset`, `ReadyState`, `Server`, `SortColumn`, `SortDirection`, `SQL`, and `URL`.

The Connect Property

The `Connect` property specifies the source of the data for the `RDS.DataControl` object. When you are authoring web pages, you can set properties at design time in HTML tags. To set the data source at design time you would use:

```
<PARAM NAME="Connect" VALUE="DSN=MyDSN;UID=UserName;PWD=password;">
```

The data source name should be a system DSN, for the data source to which you want to connect. Alternatively you can set the connection information at run time in scripting code, using:

```
objDC.Connect = "DSN=MyDSN;UID=UserName;PWD=password;"
```

The ExecuteOptions Property

With the `ExecuteOptions` property you can choose to execute recordset refreshes either synchronously or asynchronously. By default, it is set to a value of `AdcExecAsync`, which means that asynchronous execution is enabled. To execute `Refresh` synchronously you need to specify:

```
objDC.ExecuteOptions = adcExecSync
```

This is the run time syntax. As with the previous property, you could also specify this at design time. Each client-side executable file that uses these constants must provide declarations for them. You can cut and paste the constant declarations you want from the file `Adcvbs.inc`, located in the `\Program Files\Common Files\System\MSADC` folder.

The FetchOptions Property

The FetchOptions property determines the type of fetching that the RDS.DataControl object will perform. As with the previous property, by default asynchronous fetching is enabled (a value of adcFetchAsync). This means that control returns immediately to the application while records are fetched in the background.

The alternative values are adcFetchUpFront, which means that the application will wait until all the records have been fetched before continuing, or adcFetchBackground, where the application only has to wait for the first batch of records to be fetched.

In a web application, you will usually want to use adcFetchAsync (the default value), because it provides better performance. In a compiled client application, you will usually want to use adcFetchBackground.

The InternetTimeout Property

With the InternetTimeout property you can specify, in milliseconds, how long the DataControl object should wait for the server to respond to a request when the Refresh or SubmitChanges method is called. This enables your application to wait sufficiently for operations you know will take a long time. It also enables your applications to abort quickly for operations you know should execute quickly; that way, your users don't have to wait for an unacceptable length of time, or see a timeout error message displayed.

This property applies only to requests sent via HTTP or HTTPS, and its value is of datatype Long.

The ReadyState Property

As an RDS.DataControl object pulls data into its recordset, the value of its ReadyState property will change. At each change it will fire the onReadyStateChange event – we'll see this event in the *Events* section below. When the recordset is complete and ready for use, the value of this property will be adcReadyStateComplete. Confusingly enough, this will also be the value if the recordset is not initialized, or if there was an error preventing the data from being fetched.

If data is still being fetched, but some rows are ready for use, the ReadyState property will have a value of adcReadyStateInteractive. The third and final possible value, adcReadyStateLoaded, indicates that the query has not yet finished executing and that no data has been fetched into the recordset.

The Recordset and SourceRecordset Properties

These properties indicate the ADOR.Recordset object that is returned from a custom business object. You can set the SourceRecordset property or read the Recordset property at run time in scripting code (for instance, VBScript). The syntax is

```
Set objDC.SourceRecordset = objRS
```

or

```
Set objRS = objDC.Recordset
```

These properties allow an application to handle the binding process by means of a custom process. They receive a rowset wrapped in a recordset, so that you can interact directly with the recordset, performing actions such as setting properties or iterating through the recordset. (A rowset is the set of rows returned in a single fetch by a block cursor).

The Server Property

The `Server` property specifies the location of the server where server-side objects are created, as opposed to where the data is located, if they differ. You use this property to set or return the IIS URL and communication protocol, or the machine name, of the server. The syntax for using the property, whether at design time or run time, varies depending on the protocol. For each protocol, the server value should be of the following format:

HTTP	`"http://MyWebServer"`
HTTPS	`"https://MyWebServer"`
DCOM	`"machinename"`
In-process	`" "`

`MyWebServer` or `machinename` should be a string containing a valid Internet or intranet path and server name.

The SQL Property

The `SQL` property holds the query string with which we query the data source and retrieve the recordset data. You can choose to set the SQL query string at either design or run time. We must set this property (as we said above) before we can execute either the `Refresh` or the `SubmitChanges` methods.

Filtering and Sorting

The `SortColumn`, `SortDirection`, `FilterValue`, `FilterCriterion`, and `FilterColumn` properties of the `RDS.DataControl` object provide sorting and filtering functionality on the client-side cache. The sorting functionality orders records by values from one column. The filtering functionality displays a subset of records based on a criteria, while the full recordset is maintained in the cache. The `Reset` method will execute the criteria and replace the current recordset with a read-only recordset.

If there are changes to the original data that have not yet been submitted, the `Reset` method will fail. First, use the `SubmitChanges` method to save any changes in a read/write recordset, and then use the `Reset` method to sort or filter the records.

If you want to perform more than one filter on your recordset, you can use the optional Boolean argument with the `Reset` method. The following example uses the default SQL Server `Pubs` database to show how to do this:

```
MyDC.SQL = "Select au_fname from authors"
MyDC.Refresh              ' Get the rowset.
```

```
MyDC.FilterColumn = "au_fname"
MyDC.FilterCriterion = "<"
MyDC.FilterValue = "'C'"
MyDC.Reset              ' Rowset now has First Names < "C".

MyDC.FilterCriterion = ">"
MyDC.FilterValue = "'L'"

' TRUE is the default property so this call is not required.
MyDC.Reset(TRUE)        ' Rowset has First Names < "C" and > "L".

MyDC.FilterCriterion = ">"
MyDC.FilterValue = "'H'"

' Filter on the original rowset. Reset the previous filter options.
MyDC.Reset(FALSE)   ' Rowset now has all Last Names > "H".
```

Events of the RDS.DataControl Object

Two events are supported by `RDS.DataControl`, which are independent of the ADO Event Model. The `onReadyStateChange` event is called whenever the `RDS.DataControl ReadyState` property changes, thus notifying you when an asynchronous operation has completed, terminated, or experienced an error. The `onError` event is called whenever an error occurs, even if the error occurs during an asynchronous operation.

The onReadyStateChange Event Procedure

When the value of the `ReadyState` property changes this event will be fired. As we saw above, this property has three possible values, depending on whether data has been fetched into the recordset and whether the recordset is available. You should use the `onReadyStateChange` method to monitor changes in the `ReadyState` property whenever they occur. This is more efficient than periodically checking the property's value.

The onError Event Procedure

The `onerror` event was one of the features that was new with ADO 2.0, and is called whenever an error occurs during an operation. The syntax for the `onError` event procedure is

```
Sub_onError(intStatus, strDesc, strSrc, blnCancelDisplay)

End Sub
```

`intStatus` is an integer, which contains the status code of the error. `strDesc` is a string, which contains a description of the error. `strSrc` is a string containing the query or command that caused the error. `blnCancelDisplay` is a Boolean value, which when set to `False` prevents the error from being a VB-catchable error. (Defaults to `True`).

You can declare your instance of the `RDS.DataControl` as a `WithEvents` variable in the General Declarations section of a VB module:

```
Private WithEvents objDC As DataControl
```

When you declare this, notice the variable `objDC` appears in the object list in your module's code window. If you select your object, you'll see the two events: `onreadystatechange`, and `onerror`. The `onerror` event enables you to perform error trapping on your `DataControl` object without having to use VB `OnError...` code. This sample `onerror` event procedure displays the error description, status code, and source in a message box and prevents VB from seeing the error:

```
Private Sub objDC_onerror(ByVal Scode As Integer, ByVal Description As String, _
    ByVal Source As String, CancelDisplay As Boolean)
      MsgBox "Description.   " & _
             Description & vbCrLf & _
             "Scode: "    & CStr(SCode) & _
             vbCrLf &     "Source: " & _
             Source,      vbexclamation, "DataControl Error", CancelDisplay = False
    End Sub
```

Putting the Pieces Together

We have talked about so many objects, methods, and properties that you may be unclear as to exactly where each piece fits in the overall picture. I think it is time for a fly-by, looking at each piece from above. We saw this diagram earlier in the chapter – let's now describe the flow of data in detail, and see what's happening behind the scenes, as control passes from object to object.

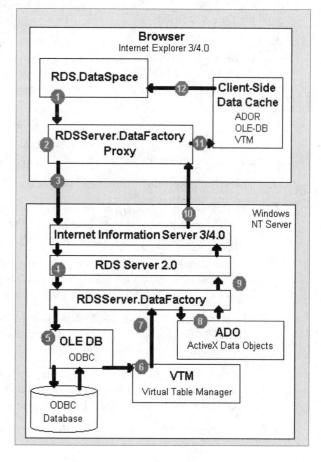

This is a representation of the process flow when the `RDSServer.DataFactory` object is used. We'll walk through and look at each step in the following list, corresponding to the numbers on the diagram.

1. The client application creates an instance of the `RDS.DataSpace` object to handle a database request.

2. The `RDS.DataSpace` object creates an instance of the `RDSServer.DataFactory` proxy.

3. The `RDSServer.DataFactory` Proxy translates the call into an HTTP request. The parameters to the method are passed across the Internet via HTTP to the Web Server specified in the `RDS.DataControl` object's `Server` property. IIS then passes the HTTP request to a server extension called the RDS Server component ADISAPI (Advanced Data Internet Server API).

4. The web server receives the request. The RDS server component examines the contents of the call. It creates an instance of the `RDSServer.DataFactory` object and makes the requested method call. When using the `RDSServer.DataFactory` object the requested method call is the Query method.

5. The `RDSServer.DataFactory` object executes the query via OLE DB or ODBC by passing in the SQL statement and DSN information. It sets the properties for the requested rowset so that OLE DB uses the Virtual Table Manger as the buffering component. The VTM manages the data before it is passed to ADO and converted to a recordset.

6. OLE DB passes the rowset containing the results of the query to the virtual table manager(VTM). The VTM populates its buffers with the rowset data and stores all of the metadata information for all base tables that are part of the resultset. It also implements the marshaling interfaces for the rowset.

7. The VTM passes the marshalable rowset back to the `RDSServer.DataFactory` object.

8. The `RDSServer.DataFactory` object creates an instance of an ADO recordset and passes it the VTM marshalable rowset. ADO wraps the rowset into a recordset, which is then returned as the return value of the original query call from step 4.

9. The `RDSServer.DataFactory` passes the recordset back to the RDS server component, which packages the return value of the recordset into MIME 64 Advanced Data Tablegram format by calling the VTM to create a tablegram stream.

10. The RDS server component (ADISAPI) sends the tablegram (it's not really a recordset when it is passed over the Internet – it's a tablegram) over HTTP, as multi-part MIME packets to the business object proxy on the client side.

11. The client-side `RDSServer.DataFactory` proxy unpacks the results of the method call from HTTP format, and recreates the recordset in the client side VTM. The VTM on the client side temporarily holds the data just before it is inserted into a recordset.

12. The application now has access to the recordset.

Summary

The purpose of this chapter was to introduce RDS and to help you begin to get familiar with the various objects that are available in RDS and the methods, properties and events that belong to those objects. A full introduction to the range of techniques is beyond the scope, but we hope this chapter should give you an idea of the possible uses for RDS.

You should now know:

> ➤ Why you would want to use RDS at all
> ➤ The structure of RDS, and where RDS fits into an n-tier architecture
> ➤ The basics of the RDS object model
> ➤ How to create business components that call and manipulate data using RDS.

For more details on RDS, and an in-depth look at delivering data across the web, we recommend Wrox's *ADO RDS Programming with ASP*, ISBN: *1-861001-64-9.*

16

A Guide to XML

For the last few years, many industry insiders have been hailing the Extensible Markup Language (XML) with its associated standards (DTD, XSL, XLL, DOM, XML Namespaces, XML Schema, etc.) as the Web standard of the future. In the first half of 1999, the World Wide Web Consortium (**W3C**) introduced a series of successive refinements of a working draft defining Extensible HTML (**XHTML**) and proved them right. Basically, XHTML is HTML 4.0 rewritten as an XML language. (So, the pundits who predicted that HTML would quickly disappear in favor of XML seem to have been mistaken.) In this short guide, we examine what XML, the "ASCII of the Future", is and how you can use it today in your web development efforts. To get the latest details of the XHTML specification, visit www.w3.org to find out the latest specifications.

XML as a second language

> **HTML is a language capable of expressing both the content and the presentation of a web page.**

You can hardly contest that hypertext markup language (HTML) is currently the ruling standard for expressing web pages. HTML is a language capable of describing both the content of a web page, and how this page is to be presented. Let us take a basic look at HTML and compare this language with the emerging standards, XML and XHTML. HTML consists of a fixed set of tags, such as html, head, meta, body, h1, td, etc. (Consequently, knowing HTML means knowing what the tags names –and their attributes, described below– are and what visual impact they have.) A tag is typically used as a paired set of markers surrounding author-defined content.

```
<TagName>Custom content goes here</TagName>
```

The following sample HTML code snippet, taken from our XML document sample below,

```
<h1>*ML Languages</h1>
```

shows the h1 tag (short for "heading level 1") and its enclosed content: "*ML Languages". The start of the tag content is marked by "<" followed by an HTML tag name and a closing ">". The end of the tag content is marked by "</" (note the forward-slash) followed by the same tag name used in the start section and a closing ">". This basic language construct also forms the building block of XML.

HTML also has standalone tags such as <hr>, for a horizontal rule, constructs that are not allowed in XML and consequently disallowed in XHTML. (In XML, you have to resort to empty tags to represent such constructs. This would take the form in the case of the hr tag, <hr><hr/>. In XHTML, the XML shorthand for empty tags, which is <hr/> as described below, will be used.) Note that the '/' character comes after the text in an empty tag.

```
<TagName Attr1="Value1" Attr2="Value2">Custom content</TagName>
```

Within a tag, you can optionally place one or more **attribute**-value pairs. These attributes are placed in the marker indicating the start of the tag. XML and XHTML also use attributes in the same manner. Attribute-value pairs are delimited by white spaces. The value must be surrounded by quotes (in XML and XHTML this is required, while in HTML this is merely a recommended good practice). In the following HTML snippet, the td tag is complemented by a width attribute with a value of 14%% (14 percent, that is)

```
<td width="14%">
```

HTML is defined using a meta-language (a language used to describe languages) called standard generalized markup language (**SGML**). HTML has fewer than 100 different tags, with each tag having a specified list of possible attributes. When the World Wide Web Consortium (W3C), the organization in charge of maintaining the HTML standard, extends this set of tags or their attributes, they call the resulting language definition a new version of HTML, such as HTML version 3.2 or 4.0. As of this writing (summer 1999), the current version of HTML is version 4.01 and, as we mentioned in the introduction, the next one in the works is XHTML version 1.0. While HTML is a standard, certain browsers also support some additional attributes not supported in the W3C standard. Also different browsers (browsers from different vendors, or different versions of a browser by a same vendor) may interpret the exact meaning of certain attributes differently –which is why certain pages can look different in different browsers.

> *You can find out the status of all these standards at the W3C site* http://www.w3.org.

Below is an example of fairly simple HTML. Notice how display information (font size, widths, etc.) is intermixed with the content of the page.

```
<html>

<head>
<meta http-equiv="Content-Language" content="en-us">
<meta http-equiv="Content-Type" content="text/html; charset=windows-1252">
<meta name="AUTHOR" content="PGB">
<title>Markup Languages</title>
```

```
</head>

<body>

<h1>*ML Languages</h1>
<hr>
<p>Here is a table with the 3 *ML languages:</p>
<table border="1" width="100%">
  <tr>
    <td width="10%"><font size="2">SGML</font></td>
    <td width="50%"><font size="2">Standard Generalized Markup Language</font></td>
    <td width="40%"><font size="2">Used to describe other languages</font></td>
  </tr>
  <tr>
    <td width="10%"><font size="2">HTML</font></td>
    <td width="50%"><font size="2">Hypertext Markup Language</font></td>
    <td width="40%"><font size="2">Used to describe web pages</font></td>
  </tr>
  <tr>
    <td width="10%"><font size="2">XML</font></td>
    <td width="50%"><font size="2">Extensible Markup Language</font></td>
    <td width="40%"><font size="2">Used to describe structured data</font></td>
  </tr>
</table>
<p><font size="2">Note: UML stands for Universal Modeling Language and does not
fit in the above category.</font></p>

</body>

</html>
```

The screenshot below shows you this HTML page opened with Internet Explorer 5. (Using another browser would give a similar result.) Only the custom content is shown. The tags and attributes are not rendered but instead used by the browser to determine the presentation of the content

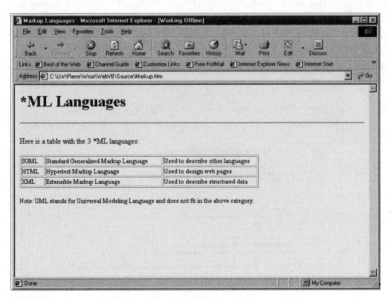

XML has been designed to provide a powerful, flexible and intuitive way of structuring data and does not contain presentation instructions used in displaying this data. XHTML combines the powerful data structuring capabilities of XML with the presentation capabilities of HTML.

XML is also defined using SGML and has been designed to provide a powerful, flexible and intuitive way of structuring data. Below is the content of our sample HTML page rewritten in XML

```
<?xml version="1.0" standalone="yes"?>
<Languages>
  <Title>Markup Languages</Title>
  <Heading1>*ML languages</Heading1>
  <Intro Text="Here is a table with the 3 *ML languages:"><Intro/>
  <Language>
   <Abbreviation>SGML</Abbreviation>
   <FullName>Standard Generalized Markup Language</FullName>
   <Description>Used to describe other languages</Description>
  </Language>
  <Language>
   <Abbreviation>HTML</Abbreviation>
   <FullName>Hypertext Markup Language</FullName>
   <Description>Used to describe web pages</Description>
  </Language>
  <Language>
   <Abbreviation>XML</Abbreviation>
   <FullName>Extensible Markup Language</FullName>
   <Description>Used to describe structured data</Description>
  </Language>
  <FootNote Text="Note: UML stands for Universal Modeling Language and does notfit
in the above category."></FootNote>
</Languages>
```

In contrast to HTML, its sibling language, XML does not contain presentation instructions used in displaying the data. At the time of writing, apart from Internet Explorer 5, few browsers support viewing of XML pages. (You will learn what is meant by support when you read about manipulating XML data later on.) Figure 2 shows you this XML page opened with Internet Explorer 5. All the XML language tokens, not just the content of the tags, are visible in the browser.

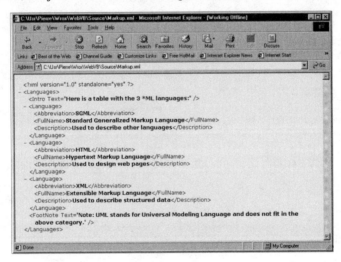

XML, as its full name suggests, lets a page creator use her or his own tag names. The tags in our sample XML page (Languages, Title, Heading1, Intro, Language, Abbreviation, FullName, Description, and FootNote) were made up by the document author and have no special meaning in XML. This is why the browser simply displays these language tokens. This distinction in presentation capabilities is perhaps also subtly expressed by the different terms used: you talk about an HTML **page** but an XML **document**.

> **XML and XHTML, unlike HTML, are case sensitive, so the tags** <language>, <Language> **and** <LANGUAGE> **are all different tag names.**

XML has a shorthand notation for tags without content. Instead of

```
<MyTag><MyTag/>
```

you may use:

```
<MyTag/>
```

White space before the closing "/>" is optional. In XHTML, this is how one writes stand-alone tags, e.g. <hr />. In XML, empty tags are most commonly used in conjunction with attributes. Just like in HTML, white space is used to separate the tag name from its attributes.

In the above sample page, for example, you could have written:

```
<Intro Text="Here is a table with the 3 *ML languages:"/>
```

instead of the slightly less readable:

```
<Intro Text="Here is a table with the 3 *ML languages:"><Intro/>
```

Finally, XML comments are delimited by "<--" and "-->"and, unlike in HTML, a comment may not contain the string "--". This restriction is imposed to simplify writing XML parsers. You can see this used below:

```
<-- XML Comments Here -->
```

Putting XML in perspective

Even in the simple XML example above, the descriptive power of XML is evident. The author-selected tags define the internal structure of the embedded XML data. (There are more rigorous ways of defining the data rules governing the XML structure contained in a document. See the discussion of DTDs and XML Schema later on.) This is analogous to a database with tables containing columns and rows. Here, a language "row" is delimited by <Language> tags. The "columns" are <Abbreviation>, <FullName> and <Description>. XML provides enough flexibility to include several "tables" in a document, and enough power to express child-parent relationships with a variable number of children. Because of this power and flexibility, the nickname "ASCII of the Future" seems appropriate, as XML proves to be a standardized data format, from which you can manipulate the data in a number of ways –you will experience the ease of programmatically reading XML data below. The icing on the cake is that the data is kept in a format relatively easy to read by humans.

Of course, all this does not mean that you should rush out and start converting all your proprietary data formats to XML. XML is not efficient enough to store data for heavy-duty processing purposes. XML is primarily meant for data communication, particularly between disparate platforms and technologies. For example, if your applications have import and export facilities for textual data, then consider adding XML to the list of supported formats.

Well-formed XML

An XML document is called **well-formed** if it obeys all the rules set forth by the XML language. You will be able to programmatically read (without errors that is) only those documents that are well-formed. You have already read some of the XML rules in the preceding section when comparing HTML and XML. The following additional rules should be enough to give you a head start writing well-formed documents:

> ➤ An XML document may optionally start with an XML declaration <?xml version="1.0"?> (I recommend you always write an XML declaration as it may protect you from future changes in the XML standard, not compatible with version 1.0..)

> ➤ The XML declaration may also contain a `standalone` attribute and an `encoding` attribute (The former is covered below, while the latter, used to indicate the character set, is not covered in this guide)

> ➤ The non-declaration part of the document must be enclosed in a tag

> ➤ Tags cannot cross over, e.g. you cannot have <X>...<Y>...</X>...</Y>

> ➤ Tag names must start with a letter, or an underscore

> ➤ You can use letters, digits and the punctuation symbols underscore, hyphen and period for the remaining characters tag names

> ➤ Tag names may not contain the string 'xml' (in any combination of lower and upper case)

In addition, certain characters cannot be represented directly in XML and need a special symbol. This concept is very similar to HTML's escape sequences, and the replacement characters use a similar form:

Character	XML Replacement
<	<
>	&gt:
&	&
'	'
"	"

DTDs and Valid XML

An XML document may also contain a **Document Type Definition** (**DTD**). A DTD lays out the rules for the data structure, such as the cardinality of elements, (or. how many of them may appear), the attribute list, the type of data they will contain, etc. You may think of a DTD as the XML equivalent of the **data definition language** (**DDL**) for tables in relational databases. We will not discuss the grammar and syntax of a DTD here, and just give you a sample corresponding to the data in the XML file shown above.

```
<!DOCTYPE Languages [
<!ELEMENT Languages (Title , Heading1, Intro?, Language+, FootNote?)>
<!ELEMENT Title (#PCDATA)>
<!ELEMENT Heading1 (#PCDATA)>
<!ELEMENT Intro (#PCDATA)>
<!ATTLIST Intro Text CDATA #REQUIRED>
<!ELEMENT Language (Abbreviation, FullName, Description)>
<!ELEMENT Abbreviation (#PCDATA)>
<!ELEMENT FullName (#PCDATA)>
<!ELEMENT Description (#PCDATA)>
<!ELEMENT FootNote (#PCDATA)>
<!ATTLIST FootNote Text CDATA #REQUIRED>
]>
```

The DTD is written in the XML file, just after the XML declaration. It can also be written in a separate file. The syntax for a separate file is putting everything between square brackets in a separate file, e.g. `Markup.dtd`.

```
<!ELEMENT Languages (Title , Header1, Intro?, Language+, FootNote?)>
<!ELEMENT Title (#PCDATA)>
<!ELEMENT Header1 (#PCDATA)>
<!ELEMENT Intro (#PCDATA)>
<!ATTLIST Intro Text CDATA #REQUIRED>
<!ELEMENT Language (Abbreviation, FullName, Description)>
<!ELEMENT Abbreviation (#PCDATA)>
<!ELEMENT FullName (#PCDATA)>
<!ELEMENT Description (#PCDATA)>
<!ELEMENT FootNote (#PCDATA)>
<!ATTLIST FootNote Text CDATA #REQUIRED>
```

Then in the XML document you place the following reference to the DTD file, again after the XML declaration:

```
<!DOCTYPE Languages SYSTEM "Markup.dtd" >
```

> **A valid XML document is well-formed and conforms to its DTD.**

If a well-formed XML document has a DTD, it is said to be **valid** if the data content conforms to the rules contained in the DTD.

As with a table and its DDL, it's possible for a DTD to affect the XML data, most commonly through the use of default values. If you don't need to load the DTD to get the expected XML data, then the XML file is called a **standalone** XML file. One can indicate this in the XML declaration using the `standalone` attribute (the values are `"yes"` and `"no"`). It is worth emphasizing that the standalone attribute does not refer to whether the DTD is internal or external.

XML Companions

Because Document Type Definitions don't use true XML syntax, they are not universally liked in the XML community. The "XML Schemas" proposal attempts to address these concerns, improving how XML handles data types and removing the necessity of creating DTDs. A first working draft on XML Schemas was released by the W3C in May of 1999. XML schemata are written in XML, eliminating the need to learn two different syntaxes to write valid XML documents.

If you wish to read more about XML, DTD and XML Schemas (as well as XSL and DOM covered in the next sections), then I recommend Paul Spencer's "Professional XML Design and Implementation", ISBN 1-861002-28-9, and the forthcoming "Professional VB6 XML ", ISBN 1-861003-32-3; both published by Wrox Press.

Obviously, the ability to describe data effectively is useful, but it hardly provides the range of functionality web programmers have come to expect. Data manipulation, data presentation and linking can be performed with HTML/DHTML and their associated script languages but not with straight XML. XML's strength is that it uses single-purpose companion standards (such as DOM, XSL, and XLL, described below) to provide these capabilities. Because of their single-minded focus, each of these associated standards provides more power in its area of specialization than HTML/DHTML. Because of their single-minded focus, each of these associated standards provides more power in its area of specialization than HTML/DHTML. You can manipulate XML data through the Document Object Model (**DOM**); present it with Extensible Style Language (**XSL**) and link through Extensible Linking Language (**XLL**). You will read about DOM and XSL in the next sections.

Finally, an important proposal handles the challenge of keeping all these author-defined tags distinct: **XML name spaces**. This is a familiar concept for C++ programmers, but new for Visual Basic programmers. The idea is to assign a qualifier to the symbols in order to avoid name collisions. In effect, one makes the "Abbreviation" tag unique by making a distinction between say Marc's "Abbreviation" tag and Sandra's "Abbreviation" tag. (In reality, XML namespaces don't use first names but unique resource identifiers (**URI**) to make this distinction. You will see namespaces in action later on.)

DOM: Manipulating XML Data

A couple of the XML rules seem unnecessarily restrictive at first: not allowing tags to cross over and requiring that all the data in the XML document (i.e. everything apart from the XML declaration section and the DTD) be enclosed in a tag. In fact, these two rules together force you to create a robust structure for your data. In this section you will learn about this data structure and show how you can navigate this structure without any knowledge of the data it may contain. This extra flexibility (not having to know the data) is crucial in creating a totally self-describing document. By using the data description contained in the document, you are able to protect an application reading a certain document type against additions to this document, such as new data previously not available.

A Tree Grows in XML

> XML data is highly structured in an n-ary tree form.

An n-ary tree is like a binary tree, a tree-like data representation with a root that has children. But while a binary tree is constrained to two children at any node, in an n-ary tree the number of children per node is not constrained at all. The diagram below shows a graphical representation of a tree.

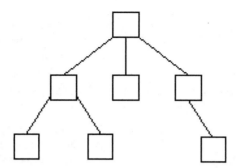

By convention, the **root** element of the tree is the document itself. This convention results in a known starting point for navigating any document. The children or off shoots of the root are called **nodes**. There are different types of nodes. The table below lists the most important node types.

Element	Handles everything but the author-defined text in a document. Elements contain attributes and can be parents to both other Elements and TextNodes.
TextNode	Handles the author-defined text in a document
Attribute	Is a property of an Element

The tree structure you're probably most familiar with is the directory tree you use to navigate the files on your hard drive. To indicate nodes in XML, XSL uses a directory-type notation, using the Unix directory forward-slash "/" as opposed to the DOS back-slash. So the root node is indicated as "/". Then, in our sample XML document, you can talk about the "/Languages", "/Languages/Language" and "/Languages/Language/Abbreviation" nodes. And, just like with directories, if the current node is "/Languages/Language", then one can simply use "Abbreviation" to indicate the "/Languages/Language/Abbreviation" node.

Above, you learned that you can programmatically traverse the data in an XML document using the Document Object Model. The Document Object Model (DOM) is a browser-independent application programmer's interface (API) that supports a tree level view of XML (and HTML) documents. (As with other standards, not all browsers support the DOM in the same way and some add their own non-standard extensions.) Microsoft exposes the DOM objects through COM interfaces. The next three tables show the methods and properties you will use in the following sections. . You may want to refer to these tables when studying the code presented in these sections. You will use each property and method in the three tables in these projects.

If you wish to read more about the IE5 DOM, then I recommend Alex Homer's "XML IE5 Programmer's Reference", ISBN 1-861001-57-6, published by Wrox Press.

Document partial Interface		
Async	Property	A read/write Boolean property that indicates whether asynchronous download should be enabled. True by default.
CreateElement(tagName)	Method	Creates an ELEMENT type node with the nodeName of tagName
Load(url)	Method	Loads an XML document from the location specified by the URL. If URL cannot be resolved or accessed or does not reference an XML document, the documentElement is set to null and an error is returned. Returns a Boolean.
Save(param)	Method	Serialize the XML. The parameter can be a filename, an ASP response, an XML document, or any other COM object that supports Istream, IpersistStream or IpersistStramInit.

ParseError Interface		
Errorcode	Property	The error code number.
Filepos	Property	The absolute file.position where the error occurred.
Line	Property	The number of the line containing the error.
Linepos	Property	The character position where the error occurred.
Reason	Property	The reason for the error.
SrcText	Property	The full text of the line containing the error.
Url	Property	The URL of the XML file containing the error.

Node Partial Interface		
AppendChild(newChild)	Method	Appends newChild as the last child of this node
TransformNode(stylesheetNode)	Method	Returns the result of processing the sourceDOMNode (the root node) and its children with the stylesheet indicated by stylesheetDOMNode.
Xml	Property	A read-only property that returns the XML representation of the node and all its descendants as a string

What is XSL?

Extensible Style Language (**XSL**) is a technology for transforming and styling XML. XSL has two components: a styling language and a transformation language. Since IE5.0 only implements the transformational components of XSL, we will ignore the styling aspect of XSL for now. (Cascading Style Sheets is a competing styling technology that may be used to style XML documents.)

The XSL transformation language takes a well-formed XML document and applies the rules in an XSL document to produce a new XML format. This new XML format could be HTML (slightly altered to become valid XML) and thus presented using a Web browser. You will see an example of this in the following section.

Transforming XML for Display Using XSL

Probably the most common use for XSL is as a way to specify how an XML document is displayed through a XSL template that transforms the XML document into an HTML. Below is a style sheet that transforms the sample XML document into an HTML document. We will limit the discussion of XSL to the essential language tokens required to perform these transformations. The output will be identical to the output of the HTML code shown in the HTML/XML comparison above. The code below is for the XSL style sheet and we will talk you through every part.

```xml
<?xml version="1.0"?>
<xsl:stylesheet
  xmlns:xsl="http://www.w3.org/TR/WD-xsl"
  xmlns="http://www.w3.org/TR/REC-html40"
  result-ns="">

<xsl:template match="text()">
   <xsl:value-of/>
</xsl:template>

<xsl:template match="/">

<HTML>

<HEAD>
<META http-equiv="Content-Language" content="en-us" />
<META http-equiv="Content-Type" content="text/html; charset=windows-1252" />
<META name="AUTHOR" content="PGB" />
<xsl:for-each select="Languages/Title">
  <TITLE>
   <xsl:value-of />
  </TITLE>
</xsl:for-each>

</HEAD>

<BODY>

<xsl:for-each select="Languages/Heading1">
  <H1>
   <xsl:value-of />
  </H1>
</xsl:for-each>
```

```
<HR />

<xsl:for-each select="Languages/Intro">
  <P>
   <xsl:value-of select="@Text" />
  </P>
</xsl:for-each>

<TABLE border="1" width="500">

<xsl:for-each select="Languages/Language">

  <TR>
   <TD width="10%">
     <FONT size="2">
      <B>
        <xsl:for-each select="Abbreviation">
         <xsl:value-of />
        </xsl:for-each>
      </B>
     </FONT>
   </TD>
   <TD width="50%">
   <FONT size="2">
      <xsl:for-each select="FullName">
       <xsl:value-of />
      </xsl:for-each>
   </FONT>
   </TD>
   <TD width="40%">
   <FONT size="2">
      <xsl:for-each select="Description">
       <xsl:value-of />
      </xsl:for-each>
   </FONT>
   </TD>
  </TR>
</xsl:for-each>
</TABLE>

<xsl:for-each select="Languages/FootNote">
  <P>
   <FONT size="2">
     <xsl:value-of select="@Text" />
   </FONT>
  </P>
</xsl:for-each>

</BODY>

</HTML>

</xsl:template>

</xsl:stylesheet>
```

Save this file as Markup.xsl and I will go through it with you in the next section.

Transforming XML for Display Using XSL: Step-by-Step

Let us now examine how the style sheet above is put together. Since a XSL style sheet is an XML document, you start with an XML declaration.

```
<?xml version="1.0"?>
```

Then we enclose the style sheet in a XSL style sheet tag, `<xsl:stylesheet>`. XSL style sheets rely on the use of an advanced XML feature called namespaces (we covered it briefly above). Typically, you always want one reference to the XSL namespace, by adding the following attribute to the XSL style sheet tag `xmlns:xsl="http://www.w3.org/TR/WD-xsl"`. Since we are generating HTML, we also include a reference to the HTML 4.0 namespace, `xmlns="http://www.w3.org/TR/REC-html40"`. The XSL processor is not accessing the web sites used to specify the name spaces; the site URLs are solely used to avoid name collisions. Because of these namespace declarations, the parser will identify everything starting with `"xsl:"` as an XSL tag, and everything not starting with `"xsl:"` as HTML. HTML and XSL tags with identical names can now be properly qualified and distinguished.

```
<xsl:stylesheet
  xmlns:xsl="http://www.w3.org/TR/WD-xsl"
  xmlns="http://www.w3.org/TR/REC-html40"
  result-ns="">

<-- Style sheet transformation goes here...-->

</xsl:stylesheet>
```

The above stylesheet is empty and would have no effect. Now, you will see how to add transformation instructions. The usual first block of XSL transformation language is an XSL line that makes the XSL processor process the text nodes. A text node, as you learned above, is the text between the tags. We indicate that we want to find text nodes with the `match=text()` attribute. The `value-of` operator returns the value stored in the node and the "/" means that we do not want to go further in the hierarchy to fetch a value.

```
<xsl:template match="text()">
   <xsl:value-of/>
</xsl:template>
```

Next, you start a template for the elements located just below the root level with a template tag, `<xsl:template>`. (An **element** is everything but text nodes.) You indicate that you want to start processing from the root node with the `match="/"` attribute. A **template** is simply a series of transformation instructions.

```
<xsl:template match="/">

<-- Template for the whole document goes here...-->

</xsl:template>
```

So far your style sheet looks as follows:

```
<?xml version="1.0"?>

<xsl:stylesheet
  xmlns:xsl="http://www.w3.org/TR/WD-xsl"
  xmlns="http://www.w3.org/TR/REC-html40"
  result-ns="">

<xsl:template match="text()">
    <xsl:value-of/>
</xsl:template>

<xsl:template match="/">
<-- Template for the whole document goes here...-->
</xsl:template>

</xsl:stylesheet>
```

We complete our XSL template by adding instructions to process the tags in the document. Except for the XSL instructions, everything in the root template (that is the instructions to transform the nodes at the root of the source document) will be copied into the resulting document.

The code fragment below, for example, does not contain any XSL instructions and will be copied verbatim to the resulting document. A discerning eye recognizes that you have reproduced the typical start of an HTML document. Since this is a XML document, you use the XML syntax for standalone tags by using "/>" instead of ">" as the tag closer.

```
<HTML>

<HEAD>
<META http-equiv="Content-Language" content="en-us" />
<META http-equiv="Content-Type" content="text/html; charset=windows-1252" />
<META name="AUTHOR" content="PGB" />
```

Next, you write templates to process the text content of specific tags. The following fragment finds the content of the tag named "MyTag" in the document with a root named "MyDoc". It results in placing the HTML tag markers around the content.

```
<xsl:for-each select="MyDoc/MyTag">
<P>
    <xsl:value-of />
</P>
</xsl:for-each>
```

When you nest XSL templates, the search to match the inner tags is performed inside the outer tags. The following fragment results in placing the HTML tag markers around the content of the "MyDoc/MyTag/MyOtherTag" tag.

```
<xsl:for-each select="MyDoc/MyTag">
    <xsl:for-each select="MyOtherTag">
    <P>
        <xsl:value-of />
    </P>
    </xsl:for-each>
</xsl:for-each>
```

You may also need to write templates to process the values of specific attributes. The following fragment finds the value of the attribute named "MyAttribute" in the tag named "MyTag" in the document with a root named "MyDoc". It results in placing the HTML tag markers around the attribute value.

```
<xsl:for-each select="MyDoc/MyTag">
  <P>
   <xsl:value-of select="@MyAttribute" />
  </P>
</xsl:for-each>
```

If you have written a stylesheet called Markup.xsl, then you can place a link to it in the XML document by placing the following line after the XML declaration.

```
<?xml-stylesheet type="text/xsl" href="Markup.xsl"?>
```

Below is the full version of your sample XML document: a valid XML document, complete with a style sheet that displays the XML document in the same manner as the HTML document.

```
<?xml version="1.0" encoding="UTF-8" standalone="yes"?>
<?xml-stylesheet type="text/xsl" href="Markup.xsl"?>
<!DOCTYPE Languages [
  <!ELEMENT Languages (Title?, Heading1, Intro?, Language+, FootNote?)>
  <!ELEMENT Title (#PCDATA)>
  <!ELEMENT Heading1 (#PCDATA)>
  <!ELEMENT Intro (#PCDATA)>
  <!ATTLIST Intro Text CDATA #REQUIRED>
  <!ELEMENT Language (Abbreviation, FullName, Description)>
  <!ELEMENT Abbreviation (#PCDATA)>
  <!ELEMENT FullName (#PCDATA)>
  <!ELEMENT Description (#PCDATA)>
  <!ELEMENT FootNote (#PCDATA)>
  <!ATTLIST FootNote Text CDATA #REQUIRED>
]>
<Languages>
  <Title>Markup Languages</Title>
  <Heading1>*ML Languages</Heading1>
  <Intro Text="Here is a table with the 3 *ML languages:" />
  <Language>
   <Abbreviation>SGML</Abbreviation>
   <FullName>Standard Generalized Markup Language</FullName>
   <Description>Used to describe other languages</Description>
  </Language>
  <Language>
   <Abbreviation>HTML</Abbreviation>
   <FullName>Hypertext Markup Language</FullName>
   <Description>Used to describe web pages</Description>
  </Language>
  <Language>
   <Abbreviation>XML</Abbreviation>
   <FullName>Extensible Markup Language</FullName>
   <Description>Used to describe structured data</Description>
  </Language>
  <FootNote Text="Note: UML stands for Universal Modeling Language and does not
fit in the above category." />
</Languages>
```

This script will produce an identical looking page to our screenshot of the HTML document shown earlier.

589

Client-side XML

As with many web technologies, you must decide where the processing is to occur: on the client or on the server. Processing on the server, may free you from requiring specific technology to be available in the client's browser, but may impose a heavy workload on the server. Processing on the client frees the server, but may require a specific browser.

Generating XML using Visual Basic 6

There are a multitude of data sources from which you could create XML data. Which one you select depends on your specific requirements. In this section, we concentrate on extracting data from a database, the most common requirement. We do not rely on any specific data base features, but instead use Active Data Objects (ADO) as a universal data access tool. It is easy to adapt the presented code to another data source (such as an Excel spreadsheet) by replacing the data navigation code (MoveFirst, MoveNext and EOF) with the code appropriate for your data source.

You will be examining three methods of creating XML from an ADO recordset. The first method, using an ADO native method, is easy to use, but in its current implementation (ADO 2.1) does not work with hierarchical recordsets and always creates an XML file (does not return the XML in a string). The two other methods work with hierarchical recordsets, but require a custom implementation. More importantly, they return the XML data in a string, which may save you the overhead of reading the data from the file.

Hierarchical recordsets (also known as "data shaping") are a new feature of ADO 2.0, letting you represent complex relationships in a hierarchical fashion (like a treeview). Hierachical recordsets are made available via a special OLE DB provider called "MSDataShape", which is implemented by the client cursor engine. Hierachical recordsets present an alternative to using the traditional JOIN syntax in SQL when accessing parent-child data. They differ from a JOIN in that with a JOIN, both the parent table fields and child table fields are represented in the same recordset. With a hierarchical recordset, the recordset contains only fields from the parent table. In addition, the recordset contains an extra field that represents the related child data, which you can assign to a second recordset variable and traverse. A new clause, SHAPE, is provided to relate SELECT statements in a hierarchical fashion. The complex syntax is summarized below:

```
SHAPE {parent-command} [[AS] name]
APPEND ({child-command} [[AS] name] RELATE parent-field TO child-field)
[,({child2-command} ...)]
```

If you wish to read more about this exciting, but complex feature of ADO, then I recommend David Sussman's "ADO 2.1 Programmer's Reference", ISBN 1-861002-68-8, published by Wrox Press.

XML from a Recordset using the ADO 2.1 Save method

In this section, you will discover the easiest way to save an ADO recordset to a file: using a method provided by recordsets in ADO 2.1. ADO 2.1 is the latest release of Active Data Objects and is included with Internet Explorer 5, Office 2000, and SQL Server 7. A service pack has also been released on the Microsoft ADO site, `http://www.microsoft.com/data/ado`. One of the features introduced in release 2.1 is the ability to persist recordsets in XML format using the `Save` method. (Unfortunately, this method does not currently work with hierarchical recordsets) In a subsequent release (version 2.5 has entered Beta at time of writing, and should be released with Windows 2000), the `GetString` method may very well also get the capability to generate an XML string. (If you cannot wait to create an XML string from a recordset, read on: in the next two sections we write VB code accomplishing exactly that.) The following code fragment shows this method in action. Most of the code you will write will be support code, since the XML generation is accomplished in a single line of code:

```
rsAuthors.Save strXMLFile, adPersistXML
```

Let us see how this works in a project. You will use SQL Server 7 as your data provider, more specifically the pubs sample database. Start up Visual Basic and select "**Standard EXE**" as the new project type. Add a reference to the ADO 2.1 library by selecting Project, then References. Locate "Microsoft ActiveX Data Obect 2.1 Library" and click on the checkbox as in the figure below.

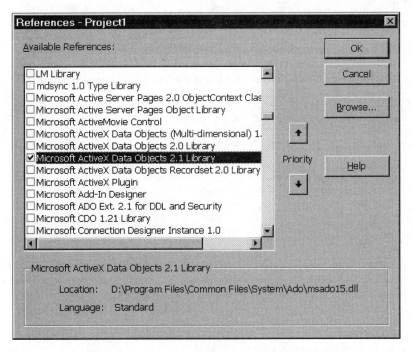

Remove the standard form from the project and add a code module instead. You will create the `Authors.xml` file in the same directory as your project, so you create a string variable containing the proper path. Then you call the `CreateAuthorsXML` function that you will implement shortly.

```
Public Sub Main()
    Dim strPath          As String

    ' Normalize Path
    strPath = App.Path
    If Right$(strPath, 1) <> "/" Then
        strPath = strPath & "/"
    End If

    CreateAuthorsXML strPath & "Authors.xml"
End Sub
```

You will need to check whether a file exists, so add the following helper function to the module.

```
Function FileExists(ByVal strFileName As String) As Boolean
    FileExists = CBool(Len(Dir$(strFileName, vbNormal _
                     + vbHidden _
                     + vbSystem _
                     + vbVolume _
                     + vbDirectory)))
End Function
```

Finally, you are ready to create your XML file: add a sub to the class module Sub CreateAuthorsXML(strXMLFile As String). The code in CreateAuthorsXML is straightforward: you declare and instantiate a recordset object:

```
Dim rsAuthors        As ADODB.Recordset

Set rsAuthors = New ADODB.Recordset
```

Then, you open the recordset object after setting the query string and the data source parameters:

```
' Open recordset with a few columns
' Limit to just a few records with WHERE clause
rsAuthors.Source = "SELECT au_id, au_fname, au_lname " _
                 & "FROM Authors WHERE au_id < 5"

' In the following, you need to change "srvr" to the
' name of your SQL Server
rsAuthors.ActiveConnection = "Provider=sqloledb;" & _
    "Data Source=srvr;Initial Catalog=pubs;User Id=sa;Password=; "

' All set to open recordset...
rsAuthors.Open
```

Since the recordset Save method returns a run-time error if the target file already exists, you determine the existence using the helper function you just wrote and, if needed, delete the target file. (Of course, in production code, you would ask the user for permission to proceed.)

```
If FileExists(strXMLFile) Then Kill strXMLFile
```

Then comes the call to the recordset save method:

```
rsAuthors.Save strXMLFile, adPersistXML
```

Finally, you close and destroy the recordset object:

```
rsAuthors.Close
Set rsAuthors = Nothing
```

Running this function creates an XML file in the following format. This example also demonstrates name spaces and an XML Schema in action.

```
<xml xmlns:s='uuid:BDC6E3F0-6DA3-11d1-A2A3-00AA00C14882'
    xmlns:dt='uuid:C2F41010-65B3-11d1-A29F-00AA00C14882'
    xmlns:rs='urn:schemas-microsoft-com:rowset'
    xmlns:z='#RowsetSchema'>
<s:Schema id='RowsetSchema'>
    <s:ElementType name='row' content='eltOnly'>
        <s:attribute type='au_id'/>
        <s:attribute type='au_fname'/>
        <s:attribute type='au_lname'/>
        <s:extends type='rs:rowbase'/>
    </s:ElementType>
    <s:AttributeType name='au_id' rs:number='1' rs:writeunknown='true'>
        <s:datatype dt:type='string' dt:maxLength='11' rs:maybenull='false'/>
    </s:AttributeType>
    <s:AttributeType name='au_fname' rs:number='2' rs:writeunknown='true'>
        <s:datatype dt:type='string' dt:maxLength='20' rs:maybenull='false'/>
    </s:AttributeType>
    <s:AttributeType name='au_lname' rs:number='3' rs:writeunknown='true'>
        <s:datatype dt:type='string' dt:maxLength='40' rs:maybenull='false'/>
    </s:AttributeType>
</s:Schema>
<rs:data>
    <z:row au_id='172-32-1176' au_fname='Johnson' au_lname='White'/>
    <z:row au_id='213-46-8915' au_fname='Marjorie' au_lname='Green'/>
    <z:row au_id='238-95-7766' au_fname='Cheryl' au_lname='Carson'/>
    <z:row au_id='267-41-2394' au_fname='Michael' au_lname='O&#x27;Leary'/>
    <z:row au_id='274-80-9391' au_fname='Dean' au_lname='Straight'/>
    <z:row au_id='341-22-1782' au_fname='Meander' au_lname='Smith'/>
    <z:row au_id='409-56-7008' au_fname='Abraham' au_lname='Bennet'/>
    <z:row au_id='427-17-2319' au_fname='Ann' au_lname='Dull'/>
    <z:row au_id='472-27-2349' au_fname='Burt' au_lname='Gringlesby'/>
    <z:row au_id='486-29-1786' au_fname='Charlene' au_lname='Locksley'/>
</rs:data>
</xml>
```

For your convenience, here is the complete code listing:

```
Option Explicit

Public Sub Main()
    Dim strPath        As String

    ' Normalize Path
    strPath = App.Path
    If Right$(strPath, 1) <> "/" Then
        strPath = strPath & "/"
    End If

    CreateAuthorsXML strPath & "Authors.xml"
End Sub
```

```
Public Sub CreateAuthorsXML(strXMLFile As String)
    Dim rsAuthors      As ADODB.Recordset

    Set rsAuthors = New ADODB.Recordset

    ' Open recordset with a few columns
    ' Limit to just a few records with WHERE clause
    rsAuthors.Source = "SELECT au_id, au_fname, au_lname " _
                    & "FROM Authors WHERE au_id < 5"

    ' In the following, you need to change "srvr" to the
    ' name of your SQL Server
    rsAuthors.ActiveConnection = "Provider=sqloledb;" & _
        "Data Source=srvr;Initial Catalog=pubs;User Id=sa;Password=; "

    ' All set to open recordset...
    rsAuthors.Open

    ' An error occurs if the target already exists,
    ' so delete target if there
    If FileExists(strXMLFile) Then Kill strXMLFile

    ' Requires ADO 2.1 or later
    rsAuthors.Save strXMLFile, adPersistXML

    ' Clean Up
    rsAuthors.Close
    Set rsAuthors = Nothing
End Sub

Function FileExists(ByVal strFileName As String) As Boolean
    FileExists = CBool(Len(Dir$(strFileName, vbNormal _
                    + vbHidden _
                    + vbSystem _
                    + vbVolume _
                    + vbDirectory)))
End Function
```

XML from a Recordset using custom code

When you want maximum flexibility, then you have to be prepared to do more coding. The most flexible way to create XML (either as a string or as a file) is by coding everything in VB. The strRS2XML function is recursive and works correctly with hierarchical recordsets. This implementation uses tags to hold field values, but it would be easy to modify this code so the field values are attributes of a "row" tag, as is the case when the Recordset Save method is used.

Again, let us see how this works in a project. As usual, you will use the pubs database in SQL Server 7. Start up Visual Basic and select "**Standard EXE**" as the new project type. Add a reference to the ADO 2.1 library by selecting Project, then References. Locate "Microsoft ActiveX Data Object 2.1 Library" and click on the checkbox. Remove the standard form from the project and add a code module instead.

Add the following constants to the general declaration section:

```
' Set to 0 for Production Mode
#Const DEMO_MODE = 1

#If DEMO_MODE = 1 Then
Private Const MAX_RECORDS = 5
#End If

Private Const DOUBLE_QUOTE = """"
Private Const CHAR_SMALLER = "<"
Private Const CHAR_GREATER = ">"
Private Const CHAR_OBLIQUE_SMALLER = "</"
Private Const CHAR_OBLIQUE_GREATER = " />"


Private Const DEFAULT_INDENTATION = 2
```

You will need to write a couple of helper functions to create valid tag names and to handle the special characters within the text nodes. The code is self-explanatory:

```
Private Function strValidXMLTag(strTagCandidate As String) As String
    ' This function only handles occurrences of "xml" and
    ' replaces white space with "_".
    ' The implementation of the remaining rules is left as
    ' an exercise for the reader. ;)

    ' Get rid of occurrences of 'xml'
    strTagCandidate = Replace(strTagCandidate, "xml", "x_m_l")
    ' Get rid of spaces
    strValidXMLTag = Replace(strTagCandidate, " ", "_")
End Function

Private Function strValidXMLContent(strContenCandidate As String) As String
    ' Get rid of occurrences of '<'
    strContenCandidate = Replace(strContenCandidate, "<", "&lt;")
    ' Get rid of occurrences of '>'
    strContenCandidate = Replace(strContenCandidate, ">", "&gt;")
    ' Get rid of occurrences of '&'
    strContenCandidate = Replace(strContenCandidate, "&", "&amp;")
    ' Get rid of occurrences of '"'
    strContenCandidate = Replace(strContenCandidate, """", "&quot;")
    ' Get rid of occurrences of "'"
    strValidXMLContent = Replace(strContenCandidate, "'", "&apos;")
End Function
```

Finally, the harder task remains: add a sub to the code module: `Public Sub CreateAuthorsXML(strXMLFile As String)`. In order to save on stack space and allocation time, declare all the variables and objects that do not need to be maintained during recursive function calls as static.

```
    Static objField       As ADODB.Field
    Static strSpaces       As String
    Static strFieldName    As String
    Static intLevel        As Integer
    Static intIndentation  As Integer
```

The variables that maintain state during recursive function calls cannot be made static.

```
Dim rsChapter      As ADODB.Recordset
Dim strXML         As String
Dim strDocName     As String
Dim lngRecCount    As Long
```

You are passing the number of spaces to use for indentation as an optional parameter. Note that you must use a variant, as required for proper functioning of the IsMissing function. The use of the IsMissing function allows us to distinguish between a zero (i.e. do not indent) and missing indentation level.

```
If IsMissing(vntIndentation) Then
    intIndentation = DEFAULT_INDENTATION
Else
    intIndentation = vntIndentation
    If intIndentation < 0 Then intIndentation = DEFAULT_INDENTATION
End If
```

Since this function is recursive, you need to take care of only writing the XML declaration once. Since your static variable intLevel starts with an initial value of zero, and is subsequently incremented as you traverse the recordset, you can use it to test whether this is the first call for this document. By the time you have processed the whole recordset, intLevel will again have the value of 0, the correct value to process another recordset in a subsequent call. You then use this variable to determine how many spaces to indent.

```
If intLevel = 0 Then    ' Only on top-level call.
    strXML = "<?xml version=" _
        & DOUBLE_QUOTE & "1.0" & DOUBLE_QUOTE _
        & " ?>" & vbCr
End If

strSpaces = Space$(intLevel * intIndentation)
```

Since the actual choice of tag names is not really relevant to understanding XML generation using VB, you can use a simple algorithm to determine the document and record tag names: you use the same noun, passed as a parameter, in the singular and plural and assume adding an 's' to the singular will produce the plural (or subtracting the 's' from the plural will give us the singular). This is not a perfect solution, but gives reasonable results.

```
strName = strValidXMLTag(strName)
If Right$(strName, 1) = "s" Then
    strDocName = strName
    strName = Left$(strName, Len(strName) - 1)
Else
    strDocName = strName & "s"
End If
```

You create a start of document tag, and increase the indentation level.

```
' Start of Document TAG
strXML = strXML & CHAR_SMALLER & strDocName & CHAR_GREATER & vbCr

intLevel = intLevel + 1
strSpaces = Space$(intLevel * intIndentation)
```

Then you move to the first record in the recordset, initializing your count of how many records you have processed so far.

```
rs.MoveFirst
lngRecCount = 1
```

You then create the loop that will iterate through all records. In demo mode, you limit the number of records that will be processed to a programmer-defined constant.

```
#If DEMO_MODE = 1 Then
    While Not rs.EOF And lngRecCount < MAX_RECORDS
#Else
    While Not rs.EOF
#End If
```

You have a record, so you create a start of record tag.

```
        strXML = strXML & strSpaces _
            & CHAR_SMALLER & strName & CHAR_GREATER & vbCr
```

Now you need to iterate through all the fields in this record.

```
        For Each objField In rs.Fields
```

You need to consider the possibility of having a hierarchical recordset. You determine this by looking at the Field Type property.

```
            If objField.Type = adChapter Then
```

If you have a hierarchical recordset, then your Field Value is actually another recordset, recognizable by the adChapter Field Type. So if this recordset is not empty, we increase the level and make a recursive call to strRS2XML, with the desired indentation level passed along. (The current indentation level is maintained through a Static variable.) You add a prefix to the Field Name to avoid creating duplicate tag names. (Another choice involves using name spaces, as Microsoft implemented in the Recordset Save method.)

```
            Set rsChapter = objField.Value
            If Not rsChapter.EOF Then
                intLevel = intLevel + 1
                strXML = strXML & strRS2XML(rsChapter, _
                        strName & "." & objField.Name, _
                        intIndentation)
                intLevel = intLevel - 1
            End If
```

If you don't have a hierarchical recordset, you can create a field tag. You are calling the `strValidXMLTag` to insure the Field Name is created according to the XML rules. `strValidXMLContent` ensures that the Field Values is conforming to the XML rules. Instead of creating empty tags for NULL values, you could elect to do nothing.

```
            Else
                ' Ensure we have a correctly formed tag name
                strFieldName = strValidXMLTag(strName & "." & objField.Name)

                If IsNull(objField.Value) Then
                    ' Empty Field tag
                    strXML = strXML & strSpaces & Space$(intIndentation) _
                        & CHAR_SMALLER & strFieldName & CHAR_OBLIQUE_GREATER & vbCr
                Else
                    ' Start of Field tag
                    strXML = strXML & strSpaces & Space$(intIndentation) _
                        & CHAR_SMALLER & strFieldName & CHAR_GREATER
                    ' Field tag Content
                    strXML = strXML & strValidXMLContent(objField.Value)
                    ' End of Field tag
                    strXML = strXML & CHAR_OBLIQUE_SMALLER _
                        & strFieldName & CHAR_GREATER & vbCr
                End If
            End If
```

You have processed this field and can go to the next one.

```
            Next objField
```

Since we have now processed all the fields, we are done with the record. We have chosen to put in a `DoEvents` call to keep the application responsive when we are processing large recordsets.

```
        strXML = strXML & strSpaces & CHAR_OBLIQUE_SMALLER _
                & strName & CHAR_GREATER & vbCr
        DoEvents
```

Since we have processed the record, we need to fetch the next one.

```
        rs.MoveNext
        lngRecCount = lngRecCount + 1
    Wend
```

We have just left the While loop, so we are done with your recordset. We need to get the `intLevel` variable back to 0 so the next call to `strRS2XML` start with an XML declaration.

```
    intLevel = intLevel - 1
    strSpaces = Space$(intLevel * intIndentation)
```

All that remains is to close our document tag.

```
    strXML = strXML & strSpaces & CHAR_OBLIQUE_SMALLER _
        & strDocName & CHAR_GREATER & vbCr
```

We return the result of our processing to the caller.

```
    strRS2XML = strXML
```

Using the `strRS2XML` function is again straightforward. In the following example, we create an XML file (as opposed to creating a string with XML data). The content of the resulting file is shown below. The key line in the code below is simply the print to file line using the sub you just wrote: `Print #intFileNumber, strRS2XML(rsAuthors, "Author")`

```
Public Sub Main()
    Dim strPath          As String

    ' Normalize Path
    strPath = App.Path
    If Right$(strPath, 1) <> "/" Then
        strPath = strPath & "/"
    End If

    CreateAuthorsXML strPath & "Authors.xml"
End Sub

Public Sub CreateAuthorsXML(strXMLFile As String)
    Dim intFileNumber   As Integer
    Dim rsAuthors       As ADODB.Recordset

    Set rsAuthors = New ADODB.Recordset

    ' Open recordset with a few columns
    ' Limit to just a few records with WHERE clause
    rsAuthors.Source = "SELECT au_id, au_fname, au_lname " _
                    & "FROM Authors WHERE au_id < 5"
```

```
    ' In the following, you need to change "srvr" to the
    ' name of your SQL Server
    rsAuthors.ActiveConnection = "Provider=sqloledb;" & _
       "Data Source=srvr;Initial Catalog=pubs;User Id=sa;Password=; "

    ' All set to open recordset...
    rsAuthors.Open
    ' Get unused file number
    intFileNumber = FreeFile
    ' Create file name
    Open strXMLFile For Output As #intFileNumber
    ' Output text
    Print #intFileNumber, strRS2XML(rsAuthors, "Author")
    ' Close file
    Close #intFileNumber

    ' Clean Up
    rsAuthors.Close
    Set rsAuthors = Nothing
End Sub
```

Below is the result of a sample run of our `strRS2XML` function.

```
<?xml version="1.0" ?>
<Authors>
  <Author>
    <Author.au_id>172-32-1176</Author.au_id>
    <Author.au_fname>Johnson</Author.au_fname>
    <Author.au_lname>White</Author.au_lname>
  </Author>
  <Author>
    <Author.au_id>213-46-8915</Author.au_id>
    <Author.au_fname>Marjorie</Author.au_fname>
    <Author.au_lname>Green</Author.au_lname>
  </Author>
  <Author>
    <Author.au_id>238-95-7766</Author.au_id>
    <Author.au_fname>Cheryl</Author.au_fname>
    <Author.au_lname>Carson</Author.au_lname>
  </Author>
  <Author>
    <Author.au_id>267-41-2394</Author.au_id>
    <Author.au_fname>Michael</Author.au_fname>
    <Author.au_lname>O&apos;Leary</Author.au_lname>
  </Author>
</Authors>
```

Below is a complete code sample to get XML from a recordset using custom code.

```
' Set to 0 for Production Mode
#Const DEMO_MODE = 1

#if DEMO_MODE = 1 then
Private Const MAX_RECORDS = 5
#endif

Private Const DOUBLE_QUOTE = """"
Private Const CHAR_SMALLER = "<"
Private Const CHAR_GREATER = ">"
Private Const CHAR_OBLIQUE_SMALLER = "</"
Private Const CHAR_OBLIQUE_GREATER = " />"

Private Const DEFAULT_INDENTATION = 2

Public Function strRS2XML(rs As ADODB.Recordset, _
                strName As String, _
                Optional vntIndentation As Variant) As String
    Static objField      As ADODB.Field
    Static strSpaces     As String
    Static strFieldName  As String
    Static intLevel      As Integer
    Static intIndentation As Integer

    ' The following variables cannot be made static!
    Dim rsChapter        As ADODB.Recordset
    Dim strXML           As String
    Dim strDocName       As String
    Dim lngRecCount      As Long

    ' Set the identation level to a positive value
    ' DEFAULT_INDENTATION is a constant defined
    ' in the general declaration section.
    If IsMissing(vntIndentation) Then
        intIndentation = DEFAULT_INDENTATION
    Else
        intIndentation = vntIndentation
        If intIndentation < 0 Then intIndentation = DEFAULT_INDENTATION
    End If

    ' Careful now, this function is recursive!
    If intLevel = 0 Then     ' Only on top-level call.
        strXML = "<?xml version=" _
            & DOUBLE_QUOTE & "1.0" & DOUBLE_QUOTE _
            & " ?>" & vbCr
    End If

    strSpaces = Space$(intLevel * intIndentation)

    ' Form a valid Document Name and Record Name
    ' The Document Name ends in "s"; the Record Name doesn't.
    strName = strValidXMLTag(strName)
    If Right$(strName, 1) = "s" Then
        strDocName = strName
        strName = Left$(strName, Len(strName) - 1)
    Else
```

```
           strDocName = strName & "s"
       End If

       ' Start of Document TAG
       strXML = strXML & CHAR_SMALLER & strDocName & CHAR_GREATER & vbCr

       intLevel = intLevel + 1
       strSpaces = Space$(intLevel * intIndentation)

       rs.MoveFirst
       lngRecCount = 1
#If DEMO_MODE = 1 Then
       While Not rs.EOF And lngRecCount < MAX_RECORDS
#Else
       While Not rs.EOF
#End If
           ' Start of Record tag
           strXML = strXML & strSpaces _
               & CHAR_SMALLER & strName & CHAR_GREATER & vbCr

           ' Record tag Content
           For Each objField In rs.Fields
               ' Is the Field a Recordset?
               If objField.Type = adChapter Then
                   ' We actually have another Recordset,
                   ' so we need to recurse
                   Set rsChapter = objField.Value
                   If Not rsChapter.EOF Then
                       intLevel = intLevel + 1
                       strXML = strXML & strRS2XML(rsChapter, _
                                   strName & "." & objField.Name, _
                                   intIndentation)
                       intLevel = intLevel - 1
                   End If
               Else
                   ' We have a regular Field,
                   ' so we add it to the XML string

                   ' Ensure we have a correctly formed tag name
                   strFieldName = strValidXMLTag(strName & "." & objField.Name)

                   If IsNull(objField.Value) Then
                       ' Empty Field tag
                       strXML = strXML & strSpaces & Space$(intIndentation) _
                           & CHAR_SMALLER & strFieldName & CHAR_OBLIQUE_GREATER & vbCr
                   Else
                       ' Start of Field tag
                       strXML = strXML & strSpaces & Space$(intIndentation) _
                           & CHAR_SMALLER & strFieldName & CHAR_GREATER
                       ' Field tag Content
                       strXML = strXML & strValidXMLContent(objField.Value)
                       ' End of Field tag
                       strXML = strXML & CHAR_OBLIQUE_SMALLER _
                           & strFieldName & CHAR_GREATER & vbCr
                   End If
               End If
           Next objField
```

```
              ' End of Record tag
          strXML = strXML & strSpaces & CHAR_OBLIQUE_SMALLER _
                  & strName & CHAR_GREATER & vbCr
          ' We may be a while, so keep UI responsive
          DoEvents

          ' We're done, with this record: fetch next
          rs.MoveNext
          lngRecCount = lngRecCount + 1
      Wend

      ' The (child) recordset has been processed,
      ' so we decrease the level.
      intLevel = intLevel - 1
      strSpaces = Space$(intLevel * intIndentation)

      ' End of Document TAG
      strXML = strXML & strSpaces & CHAR_OBLIQUE_SMALLER _
            & strDocName & CHAR_GREATER & vbCr

      ' Finally, return XML string
      strRS2XML = strXML
  End Function

  Private Function strValidXMLTag(strTagCandidate As String) As String
      ' This function only handles occurrences of "xml" and
      ' replaces white space with "_".
      ' The implementation of the remaining rules is left as
      ' an exercise for the reader. ;)

      ' Get rid of occurrences of 'xml'
      strTagCandidate = Replace(strTagCandidate, "xml", "x_m_l")
      ' Get rid of spaces
      strValidXMLTag = Replace(strTagCandidate, " ", "_")
  End Function

  Private Function strValidXMLContent(strContenCandidate As String) As String
      ' Get rid of occurrences of '<'
      strContenCandidate = Replace(strContenCandidate, "<", "&lt;")
      ' Get rid of occurrences of '>'
      strContenCandidate = Replace(strContenCandidate, ">", "&gt;")
      ' Get rid of occurrences of '&'
      strContenCandidate = Replace(strContenCandidate, "&", "&amp;")
      ' Get rid of occurrences of '"'
      strContenCandidate = Replace(strContenCandidate, """", "&quot;")
      ' Get rid of occurrences of "'"
      strValidXMLContent = Replace(strContenCandidate, "'", "&apos;")
  End Function
```

XML from a Recordset using DOM

An alternative to coding the above function in plain Visual Basic is to use Microsoft's XML parser. The MS XML parser is a COM component that is installed on your PC when you install IE5, but you may also download it as a separate component from `http://msdn.microsoft.com/xml/c-frame.htm#/xml/default.asp`. Before using the MSMXL library, you will need to add a reference to this parser from Visual Basic. This is done by selecting Projects | References | Browse and selecting Microsoft XML 1.0

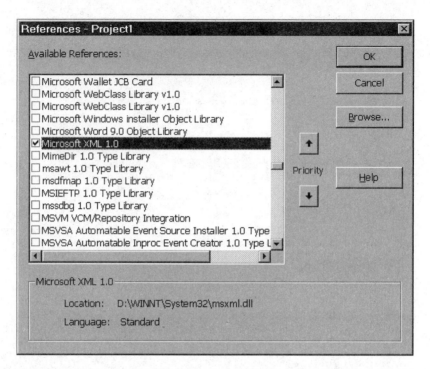

Again, let us see how this works in a project. Just as for the plain Visual Basic version, you will write an `objRS2XML_DOM` function that is recursive and works correctly with hierarchical recordsets. Again, you will use tags to hold field values. It would be just as easy to modify the code so the field values are attributes of a "row" tag, as is the case in the XML generated through the Save method of an ADO Recordset.

You know the story by now: you will use the pubs database in SQL Server 7. Start up Visual Basic and select "**Standard EXE**" as the new project type. Add a reference to the ADO 2.1 library by selecting Project, then References. Locate "Microsoft ActiveX Data Obect 2.1 Library" and click on the checkbox. Also add a reference to the XML parser as in the figure above. Remove the standard form from the project and add a code module instead. Add the code for your two helper functions as per previous project: `Private Function strValidXMLTag(strTagCandidate As String) As String` and `Private Function strValidXMLContent(strContenCandidate As String) As String`.

And now you can get to the crux of the matter: add the following Function:

```
Public Function objRS2XML_DOM(rs As ADODB.Recordset, _
                 strName As String) As MSXML.IXMLDOMElement.
```

Here is how this function works. In order to save on stack space and allocation time, you declare as static all variables and objects than do not need to be maintained during recursive function calls:

```
Static objField       As ADODB.Field
Static intLevel       As Integer
Static objXMLDocument  As MSXML.DOMDocument
Static objChild       As MSXML.IXMLDOMElement
```

The variables that maintain state during recursive function calls cannot be made static.

```
Dim objRoot           As MSXML.IXMLDOMElement
Dim objElement        As MSXML.IXMLDOMElement
Dim rsChapter         As ADODB.Recordset
Dim strDocName        As String
Dim lngRecCount       As Long
```

Since the actual choice of tag names is not really relevant to understanding XML generation using the Document Object Model, we use a simple algorithm to determine the document and record tag names: we use the same noun, passed as a parameter, in the singular and plural and assume adding an "s" to the singular will produce the plural (or subtracting the "s" from the plural will give us the singular). This is not a perfect solution, but gives reasonable results.

```
strName = strValidXMLTag(strName)
If Right$(strName, 1) = "s" Then
    strDocName = strName
    strName = Left$(strName, Len(strName) - 1)
Else
    strDocName = strName & "s"
End If
```

Since this function is recursive, you need to ensure you are only once creating the Document object. Since our static variable intLevel starts with an initial value of zero, and is subsequently incremented as we traverse the recordset, we can use it to test whether this is the first call for this document. By the time we have processed the whole recordset, intLevel will again have the value of 0, the correct value to process another recordset in a subsequent call. We increase the level for the next call.

```
If intLevel = 0 Then    ' Only on top-level call.
    Set objXMLDocument = New MSXML.DOMDocument
End If

intLevel = intLevel + 1
```

You create an element with the document name. This element is either the root of the document, in which case it does not have a parent, or it is the root of a child recordset, in which case it will be appended after the recursive call, below.

```
' Start of Document TAG
Set objRoot = objXMLDocument.createElement(strDocName)
```

Then we move to the first record in the recordset, initializing our count of how many records we have processed so far.

```
rs.MoveFirst
lngRecCount = 1
```

You will then create the loop that will iterate through all records. In demo mode, you limit the number of records that will be processed to a programmer-defined constant.

```
#If DEMO_MODE = 1 Then
    While Not rs.EOF And lngRecCount < MAX_RECORDS
#Else
    While Not rs.EOF
#End If
```

We have a record, so create a new element and append to the root object.

```
Set objElement = objXMLDocument.createElement(strName)
objRoot.appendChild objElement
```

Now you need to iterate through all the fields in this record.

```
For Each objField In rs.Fields
```

You need to consider the possibility of having a hierarchical recordset. We determine this by looking at the `Field Type` property.

```
If objField.Type = adChapter Then
```

If you have a hierarchical recordset, then our `Field Value` is actually another recordset. So if this recordset is not empty, you increase the level and make a recursive call to `objRS2XML_DOM`. You add a prefix to the `Field Name` to avoid creating duplicate tag names. (Another choice involves using name spaces, as Microsoft implemented in the `Recordset Save` method.)

```
Set rsChapter = objField.Value
If Not rsChapter.EOF Then
    objElement.appendChild objRS2XML_DOM(rsChapter, _
                    strName & "." & objField.Name)
End If
```

If you don't have a hierarchical recordset, you can create a field tag. You are calling the `strValidXMLTag` to ensure the `Field Name` is created according to the XML rules. `strValidXMLContent` ensures that the `Field Values` is conforming to the XML rules. Instead of creating empty tags for NULL values, you could elect to do nothing.

```
Else
    Set objChild = objXMLDocument.createElement( _
                strValidXMLTag(strName & "." & objField.Name))
    If Not IsNull(objField.Value) Then
        objChild.Text = strValidXMLContent(objField.Value)
    End If
    objElement.appendChild objChild
End If
```

We have processed this field and can go to the next one.

```
Next objField
```

Since we have processed all fields, we are done with the record. We have chosen to put in a DoEvents call to keep the application responsive when we are processing large recordsets.

```
        DoEvents
```

Since we have processed the record, we need to fetch the next one.

```
        rs.MoveNext
        lngRecCount = lngRecCount + 1
    Wend
```

We have just left the While loop, so we are done with our recordset. We need to get the intLevel variable back to 0 so the next call to objRS2XML_DOM creates a Document object.

```
    ' The (child) recordset has been processed,
    ' so we decrease the level.
    intLevel = intLevel - 1
```

If this is the top-level call, you need to destroy the Document object we created.

```
    If intLevel = 0 Then    ' Only on top-level call.
        Set objXMLDocument = Nothing
    End If
```

We return the result of your processing to the caller.

```
    ' Finally, return Root element
    Set objRS2XML_DOM = objRoot
```

Using the objRS2XML_DOM function is strikingly similar to using strRS2XML function. The changes required are highlighted below. You only need to add the creation of an XML document element to receive the result, since the functions differ in return types. Again, you created an XML file (as opposed to creating a string with XML data). The output of both functions is identical.

```
Public Sub Main()
    Dim strPath             As String

    ' Normalize Path
    strPath = App.Path
    If Right$(strPath, 1) <> "/" Then
        strPath = strPath & "/"
    End If

    CreateAuthorsXML strPath & "Authors.xml"
End Sub

Public Sub CreateAuthorsXML(strXMLFile As String)
    Dim intFileNumber    As Integer
    Dim rsAuthors        As ADODB.Recordset
    Dim objRoot          As MSXML.IXMLDOMElement

    Set rsAuthors = New ADODB.Recordset
```

```vb
    ' Open recordset with a few columns
    ' Limit to just a few records with WHERE clause
    rsAuthors.Source = "SELECT au_id, au_fname, au_lname " _
                    & "FROM Authors WHERE au_id < 5"

    ' In the following, you need to change "srvr" to the
    ' name of your SQL Server
    rsAuthors.ActiveConnection = "Provider=sqloledb;" & _
        "Data Source=srvr;Initial Catalog=pubs;User Id=sa;Password=; "

    ' All set to open recordset...
    rsAuthors.Open   ' Open recordset (limit to just a few records with WHERE
clause)

    ' Call objRS2XML_DOM which returns the Root element
    Set objRoot = objRS2XML_DOM(rsAuthors, "Author")

    ' Get unused file number
    intFileNumber = FreeFile
    ' Create file name
    Open strXMLFile For Output As #intFileNumber
    ' Output text
    Print #intFileNumber, objRoot.xml
    ' Close file
    Close #intFileNumber

    ' Clean Up
    rsAuthors.Close
    Set rsAuthors = Nothing
End Sub
```

Below is the complete listing for this code:

```vb
' Set to 0 for Production Mode
#Const DEMO_MODE = 1

#if DEMO_MODE = 1 then
Private Const MAX_RECORDS = 5
#endif

Public Function objRS2XML_DOM(rs As ADODB.Recordset, _
                strName As String) As MSXML.IXMLDOMElement
    Static objField       As ADODB.Field
    Static intLevel       As Integer
    Static objXMLDocument   As MSXML.DOMDocument
    Static objChild       As MSXML.IXMLDOMElement

    Dim objRoot        As MSXML.IXMLDOMElement
    Dim objElement     As MSXML.IXMLDOMElement
    Dim rsChapter      As ADODB.Recordset
    Dim strDocName     As String
    Dim lngRecCount    As Long

    ' Form a valid Document Name and Record Name
    ' The Document Name ends in "s"; the Record Name doesn't.
    strName = strValidXMLTag(strName)
    If Right$(strName, 1) = "s" Then
        strDocName = strName
        strName = Left$(strName, Len(strName) - 1)
```

```
      Else
          strDocName = strName & "s"
      End If

      ' Careful now, this function is recursive!
      If intLevel = 0 Then      ' Only on top-level call.
          Set objXMLDocument = New MSXML.DOMDocument
      End If

      ' Start of Document TAG
      Set objRoot = objXMLDocument.createElement(strDocName)

      intLevel = intLevel + 1

      rs.MoveFirst
      lngRecCount = 1
#If DEMO_MODE = 1 Then
      While Not rs.EOF And lngRecCount < MAX_RECORDS
#Else
      While Not rs.EOF
#End If
          ' Start of Record tag
          Set objElement = objXMLDocument.createElement(strName)
          objRoot.appendChild objElement

          ' Record tag Content
          For Each objField In rs.Fields
              ' Is the Field a Recordset?
              If objField.Type = adChapter Then
                  ' We actually have another Recordset,
                  ' so we need to recurse
                  Set rsChapter = objField.Value
                  If Not rsChapter.EOF Then
                      objElement.appendChild objRS2XML_DOM(rsChapter, _
                                      strName & "." & objField.Name)
                  End If
              Else
                  ' We have a regular Field,
                  ' so we add it to the XML string

                  Set objChild = objXMLDocument.createElement( _
                              strValidXMLTag(strName & "." & objField.Name))
                  If Not IsNull(objField.Value) Then
                      objChild.Text = strValidXMLContent(objField.Value)
                  End If
                  objElement.appendChild objChild
              End If
          Next objField

          ' We're done, with this record: fetch next
          DoEvents
          rs.MoveNext
          lngRecCount = lngRecCount + 1
      Wend

      ' The (child) recordset has been processed,
      ' so we decrease the level.
      intLevel = intLevel - 1
```

```
      If intLevel = 0 Then    ' Only on top-level call.
         Set objXMLDocument = Nothing
      End If


      ' Finally, return Root element
      Set objRS2XML_DOM = objRoot
      Exit Function

End Function

Private Function strValidXMLTag(strTagCandidate As String) As String
      ' This function only handles occurrences of "xml" and
      ' replaces white space with "_".
      ' The implementation of the remaining rules is left as
      ' an exercise for the reader. ;)

      ' Get rid of occurrences of 'xml'
      strTagCandidate = Replace(strTagCandidate, "xml", "x_m_l")
      ' Get rid of spaces
      strValidXMLTag = Replace(strTagCandidate, " ", "_")
End Function

Private Function strValidXMLContent(strContenCandidate As String) As String
      ' Get rid of occurrences of '<'
      strContenCandidate = Replace(strContenCandidate, "<", "&lt;")
      ' Get rid of occurrences of '>'
      strContenCandidate = Replace(strContenCandidate, ">", "&gt;")
      ' Get rid of occurrences of '&'
      strContenCandidate = Replace(strContenCandidate, "&", "&amp;")
      ' Get rid of occurrences of '"'
      strContenCandidate = Replace(strContenCandidate, """", "&quot;")
      ' Get rid of occurrences of "'"
      strValidXMLContent = Replace(strContenCandidate, "'", "&apos;")
End Function
```

Server-Side XML

A crucial question is whether you can use all these cool XML techniques without requiring an XML-capable browser on the client side (IE 5 is a fantastic browser, but its market share is still small at the present.) The great news is that the answer to this question is a resounding yes. If your web server is IIS, you can install IE 5 on the web server and use the XML parser in an IIS application to transform the XML into HTML on the server. All you need to do is ensure that the resulting HTML document will render correctly on your targeted browsers. Let's take a look at the Visual Basic code for such an IIS application.

Generating HTML from XML on the server

In this sample you will use an XSL style sheet to transform an XML document into an HTML page. You do this on the server using the IIS Applications we discussed in Chapters 12, 13 and 14. As in the previous project, you need to set a reference to MSXML.DLL in order to use the IE5 DOM objects.

Let us see how this is done. Start a new Visual Basic project and select **IIS Application** as the project type. Double-click on **WebClass1** in the Project window to bring up the WebClass designer. Change the default **WebClass1** name to "XML2HTMLonServer" and its `NameInURL` property to "XML2HTML". Right-click on Custom WebItems and select "Add Custom WebItem". Name the WebItem "XML2HTML". Double-click on this item and start adding the following helper sub.

```
Private Sub ShowParseError(objParseError As MSXML.IXMLDOMParseError)
    Response.Write "<B>Invalid XML/XSL file!</B><HR/>"

    Response.Write "<B>Please call the WebMaster @ (416) 123-4567 x890" _
        & "and report the following error info:</B><BR/><BR/>"

    Response.Write "<B>File URL :</B>" & objParseError.URL & "<BR/>"
    Response.Write "<B>Line No :</B>" & objParseError.Line & "<BR/>"
    Response.Write "<B>Character :</B>" & objParseError.linepos & "<BR/>"
    Response.Write "<B>File Position :</B>" & objParseError.filepos & "<BR/>"
    Response.Write "<B>Source Text :</B>" & objParseError.srcText & "<BR/>"
    Response.Write "<B>Error Code :</B>" & objParseError.errorCode & "<BR/>"
    Response.Write "<B>Description :</B>" & objParseError.reason & "<BR/>"
End Sub
```

Next remove all the default code from the `WebClass_Start()` event handler and start coding the following. You declare a string variable as two XML document objects: one for the XML document and one for its style sheet.

```
Dim strPath         As String
Dim objXMLDocument  As MSXML.DOMDocument
Dim objXMLStyle     As MSXML.DOMDocument
```

We ensure that our path ends with a "/" so we can append a file name to the path to get the full path name to the documents.

```
strPath = App.Path
If Right$(strPath, 1) <> "/" Then
    strPath = strPath & "/"
End If
```

Then you parse the XML document. Before calling the `Load` method, you must set the `async` property to false to get synchronous parsing.

```
Set objXMLDocument = New MSXML.DOMDocument
objXMLDocument.async = False
objXMLDocument.Load strPath & "Markup.xml"
```

Then you query the `parseError` object to ensure no errors occurred.

```
If (objXMLDocument.parseError.errorCode = 0) Then
    ' No parsing errors!
```

If no errors occurred, you repeat the loading process with the style sheet.

```
' Load the associated XSL document
Set objXMLStyle = New MSXML.DOMDocument
objXMLStyle.async = False
objXMLStyle.Load strPath & "Markup.xsl"
```

Again you query the `parseError` object to ensure no errors occurred.

```
If (objXMLStyle.parseError.errorCode = 0) Then
    ' No parsing errors!
```

Since you have successfully loaded both the XML document and its spreadsheet, you can call the `transformNode` method, which returns the transformed XML in a string. You use the Write method to show this in the browser.

```
Response.Write objXMLDocument.transformNode(objXMLStyle)
```

The remaining sections of the `If` statements, pass the `parseError` object of the document where an error occurred to a helper function that will display the error information. Along the line, you also release the XML documents.

```
    Else
        ' Show parsing errors occurring while
        ' loading the associated XSL document
        ShowParseError objXMLStyle.parseError
    End If

    ' Clean up
    Set objXMLStyle = Nothing
Else
    ' Show parsing errors occurring while loading the XML document
    ShowParseError objXMLDocument.parseError
End If

Set objXMLDocument = Nothing
```

Create an XML file with the name `Markup.xml` and an XSL file with the name `Markup.xsl`. Here, you have used the same content as shown earlier in this chapter. You are now ready to see the code in action. Run the project. A window like the one below shows up, requesting whether to start the IIS component. Click on OK.

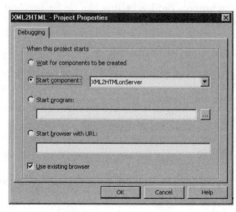

If your local web server was not started, Visual Basic will start it and shortly thereafter you will see the following page displayed in your browser.

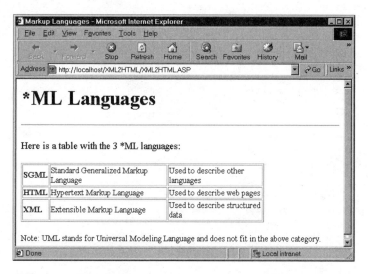

In your browser, select View|View source. As you can see below, the only hint of XML is the "/>" at the end of the standalone tags.

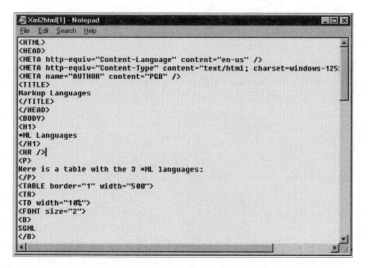

Here is the complete code listing:

```
Private Sub WebClass_Start()
    Dim strPath         As String
    Dim objXMLDocument  As MSXML.DOMDocument
    Dim objXMLStyle     As MSXML.DOMDocument
```

```
      ' Normalize Path
      strPath = App.Path
      If Right$(strPath, 1) <> "/" Then
        strPath = strPath & "/"
      End If

      ' First we load the XML document
      Set objXMLDocument = New MSXML.DOMDocument
      objXMLDocument.async = False
      objXMLDocument.Load strPath & "Markup.xml"

      ' Parsing errors while loading the XML document?
      If (objXMLDocument.parseError.errorCode = 0) Then
         ' No parsing errors!
         ' Load the associated XSL document
         Set objXMLStyle = New MSXML.DOMDocument
         objXMLStyle.async = False
         objXMLStyle.Load strPath & "Markup.xsl"

         ' Parsing errors while loading the associated XSL document?
         If (objXMLStyle.parseError.errorCode = 0) Then
            ' No parsing errors!
            ' Output the HTML text generated by transformNode
            Response.Write objXMLDocument.transformNode(objXMLStyle)
         Else
            ' Show parsing errors occurring while
            ' loading the associated XSL document
            ShowParseError objXMLStyle.parseError
         End If

         ' Clean up
         Set objXMLStyle = Nothing
      Else
         ' Show parsing errors occurring while loading the XML document
         ShowParseError objXMLDocument.parseError
      End If

      ' Clean up
      Set objXMLDocument = Nothing
End Sub

Private Sub ShowParseError(objParseError As MSXML.IXMLDOMParseError)
   Response.Write "<B>Invalid XML/XSL file!</B><HR/>"

   Response.Write "<B>Please call the WebMaster @ (416) 123-4567 x890" _
        & "and report the following error info:</B><BR/><BR/>"

   Response.Write "<B>File URL :</B>" & objParseError.URL & "<BR/>"
   Response.Write "<B>Line No :</B>" & objParseError.Line & "<BR/>"
   Response.Write "<B>Character :</B>" & objParseError.linepos & "<BR/>"
   Response.Write "<B>File Position :</B>" & objParseError.filepos & "<BR/>"
   Response.Write "<B>Source Text :</B>" & objParseError.srcText & "<BR/>"
   Response.Write "<B>Error Code :</B>" & objParseError.errorCode & "<BR/>"
   Response.Write "<B>Description :</B>" & objParseError.reason & "<BR/>"
End Sub
```

Sending XML from the client to the Server

How to send XML to the server will depend on the application-specific requirements. You will learn two methods to send XML to the server. The first one uses the IE5-specific DOM extension HTTPRequest object and is especially appropriate when you want the XML data processed as it is received. As its name indicates, an HTTPRequest object uses the HTTP protocol to send requests to the web server. You will also read how you can implement the server component that will receive this data, both using an ASP script and a Visual Basic IIS application.

Using FTP is another option to send XML data to the server. This, and similar methods such as HTTP POST, are appropriate when you simply want to put the XML document on the server, without any further server-side processing.

Putting it all together: Using the IE5 HTTPRequest Object to Send an XML File to the server

This solution requires IE5 on the client machine and relies on a server component, described in the following section, "*Receiving XML on the Server*". Once you set a reference in your project to the MSMX.DLL, you can declare and create an HttpRequest object.

```
Dim objXLMHttp          As MSXML.XMLHTTPRequest
Set objXLMHttp = New MSXML.XLMHttpRequest
```

Then, you can call the Open method to establish a connection with the web server. The URL shown here corresponds to the URL of the receiving component discussed in next section. The strXML string used as a parameter of the send method is assumed to contained well-formed XML data.

```
objXLMHttp.Open "POST", "http://localhost/ReceiveXML.ASP", False
objXLMHttp.send strXML
```

As you will see in the next section, your receiving component sends status information back. You catch and display this information in a message box.

```
MsgBox objXLMHttp.responseXML.xml, vbInformation, "Response from Server"
```

All that remains to be done is to destroy the HttpRequest object you created. That is all there is to sending.

```
Set objXLMHttp = Nothing
```

Here is a complete sample using this idea. The project, a standard EXE, contains a single form, shown below, with a Command Button (named cmdSend) and a Text Box (named txtAU_ID). For convenience, you also can add an Exit button.

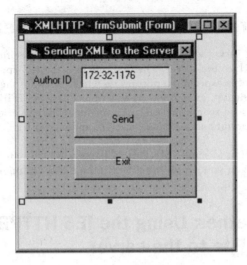

All the work is done in the `cmdSend Click` event. You start by declaring a few variables. Note that you will need to add references to both ADO 2.1 and MS XML 1.0.

```
Private Sub cmdSend_Click()
    Dim strPath          As String
    Dim strXMLFile       As String
    Dim strQuery         As String
    Dim strXML           As String
    Dim rsAuthors        As ADODB.Recordset
    Dim objXLMDocument   As MSXML.DOMDocument
    Dim objXLMHttp       As MSXML.XMLHTTPRequest
    Dim objXSLDocument   As MSXML.DOMDocument
```

Then you populate a recordset using the text box. (In production code, you would of course first validate the content of the text box.)

```
    Set rsAuthors = New ADODB.Recordset

    ' Open recordset with a few columns
    ' Limit to just a few records with WHERE clause
    rsAuthors.Source = "SELECT au_id, au_fname, au_lname " _
            & "FROM Authors WHERE au_id = '" _
            & DoQuotes(txtAU_ID.Text) & "'"

    ' In the following, you need to change "srvr" to the
    ' name of your SQL Server
    rsAuthors.ActiveConnection = "Provider=sqloledb;" & _
        "Data Source=srvr;Initial Catalog=pubs;User Id=sa;Password=; "

    ' All set to open recordset...
    rsAuthors.Open   ' Open recordset (limit to just a few records with WHERE
clause)
```

Then you use the ADO 2.1 RecordSet.Save method to make a client side temporary copy of the data.

```
' Normalize Path
strPath = App.Path
If Right$(strPath, 1) <> "\" Then
    strPath = strPath & "\"
End If

'Persist Recordset to file as XML
strXMLFile = strPath & "recordset.xml"
If FileExists(strXMLFile) Then Kill strXMLFile
rsAuthors.Save strXMLFile, adPersistXML
```

You are done with the recordset, so you can close it.

```
' Clean Up ADO objects
rsAuthors.Close
Set rsAuthors = Nothing
```

Now you use XSL to simplify the XML that will be saved on the server. The style sheet code is given below.

```
' Load the XML document we just created
Set objXLMDocument = New MSXML.DOMDocument
objXLMDocument.async = False
objXLMDocument.Load strXMLFile

' Load the stylesheet to standardize the XML
Set objXSLDocument = New MSXML.DOMDocument
objXSLDocument.async = False
objXSLDocument.Load strPath & "standard.xsl"

'Standardize the XML
strXML = objXLMDocument.transformNode(objXSLDocument)
Set objXSLDocument = Nothing
Set objXLMDocument = Nothing
```

To make sure everything is fine, you display the transformed XML in a message box.

```
MsgBox strXML, vbOKOnly, "XML"
```

Now, you are ready to send this XML to the server as described above.

```
' Create a XLMHttpRequest object
Set objXLMHttp = New MSXML.XMLHTTPRequest

' Here we ommit the optional bstrUser and bstrPassword
' of the objXLMHttp.Open method. They may be required to
' access a production Web Server.
' Use the line below for the ASP page.
'objXLMHttp.Open "POST", "http://localhost/receiveXML.asp", False
' Use the line below for the VB IIS app.
objXLMHttp.Open "POST", "http://localhost/RecvXML/VBReceiveXML.ASP", _
          False
objXLMHttp.send strXML
```

You display the server response in a message box and clean up.

```
    ' Get the response from the Server
    MsgBox objXLMHttp.responseXML.xml, vbInformation, "Response from Server"

    ' Clean Up
    Set objXLMHttp = Nothing
End Sub
```

You also need two helper functions. The helper function to properly handle quotes within quotes is not really required in this case, but is generally required when using string parameters in a query string.

```
Private Function DoQuotes(ByVal strToken As String) As String
    DoQuotes = Replace(strToken, "'", "''")
End Function

Private Function FileExists(ByVal strFileName As String) As Boolean
    FileExists = CBool(Len(Dir$(strFileName, vbNormal _
                    + vbHidden _
                    + vbSystem _
                    + vbVolume _
                    + vbDirectory)))
End Function
```

Finally, you create the XSL style sheet used to simplify the content in the server-side XML file, since, as you saw in the ADO Save section, the content generated by the ADO save method is unruly. The style sheet simply copies the proper attributes into an `<author>` tag.

```
<xsl:stylesheet xmlns:xsl="http://www.w3.org/TR/WD-xsl">

  <xsl:template match="//">
    <xsl:apply-templates/>
  </xsl:template>
  <xsl:template match="//z:row">
  <Author>
    <xsl:element name="au_id"><xsl:value-of select="@au_id"/></xsl:element>
    <xsl:element name="au_fname"><xsl:value-of select="@au_fname"/></xsl:element>
    <xsl:element name="au_lname"><xsl:value-of select="@au_lname"/></xsl:element>
  </Author>
  </xsl:template>

</xsl:stylesheet>
```

Let us test this project. Make sure both your web server and SQL Server are running and run the project. The following message box shows that the XML is successfully generated from the SQL query.

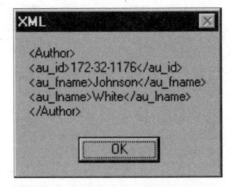

The following message box shows the server received your file.

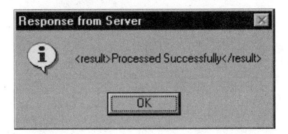

On the server, the following XML file is created.

```
<Author>
     <au_id>172-32-1176</au_id>
     <au_fname>Johnson</au_fname>
     <au_lname>White</au_lname>
</Author>
```

Here is the complete code listing:

```
Private Sub cmdSend_Click()
    Dim strPath            As String
    Dim strXMLFile         As String
    Dim strQuery           As String
    Dim strXML             As String
    Dim rsAuthors          As ADODB.Recordset
    Dim objXLMDocument     As MSXML.DOMDocument
    Dim objXLMHttp         As MSXML.XMLHTTPRequest
    Dim objXSLDocument     As MSXML.DOMDocument

    ' Create an XML Document from a SQL Query
    ' ----------------------------------------
```

```
Set rsAuthors = New ADODB.Recordset

' Open recordset with a few columns
' Limit to just a few records with WHERE clause
rsAuthors.Source = "SELECT au_id, au_fname, au_lname " _
                 & "FROM Authors WHERE au_id = '" _
                 & DoQuotes(txtAU_ID.Text) & "'"

' In the following, you need to change "srvr" to the
' name of your SQL Server
rsAuthors.ActiveConnection = "Provider=sqloledb;" & _
    "Data Source=srvr;Initial Catalog=pubs;User Id=sa;Password=; "

' All set to open recordset...
rsAuthors.Open    ' Open recordset (limit to just a few records with WHERE
clause)

' Normalize Path
strPath = App.Path
If Right$(strPath, 1) <> "\" Then
    strPath = strPath & "\"
End If

'Persist Recordset to file as XML
strXMLFile = strPath & "recordset.xml"
If FileExists(strXMLFile) Then Kill strXMLFile
rsAuthors.Save strXMLFile, adPersistXML

' Clean Up ADO objects
rsAuthors.Close
Set rsAuthors = Nothing

' Transform the created XML Document
' into a standard form
' ----------------------------------

' Load the XML document we just created
Set objXLMDocument = New MSXML.DOMDocument
objXLMDocument.async = False
objXLMDocument.Load strXMLFile

' Load the stylesheet to standardize the XML
Set objXSLDocument = New MSXML.DOMDocument
objXSLDocument.async = False
objXSLDocument.Load strPath & "standard.xsl"

'Standardize the XML
strXML = objXLMDocument.transformNode(objXSLDocument)
Set objXSLDocument = Nothing
Set objXLMDocument = Nothing

MsgBox strXML, vbOKOnly, "XML"

' Post the XML to server for processing
' -------------------------------------

' Create a XLMHttpRequest object
Set objXLMHttp = New MSXML.XMLHTTPRequest
```

```
        ' Here we ommit the optional bstrUser and bstrPassword
        ' of the objXLMHttp.Open method. They may be required to
        ' access a production Web Server.
        ' Use the line below for the ASP page.
        'objXLMHttp.Open "POST", "http://localhost/receiveXML.asp", False
        ' Use the line below for the VB IIS app.
        objXLMHttp.Open "POST", "http://localhost/RecvXML/VBReceiveXML.ASP", _
                    False
        objXLMHttp.send strXML

        ' Get the response from the Server
        MsgBox objXLMHttp.responseXML.xml, vbInformation, "Response from Server"

        ' Clean Up
        Set objXLMHttp = Nothing
    End Sub

    Private Function DoQuotes(ByVal strToken As String) As String
        DoQuotes = Replace(strToken, "'", "''")
    End Function

    Private Function FileExists(ByVal strFileName As String) As Boolean
        FileExists = CBool(Len(Dir$(strFileName, vbNormal _
                        + vbHidden _
                        + vbSystem _
                        + vbVolume _
                        + vbDirectory)))
    End Function
```

Receiving an XML File on the server

Receiving XML on the Server using an ASP script

Here is the script for an ASP page that will save the file transmitted to the server using the IE5 HTTPRequest object. Even if you decide to build a Visual Basic IIS application to handle this task, you may want to use this script for testing purposes. You need to put this script on a server that can execute ASP files and change the code in Private Sub cmdProcessCust_Click() in the code above to refer to this file. Here is the line that needs to be changed:

```
        objXLMHttp.Open "POST", "http://localhost/RecvXML/VBReceiveXML.ASP", _
                    False
```

Replace that line with:

```
        objXLMHttp.Open "POST", "http://localhost/receiveXML.asp", False
```

Here is the code for the ASP. Save this file as receiveXML.asp in the root directory of your Web site.

```
    <% @LANGUAGE=VBScript%>
    <%
        Set xmlCust = Server.CreateObject("Microsoft.XMLDOM")
        xmlCust.async = False
```

```
    xmlCust.Load (Request)
    If xmlCust.parseError.reason = "" Then
        xmlCust.Save (Server.MapPath("customer.xml"))
        Response.ContentType = "text/xml"
        Response.Write ("<result>Processed Successfully</result>")
    Else
        Response.Write ("<error/>")
    End If
%>
```

Receiving XML on the Server using a Visual Basic IIS Application

To be able to accomplish more complex tasks upon receiving XML data on the server, you may wish to write the receiving application in Visual Basic. It turns out that this is fairly straightforward.

The key idea is to create a DOMDocument in the BeginRequest event of a custom WebItem. Then, you can load the XML data sent to the server with:

```
objXMLDocument.Load Request
```

Once you have loaded the XML document, you can manipulate its data as per your requirement. In the next example, you simply save the XML data on the server using:

```
objXMLDocument.save (Server.MapPath("customer.xml"))
```

Here the complete listing for a custom WebItem that receives and saves an XML document sent using a HTTPRequest object. As usual, you need to set a reference to the MSXML.DLL in your IIS application to use the DOM objects.

```
Private Sub WebClass_BeginRequest()
    Dim objXMLDocument      As MSXML.DOMDocument
    Dim objXMLStyle         As MSXML.DOMDocument

    ' First we load the XML document received in the Request
    Set objXMLDocument = New MSXML.DOMDocument
    objXMLDocument.async = False
    objXMLDocument.Load Request

    ' Parsing errors while loading the XML document?
    If (objXMLDocument.parseError.errorCode = 0) Then
        ' No parsing errors!
        ' Save the XML document on the Server
        objXMLDocument.save (Server.MapPath("author.xml"))

        ' Say "OK!"
        Response.ContentType = "text/xml"
        Response.Write "<result>Processed Successfully</result>"
    Else
        ' Show parsing errors occurring while loading the XML document
        ShowParseError objXMLDocument.parseError
    End If

    ' Clean up
    Set objXMLDocument = Nothing
End Sub
```

```
Private Sub ShowParseError(objParseError As MSXML.IXMLDOMParseError)
    Dim strParseError       As String

    Response.ContentType = "text/xml"

    strParseError = "<Error><B>Invalid XML!</B><HR/>" & vbCr
    strParseError = strParseError & _
        "<B>File URL :</B>" & objParseError.URL & "<BR/>" & vbCr
    strParseError = strParseError & _
        "<B>Line No :</B>" & objParseError.Line & "<BR/>" & vbCr
    strParseError = strParseError & _
        "<B>Character :</B>" & objParseError.linepos & "<BR/>" & vbCr
    strParseError = strParseError & _
        "<B>File Position :</B>" & objParseError.filepos & "<BR/>" & vbCr
    strParseError = strParseError & _
        "<B>Source Text :</B>" & objParseError.srcText & "<BR/>" & vbCr
    strParseError = strParseError & _
        "<B>Error Code :</B>" & objParseError.errorCode & "<BR/>" & vbCr
    strParseError = strParseError & _
        "<B>Description :</B>" & objParseError.reason & "<BR/></Error>"

    Response.Write strParseError
End Sub
```

Here is the complete listing for this code:

```
Private Sub WebClass_BeginRequest()
    Dim objXMLDocument      As MSXML.DOMDocument
    Dim objXMLStyle         As MSXML.DOMDocument

    ' First we load the XML document received in the Request
    Set objXMLDocument = New MSXML.DOMDocument
    objXMLDocument.async = False
    objXMLDocument.Load Request

    ' Parsing errors while loading the XML document?
    If (objXMLDocument.parseError.errorCode = 0) Then
      ' No parsing errors!
      ' Save the XML document on the Server
      objXMLDocument.save (Server.MapPath("author.xml"))

        ' Say "OK!"
        Response.ContentType = "text/xml"
        Response.Write "<result>Processed Successfully</result>"
    Else
        ' Show parsing errors occurring while loading the XML document
        ShowParseError objXMLDocument.parseError
    End If

    ' Clean up
    Set objXMLDocument = Nothing
End Sub

Private Sub ShowParseError(objParseError As MSXML.IXMLDOMParseError)
    Dim strParseError       As String
    Response.ContentType = "text/xml"
```

```
        strParseError = "<Error><B>Invalid XML!</B><HR/>" & vbCr
        strParseError = strParseError & _
            "<B>File URL :</B>" & objParseError.URL & "<BR/>" & vbCr
        strParseError = strParseError & _
            "<B>Line No :</B>" & objParseError.Line & "<BR/>" & vbCr
        strParseError = strParseError & _
            "<B>Character :</B>" & objParseError.linepos & "<BR/>" & vbCr
        strParseError = strParseError & _
            "<B>File Position :</B>" & objParseError.filepos & "<BR/>" & vbCr
        strParseError = strParseError & _
            "<B>Source Text :</B>" & objParseError.srcText & "<BR/>" & vbCr
        strParseError = strParseError & _
            "<B>Error Code :</B>" & objParseError.errorCode & "<BR/>" & vbCr
        strParseError = strParseError & _
            "<B>Description :</B>" & objParseError.reason & "<BR/></Error>"

        Response.Write strParseError
    End Sub
```

Summary

In this chapter, you read everything you need to know about starting using XML in you applications. You learned how to create well-formed XML documents through a comparison with HTML. You were also briefly introduced to some of the companion standards of XML: DTD, XML Schemas, and name spaces. You used XSL to transform XML into HTML, viewable using any browser. Then, you saw how to programmatically manipulate XML using the Document Object Model (DOM). You used Visual Basic to generate XML from a recordset using a variety of methods: using native ADO, using plain Visual Basic and using the DOM. Finally, you wrote IIS applications to send and receive XML from the client to the server.

To quickly summarise, you learned:

➤ How to create valid XML documents

➤ How to create an XML Style library

➤ How to utilise DTDs

➤ How to manipulate the DOM to parse XML for output

You have also learned how to generate XML using Visual Basic 6 for these purposes:

➤ Turning the results of an ADO recordset into XML

➤ Converting the results from an ADO recordset using our own custom code

➤ Converting the results from an ADO recordset using the DOM

You have also learned how to perform a couple of functions relating to XML on the server. These are:

➤ How to use the IE5 HTTPRequest Object to convert XML to HTML on the server if the client does not have an XML enabled browser

➤ How to receive and process an XML file sent by the client to the server

Case Study : Message Board Part 1

Why a message board?

For many websites the key to success and that 7 figure hit counter heaven is getting repeat visits. Most websites have a natural subset of users, even if it's a dynamic set. Your site might be available for the whole world to see, but not everyone is interested in Star Trek, buying books or finding out about your company's latest gizmo.

To foster repeat visits requires building loyalty, a sense of community, providing something new for every visit and allowing interaction. A message board is a great way of doing this. It allows your visitors to talk to you about how good or bad the website is and it allows them to talk to each other. They'll keep visiting if only to see if someone has replied to that message they left last week.

There are plenty of freebie message boards out there, which can be set up after a quick registration process, and a few lines of HTML. However nothing says "Warning amateur website ahead" more than a free website gizmo.

This Case Study has been divided into two parts due to its large size. In this first part, we will be creating a database and a middleware business object. In the second part, we will deal with the presentation layer, in which a webclass will be created, remote scripting will be implemented, and the ASP page will be formed.

The message board of this case study is a real project, not some concocted example. It is alive and kicking and proving very successful. It was developed for a university alumni society's website and as you can imagine that's a fairly small subset of the worlds online population; therefore for them getting repeat visits is essential.

Technologies Used

In setting up this Message Board application, the following technologies are used:

MS SQL Server 7

- ➤ Creating Databases and Tables
- ➤ Creating Stored Procedures using Transact SQL

Visual Basic 6 ActiveX DLL

- ➤ Accessing SQL Server using ADO 2.1
- ➤ Applying business logic to data and returning useful information

Visual Basic 6 IIS Application

- ➤ Serving up HTML to remote browser
- ➤ Creating a business object as a VB ActiveX DLL to undertake processing
- ➤ Responding to User requests such as form posts, clicking of links and buttons
- ➤ Using HTML Frames with an IIS application

Dynamic HTML

- ➤ Creating user friendly interfaces by making full use of Internet Explorer 4 and 5's Document Object Model

Remote Scripting

- ➤ Accessing Data without page refreshes
- ➤ Remotely executing functions in an ASP page from a standard HTML page

Design Objectives

In designing the case study I had 3 major aims:

- ➤ Speed of download
- ➤ Ease of use
- ➤ Usable by widest range of internet users

Speed

Whether you're selling products from your website or not, your visitors are your customers. If you went into your favorite fast food restaurant and it took them 5 minutes to get the till up and running would you go again?

On the Internet, people's attention span is shorter than normal, they click a link and they expect results - fast. If your message board has next week's winning lottery numbers then make them wait, otherwise you had better come up with the goods now.

It was for this reason I avoided the ActiveX control route. Even the most basic control written using Visual Basic will require over a megabyte of support files such as the VB virtual machine. Okay, this would only require a download once but for those without Visual Studio installed, this is a large download even on a 56Kbps modem. Also nothing kills cross browser and platform support faster than an ActiveX control. There are also some security issues with ActiveX controls. Using unsigned controls requires the browser security setting to be set to low. Even digitally signed controls require your visitors to trust you.

It was for these reasons I took the VB Webclass route and avoided ActiveX. All that's served up in a browser is HTML. There are no downloads other than the page's HTML. Cross browser compatibility is made easier. With a couple of dozen messages, the board takes around 1 - 6 seconds to display.

It was with speed in mind that I chose Microsoft SQL Server 7 as the database as opposed to something like MS Access. Any enterprise level database would be fine, such as Oracle. MS Access is fine for very low level usage but for scalability, reliability and security you really need something more serious.

With future scalability and speed in mind, database access and information processing is contained in a VB ActiveX DLL. If we expect a lot of hits to the message board then this component can easily be put inside a Microsoft Transaction Server package. This would ensure that all transactions are either committed or rolled back to help prevent corruption even further.

Ease of use

Messages must be readable with just one click as should creating new messages and replying to existing ones.

Hopefully users will bookmark the page and quickly stop by on a regular basis just to see if new messages have been posted. Therefore, they should be able to quickly spot when there are new messages and replies.

As far as possible, everything should be immediately obvious. If it needs a 300 page online manual then something's gone badly wrong.

Accessible to Widest Range of Users

My experience is that Internet Explorer 4 and 5 currently make up 65% of browsers out there. This still means a large minority of non-IE users who can't be ignored, however tempting that may be.

However, this does leave unpleasant choices. Do you write to maximise sophistication and functionality for each and every browser and operating system? In which case cancel all holidays, you have a lot of work ahead.

Or do you aim for lowest common denominator and write something plain, boring but works with Internet Explorer 2 minor version 3b on a Unix box?

The option I have chosen is a compromise. There are two versions of the message board, one for Internet Explorer 4 and 5 and one for all other browsers. However, for this case study I am only going to concentrate on the IE version. This will exclude 35 percent of the internet population but I will leave the extra coding up to you. There is room within the code to implement support for other browsers.

With the IE version I can be a little daring in my use of technologies. It uses VBScript (and Jscript where necessary) so VB developers should feel at home when writing the client-side script. It also makes use of IE's Dynamic Html and Cascading Style Sheets.

Finally it also uses a fairly new Microsoft technology called Remote Scripting, which allows script functions in an ASP page to be executed without actually navigating to the page.

A Look at the Finished Product

To enable you to understand what we're aiming for, let's take a look at one I prepared earlier.

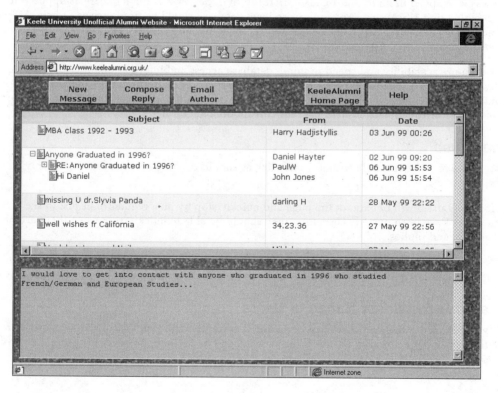

Messages are displayed within a tree-like structure with the latest messages being shown first.

Clicking on a message header line (either the Subject, From or Date area) will cause the message to be displayed in the gray text area (which is set to read-only). The message body is obtained from the database using remote scripting so there's no need to navigate to a different page.

The existence of sub messages is shown by an image depicting a plus sign. Clicking on a plus sign will cause the sub messages in the next level down to be displayed. Clicking a minus sign hides the sub level messages.

The message headers are all displayed within an **IFRAME** window. As the user's mouse runs over a message heading it changes color (using Dynamic HTML) to blue and reverts to black as the mouse moves off. A message thread is displayed in a single colored block. If a message has been posted since the user last visited, then its heading line will be in bold (which changes to normal font if clicked). If a new sub message has been posted then it will be bold and so will the top level message in the same thread. This makes it clear when there is a new sub message without the user having to open up all the messages above it.

To create a new message or reply to an existing message the user presses the buttons at the top of the page and a separate modal dialog window opens above the page in which they can type their message.

You can view a live demo version of the board at:
`http://www.keelealumni.org.uk/MessageboardDemo`

Architecture Overview

Logical View

Logically we can split the architecture into 3 tiers or layers. The data services layer storing and providing the information we need, the middleware layer containing our business objects which apply the rules of our business and the presentation layer displaying the information from the data services layer as interpreted and manipulated by the business layer.

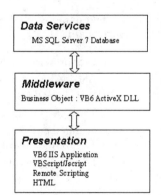

Data Services
MS SQL Server 7 Database

Middleware
Business Object : VB6 ActiveX DLL

Presentation
VB6 IIS Application
VBScript/Jscript
Remote Scripting
HTML

Physical Diagram

Though the logical view shows where the code lies conceptually, physically it's a different matter. Each of the boxes in the diagram represents a different computer, though its common for the Internet Information Server and SQL Server database to be on the same machine, although scalability will suffer. Inside the boxes, you can see what code runs on what computer.

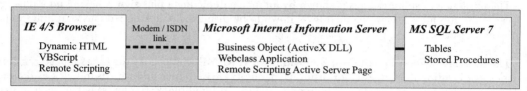

Interaction between tiers

Although the user's actions in the browser may differ, they may click a link or hit a form submit button, the basic interaction between layers remains the same as the diagram below shows.

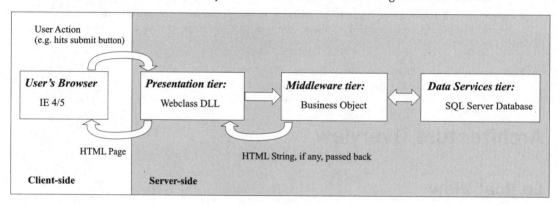

This is best demonstrated by giving a simplified example of what happens when a user browses to the message board.

> ➤ User browses to URL of webclass ASP file
> ➤ ASP file instantiates the webclass DLL
> ➤ Webclass DLL's `Start` method fires
> ➤ The `Start` method writes out the HTM template file which will contain the message
> ➤ Within the HTM Template is a Webclass Tag when the webclass arrives here it fires the Process Tag event for that Template
> ➤ Process Tag event instantiates our middleware DLL and executes its `GetMessages` method
> ➤ DLL's `GetMessages` method obtains message headers from database via stored procedure `GetMessages`
> ➤ Message header records converted into a string of HTML by `GetMessages` method
> ➤ HTML string passed back to webclass process tag method

> ➤ Webclass process tag method replaces the space between the webclass tags in the html template with the HTML string (our message headers)
> ➤ The middleware DLL is destroyed, though there may be some delay before it's released from memory
> ➤ Webclass completes writing the HTML to the client browser
> ➤ Webclass released from memory, again there may be some delay

Building the Message Board

The actual creation of the project splits nicely into the three tiers listed previously. Central to everything is the database and that's where we'll start. The order in which the layers and components within those layers will be built is as follows:

Part One:

> ➤ The database, firstly the tables, and then the four stored procedures and transaction
> ➤ Our business object, the ActiveX DLL which will act as the central focus for any server side processing

Part Two:

> ➤ The webclass code and associated HTM templates
> ➤ The client-side scripting within the templates
> ➤ The ASP page containing the method to be accessed by client-side Remote Scripting

The Database

In this section, I will explain how to set up the database components of this message board. I will guide you through setting up two tables and creating stored procedures. Finally, we shall set up a database login and a new ODBC Data Source.

Creating the message board database

First we need to use SQL Server's Enterprise Manager to create a new database.

Open Enterprise Manager and click Server group so that you can see the name of your SQL server. Click your server to expand it so you can see Databases.

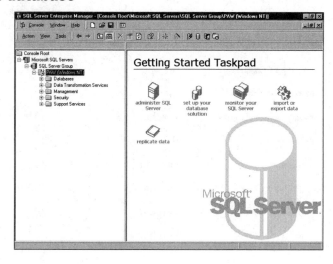

Right click
Databases and
select New
Database. This
opens a dialog box
for specifying
details for the
database. Type
MessageBoard
into the name box,
and then click OK.
The other default
values are fine for
our purposes.

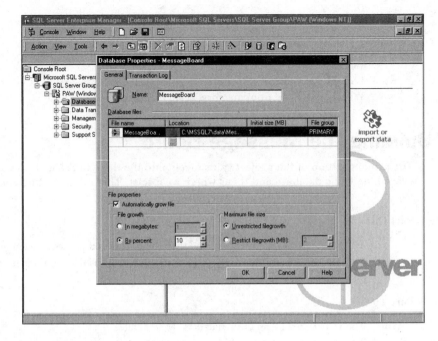

Creating the Message table

If you click Databases in Enterprise Manager, you should see MessageBoard listed. Click on the
MessageBoard database to open it up then right click Tables and select New Table. In the dialog
box that pops up, enter Message for the table name then click OK.

The field names and properties you need to enter are listed below

Column Name	Datatype	Length	Allow Nulls
MessageId	int	4	No
MessageBoardId	int	4	No
TopSection	int	4	No
MessageOrder	int	4	No
Indents	int	4	No
Remote_Address	varchar	50	No
DateSent	datetime	8	Yes
Subject	varchar	40	Yes
Message	varchar	4000	Yes
VisitorName	varchar	20	Yes
Email	varchar	50	Yes

634

It's important to make `MessageId` field an identity field by checking the **Identity** box. Also make `MessageId` and `MessageBoardId` primary key fields by clicking on `MessageId`, holding the control key down and clicking `MessageBoardId` then right clicking and selecting **Set Primary Key**. After completion your table design view should be as below.

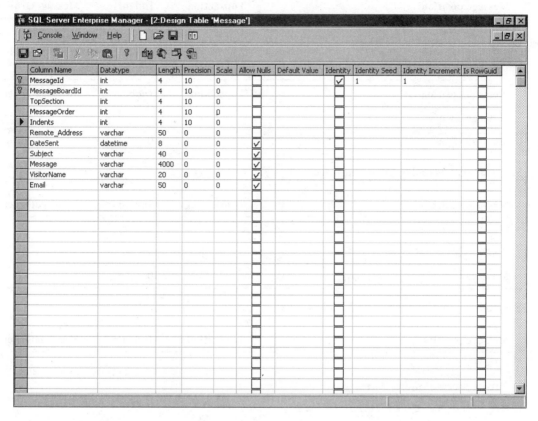

The first five columns have to be set to not allow nulls as these are important columns which are used for searching and row comparison. By not allowing nulls, we avoid the headache they can give in query writing.

The `MessageId` and `MessageBoardId` fields are used for uniquely identifying a message belonging to a particular message board. If in future we decided to add further message boards to the site then having a `MessageBoardId` allows us this room for expansion. Currently it is always set to 1.

`TopSection` field is a unique number given to the top message in a message thread and its replies. The `Indents` field indicates under which subsection of a `TopSection` field a message belongs to. The `Indents` field is also used to determine how many times to indent a message thread when creating the HTML. The `MessageOrder` field runs from 1 to the number of messages on the board, and helps determine the display order on an HTML page of each message heading. We want the latest messages to appear at the top of the board, so message headers are by `TopSection` in descending order and then by `MessageOrder` in ascending order.

Let's look at an example to clarify how the table operates.

The first message is posted.

Message position	Topsection	Indents	MessageOrder
Message One	1	0	1

A second Message is posted.

Message position	Topsection	Indents	MessageOrder
Message Two	2	0	2
Message One	1	0	1

Someone replies to the second message.

Message position	Topsection	Indents	MessageOrder
Message Two	2	0	2
Reply to Message Two	2	1	3
Message One	1	0	1

Someone replies to the reply to Message Two.

Message position	Topsection	Indents	MessageOrder
Message Two	2	0	2
Reply to Message Two	2	1	3
Reply to Reply of Message Two	2	2	4
Message One	1	0	1

Finally, someone replies to Message One.

Message position	Topsection	Indents	MessageOrder
Message Two	2	0	3
Reply to Message Two	2	1	4
Reply to Reply of Message Two	2	2	5
Message One	1	0	1
Reply to Message One	1	1	2

The MessageWrite Table

We now need to create a second table. This table's only purpose is to provide us with a way of ensuring that a SQL Server transaction, which adds a message to the Message table, is atomic. Or in other words, it succeeds completely or it fails and is rolled back completely. What we don't want is a transaction that half completes and leaves the database corrupted. We will see later how this second table is going to help us.

As before, right click on tables and select **Create New Table**. Name the table **MessageWrite**. Then add one field with the name **InAddTransaction**, data type is bit and uncheck **Allow Nulls**.

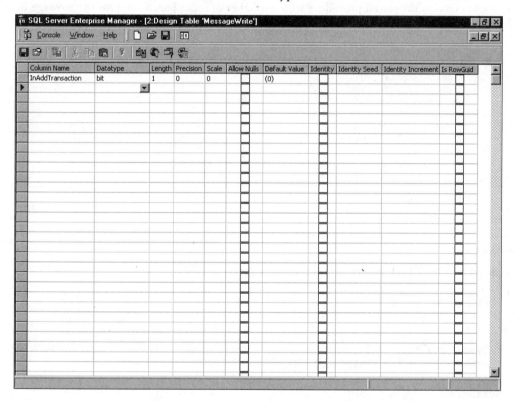

Now save and close the table. We now need to add just one record to it. In the main Enterprise manager view under `MessageBoard`'s tables right click **MessageWrite**, and select **Open Table** followed by **Return All Rows**. From here you can add the one row and give it the value 1.

Creating the Stored Procedures and Transaction

All access to and from the database tables is via stored procedures. Being pre-compiled, they offer speedy advantages over using SQL strings. They also take on some of the business logic and reduce the number of round trips necessary over the network by doing some pre-processing on the data. A further advantage is ease of maintainability of the code. If we need to change the underlying tables in the database, we need only re-write the stored procedures and not code in any business objects as long as we provide the business objects with the information they are accepting. Finally, stored procedures are easier to debug and keep your SQL statements in one place.

AddMessage

Having completed the boring administration, it's now time to move on to some real coding. The first of the five stored procedures we need is the one that adds a new message to the database. This has been designed as a multi-purpose routine. It also handles a new message being added or a reply to an existing message. This saves VB code in the DLL we will develop later and it reduces the number of stored procedures. As a result, it will be used more often on a busy message board and there is a greater chance it will be cached in memory by the SQL Server when a user adds a message – which speeds up the message board's response time.

The code creates the stored procedure with a number of input parameters for the message details to be passed. Three local variables are also declared.

```
CREATE PROCEDURE [AddMessage]
(   @VisitorName varchar(20) = "No Name",
    @Email varchar(50) = "",
    @Subject varchar(40) ="No Subject",
    @Message varchar(4000) = "No Message",
    @Remote_Address varchar(50) = "",
    @MessageBoardId int = 1,
    @ReplyToMessageId int = -1
)

AS

declare @NewOrder int
declare @Indents int
declare @TopSection int
```

GetMessage

Using a basic SELECT statement, we retrieve a message's details.

```
CREATE PROCEDURE [GetMessage]
( @MessageBoardID int, @MessageID int )
AS

SELECT Message, VisitorName, Remote_Address, DateSent, Subject, Email FROM Message
WHERE MessageID = @MessageID AND MessageBoardId = @MessageBoardId
```

GetMessages

The next stored procedure returns a recordset of all the messages on the board, in the correct display order.

However, headers are displayed in bold font if they have been posted since the user's last visit. Where there are new messages posted to one of the sub sections of a message thread then the top level message is also in bold. To minimize round trips to the database, this calculation of when a message should be in bold is made here in the stored procedure. @NewMessageId is null when no new messages and the MessageId of the new message when there are. The stored procedure starts simply enough:

```
CREATE PROCEDURE [GetMessages]
( @MessageBoardID int, @DateLastVisit datetime = "1/1/1980")
AS
SELECT    M1.MessageId,        M1.Indents,
          M1.VisitorName, M1.Email,
          M1.DateSent,    M1.Subject,
          M2.MessageID AS NewMessageID
```

But it then descends into a multiple self join and derived table.

```
FROM Message AS M1 LEFT OUTER JOIN Message AS M2
    ON   M1.MessageID = M2.MessageID   AND
         ( (M2.DateSent > @DateLastVisit)   OR
           (M2.Indents = 0 AND
           EXISTS
           (SELECT TopSection FROM Message AS M3
                    WHERE M3.TopSection = M2.TopSection AND
                          M3.DateSent > @DateLastVisit AND
                          M3.MessageOrder > M2.MessageOrder)))
WHERE M1.MessageBoardId = @MessageBoardId
ORDER BY  M1.TopSection DESC, M1.MessageOrder
```

It all makes sense when broken down in stages. Firstly, we do the self join as a LEFT OUTER JOIN. We want all the message headers from Message table as M1 even when no match exists in Message table as M2. M2 exists just to provide the message id of any new messages or sub messages. M1 and M2 tables are correlated to each other using the unique MessageId.

M2 returns a row where the message in that row was posted after @DateLastVisited (the date the message board was last viewed by the user).

```
FROM Message AS M1 LEFT OUTER JOIN Message AS M2
    ON   M1.MessageID = M2.MessageID    AND
         ( (M2.DateSent > @DateLastVisit)
```

However we also want to include M2's message id if it's the top section message in a thread, or Indents equals 0 and there are any new sub messages under it. The sub query retrieves rows which have been added since the last visit for the TopSection. We make sure M3's message order is greater than M2's to exclude sub messages under the same TopSection but prior to this particular thread and therefore unrelated.

```
OR
    (M2.Indents = 0 AND
        EXISTS
                (SELECT TopSection FROM Message AS M3
                        WHERE M3.TopSection = M2.TopSection AND
                              M3.DateSent > @DateLastVisit AND
                              M3.MessageOrder > M2.MessageOrder)))
```

NumberOfReplies

This stored procedure returns the MessageId of all messages that have sub messages below them. Its used when creating the HTML for the list of messages to determine when a plus image should be included to allow the user to open up the thread and display the next sub level of messages.

The query is an inner self join returning a MessageId from table Message as M1 when a sub message is found for it in table Message as M2. We know a sub message exists if a row has the same TopSection, the Indents are one greater and it's next in the MessageOrder.

```
CREATE PROCEDURE [NumberOfReplies]
( @MessageBoardID int )
AS
SELECT M1.MessageId FROM Message M1 JOIN Message M2
ON    (M2.TopSection = M1.TopSection) AND
      (M1.MessageOrder + 1 = M2.MessageOrder) AND
      (M1.Indents = (M2.Indents - 1))
WHERE M1.MessageBoardId = @MessageBoardID
AND M2.MessageBoardId = @MessageBoardID
GROUP BY M1.MessageID
```

Atomic transactions

It is very important that a database should never be left in a corrupted state, for example if two messages were to be given the same MessageOrder. We want our transactions which write to the database to be atomic, a single unit that succeeds or fails and doesn't affect other transactions which may be running concurrently. It is for this reason we created the WriteMessage table. A first step is putting our SQL within a Transaction. We perform error checking so that if something goes wrong at any point during the transaction, it is rolled back and our database remains free of invalid data. If all has gone okay then we commit the transaction at the very end.

Having begun the transaction the first thing we do is update the MessageWrite table's one record. The value held by the row is of no importance; it is just given its current value reversed. However what is important is that table is now locked and no changes can be made to it until we have committed our changes, which we do at the very end of the stored procedure once the new message has been added to the Message table.

If a second user tries to add a new record then their stored procedure will be unable to update the MessageWrite table and will halt at that point, waiting until the first user's stored procedure releases its lock on the MessageWrite table at which point the second user's stored procedure continues. The advantage of only locking this second table during a message add is that the Message table can still be read by users asking to view messages but not asking to write messages, limiting the danger of bottlenecks and increasing scalability. You may think this is all a lot of trouble to go to and for a message board on a low use website you would be right. On a high hit rate website however, where we might be getting a few hundred concurrent users, the possibility of two or more people trying to add a message at the same time becomes much greater.

```
BEGIN TRANSACTION
-- Updating MessageWrite Locks it during this transaction
UPDATE MessageWrite
SET InAddTransaction =  ~InAddTransAction
-- NEW MESSAGE NOT A REPLY TO EXISTING MESSAGE
```

If this is a new message rather than a reply to an existing message then @ReplyToMessageId will be −1. The TopSection will be the current highest TopSection + 1.

```
IF @ReplyToMessageId < 1
BEGIN
    SET @Indents = 0
    SELECT @TopSection = MAX(TopSection), @NewOrder = MAX(MessageOrder) FROM
      Message WHERE MessageBoardId = @MessageBoardID
    SET @TopSection = ISNULL(@TopSection,0) + 1
    SET @NewOrder =  ISNULL(@NewOrder,0) + 1
    IF (@@ERROR <> 0) GOTO on_error
END
```

The code to insert a reply to an existing message is more complex. It must be able to handle a reply to any depth of nested sub message. Firstly, the `MessageOrder` and `TopSection` of the message being replied to are retrieved, and then the order for the new message is calculated. If there are already replies to the message, then the new order is simply the maximum order of the replies plus one. Because we are in an atomic transaction and because other users are prevented from adding records until we are finished, we can be sure that our calculation of the `@NewOrder` will still be valid by the time the code reaches the end and actually inserts the new message.

```
ELSE

-- REPLY TO EXISTING MESSAGE
BEGIN

    declare @MessageOrder int
    SELECT @MessageOrder = MessageOrder,  @TopSection = TopSection, @Indents =
(Indents + 1)
    FROM Message WHERE MessageID = @ReplyToMessageID AND MessageBoardID =
@MessageBoardID

    IF (@@ERROR <> 0) GOTO on_error

    SET @NewOrder = (SELECT ISNULL(MAX(MessageOrder), -1)
                        FROM Message
                        WHERE  TopSection = @TopSection AND
                               MessageBoardId = @MessageBoardId AND
                               Indents >= @Indents) + 1
    IF (@@ERROR <> 0) GOTO on_error
```

If this is the first reply to the message then the maximum will return null. We also need to check `@NewOrder` does not relate to a reply to a message higher up the same thread. `NewOrder` is simply the `Order` of the message being replied to, plus one.

We then need to make space in the order chain by incrementing the `MessageOrder` of all messages after our message to be inserted. This is another area that would be particularly susceptible to data corruption due to concurrent users if we had not made our transaction atomic.

```
-- WHERE THE FIRST SUB MESSAGE REPLY TO A HIGHER LEVEL MESSAGE
    IF (@NewOrder = 0) OR (@NewOrder <= @MessageOrder)
    BEGIN
      SET @NewOrder = (@MessageOrder + 1)
    END

    UPDATE Message
    SET MessageOrder = MessageOrder + 1
    WHERE MessageOrder >= (@NewOrder) AND MessageBoardId = @MessageBoardId
    IF (@@ERROR <> 0) GOTO on_error
END
```

Finally, with all the values calculated we can insert the message, commit the transaction and release the locks on `MessageWrite` allowing other users to add messages.

```
INSERT INTO Message (MessageBoardId, TopSection, MessageOrder, Indents,
Remote_Address, DateSent, Subject, Message, VisitorName, Email )
VALUES (@MessageBoardId,@TopSection,@NewOrder, @Indents, @Remote_Address,
GetDate(), @Subject,@Message,@VisitorName, @Email)
IF (@@ERROR <> 0) GOTO on_error
COMMIT TRANSACTION
RETURN(0)

on_error:
ROLLBACK TRANSACTION
RETURN(1)
```

As you can see the stored procedures are more than just dumb SQL simply inserting data, they also do a lot of the calculations and decision-making. By doing this within a stored procedure we limit the number of round trips made between our business object and the database.

Creating a new database login

From within Enterprise Manager expand the tree so that you see security. Then open this up to reveal Logins.

Right click Logins and select New Login. Enter MBUser in the Name box, change Authentication to SQL Server Authentication and enter the password as inabottle

Change the default database to MessageBoard using the combo box at the bottom of the dialog box.

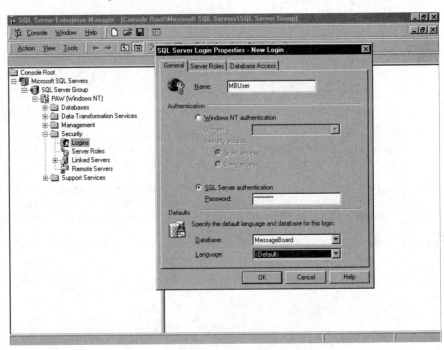

Now click the tab Database Access and under "Specify what databases can be accessed by this login" tick the box next to MessageBoard.

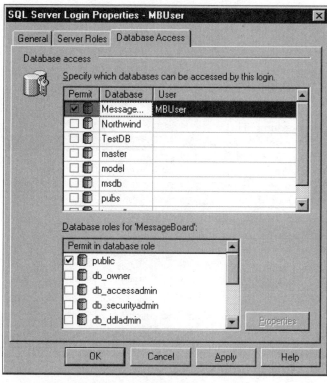

Click OK to confirm the password and return to the main Enterprise Manager screen.

Now expand the tree so we can see the MessageBoard database. Open it up to reveal Users and click on Users. Right click MBUser and select properties. A new dialog box appears, click the Permissions button.

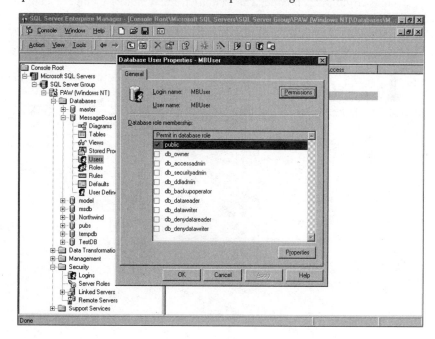

In the permissions box that's opened, tick the **Exec** (execute permission) for each of our five stored procedures. This is the only access that `MBUser` will have to our database, which helps to keeps security tight.

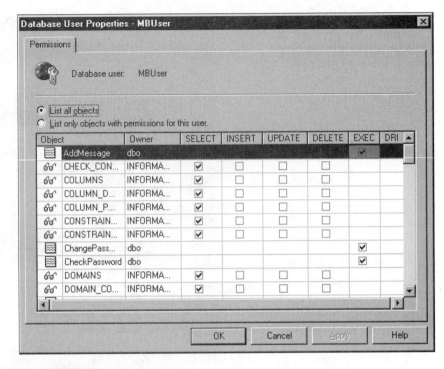

Creating a new ODBC Data Source

The final database related task is to create a new ODBC Data Source to allow us to access the database from our VB code. This is done from Windows Control Panel, by double clicking the ODBC icon

Select the System DSN tab and click **Add**. This will open the Create New Data Source Dialog. Select **SQL Server** and then click **Finish**.

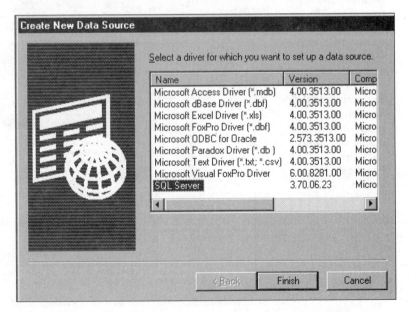

In the dialog box that appears, enter MessageBoard in Name, and then select your SQL Server from the pull down list. For development purposes this will most likely be (local).

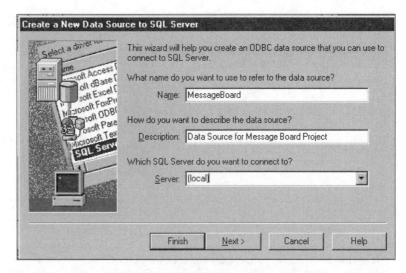

Click Next. In the dialog box that appears set the "How should SQL Server verify the authenticity of the login ID" radio button to "With SQL Server authentication". In the login ID box, enter MBUser. For the password, enter inabottle

Now click Next.

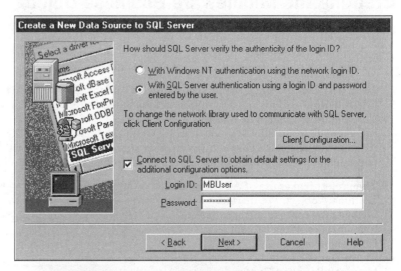

If you enter an incorrect Login ID or password, you'll see the dialog below and need to check your ID/password used.

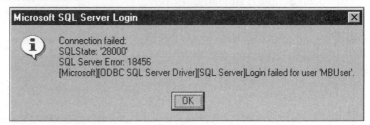

In the next screen, we may need to change the default database used to MessageBoard. This depends on how many databases MBUser has access to.

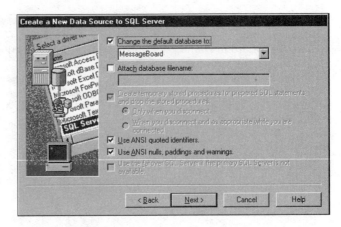

Click Next, then accept the default settings and click Finish.

If all has gone okay, you should see a Dialog box telling you that a new ODBC data source will be set up. Click Test Data Source to confirm it's working, and then click OK. The ODBC data source set-up is now complete.

Creating the Middleware Business Object

The first thing we need to do is to open Visual Basic and create a new ActiveX DLL project. VB creates one new class for us which we need to re-name to something more memorable and appropriate, so let's call it clsMBBusObject. It should have its Instancing property set to MultiUse. This will ensure that the object is creatable outside the project.

Next, we need to change the project settings. From the general tab, change the project's name to MessageBoardDB and its description to MessageBoardDB also. It's a good idea to tick the Unattended Execution box, as this makes all MsgBox commands, and any other messages to the screen, write to the App log (which in NT4 you can view using the Event Viewer under NT's Administrative Tools). Given this is a server side component, the last thing we want is a message box popping up in some corner of a deserted server room, waiting for user input that'll never happen.

The project makes use of ADO and the Dictionary object. We therefore need to include references to the appropriate type libraries. From Project, References menu select Microsoft Active Data Objects 2.1 Library and Microsoft Scripting Runtime.

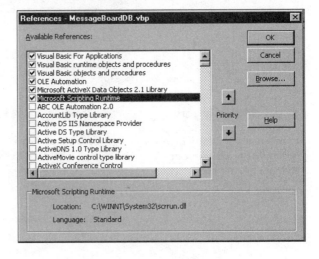

Before we continue, we need to create a new class because Visual Basic is surprisingly inefficient at concatenating strings. Using "MyString = MyString & "some more string"" is fine for limited concatenation but if you are doing a lot of concatenating then it is worth using this CStringBuffer class (which I myself inherited from a newsgroup and amended). Performance tests suggest that in bulk concatenation it's 40 – 60 times faster.

The first thing we need to do is add a new class module to your VB project. Name it CStringBuffer and set its Instancing property to Private.

The code for the module is fairly simple. It creates a string filled with spaces to act as a buffer and instead of concatenating strings, it inserts them into the string buffer using the Mid$ function. When the buffer is full, a new buffer chunk is appended to the existing buffer and insertion continues into there.

Firstly, at the top of the class the module variables are declared

```
Option Explicit

Private Const STRING_BUFFER_SIZE As Long = 4096

'class member data
Private mlBufPos  As Long  'the physical position within the buffer
Private mlBufSize As Long  'the total preallocated buffer size
Private msBuf As String    'the buffer itself
```

Next, code is added to the class initialize and terminate events.

```
Private Sub Class_Initialize()
'Initializes the buffer size and position.
    Clear
End Sub

Private Sub Class_Terminate()
'Cleans up the buffer, really unnecessary since VB will take care
    On Error Resume Next
    msBuf = vbNullString
End Sub
```

Then create the Append routine, which appends data to the buffer. It uses the current buffer position as the beginning point for insertion. If the required size of the buffer is too small to accommodate the append operation, then a new chunk of size STRING_BUFFER_SIZE is added to the current buffer size. Once expanded, the buffer will *not* shrink unless explicitly done so via the Clear member function.

```
Public Sub Append(ByVal TheText As String)

    On Error GoTo ErrorHandler

    Dim BytesToAppend As Long
    Dim TargetSize As Long

    BytesToAppend = Len(TheText)
    TargetSize = mlBufPos + BytesToAppend
```

```
      If TargetSize < mlBufSize Then
          Mid$(msBuf, mlBufPos, BytesToAppend) = TheText
          mlBufPos = TargetSize
      Else
          msBuf = msBuf & Space$(STRING_BUFFER_SIZE)
          mlBufSize = mlBufSize + STRING_BUFFER_SIZE
          Append TheText
      End If

      Exit Sub

  ErrorHandler:
      HandleError Err.Number, Err.Description, Err.Source, "CStringBuffer_Append"

  End Sub
```

The class's only property, Value, is created next. It simply allows us to get/let the buffer contents. The Let property does not resize the buffer, just sets the buffer insert position to 1 and overwrites the existing contents with the new value.

```
  Public Property Get Value() As String
      Value = Left$(msBuf, mlBufPos - 1)
  End Property

  Public Property Let Value(NewValue As String)
      mlBufPos = 1
      Append NewValue
  End Property
```

The Clear subroutine makes the buffer insertion point one, blanks out the buffer's contents with spaces and resets it to the default buffer size contained in the class constant STRING_BUFFER_SIZE.

```
  Public Sub Clear()
      On Error GoTo ErrorHandler

      'Initialize/reinitialize the buffer.
      'Sets the buffer to an "empty" state.
      mlBufSize = STRING_BUFFER_SIZE
      msBuf = Space$(mlBufSize)
      mlBufPos = 1
      Exit Sub

  ErrorHandler:
      HandleError Err.Number, Err.Description, Err.Source, "CStringBuffer_Clear"

  End Sub
```

Finally we have the all important HandleError routine which writes any errors raised in the class methods to the Windows Application event log, and then raises an error which will be caught by the MessageDB class, which passes the details on to the Webclass, which handles how the error is presented to the user (if at all).

```
Private Sub HandleError(lErrNumber As Long, sErrDesc As String, _
   sErrSource As String, sOccurredIn As String)

   App.LogEvent "Error in " & sOccurredIn & " Number = " & lErrNumber & _
      vbCrLf & " Description = " & sErrDesc & vbCrLf & " Source=" & _
      sErrSource
   Err.Raise vbObjectError + lErrNumber, sErrSource & " : " & sOccurredIn, _
      sErrDesc

End Sub
```

Creating the HTML for the Message Header List

Returning to the `clsMBBusObject` class, we need to add a number of module level constants which are used by this method. These need to be declared right at the top of our class module so they have module level scope.

```
' HTML TAG constants

Private Const PLUS_IMAGE As String = "<IMG SRC='./pageimages/plus.gif' _
   align=absMiddle "

Private Const MESSAGE_IMAGE As String = "<IMG     align=top _
   src='./pageimages/message.gif' border=0 style='MARGIN-BOTTOM : 1px'"

Private Const NONIE_MESSAGE_IMAGE As String = "<IMG  align=top _
   src='./pageimages/message.gif' border=0 "

Private Const SPAN_TAG As String = "<SPAN style='DISPLAY: none' "

Private Const IENEW_ROW_IVORY As String = "<TR bgcolor=Ivory><TD _
   NOWRAP><DL><DD "

Private Const IENEW_ROW_LACE As String = "<TR bgcolor=OldLace><TD _
   NOWRAP><DL><DD "

' Enumerator for type of message in thread
' Used in GetMessages and GetNonIEMessages methods
Private Enum MessageType
   TopLevel
   NewSubLevel
   Message
End Enum

' Connection string for ODBC datasource
Private Const DBCONNSTRING = "DSN=MessageBoard;UID=MBUser;PWD=inabottle"
```

The Images included here can obviously be whatever you choose. If you wish to use mine, then just place "http://wwww.keelealumni.org.uk/" before the src paths. Or better still, download them and save them on to your web server..

Now we can start creating the `GetMessages` function. A number of local variables are defined and then an ADO Connection is opened to the database. A separate connection object has been created, rather than using ADO Recordsets implicit connection object creation because we need to access the connection twice. Notice that the function takes a lot of parameters which is partly a consequence of our server side objects needing to be stateless, which prevents us from using public properties.

```
Public Function GetMessages(lMessageBoardID As Long, sDateFrom As String, _
    sDateTo As String, sLastVisit As String, sErrorString As String) As String

    On Error GoTo ErrorHandler

    Dim loReplies As New Dictionary ' Stores MessageId of messages with a reply
    Dim loAppendSubject As New CStringBuffer ' Contains Subject HTML String
    Dim loAppendPerson As New CStringBuffer ' Contains Person HTML String
    Dim loAppendDate As New CStringBuffer ' Contains Date HTML String
    Dim lsMessageId As String
    Dim lsNames As String    ' Used for TAG Name and ID
    Dim llPrevMessageId As Long
    Dim llPrevIndent As Long
    Dim lsFinalEndString As String ' Final end string varies depending on _
        number of replies
    Dim lsEndString As String
    Dim lsTemp As String
    Dim llMessageType As MessageType ' Enum MessageType
    Dim lsDDStyle As String
    Dim lbColour As Boolean ' Used for Thread colour block switching
    Dim llIndents As Long
    Dim lsTitle As String

    Dim llRecordCounter As Long
    Dim loConn As New ADODB.Connection
    Dim loRS As New ADODB.Recordset
    Dim vRecordsReturned() As Variant

    loConn.Open DBCONNSTRING
```

We need to know if a message has replies. A plus image is included in the HTML if there are replies so that the user can click it to open up the thread and view sub messages. The Dictionary object allows easy storage of varying amounts of data and has a useful `Exists` method, which returns whether a particular item exists within the keys of the `Dictionary`. By storing `MessageIds` of replies as keys in a `Dictionary` object we can quickly and easily search to see if a `MessageId` has replies. The `Dictionary` object uses a hash algorithm for stored keys and so is very fast and efficient in doing searches.

Also note the use of `GetRows` method of the recordset object. This populates a variant array with all the rows within a recordset and in some situations is faster than obtaining values using `RecordSet("myColumn")` and `MoveNext` to get data and move through a large recordset. However, because it pulls back all the records at once, its downside is that it does mean processing is halted until all records have been retrieved from the database. If the server is under strain then this method may prove slower. Using `MoveNext` only requires one row at a time to be retrieved from the database, which means processing can occur in between row retrieval.

```
    ' Populate loReplies Dictionary Object
    loRS.Open "NumberOfReplies " & CStr(lMessageBoardID), loConn
    If Not (loRS.BOF And loRS.EOF) Then
        vRecordsReturned = loRS.GetRows(Fields:="MessageId")

        ' returned in arrays as (Cols, Rows)
        For llRecordCounter = 0 To UBound(vRecordsReturned, 2)
            loReplies.Add CStr(vRecordsReturned(0, llRecordCounter) & ">"), ""
        Next llRecordCounter
    End If

    loRS.Close
```

Now for the meat of the method. Firstly the recordset is opened and the columns making up the message headers retrieved from the database, then the ADO `recordset.GetRows` method is used to populate a variant array. Though not strictly necessary, I have defined all the fields we want to get back from the recordset. The advantage is that it allows changes to the stored procedure without breaking the code. If we defaulted to using ordinal positions, adding a new column to our stored procedure later would result in our code failing.

```
loRS.Open "Exec GetMessages " & CStr(lMessageBoardID) & ",'" & sLastVisit _
    & "'", loConn
If Not (loRS.BOF And loRS.EOF) Then

    ' Following columns returned
    ' MessageId,Indents,MessageOrder,VisitorName
    ' Email,DateSent,Subject,Message,NewMessageID

    ' returned in arrays as (Cols, Rows)

    ' a gotcha is if you define vFieldNames to be larger than the number
    ' of columns  returned
    Dim vFieldNames(6) As Variant
    vFieldNames(0) = "MessageId"
    vFieldNames(1) = "Indents"
    vFieldNames(2) = "Email"
    vFieldNames(3) = "DateSent"
    vFieldNames(4) = "Subject"
    vFieldNames(5) = "VisitorName"
    vFieldNames(6) = "NewMessageID"

    vRecordsReturned = loRS.GetRows(Fields:=vFieldNames)
```

We loop through the variant array, row by row, creating the HTML. Lets look at the sort of HTML tags we are creating.

Our message headers are contained within a HTML table, the top of which is defined in the HTM template we'll come to when looking at the webclass. What we are doing here is building up all the individual rows (`<TR>` tags) and cells (`<TD>` tags).

All the messages for a particular thread are contained in a single row. A row is formed of 3 cells, Subject, Name and Date of Message. So in the first cell of a row we have all the subject headings for that message thread. Subject headers, except the top one, are contained in a HTML definition list tag (`<DL>`) with each subject in a list definition `<DD>` tag. Each level of replies are contained within their own `<SPAN>` tag. Initially this tag and its contents is hidden using `DISPLAY=None` property but more on this later. When the user clicks a plus sign it displays the next group of sub level messages by revealing the `<SPAN>`. For the subject cell messages we also have the message image and where necessary the plus image. The other two table cells in the row contain the person and date text inside the same type of list and span formation but with no images. A simple example may help, though note that this has had all the tag properties removed for readability.

```
<TR>
<TD>
<DL>
   <DD>
   <IMG plus image'><IMG message image>First Message
   <SPAN>
   <DL>
      <DD>
         <IMG plus image ><IMG message image>Reply To 1st Message
         <SPAN>
         <DL>
            <DD><IMG message image>RE:Reply To Reply To 1st Message
         </DL>
         </SPAN>
      <DD>
         <IMG message.gif'>2nd Reply to 1st Message
   </DL>
   </SPAN>
</DL>
</TD>
```

The font for the `<DD>` tag is set to bold for a new message posted since the user's last visit, or plain text if it's a message they have seen. We use CSS (Cascading Style Sheet) style properties to set the font.

```
' Loop through each row in array
For llRecordCounter = 0 To UBound(vRecordsReturned, 2)

' If Font Bold style for messages posted after users last visit  - Plain
' Font otherwise
lsDDStyle = IIf(vRecordsReturned(0, llRecordCounter) = _
   vRecordsReturned(6, llRecordCounter), " CLASS='clsBoldDD' ", _
   " CLASS='clsNormalDD' ")

lsMessageId = CStr(vRecordsReturned(0, llRecordCounter)) & ">"
llIndents = vRecordsReturned(1, llRecordCounter)
```

Next we determine whether a message is a new top-level message, the first message in a sub-section, or other. The distinction between them affects what end HTML tags are going to be appended. The `lsTitle` variable is populated with the message authors e-mail address if one existed, and is used as the HTML Title property for the person `<DD>` tag. In the browser, a mouse pointer over a persons name will cause a tool tip with their e-mail to be displayed.

```
' What Level of message - Top, 1st reply, or 2nd reply and greater
If llIndents = 0 Then
   llMessageType = TopLevel
Else
   llMessageType = IIf(llPrevIndent <> llIndents, NewSubLevel, Message)
End If

vRecordsReturned(2, llRecordCounter) = Trim(vRecordsReturned(2, _
   llRecordCounter))

' Setting HTML tag title to the e-mail address means it will be displayed
' when user's mouse hovers over Person name in Message Board

lsTitle = IIf(vRecordsReturned(2, llRecordCounter) = "", "", " TITLE='" _
   & vRecordsReturned(2, llRecordCounter) & "' ")
```

We deal first with creating the message header where it's the first message in a message thread. If this is not the very first message on the board, then HTML close tags are created and appended for the previous message thread's list and table cell tags.

```
If llMessageType = TopLevel Then

    ' If this is not the first message thread, then append HTML close Tags
    If llRecordCounter > 0 Then
        loAppendSubject.Append loAppendPerson.Value
        loAppendPerson.Clear

        loAppendSubject.Append loAppendDate.Value
        loAppendDate.Clear

        lsFinalEndString = "</DL></TD>"
    End If
```

First, we start with the subject part of the message header. Any close tags necessary for the previous message thread's <SPAN> and <DL> tags are added. Then we switch row background color for this thread.

The <DD> list tag with the current row's subject header is added. Using our dictionary object loReplies which we populated earlier we can determine whether this message has sub level messages and if so we insert a HTML image tag for the plus image used in the browser for opening/closing sub levels. The message image is also appended, then finally the subject title (vRecordsReturned(4, llRecordCounter)). <DD> margin sizes are set depending on the existence of the plus image; this ensures the left edge of message headers line up.

lsDDStyle determines whether the <DD> tags font will be bold or plain. Bold indicates a new message or that a new message exists in a sub section.

```
    ' Append Subject

    ' Append Close Tags for previous message Thread
    ' HTML close tags for <SPAN> and <DL>
    If llPrevIndent = 1 Then loAppendSubject.Append "</SPAN></DL>"
        loAppendSubject.Append lsFinalEndString

        ' Start new row with new colour
        lbColour = Not lbColour
        loAppendSubject.Append IIf(lbColour, IENEW_ROW_LACE, _
            IENEW_ROW_IVORY)

        ' If a message has replies - put the + sign image next to subject
        If loReplies.Exists(lsMessageId) Then
            ' Make name of tags the messageid - this will be used in browser
            ' for displaying messages
            loAppendSubject.Append lsDDStyle & _
                " STYLE='MARGIN-LEFT: 10px' id=MSGS" & lsMessageId
            loAppendSubject.Append PLUS_IMAGE & "id=ImgSub" & lsMessageId
        Else
            oAppendSubject.Append lsDDStyle & _
                " STYLE=' MARGIN-LEFT: 26px' id=MSGS" & lsMessageId
        End If
        loAppendSubject.Append MESSAGE_IMAGE & " id=MSGI" & lsMessageId
        loAppendSubject.Append vRecordsReturned(4, llRecordCounter)
```

Finally, for `TopSection` messages, we append the list, cell tags, and details of person's name, and date the message was posted. HTML Message headers for person and date have their own `CStringBuffer` object. When the message thread ends, these are concatenated to the subject HTML contained in `loAppendSubject`.

```
        ' Append Person

        lsEndString = "</DL>"
        loAppendPerson.Append lsEndString
        loAppendPerson.Append lsFinalEndString
        loAppendPerson.Append "<TD NOWRAP><DL><DD "
        loAppendPerson.Append lsTitle & lsDDStyle & _
            " STYLE=' MARGIN-LEFT: 10px' id=MSGP" & lsMessageId
        loAppendPerson.Append vRecordsReturned(5, llRecordCounter)

        ' Append Date

        loAppendDate.Append lsEndString
        loAppendDate.Append lsFinalEndString
        loAppendDate.Append "<TD NOWRAP><DL><DD STYLE=' MARGIN-LEFT: 10px' "
        loAppendDate.Append lsDDStyle & " id=MSGD" & lsMessageId
        loAppendDate.Append Format(vRecordsReturned(3, llRecordCounter), _
            "dd mmm yy hh:mm")
```

The code for dealing with non-top section messages is similar to that above. The main difference is that the HTML close tags necessary are slightly more complex. For example, a sub message thread may go any number of levels deep and then stop requiring any number of close tags.

As above for the `TopSection` the first thing we do is close the previous message's HTML tags, calculating the difference between the previous message's indents and this message's gives us how many close tags are required.

```
    Else
        ' Create the HTML close tags for last sub section(s)
        lsEndString = ""

        ' Are we moving up out of the sub messages - close off Tags if we are
        If llPrevIndent > llIndents Then
        Do While llPrevIndent <> llIndents
            lsEndString = lsEndString & "</DL></SPAN>"
            llPrevIndent = llPrevIndent - 1
        Loop
    End If
    loAppendSubject.Append lsEndString

    ' Is this the start of a new sub section higher up the message thread
    If llMessageType = NewSubLevel Then
        If llPrevIndent < llIndents Then
            loAppendSubject.Append SPAN_TAG & "id=SubjectSub" & _
                CStr(llPrevMessageId) & "><DL>"
        End If
    End If
    End If
```

Append subject header and if sub level message headers below this then include a plus image in the HTML.

```
' Append Subject
If loReplies.Exists(lsMessageId) Then
   loAppendSubject.Append "<DD STYLE='MARGIN-LEFT: 20px' " & _
      lsDDStyle & " id=MSGS" & lsMessageId
   loAppendSubject.Append PLUS_IMAGE & "id=ImgSub" & lsMessageId
Else
   loAppendSubject.Append "<DD style=' MARGIN-LEFT: 36px'" & _
      lsDDStyle & " id=MSGS" & lsMessageId
End If
loAppendSubject.Append MESSAGE_IMAGE & " id=MSGI" & lsMessageId
loAppendSubject.Append vRecordsReturned(4, llRecordCounter)
```

Now we need to append the name and date details.

```
' Append Person

' Remove <DL> tags to leave just <SPAN> tags
lsEndString = Replace(lsEndString, "</DL>", "")
loAppendPerson.Append lsEndString

If llMessageType = NewSubLevel Then
   If llPrevIndent < llIndents Then
      loAppendPerson.Append SPAN_TAG & "id=PersonSub" & _
         CStr(llPrevMessageId) & ">"
   End If
End If

loAppendPerson.Append "<DD STYLE=' MARGIN-LEFT: 10px' " & lsTitle & _
   lsDDStyle & "  id=MSGP" & lsMessageId
loAppendPerson.Append vRecordsReturned(5, llRecordCounter)

' Append Date

loAppendDate.Append lsEndString

If llMessageType = NewSubLevel Then
   If llPrevIndent < llIndents Then
      loAppendDate.Append SPAN_TAG & "id=DateSub" & _
         CStr(llPrevMessageId) & ">"
   End If
End If
loAppendDate.Append "<DD STYLE=' MARGIN-LEFT: 10px' " & lsDDStyle & _
   " id=MSGD" & lsMessageId
loAppendDate.Append Format(vRecordsReturned(3, llRecordCounter), _
   "dd mmm yy hh:mm")
End If
```

Now we have reached the end of the loop we continue looping until HTML for all message headers has been created.

```
llPrevMessageId = vRecordsReturned(0, llRecordCounter)
llPrevIndent = llIndents

Next llRecordCounter
```

Finally, we concatenate the HTML created individually for Subject, person and Date and pass the HTML string back to the webclass for inserting into an HTML template.

```
    ' Join Subject, Person and Date HTML to make final
    ' string to be passed back to webclass
    loAppendSubject.Append loAppendPerson.Value
    loAppendSubject.Append loAppendDate.Value
    GetMessages = loAppendSubject.Value & "</DL></SPAN>"
    Else
    ' Where a message board with no message - no HTML!!!
    GetMessages = ""
    End If
    Exit Function

  ErrorHandler:
    GetMessages = "Error in GetMessages " & Err.Description
    sErrorString = Err.Description

End Function
```

Retrieving an existing message

To retrieve the body text of a message in the message board, we use an ADO recordset to execute the GetMessage stored procedure created earlier. As we are only accessing the database once I have not created an explicit ADO Connection object but enabled the ADO Recordset to create one itself by passing the database connection string.

```
    Public Function GetMessage(lMessageBoardID As Long, lMessageID As Long,
    sErrorString As String) As String
    On Error GoTo ErrorHandler
        Dim       loRS As New ADODB.Recordset
        loRS.Open "Exec GetMessage " & CStr(lMessageBoardID) & "," &_
                CStr(lMessageID), DBCONNSTRING
        GetMessage = CStr(loRS("Message"))
        loRS.Close
        Set loRS = Nothing
    Exit Function
    ErrorHandler:
        GetMessage = "Error in GetMessage " & Err.Description
        sErrorString = Err.Description

    End Function
```

Adding a new message

ADO offers a sometimes-confusing range of ways of doing essentially the same thing. In this subroutine, an AddMessage stored procedure is executed to add a new record. Here I have created a Command object, manually populated its parameters and attached it to a connection object, and then executed it. One of the numerous other ways would have been to just create a Connection object and use its Execute method, passing a SQL string with the name of the stored procedure and its parameters concatenated to it. For example:

```
    loConn.Execute "myQuery " & firstparam & "," & secondparam & ""......
```

Why do it the way I have? Firstly creating a SQL string by concatenating the parameters our sub routine has been passed runs the risk of falling foul of the dreaded unclosed quotes problem. For example, if the message the user typed in contains a single quote then that causes SQL to think the string it has been passed has ended – then it wonders what the rest of the string is, and that promptly throws an error. For example, if we executed using the code:

```
loConn.Execute "myStoredProc '" & myStringParameter & "'"
```

If `myStringParameter` contains a single quote, SQL Server sees our query as `loConn.Execute "myStoredProc 'my string parameter's value'`, and thinks the string ended at parameter' rather than at value'

Using manual parameters with a `Command` object sidesteps this issue. Also, manually populating the Command object's parameters reduces the number of round trips to the database ADO has to make. When automatically populating `Parameter` objects ADO does a test query on the database with sample data to find out what type of parameters it is dealing with, using manual parameters avoids this overhead.

Okay, lets create the subroutine:

```
Public Sub AddMessage(sSubject As String, sName As String, sEmail As String, _
    sMessage As String, sRemote_Address As String, lMessageBoardID As Long, _
    sErrorString As String, Optional lMessageID As Long = -1)

    On Error GoTo ErrorHandler

    ' Prevent it failure due to a too long a string being passed
    If Len(sMessage) > 4000 Then sMessage = Left$(sMessage, 4000)
    If Len(sName) > 20 Then sName = Left$(sName, 20)
    If Len(sSubject) > 40 Then sSubject = Left$(sSubject, 40)
    If Len(sEmail) > 50 Then sEmail = Left$(sEmail, 50)


    Dim loPrm As ADODB.Parameter
    Dim loCommand As New ADODB.Command

    ' Create and open ADO connection
    Dim loConn As New ADODB.Connection
    loConn.Open DBCONNSTRING
    loConn.CursorLocation = adUseClient

    ' Create ADO command object which will execute our stored procedure
    loCommand.CommandText = "AddMessage"
    loCommand.CommandType = adCmdStoredProc
    loCommand.Name = "AddMessage"

    ' MessageID ofg -1 indicates to
    ' stored procedure used that this is a new message
    lMessageID = IIf(lMessageID = 0, -1, lMessageID)
```

Having created our command and connection object, we now populate the command object with the stored procedure's parameters.

```
' Manually Populate Command Object's parameters    Set loPrm = _
    loCommand.CreateParameter("RV", adInteger, adParamReturnValue)
LoCommand.Parameters.Append loPrm

Set loPrm = loCommand.CreateParameter("VisitorName", adVarChar,_
            adParamInput,20)
loCommand.Parameters.Append loPrm

Set loPrm = loCommand.CreateParameter("Email", adVarChar, adParamInput, 50)
loCommand.Parameters.Append loPrm

Set loPrm = loCommand.CreateParameter("Subject", adVarChar, adParamInput, _
            40)
loCommand.Parameters.Append loPrm

Set loPrm = loCommand.CreateParameter("Message", adVarChar, adParamInput, _
            4000)
loCommand.Parameters.Append loPrm

Set loPrm = loCommand.CreateParameter("Remote_Address", adVarChar, _
            adParamInput, 50)
loCommand.Parameters.Append loPrm

Set loPrm = loCommand.CreateParameter("MessageBoardId", adInteger, _
            adParamInput, 25)
loCommand.Parameters.Append loPrm

Set loPrm = loCommand.CreateParameter("ReplyToMessageId", adInteger, _
            adParamInput)
loCommand.Parameters.Append loPrm
```

Finally we execute the command object and then clear up after ourselves.

```
' Execute Command - AddMessage stored procedure will add message to the
' database
Set loCommand.ActiveConnection = loConn
loConn.AddMessage sName, sEmail, sSubject, sMessage, sRemote_Address, _
    lMessageBoardID, lMessageID

' If the new message insert failed then pass this knowledge onto
' presentation component which can let the user know
If loCommand.Parameters("RV") <> 0 Then
    Err.Raise vbObjectError, "AddMessage", "ADDFAILED"
End If
loConn.Close

Set loCommand = Nothing
Set loConn = Nothing
Exit Sub

ErrorHandler:
sErrorString = Err.Description

End Sub
```

Creating the DLL file

Create a new directory for your project and then save it. Before we can move on to the IIS application we need to make the `MessageBoardDB.DLL` file. This will allow us to reference it from our IIS application.

As we have completed the public interface of the Business object's methods, it would be a good idea to change the project's compatibility from Project Level to Binary Level. If we don't do this and we later change one of the method signatures, or delete one of the methods, then it will render the DLL incompatible with any existing applications that rely on it, such as our IIS application, and cause those applications to fail.

To enable binary compatibility:

> Make the DLL in the VB project directory.
> Call it MessageBoardDB_Reference.DLL
> In VB under Project menu select Properties
> Select the Component Tab
> Change Version Compatibility to Binary Compatibility and browse to the MessageBoardDB_Reference.DLL we just created.
> Click OK
> Make the DLL again, but call it MessageBoardDB.DLL

Now if you try any action which breaks compatibility, Visual Basic will warn you of the consequences. You can choose to break compatibility but at least you will be warned by VB that existing programs will fail and need to be recompiled.

We have finished creating the business object so you can close down Visual Basic and take a break.

Mid-Study Summary

In the first part of this Case Study, you should have learned something of SQL strings if you did not know about them already. You have learned how to use stored procedures to make your code more efficient in that they require less calls to the server and they can be cached. You have learned how to create an effective middleware business object which contains atomic transactions to help prevent corruption.

In the next section, you will learn how to implement this business object within the web application to make a secure message board that is intuitive to use and responds quickly to requests made by the client.

Now continue to the next section.

Case Study 1 :
Message Board Part 2

Creating the Presentation Layer

Having completed the data services and middleware layers in the previous section, we can start on the presentation layer. We will be creating a new IIS application, adding HTM templates and coding the client side VB. Finally, we will create the Remote Scripting functions using JScript

First open up Visual Basic and create a new IIS project. Change the webclass name to `wcMessageBoard` and the NameInURL to MessageBoard.

Under menu Project, select options and change the project name to MessageBoard and description to MessageBoard.

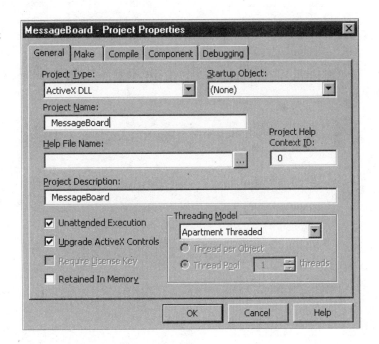

Before we start adding HTML templates we need to save the project. Create a new directory on your hard drive and save the project.

Now we need to include a reference to our business objects DLL. . From Project, references menu select MessageBoardDB.dll.

Displaying the Message Headers

Here we will learn how to make the real-time viewing of message headers possible. As you can see by going to the test website at http://www.keelealumni.org.uk/MessageBoardDemo, all of the headers are updated on the page as the client reads messages. Unread messages are shown in a bold font, and sub-messages appear quickly when the + symbol is clicked.

Creating the HTMLTemplates

Using the HTML page creator of your choice (I have used Visual Interdev 6 that comes with Visual Studio) create the HTML file below. The names used in the style tag to define CSS class attributes for the <DD> tag are important as they are used in our Business objects code. A webclass tag (<WC@...>), which fires the Process_Tag event when the page loads, has also been placed in between the <TABLE> tags. The webclass tags are replaced with the HTML text containing the message headers our webclass obtains from our Business object MessageBoardDB.DLL.

```
<HTML>
<HEAD>
<STYLE>
TABLE.clsTable
{
    BACKGROUND-COLOR: peachpuff;
    BORDER-BOTTOM: none;
    BORDER-LEFT: none;
    BORDER-RIGHT: none;
    BORDER-TOP: none;
    FONT-FAMILY: Verdana, 'MS Sans Serif';
    FONT-SIZE: 10pt;
    LIST-STYLE: none outside;
    MARGIN: 1px;

    PADDING-BOTTOM: 0px;
    PADDING-LEFT: 0px;
    PADDING-RIGHT: 0px;
    PADDING-TOP: 0px;
        POSITION : absolute;
        LEFT : 0px;
        TOP : 0px;
        WIDTH:100%;
}

DD.clsBoldDD
{

    FONT-SIZE : 9pt;
    FONT-WEIGHT: bold;
    COLOR : black;
```

```
      BORDER-BOTTOM-WIDTH : 2px;
      MARGIN: 5px;
      padding-top : 1px;

   }

   DD.clsNormalDD
   {

      FONT-SIZE : 10pt;
      FONT-WEIGHT: normal;
      COLOR : black;
         BORDER-BOTTOM-WIDTH : 2px;
         MARGIN: 5px;
         padding-top : 1px;
   }
   </STYLE>
   <TITLE></TITLE>
   </HEAD>

   <BODY bgColor=OldLace>
   <TABLE WIDTH=100% border=0 CELLSPACING=1 CELLPADDING=1 class=clsTable>
      <THEAD>
      <TR>
      <TH width=57% background="">Subject</TH>
      <TH  width=22%>From</TH>
      <TH  width=21%>Date</TH></TR>
      </THEAD>
      <!-- Webclass Tag - Message Header HTML inserted here in Process tag event -->
      <WC@MESSAGES></WC@MESSAGES>
   </TABLE>

   </BODY>
   </HTML>
```

Save the HTML file into the same directory as your webclass and give it the filename
`Messages.HTML`

> You can choose your own filename if you wish, but I find it useful to
> use the extension .HTML rather than .HTM because when you
> import your template into the IIS application, Visual Basic makes its
> own copy in the directory and names it Messages.HTM; unless you
> called yours .HTM, in which it becomes Messages1.HTM. It just
> saves confusion later.

Next we need to create the HTML template that will be used to view the text of messages when a
user clicks on a message row.

```
<html>
<body style="BACKGROUND-COLOR: silver;">
<TEXTAREA id=txtMessage name=txtMessage readOnly
style="BACKGROUND-COLOR: silver; COLOR: black; POSITION: absolute; TOP: 0; HEIGHT:
124%; LEFT: 0; WIDTH: 105%">
<WC@MessageText></WC@MessageText>
</TEXTAREA>
</body>
</html>
```

Save the template as MessageView.html

The HTML templates we just created will actually be viewed inside a frames – Internet Explorer's <IFRAME> tag. The message headers appear in the top <IFRAME> and the message text in the bottom one. We now need to create the HTM template for this top frame page.

```
<HTML>
<HEAD>
<TITLE>The Message Board</TITLE>
<STYLE>

BODY
{
    FONT-FAMILY: Verdana, 'MS Sans Serif';

}

INPUT
{
    FONT-FAMILY: Verdana;
    'MS Sans Serif';
    FONT-SIZE: 10pt;
    FONT-WEIGHT: bold;
    HEIGHT: 30px;
    WIDTH: 133px;
}

</STYLE>

</HEAD>
<!-- corkbg.jpg used as background - feel free to design your own -->
<BODY bgColor=rosybrown background="./pageimages/corkbg.jpg">
<!-- IFrame displays Message.HTM (tmpMessages) -->
<IFRAME id="messageFrame" name="messageFrame"
    src=""
    noresize
    style="BACKGROUND-COLOR: OldLace;
        BORDER : 1px;
        HEIGHT: 55%; LEFT: 1%; POSITION: absolute; TOP: 12%; WIDTH: 100%"
        marginHeight=0 marginWidth=0>

</IFRAME>
<SPAN style="LEFT: 1px; POSITION: absolute; TOP: 5px; WIDTH: 100%">
<CENTER>
<TABLE>
<TR>
    <TD>
        <INPUT id=cmdNewMessage name=cmdNewMessage type=button value="New Message">
    </TD>
    <TD>
        <INPUT id=cmdReply name=cmdReply type=button value="Compose Reply">
    </TD>
    <TD>
        <INPUT id=cmdEmail name=cmdEmail type=button value="Email Author">
    </TD>
    <TD>
        <INPUT id=cmdMainPage name=cmdMainPage type=button value="Home Page">
    </TD>
    <TD>
```

```
                <INPUT id=cmdHelp name=cmdHelp type=button value="Help">
     </TD>
   </TR>
   </TABLE>
   </CENTER>
   </SPAN> <iframe src="" name="fraMessageView"
        style="HEIGHT: 34%; LEFT: 1%; POSITION: absolute; TOP: 68%; WIDTH: 100%"
   id="fraMessageView" frameborder="No">
   </iframe>
   </BODY>
   </HTML>
```

Save this file in your IIS project directory as `message_top_frame.html`.

Incorporating the HTML Templates for GetMessages

Return to the IIS application. We need to add the three HTML templates we just created. Do so by either right clicking on **HTML Template WebItems** in the WebClass window (if the WebClass window is not open then just double click the webclass in the project view) and selecting **Add HTML Template**, or click the **Add HTML Template** icon (picture of yellow page with globe in it). Add `Messages.HTML` and call it `tmpMessages`. Visual Basic will parse the file looking for tags then create a new copy of the file for its own use called `Messages.HTM`. Add `message_top_frame.HTML` and called it **tmpMessageTopFrame**. Finally add the MessageView.html template and call it tmpMessageText The HTML files you create are no longer used so you can delete them if you wish, as it's the HTM files that VB uses.

If you click on **tmpMessageTopFrame** you'll see a list of Tags Visual Basic has identified as being connectable to Custom WebClass events or WebItems. In this case, we are interested in just one of them, the `<IFRAME>` tag `messageFrame`.

> *A little gotcha that tripped me up the first time is the WebClass's dislike of the underscore character when naming your HTML tags. My <IFRAME> tag was originally <IFRAME id=" message_frame" name=" message_frame" ..... but Visual Basic just spat it back at me and informed that this was an illegal name when I tried to connect it to a custom event. If you create a custom event then rename it to message_frame then it works but its not worth the tears later.*

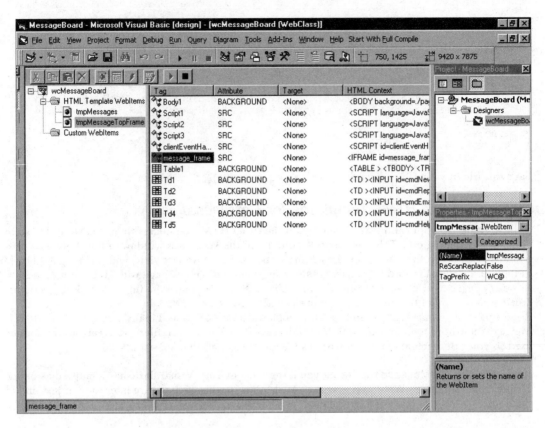

Right click messageFrame and select **Connect to Custom Event**. I used the default name VB gives us for the custom event of **messageFrame** but you can choose your own. The custom event will appear under **tmpMessageTopFrame**. Double click the event created to open up the code view. At runtime when the webclass parser reaches our IFRAME's custom event, we want it to write the tmpMessages, so lets write the code to do this.

```
Private Sub tmpMessageTopFrame_messageFrame()
On Error GoTo ErrorHandler

    tmpMessages.WriteTemplate
    Exit Sub

ErrorHandler:
    ErrorRoutine Err.Number, Err.Description, "tmpMessageTopFrame_IFrame1" &
Err.Source
End Sub
```

As you can see all we do is simply execute tmpMessage's WriteTemplate method, along with some error handling code. We'll write ErrorRoutine in a minute.

Next, lets add the code to the `Webclass.Start` method, the very first method that fires when someone browses to our WebClass's ASP page. You can access the events code by either double clicking **wcMessageBoard** in the WebClass window or going direct to the code view and using the combo boxes to access the WebClass's events. Visual Basic has already put some code in there, which we need to delete and replace with our own.

This code has two tasks. It must check which browser the client is using and if it is not IE4 or IE5 then produce the appropriate error message. If it's an appropriate browser then it must also check the client browser's cookies for the date they last visited the message board so that we can identify which messages were posted since their last visit. If they have never been before, then the cookie will not exist and we just use a nominal date of `1 Jan 1990`. The Session variable `LastVisit` is created and populated with their last visit date. Using Session variables is a very handy way of maintaining state between pages, though the client browser must support cookies and have them enabled for sessions to work.

```
Private Sub WebClass_Start()
    On Error GoTo ErrorHandler
    Dim lsBrowser As String
    ' Detect browser version
    ' write appropriate template
    lsBrowser = Request.ServerVariables("HTTP_USER_AGENT")
    ' Is this Internet Explorer 4 or 5?
    If ((InStr(lsBrowser, "IE") > 0) And ((InStr(lsBrowser, "5.") > 0) Or _
        (InStr(lsBrowser, "4.") > 0))) Then
        ' Get date of last visit
        ' to determine which messages are new to the visitor
        If Session("LastVisit") = "" Then
            Session("LastVisit") = Request.Cookies("MessageBoardLastVisit")
            ' never been before - use nominal date
            If Trim(Session("LastVisit") = "") Then
                Session("LastVisit") = "1 Jan 1990"
            End If
        End If
        tmpMessageTopFrame.WriteTemplate
        ' Update date of last visit cookie
        Response.Cookies("MessageBoardLastVisit") = Format(Now(), _
            "dd mmm yyyy hh:mm")
        Response.Cookies("MessageBoardLastVisit").Expires = _
            Format(DateAdd("m", 6, Now()), "dd mmm yyyy")
    Else
        ' NonIE browser (IE browser pre version 4)
        Response.Write "<CENTER><H2>Sorry this message board only works with
Internet
            Explorer 4 and 5</H2></CENTER>"

    End If
    Exit Sub

    ErrorHandler:
    ErrorRoutine Err.Number, Err.Description, "WebClass_Start - " & Err.Source
End Sub
```

Error Handling in a Webclass

Proper error handling in a standard Visual Basic program is important; in an IIS WebClass application it's vital. If you don't trap the errors, instead of a helpful (well possibly helpful) message giving information about source and description of the error, you'll see the following appear in the browser:

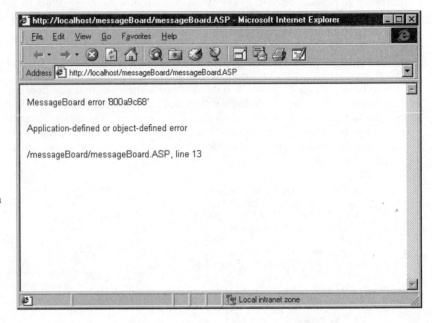

Imagine the scenario, you've deployed your webclass application to the remote server. It worked fine on your development machine so you didn't bother with error handling. The first time someone uses your application it falls over because someone forgot to copy some file or other but the only feed back you have is that above – going to be pretty tough solving the problem.

So having decided to include error handling everywhere let's create the error handling for the message board.

First we need to create another HTML Template file. Using your HTML editor create the template as below. You'll notice we have a `<WC@Errors>` WebClass tag – this is there we'll put our error messages.

```
<HTML>
<HEAD>
<TITLE>ERROR OCCURRED</TITLE>
</HEAD>
<BODY>
<P></P>
<P align=center>
    <FONT face=Verdana size=4><STRONG>
        An error has occurred in the message board
    </FONT></STRONG>
    </P>

<P>
    <FONT face=Verdana><BR>
```

```
            Please notify the Webmaster by e-mail at
                <A href="mailto:myemail@address.com">myemail@address.com</A>
        </FONT>
    </P>

    <P>
        <FONT face=Verdana>
            The error details are listed below.</P>
    <BR>
            <!-- WebClass tags for error details -->
            <WC@ERRORS>
            </WC@ERRORS>
        </FONT>
    </P>

    </BODY>
    </HTML>
```

Now save the HTML file as `Error.html` and return to the IIS project. As before add the HTML template file to the project and name it `tmpError`.

If an error occurs, each of our webclass events has code in it, which calls the subroutine `ErrorRoutine`. This takes the error message details and puts them in webclass `URLData`. `URLData` are values attached to the end of the normal URL strings and passed from page to page when navigation occurs. For example, if you have a hyperlink which you want to load a URL: `www.myname.com/mydirectory/mypage.htm`, then putting a question mark at the end and a list of value pairs separated by ampersands, allows you to pass data from one page to the next. If we want to page the value `55` for a `messageid` and `Hello` for a `Title` then the URL for the link's `href` would be: `www.myname.com/mydirectory/mypage.htm?MessageId=55&Title=Hello`.

`URLData` when used with a webclass is made easier by the ability to set `URLData` in VB code with `Webclass.URLData = "MessageId=55&Title=Hello"`. To retreive the `URLData` we just assign it to a variable, for example `MyVarString = Webclass.URLData`. If you want to manually create URL data, say if you have a link on a page or a button in a form, and fire the response event of one your webclass templates then the syntax is:

`Name_of_webclass_asp_file?WCI=name_of_template&WCU=url_data`

Using `URLData` enables state to be maintained over different pages, thus allowing us to access the error details when the `tmpError` template is written. One advantage of URLData is that it works even on browsers that don't support cookies. Session variables do require cookies so no error message would appear in a browser that does not support cookies.

Each part of the error message is stored as one string in `URLData`, but delimited using a semi colon so we can split it apart again with VB6's new `Split` function.

```
Private Sub ErrorRoutine(sErrorNum As Long, sErrorDesc As String, _
    sErrorSource As String)

    WebClass.URLData = CStr(sErrorNum) & ";" & sErrorDesc & ";" & _
        sErrorSource & ";"
    tmpError.WriteTemplate
End Sub
```

We need to add code to template `tmpError`'s Process tag event, which will write out the error details to the template for viewing in the user's browser. I have adopted a fairly simple error handling scheme, but you may wish to make it more professional by writing errors to the NT Application log and writing a different error template.

```
Private Sub tmpError_ProcessTag(ByVal TagName As String, TagContents As String, _
  SendTags As Boolean)

   Dim lsErrorDetails() As String
   lsErrorDetails = Split(WebClass.URLData, ";")
   TagContents = "<STRONG>Error Description : </STRONG>" & lsErrorDetails(1) & _
      "<BR><BR>"
   TagContents = TagContents & "<STRONG>Error Number : </STRONG>" & _
      lsErrorDetails(0) & "<BR><BR>"
   TagContents = TagContents & "<STRONG>Error Source : </STRONG>" & _
      lsErrorDetails(2)
End Sub
```

Populating tmpMessages Template's WebClass Tags

In `tmpMessages` we have two WebClass tags. `<WC@Messages>` is where the message headers are inserted and `<WC@Location>`. We will deal with populating the `<WC@Location>` tags later. We can insert HTML into the `<WC@Messages>` tag when the template's `ProcessTag` event fires by adding the code below.

```
Private Sub tmpMessages_ProcessTag(ByVal TagName As String, _
  TagContents As String, SendTags As Boolean)

   On Error GoTo ErrorHandler

   Dim lsErrorString As String
   Select Case TagName
      Case "WC@Messages"
         ' In this tag is where we put our message headers
         Dim loMessage As New clsMBBusObject
         TagContents = loMessage.GetMessages(1, "1 Jan 1990", Format(Now(), _
            "dd mmm yyyy hh:mm"), Session("LastVisit"), lsErrorString)
         If lsErrorString <> "" Then Err.Raise vbObjectError + 101, _
            "MessageDB - Function GetMessages", lsErrorString
   End Select
   Exit Sub

   ErrorHandler:
   ErrorRoutine Err.Number, Err.Description, "tmpMessages_ProcessTag" & Err.Source
End Sub
```

A Test Run

We have now done enough to actually try out the message board.

As we have not created the functionality to add a message yet you'll need to manually add test message data using SQL Server's Enterprise Manager (you can right click a table and choose return all rows then add and edit rows). Suggested data is given below.

Fields	Record One	Record Two	Record Three
MessageID	1	2	3
MessageBoardId	1	1	1
TopSection	1	1	2
MessageOrder	1	2	3
Indents	0	1	0
Remote_Address	127.0.0.1	127.0.0.7	127.0.0.1
DateSent	1999-06-19	1999-06-19	1999-06-20
Subject	Another Message	Reply to Another Message	Top Message
Message	Another Messages' body text	Reply to Another Message's body text	First in line
VisitorName	Bob	John	Paul
EMail	Some@Email.com	me@hello.com	some@else.com

It's a good idea to launch a second copy of Visual Basic and open up the Business Object project we created. Set its debugging properties to Wait for Component to be Created (under Project menu, properties and the debugging tab), then run it.

Once that's up and running, you can run your webclass and, if all goes well, the HTML pages should appear in your browser with a list of the messages you added. You can't open up sub messages yet as we've not added the script. When you first run a WebClass application Visual Basic will create a virtual directory based on the directory your IIS application is in and give it the name of your WebClass project, just accept the default it suggests and click ok.

If you find that the IIS project doesn't seem to be running the project version of MessageBoard.dll, so that setting break points in the Business object's code are never reached, then you might find you need to stop both projects, run the MessageBoardDB project, then switch to the IIS project and change the project references to reference MessageBoardDB.vbp; not MessageBoardDB.dll.

Also check under menu Tools, Options and the General tab that error trapping is set to break in the class module.

Another problem you may hit is with `localhost`, that Visual Basic uses for your server's name. When I came back from holiday, someone had decided to play with my computer's settings and as a result `localhost` has never worked since. However, I found a workaround is to change the project debugging settings from Start Component `wcMessageBoard` to start browser with URL and the URL of your Webclass's ASP file.

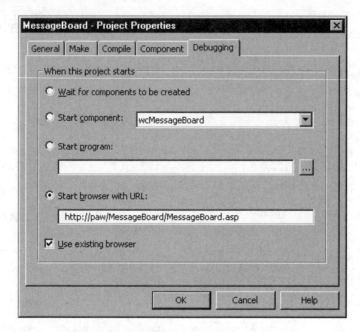

Displaying the Sub message Headers

We now need to add some client side VBScript to our `tmpMessages` HTML template to make the sub message headers appear/disappear.

From within the IIS project, right click **tmpMessages** and select **Edit HTML Template**. This will open up the HTM file in your selected HTML page editor. This defaults to notepad but you can change this to something like Visual Interdev from within Visual Basic via **Tools, Options** then select the **Advanced** Tab and enter the path to your HTML editor in the External HTML Editor box (Visual Interdev is something like `C:\Program Files\Microsoft Visual Studio\Common\IDE\IDE98\DEVENV.EXE` depending on which drive/directory you installed to).

Inside the Header tags of the template file we need to add a subroutine that displays/hides `<SPAN>` tags and also changes the image tag from a plus (indicating hidden message thread) to a minus image.

As well as the `<SPAN>` tag for the Subject being shown/hidden we also need to show/hide the related `<SPAN>` tags for Person and Date, which is what the second part of the routine achieves.

Working out which `<SPAN>`s these are is made easy because of the naming convention used for `<SPAN>`s. In **MessageBoardDB**, `<SPAN>` tags are given a name indicating their column in the table they belong to (e.g. `SubjectSub`, `PersonSub`, `DateSub`) and the `MessageId` for that row; for example, `SubjectSub23`.

So if a `<SPAN>` with an id of `SubjectSub23` is clicked to be made visible, we also know that `PersonSub23` and `DateSub23` also need to be made visible.

Add the following script to template `tmpMessages`.

```
<HTML>
<HEAD>
<SCRIPT LANGUAGE=vbscript>

' Dispalys/Hides <SPAN> tag named with name sName
' and changes image from Plus to minus when displaying and back again when hiding
' a <SPAN>
Sub SectionDisplay(sName,imgIcon)
Dim oSub
' Set oSub to referencethe subject <SPAN> being displayed/hidden
Set oSub = Document.all("Subject" & sName)

' If <SPAN> tags style.display is none then its hidden
' so make it visible
If oSub.style.display = "none" Then
    oSub.style.display = ""
    ' Change image to minus image
    imgIcon.Src = "./pageimages/minus.gif"
else
    ' <SPAN> already visible so hide
    oSub.style.display = "none"
    ' Change image to plus image
    imgIcon.Src = "./pageimages/plus.gif"
End If

' Make other <SPAN> tags for same thread as subject
' visible/hidden
Set oSub = Document.all("Person" & sName)
If oSub.style.display = "none" Then
    oSub.style.display = ""

else
    oSub.style.display = "none"
End If

Set oSub = Document.all("Date" & sName)
If oSub.style.display = "none" Then
    oSub.style.display = ""
else
    oSub.style.display = "none"
End If

End Sub

</SCRIPT>
```

The next step is to add the VBScript event handler for the `onClick` event. In Internet Explorer events bubble up from the lowest tag in the document object model to the highest. What we will do is write generic code to work for all the <SPAN>s on the page so we need to put our event handling high up the document object model in the document `onClick` event. It's the plus/minus image tag a user clicks on to show/hide sub threads so we need to make sure that's what's been clicked. We check that this is indeed an image tag (`TagName` gives us this information). Again using a naming convention we check this is an image we want to act on as we are interested only in those image tags we have given names. The name itself is a number, the `MessageId`. This allows us to find out the name of the relevant <SPAN> tag, as we know it will be called `SubjectSub` and will have the `MessageId` tacked on the end. We know the MessageId from the image name hence we have the <SPAN> name. The <SPAN> name, and a reference to the image tag, is passed to our routine for showing/hiding <SPAN>s.

Add the script inside the existing script tags

```
Sub document_onclick
Dim oSrcElement

' get HTML tag (or element) just clicked
Set oSrcElement = window.event.srcElement

' Is this a plus/minus image tag
If oSrcElement.TagName = "IMG" and oSrcElement.Id <> "" Then
    Dim sName
    Dim oSub
    sName = Right(oSrcElement.Id,Len(oSrcElement.Id) - 3)
    SectionDisplay sName,oSrcElement
    oSrcElement.scrollIntoView
End If
End Sub
</SCRIPT>
```

Row Highlighting Using Mouse Rollover

In the final version of the message board, as the user's mouse rolls over a message header the whole line is highlighted in blue; returning to black once the mouse moves away. This is a common trick and is achieved using the `mouseOver`/`mouseOut` events to change the font color, something Internet Explorer 4 and 5's dynamic HTML have made very easy.

A naming convention has been used in the Business object for creating names and Ids for <DD> tags. They all start with MSG, then have S, P or D for Subject, Person or Date column attached and finally the MessageId is put at the end. We can use Internet Explorer's Document object's `All` method to obtain a reference to any tag in the Internet Explorer document object model so long as we know its name (or ordinal position in the page). We use the `MessageId` at the end to set the <DD> tags color properties.

Again add the script inside the existing script tags.

```
Sub document_onmouseout
    ' Set colour back to black

    ' Set a reference to element to which the event happened
    Set oSrcElement = window.event.srcElement
```

```
        ' If its a <DD> tag then we know its a message row
    If oSrcElement.TagName = "DD" Then
        Dim sID
        ' Get MessageId
        sID = Right(oSrcElement.ID,LEN(oSrcElement.ID) - 4)
        ' Set <DD>s for row back to black
        document.all("MSGS" & sID).style.color="black"
        document.all("MSGP" & sID).style.color="black"
        document.all("MSGD" & sID).style.color="black"
    End If
End Sub

Sub document_onmouseover
    ' Change colour to blue

    ' Set a reference to element to which the event happened
    Set oSrcElement = window.event.srcElement

    ' If its a <DD> tag then we know its a message row
    If oSrcElement.TagName = "DD" Then
        Dim sID
        ' Get MessageId
        sID = Right(oSrcElement.ID,LEN(oSrcElement.ID) - 4)
        ' Set <DD> tags for row to blue
        document.all("MSGS" & sID).style.color="blue"
        document.all("MSGP" & sID).style.color="blue"
        document.all("MSGD" & sID).style.color="blue"
    End If

End Sub
</SCRIPT>
```

Save the template and return to our IIS project – it should automatically detect your changes and ask if your want to refresh, click Yes.

Retrieving a Message Using Remote Scripting

Remote Scripting is a fairly new Microsoft technology, which enables a client side HTML page to access functions inside a server side ASP page without requiring a page refresh.

In the server side ASP page we define a new JScript class. We list the public methods we wish to expose in your ASP page in the class's constructor. To make these methods available outside of the page we use the JScript `public_description` object. By setting this to reference our class's constructor, the methods in the constructor will be made available to Remote Scripting.

When we include references to the Remote Scripting library in our client side page, a Java applet is created and initialized for us by the Remote Scripting library files, downloadable from the Microsoft site. A lot goes on in these libraries and if you want to find out about the gory details, then `http://msdn.microsoft.com/scripting/remotescripting/` has more detail. However we need not understand the Java networking that provides the communication from our HTML page to the ASP page to use Remote Scripting.

In this project, it is used to return a message from our SQL Server database using the Business object we created, and all from the comfort of our HTML page. Furthermore, it does so asynchronously so there is no "browser freeze" while we wait for the message to be sent back. In practice, I have found that a message is usually returned in less than two seconds over a 56Kb modem link. However, there is a downside to Remote Scripting in that it uses a Java applet client side and also uses Java on the server side. Although fairly small, the server side component does use resources and the client side one means a 22k initial download. However this is still less of a strain than if we were waiting for ActiveX components to download. It also means that client browsers security must not be set to high, which prevents Java from operating. As you will see this won't prevent our message board from functioning because I have included alternatives for the situation where Remote Scripting is not working.

Installing Remote Scripting on the Server

Remote Scripting (RS) requires a number of Microsoft created support files. To get these files, either go to the Microsoft MSDN website at
`http://msdn.microsoft.com/scripting/default.htm?/scripting/remotescripting`
and download the latest Remote Scripting files from there, or you can use Visual Interdev to create the required files and folder for you (though it won't be an up to date version of RS).

To get Visual Interdev to create the required directory, go into Visual Interdev and create a new dummy web project (just accept whatever defaults it gives). When it's finished creating the project it will copy a number of files and folders over to the location you specified. One of the sub folders will be named `_ScriptLibrary`. It's this folder which contains the Remote Scripting support files which must be installed on whatever server you deploy your message board on.

For the message board I have copied this folder (leave its name as `_ScriptLibrary`) and put it as a sub folder under the virtual directory of where my IIS project files reside. This will at least allow us to develop the message board. You may decide later when putting it on the deployment server that you just want one common _ScriptLibrary and point all your Remote Scripting includes to that directory.

You'll need to use Internet Information Server's Management Console to set the permissions for that folder to Execute (including scripts)

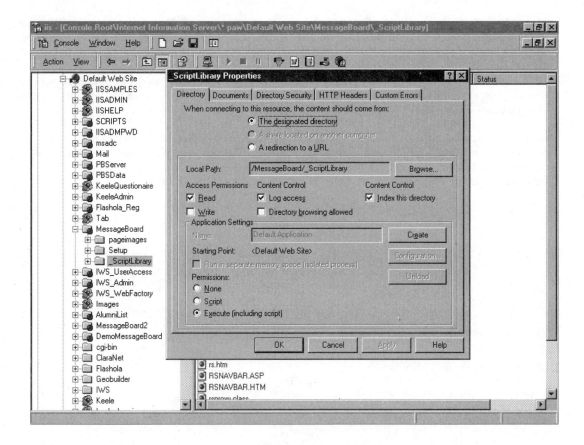

There's no set-up necessary for the client side.

Creating the ASP Page To Be Accessed Remotely

Using your HTML editor we can now create the ASP file with our remote routines in.

This uses features only available if you have downloaded and installed Scripting Engine 5 on your server, from the Microsoft site. The JScript try.catch clause is a new error handling feature brought over from Java and which finally gives us proper error handling facilities. You only need to install Script version 5 on the server – the client machines only need to have IE 4 or IE 5 installed, as the code executes on the server and not the client.

If you didn't put the _ScriptLibrary under the IIS application folder then you'll need to change the #INCLUDE to point to the correct URL.

The code firstly includes a reference to the Remote Scripting support libraries and runs RSDispatch, which enables Remote Scripting calls in the server page and only needs to be called once per page. Then we create clsMessageBoard's constructor, which declares its public interface for this class. To actually make the public interface accessible outside of this page we use the public_description object. By setting the public_discription object to reference our class we enable Remote Scripting to 'see' our class's public interface and enable Remote Scripting to create object's based on our class's template.

Finally we implement the GetMessage function. Although we declare its existence in the class constructor, we actually implement it elsewhere and set a reference to that implementation. The function creates an instance of the Business object we created earlier and uses its GetMessage function to retrieve the message text which is returned to the calling routine.

```
<%@ LANGUAGE=VBSCRIPT %>
<% RSDispatch %>
<!--#INCLUDE FILE="./_scriptlibrary/rs.asp"-->
<SCRIPT RUNAT=SERVER Language=javascript>

// Declare the class's public interface

function clsMessageBoard()
{
   // set a reference to the getMessage function we implement below
   this.getMessage = getMessage;
}
// set the public_description object to point to  a new instance of our
clsMessageBoard  class
public_description = new clsMessageBoard;

</SCRIPT>

<SCRIPT RUNAT=SERVER Language=javascript>

// implimentation of interface
function getMessage(iMessageBoardID, iMessageID)
{
     var loMessage;
     var returnValue = "ERROR";
     var lsErrorString = '';

     // Try...Catch is available with Scripting Engine 5
     try
     {

          // Create instance of our VB Business Object
          loMessage = Server.CreateObject("MessageBoardDB.clsMBBusObject");
          // Uses Business Objects getMessage function to get message text
          returnValue = loMessage.GetMessage(iMessageBoardID,
iMessageID,lsErrorString);

     // remove this if no try…catch
     if (lsErrorString != '')
               throw lsErrorString;
     }
     catch(e)
     {
          returnValue = e;
     }
```

```
        return returnValue;
    }

</SCRIPT>
```

If you don't wish to use the latest scripting engine then the code will work fine, if you remove all the try catch statement parts, but won't have the same ability to handle unexpected errors.

The `getMessage` function code for version 4 script engines will look like this

```
function getMessage(iMessageBoardID, iMessageID)
{
    var loMessage;
    var returnValue = "ERROR";
    var lsErrorString = '';

    loMessage = Server.CreateObject("MessageBoardDB.clsMBBusObject");
    returnValue = loMessage.GetMessage(iMessageBoardID, iMessageID,lsErrorString);

    return returnValue;
}
```

Now save the ASP file in the same directory as your IIS files and call it `MessageRoutines.asp`

Remote Access from the Client Side HTML

Now we can add the client side script to `tmpMessageTopFrame`.

Remote Scripting uses a Java applet, which is included as part of the `_ScriptLibrary` and included in the client web page. The first thing we need to do is create the references to the script library by adding the code below to `message_top_frame.htm` somewhere near the top of the file, ideally just below the `<BODY>` tag.

```
<BODY bgColor=rosybrown background="./pageimages/corkbg.jpg">
<script language="JavaScript" src="./_ScriptLibrary/rs.htm"></script>
<script language="JavaScript">
    RSEnableRemoteScripting("./_ScriptLibrary");
</script>
```

Next we need to add a client side VBScript block, define a few global variables and add some event handling for `window_onload`.

In `window_onload` we use function `RSGetASPObject` in the RS support library to create an object based on the class we defined in `MessageRoutines.asp`, and we set global variable `aspObject` to reference it. Although we can access it using an object on the client, the object really exists on the server and it is Remote Scripting's behind the scenes trickery that enables all this. However for the purposes of our code, on the client side it does not matter. We can access the `aspObject`'s functions as we would with any client side object.

I have found in practice that Remote Scripting fails in a small number of cases and we need to handle this gracefully. If for whatever reason our creation of the `aspObject` fails then our VBScript global variable `RSOk` will retain its default value of false. We can then check in later scripts to see if Remote Scripting is working, if it isn't then we use an alternative method to display the message. When Remote Scripting fails, the whole of the page within the bottom `<IFRAME>` tag is refreshed. The script reloads the page but adds the message id to the end of the URL, so in the webclass the pages process event can pick it up and use it to insert the message between the WC@MessageText webclass tags. So as far as the user is concerned, there has been no obvious failure. They still get to see the message when they ask for it.

```html
<HTML>
<HEAD>
<script language="JavaScript" src="./_ScriptLibrary/rs.htm"></script>
<script language="JavaScript">
     RSEnableRemoteScripting("./_ScriptLibrary");
</script>
<SCRIPT LANGUAGE=vbscript>

' Global variables

' Set by code within <IFRAME> to store subject of last message clicked on
Dim sCurrentMessageSubject
sCurrentMessageSubject = ""

' Set by code within <IFRAME> to store email address of last message clicked on
Dim msEmail
msEmail = ""

' Set in window_onload - take alternative action if for whatever reason
' Remote Scripting has failed - will be false unless Remote Scripting starts
' correctly and sets it to true
Dim RSOk
RSOk = false

Sub window_onload
     On Error Resume Next

     ' Remote Scripting requires Java to be enabled
     If window.navigator.javaEnabled = true Then
          ' Create new object based on public definition in ASP file on server
          Set aspObject = RSGetASPObject("MessageRoutines.asp")
          RSOk = true
     Else
          RSOk = false
     End If

     If Err.number <> 0 Then
          RSOk = false
     End If
End Sub

</SCRIPT>
<TITLE>The Message Board</TITLE>
```

The Message Retrieving Script

We need to use JScript for accessing Remote Scripting. Inside the HTML header of `tmpMessageTopFrame` insert the following JScript code. It's also here that we define the global variable `aspObject`, which holds a reference to our RS created ASP object.

Retrieving a message is done asynchronously using function callback. We execute JScript function `GetMessage`, which executes the `getMessage` function in our `MessageRoutines.asp` page. However `GetMessages` on the client side returns immediately without waiting for the server side `getMessages` to complete. When we called `getMessage` on the server, we also passed the address of our `DisplayMessage` routine that will be called by RS when `GetMessage` on the server has completed. Of the `GetMessage` call, the first 3 parameters are passed to our `GetMessages` function on the server side ASP page. The last two parameters are used by RS. The first is for callback for asynchronous execution, the last one is the address of our error handling routine in the client side JScript. If anything goes wrong then `showErrors` will be called by RS.

However, some errors won't be caught this way but we trap this by examining the return value passed back, if it's ERROR then something has gone wrong and we display an error message in the message text area instead of the message itself.

```
<HTML>
<HEAD>
<script language="JavaScript" src="./_ScriptLibrary/rs.htm"></script>
<script language="JavaScript">
   RSEnableRemoteScripting("./_ScriptLibrary");
</script>
<script language="JavaScript">

   var aspObject;
   var lCurrentMessageID = 0;

   function GetMessage()
   {

      // Execute getMessage in serverside asp page
      // passing it MessageBoardId, MessageId,
      // Address of DisplayMessage function, Address of showErrors function
      aspObject.getMessage(1,lCurrentMessageID,DisplayMessage, showErrors);
      fraMessageView.txtMessage.value = "Message is loading.... Please wait";
   }

   // function is called back by RS
   function DisplayMessage(objReturn)
   {
      if (objReturn.return_value == "ERROR")
      {
         fraMessageView.txtMessage.value = "An Error has occurred please email
            me@address.org.uk";
      }
      {
         fraMessageView.txtMessage.value = objReturn.return_value;
      }
   }
```

Continued on Following Page

```
    // Error routine called back by RS if something goes wrong
    function showErrors(co)
    {
        fraMessageView.txtMessage.value = "An Error has occurred please email
me@address.org.uk";
    }

</script>
<SCRIPT LANGUAGE=vbscript>
```

Responding To a User's Request to View a Message

Now we have all the code in place to actually display the message its time to write the event handling code, which reacts to the user clicking on a message headers row in the tmpMessages template. Before continuing though, save the page.

We need to amend the document_onclick routine in the tmpMessages (messages.htm), by checking the srcElement's TagName property. Every element in the IE Document Object Model has a TagName property that returns the type of tag, e.g. IMG, TABLE, being referred to. If TagName is IMG or DD, then we extract the MessageId from the tag's ID, and set the global variable in the parent frame (tmpMessageTopFrame template) to the just clicked message header's MessageID. This is used in the tmpMessageTopFrame if the user presses the Compose Reply button so we know what message they are replying to.

```
Sub document_onclick
Dim oSrcElement

' get HTML tag (or element) just clicked
' Setting a variable to reference a Document Object Element like this
' makes it easier to use as code becomes more readable
Set oSrcElement = window.event.srcElement
' Is this the message image or <DD> tag
' get MessageId from Tag's id
If (oSrcElement.TagName = "IMG" OR oSrcElement.TagName = "DD") AND _
    Left(oSrcElement.Id,3) = "MSG" Then
    Dim sMessageID
    sMessageID = CStr(oSrcElement.Id)
    sMessageID = Right(sMessageID, Len(sMessageId) - 4)

    ' Set the global variable lCurrentMessageId in top frame to id of line clicked
    window.Parent.lCurrentMessageID = Clng(sMessageID)
```

Then if Remote Scripting was initialized successfully, we can use GetMessage in the tmpMessageTopFrame template to display the message in the text area. As it's asynchronous the code continues running whilst in the background the message is being retrieved from the database for display.

To indicate when a message has been read the font is changed to normal which we defined in CSS style class clsDDNormal.

Global variables in the tmpMessageTopFrame are used to hold MessageId, message subject and e-mail address and are needed if a user composes a reply to message. If you remember in the Business object the <DD> tag for Person has its title set to the e-mail address they entered.

If the RSOk variable in tmpMessageTopFrame is false then remote scripting failed to initialize and we need to handle this error here. When they click to view a message the page within the fraMessageText <IFRAME> in the tmpMessageTopFrame has its location.href set to reload the page but with the MessageId added to the end of the URL so that we can retrieve the value using Webclass.URLData when the tmpMessageText templates Process Tag event fires. The WC@MessageText webclass tag is placed between the <TEXTAREA> start and close tags and is replaced with the message text by the Process Tag event.

```
      ' Is Remote Scripting is working
   If window.Parent.RSOk = true Then

      ' Set variable reference to the frames page of this window
      Dim oTopFrame
      Set oTopFrame = window.Parent
      ' execute GetMessage in tmpTopFrame - this will display the message in
      ' topFrames text area
      oTopFrame.GetMessage

      ' Is it a <DD> tag that was clicked
      If oSrcElement.TagName = "DD" Then

         ' To show which messages user has viewed
         ' when a message header row is clicked its font is changed
         '  from bold font to normal font
         Dim sID
         sID = Right(oSrcElement.ID,LEN(oSrcElement.ID) - 4)
         Set oSrcElement = document.all("MSGS" & sID)
         ' Set CSS class to one defined as normal font
         oSrcElement.ClassName = "clsNormalDD"
         'oTopFrame.sCurrentMessageSubject = Left(oSrcElement.innerText, _
            InStr(1,oSrcElement.innerText,vbCrLf))
         oTopFrame.sCurrentMessageSubject = oSrcElement.innerText
         Set oSrcElement = document.all("MSGP" & sID)
         oSrcElement.ClassName = "clsNormalDD"

         ' Set email address of current message in topFrame global variable
         ' For use by tmpToFrames e-mail author button
         If Trim(CStr(oSrcElement.Title)) = "" Then
            oTopFrame.msEmail = ""
         Else
            oTopFrame.msEmail = "MAILTO:" & Trim(CStr(oSrcElement.Title))
         End If
         ' Set Date <DD> to normal font
Set oSrcElement = document.all("MSGD" & sID)
         oSrcElement.ClassName = "clsNormalDD"
      End If
   Else
      ' Remote Scripting not working - so use alternative method
      ' of displaying message - URL is URL of tmpMessageText template
      window.Parent.fraMessageView.location.href = _
         "http://<WC@Location></WC@Location>?WCI=tmpMessageText&WCU=" & sMessageID
   End If
ElseIf oSrcElement.TagName = "IMG" and oSrcElement.Id <> "" Then
   ' Is this a plus/minus image tag
   Dim sName
   Dim oSub
   sName = Right(oSrcElement.Id,Len(oSrcElement.Id) - 3)
   SectionDisplay sName,oSrcElement
```

Table Continued on Following Page

```
        oSrcElement.scrollIntoView
    End If

    End Sub
```

Save the changes, close your HTML editor, and return to VB.

To populate the `<WC@Location>` tag we need to add some code to our VB IIS application's `processTag` event for the `tmpMessages`.

```
    Private Sub tmpMessages_ProcessTag(ByVal TagName As String, TagContents As String,
    SendTags As Boolean)
    On Error GoTo ErrorHandler

        Dim lsErrorString As String
        Select Case TagName
            Case "WC@Messages"
                ' In this tag is where we put our message headers
                Dim loMessage As New clsMBBusObject
                TagContents = loMessage.GetMessages(1, "1 Jan 1990", Format(Now(), "dd
    mmm yyyy hh:mm"), Session("LastVisit"), lsErrorString)
                If lsErrorString <> "" Then Err.Raise vbObjectError + 101, "MessageDB
    - Function GetMessages", lsErrorString
            Case "WC@Location"
                ' Populate
    ' Retrieve Server name and the Path to our Webclass ASP file and HTM files
                TagContents = Request.ServerVariables("Server_Name") & _
                    Request.ServerVariables("Path_INFO")
        End Select
        Exit Sub

    ErrorHandler:
        ErrorRoutine Err.Number, Err.Description, "tmpMessages_ProcessTag" &
    Err.Source
    End Sub
```

Next we must connect the `src` property of the bottom `<IFRAME>` in `tmpMessageTopFrame` to a webclass custom event. When the event fires we want it to load the `tmpMessageText` template into the frame.

As before click on `tmpMessageTopFrame`, then right click `fraMessageView` and select Connect to Custom event. The event will be created with a default name of `fraMessageView`, if not give it that name. Now double click the event in the left window and add the following code.

```
    Private Sub tmpMessageTopFrame_fraMessageView()
        tmpMessageText.WriteTemplate
    End Sub
```

Then double click the `tmpMessageText` template and add the following code to its `Respond` event.

```
    Private Sub tmpMessageText_Respond()
    WebClass.tmpMessageText.WriteTemplate
    End Sub
```

Then select the `tmpMessageText`'s Process Tag event from the **Event** box in the code window and add the code below

```
Private Sub tmpMessageText_ProcessTag(ByVal TagName As String, TagContents As
String, SendTags As Boolean)
On Error GoTo ErrorHandler
    If WebClass.URLData <> "" Then
        Dim lsError As String
        Dim loDatabase As New clsMBBusObject

        TagContents = loDatabase.GetMessage(1, CLng(WebClass.URLData), lsError)
        Set loDatabase = Nothing
        WebClass.URLData = ""
    End If
    Exit Sub

ErrorHandler:
    ErrorRoutine Err.Number, Err.Description, "tmpMessageTopFrame_IFrame1" &
Err.Source

End Sub
```

Another Test Run

You should be able to run the `MessageBoard` IIS application and view messages. Once you have recovered from the excitement, its time to write the script and add the templates to allow us to compose new messages, reply to existing ones, and e-mail message authors.

Creating a New Message

First we need to create a new HTML template file the users will use to compose and then send their messages.

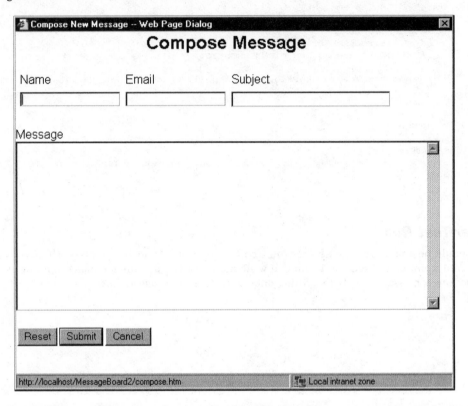

We open the dialog window using the main window object's showModalDialog method, which allows a string to be passed to the newly created dialog window which can be retrieved by script. If the user is replying to an existing message, the window will be passed a string containing the MessageId of the message we are replying to, the subject of that message, and its text. Script in the window_onload splits the string with the semi-colon being used as a delimiter and populates the form text boxes appropriately. When the user hits submit, a form post occurs, which is handled by the webclass, and the dialog window is closed and the message board refreshed. If the user cancels then the window is closed, but no submit or message board refresh occurs. We let the tmpMessageTopFrame know we have cancelled by using the return value to pass "CANCEL".

```
<HTML>
<HEAD>
<TITLE>Compose New Message</TITLE>
<SCRIPT ID=clientEventHandlersVBS LANGUAGE=vbscript>

Sub form1_onsubmit
    window.close
End Sub
```

```
Sub window_onload
    Dim oParams
    ' Params passed as string in format
    ' MessageId were replying to;
    ' Subject of message were replying to;
    ' Message Text of original message
    oParams = Split(window.dialogArguments,";")

    ' Populate form input tags

    ' Hidden input box
    form1.txtMessageID.value = oParams(0)

    ' Subject
    form1.txtSubject.value = oParams(1)

    ' Put > at beginning of line to indicate message text being replied to
    If Trim(oParams(2)) <> "" Then
        form1.txtMessage.value = vbCrLf & vbCrLF & vbCrLf & ">" & _
            Replace(oParams(2),vbCrLf,vbCrLF & ">")
    End If

End Sub

Sub cmdCancel_onclick
    ' won't tmpMessageTopFrame won't refresh
    ' canceled actions
    window.returnValue = "CANCEL"
    window.close
End Sub

</SCRIPT>

</HEAD>
<BODY>

<FORM action="" method=post id=form1 name=form1>
<BASEFONT face=sans-serif>
<H2 align=center>Compose Message</H2>

<TABLE BORDER=0 CELLSPACING=5 CELLPADDING=1>
    <TR>
        TD>Name</TD>
        <TD>Email</TD>
        <TD>Subject</TD>
    </TR>
    <TR>
        <TD><INPUT id=txtName maxLength=20 name=txtName style="HEIGHT: 20px; WIDTH:
          138px"></TD>
        <TD><INPUT id=txtEmail maxLength=50 name=txtEmail style="HEIGHT: 20px;
WIDTH:
          137px"></TD>
        <TD><INPUT id=txtSubject maxLength=40 name=txtSubject style="HEIGHT:
          21px; WIDTH: 216px" size=30></TD>
    </TR>
</TABLE>

<P>Message
<TEXTAREA   id=txtMessage name=txtMessage
```

```
            style="HEIGHT: 226px; WIDTH: 100%">
    </TEXTAREA>
    <INPUT id=txtMessageID name=txtMessageID type=hidden></P>
    </P>
    <TABLE BORDER=0 CELLSPACING=1 CELLPADDING=1>
        <TR>
            <TD><INPUT id=reset1 name=reset1 type=reset value=Reset></TD>
            <TD><INPUT id=submit1 name=submit1 type=submit value=Submit></TD>
            <TD><INPUT id=cmdCancel name=cmdCancel type=button value=Cancel></TD>
        </TR>
    </TABLE>
    </FORM>

    </BODY>
    </HTML>
```

Now save the file as `compose.html` in your IIS project directory with the other HTML files. Then add it to the IIS application as you did with the other templates, giving it the name `tmpCompose`.

While we're here we might as well add the code necessary to process the `form submit` event for `tmpCompose`. First connect the `form submit` to a custom event by going to the WebClass view, clicking on `tmpCompose` you just added, then right click **Form1** in the right hand window and select **Connect to Custom Event**.

Now go to the event for that custom event by double clicking form1 under `tmpCompose` in the left frame and add the code

```
Private Sub tmpCompose_form1()
On Error GoTo ErrorHandler

    PostMessage
    tmpSuccess.WriteTemplate
    Exit Sub

ErrorHandler:
    ErrorRoutine Err.Number, Err.Description, "tmpCompose_form1" & Err.Source

End Sub
```

The code calls sub `PostMessage` which we will write in a minute, then writes `tmpSuccess` which we also still have to create.

Storing The Message

The private subroutine `PostMessage` is used by both versions of the message board. Using `Request.Form` we access the form1 values, then use the Business object to store the new message to the database.

```
Private Sub PostMessage()
On Error GoTo ErrorHandler

    ' Our Business object
    Dim loDatabase As New clsMBBusObject
```

```
        Dim lsName As String
        Dim lsMessage As String
        Dim lsEmail As String
        Dim lsSubject As String
        Dim llMessageID As Long
        Dim lsRemoteAddress As String
        Dim lsErrorString As String

        ' Retrive message details from HTML form
        lsEmail = Trim(Request.Form("txtEmail"))
        lsMessage = Request.Form("txtMessage")
        ' replace empty subject with No Subject
        lsSubject = IIf(Trim(Request.Form("txtSubject")) = "", "No Subject",
Trim(Request.Form("txtSubject")))
        ' txtMessageId was hidden element inside form
        llMessageID = CLng(Request.Form("txtMessageId"))
        lsRemoteAddress = Request.ServerVariables("REMOTE_ADDR")
        ' If no name supplied use IP address of user
        lsName = IIf(Trim(Request.Form("txtName")) = "", lsRemoteAddress,
Trim(Request.Form("txtName")))

        ' Add message using Business object AddMessage method
        loDatabase.AddMessage lsSubject, lsName, lsEmail, lsMessage, lsRemoteAddress,
1, lsErrorString, llMessageID

    ' If lsErrorString has something in it then an error occurred -
        ' if add failure then let user know else write error template

        WebClass.URLData = "You message was added successfully"
        If lsErrorString = "ADDFAILED" Then
            WebClass.URLData = "Sorry, we were unable to add your message, please try
later"
        ElseIf lsErrorString <> "" Then
            Err.Raise vbObjectError + 101, "MessageDB - (PostMessage) Function
AddMessage", lsErrorString
        End If
        Exit Sub

ErrorHandler:
        ErrorRoutine Err.Number, Err.Description, "PostMessage - " & Err.Source
    End Sub
```

Informing the User Whether the Message Posted Successfully

`tmpSuccess` is very simple and is used to display a message informing the user if their message posted successfully or not. We insert the success or otherwise message inside the `WC@Inform` tags when the Tag Process event for this page fires. Save the html file as Success.html and add it to the IIS project and name the template `tmpSuccess`.

```
<HTML>
<HEAD>
<SCRIPT ID=clientEventHandlersJS LANGUAGE=javascript>
<!--

function button1_onclick() {
window.returnValue = true;
window.close();
return true;
```

```
}
//-->
</SCRIPT>
</HEAD>
<BODY>
<BR><BR><BR><BR>
<P align=center>
    <STRONG>
    <FONT face="" size=6>
        <WC@Inform></WC@Inform>
        <BR>
        <BR>
        <INPUT id=button1 name=button1
          type=button value="Close and Return to message board"
          LANGUAGE=javascript onclick="return button1_onclick()">
    </FONT>
    </STRONG>
</P>
</BODY>
</HTML>
```

We need to add code to its `ProcessTag` event to write out `<WC@Inform>` tags telling the user whether the message was added successfully or not.

```
Private Sub tmpSuccess_ProcessTag(ByVal TagName As String, TagContents As String,
SendTags As Boolean)
On Error GoTo ErrorHandler

If TagName = "WC@Inform" Then
    TagContents = WebClass.URLData
    WebClass.URLData = ""
End If
Exit Sub
ErrorHandler:
    ErrorRoutine Err.Number, Err.Description, "tmpSuccess_ProcessTag - " &
Err.Source
End Sub
```

Adding the Message Creation VBScript

We need to go back to `tmpMessageTopFrame` and add the event handling for the `cmdNewMessage` and `cmdReply` buttons.

Creating a New Message

We open up `tmpCompose` as a modal window and pass −1 as the `messageID` of the message being replied to which indicates this is a new message not a reply. Code execution will halt at the `window.showModalDialog` until the user closes the dialog window. The code for the event handlers can go inside the same `<SCRIPT>` tag block as our existing code.

```
Sub cmdNewMessage_onclick
    Dim Ret_Val
    Ret_Val = window.showModalDialog("compose.htm","-1; ; _
      ","status:no;center:yes;help:no;minimize:no;maximize:no; _
      border:thin;statusbar:no;dialogWidth:600px;dialogHeight:500px")
```

```
      ' Refresh messages if did not cancel
      if Ret_Val <> "CANCEL" Then location.reload true
   End Sub
</SCRIPT>
<TITLE>The Message Board</TITLE>
```

Replying to an Existing Message

The cmdReply_onclick is almost identical to the code for cmdNewMessage_onclick except that this time we pass the MessageId, subject and message text of the message being replied to. These are stored in the global variables, which were populated by tmpMessage within the <IFRAME> when the user clicks on a message headers row.

```
Sub cmdReply_onclick
   Dim Ret_Val
   Ret_Val = window.showModalDialog("compose.htm",CStr(lCurrentMessageID) & _
      ";RE:" & CStr(sCurrentMessageSubject) & ";" & _
      txtMessage.value,"status:no;center:yes;help:no;minimize:no; _
      maximize:no;border:thin;statusbar:no;dialogWidth:600px;dialogHeight:500px")
   if Ret_Val <> "CANCEL" Then location.reload true
End Sub
</SCRIPT>
```

Emailing a Message Author

We may as well take this opportunity to populate the cmdEmail_onclick event handler for the cmdEmail button. When the user clicks a message header in tmpMessage in the <IFRAME> the email address associated with that message is put in a page scope variable in tmpMessageTopFrame. When the user clicks cmdEmail it will result in the users default email program being opened in compose message view. This is achieved simply by setting document.location to a mailto hyperlink for the email address. If no email was supplied, then we just pop up a message box informing the user of that fact.

```
Sub cmdEmail_onclick
msEmail = Trim(msEmail)
If msEmail = "" Then
      Msgbox "Sorry no e-mail supplied with this message"
Else
      document.location.href=msEmail
End If
End Sub
</SCRIPT>
```

Displaying a Helpfile

I have included a simple help file that the user can view by clicking the cmdHelp button. The event code is below and can be inserted in tmpMessageTopFrame after the other VBScript.

```
Sub cmdHelp_onclick
window.open "help.htm", "Help", "scrollbars=1, resizable=1, width=600, height=450"
End Sub
</SCRIPT>
```

The HTML for the page is very simple and is not included as part of the IIS project, though there is no reason you couldn't add it. Make sure you save the file as `help.htm` in the webclass project directory.

```
<HTML>
<HEAD>
<TITLE>Message Board help File</TITLE>
</HEAD>
<BODY>
<BASEFONT face="Verdana" size=3  color=Black>
<STRONG>
<P align=center >
<FONT size=5>Message Board Help Page</FONT>
</P>

<P><FONT color=navy>View A Message</FONT>
<BR>Single click the message subject, person
or date and its text will appear in the grey textbox at the bottom of the
page.
<BR><BR>If you double click a message line it will open in a new page.
</P>

<P>
<FONT color=navy>Create a New Message</FONT>
<BR>To compose a new message click on the New Message button
at the top of the page
</P>

<P><FONT color=navy>Replying to an existing message</FONT>
<BR>To reply to a message - click the message you want to reply to,
then click the Compose Reply button
</P>

<P><FONT color=navy>E-mailing message author</FONT>
<BR>To E-mail the author of the message click the message line,
then click the Email Author button
<BR><BR>
(If they did not supply an e-mail address then you will be
notified and prevented from e-mailing)
</P>

<P>If you hold your mouse over the name of a person and
they have supplied a e-mail then their e-mail will appear
as a tool-tip
</P>

</BODY>
</HTML>
```

Save the file in the IIS project directory as help.htm

Link Back to your Web Site

On the `tmpMessageTopFrame` is a button which takes the user back to the main website, my main page is index.asp, just replace it with the URL of yours. The code for that event is below and you need to add it to `tmpMessageTopFrame` in the same <SCRIPT> block as the existing VBScript.

```
Sub cmdMainPage_onclick
     document.location.replace("index.asp")
End Sub
```

Internet Explorer Message Board Completed!

Finally we have finished the Internet Explorer message board and you are now ready to implement facilities for a non-IE message board if you want. As I stated at the beginning, although the current project on the Alumni Web Site does implement non-IE functions, I will not go into them here to try and make this case study as concise as possible.

A NonIE message board could use many of the principles of the IE message board and where it couldn't it would tend to be very much simpler. There would be no client side scripting and the HTML would want to be kept simple to maximize compatibility.

Having recompiled our code and checked its working on the development server, our next task is deploying it from the development machine and onto the live server.

Deploying the Message Board

Deployment can be one of the most stressful parts of developing web applications. A wrong move could potentially lead to registry corruption, missing DLLs and DLLs which stop existing programs from functioning. Deployment is the final stage and deadlines are looming (or have been and gone) so the pressure's on.

Visual Basic has the Package and Deployment wizard to help you, however in my experience (and that of others judging by the numerous newsgroup postings) package and deployment wizard is a tool with issues. It can be useful sometimes but following the help file instructions for its use will not necessarily lead to successful deployment. Often you need to make changes to IIS and SQL Server settings and the NT registry, which you need to do by hand.

I'll take it step by step on how to get the message board working outside the development environment.

Deploying the Database

The steps involved in deploying the database are:

> ➢ Create a blank database on deployment server

> ➢ Create new user MBUser and give access permissions to database

> ➢ On development SQL Server use Enterprise Manager to generate SQL scripts for tables and stored procedures – make sure you select Script Object Level Permission on options tab

> ➢ On the live server, use Query Analyzer to run the generated SQL scripts against the blank database

> ➢ Create ODBC Data Source Connection on server as we did for the development machine

I have covered all of the steps before except generating SQL scripts so lets take a quick look at that.

Generating SQL Scripts

Open up SQL Server Enterprise Manager on the development machine and click the tree view until you can see the message board database. If you click on the MessageBoard database you should see a list of possible tasks appear, select Generate SQL Scripts.

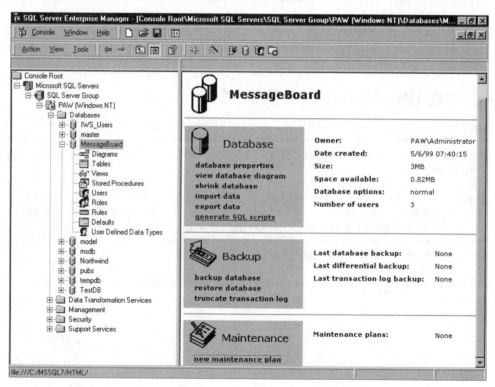

This will show the Generate SQL Scripts wizard. We can accept the defaults on the General and Formatting tabs but on the Options tab make sure you tick the Script Object Level Permissions. I have ticked all the Table Scripting options though we don't need all of these for this project it is a good habit to get into.

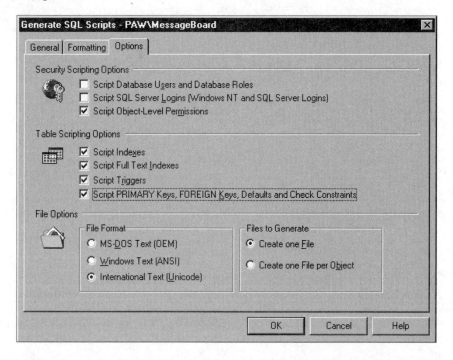

Now click OK and save the file. You then need to upload the file to the deployment SQL Server machine and open Query Analyser and load the SQL Script file. Make sure the database selected in the combobox is the Message Board, then run the scripts and all the tables and stored procedures will be created with the correct permissions.

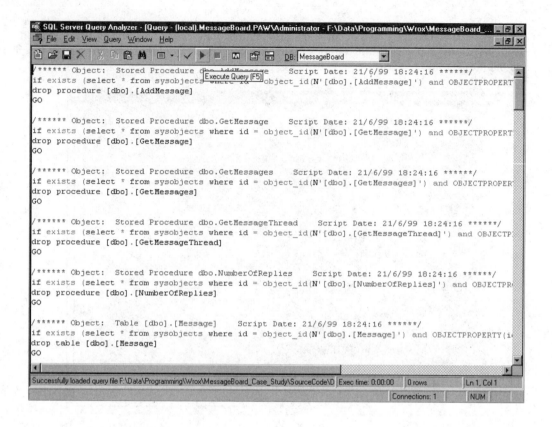

Deploying the Business Object

For any Visual Basic program or DLL to run it requires the Visual Basic support libraries installed, such as the Visual Basic virtual machine. These libraries are installed automatically with NT Service Pack 4 so this is a quick and easy way of getting them on the deployment machine, you'll also need to install ADO 2.1 service pack 2 to get the Data Access components on there. MS Office 2000 also installs the ADO 2.1 components.

Now we can use the Package and Deployment Wizard to create a set-up package for our Business Object's DLL.

First open P&D Wizard from the Windows start menu, Visual Studio, Tools, and select your project by browsing to MessageBoardDB.vbp. You can also add P&D Wizard to your add-ins menu in Visual Basic by selecting the Add-Ins, Add-in manager menu. Then click on P&D Wizard and check the Loaded/Unloaded box and the Load on Startup box.

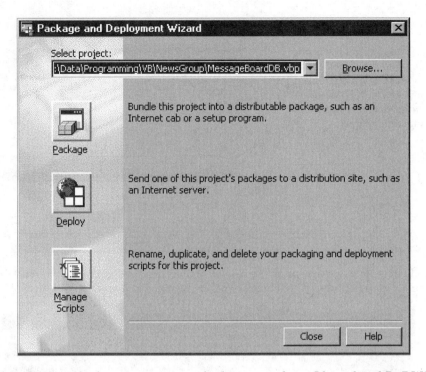

Now click Package and select to create a standard set-up package. I have found P&DW's Internet packaging to be less reliable.

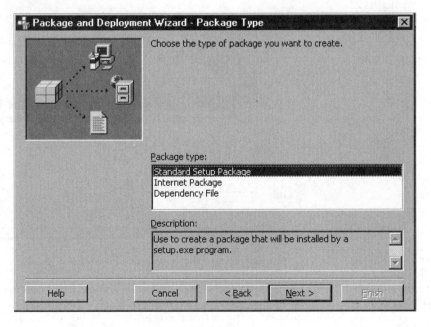

Click Next and browse to a convenient location for P&D to put the set-up package and support files.

Click Next. You may get a warning screen telling you the dependency information for scrun.dll (used for the scripting runtime's Dictionary object) is out of date. It appears safe to ignore this for our project.

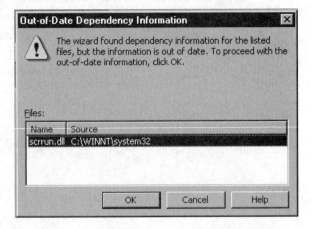

Now keep clicking Next and accepting the default options until you get to the Shared Files screen. I have chosen to share both the ADO libraries and the business objects DLL file.

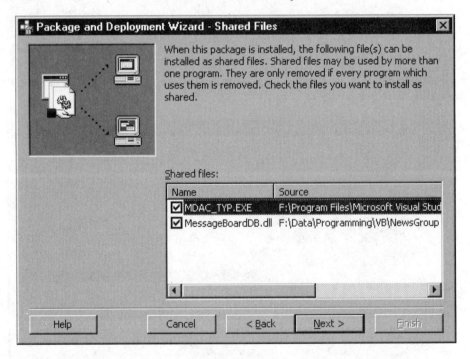

Click Next, then Finish. P&D will create the set up program you need to install on the server.

Once you have uploaded the set-up program to the deployment server and run its set up executable once, then there is no reason to use P&D again; unless you install a new Visual Studio service pack and want to update your business object on the deployment server.

If you need to update your Business object (and have not installed a new service pack) you need to

- Stop IIS
- Unregister the existing business object DLL by using regsvr32. The command line for this is:
  `regsvr32 /u drive/location of dll/MessageBoardDB.dll`
- Copy your new business object's DLL over the old one
- Register the new DLL using regsvr32 – as above but no /u on command line
- Restart IIS

Some may argue I'm being over cautious in stopping IIS rather than choosing the Unload option from within IIS Console but its better to be safe. A useful time saver is to write a DOS batch file or Windows script to perform this task automatically.

Deploying the Webclass

Having deployed the business object, deploying the webclass should be fairly simple. Although you could use the package and deployment wizard, I have had problems with it not correctly registering all the necessary components and therefore tend to do it myself by hand.

The steps involved in first installing the webclass are:

- Copy `Mswcrun.dll`, the main webclass support file, which you'll find in your windows system directory, to your live server's system directory
- Register `Mswcrun.dll` using `regsvr32`
- Copy over the IIS application's DLL to deployment server
- Register the DLL using `regsvr32`
- Copy HTML template files and IIS ASP files to the deployment server – for the message board they need to be in the same directory

And now you have yourself a working webclass. The DLL can go pretty much anywhere on the server – it doesn't need to be with the .ASP for HTML files. If security is important it may be advisable to place the DLLs in a separate directory not available to web browsing, for example the Windows System32 directory.

If you make changes to the project and want to update the deployment server then for changes to the HTML templates it's a simple matter of copying them across.

For updates to the IIS applications DLL you need to:

- Stop IIS
- Un-register existing DLL using regsvr32 /u
- Copy new DLL over old one
- Register new DLL with regsvr32
- Restart IIS

As always I'm being extra cautious and you may prefer alternative ways of installing a new DLL without stopping all of the IIS websites.

Deploying Remote Scripting

Installing Remote Scripting involves the following steps:

> Copy _ScriptLibrary to deployment server and put it under the directory you placed the .ASP and HTML files

> Ensure that under IIS the _ScriptLibrary directory permissions are set to *at least* Script. You can check this by opening up Internet Service Manage console, right clicking the _ScriptDirectory and select properties.

> Copy the MessageRoutines.ASP file to the same directory as your IIS application's .ASP file.

Updating is just a matter of copying over the new files.

Summary

In this Case Study, you should have learned a lot about programming applications on the Web without using client side ActiveX components. Although the code has been for Internet Explorer 4/5, with the exception of Remote Scripting, the browser specific coding has mostly been for cosmetic purposes and so can be updated for other browsers. To summarize, in both parts of this Case Study we have learned how to:

> Use a SQL Server database to store messages

> Create stored procedures in SQL server to implement some of the business logic

> Make the transactions within the database atomic

> Access the database using ADO 2.1

> Create an ActiveX DLL to control the business logic of the application

> Create an IIS Application in Visual Basic using the DLL to take care of the business logic

> Respond to user requests

> Use HTML frames in an IIS application

> Implement Dynamic HTML to create user friendly interfaces

> Use remote scripting to access data without page refreshes

Hopefully this case study has given you lots of ideas you can use and move on from in your own projects. There are many ways you could improve and add to the message board. Here are some suggestions:

> Adding a mechanism for security, for example a registration and logon system before adding and/or viewing messages.

> ➢ Enable users to view messages within a specified range of dates, such as all messages added in the last month.

> ➢ Administration system for the message board's owner, which allows them to approve, delete and change messages.

> ➢ Multiple message boards linked in a newsgroup like fashion.

> ➢ Allowing compatibility with far more browsers than Internet Explorer.

Case Study 2 :
Web Based Document
Management

HISTORY

"Brain-scanner" - that's how Impera Software Corporation was known among employers; it produced employee-screening software - something that recruiters loved and candidates hated. Those companies that did not trust its software, used Impera's consulting services and conducted the interview over the phone. Impera had a lot of business to deal with, a lot of sales calls to follow up on, and, most important, a lot of data to publish to their customers on the corporate web site.

Just like any other company, it had to develop some internal applications. Because these applications had to be used by the clients, most of them had to be web-enabled. There was a lot of software evaluated and nothing was found that satisfied their needs completely. The company needed a package that could track the documents, be secure, allow external users to access certain parts of the system, act as an application server, and power the whole web site; all that had to be done at the minimum cost possible and be accessible to hundreds of users. Developers started having thoughts about writing their own...

"In order to build an application, you have to think like this application"; this is how one of the meetings started one Monday morning at Impera. A couple of sleepy developers were sitting in the conference room in front of a marketing guru trying to understand what's needed. It has been common knowledge that customers needed a way to see their data on the web site, but nobody knew how to do that and what else will be needed later. In the beginning it was assumed that customers just want a simple document management system; however, it was not that easy. Most of the document management systems cost $10,000-$20,000 plus hundreds of dollars for every user you have. Impera has various types of documents. Some of those documents had to be static, some had to be generated dynamically. Some could only be accessed by certain users or be only read-only, some had to be pulled from another database or be automatically imported when sent by the customer.

At the same time, Impera had other applications to develop and they had to be integrated with the existing document management system. "What happens if we purchase this system and later find out that it does not support something we need but we did not think about this before"? After a long debate, it had been agreed that a simple document management system won't help, Impera needs a big enterprise product, perhaps a collaboration product, such as Lotus Notes. The statement "You have to think like this application" was a hint - there was no application on the market that could think exactly like Impera did and was customizable the way Impera wanted it. It has been decided to create Impera's own application.

There are several ways to solve a problem. Which way are we taking? There are lots of application servers out there, which one should we use? Impera needed an application server that would:

> Be easy to learn
> Be inexpensive
> Be easily integrated with the rest of the applications
> Allow code reuse
> Be reliable
> Be scalable
> Be easy to use
> Have an enhanced support for SQL Server
> Be very fast
> Run on Windows NT

After looking at several servers, it has been decided to use Visual Basic Web Classes. Visual Basic supported everything needed plus much more!

Design

Every application has to be designed, no matter how big or small it is, and this was no an exception. We will go through all of the design stages and see how the product was designed.

Let's go back a little bit and review what had to be done and what the marketing department requested. It has been determined that the new application should:

> Contain a storage for the documents

> Provide users with an easy way to access the documents via the browser

> Have a document-level security

> Power the web site - the whole corporate web site would be driven by this application

> Have support for integration with existing systems

Now let's review some of the above conditions to make sure we understand the details. We need to store the documents. Documents can be stored either in the database or as a file. If we store them in the file system, we may not have as much security as if it was a database, we won't be able to do easy updates, and deletes on several records at the same time and will still have to use a database to store security information. To ease this and solve all of these problems, we will store the documents in the database; after all, this is exactly why databases have been designed.

To provide users with an easy way to access the documents it can be designed so that we can use any browser to browse for the documents and view them.

We want to have a security table in the database to store usernames and passwords of all the people who will access the system. However, as this application also powers the web site, we can assume that anonymous users should be able to access some of the documents as well, even if they don't have an account set up.

To have support for integration with existing systems, we have to make sure that any developer who will come in later will be able to integrate this application and data with something else that already exists.

Where do we start?

First we have to write a plan and see how this system will organize the documents. After all, if we will have it store 1000 documents, we should have some kind of a structure. The best way to organize these documents would be to have them in a tree structure, just like files in the file system. Let's assume that your company has two products, ProductA, and ProductB. Each product has 2 modules. Each module has documentation associated with it. How do we organize it? Here's an example:

ProductA
    Module1
        Document1
        Document2
    Module2
        Document1
        Document2 (Link to Document3 of Module2 of ProductB)
ProductB
    Module1
    Module2
        Document1
        Document2
        Document3

As you see from here, Module1 of ProductA has 2 documents, Module2 of ProductA has 1 document and one link to another document, Module1 of ProductB has no documents at all, and Module2 of ProductB has 3 documents.

Just like in a regular file system, each document will have a path. For example, Document2 of Module2 of ProductB will have a path of `/ProductB/Module2/Document2`. In real life, your document path may look something like this:

`/public/clients/abc_consulting/agreement.txt`

In this case, you have a root directory called public, which has a sub-directory called clients, which has a sub-directory called abc_consulting, which contains a file called agreement.txt.

Since our files are now in a well-designed structure, we have to come up with a database design that implements this structure. Eventually, this database can be placed on an enterprise database server, such as Microsoft SQL Server or Oracle. While we are designing it, we can use Microsoft Access database - it's easier. It can later be migrated to SQL Server. We will need our final database to store only two types of object: documents and users. Users should have the following information associated with them:

> **UserID** - a unique number identifying the user (primary key)

> **UserName** - name/nickname by which user will be known

> **Password** - each user should have a password.

> **FirstName** - first name of the person using the system

> **LastName** - last name of the person using the system

Since we are not writing an operating system and are not trying to protect anything very important from ourselves, we will not encrypt the password, even though it is strongly recommended that you do so if you want to use this system to store important data. If you need help with implementing a bit more security on the system, try using a third party encryption routine that you can download from the web.

Here are the fields we will need for our documents table:

> **PageID** - an ID that uniquely identifies the document (filename+path)

> **PageTitle** - this field will store the name of the document

> **PageHeader** - header file to display before the document

> **PageFooter** - footer file to display after the document

> **PageText** - the actual document

> **PageParent** - parent folder (where this file is located)

> **NumericID** - sequence ID

> **PageCode** - a unique code to identify the document to the AppClient (will talk about it later)

`PageTitle`, and `PageText` are self-explanatory, but why do we need other fields? Remember we were talking about all documents having their own path? Well, the `PageID` field will contain just that! Since all documents are located in a certain directory, we have to be able to store the location of each document in the database (parent folder); we will use the PageParent field for that. PageHeader and PageFooter will point to the files that will contain the header and the footer of the document you are storing. NumericID is a sequence ID. We will use this field to store the order in which the documents will be displayed when browsed. We will discuss the NumericID and PageHeader/Footer fields a bit later.

Let's think about what we have so far. Right now we have a storage area where documents can be placed, but what else might we need this system to do in the future? The goal is to have all of the requirements met from the list above. As we are using the database as the storage area and we are integrating into a web browser, we have dealt with most of the requirements. We still need to deal with the third and fifth point, Since the fifth talks about integration with other applications, we can assume that we can develop the third as an external application and integrate it with this one. This would be a smart idea, because it would mean that we have to write minimum code to have the system working. Adding new features would be a matter of writing new applications and integrating them with our existing system.

How can we integrate this system with any other applications? Well, integrating them might be a huge step in advancing the product. Before integrating it, we have to make sure it's customizable within itself. To make it as customizable as possible, we will have to support macros/scripts that will run while our system will be running. This means that we also have to store scripts in our database. Of course, we can create a separate table and store them, but let's think about this: what is the difference between a directory, a document, and a script? Logically, a lot. Practically, none. A script is a *document* that can be executed and a directory is basically a *document* with no contents. Both are documents and so we can store them both in the same table! This will give us an ability to manage our objects (directories, documents, scripts) easier and will give us a centralized location where objects will be stored.

Does this mean that we are actually storing objects instead of documents? Yes and No! Yes, that's exactly what we will store. However, as we discussed before, directories and scripts are also documents, so we will store the objects in our database but will refer to them as documents (or pages).

Let's take a look at a real example:

Suppose you are developing a corporate intranet powered by this product and you are storing HTML files in the system. You would like your page to ask the user to pick a customer and then display the list of orders associated with this customer. How do you do this? Create a document structure like this:

```
CustomerName1
    Order1
            Entry1
            Entry2
    Order2
            Entry1
CustomerName2
    Order1
            Entry1
            Entry2
```

This way, if you browse a directory called `CustomerName1`, you will see Order1 and Order2, which are the orders placed by this customer. When you click on Order1, it will display the list of entries in the order. This way you can have a total billing/invoicing system without doing any programming at all.

When you display the order by opening the order directory, the system should display the list of entries in the order, which is basically the bill/invoice you have to send out. But how do you display the company information and any other billing info? This is where document header and document footer come.

```
EXAMPLE:

Header:

ABC Consulting
123 Rolling Dr.
Santa Clara, CA 12345

Document List:

Ordered Item #1
Ordered Item #2

Footer:

Total Order: $100
Due: 1/1/2000
Copyright ©1999, YourCompany
```

But what if you want to display a link to another document or a web page along with the list of documents you are displaying in the current directory? Here's an easy workaround - let's create another document object called a **Link**. `Links` will be objects that will simply point to other objects.

Now we have four different types of document objects: **directories**, **scripts**, **links**, and **documents**. In order to implement this system, we will use only these four types; however, you can implement more if you have a need for that.

Remember we talked about integration of our system with other applications and the importance of scripting? Well, now we can script, but this does not give you the full power over all of the applications features, or any other applications, and does not allow you to control the server very well. In order for us to support full integration and customize the database connectivity features of the system, we have to add support for scripts to be executed prior to making a database connection. Those scripts should be able to customize the document you are opening and limit access to it if needed. Let's call such scripts **filters**.

One good example of using filters is for security implementation. Suppose you want your web site to allow anonymous access to the system and have some private documents that can only be accessed by its owner. We can install a filter that will run every time a document is requested and check if permission is granted to use the document. If not, we can return an error message or ask the user to enter their username and password. You will see how this can be implemented later in the code.

Now that we have defined all of the features we will need, it is time to create the database. Let's create a new database using MS Access and call it appserver.mdb. This database will contain two tables as following:

Users : Table

Field Name	Data Type
UserID	Number
UserName	Text
Password	Text
FirstName	Text
lastName	Text

Pages : Table

Field Name	Data Type
NumericID	Number
PageID	Text
PageText	Memo
PageTitle	Text
PageParent	Text
PageHeader	Text
PageFooter	Text
PageCode	Text

The first table will contain the users of the system; the second one will contain the actual documents.

Let's take a close look at the scripting part of the program. We have mentioned above that our program should be able to support custom scripts. These scripts should be written in a high-level, easy to learn language. The parser for this script language should be easy to implement. In order to solve such a problem, we will use Microsoft Scripting Control.

Microsoft Scripting Control has been developed to allow programmers to make their applications scriptable (this is exactly what we need). There are several steps involved in making it work with your application:

- Add a reference to Microsoft Scripting Control from VB
- Give it the list of objects in your program that it can access
- Give it some code to execute
- Execute it!

Let's remember this for the future reference. We will need this to implement scripting.

The last stage of the design process is evaluating possible product limitations and various workarounds possible. Let's go back and look at our database. The first limitation is that PageText can be up to 64Kb. This is a temporary limitation only. We can change that by using SQL Server database instead and changing the data type of this field from Memo to Image. The second limitation is the length of the PageID. PageID should contain the actual path to a document, which can only be up to 255 characters. Again, this can be fixed by changing the data type. The same will also apply to PageParent field.

One of the features we have defined "by design" can also be considered as limitations; however, they can be carefully thought of as features as well. This feature is the actual way this application is going to be developed, by using a web class. Developing this application as a web class means that there will be a component permanently loaded into memory. This can slow down the server; after all, regular ASP scripts don't use any additional components. On the other hand, this means that our component can have a permanent/cached connection to a database, unlike ASP. Therefore we can retrieve pages from a database much faster and have some business logic in the background.

It looks like we have a design plan for the product; it's time to look at the implementation portion of it.

Implementation

As most of the computer scientists claim, it can take more time to design the product than to implement it. Even though the design we came up with seems to be complicated, implementation of the system really is not. The whole program can easily be implemented in only a few pages of code! Let's go through the implementation stage step by step and see how it can be done.

What is the first step in creating a Web application? Creating a new project! Let's run Visual Basic and create a new IIS application. Let's call it AppServer. This will be our main program. We will call it using our browser and tell it which page we would like to view. AppServer will retrieve the page for us and display it on the screen.

Let's add some references to the project. We will need to add a reference to Microsoft ActiveX Data Object and Microsoft Scripting Control. Both of them ship with Visual Basic 6.0; however, it is a good idea to make sure you have the latest version of both components by checking Microsoft's web site. Other references are added by VB automatically.

Now let's add the first web item and call it Start. As a matter of fact, this is going to be the only web item we will need. This application is too simple to contain more than one. You don't really need this item in your project, but it's considered to be a better programming practice if you do.

Let's go ahead and implement this program in several steps:

> Implement a simple **document retrieval mechanism**
> Implement **browsing directories**
> Implement **headers and footers**
> Implement **scripting**
> Implement **filters**

In order to retrieve a document from a database, we should connect to it first. Let's do so by using ADO and modifying our code as follows:

```
Dim Conn As New Connection

Private Sub WebClass_Start()
   Conn.Open "appserver"
End Sub
```

The first line should be placed in the **General Declaration** Section. It basically tells our program that we will have an instance of a connection object and it is going to be used globally. Visual Basic already knows what a Connection object is because it is a part of an ADO library, which we added a reference to. The second line basically tells us that this event will be called when an instance of a WebClass is created and started. The general syntax of an Open command is as follows:

```
Connection.Open dsn, uid, pwd

Connection : connection object
Dsn : data source name
Uid : username
Pwd : password
```

DSN is a data source name defined in the ODBC applet of the Windows Control Panel. It should point to a database you have created. In this case we will use MS Access. You don't have to specify username and password to connect to an Access database; however, you'll have to specify them if you want to connect to an enterprise database, such as SQL Server or Oracle. To create a DSN, open Windows Control Panel, double-click on the ODBC icon, click Add and follow the instructions on screen. They might vary, depending on which database you decided to use and what version your ODBC drivers are.

If you would like to use SQL Server database, your connection line can look something like this:

```
Conn.Open "appserver","sa","monkey"
```

Once we've established a database connection, we have to display a page taken from the database. Since our database can contain a lot of pages, we have to specify which page we would like to retrieve. This parameter cannot be built into our code, it will be dynamic. Therefore, we have to accept this parameter in the URL, whenever a page is called. For example, the following URL should tell us that the user wants to retrieve a page from the database called `MyPage.htm`.

```
http://localhost/appserver/app.asp?page=MyPage.htm
```

Since this parameter is passed in the Page variable of the URL, we can get the value of it by examining the `Request.QueryString` collection. This will tell us which page the user wants to display. Once we know what this page is, we can display it. Let's try to modify the following code in our program to test this:

```
Dim Conn As New Connection
Dim Rst as Recordset

Private Sub WebClass_Start()

   Conn.Open "appserver"
    Set Rst = Conn.Execute("select * from pages where PageID='" _
     & Request("Page") & "'")
    Response.Write Rst("PageText")
   Conn.Close

End Sub
```

Let's examine the above code to see what it does. First we open a database connection by calling the `Conn.Open` method. Then we execute a regular query again our database to find a page by using the `Conn.Execute` method and returning the result to the `Rst` collection. This will give us a recordset with the list of pages that matched this criteria. Since we can assume that each page has a unique name, this means that `Rst` collection will only contain one record.

Let's add some records to our test table to see if this works:

NumericID	PageID	PageText	PageTitle	PageParent	PageHeader	PageFooter	PageCode
0	MyPage.htm	Hello world	My First Page	/			ARA1010
1	MyDoc.htm	My personal doc	My doc	/			AZX0339
2	AnotherOne.htm	Another page	My page #3	/			ZS83319

Looking at the NumericID field may confuse you. Why do we need it if PageID is a key? Does NumericID identify a page? The answer is No. We can use this field in order to show the order in which our documents will be displayed when we run a query. We do not need this field to find a document but we will use it later when we would want to display the documents in a certain order. PageID field contains the actual ID of a page we want to display, PageText is the text we want to display. PageTitle contains the name of the document. PageParent should contain a parent document, but in this case it's a '/', which means it's located in the root directory. PageHeader and PageFooter are not implemented yet, so we will leave them blank for now. PageCode will be used later; this field is used exclusively by the client program. You can set it to some random text for now.

There are a couple of details to consider before trying to run this application. Firstly, create a virtual directory called `appserver` which connects to your project directory, using the IIS Management Console. Secondly, rename your `WebClass1.asp` file to `app.asp`. You can rename or copy the file using Windows NT explorer and to create your virtual directory, right click on your web site in the IIS Management Console and select to create a **New Virtual Directory**.

Now let's try executing the code again. We have records in the database to check against. Open this application in your browser window and request the following URL:
`http://localhost/appserver/app.asp?page=MyPage.htm`

When you call this page, it should take the record from the Pages table with a `PageID` of `MyPage.htm` and display it on the screen like this:

Hello World

Congratulations! You have implemented the first step of your project!

Now let's make it a little bit more complicated by adding some browsing features. When we browse a certain directory, we would like to be able to see the list of documents in a certain folder. In order to do this, we have to tell our application what the parent folder is. Let's try doing that by passing the Parent option in the URL as following:

`http://localhost/appserver/app.asp?parent=/`

Let's add some code to our function to implement this feature:

```
Private Sub WebClass_Start()

    Conn.Open "appserver"

    If Request("Parent")="" then

        Set Rst = Conn.Execute("select * from pages where PageID='" _
        & Request("Page") & "'")
        Response.Write Rst("PageText")

    Else

        WhereClause = " and PageParent='" & Request("parent") & "'"

        Set rst = conn.Execute("select * from pages where 1=1 " & _
        WhereClause & " order by NumericID")

        While Not rst.EOF
          If Left(rst("PageTitle"), 7) = "folder:" Then
            Response.Write "<img src=folder.gif> <a href='" & _
            AppPage & "?Page=" & rst("PageID") & "&Parent=" _
             & rst("PageID") & "'>" & Mid(rst("pagetitle"), 8, _
            Len(rst("pagetitle"))) & "</a><br>"
          Else
            Response.Write "<img src=document.gif> <a href='" _
             & AppPage & "?Page=" & rst("PageID") & "'>" _
             & rst("pagetitle") & "</a><br>"
          End If

        Wend

    End If

    Conn.Close

End Sub
```

There's an If statement, that basically selects if your application should display a page or browse a folder. This is determined by checking if the Parent variable was specified. If we determine that we need to display the list of documents in a folder, we do a simple SQL query to pull the list of documents in the folder specified. We dynamically build a where clause of the query and store it in the WhereClause variable. This WhereClause variable is then appended to a general query. As a result, a query that will get all of the pages from the root directory may look like this:

```
Select * from Pages Where 1=1 and PageParent='/' order by NumericID
```

Quick Note: Why do we put 1=1 as a part of the clause? 1 always equals 1, so this query will return all of the records. The answer is simple. If we don't put 1=1 there, our query will look like this:

```
Select * from Pages Where and PageParent='/' order by NumericID
```

The 'Where and' part is not valid, we have to put some kind of a dummy statement there that will be ignored. That's why we put 1=1. This is a standard trick that database programmers use in order to minimize the coding time. However, if you feel this is a bad programming practice, you can add some additional code to build the query differently.

Now that we have a recordset returned, we can display its contents on the screen. In order to do that, we create a While loop which functions until we reach the end of the recordset (EOF). For every record we have, we have to display an icon and a link to a record itself. For now we can only display two types of objects: folders and pages. Let's steal the folder and the document bitmaps from the VB Graphics directory or directly from the source code that you can download from Impera's Home Page. We have to check what kind of entry we have, a document or a folder. In order to distinguish such entries, let's add a 'folder:' prefix to each folder name like this:

	NumericID	PageID	PageText	PageTitle	PageParent	PageHeader	PageFooter	PageCode
	0	MyPage.htm	Hello world	My First Page	/			ARA1010
	1	MyDoc.htm	My personal doc	My doc	/			AZX0339
	2	AnotherOne.htm	Another page	My page #3	/			ZS83319
	0	MyDocs	My documents	folder:My Docs	/			AS29210
	0	MyOtherDoc.htm	My Other Doc	My Other Doc	MyDocs			ZW92991

Pages : Table

As you see in the table above, there are two new entries - a folder named MyDocs and page MyOtherDoc.htm, which is located in MyDocs folder. We can use these two entries to test our program.

Let's go back to our code now. As we have mentioned above, each record should either be a folder or a page. Therefore we have to include an IF statement and determine which one we have to display. What is the difference in displaying these two items? There are two differences: a different bitmap, and a different link. Pages should be viewed and directories should be browsed.

We already know how to display a link to a page and to a folder, so the only thing we have to do is build the actual link. Let's run our program and see how it works. This is what you should be getting:

> Hello world
>
> My Personal Doc
>
> Another Page
>
> My Documents

Each line should be a link. If you click on any of the three documents displayed, you will see a document itself. Clicking on a folder should display the contents of a folder.

As you can see, it is not hard at all! In only a few lines of code, you have implemented directory browsing with support for multiple levels and document viewing.

The next step in a process is adding support for headers and footers. They can be displayed in two ways: predefined in a database, or displayed by default.

Let's create four files `appheader.htm`, `appfooter.htm`, `appheader1.htm`, and `appfooter1.htm`. The first two files are going to be our default header and footer. Let's store some sample data in them:

Appheader.htm

```
<html><head><title>AppServer</title></head>
<body bgcolor=white>
<h1>Application Server</h1><hr>
```

Appfooter.htm

```
</body></html>
```

The other two files will store custom headers and footers and can be different for every page you display. They are defined in the database. Let's put some sample data in them:

Appheader1.htm

```
<html><head><title>Welcome to Impera</title></head>
<body bgcolor=white>
<h1>Welcome to Impera Software Corporation</h1><hr>
```

Appfooter1.htm

```
Copyright ©1999, Impera Software Corporation
</body></html>
```

Now let's add some code to display the default header and footer. You can create your own rules and use your own logic to determine when they should be used. In this case we will display them only when directories are being browsed. In order to ease that and promote some code reuse, let's create a function called `WriteFile`. This function will take an HTML page from your hard drive and display it on the screen. This is basically the same as retrieving it from the database, only this way it is retrieved much faster. Here it is:

```
Sub WriteFile(filename As String)

    On Error GoTo errhandler
    Dim c As Integer
    c = FreeFile
    Dim text As String
    Open App.Path & "\" & filename For Input As #c
    text = Input(LOF(c), c)
    Response.Write text
    Close #c
    Exit Sub

  errhandler:

End Sub
```

This function uses very simple logic to open a file, read it into a variable and display it using a regular `Response.Write` method. Please note, that there's an error handler created for this function. We do not want our program to crash if the file was not found. In this case we just ignore the error, however you can use your own logic here as well.

Now let's add a code that displays the default header file. This function should be placed right before the while loop that goes through the list of directories.

```
WriteFile "appheader.htm"
```

The footer file works the same way and it should be placed right after the while loop:

```
WriteFile "appfooter.htm"
```

Since the `WriteFile` function is already written, we can assume that this part works (as long as `appheader.htm` and `appfooter.htm` exist and are located in the application path).

In order to display a predefined header or footer, we have to make some more changes to the code. Go back to the very first part of your code where you display a regular page taken from the database. Add the following lines before you display a page:

```
If Not IsNull(rst("PageHeader")) Then
    WriteFile rst("PageHeader")
End If
```

Add the following lines after you display a page:

```
If Not IsNull(rst("PageFooter")) Then
    WriteFile rst("PageFooter")
End If
```

You see how useful one function can be? This `WriteFile` function allows you to display two types of headers and footers! Now open your database table and specify `appheader1.htm` and `appfooter1.htm` as your header and footer for some of the pages. Now try browsing the site to see if it works.

Now let's take a look at implementing scripting. In order for us to do that, we have to recall how the MS Scripting Model works. Do you remember which steps are involved in having a script execute? Let's take a look at this piece of code and see if it will remind us:

```
Dim Command As String
Dim SC As New MSScriptControl.ScriptControl

Command = Mid(Cmd, 8, Len(Cmd))
SC.Language = "VBScript"
SC.AllowUI = False
SC.AddObject "request", Request, True
SC.AddObject "connection", conn, True
SC.AddObject "response", Response, True
SC.AddObject "rst", rst, True
```

```
SC.AddObject "conn", conn, True
SC.AddObject "session", Session, True
SC.AddCode Command
SC.Run "Main"
```

In the beginning we simply create an instance of the MSScriptingControl. Then we determine a command or a piece of code to run and add references to various objects we have.

Use the following command to add an object:

```
Control.AddObject Name, Object, AddMembers
```

Control - MS Scripting control
Name - Name under which your script will know this object
Object - The actual object you are adding
AddMembers - If set to true, adds all objects under this object as well.

When objects are added, we can execute a script by issuing a Run method and telling it which function to execute. In this particular case we will execute a `Main()` function.

This part seems to be easy, doesn't it? But how do you insert it into your code and how does your program know if the page requested is a document or a script? Remember how we could tell the difference between a page and a folder? The same way we distinguished a script, only this script prefix will be stored in the body of the message. Here's a simple script:

```
script:

Sub Main()
    Response.Write "Hello World"
End Sub
```

Go back to your code for one second. Remember how you determine the code to run and use the `Mid` function to cut the first 8 characters out? This is done because of this script prefix in the beginning. We don't want to execute that, so after we run a `Mid` function, we will only have a sub called `Main` to execute.

Let's add some code to tell our program the difference between a page and a script:

```
Dim Cmd As String
Cmd = rst("Pagetext")

If Left(Cmd, 7) <> "script:" Then
    Response.Write Cmd
Else
    Dim Command As String
    Dim SC As New MSScriptControl.ScriptControl

    Command = Mid(Cmd, 8, Len(Cmd))
    SC.Language = "VBScript"
    SC.AllowUI = False
```

```
    SC.AddObject "request", Request, True
    SC.AddObject "connection", conn, True
    SC.AddObject "response", Response, True
    SC.AddObject "rst", rst, True
    SC.AddObject "conn", conn, True
    SC.AddObject "session", Session, True
    SC.AddObject "server", Server, True
    SC.AddCode Command

    SC.Run "Main"
End If
```

Do you remember how it worked before? The only line we had was:

```
Response.Write Rst("PageText")
```

Now this code is more advanced, we replaced it with code above.

> Note: **One of the objects we added with the AddObject method is a Connection
> object. The reason this was done is so that our script could use our database
> directly. This way it does not have to create a separate connection to the database.**

You have just completed another part of the program - you can now support scripting. Filters are next in the list.

Before continuing our work and implementing filters, let's review what they are. Suppose you have a knowledge base, which is a collection of articles that talk about how your product works. There are a number of articles that should only be accessible to certain users, for example, customers who paid for technical support. In order to do that, we will create a page that will load every time you request any document in the system and check if you have permissions to do so. This page will filter the pages we will display; therefore we will call it a **filter**.

This part is probably the most complicated. The initial idea of the program was to have a centralized storage system for all of the documents. Every time you request a page, the database is queried and the page is displayed. This means that we only display one page at a time but that is fine for use on the Web. Filters are a little different. They should be requested every single time, for every page. Making a call to a database will make it slow. In order to make it a little bit faster, we will store the filters as files on the server. This is not going to cause a big problem as far as management, because we will not have a lot of filters.

Let's take a look at how we can implement filters as files located on the server. In order to manage them easily, we will place each filter in a separate file. Each file will contain the code to execute with a Main() function. This gives us the whole idea on how to process filters logically:

```
For Every Filter in the filesystem
    ReadFilterFile
    ExecuteMainFunction
Next
```

How do we know which files are filter files? There are several ways we can do that. We can either give them a particular extension, place them all in a separate directory on the file system, or we can have a directory of filters in a separate file. Let's look at the three ways to find out which one is better. Having a directory is good because we don't need to have a separate file with the list. However, reading the contents of a directory is slower than reading a file as it can contain lots of files. Also if we decide to disable a filter we will have to either move it or remove it.

The same arguments can apply to having files of a fixed extension. If we have a filter list file, it is faster to read and if a filter wants to be removed, the reference to it only needs to be removed. For these reasons, we will choose to implement a directory of filters in a separate file. Let's create a filter file:

Filters.lst

```
C:\Projects\AppServer\myfilter.fi
C:\Projects\AppServer\privatefiles.fi
```

As you see, this file contains a physical location of two filters we will use. Let's create one of those filters. Our filter will disable web access to all pages that start with letter 'M':

Myfilter.fi

```
Sub Main()

    If UCase(Left(Request("Page")),1)="M" Then
      Response.Write "Permission denied"
      Response.End
    End If

End Sub
```

This is a very simple filter. As you can see by its code, it checks for the first symbol of the Page path and displays a message if the first symbol is letter "M".

Now, let's think about it. What is the difference between this filter page and a regular script we execute? The only difference is location. This means that both scripts can be executed using the same exact code. Let's try doing it by creating the following two functions:

```
Sub RunFilters()
    On Error GoTo errhandler
    c = FreeFile 'get the next available file #
    Open App.Path & "\filters.lst" For Input As #c
    While Not EOF(c)
      Line Input #c, filename
      ProcessFilter filename
    Wend
    Close #c
    Exit Sub
  errhandler:
    'ignore errors
End Sub

Sub ProcessFilter(filterfile)
    On Error GoTo errhandler
    q = FreeFile
```

```
      Open filterfile For Input As #q
        text = Input(LOF(q), q)
      Close #q

      Dim Command As String
      Dim SC As New MSScriptControl.ScriptControl

      Set rst = conn.Execute("select * from pages")

      Command = text
      SC.Language = "VBScript"
      SC.AllowUI = False
      'SC.Timeout = 100
      SC.AddObject "request", Request, True
      'SC.AddObject "ADOConnection", ADODB.Connection, True
      SC.AddObject "connection", conn, True
      'SC.AddObject "script", MSScriptControl, True
      SC.AddObject "response", Response, True
      SC.AddObject "rst", rst, True
      SC.AddObject "conn", conn, True
      SC.AddObject "session", Session, True
      SC.AddObject "server", Server, True
      SC.AddCode Command

      SC.Run "Main"

      Exit Sub

errhandler:
      'ignore errors

End Sub
```

As you see, the first function opens the filters.lst file and reads it line by line. It assumes that every line is a path to a filter file. It takes each filter and makes a call to the second function, which runs the filter by using the same method as we used before to run the scripts.

Since scripts are very similar to filters, you can have them share the code that specifies which objects they can reference. However, you might want to give filters more power. For example, you can add a reference to the Scripting Control, so that filters can control how scripts are executed.

> Note: as an example, we have added a call to open a recordset with the list of pages. This is done in order to pass the Recordset object to a filter, support more features and have better control over your code. You can eliminate this code if you want.

We now have two functions that support filters. All we need to do now is to call them when required from the main program. In order to do that, let's insert the following code in our program right after we make a connection to the database:

```
Dim Conn As New Connection
Dim Rst as Recordset

Private Sub WebClass_Start()
```

```
       Conn.Open "appserver"
    RunFilters
    Set Rst = Conn.Execute("select * from pages where PageID='" _
     & Request("Page") & "'")
    Response.Write Rst("PageText")
    Conn.Close

End Sub
```

There are lots of changes you can make to this program to satisfy your needs. The code above only displayed pages when browsing folders; you can have it display links, folders, scripts, and any other objects you can think of. You can have this program support additional objects, such as email, just by adding another reference to the SC object (see how it was used above).

In case you are wondering how to implement some other modifications to your program, take a look at the full source code:

```
'Option Explicit
Option Compare Text
Public AppPage As String
Dim rst As Recordset
Dim conn As New Connection

Private Sub WebClass_Start()
   On Error GoTo errhandler
   AppPage = "/appserver/app.asp"

   'Write a reply to the user

   Dim WhereClause As String

   If Request("parent") <> "" Then
    WhereClause = " and PageParent='" & Request("parent") & "'"
   End If

   conn.Open "appserver"

   RunFilters

   If Request("Page") = "" Or Request("Parent") <> "" Then
    Set rst = conn.Execute("select * from pages where 1=1 " & WhereClause & "
order by NumericID")

    WriteFile "appheader.htm"
    While Not rst.EOF
     If Left(rst("PageTitle"), 5) = "link:" Then
     Response.Write "<img src=link.gif> <a href='" & AppPage & "?Page=" & _
      rst("PageID") & "'>" & Mid(rst("pagetitle"), 6, Len(rst("pagetitle"))) _
      & "</a><br>"
     Else
      If Left(rst("PageTitle"), 7) = "folder:" Then
       Response.Write "<img src=folder.gif> <a href='" & AppPage & "?Page=" & _
        rst("PageID") & "&Parent=" & rst("PageID") & "'>" & _
        Mid(rst("pagetitle"), 8, Len(rst("pagetitle"))) & "</a><br>"
      Else
```

```
                Response.Write "<img src=document.gif> <a href='" & AppPage & "?Page=" _
                   & rst("PageID") & "'>" & rst("pagetitle") & "</a><br>"
             End If
           End If
         rst.MoveNext
       Wend
       WriteFile "appfooter.htm"
     Else

       Set rst = conn.Execute("select * from pages where PageID='" & Request("Page") &
                          "'" & " order by NumericID")
       If Left(rst("PageTitle"), 5) = "link:" Then
         Response.Redirect rst("PageText")
         Response.End
       End If

       Dim Cmd As String
       Cmd = rst("Pagetext")

       'WriteFile "appheader.htm"
       If Not IsNull(rst("PageHeader")) Then
         WriteFile rst("PageHeader")
       End If
       If Left(Cmd, 7) <> "script:" Then
         Response.Write Cmd
       Else
         Dim Command As String
         Dim SC As New MSScriptControl.ScriptControl

         Command = Mid(Cmd, 8, Len(Cmd))
         SC.Language = "VBScript"
         SC.AllowUI = False
         'SC.Timeout = 100
         SC.AddObject "request", Request, True
         'SC.AddObject "ADOConnection", ADODB.Connection, True
         SC.AddObject "connection", conn, True
         'SC.AddObject "script", MSScriptControl, True
         SC.AddObject "response", Response, True
         SC.AddObject "rst", rst, True
         SC.AddObject "conn", conn, True
         SC.AddObject "session", Session, True
         SC.AddObject "server", Server, True
         SC.AddCode Command

         SC.Run "Main"
       End If
       If Not IsNull(rst("PageFooter")) Then
         WriteFile rst("PageFooter")
       End If

   '    WriteFile "appfooter.htm"
       Response.End

     End If
     Exit Sub
   errhandler:
     Response.Write "<hr><br><b>AppServer error " & Err.Number & ":</b> " & _
       Err.Description
End Sub
```

```
Sub WriteFile(filename As String)
    On Error GoTo errhandler
    Dim c As Integer
    c = FreeFile
    Dim text As String
    Open App.Path & "\" & filename For Input As #c
    text = Input(LOF(c), c)
    Response.Write text
    Close #c
    Exit Sub

  errhandler:

End Sub

Sub RunFilters()
    On Error GoTo errhandler
    c = FreeFile
    Open App.Path & "\filters.lst" For Input As #c
    While Not EOF(c)
     Line Input #c, filename
     ProcessFilter filename
    Wend
    Close #c
    Exit Sub

  errhandler:
   'ignore errors
End Sub

Sub ProcessFilter(filterfile)
    On Error GoTo errhandler
    q = FreeFile
    Open filterfile For Input As #q
     text = Input(LOF(q), q)
    Close #q

    Dim Command As String
    Dim SC As New MSScriptControl.ScriptControl

    Set rst = conn.Execute("select * from pages")

    Command = text
    SC.Language = "VBScript"
    SC.AllowUI = False
    'SC.Timeout = 100
    SC.AddObject "request", Request, True
    'SC.AddObject "ADOConnection", ADODB.Connection, True
    SC.AddObject "connection", conn, True
    'SC.AddObject "script", MSScriptControl, True
    SC.AddObject "response", Response, True
    SC.AddObject "rst", rst, True
    SC.AddObject "conn", conn, True
    SC.AddObject "session", Session, True
    SC.AddObject "server", Server, True
    SC.AddCode Command
```

```
    SC.Run "Main"

    Exit Sub
errhandler:
    'ignore errors

End Sub
```

There's one more useful feature you can add. This feature will redirect you to a certain page when `app.asp` is referenced without any parameters. This can be implemented by adding these three lines of code of the `app.asp` page:

```
If Request("QUERY_STRING") = "" Then
    Response.Redirect app.asp?parent=/"
End If
```

In this case the user will be redirected to a page that will display the list of objects in the parent folder.

It is hard to believe, but this should be it as far as development. The code is very small but it does everything we wanted. Now everything is just a matter of configuration!

Configuration

The best way to test the whole system is to try using it. The best thing to do is to create a sample web application that will be powered by our system. Let's take a look at a sample web site.

ABC Technologies needs to create a web-based knowledge base. Most of the articles should be available publicly; however, some should only be accessible to registered users of the system. All articles are sorted by categories. The following structure should be used:

```
Public Pages
     Product Installation
            Documents
     Product Documentation
            Documents
     Product Troubleshooting
            Documents
Private Pages
     Troubleshooting
            Documents
     Updates
            Documents
```

This structure is very easy to implement. We have support for folders and documents; therefore adding documents to the system will be just a matter of adding database records. We implement security and make sure that only registered users can access our private pages by using filters!

Note that public and private pages are located in different directories. We can create a filter that checks for a document requested; if the document is in a private directory, we will check who this user is and will redirect the user to a custom login page, if the user is unknown. How do we know who this user is? Go back to the ProcessFilter function. It looks like one of the objects we are passing to a filter is a Session object. Session objects have an ability to store variables and pass them across pages. We can check the Username variable stored in the Session object. If it is unknown, we will redirect to a login page and ask the user to enter their username and then store it in the Session object.

Sounds complicated? Actually it is not as complicated as it sounds. Here's the filter code itself:

> Note: **The filter has to be created in a new file and registered with the filter list.**

```
sub Main()
    if instr(Request("page"),"private")=0 then
     exit sub
    end if

    if Session("username")="" or Session("password")="" then
     Session("redir")=Request("page")
     response.redirect "app.asp?Page=pages/public/login"
    end if

    dim rst1
    set rst1=conn.execute ("select * from users where username='" & _
     Session("username") & "' and password='" & Session("password") & "'")

    if rst1.eof then
     Session("redir")=Request("page")
     response.redirect "app.asp?page=pages/public/login"
    end if
end sub
```

This example assumes that all private pages contain the word "Private" in its path. In fact, if you follow the structure outlined above, it will work this way.

Let's step through the code and see what it does.

The first three lines of the sub check if the page is private. If not, the filter is not processed any further. The next three lines check if the username and password session variables are set. If one of them is not set (or unknown), we redirect the user to our login page. If our program runs beyond that point, it means that the user actually logged in. Now we have to check who this user is and if he has permissions to access the system.

As we mentioned above, we assume the user has access to our documents if he is registered. Remember we have a user table in our database? This is exactly what we need this table for. The next few lines of code query the user table and attempt to find a user with credentials supplied. If no records were found, the user is redirected to a login page. If for any reason the user is redirected to a login page, we store a page requested in the Redir session variable, so that we can redirect the user back to the page later.

⊞ Users : Table				
UserID	**UserName**	**Password**	**FirstName**	**LastName**
1	joe	joe123	Joseph	Robinson
2	mike	impera09	Michael	Smith
▶ 0				

Let's test our theory. Try entering a couple of users into your users table. You can use users from an example above. Create a login page in the system under pages/public/login with the following code:

```
<form>
<input type=hidden name=Page value="pages/public/Authenticate">
Username: <input name=username><br>
Password: <input type=password name=password><br>
<input type=submit name=submit value=Login>
</form>
```

This is a very simple page. It should display two fields in your browser, one for username and one for password. When you click Login, you will be redirected to a page specified by the Page hidden field. In this case it would be pages/public/Authenticate.

Now create a script under pages/public/Authenticate with the following code:

```
Script:

Sub Main()
    Session("Username")=Request("Username")
    Session("Password")=Request("Password")
    Response.Redirect "app.asp?Page=" & Session("Redir")
End Sub
```

This script sets the username and password session variables and redirects the user to a page that was initially requested.

Try adding some sample pages to your database and test this little program. The best way to test it is to add several categories under the public and private folders with several pages per category. After you are done, try browsing the folders. Browse some of the public folders at first, and then try browsing some private ones. Note, once you authenticate and let the system know who you are, you don't have to authenticate again to view another private page. This is happening because your session variables will remain in memory until you close your browser or the session object is destroyed.

Real Life Examples

Let's take a look at some real life uses of the system. One of the major users of the system right now is Impera Software Corporation. This system is installed on several servers; some are powered by SQL Server 7, others use MS Access 97 and MS Access 2000. Most of the applications are used internally; however, some of them are accessible by our clients.

Since the main purpose of this application is a document management system, Impera used it to store the customer support knowledge base, which is basically a collection of searchable documents in HTML format. Most of the features of a regular knowledge base are already built into the system. Features that had to be added were authentication (so that documents were only accessible to certain clients), and search. We have discussed how to implement all of the features mentioned above except for searching.

Searching involves using a small script that queries a database to find certain pages in a certain location. The code below shows how searching works:

```
script:

sub Main()

    on error resume next
    dim rst1
    if Request("query")="" then
     response.redirect "app.asp?page=pages/kb/Search"
    end if

    set rst1=conn.execute ("select * from pages where PageParent like" & _
                    "'pages/kb%' and PageText like '%" & Request("query") & "%'")
    if rst1.eof then
     response.write "Nothing found."
    else
     while not rst1.eof
      response.write "<img src=document.gif><a href='app.asp?page=" & _
       rst1("PageID") & "'>" & rst1("PageTitle") & "</a><br>"
      rst1.movenext
     wend
    end if

end sub
```

As you see, this code is somewhat similar to what we had before when we implemented browsing features. The only difference is a query. In browsing code, we have to ask to retrieve a list of documents in a certain folder. In this one, we ask to retrieve all documents located in the knowledge base folder and all of its subfolders.

What needs to be implemented in a knowledge base? A knowledge base is usually a collection of searchable articles. Most of the existing knowledge base applications use regular files to store articles. An example of such an application is Microsoft TechNet. In order to search such a knowledge base, we have to create an index file, which will contain the list of keywords we can search on. In our case we do not need to create an index list since all articles are stored in the same central location. By using regular SQL, we can query our database and find articles without having any keywords table. Of course, it might become slow if we have too many articles to search on. However, it is going to be pretty fast for an average size knowledge base, considering we will use an enterprise database to store them.

In order to implement a knowledge base, all we need to do is have a collection of articles, which are basically regular document objects that our system already knows about. We should be able to search these articles, and we already have code written to do that. All we need is to create a web page with a query field (you can use the example with authentication to do so) and create a page with search script. It's that easy!

Another application Impera implemented was its technical support application. This application was supposed to:

> ➤ Be accessible to only registered users
>
> ➤ Be integrated with an existing knowledge base
>
> ➤ Allow users to submit bugs and issues
>
> ➤ Allow technical support staff to access those issues

You could probably think: "This application is too complex. You can't implement it using a document management system." Well, you can't implement it with a regular one, but you can with this one.

Think about this. Each issue or a bug can be stored in the system as a document. When a user submits an issue, all we do is create a document in the "Current Issues" folder. The structure of the documents in the system can look something like this:

```
Support Application
     Submitted Issues
            Issues
     Resolved Issues
            Issues
     Staff
            Alex
                    Issues
            Dave
                    Issues
            Mark
                    Issues
```

As you see, we have a directory with submitted issues. Every time an issue is submitted, we create a document containing this issue in the Submitted Issues folder. Later, one of the staff members will pick one of the pending issues and place it in his personal folder. This means that they are working on an issue. When the issue is resolved, it is placed in the Resolved Issues Folder.

Sounds simple, doesn't it? In this case you have to implement security, using filters as we discussed above. The document management part is already implemented; the only item yet to be implemented is Issue Submission and a script that moves issues from one directory to another. How do we do that?

Let's take a look at both of these parts.

To think about it, moving an issue from one folder to another is just a matter of giving it another parent folder. Therefore, when you display an issue on the screen, you can put a link in the footer that will take you to one of the two scripts. One moves pages to the Resolved Issues directory, and one moves it to your personal directory. Your footer page can contain the following:

```
<a href="app.asp?page=pages/SupportSystem/Resolved">Move to Resolved</a>
```

As you see, this is a link to a page that will move your currently opened issue to another folder. How does this script know which issue was selected? Easy! Since your scripts have access to the Request object (remember, this was implemented earlier), you can use it to retrieve an `HTTP_REFERER` server variable. This variable will contain a page that requested the `SupportSystem/Resolved` page to be opened. By parsing this variable, you can find out what issue this request came from and then run a query to update its parent:

```
Conn.Execute "update pages set PageParent='pages/SupportSystem/ResolvedIssues' _
    where PageID='" & PageID & "'"
```

Assuming you parsed the URL and placed the issue ID in the `PageID` variable, the code above should update the parent and move an issue to another folder in the same manner you have this issue moved to your personal folder.

Issue submission is a little bit more complicated, but it's not as complicated as it seems to be. In order to submit an issue, all you have to do is run an `INSERT` statement against your database. Since you designed the document management system, you know all of the fields used, and adding a new record is just a matter of running a simple SQL query, which is Database Management 101.

Now you can see some of the power of this document management system. It looks like it can do much more than just store documents.

After this application has been implemented (and it only took 30 min. to implement it with all the bells and whistles), the staff at Impera were so excited to have the system, they decided to implement a small collaboration tool. The main purpose of this project was to show the power of the system.

This tool has to replace a regular mail client. Imagine sitting down and writing an email client from scratch, that should be a pretty big application. However, in this case, most of it was already written, because most of the application is just a collection of documents. In fact, every email message is a document.

A system like this would have the following structure:

```
Inbox
      Alex
            Messages
      Mark
            Messages
      Login Script
```

Each user will have his own folder that will contain his personal messages. In order to retrieve a new mail message and show it on the screen, all you have to do is display the list of documents in a user's folder. When the message is sent from user Alex to user Mark, all you do is create a new entry in Mark's folder with a message entered by Alex.

There are several things you have to implement when designing such a system:

> **Security** - users can only see their own messages

> **User friendliness** - display messages in a user-friendly format. Users want to see who the message is from and when it was sent.

> **Mail Transfer** - Sending email from one person to another as well as sending messages externally

Security is the easiest part to implement. We can use a standard filter that we used before. This filter will ensure that if you access the "pages/Inbox/something" folder this something must start with your username. If not, you will be redirected to a login page that will ask you to authenticate and then redirect you back to the page requested.

The idea of a user-friendly format can cause some confusion. A message will normally be stored like this:

PageID: `pages/Inbox/username/message1`
PageTitle: *The actual subject of the message*
PageText: *body of the message*

When you display a list of messages, you have to figure out how to display from whom this message is from. As you see, there's no field here that actually contains that. How do we solve this problem?

Let's look at the design of `appserver`. What is `PageID`? Logically, `PageID` contains a path to a document, including the document name itself. Physically, it can contain anything we wish. We did not define a standard for this field. Therefore, instead of storing `PageID` as we mentioned above, we can do something like this:

PageID: `pages/Inbox/username/from=me@mydomain.com/message1`

or

PageID: `pages/Inbox/username/message1/from=me@mydomain.com`

What we did is we specified an additional parameter to a page. For `appserver`, this is just a Page ID, for us it's a logical string that contains the sender of the message. When displaying the list of messages in the folder, we can parse out the 'from' part of `PageID` and display it on the screen. This way we can proudly say that viewing of messages is done.

How do we send messages? It can seem to be a hard job but it's actually not. The task of sending a message can be divided into two parts though: sending an internal or external message. To send an internal message, all you need to do is create an entry in the recipient's mailbox (this can be done using regular document submission algorithms). Sending an external message is a little bit more complicated. In order to do so, you will have to obtain a third-party component (an ActiveX Control or a COM Object). We can also use the CDONTS object supplied with IIS. Details are given in an appendix at the end of this book. Depending on what kind of component it is, your code can look approximately like this:

```
Set MyMail=Server.CreateObject("MyMail.SMTPMail")

MyMail.Sender="me@imperasoft.com"
MyMail.Recipient="info@imperasoft.com"
MyMail.Subject="This is a test"
MyMail.Body="Hello world"
MyMail.Server="mail.imperasoft.com"
MyMail.SendMessage

Set MyMail = Nothing
```

As you see, an Inbox application is not as easy as other applications. However, because you used `appserver`'s document management features, it took very little time to implement this.

By looking at these three examples, one can make a conclusion that `appserver` is pretty good for applications that use documents. But how good is it for other applications? If you understand the design of `appserver` pretty well, you see that you can develop virtually any application using it and use it's powerful features. The worst-case scenario is when you have to develop an application that is not related to document management in any way. In this case, the only difference between `appserver` and a regular web application written using ASP or any other scripting language is that `appserver` stores all scripts in the same centralized database. You are not losing anything if you do so, however, if you can use `appserver`'s features you can gain a lot. Therefore, using `appserver` will either work with the same effectiveness as other scripting languages or better.

Let's take a look at one last example of using this application. One of the most popular applications used on the Internet right now deals with e-commerce. Can you write a front end for a store using `appserver`?

Of course you can! Not only can you use its powerful scripting features, but also use document management to store a lot of the information about your electronic store. A document structure might look like this:

```
My Store
    Product Categories
        Category 1
            Product1
                    Option 1
                    Option 2
        Category 2
            Products
    Basket
        Basket 1
            Item 1
            Item 2
        Basket 2
            Items
    Orders
        Order 1
            Item 1
            Item 2
        Order 2
            Items
    Reports
        Report 1
        Report 2
```

It looks complicated compared with other applications written so far, however, because you can use `appserver`'s document management features, you can structure your application the way shown above (or any other way you wish) and ease the development.

As you see from the diagram, the first part is a product storage area. An example of data that can be stored there is this:

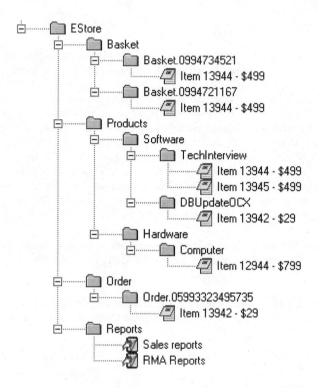

This tree will contain the category under which this product, product information and its options can be listed.

The second part of the storage is a basket. Every time a new user comes to the online store (when a new session is created), we create a new basket folder for the user. Every time a user wants to add something to a basket, we add an item with information about what was added to the user's basket. When the user places an order, his basket is moved to an Orders folder. Since folders can also be documents (a folder can contain text), we can store order information such as name, address, etc. in the folder itself.

The last part is the reports. This is a collection of scripts needed to run the store. It can contain any reports store managers might want to have as well as any scripts that users might want to execute.

As you see, implementing an e-commerce solution is pretty easy.

AppClient

You can come up with a lot of various applications you can write. However, the more you write the harder they will be, and there will be a point when you will simply say that applications are too complex and you can't use Microsoft Access to create folders and scripts. Therefore, you need to ease the way you edit documents in appserver by creating an AppClient.

We wrote a server part of our application and saw how it works. Now we need a client that can edit documents and present them to us in an easy to understand form.

Our client software will be known as AppClient. It will basically be a development tool for the appserver. It will have the following specifications:

- It will be user friendly
- It will display a directory of all the documents in a tree style (just like Windows Explorer)
- It will enable the user to add various types of objects to the system.
- It will allow users to add filters
- It will allow users to view how resulting pages will look in a browser
- It will allow users to have their own personal directories which can only be accessible by them

In the beginning, when you just look at developing simple applications for appserver, you might want to implement AppClient in a quick and dirty way. This quick and dirty AppClient will allow you to simply edit documents in your system. Later, when you decide to use some of the advanced features of the system, you might want to add more features to your program and have it work in any way you want.

Initially, Impera implemented AppClient the quick and dirty way. This was done simply because there was a need to develop some small applications and store some documents and using MS Access wasn't very intuitive in this case. Other features were added later, which turned AppClient into an enterprise software development product.

Let's take a look at a quick and dirty way of writing this application. However, in our case this application will be quick and dirty not because of the feature set, but because we need to write it fairly quickly. The front end for our application should look approximately like this:

The left panel of the application will allow you to browse for a document to modify. The right panel will allow you to view the actual document and modify its properties. AppClient will also have a pull down menu that will have a number of actions you can perform with your appserver database.

Let's create a new project. Make it a standard VB application. Add a reference to Microsoft Windows Common Controls. Drop a TreeView control on the form and name it TreeView1. Drop three text boxes and name them Text1, Text2, and Text3. Text1 will contain the document, Text2 will contain a short name of the document (PageID), and Text3 will have a title. Place controls on the form as displayed above with the entire left pane being the TreeView control.

Add a menu to your project. You will need the following menu items:

Item Name	Caption
MnuFile	&File
MnuFileConnect	Connect to server
MnuFileExit	E&xit
MnuView	&View
MnuViewAdd	Add
MnuViewAddFolder	Folder
MnuViewAddLink	Link
MnuViewAddScript	Script
MnuViewAddPage	Page
MnuViewSave	Save
MnuViewBrowse	Browse
MnuViewViewFolder	View folder
MnuViewShortcut	View shortcut
MnuViewFollowLink	Follow Link
MnuEdit	Edit
MnuEditCut	Cut
MnuEditCopy	Copy
MnuEditPaste	Paste
MnuSplitter	Splitter
MnuSplitterLeft	Left
MnuSplitterRight	Right
MnuTools	Tools
MnuToolsInstallFilter	Install Filter
MnuToolsCommandFile	Browser File
MnuToolsFind	Find
MnuHelp	Help
MnuHelpAbout	About

You can determine the level of each menu item by looking at its name.

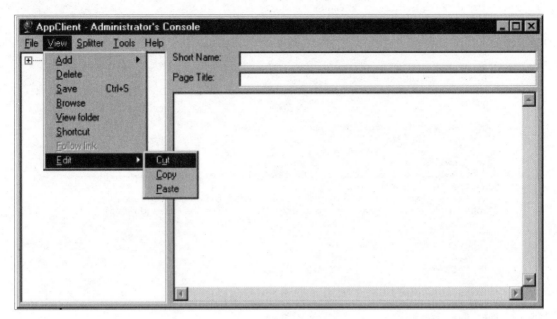

The picture above shows how your resulting menu should look.

Now let's take a look at the code. This code is very simple. It basically loads the list of documents into the TreeView1 control. When a certain document is selected, it is displayed in the right pane. You can edit it and click **Save** in the **View** menu to save it. Here's a quick and dirty code:

```
Const AdminUser = "admin"     'specify a network user who can administer the system

Dim CurrentTitle As String
Dim Conn As New Connection

Dim rst As Recordset
Dim rst1 As Recordset
Dim FilterCounter As Integer
Dim uid As String
Dim TheLink As String
Dim ClipBoardText1 As String, ClipBoardText2 As String, ClipBoardText3 As String
Dim ClipBoardImageID As Integer

Private Sub Form_Load()
    'this function will connect to the database and load the directory structure
    'into a tree control
    On Error Resume Next
    Dim sBuffer As String
    Dim lSize As Long


    sBuffer = Space$(255)
    lSize = Len(sBuffer)
    GetUserName sBuffer, lSize
```

```
    If lSize > 0 Then
     uid = Left$(sBuffer, lSize - 1)
    Else
     uid = vbNullString
    End If

    'if user is an administrator, note that in the caption of the window
    If uid = AdminUser Then
     frmClientMain.Caption = frmClientMain.Caption & " - Administrator's Console"
    End If

    'connect to the Access database
    Conn.Open "appserver"

    TreeView1.Nodes.Add , , "localhost", "LocalHost", 1
    TreeView1.Nodes.Add "localhost", tvwChild, "BadLinks", "Bad Links", 5
    On Error GoTo errhandler
    Set rst = Conn.Execute("select * from pages order by PageID")
    'loop through the documents and load them into the tree control

    While Not rst.EOF
     pagetitle = rst("PageTitle")
     ImageID = 2
     If Left(pagetitle, 7) = "folder:" Then
      ImageID = 5
      pagetitle = Mid(pagetitle, 8, Len(pagetitle))
     End If
     If Left(pagetitle, 5) = "link:" Then
      ImageID = 4
      pagetitle = Mid(pagetitle, 6, Len(pagetitle))
     End If
     If Left(rst("PageText"), 7) = "script:" Then
      ImageID = 3
     End If
     If rst("PageParent") = "/" Then
      TreeView1.Nodes.Add "localhost", tvwChild, rst("PageCode"), " & _
                          "pagetitle, ImageID
     Else
      TreeView1.Nodes.Add FindParentCode(rst("PageParent")), tvwChild, _
      rst("PageCode"), pagetitle, ImageID
     End If
     rst.MoveNext
    Wend

    'add filters
    TreeView1.Nodes.Add "localhost", tvwChild, "Localhost_Filters", "Filters", 7

    'load the list of filters and display them in the tree control

    On Error GoTo NoFilters
    filterfile = GetSetting(App.Title, "Settings", "FilterFile", App.Path & _
     "\filters.lst")
    g = FreeFile
    Open filterfile For Input As #g
    FilterCounter = 1
    While Not EOF(g)
     Line Input #g, TheLine
     TheLine = Trim(TheLine)
     If TheLine <> "" Then
```

```
                TreeView1.Nodes.Add "Localhost_Filters", tvwChild, "Filter" & _
                  Trim(Str(FilterCounter)), TheLine, 8
                    FilterCounter = FilterCounter + 1
                End If
            Wend
            Close #g
            Exit Sub

        errhandler:

            'if page cannot be added, add it to the Bad Links folder
            'this might happen if document's parent has been accidentally deleted

            TreeView1.Nodes.Add "BadLinks", tvwChild, rst("PageCode"), pagetitle, ImageID
            Resume Next
            Exit Sub
        NoFilters:
            TreeView1.Nodes.Add "Localhost_Filters", tvwChild, "Problem", "No filter file"

        End Sub
```

```
        Function FindParentCode(ParentName)

            'small function that returns a unique parent code for a parent
            'the reason this code exists is so that we can have a unique field to use a
            'key in the tree control

            On Error Resume Next
            Set rst1 = Conn.Execute("select * from pages where PageID='" & ParentName & _
                              "'")
            If rst1.EOF Then
              FindParentCode = ""
            Else
              FindParentCode = rst1("PageCode")
            End If

        End Function
```

```
        Function FindParentID(ParentCode)
            'this function returns a ParentCode by ParentID

            On Error Resume Next
            Set rst1 = Conn.Execute("select * from pages where PageCode='" & ParentCode & _
                              "'")
            If rst1.EOF Then
              FindParentID = "/"
            Else
              FindParentID = rst1("PageID")
            End If

        End Function
```

```
        Private Sub Form_Resize()

            On Error Resume Next
            TreeView1.Height = frmClientMain.Height - 720
            Text1.Height = frmClientMain.Height - 1450
            Text1.Width = frmClientMain.Width - 2925
            Text2.Width = Text1.Width - 1200
```

```
    Text3.Width = Text2.Width

End Sub

'Functions that add folders, scripts, etc. are very similar

Private Sub mnuAddFolder_Click()
   On Error Resume Next
  firststep:
   Randomize Timer
   Parent = TreeView1.SelectedItem.Key
   TheKey = "A"

'make up a unique ID to use as a ParentCode

   For s = 1 To 9 '49
    TheKey = TheKey & Chr(Asc("A") + Int(Rnd * 26))
   Next

   TheKey = FindParentID(Parent) & "/" & TheKey

   The2Key = "A"
   For s = 1 To 49
    The2Key = The2Key & Chr(Asc("A") + Int(Rnd * 26))
   Next

   'see if this key already exists
   Set rst = Conn.Execute("select * from pages where PageCode='" & TheKey & "'")
   If Not rst.EOF Then GoTo firststep
   Conn.Execute "insert into pages _
    (PageCode,PageID,PageParent,PageTitle,PageText) values('" & The2Key & "','" _
    & TheKey & "','" & FindParentID(Parent) & "','folder:New Key','New folder')"

   TreeView1.Nodes.Add Parent, tvwChild, The2Key, "New Key", 5

End Sub

   Private Sub mnuAddLink_Click()

    On Error Resume Next
    firststep:
    Randomize Timer
    Parent = TreeView1.SelectedItem.Key
    TheKey = "A"
    For s = 1 To 9 ' 49
     TheKey = TheKey & Chr(Asc("A") + Int(Rnd * 26))
    Next

    The2Key = "A"
    For s = 1 To 49
     The2Key = The2Key & Chr(Asc("A") + Int(Rnd * 26))
    Next

    TheKey = FindParentID(Parent) & "/" & TheKey

    'see if this key already exists
    Set rst = Conn.Execute("select * from pages where PageCode='" & TheKey & "'")
    If Not rst.EOF Then GoTo firststep
    Conn.Execute "insert into pages _
     (PageCode,PageID,PageParent,PageTitle,PageText) values('" & The2Key & "','" _
```

```
          & TheKey & "','" & FindParentID(Parent) & "','link:New Key','http://url')"

      TreeView1.Nodes.Add Parent, tvwChild, The2Key, "New Key", 4

End Sub


Private Sub mnuAddPage_Click()
   On Error Resume Next
   firststep:
   Randomize Timer
   Parent = TreeView1.SelectedItem.Key
   TheKey = "A"
   For s = 1 To 9 '49
    TheKey = TheKey & Chr(Asc("A") + Int(Rnd * 26))
   Next
   TheKey = FindParentID(Parent) & "/" & TheKey

   The2Key = "A"
   For s = 1 To 49
    The2Key = The2Key & Chr(Asc("A") + Int(Rnd * 26))
   Next

   'see if this key already exists
   Set rst = Conn.Execute("select * from pages where PageCode='" & TheKey & "'")
   If Not rst.EOF Then GoTo firststep
   Conn.Execute "insert into pages _
    (PageCode,PageID,PageParent,PageTitle,PageText) values('" & The2Key & "','" _
    & TheKey & "','" & FindParentID(Parent) & "','New page','new page')"

   TreeView1.Nodes.Add Parent, tvwChild, The2Key, "New Key", 2

End Sub

Private Sub mnuAddScript_Click()

   On Error Resume Next
   firststep:
   Randomize Timer
   Parent = TreeView1.SelectedItem.Key
   TheKey = "A"
   For s = 1 To 9 '49
    TheKey = TheKey & Chr(Asc("A") + Int(Rnd * 26))
   Next

   TheKey = FindParentID(Parent) & "/" & TheKey

   The2Key = "A"
   For s = 1 To 49
    The2Key = The2Key & Chr(Asc("A") + Int(Rnd * 26))
   Next


   'see if this key already exists
   Set rst = Conn.Execute("select * from pages where PageCode='" & TheKey & "'")
   If Not rst.EOF Then GoTo firststep
   Conn.Execute "insert into pages _
    (PageCode,PageID,PageParent,PageTitle,PageText) values('" & The2Key & "','" _
    & TheKey & "','" & FindParentID(Parent) & "','New script','script:')"

   TreeView1.Nodes.Add Parent, tvwChild, The2Key, "New Key", 3
```

```
End Sub

'we want to be able to copy and paste the documents, so let's
'create our own version of the Clipboard (can't use Windows
'system clipboard because of some incompatibility issues


Private Sub mnuEditCopy_Click()
   On Error Resume Next
   ClipBoardText1 = Text1.text
   ClipBoardText2 = Text2.text
   ClipBoardText3 = Text3.text
   ClipBoardImageID = TreeView1.SelectedItem.Image

   'now find the actual FileName
   For s = Len(ClipBoardText2) To 1 Step -1
    If Mid(ClipBoardText2, s, 1) = "/" Then
     Exit For
    End If
    zz = Mid(ClipBoardText2, s, 1) & zz
   Next
   ClipBoardText2 = zz

End Sub

Private Sub mnuEditCut_Click()
   On Error Resume Next
   mnuEditCopy_Click
   mnuViewDelete_Click
End Sub

Private Sub mnuEditPaste_Click()
On Error GoTo errhandler
  firststep:
   Randomize Timer
   Parent = TreeView1.SelectedItem.Key
   TheKey = "A"
   For s = 1 To 9
    TheKey = TheKey & Chr(Asc("A") + Int(Rnd * 26))
   Next

   The2Key = "A"
   For s = 1 To 49
    The2Key = The2Key & Chr(Asc("A") + Int(Rnd * 26))
   Next

   TheKey = FindParentID(Parent) & "/" & ClipBoardText2 '& "/" & TheKey

   'see if this key already exists
   Set rst = Conn.Execute("select * from pages where PageCode='" & TheKey & "'")
   If Not rst.EOF Then GoTo firststep
   Conn.Execute "insert into pages _
    (PageCode,PageID,PageParent,PageTitle,PageText) values('" & The2Key & "','" _
    & TheKey & "','" & FindParentID(Parent) & "','" & _
    DoubleQuote(ClipBoardText3) & "','" & DoubleQuote(ClipBoardText1) & "')"

   Dim TheNode As Node
   Set TheNode = TreeView1.Nodes.Add(Parent, tvwChild, The2Key, ClipBoardText3, _
```

```
        ClipBoardImageID)
    TheNode.EnsureVisible
    Exit Sub

errhandler:
    MsgBox Error$

End Sub


Private Sub mnuFileConnect_Click()

    'we'll add support for multiple servers in the future
    MsgBox "This version of the product does not support multiple servers."

End Sub


Private Sub mnuFileExit_Click()

    End

End Sub


Private Sub mnuHelpAbout_Click()

    'There's no application in this world that does not have an About box

    MsgBox "Impera AppClient v" & App.Major & "." & App.Minor & "." & _
    App.Revision & vbLf & "Copyright (C)1999, Impera Software Corporation." _
    & vbLf & vbLf & "Current user: " & uid, vbInformation, "About"

End Sub


Private Sub mnuSplitterLeft_Click()

    On Error Resume Next
    'since we are implementing a quick and dirty version of this app, we do not
    'want to add any complex GUI code to move the splitter, let's make it simple

    TreeView1.Width = TreeView1.Width - 500
    Text1.Width = Text1.Width + 500
    Text1.Left = Text1.Left - 500
    Text2.Width = Text1.Width - 1200
    Text3.Width = Text2.Width
    Label1.Left = Text1.Left
    Label2.Left = Text1.Left
    Text2.Left = Text1.Left + 1000
    Text3.Left = Text2.Left

End Sub


Private Sub mnuSplitterRight_Click()

    On Error Resume Next
    TreeView1.Width = TreeView1.Width + 500
    Text1.Width = Text1.Width - 500
    Text1.Left = Text1.Left + 500
    Text2.Width = Text1.Width - 1200
    Text3.Width = Text2.Width
    Label1.Left = Text1.Left
```

```
      Label2.Left = Text1.Left
      Text2.Left = Text1.Left + 1000
      Text3.Left = Text2.Left

End Sub

Private Sub mnuToolsCommandFile_Click()

   'let's ask the user for the location of the browser they want to use

   On Error Resume Next
   cmd = GetSetting(App.Title, "Settings", "Cmd", "start")
   cmd = InputBox _
     ("Please enter the path to the browser:", "Application Launcher", cmd)
   If cmd = "" Then Exit Sub
   SaveSetting App.Title, "Settings", "Cmd", cmd

End Sub

Private Sub mnuToolsFind_Click()

   On Error Resume Next

   'Simple Page Search. Can search by PageID

   PageID = InputBox("Please enter a page to look for:", "Search", TheLink)
   If PageID = "" Then Exit Sub
   Set keyrst = Conn.Execute("select * from pages where PageID='" & PageID & "'")
   If keyrst.EOF Then
      MsgBox "Page not found"
      Exit Sub
   End If
   For s = 1 To TreeView1.Nodes.Count
    If TreeView1.Nodes(s).Key = keyrst("PageCode") Then
     TreeView1.Nodes(s).EnsureVisible
     TreeView1.Nodes(s).Selected = True
     TreeView1_Click
     Exit Sub
    End If
   Next
   MsgBox "Document has been found in the database, however, it was not possible _
    to display it. Please refresh the list of documents and try searching again."

End Sub

Private Sub mnuToolsInstallFilter_Click()

   'allow users to add/register new filters

   On Error Resume Next

   filterfile = GetSetting(App.Title, "Settings", "FilterFile", App.Path & _
                       "\filters.lst")
   filterfile = InputBox("Please confirm the location of the filter index file:" _
                    , "Filters", filterfile)
   If filterfile = "" Then Exit Sub
   SaveSetting App.Title, "Settings", "FilterFile", filterfile
   On Error GoTo ExitThis
   CommonDialog1.ShowOpen
```

```
      On Error GoTo errhandler
      g = FreeFile
      Open filterfile For Append As #g
      Print #g, CommonDialog1.FileName
      Close #g
      TreeView1.Nodes.Add "Localhost_Filters", tvwChild, "Filter" & _
       Trim(Str(FilterCounter)), CommonDialog1.FileName, 8
      MsgBox "Filter has been successfully installed", vbInformation, "Filters"
      Exit Sub

errhandler:
      MsgBox "There was an error installing a filter: " & Error$

ExitThis:

End Sub

Private Sub mnuViewBrowser_Click()

      'display this page on the screen
      On Error Resume Next
      cmd = GetSetting(App.Title, "Settings", "Cmd", "start")
      If TreeView1.SelectedItem.Key = "localhost" Then
       Shell cmd & " http://localhost/appserver/app.asp", vbNormalFocus
       Exit Sub
      End If
      Set rst = Conn.Execute("select * from pages where PageCode='" & _
       TreeView1.SelectedItem.Key & "'")
      If rst.EOF Then
       MsgBox "Page can no longer be found"
      Else
      Shell cmd & " http://localhost/appserver/app.asp?page=" & rst("PageID"), _
       vbNormalFocus
      End If

End Sub

Private Sub mnuViewDelete_Click()

      'delete the selected item

      On Error Resume Next
      If TreeView1.SelectedItem.text = "Bad Links" Then
       MsgBox "'Bad Links' is a system folder and cannot be deleted."
       Exit Sub
      End If
      If TreeView1.SelectedItem.text = "LocalHost" Then
       MsgBox "Sorry, but you cannot remove all files from the system this way."
       Exit Sub
      End If
      If InStr(TreeView1.SelectedItem.Key, "Filter") <> 0 Then
       MsgBox _
       "To remove a filter, please remove it's entry from the filter list file."
       Exit Sub
      End If


      If MsgBox("Delete this item?", vbYesNo, "Delete") = vbNo Then Exit Sub
      Conn.Execute "delete * from pages where PageCode='" & _
```

```
        TreeView1.SelectedItem.Key & "'"
      TreeView1.Nodes.Remove TreeView1.SelectedItem.Index

End Sub

Private Sub mnuViewFollowLink_Click()

   'show the user where the currently selected link points to

   On Error Resume Next
   If Left(Text3.text, 5) = "link:" Then
    TheLink = Trim(Text1.text)
    If Left(TheLink, 7) = "app.asp" Then
     TheLink = Mid(TheLink, 14, Len(TheLink))
     mnuToolsFind_Click
    End If
   End If

End Sub

Private Sub mnuViewSave_Click()

   'save the current document

   On Error GoTo errhandler
   Pagetext = DoubleQuote(Text1.text)
   PagePath = DoubleQuote(Text2.text)
   pagetitle = DoubleQuote(Text3.text)
   Conn.Execute "update pages set PageID='" & PagePath & "',Pagetitle='" & _
    pagetitle & "',PageText='" & Pagetext & "' where PageCode='" & _
    TreeView1.SelectedItem.Key & "'"
   Exit Sub

errhandler:
   MsgBox Error$

End Sub

Private Sub mnuViewShortcut_Click()

   'just display an input box so that user can cut and paste the location
   'of the document

   On Error Resume Next
   InputBox "Shortcut", , "app.asp?page=" & rst("PageID")

End Sub

Private Sub mnuViewViewFolder_Click()

   'browse the folder (display the list of items in it)
   On Error Resume Next
   cmd = GetSetting(App.Title, "Settings", "Cmd", "start")
   If TreeView1.SelectedItem.Key = "localhost" Then
    Shell cmd & " http://localhost/appserver/app.asp", vbNormalFocus
    Exit Sub
   End If
   Set rst = Conn.Execute("select * from pages where PageCode='" & _
```

```
      TreeView1.SelectedItem.Key & "'")
    If rst.EOF Then
     MsgBox "Page can no longer be found"
    Else
     Shell cmd & " http://localhost/appserver/app.asp?page=" & rst("PageID") & _
     "&parent=" & rst("PageID"), vbNormalFocus
    End If

End Sub

Private Sub Text1_MouseDown(Button As Integer, Shift As Integer, X As Single, _
                           Y As Single)
   On Error Resume Next
   If Button = 2 Then
    If Left(Text3.text, 5) = "link:" And Left(Text1.text, 7) = "app.asp" Then
    mnuViewFollowLink.Enabled = True
    Else
     mnuViewFollowLink.Enabled = False
    End If
    PopupMenu mnuView
   End If

End Sub

Private Sub Text3_Change()

   'some fancy GUI stuff, modifies the data in the tree as you are typing it

   On Error Resume Next
   'pagetitle = Text3.text
   If UCase(TreeView1.SelectedItem.text) = "LOCALHOST" Then Exit Sub
   If TreeView1.SelectedItem.text = "Bad Links" Then Exit Sub
   If pagetitle = TreeView1.SelectedItem.text Then Exit Sub
   If InStr(TreeView1.SelectedItem.Key, "Filter") <> 0 Then Exit Sub
   If Left(pagetitle, 7) = "folder:" Then
    pagetitle = Mid(pagetitle, 8, Len(pagetitle))
   End If
   If Left(pagetitle, 5) = "link:" Then
    pagetitle = Mid(pagetitle, 6, Len(pagetitle))
   End If

   TreeView1.SelectedItem.text = pagetitle
End Sub

Private Sub TreeView1_Click()
   'this function opens the selected document in the right pane
   'makes sure that you can only open your own private folder, unless you
   'are an administrator

   On Error Resume Next
   If InStr(TreeView1.SelectedItem.Key, "Filter") <> 0 Then
    Text1.text = "Filters can not be edited using this application."
    Text1.Enabled = False
    Text2.text = TreeView1.SelectedItem.text
    Text3.text = ""
    Exit Sub
   End If
   Set rst = Conn.Execute("select * from pages where PageCode='" & _
    TreeView1.SelectedItem.Key & "'")
```

```
    If rst.EOF Then
      Text1.text = "Item does not exist. Has it been deleted?"
      Text1.Enabled = False
      Text2.text = ""
      Text3.text = ""
    Else
      If LCase(Left(rst("PageID"), 15)) = "pages/personal/" _
          And uid <> AdminUser Then
      ShouldBe = "pages/personal/" & uid & "/"
      If Left(rst("PageID") & "/", Len(ShouldBe)) <> ShouldBe Then
       TreeView1.Nodes.Remove TreeView1.SelectedItem.Index
       MsgBox "Permission denied, this object belongs to another user. It will now _
        be removed from your profile."
       Exit Sub
      End If
    End If

    Text1.Enabled = True
    Text1.text = rst("PageText")
    Text2.text = rst("PageID")
    Text3.text = rst("PageTitle")
    CurrentTitle = Text3.text
    End If
    Text2.Enabled = Text1.Enabled
    Text3.Enabled = Text1.Enabled
    If Left(Text3.text, 5) = "link:" And Left(Text1.text, 7) = "app.asp" Then
     mnuViewFollowLink.Enabled = True
    Else
     mnuViewFollowLink.Enabled = False
    End If

End Sub

Private Sub TreeView1_Expand(ByVal Node As MSComctlLib.Node)

  'if user expands the tree, make sure he is not expensing someone's personal
  'folder.

  On Error GoTo IgnoreAll
  Set rst = Conn.Execute("select * from pages where PageCode='" & Node.Key & "'")
  If LCase(Left(rst("PageID"), 15)) = "pages/personal/" And uid <> AdminUser Then
   ShouldBe = "pages/personal/" & uid & "/"
   If Left(rst("PageID") & "/", Len(ShouldBe)) <> ShouldBe Then
    TreeView1.Nodes.Remove Node.Index
    MsgBox _
     "Permission denied, this object belongs to another user. It will now be _
      removed from your profile."
    Exit Sub
   End If
  End If
 IgnoreAll:
End Sub

Private Sub TreeView1_MouseDown(Button As Integer, Shift As Integer, X As Single,
Y As Single)
  If Button = 2 Then
   If Left(Text3.text, 5) = "link:" And Left(Text1.text, 7) = "app.asp" Then
   mnuViewFollowLink.Enabled = True
```

```
      Else
        mnuViewFollowLink.Enabled = False
      End If
      PopupMenu mnuView
    End If
End Sub


Function DoubleQuote(text) As String

    'a very useful function that you can probably reuse later in any program
    'this function parses the string and converts all single-quotes into
    'double-quotes
    'the reason this is done is to avoid any SQL errors that might appear if
    'you try to run an SQL query with a single quote in the varchar field

    txt1 = ""
    For s = 1 To Len(text)
      If Mid(text, s, 1) = "'" Then
        txt1 = txt1 & "''"
      Else
        txt1 = txt1 & Mid(text, s, 1)
      End If
    Next
    DoubleQuote = txt1

End Function
```

This program looks longer and more complex than `appserver`. It is, in fact, longer and more complicated. However, this is a regular Windows application and it is not a main idea of a book to describe how this particular application works. The only reason you are given this application is so that you can use it as a helpful tool in appserver development. As this code is so large, you can also download it from the Wrox website - `www.wrox.com`. You can also download a copy of AppDeveloper, which is a more sophisticated, enterprise version of AppClient.

As you see from this case study, one little web application written in Visual Basic can solve lots of programming problems. Now, that you have both AppServer and AppClient, you can develop almost any application using them easily and cut on development cost.

Good luck with your web development!

Summary

In this Case Study we have learned about a different way of approaching standard network and office functions using a database as a file management system. During this study we have learned:

> How to use a database as a file system

> How to use the database as the structure for a Web server

> How to implement a document retrieval system on a Web site

> How to implement a client program to make full use of this system.

We have also discussed how we could modify the code to add e-mail and other functions to the application and so create an entirely new front end for a business's operating system.

Case Study 3: DHTML Applications

The Employee Data-Entry Application (EDA)

The goal of this case study is to demonstrate several techniques in building applications using the VB's new DHTML Application Project. As you will soon see, the combination of DHTML and VB allows extremely dynamic web content without the hassles (and limitations) of a web scripting language. In fact, DHTML enables the VB programmer to control the events on a web page much like events are controlled on a standard VB form.

Case Study Road Map

This case study is divided into 4 sections.

- ➤ **The Employee Data-Entry Application** – This section defines the project scope, specifies the requirements, and documents the design strategy.

- ➤ **Implementing EDA** – This section describes how to build a DHTML Application with VB. It demonstrates the techniques for binding VB code with elements on the web page, and how to take advantage of the "Dynamic" in Dynamic HTML.

- ➤ **Implementing EDA – Take 2** – This section demonstrates how to add an ActiveX control to the web page, and control it using VB code. It also describes how to persist the employee data by using ADO to save the information to an Access database. Finally, this section explains how to save and restore state information related to the web page.

- ➤ **Where to Go from Here** – This section suggests other enhancements you can try on your own.

EDA Requirements

To demonstrate the key aspects of DHTML Applications, we will be building a simple employee data entry application. Every project needs a name, not to mention a corresponding acronym. So we will dub this the **Employee Data-Entry Application**, or **EDA**.

First, let's define the requirements for EDA. The system will be used to enter, save, and retrieve employee information. The exact requirements are:

- The application will query for and store employee information.
- Employee data will include Name, Id, the hourly pay, the number of hours worked per week, and the start date.
- The user will input employee data via a form displayed on Internet Explorer 4.0 (or greater).
- The data entry form will allow the user to view all the employees currently in the company.
- The application will be written entirely in Visual Basic 6, using the new DHTML Application project type.
- Employee information will be stored in a Microsoft Access database.

EDA Design

We will keep the design and implementation as simple as possible, so that we can focus on DHTML instead of the underlying business rules of the project.

First we will create the proper HTML form, which will present the user with a simple data entry interface. The form will gather all the data for the employee. The form will also display three buttons, Save, Reset, and Display All.

All the necessary logic for the form will be contained within the DHTML Application. It will be responsible for validating the data entered and providing the appropriate feedback to the user. It will also handle the implementation for all the buttons on the form. To implement the save feature, we will store the employee information in an Access database containing a predefined Employees table.

When Internet Explorer loads the EDA HTML form, it will also load the DHTML Application (as an ActiveX DLL). User events on the form will be delegated to the DHTML Application for processing, triggering the core business logic contained within.

Implementing EDA

Now that we have a clear understanding of what we are trying to accomplish, let's get started! The implementation has been broken into two sections. This first section steps through most of the core functionality, temporarily implementing a simple but non-persistent storage technique. The next section, "Implementing EDA – Take 2" demonstrates the use of an ActiveX control, and implements true persistence using an Access database and cookies.

Create a DHTML Application project

First, we create a new VB project by selecting the DHTML Application project type from the New Project window.

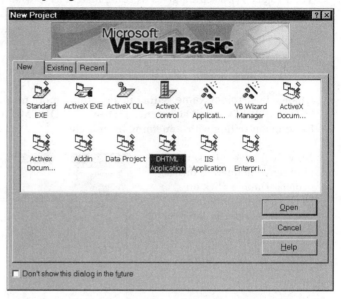

Visual Basic now works its magic, creating the project shell we need to get started with our program. A quick look at the Project Explorer window shows us what exactly has occurred on our behalf. Two modules have been created, a standard module called `modDHTML.bas`, and a designer called `DHTMLPage1.dsr`.

Before we get too involved in these modules though, let's give this project a proper name and set up some other project properties. Select the menu item Project | DHTMLProject Properties to open the Project Properties dialog box.

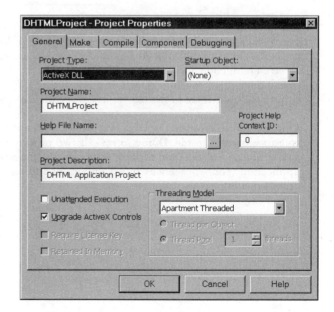

The Project Type setting gives us some insight as to what a DHTML Application really is - an ActiveX DLL. When we compile this project, a DLL will be created and Internet Explorer will automatically load this DLL into its process space whenever the web page is loaded. In other words, the DHTML Application actually becomes part of the browser. You might be tempted to change the Project Type setting to one of the other options like "ActiveX EXE". *This is not a good idea.* Doing so will effectively make your project inoperable. The fact that VB even allows this is a bit perplexing.

Change the Project Name setting to something more meaningful, like EmpDataDH (the appended "DH" will help you tell at a glance that this is a DHTML Application project). Also fill in the Project Description setting with something meaningful.

Now we'll have a look at the modules contained in this project. Double click on DHTMLPage1 under the Designers folder in the Project Explorer window to display it.

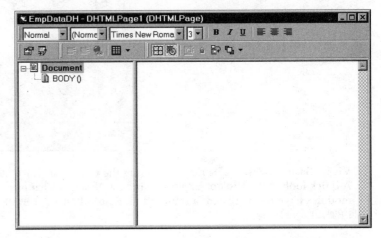

DHTMLPage1 is not a very meaningful name, so we will change it to htmEmpData. In the Properties window, choose IHTMLPageDesigner from the drop down list and set both the Name and the Id properties to htmEmpData. As you might suspect, the Name property specifies how the item will be referred to in code, just as it does for a form. The Id property is used when the HTML is generated. When this project is built, VB will insert an OBJECT tag into the HTML file, and use this setting to fill in the Id attribute of the tag. You will see this later when we build this project.

Our final act in creating the DHTML project is to open the standard module, modDHTML, to see what treasures it holds inside. Doing so reveals two procedures, PutProperty() and GetProperty(). These procedures are used to store state information when implementing a multiple page web application. You will see why this is important and also the actual implementation used in "**Implementing EDA – Take 2**".

Importing the HTML file

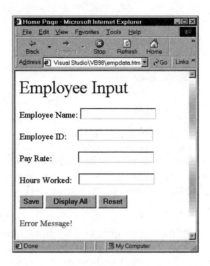

Our HTML document is going to be very simple and to the point. It will be a short form with 4 input boxes and 3 buttons. The easiest way to create this HTML document is to import it from the Wrox website. Copy the EmpData.htm file to your project directory. In the DHTML Designer window, click on the **Properties** icon to bring up the Designer's **Properties** dialog. Choose "**Save HTML in an External File:**" and click **Open** to browse for and select the EmpData.htm file copied into your project directory. Now the Designer can be used to edit this HTML file. It shows the HTML rendered in the right pane, and has a tree view in the left pane that shows the document in outline form. The HTML for this form is shown below. Many formatting tags have been removed in order to make it readable, so if you type it in verbatim, you might end up with an oddly formatted form.

```
<html> <head>
<title>Home Page</title>
<meta name="Microsoft Theme" content="none">
</head>

<body>
<p align="left"><big><big><big>Employee Input</big></big></big></p>

<p>Employee Name:
<input ID="EmpName" name="T1" Title="Enter the Employee Name" >
<br><br>

Employee ID:
<input ID="EmpID" name="T2" Title="Enter the Employee ID">
<br><br>

Pay Rate:
<input ID="EmpPay" name="T3" Title="Enter the Employee's pay rate">
<br><br>

Hours Worked:
<input ID="EmpHours" name="T4" Title = "Enter the hours per week">
```

Continued on Following Page

```
</p>

<p><input ID="Save" type="button" value="Save" name="B1">
<input ID="Display" type="button" value="Display All" name="B2">
<input ID="Reset" type="reset" value="Reset" name="B3"></p>

<span ID="ErrorMsg" align = "left" alt = "Error Message here"><font
color="#ff0000">
<p>Error Message!</font><br></P></span>

</body></html>
```

Notice that each HTML element has been given an ID. For instance, the input box associated with the employee name has been given the ID of EmpName. This is important, because the VB code in the DHTML application will use the ID to refer to this element. Every time we want to respond to an event that occurs on this element, or set a property for this element, it is this ID that allows us to do it. In fact, the ID property of HTML elements is analogous to the Name property of standard VB controls.

We have created the DHTML Application project and we have imported an HTML document which will act as our user interface. So far, we have not seen anything that sets this DHTML application apart from other web applications. In the next section however, we will start adding VB code that will respond to events that occur on this web page. We will also write code that will dynamically alter the appearance of the web page.

Implementing the User Interface

We have reached the point where we can start connecting the elements in the HTML document to VB code. We will start by writing code that will execute when the Reset button on the web page is clicked. Like VB forms, the DHTML Designer has two views, the "visual" view and the "code" view. And like VB forms, you can quickly get to the code view by double clicking on an element in the Designer.

In the Designer, double click on the Reset button. This will bring up a code window with the stub for the onclick() event. Enter the following code:

```
'User clicked on the Reset button.  Looks almost like a Click() event
'on a form button!
Private Function Reset_onclick() As Boolean
    Call ClearForm
End Function

' Clear all the text boxes
Private Sub ClearForm()

    EmpName.Value = ""
    EmpID.Value = ""
    EmpPay.Value = "0"
    EmpHours.Value = "0"

End Sub
```

Notice that the input boxes have a `Value` property that is similar to the `Text` property of a `TextBox` control.

This is a good point to build the project and run it to see what we have achieved. Under the **File** menu, select "**Make EmpDataDH.dll ...**". Now run the project. The first time you run the project you will see the **Project Properties** window appear with the **Debugging** tab selected. Fill the window with the start component shown to be htmEmpData.

Now click **OK** and watch it go! Internet Explorer will start and show the Employee Data Entry form. Test it out by filling in some text and clicking on the "**Reset**" button. You will see the initial values placed in the input boxes. You can even set a breakpoint on the `Reset_onclick()` to debug the code. Not only can we control web events using VB code, we can debug our web application using the powerful VB IDE.

Before we go on, lets investigate the source HTML that Internet Explorer is using to render this form. We might expect it to be exactly the same as `EmpData.htm`, but when we view the source, we see the following inserted towards the top of the document:

```
<!--METADATA TYPE="MsHtmlPageDesigner" startspan-->
<object id="htmEmpData" classid="clsid:F64A375F-1633-11D3-9321-00A0C99DFEFC"
width=0 height=0>
</object><!--METADATA TYPE="MsHtmlPageDesigner" endspan-->
```

This is how Internet Explorer knows that it must load the `EmpDataDH.dll` when it loads this web page. The `classid` attribute is a GUID that uniquely identifies the `htmEmpData` class and the DLL in which it resides. So it's not all magic after all, just COM.

One of the key features of the DHTML Applications is the ability to incorporate input validation logic on the client side. We will implement this by executing validation code every time the user enters data in the input boxes. In a normal VB application we might use the `LostFocus()` event to do this. In a DHTML application we use the `onblur()` event. Start by coding the `onblur()` event for the `EmpName` input box:

```
Private Sub EmpName_onblur()
    If Trim(EmpName.Value) = "" Then
        ErrorMsg.innerText = "Employee Name Required!"
    Else
        ErrorMsg.innerText = ""
    End If
End Sub
```

This code verifies that there is some text in the input box. If not, then the span named `ErrorMsg` will be set to show the text "Employee Name Required!". Notice that a span element uses the `innerText` property instead of the Value property. Like learning to use VB controls, learning DHTML requires us to become familiar with a new set of objects, their properties, and their methods. Thankfully, Visual Basic eases the burden with IntelliSense.

Like VB forms, there is an event which fires when the page is initially loaded. It is the `DHTMLPage_Loaded()` event. We will use this event to call the `ClearForm()` routine and to set the focus to the `EmpName` input box.

```
Private Sub DHTMLPage_Load()
    ClearForm
    EmpName.focus
End Sub
```

Run the project again to test this new code. The page will load and the **Employee Name** input box will have the focus. Trying to tab away from the box will cause the error message to appear at the bottom. Adding some text to the box before tabbing away will clear the error message.

Next we add validation code for all of the input boxes. The `EmpID` validation will be much like `EmpName`. For `EmpHours` and `EmpPay` we will validate that the value entered was a number.

```
Private Sub EmpID_onblur()
    If Trim(EmpID.Value) = "" Then
        ErrorMsg.innerText = "Employee ID Required!"
    Else
        ErrorMsg.innerText = ""
    End If
End Sub

Private Sub EmpHours_onblur()
    If Not IsNumeric(EmpHours.Value) Then
        ErrorMsg.innerText = "Hours must be a number"
    Else
        ErrorMsg.innerText = ""
    End If
End Sub

Private Sub EmpPay_onblur()
    If Not IsNumeric(EmpPay.Value) Then
        ErrorMsg.innerText = "Pay Rate must be a number"
    Else
        ErrorMsg.innerText = ""
    End If
End Sub
```

There is still one small problem. When the page is initially loaded the message "Error Message!" appears at the bottom. This is coming from the HTML source where we've set the span element to contain this text. So we need to update the `ClearForm()` routine to clear this span message too. We also want to make this error message very noticeable, so we'll change the color of the text to red. Here is the `ClearForm()` sub again with the new lines inserted:

```
Private Sub ClearForm()

    ErrorMsg.Style.Color = "red"
    ErrorMsg.innerText = ""

    EmpName.Value = ""
    EmpID.Value = ""
    EmpPay.Value = "0"
    EmpHours.Value = "0"

End Sub
```

The `Style` property used above gives us access to many different text attributes such as color, font size, font style, etc. This allows us to dynamically change the look of the text during runtime. This is called "dynamic text" and can be a very useful user interface tool. For instance, you can change the text color and size when the mouse pointer hovers over it.

We will try this technique out on the `ErrorMsg` span. When the mouse pointer is over an element the `onmouseover()` event is fired. Likewise, when the mouse pointer moves away from the element the `onmouseout()` event is fired. Using these two events, we can change the error message text to turn blue and increase in size when the mouse pointer hovers over it. Here is the code:

```
Private Sub ErrorMsg_onmouseover()
    ErrorMsg.Style.Color = "blue"
    ErrorMsg.Style.FontSize = "150%"
End Sub

Private Sub ErrorMsg_onmouseout()
    ErrorMsg.Style.Color = "red"
    ErrorMsg.Style.FontSize = "100%"
End Sub
```

The `FontSize` property used above is very flexible. Here we are using percentages to indicate the size, but we can also specify an exact size with "18pt", or we can use keywords such as `x-small`, `small`, `medium`, `large`, etc.

Now test the application. Cause an error message to appear at the bottom and move the mouse pointer over it. You will see the text turn blue and increase in size by 50 percent. Move the pointer away, and the text returns back to normal.

We can dynamically change the styles of other elements on the page as well. In order to give the user a better visual indication of what input element currently has the focus, we will change the style of an input box to make it appear highlighted when it has the focus. As you might have guessed, we will need another event, the `onfocus()` event. Recognizing that every input box will change its style in the same way, we will write a common routine called `InputGotFocus()` which will take any text input element and change the style. Here is the routine:

```
Private Sub InputGotFocus(htmInput As HTMLInputTextElement)
    htmInput.Style.BorderStyle = "double"
    htmInput.Style.BorderColor = "blue"
End Sub
```

Now in the `onfocus()` event of each input element, we simply need to call this sub, passing the input element.

```
Private Sub EmpName_onfocus()
    InputGotFocus EmpName
End Sub

Private Sub EmpID_onfocus()
    InputGotFocus EmpID
End Sub

Private Sub EmpHours_onfocus()
```

Continued on Following Page

```
        InputGotFocus EmpHours
    End Sub

    Private Sub EmpPay_onfocus()
        InputGotFocus EmpPay
    End Sub
```

We also need to make sure the style gets restored back to normal when the input element loses focus. So we write another common routine called `InputLostFocus()`, which will set both the `BorderStyle` and `BorderColor` properties to their respective defaults.

```
    Private Sub InputLostFocus(htmInput As HTMLInputTextElement)
        htmInput.Style.BorderStyle = ""
        htmInput.Style.BorderColor = ""
    End Sub
```

Of course, we have to call this routine from every `onblur()` event. Below is the updated version of `EmpName_onblur()` with the new line inserted.

> **Ensure you make the same update for** `EmpID`, `EmpHours`, **and** `EmpPay`.

```
    Private Sub EmpName_onblur()

        InputLostFocus EmpName

        If Trim(EmpName.Value) = "" Then
            ErrorMsg.innerText = "Employee Name Required!"
        Else
            ErrorMsg.innerText = ""
        End If
    End Sub
```

Now if you test the application, you will see the border for each input box turn blue as it gets the focus, and go back to normal when it loses focus. Now that's slick!

Saving the Employee Data

All that is left to do now is to implement the **Save** and **Display** buttons. In the real world, clicking **Save** would save the information to a database. We will be getting there, but for now let's just save each employee in a collection maintained by our `dhEmpData` module.

First add a `Collection` object as a private member variable in `dhEmpData`. Then modify the `DHTMLPage_Load()` event to instantiate the `Collection`

```
    'Create a collection to hold the Employee objects.
    Private m_Staff As Collection

    Private Sub DHTMLPage_Load()
        Set m_Staff = New Collection
```

```
        ClearForm
        EmpName.focus
End Sub
```

As a rule of thumb, whenever we are done using an object variable, we should set that object variable to **Nothing**. We will not be done using the Collection object until this page is unloaded. Since we have a `DHTMLPage_Load()` event, it only follows that a `DTHMLPage_Unload()` event exists as well. And it does. We will use it to set the Collection variable to **Nothing**:

```
Private Sub DHTMLPage_Unload()
    Set m_Staff = Nothing
End Sub
```

Before we can save the employee data into the collection, we will need to organize all the data for each employee into one entity. Of course, I am talking about creating a class, in this case named `CEmployee`. This class will represent the data for any given employee, so it will have 4 properties: `Name`, `ID`, `PayRate`, and `Hours`. We will also implement one method in this class, called `AsString()`, which will convert the current employee data into a nicely formatted string.

Add a new class module to the project called `CEmployee`. Open the class and enter the code below.

```
Option Explicit

Private m_Name As String
Private m_SSN As String
Private m_PayRate As Double
Private m_Hours As Double

'*****************************************************************
' Employee Properties
'*****************************************************************
Public Property Let Name(NewName As String)
    m_Name = NewName
End Property
Public Property Get Name() As String
    Name = m_Name
End Property

Public Property Let SSN(sData As String)
    m_SSN = sData
End Property
Public Property Get SSN() As String
    SSN = m_SSN
End Property

Public Property Let PayRate(sData As Double)
    m_PayRate = sData
End Property
Public Property Get PayRate() As Double
    PayRate = m_PayRate
End Property

Public Property Let Hours(sData As Double)
    m_Hours = sData
```

Continued on Following Page

```
End Property
Public Property Get Hours() As Double
    Hours = m_Hours
End Property

'*********************************************************************
' Employee methods
'*********************************************************************
Public Function AsString() As String
    Dim sEmp As String

    sEmp = "Name: " & vbTab & m_Name & vbCrLf
    sEmp = sEmp & "ID: " & vbTab & m_SSN & vbCrLf
    sEmp = sEmp & "PayRate: " & vbTab & m_PayRate & vbCrLf
    sEmp = sEmp & "Hours: " & vbTab & m_Hours & vbCrLf

    AsString = sEmp
End Function
```

The CEmployee class looks very much like a business object. Indeed it is. Later, we will modify this class to implement all the data access procedures required to save and load the employee data.

Now we are ready to implement the Save_onclick() event.

```
Private Function Save_onclick() As Boolean

    If IsPageValid() Then
        ErrorMsg.innerText = ""
        SaveEmployee
        BaseWindow.alert "Employee Saved!"
    Else
        BaseWindow.alert "Some Employee information is missing or invalid."
    End If

End Function
```

A close investigation of this function shows that it really does not do much. Like good UI developers, we have moved the grunt work out from the event handler and into helper routines, in this case IsPageValid() and SaveEmployee(). Also, we are using the alert() method of the BaseWindow object to display a message to the user much like VB's MsgBox() procedure. The first such call will bring up the dialog below:

IsPageValid() implements one last pass through the form data to ensure everything is valid before attempting to save. It will return **True** if all the required data is present and valid, it will return **False** otherwise.

```
Private Function IsPageValid() As Boolean
    ErrorMsg.innerText = ""
    If Trim(EmpName.Value) = "" Then
        ErrorMsg.innerText = "Employee Name Required!"
    ElseIf Trim(EmpID.Value) = "" Then
        ErrorMsg.innerText = "Employee ID Required!"
    ElseIf Not IsNumeric(Trim(EmpPay.Value)) Then
        ErrorMsg.innerText = "Pay Rate must be a number!"
    ElseIf Not IsNumeric(Trim(EmpHours.Value)) Then
        ErrorMsg.innerText = "Hours worked must be a number!"
```

```
        End If

        IsPageValid = (ErrorMsg.innerText = "")

End Function
```

`SaveEmployee()` does the work of actually saving the data to the collection. We need to create a temporary `Employee` object, then set that object's properties using the information in each of the input boxes. The `Employee` object can then be added to the collection. Here is the code:

```
Private Sub SaveEmployee()
    Dim Emp As New CEmployee

    With Emp
        .Name = EmpName.Value
        .SSN = EmpID.Value
        .PayRate = EmpPay.Value
        .Hours = EmpHours.Value
    End With

    m_Staff.Add Emp
    Set Emp = Nothing
End Sub
```

We have added a significant amount of code, so now is a good time to run the project and test out the new features.

You can now enter employee data and save, but unfortunately we currently have no way of verifying the contents of the collection. So, our final task for this section is to implement the **Display All** button. When this is clicked, every saved employee should be displayed in a message box. This is just a temporary implementation in order to ensure that our Save button is working as expected.

```
Private Function Display_onclick() As Boolean
    Dim sStaff As String

    sStaff = StaffToString()
    BaseWindow.alert sStaff

End Function
```

As before, the event code delegates most of the work to a helper routine. The `StaffToString()` function formats the Collection into one long string.

```
Private Function StaffToString() As String
    Dim Emp As CEmployee
    Dim sMsg As String

    sMsg = ""
    For Each Emp In m_Staff
        sMsg = sMsg & vbCrLf & Emp.AsString & vbCrLf
    Next Emp

    StaffToString = sMsg
End Function
```

Let's pause for a moment to look back at what we have accomplished.

> We have created a DHTML Application.

> We have imported an HTML document composed of several elements to create an Employee Data Entry form.

> We have seen how to tie those HTML elements to VB code.

> We have implemented VB code to respond to user actions on the HTML document.

Not bad! With a little imagination we can envision saving the employee information to a database instead of a `Collection`. We could also implement the "Display All" button to read from the database and display the information in an HTML document instead of a crude message box. We could even spice up the user interface by using ActiveX Controls to gather the employee information. To see how all this can be done, then continue to the next section "**Implementing EDA – Take 2**"

Implementing EDA - Take 2

In this section, we will implement some more advanced features for our DHTML Application. First, we will add an ActiveX control to the form that will help us query for the employee's start date. We will also change the application to save the employee information to a database, which will make it much more useful.

Adding an ActiveX Control to the Web Page

If you look at the original requirements for this application, you will see that we are missing one piece of employee data, and that is the start date. We could implement this by adding another text input box, but forcing the user to enter a date with raw text is awkward at best. Furthermore, we have to consider what the proper format of the date will be. Is it MM/DD/YYYY, or DD/MM/YYYY? Do we accept long dates like "September 1, 1999"? It seems this simple requirement has opened a few thorny issues.

This is where the **DTPicker** control comes to the rescue. You may have used this new control in your VB forms to query users for date information. It provides a simple calendar like interface to allow the user to select a date. The important fact about DTPicker is that it is an ActiveX control. ActiveX controls can be hosted in any ActiveX aware container. A VB form is one such container. So is Internet Explorer. Therefore, we can use the DTPicker control in our DHTML Application and refer to it in our VB code much like we do with the other HTML elements on the page.

First we have to add the control to the projects Toolbox. The `DTPicker` control is bundled with "Microsoft Windows Common Controls-2 6.0". From the Project menu, select **Components** and find this listing in the **Controls** tab of the **Components** dialog box.

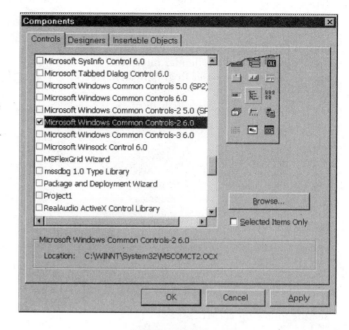

The `DTPicker` control now should now appear in the Toolbox under **General**.

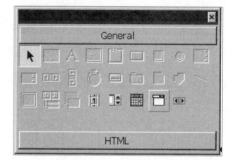

Now, using the DHTML Designer, add a new line after the **Hours Worked** text input box and add the label "**Start Date:** ". Then double click on the `DTPicker` icon in the Toolbox to add the control to the web page. You might have to experiment a bit to get the control aligned properly next to the text. It will be easier if you right click on the control and select **Absolute Position** in the popup menu.

Now when you run the application, the control appears just like the other text input boxes except that it has a drop down item. Click on the drop down, and a Calendar interface appears, allowing the user to graphically select the date.

In the View menu of your browser, click on Source to view the HTML source. Scroll down until you see the following HTML:

```
<p>Start Date:
<OBJECT classid=CLSID:20DD1B9E-87C4-11D1-8BE3-0000F8754DA1 height=29
id=DTPicker1
style="HEIGHT: 29px; LEFT: 161px; POSITION: absolute; TOP: 303px; WIDTH: 187px; Z-
INDEX: 100"
width=187>
    <PARAM NAME="_ExtentX" VALUE="3958">
    <PARAM NAME="_ExtentY" VALUE="614">
    <PARAM NAME="_Version" VALUE="393216">
    <PARAM NAME="MousePointer" VALUE="0">
    <PARAM NAME="Enabled" VALUE="1">
    <PARAM NAME="OLEDropMode" VALUE="0">
    <PARAM NAME="CalendarBackColor" VALUE="-2147483643">
    <PARAM NAME="CalendarForeColor" VALUE="-2147483630">
    <PARAM NAME="CalendarTitleBackColor" VALUE="-2147483633">
    <PARAM NAME="CalendarTitleForeColor" VALUE="-2147483630">
    <PARAM NAME="CalendarTrailingForeColor" VALUE="-2147483631">
    <PARAM NAME="CheckBox" VALUE="0">
    <PARAM NAME="CustomFormat" VALUE="">
    <PARAM NAME="DateIsNull" VALUE="0">
    <PARAM NAME="Format" VALUE="662831105">
    <PARAM NAME="UpDown" VALUE="0">
    <PARAM NAME="CurrentDate" VALUE="36311">
    <PARAM NAME="MaxDate" VALUE="2958465">
    <PARAM NAME="MinDate" VALUE="-109205">
</OBJECT>
</p>
```

This is the HTML that has been added to support the DTPicker control. The <OBJECT> tag is used to define the control. The classid attribute is set to the GUID which uniquely identifies the DTPicker control. The <PARAM> tags contain name-value pairs that correspond to properties supported by the control. This allows us to initialize the properties to the appropriate values.

The most important setting, however, is found right after the `classid` attribute. It is the `id` attribute. Just like with other HTML elements, the `id` specifies the name that we will use in our VB code to refer to this ActiveX control. Currently, the `id` is set to `"DTPicker1"`. That is not very informative, so we will give it a better name. Stop the application and in the DTHML Designer window, select the `DTPicker` control. In the **Properties** window, simply change the `id` property to `"EmpStartDt"`.

Using ActiveX Controls in VB

When the **Save** button is clicked, we need to retrieve the date setting from the `DTPicker` control and save it as part of the employee information. To implement this, we need to make two simple updates.

First, we need to add the `StartDate` property to the `CEmployee` class and update the `AsString()` method. Add the following code to the `CEmployee.cls` module:

```
'In the general declarations add
Private m_StartDate As Date

Public Property Let StartDate(dtDate As Date)
    m_StartDate = dtDate
End Property
Public Property Get StartDate() As Date
    StartDate = m_StartDate
End Property

Public Function AsString() As String
    Dim sEmp As String

    sEmp = "Name: " & vbTab & m_Name & vbCrLf
    sEmp = sEmp & "ID: " & vbTab & m_SSN & vbCrLf
    sEmp = sEmp & "PayRate: " & vbTab & m_PayRate & vbCrLf
    sEmp = sEmp & "Hours: " & vbTab & m_Hours & vbCrLf
    sEmp = sEmp & "Start Date: " & Format(m_StartDate, "long date") & vbCrLf
    AsString = sEmp
End Function
```

Second, we need to modify the `SaveEmployee()` routine to query the `DTPicker` control for the current date setting, and use that to set the `StartDate` property of the `CEmployee` object. All that translates into one additional line of code emphasised below:

```
Private Sub SaveEmployee()
    Dim Emp As New CEmployee

    With Emp
        .Name = EmpName.Value
        .SSN = EmpID.Value
        .PayRate = EmpPay.Value
        .Hours = EmpHours.Value
        .StartDate = EmpStartDt.Value
    End With

    m_Staff.Add Emp
    Set Emp = Nothing
End Sub
```

Run the application to test these new features. You should be able to save several employees using the control to select the start dates. Clicking on the Display All button should display a message box showing all the information for all the employees added, including the start date shown in "long" format.

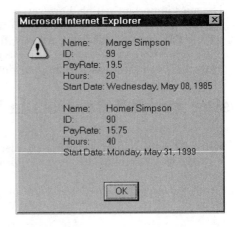

Persisting the Employee Data

For all the work we have put into this project there is still one fatal flaw. It can be demonstrated with this simple test. Run the application and enter a couple of employees. Now, using the same instance of the IE program, surf to your favorite web site. Use the "Back" button to go back to the employee form and click "Display All". What happened to all the employees entered? I am afraid they went to the great big bit bucket up in the sky. When the browser is directed to load another web page, our employee data entry form will be unloaded, the DHTMLPage_Unload() event will fire, and the Collection will be destroyed along with all of our employee data.

In order to make this application useful, we will have to find a way to persist the Employee data. In this example, we will use a local MS Access database as our repository. We will put all the data access code inside of the CEmployee class, so if you want to experiment with remote or web data access you just need to update the class. It would be more effective if we stored the information on a database on the server but, as we are looking at client side programming, we will use this local Access database

The first thing we need to do is create the database. Use Access to create a new database and add a table called Employees. The table should have a field for each of the input boxes on the form. See the diagram:

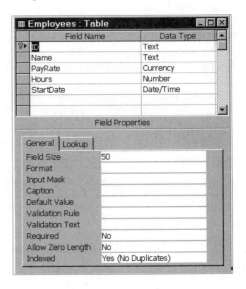

Save the database as "EmpData.mdb".

Back in the VB project, we will make use of a Data Environment Designer to establish the connection to this database. From the Project menu, select More ActiveX Designers, and Data Environment. A window like the following will be displayed showing the Data Environment and also the project has automatically referenced the ADO dll as we will need this later.

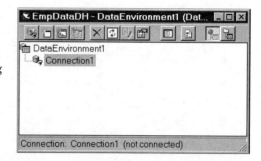

First we need to give the items in the Tree View some better names. With "DataEnvironment1" selected, go to the Properties window and change its name to deEmpData. Then select "Connection1" from the Tree View and change its name to cnnEmpData. Right click on cnnEmpData and select Properties from the popup menu. You will see the following window displayed:

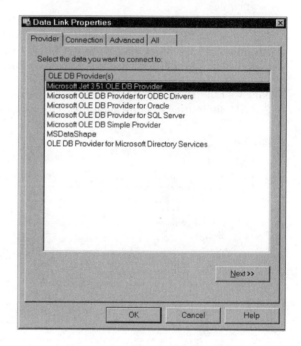

Select the "Microsoft Jet 3.51 OLE DB Provider" item (or the most recent version present on your system) and click on "Next". This will take you to the Connection tab where you can specify the Access database file to use. In our case, that would be EmpData.mdb. Click on "Test Connection" to verify the settings. Now click on OK to save the changes.

Now that we have the project ready, we can start adding code to the CEmployee class to implement the data access features. First we will establish an ADO Recordset object in the Initialize() event.

```
'In the declaration section add this member variable
Private m_rsEmps As ADODB.Recordset

Private Sub Class_Initialize()
    deEmpData.cnnEmpData.Open

    Set m_rsEmps = New ADODB.Recordset
    With m_rsEmps
        .ActiveConnection = deEmpData.cnnEmpData
        .LockType = adLockOptimistic
        .CursorType = adOpenKeyset
    End With

End Sub
```

The Initialize() event uses the Connection object defined in the Data Environment Designer. It also initializes the properties of the Recordset variable. The settings of the LockType and CursorType properties make this Recordset fully updateable.

Now we can use this Recordset to save the current Employee information. We will add a public Save() subroutine to implement this. The code for the Save() routine is shown below.

```
Public Sub Save()
    Dim sSQL As String

    sSQL = "Select * from Employees where ID = '" & m_SSN & "'"
    m_rsEmps.Open sSQL
    If m_rsEmps.BOF Then
        m_rsEmps.AddNew
        m_rsEmps.Fields("ID") = m_SSN
    End If

    With m_rsEmps
        .Fields("Name") = m_Name
        .Fields("Hours") = m_Hours
        .Fields("PayRate") = m_PayRate
        .Fields("StartDate") = m_StartDate
    End With

    m_rsEmps.Update
    m_rsEmps.Close

End Sub
```

This routine dynamically builds an SQL query string based on the employee's ID. This query is used to open the recordset and fills in the data for the employee identified. Each individual field of the record is changed based on the current property settings and then Update() is called to save the changes. Also notice that if the recordset is empty (the ID does not exist), a new record is created. For more information on passing SQL strings like this with ADO, read the relevant appendix at the end of this book or Wrox publishes a few good books on the subject.

Next we need to update the `SaveEmployee()` routine in `dhEmpInput.dsr`. Instead of adding the `Employee` object to the collection, we will invoke the `Save()` routine on the `Employee` object. Here is the new `SaveEmployee()` subroutine with the changed line indicated:

```
Private Sub SaveEmployee()
    Dim Emp As New CEmployee

    With Emp
        .Name = EmpName.Value
        .SSN = EmpID.Value
        .PayRate = EmpPay.Value
        .Hours = EmpHours.Value
        .StartDate = EmpStartDt.Value
    End With

    Emp.Save
    Set Emp = Nothing
End Sub
```

You can test the application now. In order to verify that the data is being saved in the database, you will have to open Access and view the table.

The last task for this section is to update the "Display All" feature. Currently it is still using the Collection mechanism from before. Now it should read the all the employees from the database. Again, we will put the brunt of the implementation inside of the `CEmployee` class.

The first step is to implement a `Load()` method for the class. This method will take an `ID`, and search the database for the associated employee data, and set all the class properties.

```
Public Sub Load(ID As String)
    Dim sSQL As String

    sSQL = "Select * from Employees where ID = '" & ID & "'"
    With m_rsEmps
        .Open sSQL
        If Not .BOF Then
            m_Name = .Fields("Name")
            m_SSN = .Fields("ID")
            m_PayRate = .Fields("PayRate")
            m_Hours = .Fields("Hours")
            m_StartDate = .Fields("StartDate")
        End If
        .Close
    End With

End Sub
```

Like the `Save()` method, this method dynamically builds an SQL statement based on the provided ID. The record returned form the query is used to set all the properties of the employee object.

Now we will make use of the `Load()` method, plus the `AsString()` method previously defined, to iterate through every Employee ID in the database, load the Employee object for each, and call `AsString()`. Place this in a method called `AllAsString()`.

```
Public Function AllAsString() As String
    Dim rs As New ADODB.Recordset
    Dim sMsg As String

    rs.Open "SELECT ID FROM Employees", deEmpData.cnnEmpData
    Do While Not rs.EOF
        Load rs.Fields("ID")
        sMsg = sMsg & AsString() & vbCrLf
        rs.MoveNext
    Loop

    rs.Close
    AllAsString = sMsg

End Function
```

Admittedly, this is not the most efficient method. However, it does make the most use of existing functions, and the performance is adequate for local databases. If you plan on accessing data on a remote machine, you would want to minimize the number of queries to the data server.

The next step is to modify the `Display_onclick()` event itself. Before, we delegated the responsibility of creating the display string to the `StaffToString()` function implemented within dhEmpInput. Now we just invoke the `AllAsString()` method on the employee object. Here is the new updated `Display_onclick()` function:

```
Private Function Display_onclick() As Boolean
    Dim sStaff As String
    Dim Emp As New CEmployee

    sStaff = Emp.AllAsString()
    BaseWindow.alert sStaff

End Function
```

Finally, we need to add a class terminate event to empty the reference to the recordset and close the data connection. Here is the code:

```
Private Sub Class_Terminate()
    Set m_rsEmps = Nothing
    deEmpData.cnnEmpData.Close
End Sub
```

Now test the application. You will see that surfing to other sites now has no effect on the employees you add. In fact, you can add new employees and restart the whole application without losing your updates. This of course, is how it should be.

Saving State Information

One last feature and our application will be complete. EDA has yet another problem. To see the problem for yourself, start the project and fill in the input boxes but do not save. Now surf to another web site. Hit the "Back" button to return to the employee input form. What happened to the values in the form? When the browser loads another web site, it unloads all the information associated with this form including the values entered in the input boxes. Put yourself in the shoes of a the data entry clerk who has just filled out this form and decided to check out the weather forecast at www.weather.com before saving. On returning back to the form, the clerk will not be happy to discover the form data missing.

This brings us all the way back to the modDHTML.bas module that VB created when we started this project. Inside the module are two procedures which we can use to solve this problem, PutProperty() and GetProperty(). These procedures associate a property name with a value, essentially creating a name-value pair, which is stored in a file called a cookie. Browsers know how to handle cookies. It is a common mechanism for persisting data on the web. PutProperty() and GetProperty() exposes this functionality in a manner that is easier to use than directly manipulating the cookie.

Using the procedures is simple. When we want to store some data, we call PutProperty() passing the current Document object, the Name of the property, and the value. In our employee data entry form, it makes sense to do this whenever an input box loses focus, i.e. in the onblur() event. The code below shows the updated EmpName_onblur() event which calls PutProperty() to store the current EmpName value:

```
Private Sub EmpName_onblur()
    InputLostFocus EmpName
    PutProperty BaseWindow.Document, "EmpName", EmpName.Value
    If Trim(EmpName.Value) = "" Then
        ErrorMsg.innerText = "Employee Name Required!"
    Else
        ErrorMsg.innerText = ""
    End If
End Sub
```

The first argument to PutProperty() is the Document object. This object provides programmatic access to the cookie jar. Most of the time you will use "BaseWindow.Document" for this argument.

The second argument is a string representing the name of the value. Since the property name is a string value, we can assign any name we like to the value. For instance, we could have called the EmpName value "Foo" if we wanted. We just have to make sure that we use the same name for the corresponding call to GetProperty().

The third argument is the actual value. Here are the rest of the onblur events:

```
Private Sub EmpID_onblur()
    InputLostFocus EmpID
    PutProperty BaseWindow.Document, "EmpID", EmpID.Value
    If Trim(EmpID.Value) = "" Then
        ErrorMsg.innerText = "Employee ID Required!"
```

Continued on Following Page

```
        Else
            ErrorMsg.innerText = ""
        End If
    End Sub

    Private Sub EmpHours_onblur()
        InputLostFocus EmpHours
        PutProperty BaseWindow.Document, "EmpHours", EmpHours.Value
        If Not IsNumeric(EmpHours.Value) Then
            ErrorMsg.innerText = "Hours must be a number"
        Else
            ErrorMsg.innerText = ""
        End If
    End Sub

    Private Sub EmpPay_onblur()
        InputLostFocus EmpPay
        PutProperty BaseWindow.Document, "EmpPay", EmpPay.Value
        If Not IsNumeric(EmpPay.Value) Then
            ErrorMsg.innerText = "Pay Rate must be a number"
        Else
            ErrorMsg.innerText = ""
        End If
    End Sub
```

The other aspect of maintaining the state is to restore the last known state when the page is loaded. This involves updating the DHTMLPage_Load() event to call GetProperty() to retrieve the values stored in the cookies. Actually, in the following code, the event delegates this to a helper routine called FillForm() which replaces the previous call to ClearForm().

```
    Private Sub DHTMLPage_Load()
        Set m_Staff = New Collection

        FillForm
        EmpName.focus

    End Sub

    Private Sub FillForm()
        Dim sValue As String
        ErrorMsg.Style.Color = "red"
        ErrorMsg.innerText = ""

        EmpName.Value = GetProperty(BaseWindow.Document, "EmpName")

        EmpID.Value = GetProperty(BaseWindow.Document, "EmpID")

        sValue = GetProperty(BaseWindow.Document, "EmpHours")
        EmpHours.Value = IIf(sValue <> "", sValue, "0")

        sValue = GetProperty(BaseWindow.Document, "EmpPay")
        EmpPay.Value = IIf(sValue <> "", sValue, "0")

    End Sub
```

The first argument to GetProperty() is the Document object. Like PutProperty(), this will generally be "BaseWindow.Document".

The second argument is the name of the property to retrieve. Notice that we have to specify the same string used in the corresponding calls to PutProperty().

The function returns the value for the specified property name. If the property does not exist, GetProperty() will turn an empty string. Therefore, the FillForm() routine makes sure that EmpPay and EmpHours are initialized to "0" if GetProperty() returns an empty string. That takes care of the input boxes, but what about the DTPicker ActiveX Control? This control does not have an onblur() event, so we need to use another event. The control does fire a Change() event whenever the date setting changes. This will be a good place to call PutProperty().

```
Private Sub EmpStartDt_Change()
    PutProperty BaseWindow.Document, "EmpStartDt", EmpStartDt.Value
End Sub
```

Finally, we need to update the FillForm routine to retrieve the EmpStartDt property value. The added code is shown below:

```
Private Sub FillForm()
    Dim sValue As String

    ErrorMsg.Style.Color = "red"
    ErrorMsg.innerText = ""

    EmpName.Value = GetProperty(BaseWindow.Document, "EmpName")

    EmpID.Value = GetProperty(BaseWindow.Document, "EmpID")

    sValue = GetProperty(BaseWindow.Document, "EmpHours")
    EmpHours.Value = IIf(sValue <> "", sValue, "0")

    sValue = GetProperty(BaseWindow.Document, "EmpPay")
    EmpPay.Value = IIf(sValue <> "", sValue, "0")

    sValue = GetProperty(BaseWindow.Document, "EmpStartDt")
    EmpStartDt.Value = IIf(sValue <> "", sValue, Now)

End Sub
```

Now test the application. Your web page should always restore the last values entered in the input boxes no matter how often you unload the page by going to another site. This will be true while you are using the current instance of IE.

Where To Go From Here

Congratulations, you have applied many of the key aspects of developing DHTML Applications with Visual Basic. Believe it or not, we have only scratched the surface of what can be done, and how far even this simple application can be taken. Here are some ideas for further experimentation:

> Instead of using the alert message to display all the employees format them into an HTML table and display them in a separate web page.

> Allow the user to select the Employee name from a drop down list of all the names in the database.

> Try serving the Employee database over the web. Use one or more of the following techniques: ASP, server side scripting, Web Classes, RDS, etc.

> For the ultimate experiment, create and deploy an EDA MTS component to handle the data access and send back results via the web server.

Case Study 4 : CGI Integration

CGI Overview

We owe a lot to the first generation of computer pioneers. It is hard to imagine what they had to go through just to enter a program with punch cards. After I talk with someone who blazed the computing trail decades before, I sometimes wonder what stories I will be able to pass on to future generations. I have imagined the conversation to go something like the dialog below. The participants are ME - myself 5 years older, wiser, and more cynical, and NEWBIE - a new hire right out of college, fresh with dreams of conquering the world with better programming.

ME: Back in my day, we didn't have any of this fancy ASP, IIS, MTS, MSMQ, or DHTML stuff.
NEWBIE: But how did you create dynamic web applications without them?
ME: We did it the way it was MEANT to be, with the Common Gateway Interface (CGI).
NEWBIE: <GROANS> Not this story again!
ME: <Rambles on about the joys of CGI programming and buying ice cream cones for a nickel.>

Drawing the analogy of CGI programming to punch card program entry really does not do CGI justice though. Sure it is old, but not THAT old. And when it was new it was the *only* way to create dynamic web applications, and companies jumped on the technology quickly. Hence there are still thousands of CGI applications serving important data over the Internet today.

CGI resembles COM in that it really is just a specification. The CGI specification defines how a web server passes the details of an HTTP request to another application. What the application does with the information is up to it, but typically the application will dynamically generate an HTML document based on the parameters contained in the request. To generate the HTML, the application could potentially access a local or remote database, execute yet another application, email a notification to an administrator, etc. The possibilities are endless. Ultimately, the dynamically generated HTML is sent back to the browser via the web server. To the end user, the resulting document looks no different than a static HTML page.

If you are saying "Sounds like server side scripting" or "Sounds like Web Classes", then you have the right idea. In fact, these technologies were developed to replace CGI as a means of providing dynamic web content.

Advantages and Disadvantages

Even though it is ancient technology by web standards, CGI still offers several important benefits.

> ➤ CGI is language independent. Since it is a specification only, CGI programs can be written in nearly any language. This includes languages that are compiled, as well as interpreted scripting languages. Many early CGI programs were even written using Unix shell command languages like csh or ksh. To a large degree, the need for a powerful scripting language for implementing CGI programs fueled the popularity of Perl. Since so many CGI programs were implemented with a scripting language, the term "CGI Script" came to describe any program that supported CGI, even if it was actually a compiled program.

> ➤ CGI is almost universally supported. Nearly every web server ever made can execute CGI programs. So if your application needs to work with Apache, Netscape, and Microsoft web servers, CGI is your one and only option.

> ➤ CGI is robust. CGI programs run in a separate process from the web server. This makes it nearly impossible for an out of control CGI program to harm anything other than itself.

> ➤ CGI is easy. When you really boil it down, all CGI is really, is a set of operation system environmental variables and a string containing a number of name-value pairs. All we have to do as CGI program developers is investigate the information available to us in these items and generate the appropriate HTML.

Well if CGI is so great, why is Microsoft and others trying so hard to develop something to replace it? Good question. Here are two possible answers:

> ➤ CGI is slow. Whenever the HTTP request gets routed to a CGI program, the web server must create a new process to run it in. When the CGI program is done, the process ends and is destroyed. Creating and destroying processes is very time consuming and can quickly bog down a server if many concurrent requests are frequently made. This lack of scalability is probably the Achilles heel of CGI.

> CGI programs "hard code" HTML. Don't quite like the font being used in the generated HTML? Does the formatting need tweaking a little bit? If so, don't bother opening FrontPage to change it because it is not going to do any good. Since CGI programmatically creates the HTML, if you need to change the look of the document, you usually have to change the program. With a compiled language, that of course means recompiling the executable.

Visual Basic and CGI

I will be the first to admit that the combination of VB and CGI is not exactly the programming equivalent of peanut butter and jelly. Why not? Well, in order to be a good candidate to implement CGI programs, a language must:

> Have good string handling functionality. HTML is simply text, so programmatically generating HTML will require lots of string manipulation. Plus, most of the important information is passed into the CGI program via a delimited string called a *query string*. To get at the data in the string, we must know how to parse it appropriately.

> Be able to read environmental variables. Along with the query string, other important information is available through several environmental variables.

> Be able to read from standard input and write to standard output. When the CGI program starts, it can read the query string by reading the standard input stream. All HTML generated by the program is then written to the standard output stream.

Whoops, everything was looking good for VB up to that last point. This final CGI requirement reveals its Unix heritage where redirecting standard I/O is a common form of interprocess communication. Windows also has the same concept, but Windows tries very hard to steer away from it while Unix embraces it. In fact, VB has no built in functionality to either write to standard output or read standard input.

This limitation is unfortunate, since VB would otherwise provide a very nice environment for developing CGI programs. String handling is a breeze in VB, especially with all the new functions added in version 6 like `Split()`, `Replace()`, and `Join()`. Reading an environmental variable is a simple call to the `Environ()` function. Furthermore, the main objective of many CGI programs is to build HTML based upon database queries and VB thrives on data access.

Recognizing the potential for developing CGI programs with VB, a specification called **WinCGI** was created. WinCGI represents an effective workaround but is hardly a solution. The main disadvantage of WinCGI is that, unlike standard CGI, it is not supported by all web servers. In fact, not even all Microsoft built web servers support WinCGI.

The *real* solution lies within the Win32 API. Section 2 of this case study details how to use the `WriteFile()` and `ReadFile()` API functions to implement standard I/O in VB. The section goes on to explain how you can use VB to implement a CGI Framework which you can use to rapidly implement custom CGI programs.

Even if you are not interested in building CGI applications with VB, someday you may have to execute a CGI application with VB. Consider for example a scenario where a company has implemented an e-commerce system using CGI. The resulting HTML is fine for customers browsing and buying over the web, but the company wishes to give sales people out in the field a more sophisticated, non-browser based interface. A simple but effective solution is to put a VB front end on the CGI application. Essentially you are using a standard VB application to trigger the CGI program instead of a web browser. This scenario is detailed in Section 3, where a VB front end is created that uses the WebBrowser control to send HTTP requests to a CGI program.

CGI Fundamentals

To demonstrate how CGI works, let's look at a simple example. Consider the following HTML form:

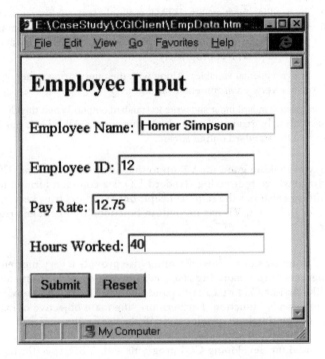

The HTML for this form is:

```html
<html>
<body>

<h2 align="left">Employee Input</h2>

<form method = "POST" action = "/cgi-bin/cgitest.exe">
<p>Employee Name: <input type="text" name="EmpName"> <br><br>
   Employee ID: <input type="text" name="EmpID" > <br><br>
   Pay Rate: <input type="text" name="EmpPay" > <br><br>
   Hours Worked: <input type="text" name="EmpHours" > <br><br>
</p>
<p><input type="submit" value="Submit" name="Submit">
<input     type="reset"  value="Reset" name = "Reset"></p>
```

780

```
    </form>
    </body>
    </html>
```

Notice the action parameter specified in the <FORM> tag. When the Submit button is pressed, the information in the form will be packaged into a query string and sent to the server. The server will execute the CGI program specified and pass it the query string.

Composing the Query String

This all should look very familiar, since this mechanism of packaging the form information into a query string is the same mechanism used in ASP scripting. In the case of ASP, most of the details about the how the string is formed is hidden within the ASP Request object. We have no such luxury in CGI programs though, so we need to know the exact format of the query string.

The format of the query string is defined as follows:

```
Name1=Value1&Name2=Value2&Name3=Value3&  ...  &Namen=Valuen
```

As you can see, the query string is a set of name-value pairs delimited by an ampersand (&). The name-value pairs are in turn separated by an equal sign. For the form shown above, the resulting query string would be

```
EmpName=Homer+Simpson&EmpID=12&EmpPay=12.75&EmpHours=40
```

Look closely, and you will notice another detail. The space character in the employee name "Homer Simpson" has been converted to a plus sign. In fact, all spaces in the fields are converted into plus signs when packaged into the query string. Our CGI program will need to recognize this, and convert the plus signs in the values to spaces.

But what if the field itself contains a plus sign? Or what if it contains an ampersand? Query string syntax handles this situation by converting all plus sign, ampersands, and other special characters to their equivalent hexadecimal code from the ASCII table. Lets look at an example. In the form below we have added an ampersand to the Employee name field and a plus sign to the ID field.

The query string that is generated when the Submit button is selected is:

```
EmpName=Homer%26Simpson&EmpID=12%2B&EmpPay=12.75&EmpHours=40
```

The ampersand has been replaced with %26. The plus sign has been replaced with %2B. So the special characters are replaced with %XX where XX is the ASCII value of the character in hexadecimal.

POST vs. GET

Now that we know the format of the query string, we can parse the string to retrieve specific pieces of information to use in our CGI program. However, before we do that, we have to know where the query string is and how we can read it.

In the example form, the method attribute of the <FORM> tag has been set to "POST". This instructs the web server to write the query string to the **standard input stream** of the CGI program. So all the CGI program needs to do is read the query string from the standard input, parse it, and then do whatever it is designed to do with the information. Piece of cake, as long as the programming language supports the concept of standard input.

The method attribute of the <FORM> tag could also have been set to "GET". In this case, the web server places the query string contents into an environmental variable named QUERY_STRING. In VB, we can easily retrieve the query string using the built in Environ() function:

```
sQueryString = Environ("QUERY_STRING")
```

Great, now we don't have to worry about that silly standard input mechanism ... right? Not so fast! Most HTML forms use the POST action method. In fact, it is the preferred way of passing the query string. In reality, a CGI program should support both POST and GET methods.

CGI Environmental Variables

In addition to the query string, the web server passes information to the CGI application through several known environmental variables. These variables contain additional information about the web server, the remote user, and the method used to make the request (e.g. POST or GET). The table below is a partial list of the available environmental variables. Complete listings can be found on several web sights, such as http://hoohoo.ncsa.uiuc.edu/cgi/env.html.

Variable Name	Description
GATEWAY_INTERFACE	The revision level of the CGI specification supported by the web server. Example: **CGI/1.1**
SERVER_NAME	The server's hostname, DNS alias, or IP address.
SERVER_SOFTWARE	Name and version of the web server software.
CONTENT_TYPE	For POST or PUT requests, this describes the data attached to the request.
CONTENT_LENGTH	The length in bytes of the attached data.
REMOTE_ADDR	IP address of the remote host making the request.
REMOTE_HOST	The hostname making the request.
QUERY_STRING	The query string portion of the URL. Used for GET requests.
REQUEST_METHOD	The request method used by the client to issue the request. Usually POST or GET.

Generating the Response

Typically, the CGI program will use all the information from the query string and the environmental variables to generate a response in the form of an HTML document. The CGI program does this by writing the HTML code to standard output. The web server intercepts this output and sends it back down to the requesting web browser. ASP programmers can use the Response object to handle the details of building the appropriate response, but if we are using CGI we need to know the specifics.

HTTP specifies **Response Codes** and **Response Headers**, which act to describe the response status and contents. Like with the query string, there is a strict protocol for specifying these correctly. Luckily, most web servers assist in the process of creating the response codes and headers. So all we generally need to do is start our output stream with the following:

```
Content-type: text/html
```

This describes the type of data we are returning. In this example, as is typically the case, we are returning HTML. The web server will complete the rest of the response headers for us.

Project Description

Now that we understand the CGI specification, it's time to put it to use with a VB application. This case study is broken into two parts:

> **Building a CGI Application Using VB.** If you despise artificial limitations, then this section is for you! It describes how you can build a `CStdIO` class in VB to add standard I/O capabilities to the language. Then you will see how to build on this to create an entire framework for creating CGI applications. I call this the **CGI Application Framework**, or **CAF**.

> **Building a CGI Client Using VB.** This section describes the steps necessary to replace the browser interface to a CGI application with a VB front end. This allows us to provide a more sophisticated, business oriented user interface to users who need it, while still leveraging legacy work done with CGI.

For the first part of the case study, you will need the `CEmployee.cls` class module, `deEmpData.dsr` Data Designer file, and the `EmpData.mdb` Access database created in the DHTML case study. Either do these parts of this case study first, or get the required files from the Wrox website.

Building a CGI Application Using VB

Unfortunately, VB does not have any built in support for the concept of standard input and output, but this is essential for implementing CGI. So the first thing we must do is build a custom class called `CStdIO` that encapsulates the Win32 API calls necessary to support standard I/O in a VB program.

We won't stop there though. Recognizing that *all* CGI programs will have to share many common tasks, we will create a **CGI Application Framework (CAF)**. The framework will provide all the services a CGI program will need. This includes error and event logging, parsing the query string, retrieving CGI environmental variable settings, and creating the standard I/O object. We will compile this all to an ActiveX DLL called `CGILibrary.dll`. Then when we need to create a new CGI program, we simply start a new VB project and add a reference to this DLL.

Breaking the Standard I/O Barrier with CStdIO

Our first task is to create the `CStdIO` class. This class will hide all the Win32 API calls and expose a VB friendly interface. First let's define the public interface for the class.

Property or Method	Description
Function ReadIn	Reads standard input. Returns a string.
	`sInput = StdIO.ReadIn()`
Function WriteOut	Writes a string to standard output. Returns a long representing the number of bytes written.
	`lCount = StdIO.WriteOut(sData)`

For now, we will create this class within a standard VB project. This will allow us to test it before copying it to the `CGILibrary` DLL project. After we create the standard VB project, we will add a class module named `CStdIO`.

CStdIO API Declarations

The `CStdIO` class will need 4 API functions to be declared.

> **GetStdHandle** is used to get the appropriate file handles for the standard input and output.

> **ReadFile** is used to read from standard input. We pass in the standard input handle returned from `GetStdHandle`.

> **WriteFile** is used to write to standard output. We pass in the standard output handle returned from `GetStdHandle`.

> **CloseHandle** is used to close the standard input and output handles.

The declarations are shown below. They are added as part of the General Declarations section of the class.

```
Option Explicit

'Declare the Win API functions
Private Declare Function GetStdHandle Lib "kernel32" _
                    (ByVal nStdHandle As Long) As Long

Private Declare Function ReadFile Lib "kernel32" _
                    (ByVal hFile As Long, _
                    ByVal lpBuffer As String, _
                    ByVal nNumberOfBytesToRead As Long, _
                    lpNumberOfBytesRead As Long, _
                    ByVal lpOverlapped As Any) As Long

Private Declare Function WriteFile Lib "kernel32" _
                    (ByVal hFile As Long, _
                    ByVal lpBuffer As String, _
                    ByVal nNumberOfBytesToWrite As Long, _
                    lpNumberOfBytesWritten As Long, _
                    ByVal lpOverlapped As Any) As Long

Private Declare Function CloseHandle Lib "kernel32" _
                    (ByVal hObject As Long) As Long

'System Standard Handle Constants. Passed into GetStdHandle() API.
Private Const STD_OUTPUT_HANDLE As Long = -11
Private Const STD_INPUT_HANDLE As Long = -10

'Constant overlapped argument value.  Passed into ReadFile() and WriteFile() API
functions.
Private Const SIO_OVERLAPPED As Long = 0
```

In addition to the declare statements, the code also creates several constants that will be needed to call these API functions.

Now we can complete the General Declaration by entering the code below:

```
'CStdIO Errors.
Public Enum StdIOErrors
    sioSTDIN_HANDLE = 9000    'Failed to allocate standard input handle
    sioSTDOUT_HANDLE          'Failed to allocate standard output handle
    sioREAD_FAILURE           'Failed to read standard input.
    sioWRITE_FAILURE          'Failed to write to standard output.
End Enum

'Standard in and out handles
Private m_hStdOut As Long
Private m_hStdIn As Long
```

Here we are creating an enumeration for the errors that the class may raise. We have to handle errors carefully when creating CGI applications since they run unattended on the server. Later we will look at an event logging class that we can use to log the errors that occur. Note that we are also creating two member variables to contain the standard input and standard output handles.

CStdIO Initialize and Terminate

We will call the GetStdHandle API function in the class Initialize event to retrieve the standard input and output handles and store them in the corresponding member variables. If for some reason we cannot retrieve the handles, an error will be raised. Note that a Debug.Print statement is added to print the results to the **Immediate** window of the VB IDE. It is placed there as a recommendation only, in order to assist in debugging if the need arises. All Debug statements are removed automatically when the project is compiled.

```
Private Sub Class_Initialize()

    'Get the standard input handle.  Raise an error if unsuccessful.
    m_hStdIn = GetStdHandle(STD_INPUT_HANDLE)
    If (m_hStdIn = 0) Then
        Err.Raise sioSTDIN_HANDLE Or vbObjectError, "CStdIO.Inititialize()", _
                  "Failed to allocate standard input handle"
    End If

    'Get the standard output handle.  Raise an error if unsuccessful.
    m_hStdOut = GetStdHandle(STD_OUTPUT_HANDLE)
    If (m_hStdOut = 0) Then
        Err.Raise sioSTDOUT_HANDLE or vbObjectError, "CStdIO.Inititialize()", _
                  "Failed to allocate standard output handle"
    End If

    Debug.Print "StdIO class initialized: StdIn = " & m_hStdIn & _
                " StdOut = " & m_hStdOut

End Sub
```

In the class `Terminate` event, we need to close the standard input and output handles.

```
Private Sub Class_Terminate()
    'Close the handles.
    CloseHandle m_hStdIn
    CloseHandle m_hStdOut
    Debug.Print "CStdIO class terminating"
End Sub
```

CStdIO WriteOut Method

The `WriteOut` method uses the `WriteFile` API function to write the given string to standard output. It will return a `Long` representing the number of bytes written. If the call to `WriteFile` fails then we will raise the appropriate error.

```
Public Function WriteOut(ByVal sBuf As String) As Long
    Dim lByteCnt As Long
    Dim bResult As Boolean

    Debug.Print "To Standard Out: " & sBuf

    bResult = WriteFile(m_hStdOut, sBuf, Len(sBuf), lByteCnt, SIO_OVERLAPPED)
    WriteOut = lByteCnt
    If Not bResult Then
        Err.Raise sioWRITE_FAILURE or vbObjectError, "CStdIO.WriteOut()", _
                  "Failed to write to standard output."
    End If
End Function
```

CStdIO ReadIn Method

The ReadIn method uses the `ReadFile` API function to read from standard input. It returns a string representing the data it retrieved from standard input. If the API call fails, then the appropriate error will be raised.

```
Public Function ReadIn() As String
    Dim sBuf As String
    Dim lByteCnt As Long
    Dim bResult As Boolean

    'Prepare a 10K string
    sBuf = String$(10000, 0)

    bResult = ReadFile(m_hStdIn, sBuf, Len(sBuf) - 1, lByteCnt, SIO_OVERLAPPED)
    If bResult Then
        sBuf = Left$(sBuf, lByteCnt)
        ReadIn = sBuf
    Else
        ReadIn = ""
        Err.Raise sioREAD_FAILURE or vbObjectError, "CStdIO.ReadIn()", _
                  "Failed to read standard input."
    End If
End Function
```

Testing the CStdIO Class

Since this is a fundamental piece to the rest of this case study, I recommend testing this class before moving on in order to catch any bugs early. To test the class, we can add a standard module to the project and insert the following code.

```
Option Explicit

Private Sub Main()

    Dim sInput As String
    Dim stdio As New CStdIO

    sInput = stdio.ReadIn()
    stdio.WriteOut "The contents of standard input are: " & vbCrLf
    stdio.WriteOut sInput

End Sub
```

When this program runs, it will read the contents of standard input and write an informational message to standard output.

> **Before continuing, set the startup object in Project Properties to Sub Main.**

Next, make an executable named stdio.exe. In order to execute the program, we will go to the command prompt, navigate to the directory where the executable was built, and enter a command similar to the following:

```
C:\CGIProjects> echo "This is a test of Standard IO" | stdio.exe > test.out
```

This command forces the text "This is a test of Standard IO" into the standard input stream of the stdio program. The program then writes the message to standard output, but the command line redirects the output to a file called test.out. If you open this file with notepad, you should see the following:

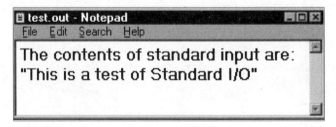

Now that we have Standard IO working in Visual Basic, we are ready to take on CGI programming!

Designing the CGI Application Framework (CAF)

CGI programs are radically different than standard VB programs. There are no user interface controls, no event handling, and no dialog boxes. CGI programs just take a request, process it, and return the result. Furthermore, CGI programs run on the server, so if the application does display a message box of some sort, there will probably be no one around to click the OK button.

Therefore, it is important that we implement some sort of global error-handling scheme to trap all errors. It is also important that we implement a logging mechanism to log all errors and important events. If our CGI program is failing intermittently, the log file might be our only way of tracking down the problem.

All of the CGI programs we write in VB will have to overcome the same issues:

> Global error management

> Error and event logging

> Implementing standard I/O

> Processing the HTTP request

> Retrieving information from the CGI environmental variables

> Generating and sending the HTTP response

So the challenge is not simply to write a CGI program in VB, but to do it in such a way that we never have to do this amount of work again! To meet this challenge we will develop the **CGI Application Framework** (henceforth **CAF**). A framework is more than simply an API or class library. Like class libraries, frameworks often provide utility classes, but they also control the execution sequence of the application. To write a custom application using a framework, you write classes that "plug-in" to the framework. The diagram below illustrates the differences between building an application from a class library versus building an application from a framework:

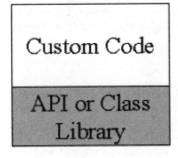
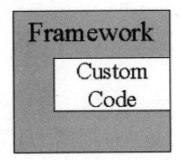

You can see the framework wraps the custom code completely, controlling what methods are called in the custom code and when they are called. This enables the programmer to develop custom applications with much less time and effort.

However, in order for us to write the custom code, we must know what methods the framework will expect our custom classes to implement. Visual Basic provides the perfect mechanism for defining what methods a class is expected to implement – the **Interface**. An Interface is a class module that declares the methods and properties without providing any implementation. Our custom class can then inherit this interface, but in doing so it is guaranteeing that it will implement the methods in the interface.

The ICGIApp Interface

The CGI Application Framework will publish the ICGIApp interface. To create a CGI Application using the framework, all we need to do is create a class that implements this interface. The table below describes the methods and properties of ICGIApp.

Property or Method	Description
Function Create	Called by CAF to initialize the CGIApp object. The function takes two arguments: a reference to a CGI object, and a reference to a Log object. Both of these objects are created and maintained by the framework.
Function PreProcess	Called by CAF to allow the CGIApp object to do any pre processing activities.
Function Process	Called by CAF to process the CGI request.
Function PostProcess	Called by CAF to allow the CGIApp object to do any post processing activities.
Property CGI	Read only. Returns the CGI context object.
Property Log	Read only. Returns the Log object.

So we see that the framework will call our CGI Application object in the following order: Create, PreProcess, Process, and PostProcess. As we will discover, it also provides us with two service classes to simplify our processing tasks, CCGI and CEventLog. These classes are described in the next section.

CAF Classes

The CAF acts as an object factory for two useful classes: CCGI and CEventLog. The instancing properties of these classes are set to PublicNotCreatable, which means that our custom code can use their methods, but the framework must create them. When the framework calls the Create method on our custom CGI Application object, it will pass a reference to an instance of each. This gives us the opportunity to store these references in member variables and use them throughout the processing cycle.

The CCGI Class

The CCGI class encapsulates all the information associated with this CGI request. This includes the query string and all CGI environmental variables. It also contains a `CStdIO` object. The table below describes the public interface of this class.

Property or Method	Description
Property `QueryString`	Read only. Returns the HTTP query string. `sQuery = m_CGI.QueryString`
Property `Params`	Read only. Returns a dictionary containing all the name-value pairs in the query string. `sEmpID = m_CGI.Params("EmpID")`
Property `Environs`	Read only. Returns a dictionary containing all the CGI environmental variables. `sServerName = m_CGI.Environs("SERVER_NAME")`
Property `StdIO`	Read only. Returns a reference to a CStdIO object. `Set oStdIO = m_CGI.StdIO`

The CEventLog Class

This class encapsulates event-logging functionality. The framework will create this object, initializing it to write to a log file called `xxx.log`, where `xxx` is the name of the CGI executable. This file will be created in the same directory as the CGI program. The table below describes the public interface of this class:

Property or Method	Description
Public Sub `NewEntry`	Prepares and opens a new entry in the log file. Writes entry header information.
Public Sub `WriteLn`	Writes a line to the log file. `NewEntry()` must be called first.
Public Sub `CloseEntry`	Closes the current log entry.
Public Sub `WriteEntry`	Opens, writes, and closes an entry. If an entry is open, it is closed.

Here is a code example demonstrating how these methods can be used:

```
With m_Log
        .NewEntry
        .WriteLn "Error Number: " & nErrNum
        .WriteLn "Description : " & sErrMsg
        .WriteLn "Source      : " & sErrSrc
        .CloseEntry
End With

m_Log.WriteEntry "CGI App " & sAppName & " Terminating: ErrCode = " & nErrNum
```

So we can choose to either "stream" output to the log using `WriteLn`, or we can write an entire entry in one shot using `WriteEntry`.

The CGILibGlobal Class

The `CGILibGlobal` class is the one entry point into the framework. It is a `GlobalMultiUse` class, meaning that our custom code does not have to create an instance of this object in order to use it. This class exposes only one public method, Run. The method signature and description of the arguments are shown below:

```
Public Sub Run(CGIApp As ICGIApp, sAppPath As String, sAppName As String,
lAppThread As _ Long)
```

> **CGIApp** is a reference to our custom CGI Application object.
> **sAppPath** is a string containing the current application path
> **sAppName** is a string containing the application name.
> **lAppThread** is a long representing the thread id of the application.

How is this used? Well, this method actually kick-starts the entire application. We simply add a standard VB module to our CGI Application project and implement `Sub Main` as shown below:

```
Private Sub Main()

    'Change this to your custom CGI Application class.
    Dim MyApp As New CCGIEmp

    'Run the CGI Application.
    CGILibGlobal.Run MyApp, App.Path, App.EXEName, App.ThreadID

End Sub
```

First we create an instance of our custom CGI application object. Then we pass that object into the Run method, along with information about the application. The framework does all the rest, with some help from our custom CGI Application object, of course.

Implementing the CGI Application Framework

Well, lets start coding this thing already. We will open a new ActiveX DLL project called `CGILibrary.vbp`. Change the name of the provided class to `CGILibGlobal`, and set its Instancing property to GlobalMultiUse. This will allow clients to use the class without creating it.

Implementing the CGILibGlobal Class

Now that we have the class created, we will add the following code to the General Declarations section:

```
Option Explicit

'Error logging class to log events
Private m_Log As CEventLog
```

We will also add one read only property called `CGILibGlobal` that returns a reference to the current object.

```
Public Property Get CGILibGlobal() As CGILibGlobal
    Set CGILibGlobal = Me
End Property
```

This little trick allows the methods of a `GlobalMultiUse` class to be invoked using the actual name of the class. Otherwise, we would have to use the `ProgID` of the `DLL` (`CGILibrary`), or call the method without specifying an object. Consider the following examples:

```
'Invoke method using class name.  This is preferred.
CGILibGlobal.Run( …)

'Use the ProgID of the DLL.  Yuck!
CGILibrary.Run(…)

'Don't use an object at all.  Someone else reading the code might think, "Is this
a new built in VB function?"
Run(…)
```

Now we are ready to implement the Run method. Here is the code:

```
Public Sub Run(CGIApp As ICGIApp, sAppPath As String, _
               sAppName As String, lAppThread As Long)

    Dim CGI As CCGI
    Dim sLogFile As String

    On Error GoTo LogCreateError

    'Create the event log. Use the app name to name the file
    Set m_Log = New CEventLog
    sLogFile = sAppPath & "\" & sAppName & ".log"
    m_Log.Create sLogFile, sAppName, lAppThread

    On Error GoTo GlobalHandler

    'Log initial info
    LogAppInfo sAppPath, sAppName, lAppThread

    'Create the CGI object and log all the info
    Set CGI = New CCGI
    LogCGIInfo CGI

    'Now run the client's CGI application
    CGIMain CGIApp, CGI

    m_Log.WriteEntry "CGI App " & sAppName & " Terminating: ErrCode = 0"
    Exit Sub
```

Before we add the error handlers, let's study what this is doing. The first thing it does is to create a `CEventLog` object. The actual log file name is generated using the application and path information passed into the procedure. Hence, for this case study, a `CGIEmpData.log` file will be generated in the same directory as the `EXE` file. Notice that if an error occurs during this process, we jump to the `LogCreateError` label.

Next, the procedure calls the private method `LogAppInfo` to add a start up entry to the log file, and then creates a `CCGI` object. The `CCGI` object will read all the CGI context information in its initialize event. The procedure also logs all the CGI information by calling the private method `LogCGIInfo`.

Finally, this procedure calls the private method `CGIMain` and passes it the CGI Application object. `CGIMain` will execute the `Create`, `PreProcess`, `Process`, and `PostProcess` methods of the CGI Application object.

Now we can add the code for the error handler routines. Note that if an error occurs before the `CEventLog` object can be properly created, we will log the event to the NT Event Log using the global VB `App` object.

```
LogCreateError:
    'Errors occured while creating the log, so log to NT Event Log.
    'Assert condition if in debug mode
    Debug.Assert False

    Dim sErr As String
    sErr = "A fatal error has occured in the CGI Application before" _
        & " the event log, " & sLogFile & ", could be created." _
        & vbCrLf & "CGI Error: " & BasicError(Err.Number) _
        & " = " & Err.Description

    App.LogEvent sErr, vbLogEventTypeError

    Exit Sub
GlobalHandler:
    Dim sErrMsg As String, lErrNum As Long, sErrSrc As String
    Dim sLogMsg As String
    sErrMsg = Err.Description
    lErrNum = BasicError(Err.Number)
    sErrSrc = Err.Source

    With m_Log
        .NewEntry
        .WriteLn "Error Number: " & lErrNum
        .WriteLn "Description : " & sErrMsg
        .WriteLn "Source      : " & sErrSrc
        .CloseEntry
    End With

    m_Log.WriteEntry "CGI App " & sAppName & " Terminating: ErrCode = " & lErrNum
    Exit Sub
End Sub
```

Here is the code for the `CGIMain` method. This method turns out to be very straightforward.

```
Private Sub CGIMain(CGIApp As ICGIApp, CGI As CCGI)
    With CGIApp
        'Create the CGI Application class
        .Create CGI, m_Log

        'Now process the CGI Request.
        .PreProcess
        .Process
```

```
            .PostProcess
        End With
    End Sub
```

The rest of the code for the `CGILibGlobal` class is shown below.

```
'******************************************************************
'Helper function which converts a dictionary to a nicely
'formatted string.
'******************************************************************
Private Function DictionaryToString(Dict As Dictionary) As String
    Dim sResult As String
    Dim vKey As Variant
    For Each vKey In Dict
        sResult = sResult & vKey & " = " & Dict(vKey) & vbCrLf
    Next vKey
    DictionaryToString = sResult
End Function


'******************************************************************
'Logs all the CGI information.
'******************************************************************
Private Sub LogCGIInfo(CGI As CCGI)
    With m_Log
        .NewEntry
        .WriteLn "Query String Parameters:" & vbCrLf & "-------------------------"
        .WriteLn "Query String: " & CGI.QueryString
        .WriteLn DictionaryToString(CGI.Params)
        .WriteLn "Environmental Variables:" & vbCrLf & "-------------------------"
        .WriteLn DictionaryToString(CGI.Environs)
        .CloseEntry
    End With
End Sub


'******************************************************************
'Logs all application information
'******************************************************************
Private Sub LogAppInfo(sAppPath As String, sAppName As String, lAppThread As Long)
    With m_Log
        .NewEntry
        .WriteLn "CGI Application Startup Details:"
        .WriteLn "--------------------------------------"
        .WriteLn "Executable: " & sAppPath & "\" & sAppName
        .WriteLn "Thread ID:" & lAppThread
        .CloseEntry
    End With
End Sub


'******************************************************************
'Reformats the Error code to make it more presentable
'******************************************************************
Private Function BasicError(lErrNum As Long)
    BasicError = lErrNum And &HFFFF&
End Function
```

Implementing the CCGI Class

The CCGI class reads and stores all the CGI information available from the HTTP query string and the environmental variables. We will add a new class to the project and set its name to CCGI and its Instancing property to PublicNotCreatable.

Then, we add the following code to the General Declarations section of the class:

```
'The raw query string recieved by the CGI application.
Private m_sQueryString As String

'Dictionary containing all the Name/Value pairs in the query string.
Private m_dicParams As Scripting.Dictionary

'Dictionary Containing all the environmental variables
Private m_dicEnvVars As Scripting.Dictionary

'Standard I/O object
Private m_StdIo As CStdIO

'CStdIO Errors.
Public Enum enCGI_ERRORCODES
    cgiQUERY_STRING_EMPTY = 9020   'No data in query string
    cgiQUERY_STRING_PARSE          'Could not parse the query string. Check format.
    cgiINVALID_REQUEST_METHOD      'Invalid Request Method.
End Enum

'CGI Environmental Variables.  These also have corresponding strings
'in the string table resource.
Public Enum enCGI_ENVIRONMENT_VARS
    cgiGATEWAY_INTERFACE = 20000
    cgiSERVER_NAME
    cgiSERVER_SOFTWARE
    cgiCONTENT_LENGTH
    cgiCONTENT_TYPE
    cgiSCRIPT_NAME
    cgiQUERY_STRING
    cgiREMOTE_HOST
    cgiREMOTE_USER
    cgiSERVER_PROTOCOL
    cgiREQUEST_METHOD
End Enum

'This is an error code returned by a dictionary if we
'attempt to add a key that already exists.
Private Const KEY_EXISTS As Integer = 457
```

Like the CQueryString class we will see in the next section, the CCGI class uses the Dictionary object to manage the name-value pairs. It also uses a separate dictionary object to manage the environmental variables.

An enumeration is used to give a unique numeric ID to each of the environmental variables. Note this is just a sub set of all the variables available, but it is easy to add more if you need to. These IDs correspond to a string table resource file.

We can use the Visual Basic Resource Editor tool to create a new resources file (.res) with the string table as shown below. When we finish entering the strings, we save the resource file and add it to the project

Next, we will implement the `Initialize` event. A lot happens in the `Initialize` event. It creates both dictionaries. It reads standard input or the `QUERY_STRING` variable for the query string, parses it, and fills the parameter dictionary with the resulting name-value pairs. It also reads all the CGI environmental variables and places them in another dictionary. Most of these activities are delegated to private helper functions. Here is the `Initialize` event code, and all its supporting methods:

```
Private Sub Class_Initialize()
    Debug.Print "CCGI Initialize"

    'Instatiate the dictionaries and the Standard I/O object
    Set m_dicParams = New Scripting.Dictionary
    Set m_dicEnvVars = New Scripting.Dictionary
    Set m_StdIo = New CStdIO

    'Load the CGI evironmental variables into dictionary
    SetEnvirons m_dicEnvVars

    'Retrieve the query string and load into dictionary
    SetParams
End Sub

'****************************************************************
'Sets up the parameter dictionary
'****************************************************************
Private Sub SetParams()
    m_sQueryString = GetQueryString()
    ParseQueryString m_sQueryString, m_dicParams
End Sub
```

```
'*******************************************************************
'Gets the query string from either standard input or the
'QUERY_STRING environmental variable.
'*******************************************************************
Private Function GetQueryString() As String
    Dim sResult As String
    Select Case m_dicEnvVars("REQUEST_METHOD")
        Case "GET", "PUT", "HEAD":
            sResult = Environ("QUERY_STRING")
        Case "POST":
            sResult = m_StdIo.ReadIn()
        Case Else
            'Should be one of the above methods
            Debug.Assert False
            Err.Raise cgiINVALID_REQUEST_METHOD Or vbObjectError, _
                    "CCGI.GetQueryString()", _
                    "Invalid Request Method."
    End Select
    GetQueryString = sResult
End Function


'*******************************************************************
'Parses the Query String and puts the Name-Value pairs into the
'parameter dictionary.
'*******************************************************************
Private Sub ParseQueryString(ByVal sQuery As String, Params As Dictionary)
    Dim arParams() As String
    Dim I As Long

    On Error GoTo Handler:

    arParams = Split(sQuery, "&")

    For I = 0 To UBound(arParams)
        Params.Add GetParamName(arParams(I)), GetParamValue(arParams(I))
    Next I

    Exit Sub

Handler:
    Dim lErr As Long
    lErr = Err.Number
    Select Case lErr
        Case KEY_EXISTS        'Duplicate key, just skip it
            Resume Next
        Case Else
            Debug.Assert False
            Err.Raise cgiQUERY_STRING_PARSE Or vbObjectError, _
                    "CCGI.ParseQueryString()", _
                    "Could not parse the query string. Check format."
    End Select
End Sub


'*******************************************************************
'Returns the Value portion of a Name=Value pair
'*******************************************************************
Private Function GetParamValue(ByVal sParam As String) As String
    Dim arPair() As String
    Dim sResult As String
```

```
        arPair = Split(sParam, "=")

        'Replace each + char with a space
        sResult = Replace(arPair(1), "+", " ")

        'Convert all %XX hex codes
        GetParamValue = ReplaceHex(sResult)
End Function

'*****************************************************************
'Replace the %XX Hex codes with their ASCII equivilant
'*****************************************************************
Private Function ReplaceHex(ByVal sValue As String) As String
    Dim I As Integer
    Dim sHex As String
    Dim sResult As String

    sResult = sValue
    Do
        I = InStr(I + 1, sResult, "%")
        If (I = 0) Then Exit Do
        sHex = "&H" + Mid(sResult, I + 1, 2)
        sResult = Left(sResult, I - 1) & Chr(CInt(sHex)) _
                    & Mid(sResult, I + 3)
    Loop

    ReplaceHex = sResult

End Function

'*****************************************************************
'Returns the Name portion of a Name=Value pair
'*****************************************************************
Private Function GetParamName(ByVal sParam As String) As String
    Dim arPair() As String
    arPair = Split(sParam, "=")
    GetParamName = arPair(0)
End Function

'*****************************************************************
'Initialize the environmental variables dictionary
'*****************************************************************
Private Sub SetEnvirons(Environs As Dictionary)
    Dim I As Long
    Dim sVar As String
    Dim sValue As String
    For I = cgiGATEWAY_INTERFACE To cgiREQUEST_METHOD
        sVar = LoadResString(I)
        sValue = Environ(sVar)
        If sValue = "" Then sValue = " "
        Debug.Print sVar & " = " & sValue
        Environs.Add sVar, sValue
    Next I
End Sub
```

Notice that in the SetEnvirons function above, we are retrieving the string representing the environmental variable's name from the resource file, using the built in LoadResString function.

All that is left to implement now are the read only properties and the `Terminate` event.

```
'**************************************************************
'Returns the query string
'**************************************************************
Public Property Get QueryString() As String
    QueryString = m_sQueryString
End Property


'**************************************************************
'Returns the parameter dictionary.
'**************************************************************
Public Property Get Params() As Dictionary
    Set Params = m_dicParams
End Property


'**************************************************************
'Returns the environmental variables dictionary
'**************************************************************
Public Property Get Environs() As Dictionary
    Set Environs = m_dicEnvVars
End Property


'**************************************************************
'Returns the Standard input/output object.
'**************************************************************
Public Property Get StdIO() As CStdIO
    Set StdIO = m_StdIo
End Property
```

Finally, here's the `Terminate` event.

```
Private Sub Class_Terminate()
    Debug.Print "CCGI Terminated"

    Set m_dicParams = Nothing
    Set m_dicEnvVars = Nothing
    Set m_StdIo = Nothing
End Sub
```

Implementing the CEventLog Class

For this case study, the CEventLog class is a necessary evil. It really does not have anything to do with CGI, but if we did not log events it would be nearly impossible to debug our CGI Applications. Since it not essential to understanding CGI, the code is presented here with minimal explanation.

```
Option Explicit

Public Enum enLOG_ERRORCODES
    logFILE_OPEN_FAILED = 9040    'Could not open specified event log.
    logWRITE_WITHOUT_CREATE       'Event log write operation attempted before
                                  'log was created.
    logWRITE_WITHOUT_ENTRY        'Event log write operation attempted before
                                  'log entry created.
    logWRITE_FAILED               'Event log write operation failed.
End Enum
```

```vb
Private m_hFile As Long          'Log file handle
Private m_sAppName As String     'Application Name
Private m_lThreadID As Long      'Application thread id

'Used to ensure the Create() method is called.
Private m_bIsCreated As Boolean

'True if there is a current log entry.
Private m_bIsEntryOpen As Boolean

'Some useful String Constants
Private Const WRITE_FAILED As String = "Event log write operation failed."
Private Const APP_NAME As String = "*AppName: "
Private Const THREAD_ID As String = "*ThreadID: "
Private Const TIME_STAMP As String = "*TimeStamp: "
Private Const ENTRY_TYPE As String = "*Entry Type: "
Private Const ENTRY_SEPARATOR As String = _
"********************************************************************"

'********************************************************************
'Initialize the class
'********************************************************************
Private Sub Class_Initialize()
    m_bIsCreated = False
    m_bIsEntryOpen = False
End Sub


'********************************************************************
'Class Terminate
'********************************************************************
Private Sub Class_Terminate()
    Close m_hFile
End Sub


'********************************************************************
'Create the log file.  Set data members.
'********************************************************************
Friend Sub Create(sPath As String, _
                  sAppName As String, _
                  lAppThread As Long)

    On Error GoTo ErrorHandler
    m_hFile = FreeFile
    Open sPath For Append As #m_hFile

    m_sAppName = sAppName
    m_lThreadID = lAppThread
    m_bIsCreated = True

    Exit Sub

ErrorHandler:
    Dim sErr As String
    sErr = "Could not open specified event log." & vbCrLf & vbCrLf _
          & "System Error: " & Err.Number & " = " & Err.Description
    Err.Raise logFILE_OPEN_FAILED Or vbObjectError, "CEventLog.Create", sErr
    m_bIsCreated = False
End Sub
```

801

```
'******************************************************************
'Writes an entire entry to the log file.  If a previous entry
'is still open, then it is closed.
'******************************************************************
Public Sub WriteEntry(sLog As String)

    If m_bIsEntryOpen Then
        CloseEntry
    End If

    NewEntry
    WriteLn sLog
    CloseEntry

End Sub

'******************************************************************
'Writes a line to the log file.
'******************************************************************
Public Sub WriteLn(sLine As String)

    'Make sure the Create() method has been called.
    If Not m_bIsCreated Then
        Debug.Assert False 'Assert condition in debug mode
        Err.Raise logWRITE_WITHOUT_CREATE Or vbObjectError, _
                "CEventLog.WriteLn()", _
                "Event log write operation attempted before log was created."
    End If

    'Make sure NewEntry() method has been called.
    If Not m_bIsEntryOpen Then
        Debug.Assert False 'Assert condition in debug mode
        Err.Raise logWRITE_WITHOUT_ENTRY Or vbObjectError, _
                "CEventLog.WriteLn()", _
                "Event log write operation attempted before log entry
created."
    End If

    PrivateWrite sLine

End Sub

'******************************************************************
'Creates a new entry in the log file.  Writes the log headers
'and sets various member variables.
'******************************************************************
Public Sub NewEntry()

    'Make sure the Create() method has been called.
    If Not m_bIsCreated Then
        Debug.Assert False 'Assert condition in debug mode
        Err.Raise logWRITE_WITHOUT_CREATE Or vbObjectError,
"CEventLog.OpenEntry()", _
            "Event log write operation attempted before log was created."
    End If
```

```
      PrivateWrite ENTRY_SEPARATOR
      PrivateWrite APP_NAME & vbTab & m_sAppName
      PrivateWrite THREAD_ID & vbTab & m_lThreadID
      PrivateWrite TIME_STAMP & vbTab & Format(Now, "general date")
      PrivateWrite ENTRY_SEPARATOR
      m_bIsEntryOpen = True

  End Sub

  '*************************************************************
  'Closes the log entry.
  '*************************************************************
  Public Sub CloseEntry()
      WriteLn ""
      m_bIsEntryOpen = False
  End Sub

  '*************************************************************
  'Performs the actual write to the log file.
  '*************************************************************
  Private Sub PrivateWrite(sLine As String)
      On Error GoTo WriteError
      Print #m_hFile, sLine
      Exit Sub

  WriteError:
      Dim sErrMsg As String
      sErrMsg = WRITE_FAILED & vbCrLf & "System Error: " & Err.Description
      Err.Raise logWRITE_FAILED Or vbObjectError, _
                "CEventLog.WriteLn()", sErrMsg
  End Sub
```

Implementing the CStdIO Class

We already did this earlier. We just need to copy the `CStdIO.cls` created previously to the current project directory. Then add it to the project. In the `Properties` window, we change the Instancing property to PublicNotCreatable.

Defining the ICGIApp Interface

The final task is to define the `ICGIApp` interface. Recall that an interface is just a collection of empty methods and properties. We need to add a new class to the project, name it `ICGIApp` and set its Instancing property to PublicNotCreatable. Then we add all the method and property "stubs" as shown below:

```
  Option Explicit

  Public Function Create(CGI As CCGI, Log As CEventLog) As Boolean
  End Function

  Public Function PreProcess() As Boolean
  End Function

  Public Function Process() As Boolean
  End Function
```

```
Public Function PostProcess() As Boolean
End Function

Public Property Get CGI() As CCGI
End Property

Public Property Get Log() As CEventLog
End Property
```

Although the methods all return a Boolean value, the current implementation of the CAF ignores the return values (see the `CGIMain` method of `CGILibGlobal`).

Summary

It was a long journey, but the CGI Application Framework is now complete. We have implemented all the services required from a CGI program, event logging, standard input and output, and retrieval of the CGI context information. The next section describes how we can use all this to create a custom CGI application.

> **Before moving on, make sure you compile this project to make the DLL.**

Using CAF to Implement CGIEmpData

In order to write a custom CGI Application using the framework we need to perform the following steps:

> ➢ Create an ActiveX EXE VB project
> ➢ Set the Unattended Execution option in the Project Properties dialog.
> ➢ Add a reference to the CGI Application Framework DLL.
> ➢ Add a standard module and implement Sub Main as shown in another section under "The CGILibGlobal Class"
> ➢ Add a class module that implements the `ICGIApp` interface to perform the required application logic.

We will do steps 1-4 and save the project as `CGIEmpData.vbp`. Step 5 is the complicated part. It is described in detail below.

Implementing ICGIApp with the CCGIEmp Class

This section describes the implementation of the `CCGIEmp` class. This class contains all the logic for the Employee Data Entry application. It implements the `ICGIApp` interface so that CGI Framework can drive the application and provide useful services.

First, we add a new class to the project and name it CCGIEmp. In the General Declarations section we add the following code:

```
Option Explicit

Implements ICGIApp

'The following objects are created and maintained by the CGILibrary
'DLL. The CGILibrary passes these objects through the Create() method.
Private m_Cgi As CCGI        'Encapsulates CGI information
Private m_Log As CEventLog   'Used to write to the application log file
Private m_StdIo As CStdIO    'Used to write to standard output

Private m_bIsCreated As Boolean

'******* Application specific member variables *******

'The employee business object
Private m_Emp As CEmployee

'Action enumeration
Private Enum Action
    acSave
    acRetrieveAll
End Enum

'Useful constants
Private Const MISSING_INFO As String = "Some employee information is missing or
invalid"

'Note that everything below should be on same line
Private Const TABLE_HEADER As String = "<TABLE BORDER=1><THEAD BGCOLOR=GRAY
FGCOLOR=WHITE><TD WIDTH=65>ID</TD><TD>NAME</TD><TD>PAY
RATE</TD><TD>HOURS</TD><TD>START DATE</TD></THEAD>"
```

Notice how the Implements keyword is used to state that the class will implement the ICGIApp interface. The first method we implement is Create:

```
'**************************************************************
'Initializes the CGI, Error log, and standard IO references.
'These objects are created by the CGILibrary.
'**************************************************************
Private Function ICGIApp_Create(CGI As CCGI, Log As CEventLog) As Boolean
    Set m_Cgi = CGI
    Set m_Log = Log
    Set m_StdIo = CGI.StdIO
    m_bIsCreated = True

    ICGIApp_Create = True
End Function
```

Remember the framework is creating the CGI and Log objects on our behalf. We just keep a reference to each object in the corresponding member variables.

Now we implement the `PreProcess` method. Typically, we will send the HTTP response headers and validate the query string. The code below also initializes the `CEmployee` business object. The `CEmployee` class is defined later. If the Debug parameter in the query string is set to 1, then private helper methods `WriteParams` and `WriteEnvirons` are called to send the CGI context information to the browser for display.

```
Private Function ICGIApp_PreProcess() As Boolean
    'Assert if Create() has not been called
    Debug.Assert m_bIsCreated

    m_Log.WriteEntry "PreProcess()"

    'Send the response header.
    m_StdIo.WriteOut "Content-type: text/html" & vbCrLf & vbCrLf
    m_StdIo.WriteOut "<HTML>"
    m_StdIo.WriteOut "<BODY>"

    'Verify the Action parameter exists.
    If IsParamsValid() Then

        'Initialize the Employee bus obj.
        Set m_Emp = New CEmployee

        'If Debug parameter is 1 then return CGI info.
        If m_Cgi.Params("Debug") = 1 Then
            m_StdIo.WriteOut "<H1>CGI Info Received</H1><br>"
            WriteParams
            WriteEnvirons
            m_StdIo.WriteOut "<hr>"          'Horizontal Line
        End If

    Else
        'Action parameter does not exist.  Return an error message.
        m_StdIo.WriteOut "<h1>Invalid Query String!</h1>"
        m_StdIo.WriteOut "<p>Query string does not contain a valid Action
 value.<p>"

        'Raising an error to stop processing.  Error handled in the
        'CGILibrary and logged to the log file.
        Err.Raise 10000, "CGIEmpMain.PreProcess()", "Invalid query string"

    End If

    ICGIApp_PreProcess = True
End Function
```

The `WriteEnvirons`, `WriteParams`, and `IsParamsValid` code is shown below:

```
'****************************************************************
'Format and send the CGI environmental variables.  Used when the
'Debug parameter is set.
'****************************************************************
Private Sub WriteEnvirons()
    Dim vKey As Variant

    m_StdIo.WriteOut "<H2>Environmental Variables:</H2>"
    m_StdIo.WriteOut "<p>"
    For Each vKey In m_Cgi.Environs
        m_StdIo.WriteOut vKey & " = " & m_Cgi.Environs(vKey) & "<br>"
    Next vKey
    m_StdIo.WriteOut "</p>"
```

```
End Sub

'*******************************************************************
'Format and send the CGI query string parameters.  Used when the
'Debug parameter is set.
'*******************************************************************
Private Sub WriteParams()
    Dim vKey As Variant

    m_StdIo.WriteOut "<H2>Parameters:</H2>"
    m_StdIo.WriteOut "<p>"
    m_StdIo.WriteOut "Query String: " & m_Cgi.QueryString & "<br>"
    For Each vKey In m_Cgi.Params
        m_StdIo.WriteOut vKey & " = " & m_Cgi.Params(vKey) & "<br>"
    Next vKey
    m_StdIo.WriteOut "</p>"
End Sub


'*******************************************************************
'Validate Action parameter is present and is a number.
'*******************************************************************
Private Function IsParamsValid() As Boolean
    Dim vAction As Variant

    vAction = m_Cgi.Params("Action")

    If (IsNumeric(vAction) And Not IsEmpty(vAction)) Then
        IsParamsValid = True
    Else
        IsParamsValid = False
    End If

End Function
```

The next method we need to implement is Process. This is where the request is actually processed and most of the work is done.

```
Private Function ICGIApp_Process() As Boolean
    'Assert if Create() has not been called
    Debug.Assert m_bIsCreated

    m_Log.WriteEntry "Process()"

    If m_Cgi.Params("Action") = acSave Then
        SaveEmployee
    Else
        RetrieveEmps
    End If

    ICGIApp_Process = True
End Function
```

The actual processing action is determined by the value of the Action parameter. If it is 0, then SaveEmployee is called to save all the employee data to a database. If the Action value is 1, then RetrieveEmps is called which formats information on all the current employees into an HTML table and sends it back to the browser for display.

The `RetrieveEmps()` method is shown below. Note is uses the employee business object to invoke a method called `GetAll`; this returns a recordset that we can use to generate the HTML table.

```
Private Sub RetrieveEmps()
    Dim sMsg As String
    Dim rs As ADODB.Recordset

    m_Log.WriteEntry "RetrieveEmps()"

    'Get the recordset from the employee object
    Set rs = m_Emp.GetAll()
    rs.Open
    With m_StdIo
        'Begin Table
        .WriteOut TABLE_HEADER
        Do While Not rs.EOF
            .WriteOut "<TR>"
            .WriteOut "<TD>" & rs("ID") & "</TD>"
            .WriteOut "<TD>" & rs("Name") & "</TD>"
            .WriteOut "<TD>" & FormatCurrency(rs("PayRate")) & "</TD>"
            .WriteOut "<TD>" & rs("Hours") & "</TD>"
            .WriteOut "<TD>" & Format(rs("StartDate"), "mm/dd/yyyy") & "</TD>"
            .WriteOut "</TR>"
            rs.MoveNext
        Loop
        .WriteOut "</TABLE>"
    End With

    rs.Close
End Sub
```

`SaveEmployee` is a little more complicated. We use the `Params` dictionary exposed by the CGI object to set the properties of the employee object. Then we call the `Save` method of the employee object to write the information to the database.

```
Private Sub SaveEmployee()
    Dim sEmployee As String

    m_Log.WriteEntry "SaveEmployee()"

    'Ignore errors while setting the employee properties. This is
    'to avoid "Type Mismatch" errors if some parameters are missing.
    On Error Resume Next

    With m_Emp
        .Name = m_Cgi.Params("Name")
        .SSN = m_Cgi.Params("ID")
        .Hours = m_Cgi.Params("Hours")
        .PayRate = m_Cgi.Params("PayRate")
        .StartDate = m_Cgi.Params("StartDate")
    End With

    'Stop ignoring errors
    On Error GoTo 0
```

```
        'If employee object is valid then save it
    If m_Emp.IsValid() Then
        m_StdIo.WriteOut "<h2>Employee Saved!</h2>"
        m_StdIo.WriteOut m_Emp.AsHTML()
        m_Log.WriteEntry "SaveEmployee()" & vbCrLf & m_Emp.AsString()
    Else
        'Employee is missing some data or data is invalid.
        m_StdIo.WriteOut "<h2>Employee Save Failed!</h2>"
        m_StdIo.WriteOut "<p>" & MISSING_INFO & "</p>"

        'Log the error too.
        m_Log.WriteEntry "Save Error: " & MISSING_INFO
    End If
End Sub
```

After the Process method completes, the framework will call the PostProcess method. In this case, we make sure to release the reference to the employee object and then write the closing HTML tags.

```
Private Function ICGIApp_PostProcess() As Boolean
    'Assert if Create() has not been called
    Debug.Assert m_bIsCreated

    m_Log.WriteEntry "PostProcess()"

    m_StdIo.WriteOut "</BODY>"
    m_StdIo.WriteOut "</HTML>"
    m_StdIo.WriteOut ""
    Set m_Emp = Nothing

    ICGIApp_PostProcess = True
End Function
```

To complete the ICGIApp interface, all we need is to implement the CGI and Log properties:

```
Private Property Get ICGIApp_CGI() As CCGI
    Set ICGIApp_CGI = m_Cgi
End Property

Private Property Get ICGIApp_Log() As CEventLog
    Set ICGIApp_Log = m_Log
End Property
```

The only thing missing now is the Initialize and Terminate events. Initialize sets the m_bIsCreated member variable to false in order to force the Create method to always be the first method called. Terminate releases the references to the CGI, Log, and StdIO objects.

```
Private Sub Class_Initialize()
    m_bIsCreated = False
End Sub

Private Sub Class_Terminate()
    Set m_Cgi = Nothing
    Set m_Log = Nothing
    Set m_StdIo = Nothing
End Sub
```

Implementing the CEmployee Class

The CEmployee class used here is very similar to the one defined in the DHTML Applications case study. In fact, all we need to do is add three new methods, IsValid, AsHTML, and GetAll.

First, we copy the CEmployee class module created in the DHTML Application to the current project directory and add it to the project. This module can also be found on the Wrox website.

> **CEmployee uses the Data Designer for data access, so we also need to copy the deEmpData.dsr file and add it to the project.**

Finally, we copy the EmpData.mdb file into the current directory.

The IsValid method does a simple sanity check on the current state of the employee object. It makes sure that all the properties of the employee are set and valid. If so, it returns true. The fact that this function is needed here in the CGI version of the class and not in the DHTML version highlights one of the key differences between DHTML programming and CGI or any other form of server side web programming. In the DHTML case study we could put this validation logic on the client side, so it did not have to call the server just to find out the data was invalid.

```
Public Function IsValid() As Boolean
    Dim bIsValid As Boolean
    bIsValid = True

    If m_Name = "" Then
        bIsValid = False
    ElseIf m_SSN = "" Then
        bIsValid = False
    ElseIf Not IsNumeric(Trim(m_PayRate)) Then
        bIsValid = False
    ElseIf Not IsNumeric(Trim(m_Hours)) Then
        bIsValid = False
    ElseIf Not IsDate(Trim(m_StartDate)) Then
        bIsValid = False
    End If

    IsValid = bIsValid

End Function
```

The AsHTML method places all the current employee information into a string with HTML formatting tags.

```
Public Function AsHTML() As String
    Dim sResult As String

    sResult = "<table border=0 width=500>"
    sResult = sResult & "<tr><td width=100>Name:</td><td width=400>" & m_Name &
"</td></tr>"
```

```
        sResult = sResult & "<tr><td>ID:</td><td>" & m_SSN & "</td></tr>"
        sResult = sResult & "<tr><td>Pay Rate:</td><td>" & m_PayRate & "</td></tr>"
        sResult = sResult & "<tr><td>Hours:</td><td>" & m_Hours & "</td></tr>"
        sResult = sResult & "<tr><td>Start Date:</td><td>" & m_StartDate &
"</td></tr>"
        sResult = sResult & "</table>"

        AsHTML = sResult
End Function
```

The final method we need to add to the CEmployee class is GetAll. This method creates and prepares a recordset object to retrieve all the employees in the database. The method returns a reference to this recordset. Note, however, that the recordset is not opened. Instead, that is left to the calling code.

```
Public Function GetAll() As ADODB.Recordset
    Dim rs As New Recordset
    With rs
        .Source = "Select * FROM Employees"
        .ActiveConnection = deEmpData.cnnEmpData
        .LockType = adLockReadOnly
        .CursorType = adOpenStatic
    End With

    Set GetAll = rs

End Function
```

Finally, we have finished the program. Now all we need to do is try it out.

Testing the CGIEmpData Program

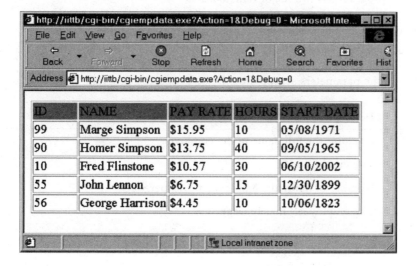

To run the `CGIEmpData` program, copy the executable and the Access database to the CGI directory of the web server. Typically this will be something like `c:\InetPub\wwwroot\cgi-bin`. We can use the Employee Date Entry client we will create in the next section to kick off the CGI process. Alternately, we can use a web browser to fire the program. We just need to add the query string manually at the end of the URL:

As illustrated in the screenshot, to do this you enter the URL of the program and, without spaces, enter a question mark followed by the CGI query string. This calls the CGI program with the action method set to `GET` instead of `POST`, but that's fine since the CGI Framework can handle both.

Building a CGI Client using VB

This section describes how to build a Visual Basic front end to a CGI application. The key problem we have to solve is how to build the query string. In order to do that in a generic fashion, we build a class called `CQueryString`. We will also use the `WebBrowser` control to send the HTTP request to the web server, and display the response from the CGI program.

Preparing the Environment

This project puts a Visual Basic front end on the CGIEmpData program created in the last section. For this to work, the CGIEmpData executable and the associated Access database must be copied to the CGI directory of the web server.

The Employee Data Entry Application Client

Before we can effectively build an interface for a CGI program, we must know all the capabilities of the program, the parameters it expects, and how the values of the parameters affect the final HTML outcome. The `CGIEmpData` program has two major functions:

➢ Save the employee information to a database.
➢ Retrieve a listing of all the employees in the database.

The table below describes all the parameters accepted by the `CGIEmpData` program:

Parameter Name	Description
Name	Contains the full name of the employee
ID	The employee ID
Hours	Number of hours the employee works per week
PayRate	The employee's hourly wage

Parameter Name	Description
StartDate	The employee's start date
Action	This is required. If 0, the program will save the employee (all the above parameters are required). If 1, the program will retrieve all the current employees from the database.
Debug	If 1, the CGIEmpData will report all the query string parameters and environmental variables used to fill the request.

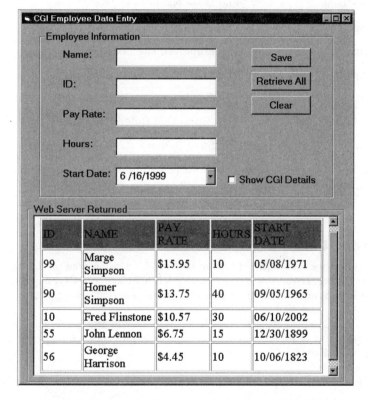

This can all be mapped to a fairly standard VB form. Here is a possible Visual Basic client interface to the CGI program:

To implement the client, we first create a new standard project and call it CGIClient.vbp. Then design the form shown above. Here are a few details about this form:

> The **Web Server Returned** section on the bottom is actually a WebBrowser control. We will use this to control the request to the CGI program and to display the response. We could also have opted to use the HTTP protocol features of the Internet Transfer control. This would allow us to retrieve the response, parse out the HTML tags, and display the data in any format we desired. For example, instead of displaying the Retrieve All response as a simple HTML table, we could have displayed the results in a grid control.

> ➢ The **Show CGI Details** check box maps to the `Debug` parameter of the CGI program. If checked, then `Debug` will be set to `1`.

> ➢ The **Start Date** field is a `dtPicker` control. Feel free to use any other means to enter the employee start date.

Below are the object names used on the form in this project:

Object Name	Description
txtEmpName	Employee Name TextBox
txtEmpID	Employee ID TextBox
txtEmpPay	The Employee Pay TextBox
txtEmpHours	The Employee Hours TextBox
dtStartDt	The Employee Start Date dtpicker control
chkDebug	The "Show CGI Details" Checkbox
cmdSave	The Save Button
cmdRetrieveAll	The Retrieve All Button
cmdClear	The Clear button

The CQueryString Class

The primary problem we must solve is how to take all the data entered on the form and package it into a valid query string. If you think about it, any VB interface to a CGI application will have the exact same problem. Sounds like a good candidate for a generic class – the `CQueryString` class.

We want the `CQueryString` class to provide a simple way to add name-value pairs to the query string. We also want it to automatically convert spaces to plus signs, and special characters to their hexadecimal ASCII values.

To do all the above, we will implement the following public interface for the class:

Property or Method	Description
Sub SetParam	Adds/sets the name-value pair in the query string. If the Named parameter does not exist in the query string, it will be added. `QStr.SetParamHours txtHours.Text`
Function GetParam	Retrieves the value of the named parameter. If the parameter does not exist in the query string, a zero length string will be returned. `SEmpName = QStr.GetParam(Name)`

Property or Method	Description
Property QueryString	*Read Only* Returns a fully formatted query string with all the name-value pairs added via the SetParam method. `sQryStr = QStr.QueryString`
Property QueryByteArray	*Read Only* Returns the query string as a byte array. `bytQuery = QStr.QueryByteArray`
Public Sub Clear	Empties the query string. QStr.Clear

CQueryString General Declarations

First, we need to add a class module to the project and set its `Name` to `CQueryString`. Then we add the following code to the General Declarations section:

```
Option Explicit

'The query string
Private m_sQryStr As String

'Dictionary containing the name-value pairs
Private m_dicParams As Dictionary

'If true, the name-value pair dictionary has been updated and
'the m_sQryStr variable has NOT been updated.
Private m_bIsDirty As Boolean
```

As you can see, the internal storage mechanism we will use to maintain the name-value pairs is the Dictionary object. This object is ideally suited to for this task, but to use it we will have to reference the **Microsoft Scripting Runtime** library. Remember that the `CQueryString` user could possibly add a few name-value pairs via the `SetParam` method, then retrieve the resulting query string, add a few more name-value pairs, and retrieve the query string again. We will cache the query string in the member variable `m_sQryStr`, but we will need to know when the Dictionary has been modified so that the query string will be recreated when the `QueryString` property is used. The `m_bIsDirty` member variable is the flag that will be set when the `Dictionary` has been modified. Of course it will be cleared when the query string has been updated to reflect the latest contents of the `Dictionary`.

CQueryString Initialize and Terminate Events

Next we will write the `Initialize` and `Terminate` event procedures.

```
Private Sub Class_Initialize()
    Set m_dicParams = New Dictionary
    m_sQryStr = ""
    m_bIsDirty = False
End Sub

Private Sub Class_Terminate()
    Set m_dicParams = Nothing
End Sub
```

`Initialize` simply instantiates the `Dictionary` object, initializes the query string as a zero length string, and sets the dirty flag to false. `Terminate` needs only to release the reference to the `Dictionary` object.

CQueryString Properties: QueryString and QueryByteArray

The `QueryString` property is read only. So we only need to implement the `Property Get` procedure. This is not as simple as just returning the `m_sQryStr` member variable, since the `Dictionary` could contain new and updated name-value pairs. We could regenerate the query string based on the current contents of the `Dictionary` every time this property is called, but that is not very efficient. Instead, we will check the `m_bIsDirty` flag. If this is true, then we will call the private method `MakeQueryString` to iterate through the dictionary and recreate the query string. The code for `MakeQueryString` method is shown later. On the other hand, if the flag is false we can simply return the current query string.

```
Public Property Get QueryString() As String
    If m_bIsDirty Then
        MakeQueryString
    End If
    QueryString = m_sQryStr
End Property
```

Actually for this particular case study, the `QueryByteArray` property is more useful. This is because the `WebBrowser` control's `Navigate2` method takes the query string as a byte array. We will see how this works momentarily. For now, we just need to be able to convert the query string from a VB string to a byte array. The built in VB function `StrConv` is used to do the actual conversion. Again, we use the `m_bIsDirty` flag to determine if we have to call the `MakeQueryString` method before returning the query string.

```
Public Property Get QueryByteArray() As Byte()
    If m_bIsDirty Then
        MakeQueryString
    End If
    QueryByteArray = StrConv(m_sQryStr, vbFromUnicode)
End Property
```

CQueryString Public Methods: GetParam, SetParam and Clear

To implement `GetParam`, we first check to see if the provided parameter name currently exists in the dictionary. If so, we return the `Value` associated with the parameter name. Otherwise, we return a zero length string.

```
Public Function GetParam(ByVal sName As String) As String
    If m_dicParams.Exists(sName) Then
        GetParam = m_dicParams.Item(sName)
    Else
        GetParam = ""
    End If
End Function
```

For the `SetParam` method, all we need to do is add the provided `Name` and `Value` to the dictionary. The parameter `Name` will be set as the dictionary key, while the `Value` will be the item. Also, since this is updating the dictionary, we must set the `m_bIsDirty` flag to true to make sure the query string will be regenerated the next time the `QueryString` property is used.

```
Public Sub SetParam(ByVal sName As String, ByVal sValue As String)
    m_dicParams.Item(sName) = sValue
    m_bIsDirty = True
End Sub
```

The `Clear` method is trivial. It removes all the entries from the dictionary and clears the query string. It also sets the `m_bIsDirty` flag to false.

```
Public Sub Clear()
    m_dicParams.RemoveAll
    m_sQryStr = ""
    m_bIsDirty = False
End Sub
```

CQueryString Private Methods: MakeQueryString and ConvertSpecial

Most of the grunt work in this class is contained in the `MakeQueryString` method. This method iterates through all the name-value pairs contained in the dictionary to construct a properly formatted query string. This includes replacing all the spaces with the plus sign, converting special characters to their ASCII hexadecimal code, and delimiting name-value pairs with the ampersand character. Here is the implementation:

```
Private Sub MakeQueryString()
    Dim sResults As String
    Dim sName As Variant
    Dim sValue As String

    'Iterate the dictionary
    For Each sName In m_dicParams
        sValue = ConvertSpecial(m_dicParams(sName))
        sResults = sResults & sName & "=" & sValue & "&"
    Next sName

    'Chop off the extra & on the end
    sResults = Left(sResults, Len(sResults) - 1)

    'Replace the spaces with +
    m_sQryStr = Replace(sResults, " ", "+")

    m_bIsDirty = False
End Sub
```

The procedure iterates through the keys in the dictionary using the For Each looping construct. The key is used to retrieve the Value, which is sent to another private method called `ConvertSpecial` to convert any special characters in the string to ASCII code. The Name and Value strings are then appended to the query string. To replace the space characters with plus signs, we simply call the VB `Replace` function. Finally, we set the `m_bIsDirty` flag to false to indicate that the query string does not need to be regenerated.

The last thing we need to implement is the `ConvertSpecial` private method. This method iterates through a provided string and substitutes each special character with %XX where XX is the character ASCII code in hexadecimal.

```
Private Function ConvertSpecial(ByVal sData As String) As String
    Dim sResult As String
    Dim i As Integer
    Dim iAsc As Integer

    'Iterate the entire string, one character at a time
    For i = 1 To Len(sData)
        iAsc = Asc(Mid(sData, i, 1))
        Select Case iAsc
            Case 33 To 47, 58 To 63, 123 To 126
                sResult = sResult & "%" & Hex$(iAsc)
            Case Else
                sResult = sResult & Chr(iAsc)
        End Select
    Next i

    ConvertSpecial = sResult

End Function
```

Implementing the Employee Data Entry Form

Remember the above discussion about the `CQueryString` started with the realization that we needed some generic mechanism to create a query string based on the information entered in the form. Now its time to use the class to do just that.

frmEmpInput General Declarations

First we will open the code view of the form and add the following to the General Declarations section:

```
Option Explicit

'Enumeration for the Action parameter
Private Enum enAction
    acSAVE
    acRETRIEVE_ALL
End Enum

'Action Setting
Private m_Action As enAction

'Query string object
Private m_QryStr As CQueryString
```

The `m_Action` form variable will be used to specify whether the requested action is either a save (`acSAVE`), or a retrieve all (`acRETRIEVE_ALL`). Below that we see the `m_QryStr` variable defined as a reference to a `CQueryString` object.

frmInput Form and Control Events

The `Form_Load` and `cmdClear_Click` events are pretty mundane and do not need much explanation. The load event instantiates the `CQueryString` object and the `cmdClear_Click` event clears all the text boxes and sets the start date to the current date.

```
Private Sub Form_Load()
    cmdClear_Click
    Set m_QryStr = New CQueryString
End Sub

Private Sub cmdClear_Click()
    txtEmpName.Text = ""
    txtEmpID.Text = ""
    txtEmpPay.Text = ""
    txtEmpHours.Text = ""
    dtStartDt.Value = Now
End Sub
```

The click events for the **Save and Retrieve All** buttons are only slightly more interesting. In `cmdSave_Click`, we set the form variable `m_Action` to `enSAVE(0)`. Likewise in `cmdRetrieveAll_Click`, we set `m_Action` to `enRETRIEVE_ALL(1)`. In both events, after we set the action type we call the private `SubmitRequest` method to take care of the rest of the details.

```
Private Sub cmdRetrieveAll_Click()
    m_Action = acRETRIEVE_ALL   'Enumeration, Action = 1
    SubmitRequest
End Sub

Private Sub cmdSave_Click()
    m_Action = acSAVE    'Enumeration, Action = 0
    SubmitRequest
End Sub
```

frmEmpInput Helper Routines

Now we can get to the core of the issue. The `SubmitRequest` procedure calls another private procedure, `BuildQuery`, to take care of the details of adding the form data to the query string. Then the routine retrieves the query string as a byte array using the `CQueryString`'s `QueryByteArray` property. This byte array is passed as the `PostData` argument to the `Navigate2` method of the `WebBrowser` control. Here is the source:

```
Private Sub SubmitRequest()
    Dim sQuery As String
    Dim sHeaders As String
    Dim bytPostData() As Byte

    'Add all the form info to the query string.
    BuildQuery

    'Convert the query string into a byte array.  The Web Browser
    'control requires that the post data be in byte form.
    bytPostData = m_QryStr.QueryByteArray
```

```
      sHeaders = "Content-Type: application/x-www-form-urlencoded" & vbCrLf

      WebBrowser1.Navigate2 "http://www.someserver.com/cgi-bin/cgiempdata.exe", _
                        0, "", bytPostData, sHeaders    '**Enter correct URL
  above**
  End Sub
```

The `Navigate2` method directs the browser to open the given URL. The header information describes the data contained in the `PostData` argument. All we need to do now is implement the `BuildQuery` routine. This procedure takes all the data from each control on the form and adds it to the query string while associating the appropriate name. For both save and retrieve actions, it will add the `Action`, and `Debug` parameters to the query string. If the Action is to save, then it will add all the data from the text boxes and the `dtPicker` control.

```
Private Sub BuildQuery()

    m_QryStr.Clear

    m_QryStr.SetParam"Action", CStr(m_Action)
    m_QryStr.SetParam "Debug", chkDebug.Value

    'If this is a Save action, add the form data to the query string
    If m_Action = acSAVE Then
        m_QryStr.SetParam "Name", txtEmpName.Text
        m_QryStr.SetParam "ID", txtEmpID.Text
        m_QryStr.SetParam "PayRate", txtEmpPay.Text
        m_QryStr.SetParam "Hours", txtEmpHours.Text
        m_QryStr.SetParam "StartDate", FormatDateTime(dtStartDt.Value, _
vbShortDate)
    End If

End Sub
```

Running the Employee Data Client

The client application is complete. Give it a test run and try a save and a retrieve operation. Select Show CGI Details to see all the information the CGI program is using to process the request. The diagram below shows the results from this. Also try saving a new employee, and then retrieving all again to verify the employee was added.

> You will need to have the CGIEmpData program and database available on your web server NOW for this to work. See "Testing the CGIEmpData Program" for details.

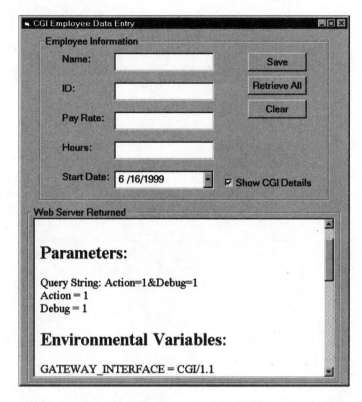

Keep in mind that this little trick of making a standard Visual Basic form act like a web page is not restricted to CGI applications. In ASP scripts, the query string is read from the HTTP request and placed into the `Request` object's `Form` collection. So this same mechanism could be used to kick off an ASP application. Indeed, it could be used to drive nearly any server side web technology.

Summary

This case study has demonstrated how we can build CGI programs with VB and how we can build VB clients that communicate with CGI programs. Along the way, we have:

> Learned about the query string, response headers, and other CGI and HTTP fundamentals
> Developed the `CStdIO` class to facilitate standard input and output support in Visual Basic
> Designed and implemented an application framework for VB based CGI programs
> Used the CGI Application Framework to create an Employee Data Entry CGI program
> Seen how to send data to the web browser and CGI program using the WebBrowser control.

Common HTML Tags by Category

Here, we have listed some of the more commonly used HTML tags by the following categories:

Document Structure	Titles and Headings	Paragraphs and Lines
Text Styles	Lists	Tables
Links	Graphics, Objects, Multimedia and Scripts	
Forms	Frames	

When you know what you want to do, but you're not sure which tag will achieve the desired effect, use the reference tables below to put you on the right track.

Document Structure

Tag	Meaning
`<!>`	Allows authors to add comments to code.
`<!DOCTYPE>`	Defines the document type. This is required by all HTML documents.
`<BASE>`	Specifies the document's base URL – its original location. It's not normally necessary to include this tag. It may only be used in `HEAD` section.
`<BODY>`	Contains the main part of the HTML document.

Table Continued on Following Page

Tag	Meaning
<COMMENT>	Allows authors to add comments to code. No longer recommended, use < ! >.
<DIV>	Defines a block division of the BODY section of the document.
<HEAD>	Contains information about the document itself.
<HTML>	Signals the beginning and end of an HTML document.
<LINK>	Defines the current document's relationship with other resources. Used in HEAD section only.
<META>	Describes the content of a document.
<NEXTID>	Defines a parameter in the HEAD section of the document
<SPAN>	Defines an area for reference by a style sheet
<STYLE>	Specifies the style sheet for the page.
<XML>	defines an XML data island on the HTML page.

Titles and Headings

Tag	Meaning
<H1>	Heading level 1
<H2>	Heading level 2
<H3>	Heading level 3
<H4>	Heading level 4
<H5>	Heading level 5
<H6>	Heading level 6
<TITLE>	Identifies the contents of the document.

Paragraphs and Lines

Tag	Meaning
 	Inserts a line break.
<CENTER>	Centers subsequent text/images.

Tag	Meaning
`<HR>`	Draws a horizontal rule.
`<NOBR>`	Prevents a line of text breaking.
`<P>`	Defines a paragraph.
`<WBR>`	Inserts a soft line break in a block of `NOBR` text.

Text Styles

Tag	Meaning
`<ACRONYM>`	Indicates an acronym.
`<ADDRESS>`	Indicates an address, typically displayed in italics.
`<B>`	Emboldens text.
`<BASEFONT>`	Sets font size to be used as default.
`<BIG>`	Changes the physical rendering of the font to one size larger.
`<BLOCKQUOTE>`	Formats a quote – typically by indentation
`<BDO>`	Allows the Unicode bidirectional algorithm (which reverses the order of embedded character sequences) to be disabled.
`<CITE>`	Renders text in italics.
`<CODE>`	Renders text in a font resembling computer code.
`<DEL>`	Denotes text that has been deleted from the document.
`<DFN>`	Indicates the first instance of a term or important word.
`<EM>`	Emphasized text – usually italic.
`<FONT>`	Changes font properties.
`<I>`	Defines italic text.
`<INS>`	Denotes text that has been inserted into the document.
`<KBD>`	Indicates typed text. Useful for instruction manuals etc.
`<LISTING>`	Renders text in a fixed-width font. No longer recommended - use `<PRE>`.

Table Continued on Following Page

Tag	Meaning
`<PLAINTEXT>`	Renders text in a fixed-width font without processing any other tags it may contain. May not be consistently supported across browsers - use `<PRE>`.
`<PRE>`	Pre-formatted text. Renders text exactly how it is typed, i.e. carriage returns, styles etc., *will* be recognized.
`<Q>`	Sets a quotation.
`<RT>`	Specifies the ruby text (i.e. the annotation text) that annotates the content of the RUBY tag.
`<RUBY>`	Defines an pronunciation guide through which a block of text can be annotated using the RT tag.
`<S>` `<STRIKE>`	Strike through. Renders the text as 'deleted' (crossed out).
`<SAMP>`	Specifies sample code and renders it in small font.
`<SMALL>`	Changes the physical rendering of a font to one size smaller.
`<STRONG>`	Strong emphasis – usually bold.
`<STYLE>`	Specifies the style sheet for the page.
`<SUB>`	Subscript.
`<SUP>`	Superscript.
`<TT>`	Renders text in fixed width, typewriter style font.
`<U>`	Underlines text. Not widely supported at present, and not recommended, as it can cause confusion with hyperlinks, which also normally appear underlined.
`<VAR>`	Indicates a variable.
`<XMP>`	Renders text in fixed width type, used for example text. No longer recommended, use `<PRE>` or `<SAMP>`.

Lists

Tag	Meaning
`<DD>`	Definition description. Used in definition lists with DT to define the term.
`<DIR>`	Denotes a directory list by indenting the text.

Tag	Meaning
<DL>	Defines a definition list.
<DT>	Defines a definition term within a definition list.
<LI>	Defines a list item in any type of list other than a definition list.
<MENU>	Defines a menu list.
<OL>	Defines an ordered (numbered) list.
<UL>	Defines an unordered (bulleted) list.

Tables

Tag	Meaning
<CAPTION>	Puts a title above a table.
<COL>	Defines column width and properties for a table.
<COLGROUP>	Defines properties for a group of columns in a table.
<TABLE>	Defines a series of columns and rows to form a table.
<TBODY>	Defines the table body.
<TD>	Specifies a cell in a table.
<TFOOT>	Defines table footer.
<TH>	Specifies a header column. Text will be centered and bold.
<THEAD>	Used to designate rows as the table's header.
<TR>	Defines the start of a table row.

Links

Tag	Meaning
<A>	Used to insert an anchor, which can be either a local reference point or a hyperlink to another URL.
<A HREF="url">	Hyperlink to another document.
<A NAME="name">	Link to a local reference point.

Graphics, Objects, Multimedia and Scripts

Tag	Meaning
`<APPLET>`	Inserts an applet.
`<AREA>`	Specifies the shape of a "hot spot" in a client-side image map.
`<BGSOUND>`	Plays a background sound.
`<EMBED>`	Defines an embedded object in an HTML document.
`<IMG>`	Embeds an image or a video clip in a document.
`<MAP>`	Specifies a collection of hot spots for a client-side image map.
`<MARQUEE>`	Sets a scrolling marquee.
`<NOSCRIPT>`	Specifies HTML to be displayed in browsers which don't support scripting.
`<OBJECT>`	Inserts an object.
`<PARAM>`	Sets the property value for a given object.
`<SCRIPT>`	Inserts a script.

Forms

Tag	Meaning
`<BUTTON>`	Creates an HTML-style button.
`<FIELDSET>`	Draws a box around a group of controls.
`<FORM>`	Defines part of the document as a user fill-out form.
`<INPUT>`	Defines a user input box. There are input controls: `button`, `checkbox`, `file`, `hidden`, `image`, `password`, `radio`, `reset`, `submit`, `text`
`<ISINDEX>`	Causes the borwser to display a dialog containing a single-line prompt. (Depreciated in HTML 4.0 – use `INPUT` instead.)
`<LABEL>`	Defines a label for a control.

Tag	Meaning
<LEGEND>	Defines the text label to use in box created by a FIELDSET tag.
<OPTION>	Used within the SELECT tag to present the user with a number of options.
<SELECT>	Denotes a list box or drop-down list.
<TEXTAREA>	Defines a text area inside a FORM element.

Frames

Tag	Meaning
<FRAME>	Defines a single frame in a frameset.
<FRAMESET>	Defines the main container for a frame.
<IFRAME>	Defines a 'floating' frame within a document.
<NOFRAMES>	Allows for backward compatibility with non-frame compliant browsers.

B

A Tutorial in VBScript

In this appendix, we'll walk through the fundamentals, and along the way you will learn the structure of the VBScript language, and how to use **event-driven** programming within your HTML documents. This tutorial can be used as a refresher course, and should make the differences between VB and VBScript evident to you.

What is VBScript?

VBScript, Microsoft's Visual Basic Scripting Edition, is a scaled down version of Visual Basic. While it doesn't offer the full functionality of Visual Basic, it does provide a powerful, easy to learn tool that can be used to add interaction to your web pages. If you are already experienced in either Visual Basic or Visual Basic for Applications, you will find working with VBScript easy and should be immediately productive. Don't be concerned if you haven't worked in another version of Visual Basic. VBScript is easy to learn, even for the novice developer.

How to Use this Tutorial

This tutorial is a stand-alone introduction to VBScript. It is laid out in a series of five lessons. Each lesson introduces you to a new segment of the VBScript language. Along the way you will learn how to add calculations, formatting and validations to your web pages. At the end of each lesson is an exercise where you, the reader, get to try out your newly acquired knowledge by building web pages utilizing VBScript. The topics of the lessons are:

- ➤ **An Introduction to VBScript.** You will learn how to add VBScript to a web page, and different methods for linking scripts with HTML

- ➤ **Working with Variables.** What would any language be without variables? Here you learn how to define and use variables in your script routines

> ➤ **Using Objects with VBScript.** Java applets and ActiveX controls extend the HTML environment. In this lesson you will learn how to tie these objects together using VBScript

> ➤ **Controlling Your VBScript Routines.** Conditional statements (If...Then...Else, Select...Case) and looping (For...Next and Do...Loop) are the topic of this section

> ➤ **Using VBScript with Forms.** With VBScript you can validate forms before they are submitted. You'll see how in this final lesson

Step-by-Step Exercises

As mentioned above, each of the five lessons has a worked exercise, which demonstrates how to use the topics that were presented. Along the way you will find descriptions of each component of the example, so that by the end you will have a sound understanding of the lesson's topic.

A copy of the completed exercises can be found on the Wrox Press web site at http://webdev.wrox.co.uk/books/1746. Each lesson will have two or more completed examples that are referenced in the step-by-step instructions.

Lesson 1: Adding VBScript to Web Pages

Scripting languages like JScript and VBScript are designed as an extension to HTML. The web browser receives scripts along with the rest of the web document, and it is the browser's responsibility to parse and process the scripts. HTML was extended to include a tag that is used to incorporate scripts into HTML – the <SCRIPT> tag.

The <SCRIPT> Tag

You add scripts into your web pages within a pair of <SCRIPT> tags. The <SCRIPT> tag signifies the start of the script section, while </SCRIPT> marks the end. An example of this is shown below:

```
<HTML>
<HEAD>
<TITLE>Working With VBScript</TITLE>
<SCRIPT LANGUAGE="VBScript">
  MsgBox "Welcome to my Web page!"
</SCRIPT>
</HEAD>
</HTML>
```

The beginning <SCRIPT> tag includes a LANGUAGE argument that indicates the scripting language that will be used. The LANGUAGE argument is required because there is more than one scripting language. Without the LANGUAGE argument, a web browser would not know if the text between the tags was JavaScript, VBScript, or another scripting language.

While technically you can place scripts throughout an HTML document using pairs of <SCRIPT> tags, scripts are typically found at either the top or bottom of a Web document. This provides for easy reference and maintenance. Placing script at the top guarantees that the script is fully loaded before it needs to be called.

Handling Non-Supporting Browsers

Not all browsers support scripting languages. Some only support JavaScript. Only Microsoft's Internet Explorer supports VBScript. You might be wondering what happens to your scripts when non-supporting browsers encounter them. Usually, browsers will do what they do most frequently with text: they will display your scripts as part of the web page. Obviously, this isn't the result you had hoped for. One simple way to address this problem is to encase your scripts in comment tags (<!-- and -->). Below is our example script as it appears with the addition of the comment tags:

```
<HTML>
<HEAD>
<TITLE>Working With VBScript</TITLE>
<SCRIPT LANGUAGE="VBScript">
<!--
  MsgBox "Welcome to my Web page!"
-->
</SCRIPT>
</HEAD>
</HTML>
```

Now, when a browser that does not support VBScript processes this page, it will view your script as a comment and simply ignore it.

Exercise 1: Adding VBScript to a Web page

The easiest way to learn any language is to work with it. So let's get right into Exercise 1 and expose you to the process of using VBScript in your web pages. Just follow along with the step-by-step instructions to create your first script-enabled web page.

In this exercise, you will create an HTML document and add a simple script to respond to a click event generated by a command button. You will need to be familiar with creating and testing an HTML document. A completed copy of this part of the exercise can be found in the file exer1_v1.htm.

Part 1: Creating the HTML Document

1 Open up a text editor application and insert the following HTML code:

```
<HTML>
<HEAD>
<TITLE>Working With VBScript: Exercise 1</TITLE>
</HEAD>
<BODY>
  <H1>Your First VBScript Exercise</H1>
  <P> By utilizing VBScript you can give your web pages actions.
```

```
" Click on the button below to see what we mean. </P>
  <FORM NAME="frmExercise1">
    <INPUT TYPE="Button" NAME="cmdClickMe" VALUE="Click Me">
  </FORM>
</BODY>
</HTML>
```

2 Save the file and test it by loading it into Internet Explorer. The resulting page should be similar to the screenshot.

Try out the Click Me button. Does anything happen?

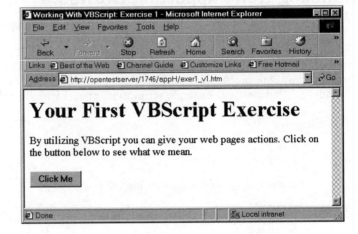

In the next part we will add a script to provide functionality for the Click Me command button. A completed copy of this part of the exercise can be found in the file exer1_v2.htm.

Part 2: Adding VBScript

3 Re-open the HTML document that you created in Part 1, if necessary. Modify the document adding the lines shown with shading below:

```
<HTML>
<HEAD>
<TITLE>Working With VBScript: Exercise 1</TITLE>
</HEAD>
<BODY>
  <H1>Your First VBScript Exercise</H1>
  <P> By utilizing VBScript you can give your Web pages actions.
  Click on the button below to see what we mean. </P>
  <FORM NAME="frmExercise1">
    <INPUT TYPE="Button" NAME="cmdClickMe" VALUE="Click Me">
    <SCRIPT FOR="cmdClickMe" EVENT="onClick" LANGUAGE="VBScript">
      MsgBox "A simple example of VBScript in action."
    </SCRIPT>
  </FORM>
</BODY>
</HTML>
```

4 Save the file and test it by loading it into Internet Explorer. Then try out the **Click Me** button. The result is shown here.

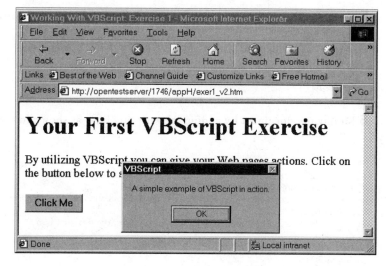

How It Works

Let's take a look at the three lines of code that you added. We want you to have a firm understanding of what the VBScript code is doing and how it is implemented within the HTML document. The first line defines a script:

```
<SCRIPT FOR="cmdClickMe" EVENT="onClick" LANGUAGE="VBScript">
```

The FOR argument specifies that this script is for the button named cmdClickMe, the name we have given our command button with the HTML <INPUT> tag. The EVENT argument says that this script should be run when the button is clicked. The LANGUAGE argument states that this is a VBScript module.

The second line is the only line of VBScript in this HTML document. The MsgBox function simply displays a message dialog. You will see more of the MsgBox function later in this tutorial. The third line marks the end of our script.

Part 3: Preferred Method of Including VBScript

In the code above, we simply inserted the VBScript module right after the HTML tag that defined the command button. While this method is functional, it is not the preferred approach. The HTML alone can be confusing to read with all of its tags and text; adding VBScript into the middle of all this just makes it even more complicated. A more organized alternative is to place all of your script together within the HTML document. The following steps introduce you to this approach.

A completed copy of this part of the exercise can be found in the file exer1_v3.htm.

5 Re-open the HTML document that you created in Part 2, if necessary, and remove the lines that you added there:

```
<SCRIPT FOR="cmdClickMe" EVENT="onClick" LANGUAGE="VBScript">
  MsgBox "A simple example of VBScript in action."
</SCRIPT>
```

6 Modify the document by adding the scripting lines as shown in the light shading below:

```
<HTML>
<HEAD>
<TITLE>Working With VBScript: Exercise 1</TITLE>
<SCRIPT LANGUAGE="VBScript">
<!-- Instruct non-IE browsers to skip over VBScript modules.
  Sub cmdClickMe_OnClick
     MsgBox "A simple example of VBScript in action."
  End Sub
-->
</SCRIPT>
</HEAD>
<BODY>
  <H1>Your First VBScript Exercise</H1>
  <P> By utilizing VBScript you can give your Web pages actions.
  Click on the button below to see what we mean. </P>
  <FORM NAME="frmExercise1">
    <INPUT TYPE="Button" NAME="cmdClickMe" VALUE="Click Me">
  </FORM>
</BODY>
</HTML>
```

7 Save the file and test it by loading it into Internet Explorer. When you try out the Click Me button, the result is the same as the previous code.

How It Works

This second method starts with the same `<SCRIPT>` tag as the previous example. At the center of this script are three lines that provide the functionality for our page. The first line defines a sub-procedure called `cmdClickMe_OnClick`, which will be executed any time that the control `cmdClickMe` is clicked:

```
Sub cmdClickMe_OnClick
```

This type of procedure is referred to as an **event** procedure. The event is the user clicking the button, and the procedure that we associate with this event is executed every time the button is clicked.

On the second line we find the `MsgBox` function again, while the third line marks an end to our subroutine.

Don't get too hung up on understanding all of the details of this right now – you will see plenty more examples along the way.

Summary

That's it – you just created your first VBScript-enabled web page. Along the way you have learned:

> How to add VBScript into your web pages

> Ways to tie HTML and VBScript together to provide functionality to your pages

> Why you should encase your VBScript modules within HTML comments

Next up, we will look at what VBScript has to offer in the way of variables.

Lesson 2: Working with Variables

A **variable** is a named location in computer memory that you can use for the storage of data during the execution of your scripts. You can use variables to:

> Store input from the user gathered via your web page

> Save data returned from functions

> Hold results from calculations

An Introduction to Variables

Let's look at a simple VBScript example to clarify the use of variables:

```
Sub cmdVariables_OnClick
   Dim Name
   Name = InputBox("Enter your name: ")
   MsgBox "The name you entered was " & Name
End Sub
```

The first line of this example defines a sub procedure named `cmdVariables`, which is associated with the `onclick` event of a command button.

On the second line we declare a variable called `Name`. We are going to use this variable to store the name of the user when it is entered. The third line uses the `InputBox` function to first prompt for, and then return, the user's name. You'll see more of the `InputBox` function later in this tutorial. The name it returns is stored in the `Name` variable.

The fourth line uses the `MsgBox` function to display the user's name. The sub procedure completes on the fifth line.

Exactly how and where variables are stored is not important. What is important is what you use them for, and how you use them. That's what we will be looking at next.

Declaring Variables

There are two methods for declaring variables in VBScript – **explicitly** and **implicitly**. You usually declare variables explicitly with the Dim statement:

```
Dim Name
```

This statement declares the variable Name. You can also declare multiple variables on one line as shown below:

```
Dim Name, Address, City, State
```

Variables can be declared implicitly by simply using the variable name within your script. This practice is not recommended. It leads to code that is prone to errors and more difficult to debug.

You can force VBScript to require all variables to be explicitly declared by including the statement Option Explicit at the start of every script. Any variable that is not explicitly declared will then generate an error.

Variable Naming Rules

When naming variables the following rules apply:

- ➢ They must begin with an alphabetic character.
- ➢ They cannot contain embedded periods.
- ➢ They must be unique within the same scope. (There's more on scopes later in this lesson.)
- ➢ They must be no longer than 255 characters.

Variants and Subtypes

VBScript has a single data type called a **variant**, which has the ability to store different types of data. The types of data that a variant can store are referred to as **subtypes**. The table below describes the subtypes supported by VBScript.

Subtype	Description of Uses for Each Subtype
Byte	Integer numbers between 0 to 255
Boolean	True and False
Currency	Monetary values
Date	Date and time
Double	Extremely large numbers with decimal points
Empty	Indicates that a Variant has been declared, but not assigned a value

Subtype	Description of Uses for Each Subtype
Error	An error number
Integer	Large integers between –32,768 and 32,767
Long	Extremely large integers (between –2,147,483,648 and 2,147,483,647)
Object	Objects
Null	No valid data
Single	Large numbers with decimal points
String	Character strings

Assigning Values

You assign a value to a variable by using the following format:

```
Variable_name = value
```

The following examples demonstrate assigning values to variables:

```
Name = "Larry Roof"
HoursWorked = 50
Overtime = True
```

Scope of Variables

The scope of a variable dictates where it can be used in your script. A variable's scope is determined by where it is declared. If it is declared within a procedure, it is referred to as a **procedure-level** variable and can only be used within that procedure. If it is declared outside of any procedure, it is a **script-level** variable and can be used throughout the script.

The example below demonstrates both script-level and procedure-level variables:

```
<SCRIPT>
  Dim counter
  Sub cmdButton_onClick
    Dim temp
  End Sub
</SCRIPT>
```

The variable counter is a script-level variable and can be utilized throughout the script. The variable temp exists only within the cmdButton_onClick sub-procedure.

Constants

Constants can be declared in VBScript using the following syntax:

```
Const constname = expression
```

For example, we can assign values or strings as follows:

```
Const MyNumber = 99.9
Const MyString = "constant"
```

You could also assign constant values to variables that you have defined, as shown in the example below. Here, TAX_RATE is our constant:

```
<SCRIPT>
  Dim TAX_RATE
  TAX_RATE = .06
  Function CalculateTaxes
    CalculateTaxes = CostOfGoods * TAX_RATE
  End Function
</SCRIPT>
```

Arrays

The VBScript language provides support for arrays. You declare an array using the Dim statement, just as you did with variables:

```
Dim States(50)
```

The statement above creates an array with 51 elements. Why 51? Because VBScript arrays are **zero-based**, meaning that the first array element is indexed 0 and the last is the number specified when declaring the array.

You assign values to the elements of an array just as you would a variable, but with an additional reference (the **index**) to the element in which it will be stored:

```
States(5) = "California"
States(6) = "New York"
```

Arrays can have multiple dimensions – VBScript supports up to 60 dimensions. Declaring a two-dimensional array for storing 51 states and their capitals could be done as follows:

```
Dim StateInfo(50,1)
```

To store values into this array you would then reference both dimensions.

```
StateInfo(18,0) = "Michigan"
StateInfo(18,1) = "Lansing"
```

VBScript also provides support for arrays whose size may need to change as the script is executing. These arrays are referred to as **dynamic arrays**. A dynamic array is declared without specifying the number of elements it will contain:

```
Dim Customers()
```

The `ReDim` statement is then used to change the size of the array from within the script:

```
ReDim Customers(100)
```

There is no limit to the number of times an array can be re-dimensioned during the execution of a script. To preserve the contents of an array when you are re-dimensioning, use the `Preserve` keyword:

```
ReDim Preserve Customers(100)
```

Exercise 2: Working with Variables

We will now create a page that performs a simple calculation involving sub-totals, sales tax and final totals. Follow the step-by-step instructions that will introduce you to using variables with VBScript.

In this exercise you will create an HTML document which contains a script that will retrieve data from a web page, perform calculations, and output a result.

Part 1: Creating the HTML Document

A completed copy of this part of the exercise can be found in the file `exer2_v1.htm`.

1 Open up a text editor and insert the following HTML code:

```
<HTML>
<HEAD>
<TITLE>Working With VBScript: Exercise 2</TITLE>
</HEAD>
<BODY>
<H1>Your Second VBScript Exercise</H1>
<P> Variables can be used to store and manipulate values. To
see a demonstration of this enter a quantity and unit price
in the fields below and click the "Calculate Cost" button.</P>
<FORM NAME="frmExercise2">
  <TABLE>
    <TR>
      <TD><B>Quantity:</B></TD>
      <TD><INPUT TYPE="Text" NAME="txtQuantity" SIZE=5></TD>
    </TR>
    <TR>
      <TD><B>Unit price:</B></TD>
      <TD><INPUT TYPE="Text" NAME="txtUnitPrice" SIZE=5></TD>
    </TR>
```

Continued on Following Page

```
  </TABLE>
  <BR>
  <INPUT TYPE="Button" NAME="cmdCalculate" VALUE="Calculate Cost">
</FORM>
</BODY>
</HTML>
```

2 Save the file, and load it into Internet Explorer. The result is shown is this screenshot.

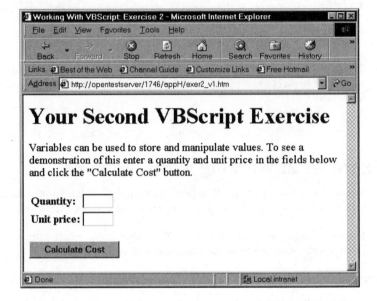

Part 2: Adding VBScript

In the following section, we will be adding a script to provide functionality for when the Calculate Cost command button is clicked. A completed copy of this part of the exercise can be found in the file exer2_v2.htm.

3 Re-open the HTML document that you created in Part 1, if necessary. Modify the document adding the scripting lines as shown by the shading:

```
<HTML>
<HEAD>
<TITLE>Working With VBScript: Exercise 2</TITLE>
<SCRIPT LANGUAGE="VBScript">
<!-- Add this to instruct non-IE browsers to skip over VBScript modules.
Option Explicit

Sub cmdCalculate_OnClick
  Dim AmountofTax
  Dim CRLF
  Dim Message
  Dim Subtotal
  Dim TABSPACE
  Dim TAX_RATE
```

```
    Dim TotalCost

' Define our constant values.
    TAX_RATE = 0.06
    CRLF = Chr(13) & Chr(10)
    TABSPACE = Chr(9)

' Perform order calculations.
    Subtotal = document.frmExercise2.txtQuantity.value _
            * document.frmExercise2.txtUnitPrice.value
    AmountofTax = Subtotal * TAX_RATE
    TotalCost = Subtotal + AmountofTax

' Display the results.
    Message = "The total for your order is:"
    Message = Message & CRLF & CRLF
    Message = Message & "Subtotal:" & TABSPACE & "$" & Subtotal & CRLF
    Message = Message & "Tax:" & TABSPACE & "$" & AmountofTax & CRLF
    Message = Message & "Total:" & TABSPACE & "$" & TotalCost
    MsgBox Message,,"Your Total"
End Sub
-->
</SCRIPT>
</HEAD>
<BODY>
...
```

The apostrophes (') are there to comment out code – there's more on this in a moment. The underscore (_) at the end of the line
`Subtotal = document.frmExercise2.txtQuantity.value _` *is a coding convention which is used to instruct VBScript to join this line and the next one together for processing. This has the same effect as typing the code of these two lines on a single line, discarding the _.*

4 Save the file and test it by loading it into Internet Explorer. Enter 100 into the **Quantity** field and 10 into the **Unit Price** field. Try out the **Calculate Cost** button. The result is shown in the screenshot.

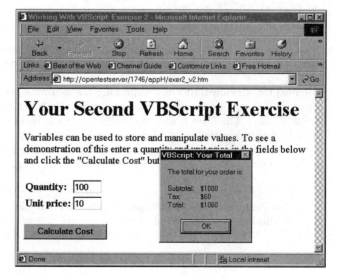

How It Works

What should be obvious right from the start is that this script is far more involved than the one used with Exercise 1. Don't be intimidated by its size – as with the previous lesson, we will work through this script line-by-line.

After the starting <SCRIPT> tag and HTML comment we find:

```
Option Explicit
```

Remember what this statement does: it forces you to declare all of your variables.

Next we create a sub procedure for the click event of the cmdCalculate button:

```
Sub cmdCalculate_OnClick
```

Following that we declare seven variables, three of which we are going to use as constants. The constants can be identified by the fact that they are all in uppercase. Case doesn't matter in VBScript (although it does in JavaScript) – we are using it to make the script easier to read. Are the variables procedure-level or script-level variables? They are procedure-level since they are declared within a procedure.

In VBScript, anything to the right of an apostrophe is a comment. These comments are ignored when the script is processed. A comment can appear on a line by itself or at the end of a line of script. Comments at the end of a line are referred to as inline comments:

```
' Define our constant values.
```

The constants are assigned values in the following lines:

```
CRLF = Chr(13) & Chr(10)
TABSPACE = Chr(9)
```

Chr() is a VBScript function that returns the character associated with a specified ANSI code. ANSI codes 13, 10 and 9 are carriage return, line feed and tab, respectively.

The next line demonstrates how values are taken from a form on a web page, and used within a script. The two fields on our form were named txtQuantity and txtUnitPrice in their HTML <INPUT> tags. The form is named frmExercise2. Here we are referencing our web document, then the form, then the input field, and finally the value of that field. The value associated with each field contains what the user entered into that field on the web page. The * says to multiply the value of the first field, txtQuantity, by the second field, txtUnitPrice.

> The commonly-used VBScript operands are + for addition, – for subtraction, * for multiplication and / for division.

The result of this calculation is then stored in the variable `Subtotal`. Next we perform some additional calculations. Finally, we display the result of our calculations using the `MsgBox` function. The ampersand character, `&`, is used to concatenate two strings.

As we said in Lesson 1, don't get too worried about understanding all of the details of this example right now. You will pick up the language as you continue to work with VBScript.

Summary

That completes Exercise 2. You just created a web page that interacts with the user to gather data, perform calculations and present results – the fundamental components of most applications. Along the way you have learned:

> The types of variables that VBScript supports

> How to declare and use variables within a script

> A technique to work around the absence of constants in VBScript

> What a comment line is in a script

In the next lesson we'll look at objects. You will learn what they are and how they are used with VBScript.

Lesson 3: Objects and VBScript

Objects, both in the form of Java applets and ActiveX controls, enhance the functionality that is provided with HTML. By using VBScript you can extend the capabilities of these controls, integrating and manipulating them from within your scripts. In this lesson we will look at how you can utilize the power of objects with VBScript.

Scripting with objects involves two steps:

> Adding the object to your web page using HTML

> Writing script procedures to respond to events that the object provides

Adding Objects to Your Web Pages

Since this is a VBScript tutorial (rather than an HTML tutorial), we will offer only a limited discussion of how to add an object to a web page. Objects (whether they're Java applets or ActiveX controls) are added to a page with the `<OBJECT>` tag. The properties, or characteristics, of the object are configured using the `<PARAM>` tag. Typically you will see an object implemented using a single `<OBJECT>` tag along with several `<PARAM>` tags. The following HTML code demonstrates how an ActiveX control might appear when added to a page:

```
<OBJECT ID="lblTotalPay" WIDTH=45 HEIGHT=24
        CLASSID="CLSID:978C9E23-D4B0-11CE-BF2D-00AA003F40D0">
  <PARAM NAME="ForeColor" VALUE="0">
  <PARAM NAME="BackColor" VALUE="16777215">
```

```
      <PARAM NAME="Caption" VALUE="">
      <PARAM NAME="Size" VALUE="1582;635">
      <PARAM NAME="SpecialEffect" VALUE="2">
      <PARAM NAME="FontHeight" VALUE="200">
      <PARAM NAME="FontCharSet" VALUE="0">
      <PARAM NAME="FontPitchAndFamily" VALUE="2">
      <PARAM NAME="FontWeight" VALUE="0">
   </OBJECT>
```

Linking VBScript with Objects

Once you have added a control to your web page, it can be configured, manipulated and responded to through its properties, methods and events. **Properties** are the characteristics of an object. They include items like a caption, the foreground color and the font size. **Methods** cause an object to perform a task. **Events** are actions that are recognized by an object. For instance, a command button recognizes an `onclick` event.

For the most part, you will be focusing on properties and events. The following is an example of setting properties for a label control:

```
<SCRIPT LANGUAGE="VBScript">
Sub cmdCalculatePay_onClick
   Dim HoursWorked
   Dim PayRate
   Dim TotalPay

   HoursWorked = InputBox("Enter hours worked: ")
   PayRate = InputBox("Enter pay rate: ")
   TotalPay = HoursWorked * PayRate

   document.lblTotalPay.caption = TotalPay
End Sub
</SCRIPT>
```

The `caption` property of the label control `lblTotalPay` is set equal to the results of our calculation with the script line:

```
document.lblTotalPay.caption = TotalPay
```

Object properties are referenced within your scripts using the same format shown in Exercise 2.

Exercise 3: Working with Objects

In Exercise 3 we modify the web page created in Exercise 2. These modifications will be made so that we can display the results of our calculations not with the `MsgBox` function, but rather to ActiveX objects that are part of the page. Just follow the step-by-step instructions below to begin learning how to use VBScript with ActiveX.

In this exercise, you will create an HTML document that contains a script that will retrieve data from a web page, perform calculations and output a result back to the web page.

Part 1: Testing the HTML Document

1 Load the file `exer3_v1.htm` into a text editor. This is the HTML component of this exercise already typed in for you. Look over the HTML document. It contains three ActiveX label controls named `lblSubtotal`, `lblTaxes` and `lblTotalCost`. Save the file under a different name. We are going to be modifying this source and wouldn't want to work with the original.

2 Test the file by loading it into Internet Explorer. The result is shown below. I'd have you try out the **Calculate Cost** button, but you have probably already figured out from the previous two exercises that it doesn't do anything.

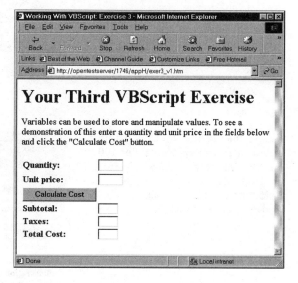

Part 2: Adding VBScript

As we did in Exercise 2, we will now add a script to provide functionality for the **Calculate Cost** command button's click event. A completed copy of this part of the exercise can be found in the file `exer3_v2.htm`.

3 We're going to modify the document, by adding the scripting lines as shown by the shading below:

```
<HTML>
<HEAD>
<TITLE>Working With VBScript: Exercise 3</TITLE>
<SCRIPT LANGUAGE="VBScript">
<!-- Add this to instruct non-IE browsers to skip over VBScript modules.
Option Explicit

Sub cmdCalculate_OnClick
   Dim AmountofTax
   Dim Subtotal
   Dim TAX_RATE
   Dim TotalCost
```

Continued on Following Page

847

```
    ' Define our constant values.
    TAX_RATE = 0.06

    ' Perform order calculations.
    Subtotal = document.frmExercise3.txtQuantity.value _
            * document.frmExercise3.txtUnitPrice.value
    AmountofTax = Subtotal * TAX_RATE
    TotalCost = Subtotal + AmountofTax

    ' Display the results.
    document.frmExercise3.lblSubtotal.caption = Subtotal
    document.frmExercise3.lblTaxes.caption = AmountofTax
    document.frmExercise3.lblTotalCost.caption = TotalCost
End Sub
-->
</SCRIPT>
</HEAD>
...
```

4 Save the file and test it by loading it into Internet Explorer. Enter 100 into the **Quantity** field and 10 into the **Unit Price** field. Try out the **Calculate Cost** button. The result is shown in the screenshot.

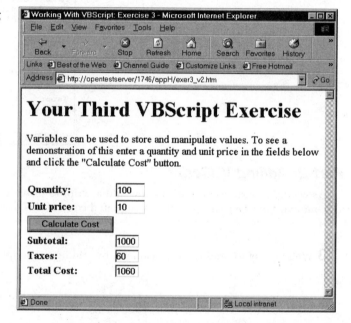

How It Works

Exercise 3 is just a modification of Exercise 2. As such, we will focus on what's different, rather than going over the script line by line again.

There were minimal changes involving variable declarations and the defining of constant values. We simply didn't need them in this version, so they were removed:

```
Dim AmountofTax
Dim Subtotal
Dim TAX_RATE
```

```
    Dim TotalCost

  ' Define our constant values.
    TAX_RATE = 0.06
```

We won't discuss the method used to calculate the subtotal, taxes and total amount, as it is identical in both exercises.

The way results are displayed is different in Example 3. The script has been modified to remove the MsgBox function, and in its place we set the caption property of three label controls:

```
  ' Display the results.
    document.frmExercise3.lblSubtotal.caption = Subtotal
    document.frmExercise3.lblTaxes.caption = AmountofTax
    document.frmExercise3.lblTotalCost.caption = TotalCost
```

The format used when referencing these properties is:

document	Our web document
frmExercise3	The form on which the ActiveX controls were placed
lblTaxes	The name of the control
caption	The property to set

Hopefully, by this point you are starting to get comfortable reading and working with VBScript. The best way to strengthen your knowledge of VBScript is to take some of the examples that we have been working with in the first three lessons and modify them to suit your own needs.

Summary

Well, that's it for Exercise 3. I know, objects are a pretty hefty topic for a small lesson. What we wanted to do was to give you an exposure to objects and how they can be utilized in VBScript. Along the way, you have learned:

➤ What objects are and how they could be used with VBScript

➤ About properties, methods and events

Next is a lesson in how you can control your script files using conditional and looping statements.

Lesson 4: Controlling Your VBScript Routines

VBScript allows you to control how your scripts process data through the use of **conditional** and **looping** statements. By using conditional statements you can develop scripts that evaluate data and use criteria to determine what tasks to perform. Looping statements allow you to repetitively execute lines of a script. Each offers benefits to the script developer in the process of creating more complex and functional web pages.

Conditional Statements

VBScript provides two forms of conditional statements: `If..Then..Else` and `Select..Case`.

If..Then..Else

The `If..Then..Else` statement is used to evaluate a condition to see if it is true or false and then, depending upon this result, to execute a statement or set of statements. Rather than discussing an `If` statement in theory, we will examine some examples to see how they work.

The simplest version of an `If` statement is one that contains only a condition and a single statement:

```
If AmountPurchased > 10000 Then DiscountAmount = AmountPurchased * .10
```

In this example statement the condition is:

```
If AmountPurchased > 10000
```

which simply checks to see if the contents of the variable `AmountPurchased` is greater than 10,000. If it is, the condition is true. In this simple version of the `If` statement, when the condition is true the following statement is executed:

```
DiscountAmount = AmountPurchased * .10
```

Now let's look at a more complicated version of the `If` statement. In this version we will perform a series of statements when the condition is true:

```
If AmountPurchased > 10000 Then
   DiscountAmount = AmountPurchased * .10
   Subtotal = AmountPurchased - DiscountAmount
End If
```

In this form of the `If` statement, one or more statements can be executed when the condition is true, by placing them between the `If` statement on the top and the `End If` statement on the bottom.

The next form of the `If` statement uses the `If..Then..Else` format. This version of the `If` statement differs from the two previous versions in that it will perform one set of statements if the condition is true and another set when the condition is false:

```
If AmountPurchased > 10000 Then
   DiscountAmount = AmountPurchased * .10
   Subtotal = AmountPurchased - DiscountAmount
Else
   HandlingFee = AmountPurchased *.03
   Subtotal = AmountPurchased + HandlingFee
End If
```

In this example, when the customer's order is over $10,000 (that is, the condition is true) they receive a 10% discount. When the order is under $10,000, they are charged a 3% handling fee.

The final version of the `If` statement that we will look at is the `If..Then..ElseIf`. In this form the `If` statement checks each of the conditions until it finds either one that is true or an `Else` statement:

```
If AmountPurchased > 10000 Then
   DiscountAmount = AmountPurchased * .10
   Subtotal = AmountPurchased - DiscountAmount
ElseIf AmountPurchased > 5000 Then
   DiscountAmount = AmountPurchased * .05
   Subtotal = AmountPurchased - DiscountAmount
Else
   HandlingFee = AmountPurchased *.03
   Subtotal = AmountPurchased + HandlingFee
End If
```

In this example the customer receives a 10%discount for orders over $10,000, a 5% discount for orders over $5000 or a handling fee of 3% for orders under $5000. Note that only *one* of these three possibilities is actually executed.

As you see, VBScript offers you plenty of options when it comes to `If` statements.

Select Case

The `Select Case` statement provides an alternative to the `If..Then..Else` statement, providing additional control and readability when evaluating complex conditions. It is well suited for situations where there are a number of possible conditions for the value being checked. Like the `If` statement, the `Select Case` structure checks a condition and, based upon that condition being true, executes a series of statements.

The syntax of the `Select Case` statement is:

```
Select Case condition
  Case value
    Statements
...
  Case value
    statements
  ...
  Case Else
    statements
End Select
```

For example, the following `Select` statement assigns a shipping fee based upon the state where the order is being sent:

```
Select Case Document.frmOrder.txtState.Value
   Case "California"
     ShippingFee= .04
   Case "Florida"
```

```
      ShippingFee = .03
   Case Else
      ShippingFee = .02
End Select
```

The `Select Case` statement checks each of the `Case` statements until it finds one that will result in the condition being true. If none are found to be true, it executes the statements within the `Case Else`.

> Even though it is not required, always include a `Case Else` when working with `Select Case` statements to process conditions that you may not have considered possible. For these conditions you can display something as simple as a message dialog, informing you that a branch was executed that you hadn't planned for.

Looping Statements

VBScript provides four forms of looping statements, which can be divided into two groups. The `For..Next` and `For Each..Next` statements are best used when you want to perform a loop a specific number of times. The `Do..Loop` and `While..Wend` statements are best used to perform a loop an undetermined number of times.

For..Next

The `For..Next` structure is used when you want to perform a loop a specific number of times. It uses a counter variable, which is incremented or decremented with each repetition of the loop. The following example demonstrates a simple `For` loop, with a counter that is incremented with each iteration:

```
For counter = 1 To 12
   result = 5 * counter
   MsgBox counter & " times 5 is " & result
Next
```

The variable `counter` is the numeric value being incremented or decremented. The number 1 defines the start of the loop, 12 the end of the loop. When this loop executes it will display twelve dialog box messages, each containing the product of multiplying five times the counter as it runs from 1 to 12.

In this example, the variable `counter` is incremented by 1 with each loop. Optionally, we could control how we wanted the counter to be modified through the addition of the `Step` argument:

```
For counter = 1 To 12 Step 2
   result = 5 * counter
   MsgBox counter & " times 5 is " & result
Next
```

This slight modification to the loop results in only the products of the odd numbers between 1 and 12 being displayed. If you want to create a countdown loop (where the number is decremented with each loop), simply use a negative value with the `Step` argument as shown in the following example:

```
For counter = 12 To 1 Step -1
   result = 5 * counter
   MsgBox counter & " times 5 is " & result
Next
```

Note that, in a decrementing loop, the starting number is greater than the ending number.

For Each..Next

The `For Each..Next` is similar to the `For..Next` loop, but instead of repeating a loop for a certain number of times, it repeats the loop for each member of a specified collection. The discussion of collections and their use is outside of the scope of this tutorial. The `For Each..Next` structure is detailed elsewhere in the book.

Do..Loop

The `Do..Loop` structure repeats a block of statements until a specified condition is met. Normally, when using a `Do..Loop`, the condition being checked is the result of some operation being performed within the structure of the loop. Two versions of this structure are provided – the `Do..While` and the `Do..Until`.

Do..While

A `Do` loop that contains the `While` keyword will be performed as long as the condition being tested is true. You have the option of checking the condition at the start of the loop, as in the form:

```
Do While condition
   statements
Loop
```

or at the end of the loop, as shown in the following example:

```
Do
   statements
Loop While condition
```

The difference between these two formats is that the first example may never perform the statements included within its structure, while the second example will always perform its statements at least once.

Do..Until

A `Do` loop that contains the `Until` keyword will continue to loop as long as the condition being tested is false.

As with the `Do..While` structure, you have the option of checking the condition at the start of the loop, as in the form:

```
Do Until condition
  statements
Loop
```

or at the end of the loop, as shown in the following example:

```
Do
  statements
Loop Until condition
```

One use for a `Do Until..Loop` is shown in the example below:

```
password = InputBox("Enter your password:")
Do Until password = "letmein"
  Msgbox "Invalid password - please try again."
  password = InputBox("Enter you password:")
Loop
```

In this example we ask the user to enter a password before performing the conditional part of the `Do..Loop` the first time. The result is that, if they enter the correct password the first time, the statements within the loop's structure will never be performed. If the user were to enter an invalid password then the statements within the `Do..Loop` structure would be performed, a message would be displayed and the user would be prompted to re-enter their password.

While..Wend

The `While..Wend` structure loops as long as the condition being checked is true. If the condition is true, the `While..Wend` statement operates similar to the `Do..Loop` structure, but without its flexibility. The structure for the `While..Wend` statement is:

```
While condition
  statements
Wend
```

Exercise 4: Working with Conditional and Looping Statements

In this exercise we continue to extend the functionality of our web page. New features provided by this exercise are:

> A combo box from which the user can select products

> Automatic pricing of products as they are selected

> Discounting purchase prices based upon the size of the order

As with the first three exercises simply follow the step-by-step instructions below to begin to learn how to use conditional and looping statements with your scripts.

We will create an HTML document containing a script that will retrieve data from a web page, perform calculations and output a result back to the web page. In addition, it will look up prices for products and provide discounts based upon the order size.

Part 1: Testing the HTML Document

1 Open up a text editor application and load the file `exer4_v1.htm`. This is the HTML component of this exercise already typed in for you.

2 Look over the HTML document. Note the addition of an ActiveX combo box control, `cmbProducts`, and additional label controls. Scroll to the bottom of the document where you will find a script that fills the combo box with the available products as shown in the following code fragment:

```
<SCRIPT LANGUAGE="VBScript">
<!--
  Document.frmExercise4.cmbProducts.Additem "NEC MultiSync E1100"
  Document.frmExercise4.cmbProducts.Additem "NEC MultiSync P1150"
  Document.frmExercise4.cmbProducts.Additem "NEC MultiSync E750"
-->
</SCRIPT>
```

3 Test the file by loading it into Internet Explorer. The resulting page is shown here. You can forget about testing the **Calculate Cost** button: we've been down that road before.

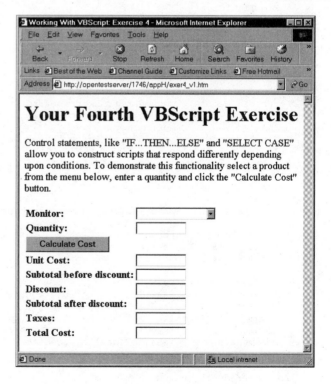

Part 2: Adding VBScript

We will now add a script to provide functionality for the **Calculate Cost** command button, as well as when a product is selected from the combo box control. A completed copy of this part of the exercise can be found in the file `exer4_v2.htm`.

4 Modify the document by adding the shaded lines of script:

```
<HTML>
<HEAD>
<TITLE>Working With VBScript: Exercise 4</TITLE>
<SCRIPT LANGUAGE="VBScript">
<!-- Add this to instruct non-IE browsers to skip over VBScript modules.
Option Explicit

Sub cmdCalculate_OnClick
    Dim AmountofDiscount
    Dim AmountofTax
    Dim DISCOUNT_LIMIT
    Dim DISCOUNT_RATE
    Dim SubtotalBefore
    Dim SubtotalAfter
    Dim TAX_RATE
    Dim TotalCost

' Define our constant values.
    DISCOUNT_LIMIT = 1000
    DISCOUNT_RATE = .10
    TAX_RATE = 0.06

' Calculate the subtotal for the order.
    SubtotalBefore = document.frmExercise4.txtQuantity.value _
                   * document.frmExercise4.lblUnitCost.caption

' Check to see if the order is large enough to offer discounts.
    If (SubtotalBefore > DISCOUNT_LIMIT) Then
      AmountofDiscount = SubtotalBefore * DISCOUNT_RATE
    Else
      AmountofDiscount = 0
    End If
    SubtotalAfter = SubtotalBefore - AmountofDiscount

' Calculate taxes and total cost.
    AmountofTax = SubtotalAfter * TAX_RATE
    TotalCost = SubtotalAfter + AmountofTax

' Display the results.
    document.frmExercise4.lblSubtotalBefore.caption = SubtotalBefore
    document.frmExercise4.lblDiscount.caption = AmountofDiscount
    document.frmExercise4.lblSubtotalAfter.caption = SubtotalAfter
    document.frmExercise4.lblTaxes.caption = AmountofTax
    document.frmExercise4.lblTotalCost.caption = TotalCost
End Sub

Sub cmbProducts_Change()
    Select Case document.frmExercise4.cmbProducts.value
      Case "NEC MultiSync E1100"
```

```
         document.frmExercise4.lblUnitCost.caption = 1590
      Case "NEC MultiSync P1150"
         document.frmExercise4.lblUnitCost.caption = 880
      Case "NEC MultiSync E750"
         document.frmExercise4.lblUnitCost.caption = 1940
      Case Else
         document.frmExercise4.lblUnitCost.caption = 0
   End Select
End Sub
-->
</SCRIPT>
</HEAD>
...
```

5 Save the file, and test it in Internet Explorer. Select a product (say NEC MultiSync E1100) from the combo box. Notice how the Unit Cost field is automatically updated as shown in the screenshot.

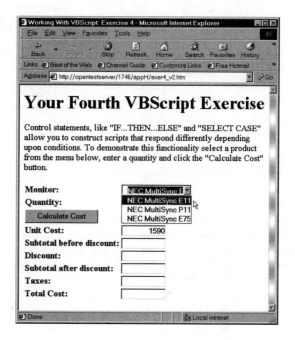

6 Enter 10 into the Quantity field, and try out the Calculate Cost button. The result is shown here.

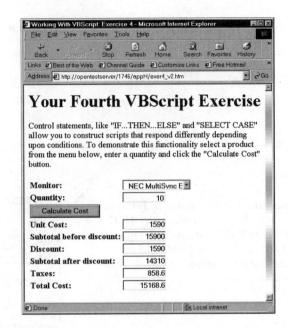

Exercise 4 has two new features: the automatic price lookup and the discount feature. We will look at how each is implemented separately.

Product Lookup: How It Works

The lookup feature is implemented via the cmbProducts_Change event procedure. As you might have remembered, the ActiveX combo box control that we added to your HTML document was given the name cmbProducts. This control supports a change event, which is triggered every time the user selects an item from the list. We simply make use of the Select Case statement to check the value of the control:

```
Sub cmbProducts_Change()
   Select Case document.frmExercise4.cmbProducts.value
      Case "NEC MultiSync E1100"
         document.frmExercise4.lblUnitCost.caption = 1590
      Case "NEC MultiSync P1150"
         document.frmExercise4.lblUnitCost.caption = 880
      Case "NEC MultiSync E750"
         document.frmExercise4.lblUnitCost.caption = 1940
      Case Else
         document.frmExercise4.lblUnitCost.caption = 0
   End Select
End Sub
```

Now, in our example, these values are hard coded. In a real life application we would normally pull these from a data source.

> *Even though the combo box control can only contain one of the three monitors, we still employ a Case Else branch. This is simply a good programming habit to develop.*

Discounting Orders: How It Works

The script used to implement discounts begins by defining some constants, setting the discount limit at $1000 and a discount rate of 10%. Our discounting process begins by calculating the subtotal of the order before discounts and taxes are applied.

Discounting is then applied through the use of an `If..Then..Else` statement. We compare our subtotal amount against the constant `DISCOUNT_LIMIT`. If our amount is greater than the limit, the discount amount is calculated and stored in the variable `AmountofDiscount`. If it is less than, or equal to, the limit, the discount amount is set to 0:

```
' Check to see if the order is large enough to offer discounts.
  If (SubtotalBefore > DISCOUNT_LIMIT) Then
    AmountofDiscount = SubtotalBefore * DISCOUNT_RATE
  Else
    AmountofDiscount = 0
  End If
  SubtotalAfter = SubtotalBefore - AmountofDiscount
```

The value of the variable `AmountofDiscount` is subsequently subtracted from the subtotal. Next we calculate the taxes and total cost of the order. We complete the script by displaying the order information on the web page.

Extending this application

In this example I set the discount limit at $1,000. What would we have to change in our script to set the limit at a more reasonable amount of say, $100,000?

Summary

Can you believe how far our original application has progressed? Now we have a page that receives user input, performs price lookups, calculates discount amounts and displays the complete order information on the web page, all without having to go back to the web server.

In this section you were introduced to:

> Conditional statements, which allow you to selectively execute blocks of statements

> Looping statements, which provide you with a way to repetitively execute blocks of statements

Now that we can input, manipulate and display data, it is time to learn how to validate the data, before sending it on to a web server.

Lesson 5: Using VBScript with Forms

As the popularity of web page forms increase, so does the need to be able to validate data before the client browser submits it to the web server. As a scripting language, VBScript is well suited for this task. Once the form has been validated, the same script can be used to forward the data on to the server. In this lesson we will look at both the process of validating and submitting forms.

Validating Your Forms

The process of validating forms involves checking the form to see if:

> ➤ All of the required data is proved
> ➤ The data provided is valid

Meticulous data validation scripts can be tedious to code but are well worth their return in verifying the quality of the data.

The validation example that we will be examining does not contain anything new in the way of VBScript. We are simply using the elements that we have learned in the previous lessons in a new way. Before reading any further you may find it beneficial to ponder how you would validate an HTML form using the VBScript techniques that you have learned.

Okay, are you through pondering? Let's look at an example to give you an idea of what is possible when it comes to validating forms.

Checking Form Input

This example is pretty simple. It has a single field in which the user can enter their age, and a single command button that is used to submit their age to the server. A copy of this example can be found in exam_5a.htm.

```
<HTML>
<HEAD>
<TITLE>Working With VBScript: Example 5a</TITLE>

<SCRIPT LANGUAGE="VBScript">
<!-- Add this to instruct non-IE browsers to skip over VBScript modules.
Option Explicit

Sub cmdSubmit_OnClick

' Check to see if the user entered anything.
  If (Len(Document.frmExample5a.txtAge.Value) = 0) Then
    MsgBox "You must enter your age before submitting."
    Exit Sub
  End If

' Check to see if the user entered a number.
  If (Not(IsNumeric(Document.frmExample5a.txtAge.Value))) Then
    MsgBox "You must enter a number for your age."
    Exit Sub
  End If

' Check to see if the age entered is valid.
  If (Document.frmExample5a.txtAge.Value < 0) OR _
     (Document.frmExample5a.txtAge.Value > 100) Then
    MsgBox "The age you entered is invalid."
    Exit Sub
  End If
```

```
' Data looks okay so submit it.
  MsgBox "Thanks for providing your age."
  Document.frmExample5a.Submit

End Sub

-->
</SCRIPT>

</HEAD>

<BODY>
<H1>A VBScript Example on Variables</H1>
<P>
This example demonstrates validation techniques in VBScript.
</P>
<FORM NAME="frmExample5a">
  <TABLE>
    <TR>
      <TD>Enter your age:</TD>
      <TD><INPUT TYPE="Text" NAME="txtAge" SIZE="2"></TD>
    </TR>
    <TR>
      <TD><INPUT TYPE="Button" NAME="cmdSubmit" VALUE="Submit"></TD>
      <TD></TD>
    </TR>
  </TABLE>
</FORM>

</BODY>
</HTML>
```

How It Works

The heart of this validation script is found in the click event procedure for the cmdSubmit command button. We start by checking if the user entered anything at all into the field using VBScript's Len function. This function returns the length of a string. If the length is 0, the data is invalid. We inform the user and exit the submit procedure via the Exit Sub statement:

```
' Check to see if the user entered anything.
  If (Len(Document.frmExample5a.txtAge.Value) = 0) Then
    MsgBox "You must enter your age before submitting."
    Exit Sub
  End If
```

Next we check to see if what the user entered is a numeric value. The VBScript function IsNumeric returns a true value when it is a number. If not, we tell the user and exit:

```
' Check to see if the user entered a number.
  If (Not(IsNumeric(Document.frmExample5a.txtAge.Value))) Then
    MsgBox "You must enter a number for your age."
    Exit Sub
  End If
```

Our final check involves verifying that the age they entered seems reasonable for our environment. I have determined that no age less than 0 or greater than 100 is acceptable. Using an `If..Then` statement, we can check the value of the input field against this criteria:

```
' Check to see if the age entered is valid.
  If (Document.frmExample5a.txtAge.Value < 0) OR _
     (Document.frmExample5a.txtAge.Value > 100) Then
    MsgBox "The age you entered is invalid."
    Exit Sub
  End If
```

That's it. While this example is by no means the most detailed validation script you will encounter, it provides you with a basis of what is possible with VBScript.

Submitting Your Forms

Compared to validation, the process of submitting a form is simple. In our example we've used a normal HTML button with the Submit caption that is tied to an event procedure that both validates and, at the same time, submits the form.

The code that we would have to add to our previous example to submit the form is shown below:

```
' Data looks okay so submit it.
  MsgBox "Thanks for providing your age."
  Document.frmExample5a.Submit
```

The `MsgBox` statement lets the user know that their data has been processed. The form is then submitted by invoking the Submit method of the form object. As we saw in Lesson 3 on objects, methods cause an object to perform a task. Here we are using the `submit` method of our form to cause the form to submit its data, just as if we had used a `submit` control.

Exercise 5: How to Validate and Submit a Form

With this exercise we will add scripts to validate and submit the form that we have been constructing in the previous four lessons.

In this exercise you will create an HTML document containing a script that will retrieve data from a web page, perform calculations, and output results back to the web page. Additionally it will lookup prices for products and provide discounts based upon the order size. Finally, it will validate data and submit the web page form to a server.

Part 1: Testing the HTML Document

1 Open up the file `exer5_v1.htm` in a text editor. This is the HTML component of this exercise. Look over the HTML document. Note the addition of a command button `cmdSubmit`, which will be used to submit our form to a web server, after validation. Load the file up into Internet Explorer and it should look like the illustration below:

Part 2: Adding VBScript

Next, we will add the script that will handle the validation and submit our form. A completed copy of this part of the exercise can be found in the file `exer5_v2.htm`.

2 Modify the document by adding the shaded lines of script:

```
Sub cmdCalculate_OnClick
   Dim AmountofDiscount
   Dim AmountofTax
   Dim DISCOUNT_LIMIT
   Dim DISCOUNT_RATE
   Dim SubtotalBefore
   Dim SubtotalAfter
   Dim TAX_RATE
   Dim TotalCost


' Perform validation checks before process anything. While this is not
' everything that we could check, it provides an example of how you can
' validate data.
   If (Len(document.frmExercise5.txtQuantity.value) = 0) Then
```

```
      MsgBox "You must enter a quantity."
      Exit Sub
   End If

   If (Not IsNumeric(document.frmExercise5.txtQuantity.value)) Then
      MsgBox "Quantity must be a numeric value."
      Exit Sub
   End If

   If (Len(document.frmExercise5.cmbProducts.value) = 0) Then
      MsgBox "You must select a product."
      Exit Sub
   End If

' Define our constant values.
   DISCOUNT_LIMIT = 1000
   DISCOUNT_RATE = .10
   TAX_RATE = 0.06

' Calculate the subtotal for the order.
   SubtotalBefore = document.frmExercise5.txtQuantity.Value _
                    * document.frmExercise5.lblUnitCost.Caption

' Check to see if the order is large enough to offer discounts.
   If (SubtotalBefore > DISCOUNT_LIMIT) Then
      AmountofDiscount = SubtotalBefore * DISCOUNT_RATE
   Else
      AmountofDiscount = 0
   End If
   SubtotalAfter = SubtotalBefore - AmountofDiscount

' Calculate taxes and total cost.
   AmountofTax = SubtotalAfter * TAX_RATE
   TotalCost = SubtotalAfter + AmountofTax

' Display the results.
   Document.frmExercise5.lblSubtotalBefore.Caption = SubtotalBefore
   Document.frmExercise5.lblDiscount.Caption = AmountofDiscount
   Document.frmExercise5.lblSubtotalAfter.Caption = SubtotalAfter
   Document.frmExercise5.lblTaxes.Caption = AmountofTax
   Document.frmExercise5.lblTotalCost.Caption = TotalCost
End Sub

' Submit this order for processing.
Sub cmdSubmit_onClick
   MsgBox "Your order has been submitted."
   document.frmExercise5.submit
End Sub

Sub cmbProducts_Change()
   Select Case Document.frmExercise5.cmbProducts.Value
      Case "NEC MultiSync E1100"
         Document.frmExercise5.lblUnitCost.Caption = 1590
      Case "NEC MultiSync P1150"
         Document.frmExercise5.lblUnitCost.Caption = 880
      Case "NEC MultiSync E750"
         Document.frmExercise5.lblUnitCost.Caption = 1940
      Case Else
         Document.frmExercise5.lblUnitCost.Caption = 0
```

```
      End Select
   End Sub
```

3 Save the file and test it by loading it into Internet Explorer. Without entering anything into the Quantity field click the Calculate Costs button. This dialog will be displayed.

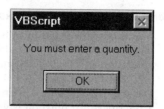

4 Enter the letter A into the Quantity field and click the Calculate Costs button. Now you'll see this dialog.

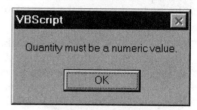

5 Enter a value of 10 into the Quantity field and once again click the Calculate Costs button. This time you will see this dialog.

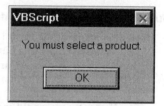

6 Finally, select the NEC MultiSync E1100 monitor from the combo box. Clicking the Calculate Costs button followed by the Submit Order button will leave you with the following:

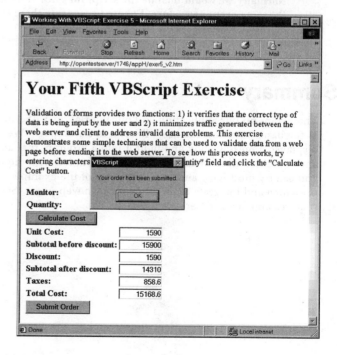

The script that was added to Exercise 5 has two components, one which validates the form and one that submits the form. We will look at each component separately.

Form Validation: How It Works

The validation of our form is handled by the event procedure associated with the button named `cmdCalculate`. You should note that this is only an example of what is possible in the way of validation and is by no means a comprehensive validation script.

We start by checking the length of the Quantity field to determine if the user has entered anything. VBScript's `Len` function is well suited for this purpose. If we find that the length is zero, the user is informed and we exit the event procedure.

Next we check to make sure that the Quantity field contains a numeric value. For this we use VBScript's `IsNumeric` function. An order would never be valid without selecting a product first, so we check the value of the Monitor combo box, again using the `Len` function.

If we pass all of these validations the cost of the order is calculated and displayed.

Submitting the Form How It Works

The submitting of the form is handled within the event procedure for the button named `cmdSubmit`. When the user clicks this button, first a message box is displayed to confirm with the user that the order has been processed, and then the form is submitted.

> Normally we would include the script for both validating a form and submitting it in the same event procedure. I chose to separate them in this example so that it would be easier to understand.

Summary

That wraps up our application and our tutorial on VBScript. In this short space we've covered some of the basic ways you can use VBScript in a web page. We started with a simple example that displayed a message box and built it into a program that accepted, processed, displayed, validated and submitted data. What's left for you? Coupled with the reference and the examples in the book, you can try modifying and tweaking some of the examples. Take some of the techniques that were presented and integrate them into your own web pages. Script writing, like any development skill, requires practice and perseverance.

VBScript Reference

This appendix is intended as a reference aid to VB programmers who might need to know what is present in the subset of Visual Basic known as VBScript.

Array Handling

Dim – declares a variable. An array variable can be static, with a defined number of elements, or dynamic, and can have up to 60 dimensions.

ReDim – used to change the size of an array variable which has been declared as dynamic.

Preserve – keyword used to preserve the contents of an array being resized (otherwise data is lost when ReDim is used). If you need to use this then you can only re-dimension the rightmost index of the array.

Erase – reinitializes the elements of a fixed-size array or empties the contents of a dynamic array:

```
Dim arEmployees ()
ReDim arEmployees (9,1)

arEmployees (9,1) = "Phil"

ReDim arEmployees (9,2)              'loses the contents of element (9,1)
arEmployees (9,2) = "Paul"

ReDim Preserve arEmployees (9,3)     'preserves the contents of (9,2)
arEmployees (9,3) = "Smith"

Erase arEmployees                    'now we are back to where we started - empty
array
```

LBound – returns the smallest subscript for the dimension of an array. Note that arrays always start from the subscript zero so this function will always return the value zero.
UBound – used to determine the size of an array:

```
Dim strCustomers (10, 5)
intSizeFirst = UBound (strCustomers, 1)      'returns SizeFirst = 10
intSizeSecond = UBound (strCustomers, 2)     'returns SizeSecond = 5
```

> **The actual number of elements is always one greater than the value returned by** UBound **because the array starts from zero.**

Assignments

Let – used to assign values to variables (optional).
Set – used to assign an object reference to a variable.

```
Let intNumberOfDays = 365

Set txtMyTextBox = txtcontrol
txtMyTextBox.Value = "Hello World"
```

Constants

Empty – an empty variable is one that has been created, but has not yet been assigned a value.
Nothing – used to remove an object reference:

```
Set txtMyTextBox = txtATextBox      'assigns object reference
Set txtMyTextBox = Nothing          'removes object reference
```

Null – indicates that a variable is not valid. Note that this isn't the same as Empty.
True – indicates that an expression is true. Has numerical value –1.
False – indicates that an expression is false. Has numerical value 0.

Error constant

Constant	Value
vbObjectError	&h80040000

System Color constants

Constant	Value	Description
vbBlack	&h000000	Black
vbRed	&hFF0000	Red
vbGreen	&h00FF00	Green
vbYellow	&hFFFF00	Yellow
vbBlue	&h0000FF	Blue
vbMagenta	&hFF00FF	Magenta
vbCyan	&h00FFFF	Cyan
vbWhite	&hFFFFFF	White

Comparison constants

Constant	Value	Description
vbBinaryCompare	0	Perform a binary comparison.
vbTextCompare	1	Perform a textual comparison.

Date and Time constants

Constant	Value	Description
vbSunday	1	Sunday
vbMonday	2	Monday
vbTuesday	3	Tuesday
vbWednesday	4	Wednesday
vbThursday	5	Thursday
vbFriday	6	Friday
vbSaturday	7	Saturday

Table Continued on Following Page

Constant	Value	Description
vbFirstJan1	1	Use the week in which January 1 occurs (default).
vbFirstFourDays	2	Use the first week that has at least four days in the new year.
vbFirstFullWeek	3	Use the first full week of the year.
vbUseSystem	0	Use the format in the regional settings for the computer.
vbUseSystemDayOfWeek	0	Use the day in the system settings for the first weekday.

Date Format constants

Constant	Value	Description
vbGeneralDate	0	Display a date and/or time in the format set in the system settings. For real numbers display a date and time. For integer numbers display only a date. For numbers less than 1, display time only.
vbLongDate	1	Display a date using the long date format specified in the computer's regional settings.
vbShortDate	2	Display a date using the short date format specified in the computer's regional settings.
vbLongTime	3	Display a time using the long time format specified in the computer's regional settings.
vbShortTime	4	Display a time using the short time format specified in the computer's regional settings.

Message Box Constants

Constant	Value	Description
vbOKOnly	0	Display OK button only.
vbOKCancel	1	Display OK and Cancel buttons.
vbAbortRetryIgnore	2	Display Abort, Retry, and Ignore buttons.
vbYesNoCancel	3	Display Yes, No, and Cancel buttons.

Constant	Value	Description
vbYesNo	4	Display Yes and No buttons.
vbRetryCancel	5	Display Retry and Cancel buttons.
vbCritical	16	Display Critical Message icon.
vbQuestion	32	Display Warning Query icon.
vbExclamation	48	Display Warning Message icon.
vbInformation	64	Display Information Message icon.
vbDefaultButton1	0	First button is the default.
vbDefaultButton2	256	Second button is the default.
vbDefaultButton3	512	Third button is the default.
vbDefaultButton4	768	Fourth button is the default.
vbApplicationModal	0	Application modal.
vbSystemModal	4096	System modal.

String constants

Constant	Value	Description
vbCr	Chr(13)	Carriage return only
vbCrLf	Chr(13) & Chr(10)	Carriage return and linefeed (Newline)
vbFormFeed	Chr(12)	Form feed only
vbLf	Chr(10)	Line feed only
vbNewLine	-	Newline character as appropriate to a specific platform
vbNullChar	Chr(0)	Character having the value 0
vbNullString	-	String having the value zero (not just an empty string)
vbTab	Chr(9)	Horizontal tab
vbVerticalTab	Chr(11)	Vertical tab

Tristate constants

Constant	Value	Description
TristateUseDefau lt	-2	Use default setting
TristateTrue	-1	True
TristateFalse	0	False

VarType constants

Constant	Value	Description
vbEmpty	0	Uninitialized (default)
vbNull	1	Contains no valid data
vbInteger	2	Integer subtype
vbLong	3	Long subtype
vbSingle	4	Single subtype
vbDouble	5	Double subtype
vbCurrency	6	Currency subtype
vbDate	7	Date subtype
vbString	8	String subtype
vbObject	9	Object
vbError	10	Error subtype
vbBoolean	11	Boolean subtype
vbVariant	12	Variant (used only for arrays of variants)
vbDataObject	13	Data access object
vbDecimal	14	Decimal subtype
vbByte	17	Byte subtype
vbArray	8192	Array

Control Flow

`For...Next` – executes a block of code a specified number of times:

```
Dim intSalary (10)
For intCounter = 0 to 10
    intSalary (intCounter) = 20000
Next
```

`For Each...Next` – repeats a block of code for each element in an array or collection:

```
For Each Item In Request.QueryString("MyControl")
    Response.Write Item & "<BR>"
Next
```

`Do...Loop` – executes a block of code while a condition is true or until a condition becomes true. Note that the condition can be checked either at the beginning or the end of the loop: the difference is that the code will be executed at least once if the condition is checked at the end.

```
Do While strDayOfWeek <> "Saturday" And strDayOfWeek <> "Sunday"
    MsgBox ("Get Up! Time for work")
    ...
Loop
```

```
Do
    MsgBox ("Get Up! Time for work")
    ...
Loop Until strDayOfWeek = "Saturday" Or strDayOfWeek = "Sunday"
```

We can also exit from a `Do...Loop` using `Exit Do`:

```
Do
    MsgBox ("Get Up! Time for work")
    ...
    If strDayOfWeek = "Sunday" Then
        Exit Do
    End If
Loop Until strDayOfWeek = "Saturday"
```

`If...Then...Else` – used to run various blocks of code depending on conditions:

```
If intAge < 20 Then
    MsgBox ("You're just a slip of a thing!")
ElseIf intAge < 40 Then
    MsgBox ("You're in your prime!")
Else
    MsgBox ("You're older and wiser")
End If
```

`Select Case` – used to replace `If...Then...Else` statements where there are many conditions:

```
Select Case intAge
Case 21,22,23,24,25,26
   MsgBox ("You're in your prime")
Case 40
   MsgBox ("You're fulfilling your dreams")
Case Else
   MsgBox ("Time for a new challenge")
End Select
```

While...Wend – executes a block of code while a condition is true:

```
While strDayOfWeek <> "Saturday" AND strDayOfWeek <> "Sunday"
   MsgBox ("Get Up! Time for work")
   ...
Wend
```

With – executes a series of statements for a single object:

```
With myDiv.style
   .posLeft = 200
   .posTop = 300
   .color = Red
End With
```

Functions

VBScript contains several inbuilt functions that can be used to manipulate and examine variables. These have been subdivided into these general categories:

- Conversion functions
- Date/time functions
- Math functions
- Object management functions
- Script engine identification functions
- String functions
- Variable testing functions

For a full description of each function and the parameters it requires, see the Microsoft web site at http://msdn.microsoft.com/scripting/.

Conversion Functions

These functions are used to convert values in variables between different types:

Function	Description
Abs	Returns the absolute value of a number.
Asc	Returns the numeric ANSI (or ASCII) code number of the first character in a string.
AscB	As above, but provided for use with byte data contained in a string. Returns result from the first byte only.
AscW	As above, but provided for Unicode characters. Returns the Wide character code, avoiding the conversion from Unicode to ANSI.
Chr	Returns a string made up of the ANSI character matching the number supplied.
ChrB	As above, but provided for use with byte data contained in a string. Always returns a single byte.
ChrW	As above, but provided for Unicode characters. Its argument is a Wide character code, thereby avoiding the conversion from ANSI to Unicode.
CBool	Returns the argument value converted to a Variant of subtype Boolean.
CByte	Returns the argument value converted to a Variant of subtype Byte.
CCur	Returns the argument value converted to a Variant of subtype Currency
CDate	Returns the argument value converted to a Variant of subtype Date.
CDbl	Returns the argument value converted to a Variant of subtype Double.
CInt	Returns the argument value converted to a Variant of subtype Integer.
CLng	Returns the argument value converted to a Variant of subtype Long
CSng	Returns the argument value converted to a Variant of subtype Single
CStr	Returns the argument value converted to a Variant of subtype String.

Table Continued on Following Page

Function	Description
Fix	Returns the integer (whole) part of a number. If the number is negative, Fix returns the first negative integer greater than or equal to the number
Hex	Returns a string representing the hexadecimal value of a number.
Int	Returns the integer (whole) portion of a number. If the number is negative, Int returns the first negative integer less than or equal to the number.
Oct	Returns a string representing the octal value of a number.
Round	Returns a number rounded to a specified number of decimal places.
Sgn	Returns an integer indicating the sign of a number.

Date/Time Functions

These functions return date or time values from the computer's system clock, or manipulate existing values:

Function	Description
Date	Returns the current system date.
DateAdd	Returns a date to which a specified time interval has been added.
DateDiff	Returns the number of days, weeks, or years between two dates.
DatePart	Returns just the day, month or year of a given date.
DateSerial	Returns a Variant of subtype Date for a specified year, month and day.
DateValue	Returns a Variant of subtype Date.
Day	Returns a number between 1 and 31 representing the day of the month.
Hour	Returns a number between 0 and 23 representing the hour of the day.
Minute	Returns a number between 0 and 59 representing the minute of the hour.
Month	Returns a number between 1 and 12 representing the month of the year.

Function	Description
MonthName	Returns the name of the specified month as a string.
Now	Returns the current date and time.
Second	Returns a number between 0 and 59 representing the second of the minute.
Time	Returns a Variant of subtype Date indicating the current system time.
TimeSerial	Returns a Variant of subtype Date for a specific hour, minute, and second.
TimeValue	Returns a Variant of subtype Date containing the time.
Weekday	Returns a number representing the day of the week.
WeekdayName	Returns the name of the specified day of the week as a string.
Year	Returns a number representing the year.

Math Functions

These functions perform mathematical operations on variables containing numerical values:

Function	Description
Atn	Returns the arctangent of a number.
Cos	Returns the cosine of an angle.
Exp	Returns e (the base of natural logarithms) raised to a power.
Log	Returns the natural logarithm of a number.
Randomize	Initializes the random-number generator.
Rnd	Returns a random number.
Sin	Returns the sine of an angle.
Sqr	Returns the square root of a number.
Tan	Returns the tangent of an angle.

Miscellaneous Functions

Function	Description
Eval	Evaluates an expression and returns a boolean result (e.g. treats x=y as an *expression* which is either true or false).
Execute	Executes one or more statements (e.g. treats x=y as a *statement* which assigns the value of y to x).
RGB	Returns a number representing an RGB color value

Object Management Functions

These functions are used to manipulate objects, where applicable:

Function	Description
CreateObject	Creates and returns a reference to an ActiveX or OLE Automation object.
GetObject	Returns a reference to an ActiveX or OLE Automation object.
LoadPicture	Returns a picture object.

Script Engine Identification

These functions return the version of the scripting engine:

Function	Description
ScriptEngine	A string containing the major, minor, and build version numbers of the scripting engine.
ScriptEngineMajorVersion	The major version of the scripting engine, as a number.
ScriptEngineMinorVersion	The minor version of the scripting engine, as a number.
ScriptEngineBuildVersion	The build version of the scripting engine, as a number.

String Functions

These functions are used to manipulate string values in variables:

Function	Description
Filter	Returns an array from a string array, based on specified filter criteria.
FormatCurrency	Returns a string formatted as currency value.
FormatDateTime	Returns a string formatted as a date or time.
FormatNumber	Returns a string formatted as a number.
FormatPercent	Returns a string formatted as a percentage.
InStr	Returns the position of the first occurrence of one string within another.
InStrB	As above, but provided for use with byte data contained in a string. Returns the byte position instead of the character position.
InstrRev	As InStr, but starts from the end of the string.
Join	Returns a string created by joining the strings contained in an array.
LCase	Returns a string that has been converted to lowercase.
Left	Returns a specified number of characters from the left end of a string.
LeftB	As above, but provided for use with byte data contained in a string. Uses that number of bytes instead of that number of characters.
Len	Returns the length of a string or the number of bytes needed for a variable.
LenB	As above, but is provided for use with byte data contained in a string. Returns the number of bytes in the string instead of characters.
LTrim	Returns a copy of a string without leading spaces.
Mid	Returns a specified number of characters from a string.
MidB	As above, but provided for use with byte data contained in a string. Uses that numbers of bytes instead of that number of characters.

Table Continued on Following Page

Function	Description
Replace	Returns a string in which a specified substring has been replaced with another substring a specified number of times.
Right	Returns a specified number of characters from the right end of a string.
RightB	As above, but provided for use with byte data contained in a string. Uses that number of bytes instead of that number of characters.
RTrim	Returns a copy of a string without trailing spaces.
Space	Returns a string consisting of the specified number of spaces.
Split	Returns a one-dimensional array of a specified number of substrings.
StrComp	Returns a value indicating the result of a string comparison.
String	Returns a string of the length specified made up of a repeating character.
StrReverse	Returns a string in which the character order of a string is reversed.
Trim	Returns a copy of a string without leading or trailing spaces.
UCase	Returns a string that has been converted to uppercase.

Variable Testing Functions

These functions are used to determine the type of information stored in a variable:

Function	Description
IsArray	Returns a Boolean value indicating whether a variable is an array.
IsDate	Returns a Boolean value indicating whether an expression can be converted to a date.
IsEmpty	Returns a Boolean value indicating whether a variable has been initialized.
IsNull	Returns a Boolean value indicating whether an expression contains no valid data
IsNumeric	Returns a Boolean value indicating whether an expression can be evaluated as a number.
IsObject	Returns a Boolean value indicating whether an expression references a valid ActiveX or OLE Automation object.

Function	Description
TypeName	Returns a string that provides `Variant` subtype information about a variable.
VarType	Returns a number indicating the subtype of a variable.

Variable Declarations

`Class` – Declares the name of a class, as well as the variables, properties, and methods that comprise the class.
`Const` – Declares a constant to be used in place of literal values.
`Dim` – declares a variable.

Error Handling

`On Error Resume Next` –indicates that if an error occurs, control should continue at the next statement.
`Err` – this is the error object that provides information about run-time errors.

Error handling is very limited in VBScript and the `Err` object must be tested explicitly to determine if an error has occurred.

Input/Output

This consists of `Msgbox` for output and `InputBox` for input:

MsgBox

This displays a message, and can return a value indicating which button was clicked.

```
MsgBox "Hello There",20,"Hello Message","c:\windows\MyHelp.hlp",123
```

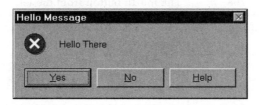

The parameters are:
`"Hello There"` – this contains the text of the message (the only obligatory parameter).
`20` – this determines which icon and buttons appear on the message box.
`"Hello Message"` – this contains the text that will appear as the title of the message box.

`"c:\windows\MyHelp.hlp"` – this adds a **Help** button to the message box and determines the help file that is opened if the button is clicked.

`123` – this is a reference to the particular help topic that will be displayed if the **Help** button is clicked.

The value of the icon and buttons parameter is determined using the following tables:

Constant	Value	Buttons
`vbOKOnly`	0	
`vbOKCancel`	1	
`vbAbortRetryIngnore`	2	
`vbYesNoCancel`	3	
`vbYesNo`	4	
`vbRetryCancel`	5	

Constant	Value	Buttons
`vbDefaultButton1`	0	The first button from the left is the default.
`vbDefaultButton2`	256	The second button from the left is the default.
`vbDefaultButton3`	512	The third button from the left is the default.
`vbDefaultButton4`	768	The fourth button from the left is the default.

Constant	Value	Description	Icon
`vbCritical`	16	Critical Message	
`vbQuestion`	32	Questioning Message	

Constant	Value	Description	Icon
vbExclamation	48	Warning Message	⚠
vbInformation	64	Informational Message	ⓘ

Constant	Value	Description
vbApplicationModal	0	Just the application stops until user clicks a button.
vbSystemModal	4096	On Win16 systems the whole system stops until user clicks a button. On Win32 systems the message box remains on top of any other programs.

To specify which buttons and icon are displayed you simply add the relevant values. So, in our example we add together 4 + 0 + 16 to display the **Yes** and **No** buttons, with **Yes** as the default, and the Critical icon. If we used 4 + 256 + 16 we could display the same buttons and icon, but have **No** as the default.

You can determine which button the user clicked by assigning the return code of the MsgBox function to a variable:

```
intButtonClicked = MsgBox ("Hello There",35,"Hello Message")
```

Notice that brackets enclose the MsgBox parameters when used in this format. The following table determines the value assigned to the variable intButtonClicked:

Constant	Value	Button Clicked
vbOK	1	OK
vbCancel	2	Cancel
vbAbort	3	Abort
vbRetry	4	Retry

Constant	Value	Button Clicked
vbIgnore	5	Ignore
vbYes	6	Yes
vbNo	7	No

InputBox

This accepts text entry from the user and returns it as a string.

```
strName = InputBox ("Please enter your name","Login","John Smith",500,500)
```

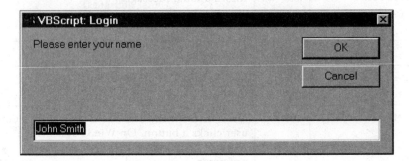

The parameters are:

"Please enter your name" – this is the prompt displayed in the input box.

"Login" – this is the text displayed as the title of the input box.

"John Smith" – this is the default value displayed in the input box.

500 – specifies the x position of the input box in relation to the screen.

500 – specifies the y position of the input box in relation to the screen.

As with the MsgBox function, you can also specify a help file and topic to add a Help button to the input box.

Procedures

Call – optional method of calling a subroutine.

Function – used to declare a function.

Sub – used to declare a subroutine.

Other Keywords

Rem – old style method of adding comments to code (it's now more usual to use an apostrophe (').)

Option Explicit – forces you to declare a variable before it can be used. If keyword used, it must appear before any other statements in a script.

Visual Basic Run-time Error Codes

The following error codes also apply to VBA code and many will not be appropriate to an application built completely around VBScript. However, if you have built your own components then these error codes may well be brought up when such components are used.

Code	Description	Code	Description
3	Return without GoSub	502	Object not safe for scripting
5	Invalid procedure call	503	Object not safe for initializing
6	Overflow	504	Object not safe for creating
7	Out of memory	505	Invalid or unqualified reference
9	Subscript out of range	506	Class not defined
10	This array is fixed or temporarily locked	1001	Out of memory
11	Division by zero	1002	Syntax error
13	Type mismatch	1003	Expected ':'
14	Out of string space	1004	Expected ';'
16	Expression too complex	1005	Expected '('
17	Can't perform requested operation	1006	Expected ')'
18	User interrupt occurred	1007	Expected ']'
20	Resume without error	1008	Expected '{'
28	Out of stack space	1009	Expected '}'
35	Sub or Function not defined	1010	Expected identifier
47	Too many DLL application clients	1011	Expected '='
48	Error in loading DLL	1012	Expected 'If'
49	Bad DLL calling convention	1013	Expected 'To'
51	Internal error	1014	Expected 'End'
52	Bad file name or number	1015	Expected 'Function'
53	File not found	1016	Expected 'Sub'
54	Bad file mode	1017	Expected 'Then'
55	File already open	1018	Expected 'Wend'
57	Device I/O error	1019	Expected 'Loop'
58	File already exists	1020	Expected 'Next'

Table Continued on Following Page

Code	Description	Code	Description
59	Bad record length	1021	Expected 'Case'
61	Disk full	1022	Expected 'Select'
62	Input past end of file	1023	Expected expression
63	Bad record number	1024	Expected statement
67	Too many files	1025	Expected end of statement
68	Device unavailable	1026	Expected integer constant
70	Permission denied	1027	Expected 'While' or 'Until'
71	Disk not ready	1028	Expected 'While', 'Until' or end of statement
74	Can't rename with different drive	1029	Too many locals or arguments
75	Path/File access error	1030	Identifier too long
76	Path not found	1031	Invalid number
91	Object variable not set	1032	Invalid character
92	For loop not initialized	1033	Un-terminated string constant
93	Invalid pattern string	1034	Un-terminated comment
94	Invalid use of Null	1035	Nested comment
322	Can't create necessary temporary file	1036	'Me' cannot be used outside of a procedure
325	Invalid format in resource file	1037	Invalid use of 'Me' keyword
380	Invalid property value	1038	'loop' without 'do'
423	Property or method not found	1039	Invalid 'exit' statement
424	Object required	1040	Invalid 'for' loop control variable
429	OLE Automation server can't create object	1041	Variable redefinition
430	Class doesn't support OLE Automation	1042	Must be first statement on the line
432	File name or class name not found during OLE Automation operation	1043	Cannot assign to non-ByVal argument

Code	Description	Code	Description
438	Object doesn't support this property or method	1044	Cannot use parentheses when calling a Sub
440	OLE Automation error	1045	Expected literal constant
442	Connection to type library or object library for remote process has been lost. Press OK for dialog to remove reference	1046	Expected 'In'
443	OLE Automation object does not have a default value	1047	Expected 'Class'
445	Object doesn't support this action	1048	Must be defined inside a Class
446	Object doesn't support named arguments	1049	Expected Let or Set or Get in property declaration
447	Object doesn't support current locale setting	1050	Expected 'Property'
448	Named argument not found	1051	Number of arguments must be consistent across properties specification
449	Argument not optional	1052	Cannot have multiple default property/method in a Class
450	Wrong number of arguments or invalid property assignment	1053	Class initialize or terminate do not have arguments
451	Object not a collection	1054	Property set or let must have at least one argument
452	Invalid ordinal	1055	Unexpected 'Next'
453	Specified DLL function not found	1056	'Default' can be specified only on 'Property' or 'Function' or 'Sub'
454	Code resource not found	1057	'Default' specification must also specify 'Public'
455	Code resource lock error	1058	'Default' specification can only be on Property Get

Table Continued on Following Page

Code	Description	Code	Description
457	This key is already associated with an element of this collection	5016	Regular Expression object expected
458	Variable uses an OLE Automation type not supported in Visual Basic	5017	Syntax error in regular expression
462	The remote server machine does not exist or is unavailable	5018	Unexpected quantifier
481	Invalid picture	5019	Expected ']' in regular expression
500	Variable is undefined	5020	Expected ')' in regular expression
501	Cannot assign to variable	5021	Invalid range in character set
		32811	Element not found

For more information about VBScript, visit Microsoft's VBScript site, at
http://msdn.microsoft.com/scripting.

D

JScript Tutorial

This appendix should be used as a reference guide for programming in JScript.

General Information

JScript is included in an HTML document with the `<SCRIPT>` tag. Here's an example:

```
<HTML>
<HEAD>

<SCRIPT LANGUAGE = "JScript">
<!-- wrap script in comments
        script code goes here
-->
</SCRIPT>

</HEAD>
<BODY>
        HTML goes here
</BODY>
</HTML>
```

The following points should be kept in mind:

> By placing JScript code in the `<HEAD>` section of the document you ensure that all the code has been loaded before an attempt is made to execute it.

➤ The script code should be wrapped in an HTML comment tag to stop older (non-JScript) browsers from displaying it.

➤ JScript is case sensitive.

Values

JScript recognizes the following data types:

➤ **strings** – e.g. "Hello World"

➤ **numbers** – both integers (86) and decimal values (86.235)

➤ **boolean** – `true` or `false` (case sensitive)

A null (*no value*) value is assigned with the keyword `null`.

JScript also makes use of 'special characters' in a similar way to the C++ programming language:

Character	Function
\n	newline
\t	tab
\f	form feed
\b	backspace
\r	carriage return

You may 'escape' other characters by preceding them with a backslash (\), to prevent the browser from trying to interpret them. This is most commonly used for quotes and backslashes, or to include a character by using its octal (base 8) value:

```
document.write("This shows a \"quote\" in a string.");
document.write("This is a backslash: \\");
document.write("This is a space character: \040.");
```

Variables

JScript is a **loosely typed** language. This means that variables do not have an explicitly defined variable type. Instead, every variable can hold values of various types. Conversions between types are done automatically when needed, as this example demonstrates:

```
x = 55;      // x is assigned to be the integer 55
y = "55";    // y is assigned to be the string "55"
y = '55';    // an alternative using single quotes
```

```
z = 1 + y;

/* because y is a string, 1 will be automatically
 converted to a string value, so the result is z = 155. */

document.write(x);
/* the number 55 will be written to the screen. Even
 though x is an integer and not a string, JScript will
 make the necessary conversion for you. */

n = 3.14159;  // assigning a real (fractional) number
n = 0546;     // numbers starting 0 assumed to be octal
n = 0xFFEC;   // numbers starting 0x assumed to be hex
n = 2.145E-5; // using exponential notation
```

The `parseInt()` and `parseFloat()` functions (discussed later in this appendix) can be used to convert strings for numeric addition.

Variable names must start with either a letter or an underscore. Beyond the first letter, variables may contain any combination of letters, underscores, and digits. JScript is case sensitive, so `this_variable` is not the same as `This_Variable`.

Variables do not need to be declared before they are used. However, you may use the `var` keyword to explicitly define a variable. This is especially useful when there is the possibility of conflicting variable names. When in doubt, use `var`.

```
var x = "55";
```

Assignment Operators

The following operators are used to make assignments in JScript:

Operator	Example	Result
=	x = y	x equals y
+=	x += y	x equals x plus y
-=	x -= y	x equals x minus y
*=	x *= y	x equals x multiplied by y
/=	x /= y	x equals x divided by y
%=	x %= y	x equals x modulus y

Each operator assigns the value on the right to the variable on the left.

```
x = 100;
y = 10;
x += y;   // x now is equal to 110
```

Equality Operators

Operator	Meaning
==	is equal to
!=	is not equal to
>	is greater than
>=	is greater than or equal to
<	is less than
<=	is less than or equal to

Other Operators

Operator	Meaning
+	Addition
-	Subtraction
*	Multiplication
/	Division
%	Modulus
++	Increment
--	Decrement
-	Unary Negation
&	Bitwise AND
|	Bitwise OR
^	Bitwise XOR
<<	Bitwise left shift
>>	Bitwise right shift
>>>	Zero-fill right shift

Operator	Meaning
&&	Logical AND
||	Logical OR
!	Not

String Operators

Operator	Meaning
+	Concatenates strings, so `"abc"` + `"def"` is `"abcdef"`
==	
!=	Compare strings in a case-sensitive way. A string is 'greater' than another based on the Latin ASCII code values of the characters, starting from the left of the string. So `"DEF"` is greater than `"ABC"` and `"DEE"`, but less than `"abc"` (uppercase letters are before lowercase ones in the ASCII character set).
>	
>=	
<	
<=	

Comments

Operator	Meaning
`// a comment`	A single line comment
`/* this text is a`	A multi-line comment
`multi-line comment */`	

Input/Output

In JScript, there are three different methods of providing information to the user and getting a response back. (Note that these are methods of the window object, and not JScript function calls.)

Alert

This displays a message with an OK button:

```
alert("Hello World!");
```

Confirm

Displays a message with both an OK and a Cancel button. True is returned if the OK button is pressed, and false is returned if the Cancel button is pressed:

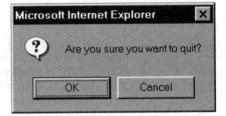

```
confirm("Are you sure you want to quit?");
```

Prompt

Displays a message and a text box for user input. The first string argument forms the text that is to be displayed above the text box. The second argument is a string, integer, or property of an existing object, which represents the default value to display inside the box. If the second argument is not specified, "<undefined>" is displayed inside the text box.

The string typed into the box is returned if the OK button is pressed. False is returned if the Cancel button is pressed:

```
prompt("What is your name?", "");
```

Explorer User Prompt		☒
JavaScript Prompt: What is your name?		OK Cancel
Gina Mackinroe		

Control Flow

There are two ways of controlling the flow of a program in JScript. The first involves **conditional** statements, which follow either one branch of the program or another. The second way is to use a **repeated iteration** of a set of statements.

Conditional Statements

JScript has two conditional statements:

`if..then..else` – used to run various blocks of code, depending on conditions. These statements have the following general form in JScript:

```
if (condition)
{
  code to be executed if condition is true
}
else
{
  code to be executed if condition is false
};
```

In addition:

> ➤   The `else` portion is optional.
> ➤   `if` statements may be nested.
> ➤   Multiple statements must be enclosed by braces.

Here is an example:

```
person_type = prompt("What are you ?", "");
if (person_type == "cat")
  alert("Here, have some cat food.");
else
{
  if (person_type == "dog")
    alert("Here, have some dog food.");
  else
  {
    if (person_type == "human")
      alert("Here have some, er, human food!");
  }
};
```

Notice that the curly brackets are only actually required where there is more than one statement within the block. Like many other constructs, they can be omitted where single statements are used. (Although not necessary, it can sometimes be a good idea to include all of the semi-colons and brackets that could be used, as this makes the code easier to modify.)

All statements in JScript are supposed to have a semi-colon line terminator, because a statement can span more than one line without special continuation markers. However, JScript lets you leave it out in quite a few areas, as long as it can tell where a statement is supposed to end. The final semicolon is therefore not mandatory.

switch – used to run various blocks of code, depending on conditions. These statements have the following general form in JScript:

```
switch (expression) {
  case label1 :
    code to be executed if expression is equal to label1
    break;
  case label2 :
    code to be executed if expression is equal to label2
  ...
  default :
    code to be executed if expression is not equal to any of the
    case labels.
}
```

break; can be inserted following the code for a case, to prevent execution of the code running into the next case automatically

Loop Statements

for – executes a block of code a specified number of times:

```
for (initialization; condition; increment)
{
  statements to execute...
}
```

In the following example, i is initially set to zero, and is incremented by 1 at the end of each iteration. The loop terminates when the condition i < 10 is false:

```
for (i = 0; i < 10; i++)
{
  document.write(i);
}
```

while – executes a block of code while a condition is true:

```
while (condition)
{
  statements to execute ...
}
```

`do...while` – executes a statement block once, and then repeats execution of the loop while a condition is true:

```
do
{
   statements to execute ...
}
while (condition);
```

`break` – will cause an exit from a loop regardless of the condition statement:

```
x = 0;
while (x != 10)
{
   n = prompt("Enter a number or 'q' to quit", "");
   if (n == "q")
   {
      alert("See ya");
      break;
   }
}
```

`break` can also be used in `switch`, `for` and `do…while` loops.

`continue` – will cause the loop to jump immediately back to the condition statement.

```
x = 0;
while (x != 1)
{
   if (!(confirm("Should I add 1 to n ?")))
   {
      continue;
      // the following x++ is never executed
      x++;
   }
   x++;
}
alert("Bye");
```

`with` – Establishes a default object for a set of statements. The code:

```
x = Math.cos(3 * Math.PI) + Math.sin(Math.LN10)
y = Math.tan(14 * Math.E)
```

can be rewritten as:

```
with (Math)
{
   x = cos(3 * PI) + sin (LN10)
   y = tan(14 * E)
}
```

When you use the `with` statement, the object passed as the parameter is the default object. Notice how this shortens each statement.

Error Handling Statements

JScript 5 now includes built-in error handling. This is done using the try...catch statement. It allows the developer to anticipate certain error messages, and provide a different code path to follow if that error occurs.

```
function ErrorHandler(x)
{
  try {
    try {
      if (x == 'OK')              // Evalute argument
        throw "Value OK";         // Throw an error
      else
        throw "Value not OK";     // Throw a different error
    }
    catch(e) {                    // Handle "x = OK" errors here
      if (e == "Value OK")        // Check for an error handled here
        return(e + " successfully handled.");
                                  // Return error message
      else                        // Can't handle error here
        throw e;                  // Rethrow the error for next
    }                             // error handler
  }
  catch(e) {                      // Handle other errors here
    return(e + " handled elsewhere.");
                                  // Return error message
  }
}
document.write(ErrorHandler('OK'));
document.write(ErrorHandler('BAD'));
```

The `throw` statement is used to generate error conditions that can then be handled by a `try...catch` block. The value that you throw can be any expression, including a string, Boolean or number.

Built-in Functions

JScript provides a number of built-in functions that can be accessed within code.

Function	Description
`escape(char)`	Returns a new string with all spaces, punctuation, accented characters and any non–ASCII characters encoded into the format %XX, where XX is their hexadecimal value.

Function	Description
eval (expression)	Returns the result of evaluating the JScript expression expression
isFinite (value)	Returns a Boolean value of true if value is any value other than NaN (not a number), negative infinity, or positive infinity.
isNaN (value)	Returns a Boolean value of true if value is not a legal number.
parseFloat (string)	Converts string to a floating-point number.
parseInt (string, base)	Converts string to an integer number with the base of base.
typeOf (object)	Returns the data type of object as a string, such as "boolean", "function", etc.
unescape (char)	Returns a string where all characters encoded with the %XX hexadecimal form are replaced by their ASCII character set equivalents.

Built-in Objects

JScript provides a set of built-in data-type objects, which have their own set of properties, and methods – and which can be accessed with JScript code.

ActiveXObject Object

The ActiveXObject object creates and returns a reference to an automation object. To create a new ActiveXObject object, use:

```
ExcelSheet = new ActiveXObject("Excel.Sheet");
    // create an automation object referring to an Excel Spreadsheet
```

Once you have created the object reference, you can interact with the object using it's methods and properties.

Array Object

The Array object specifies a method of creating arrays and working with them. To create a new array, use:

```
cats = new Array();       // create an empty array
cats = new Array(10);     // create an array of 10 items

// or create and fill an array with values in one go:
cats = new Array("Boo Boo", "Purrcila", "Sam", "Lucky");
```

Properties	Description
length	A read/write integer value specifying the number of elements in the array.

Methods	Description
array1.concat(array2)	Returns a new array consisting of the contents of two arrays.
join([string])	Returns a string containing each element of the array, optionally separated with string.
reverse()	Reverses the order of the array, without creating a new object.
slice(start, [end])	Returns a section of an array, starting at position start and going up to and including position end.
sort([function])	Sorts the array, optionally based upon the results of a function specified by function.
toString()	Returns the elements of an array converted to strings and concatenated, separated by commas.
valueOf()	Returns the elements of an array converted to strings and concatenated, separated by commas. Like toString.

Early versions of JScript had no explicit array structure. However, JScript's object mechanisms allow for easy creation of arrays:

```
function MakeArray(n)
{
  this.length = n;
  for (var i = 1; i <= n; i++)
    this[i] = 0;
  return this
}
```

With this function included in your script, you can create arrays with:

```
cats = new MakeArray(20);
```

You can then populate the array like this:

```
cats[0] = "Boo Boo";
cats[1] = "Purrcila";
cats[2] = "Sam";
cats[3] = "Lucky";
```

Boolean Object

The `Boolean` object is used to store simple yes/no, true/false values. To create a new Boolean object, use the syntax:

```
MyAnswer = new Boolean([value])
```

If *value* is 0, `null`, `omitted`, or an empty string the new Boolean object will have the value `false`. All other values, *including the string* `"false"`, create an object with the value `true`.

Methods	Description
toString()	Returns the value of the Boolean as the string true or false.
valueOf()	Returns the primitive numeric value of the object for conversion in calculations.

Date Object

The `Date` object provides a method for working with dates and times inside of JScript. New instances of the `Date` object are invoked with:

```
newDateObject = new Date([dateInfo])
```

dateInfo is an optional specification for the date to set in the new object. If it is not specified, the current date and time are used. *dateInfo* can use any of the following formats:

`milliseconds` (since midnight GMT on January 1, 1970)
`year, month, day` (e.g. `1997, 0, 27` is January 27, 1997)
`year, month, day, hours, minutes, seconds`
    (e.g. `1997, 8, 23, 08, 25, 30` is September 23 1997 at 08:25:30)

Times and dates are generally in **local time**, but the user can also specify Universal Coordinated Time (**UTC**, previously GMT).

Methods	Description
getDate() getUTCDate	Returns the day of the month as an Integer between 1 and 31, using local time or UTC.
getDay() getUTCDay()	Returns the day of the week as an Integer between 0 (Sunday) and 6 (Saturday), using local time or UTC.
getFullYear() getUTCFullYear()	Returns the year as an Integer, using local time or UTC.
getHours() getUTCHours()	Returns the hours as an Integer between 0 and 23, using local time or UTC.
getMilliseconds() getUTCMilliseconds()	Returns the milliseconds as an integer between 0 and 999, using local time or UTC.
getMinutes() getUTCMinutes()	Returns the minutes as an Integer between 0 and 59, using local time or UTC.
getMonth() getUTCMonth()	Returns the month as an Integer between 0 (January) and 11 (December), using local time or UTC.
getSeconds() getUTCSeconds()	Returns the seconds as an Integer between 0 and 59, using local time or UTC.
getTime()	Returns the number of milliseconds between January 1, 1970 at 00:00:00 UTC and the current Date object as an Integer.
getTimeZoneOffset()	Returns the number of minutes difference between local time and UTC as an Integer.
getVarDate()	Returns the date in VT_DATE format, which is used to interact with ActiveX objects.
getYear()	Returns the year minus 1900 - i.e. only two digits) as an Integer.

Methods	Description
parse (*dateString*)	Returns the number of milliseconds in a date string, since Jan. 1, 1970 00:00:00 UTC.
setDate (*dayValue*) setUTCDate (*dayValue*)	Sets the day of the month where *dayValue* is an Integer between 1 and 31, using local time or UTC.
setFullYear (*yearValue*) setUTCFullYear (*yearValue*)	Sets the year where *yearValue* indicates the 4 digit year, using local time or UTC.
setHours (*hoursValue*) setUTCHours (*hoursValue*)	Sets the hours where *hoursValue* is an Integer between 0 and 59, using local time or UTC.
setMilliSeconds (*msValue*) setUTCMilliSeconds (*msValue*)	Sets the milliseconds where *msValue* is an Integer between 0 and 999, using local time or UTC.
setMinutes (*minutesValue*) setUTCMinutes (*minutesValue*)	Sets the minutes where *minutesValue* is an integer between 0 and 59, using local time or UTC.
setMonth (*monthValue*) setUTCMonth (*monthValue*)	Sets the month where *monthValue* is an integer between 0 and 11, using local time or UTC.
setSeconds (*secondsValue*) setUTCSeconds (*secondsValue*)	Sets the seconds where *secondsValue* is an integer between 0 and 59, using local time or UTC.
setTime (*timeValue*)	Sets the value of a Date object where *timeValue* is and integer representing the number of milliseconds in a date string, since Jan. 1, 1970 00:00:00 GMT.
setYear (*yearValue*)	Sets the year where *yearValue* is an integer (generally) greater than 1900.

Table Continued on Following Page

Methods	Description
toGMTString()	Converts a date to a string using GMT. Equivalent to toUTCString, and included only for backwards compatibility.
toLocaleString()	Converts a date to a string using local time.
toUTCString()	Converts a date to a string using UTC.
UTC(*year*, *month*, *day* [, *hrs*] [, *min*] [, *sec*])	Returns the number of milliseconds in a date object, since Jan. 1, 1970 00:00:00 UTC.

Enumerator Object

The Enumerator object is used to enumerate, or step through, the items in a collection. The Enumerator object provides a way to access any member of a collection, and behaves similarly to the For...Each statement in VBScript.

```
newEnumeratorObj = new Enumerator(collection)
```

Methods	Description
atEnd()	Returns a boolean value indicating if the enumerator is at the end of the collection.
item()	Returns the current item in the collection.
moveFirst()	Resets the current item to the first item in the collection.
moveNext()	Changes the current item to the next item in the collection.

Error Object

The Error object contains information about run-time errors generated in JScript code. The scripting engine automatically generates this object. You can also create it yourself if you want to generate your own custom error states.

```
newErrorObj = new Error(number)
```

Properties	Description
description	The descriptive string associated with a particular error.
number	The number associated with a particular error.

Function Object

The Function object provides a mechanism for compiling JScript code as a function. A new function is invoked with the syntax:

```
functionName = new Function(arg1, arg2, ..., functionCode)
```

where *arg1*, *arg2*, etc. are the argument names for the function object being created, and *functionCode* is a string containing the body of the function. This can be a series of JScript statements separated by semi-colons.

Properties	Description
arguments[]	A reference to the arguments array that holds the arguments that were provided when the function was called.
caller	Returns a reference to the function that invoked the current function.
prototype	Provides a way for adding properties to a Function object.

Methods	Description
toString()	Returns a string value representation of the function.
valueOf()	Returns the function.

Arguments Object

The arguments object is a list (array) of arguments in a function.

Properties	Description
length	An Integer specifying the number of arguments provided to the function when it was called.

Math Object

Provides a set of properties and methods for working with mathematical constants and functions. Simply reference the Math object, then the method or property required:

```
MyArea = Math.PI * MyRadius * MyRadius;
MyResult = Math.floor(MyNumber);
```

Properties	Description
E	Euler's Constant e (the base of natural logarithms).
LN10	The value of the natural logarithm of 10.
LN2	The value of the natural logarithm of 2.
LOG10E	The value of the base 10 logarithm of E.
LOG2E	The value of the base 2 logarithm of E.
PI	The value of the constant π (pi).
SQRT1_2	The value of the square root of a half.
SQRT	The value of the square root of two.

Methods	Description
abs(number)	Returns the absolute value of number.
acos(number)	Returns the arc cosine of number.
asin(number)	Returns the arc sine of number.
atan(number)	Returns the arc tangent of number.
atan2(x, y)	Returns the angle of the polar coordinate of a point x, y from the x-axis.
ceil(number)	Returns the next largest Integer greater than number, i.e. rounds up.
cos(number)	Returns the cosine of number.
exp(number)	Returns the value of number as the exponent of e, as in e^{number}.
floor(number)	Returns the next smallest Integer less than number, i.e. rounds down.
log(number)	Returns the natural logarithm of number.

Methods	Description
max(num1, num2)	Returns the greater of the two values num1 and num2.
min(num1, num2)	Returns the smaller of the two values num1 and num2.
pow(num1, num2)	Returns the value of num1 to the power of num2.
random()	Returns a random number between 0 and 1.
round(number)	Returns the closest Integer to number i.e. rounds up or down to the nearest whole number.
sin(number)	Returns the sin of number.
sqrt(number)	Returns the square root of number.
tan(number)	Returns the tangent of number.

Number Object

The Number object provides a set of properties that are useful when working with numbers:

```
newNumberObj = new Number(value)
```

Properties	Description
MAX_VALUE	The maximum numeric value represented in JScript (~1.79E+308).
MIN_VALUE	The minimum numeric value represented in JScript (~2.22E-308).
NaN	A value meaning 'Not A Number'.
NEGATIVE_INFINITY	A special value for negative infinity ("-Infinity").
POSITIVE_INFINITY	A special value for infinity ("Infinity").

Methods	Description
toString([radix_base])	Returns the value of the number as a string to a radix (base) of 10, unless specified otherwise in radix_base.
valueOf()	Returns the primitive numeric value of the object.

RegularExpression Object

The RegularExpression object contains a regular expression. A regular expression is used to search strings for character patterns.

```
function RegExpDemo()
{
  var s = "AaBbCcDdEeFfGgHhIiJjKkLlMmNnOoPp"
  var r = new RegExp("g", "i");
  var a = r.exec(s);
  document.write(a);
  r.compile("g");
  var a = r.exec(s);
  document.write(a);
}
```

Properties	Description
lastIndex	Character position at which to start the next match.
source	Text of the regular expression.

Methods	Description
compile()	Converts the regular expression into an internal format for faster execution.
exec()	Executes the search for a match in a particular string.
test()	Returns a boolean value indicating whether or not a pattern exists within a string.

RegExp Object

The RegExp object stores information about regular expression pattern searches. It works in conjunction with the RegularExpression object.

In the example below, even though the new method was called with the RegExp object as a parameter, a RegularExpression object was actually created:

```
function regExpDemo()
{
  var s;
  var re = new RegExp("d(b+)(d)","ig");
  var str = "cdbBdbsbdbdz";
  var arr = re.exec(str);
  s = "$1 contains: " + RegExp.$1 + "<BR>";
  s += "$2 contains: " + RegExp.$2 + "<BR>";
  s += "$3 contains: " + RegExp.$3;
  return(s);
}
```

Notice that when checking the properties for the RegExp object, we don't refer to an instance of that object. Rather the reference is made directly to the static RegExp object.

Properties	Description
$1...$9	The 9 most recently found portions during pattern matching.
index	Character position where the first successful match begins.
input	String against which the regular expression is searched.
lastIndex	Character position where the last successful match begins.

String Object

The String object provides a set of methods for text manipulation. To create a new string object, the syntax is:

```
MyString = new String([value])
```

where value is the optional text to place in the string when it is created. If this is a number, it is converted into a string first.

Properties	Description
length	An Integer representing the number of characters in the string.

Methods	Description
anchor ("nameAttribute")	Returns the original string surrounded by <A> and </A> anchor tags, with the NAME attribute set to "nameAttribute".
big()	Returns the original string enclosed in <BIG> and </BIG> tags.
blink()	Returns the original string enclosed in <BLINK> and </BLINK> tags.
bold()	Returns the original string enclosed in <B> and </B> tags.
charAt (index)	Returns the single character at position index within the String object.
charCodeAt (index)	Returns the Unicode encoding of the character at position index.
concat (string2)	Returns a string containing string2 added to the end of the original string.
fixed()	Returns the original string enclosed in <TT> and </TT> tags.
fontcolor ("color")	Returns the original string surrounded by <FONT> and </FONT> tags, with the COLOR attribute set to "color".
fontsize ("size")	Returns the original string surrounded by <FONT> and </FONT> anchor tags, with the SIZE attribute set to "size".
fromCharCode (code1, ...coden)	Returns the string from a number of Unicode character values.
indexOf (searchValue [, fromIndex])	Returns first occurrence of the string searchValue starting at index fromIndex.
italics()	Returns the original string enclosed in <I> and </I> tags.
lastIndexOf (searchValue [, fromIndex])	Returns the index of the last occurrence of the string searchValue, searching backwards from index fromIndex.
link ("hrefAttribute")	Returns the original string surrounded by <A> and </A> link tags, with the HREF attribute set to "hrefAttribute".

Methods	Description
match(regExp)	Returns an array containing the results of a search using the regExp RegularExpression object.
replace(regExp, replaceText)	Returns a string with text replaced using a regular expression.
search(regExp)	Returns the position of the first substring match in a regular expression search.
slice(start, [end])	Returns a section of a string starting at position start and ending at position end.
small()	Returns the original string enclosed in <SMALL> and </SMALL> tags.
split(separator)	Returns an array of strings created by separating the String object at every occurrence of separator.
strike()	Returns the original string enclosed in <STRIKE> and </STRIKE> tags.
sub()	Returns the original string enclosed in _{and} tags.
substr(start, [length])	Returns a substring starting at position start and having a length of length characters.
substring(indexA, indexB)	Returns the sub-string of the original String object from the character at indexA up to and including the one before the character at indexB.
sup()	Returns the original string enclosed in ^{and} tags.
toLowerCase()	Returns the original string with all the characters converted to lowercase.
toUpperCase()	Returns the original string with all the characters converted to uppercase.
toString()	Returns the value of the String object.
valueOf()	Returns the string.

VBArray Object

Provides access to an array created in VBScript. Since these arrays use a different memory structure than JScript arrays, it is necessary to use this object to access them. This object only provides read-only access.

```
<SCRIPT LANGUAGE="VBScript">
<!--
dim arVBArray
' populate this VBScript array…
-->
</SCRIPT>
<SCRIPT LANGUAGE="JScript">
<!--
function useVBArray()
{
  var arJSArray = new VBArray(arVBArray);
  var arArray = arJSArray.toArray();
// now arArray can be used like a JScript array
}
-->
</SCRIPT>
```

Methods	Description
dimensions()	Returns the number of dimensions in the VBArray.
getItem(dim1, dim2,... dimn)	Returns the item at the specified location.
lbound(dimension)	Returns the lowest index value used at the dimension specified by dimension.
toArray()	Returns a standard JScript array converted from the VBArray object.
ubound(dimension)	Returns the highest index value used at the dimension specified by dimension.

Reserved Words

The following are reserved words that can't be used for function, method, variable, or object names. Note that while some words in this list are not currently used as JScript keywords, they have been reserved for future use.

abstract	else	int	super
boolean	extends	interface	switch
break	false	long	synchronized
byte	final	native	this
case	finally	new	throw
catch	float	null	throws
char	for	package	transient
class	function	private	true
const	goto	protected	try
continue	if	public	typeof
default	implements	reset	var
delete	import	return	void
do	in	short	while
double	instanceof	static	with

Active Server Pages Object Model

This appendix offers a handy reference to the Active Server Pages **object model**, and in each case provides the properties, methods and events for the object, along with their collections.

The Request Object

Together, the Request object and the Response object form the 'conversational mechanism' of ASP. The Request object is responsible for controlling how the user sends information to the server. Using the Request object, the server can obtain information about what the user wants – either explicitly (e.g. through programmed ASP code) or implicitly (e.g. through the HTTP headers).

Collections	Description
ClientCertificate	Client certificate values sent from the browser. Read Only
Cookies	Values of cookies sent from the browser. Read Only
Form	Values of form elements sent from the browser. Read Only
QueryString	Values of variables in the HTTP query string. Read Only
ServerVariables	Values of the HTTP and environment variables. Read Only

Property	Description
TotalBytes	Specifies the number of bytes the client is sending in the body of the request. Read Only

Method	Description
BinaryRead	Used to retrieve data sent to the server as part of the POST request

The Response Object

The Response object is responsible for sending the server's output to the client. In this sense, the Response object is the counterpart to the Request object: the Request object gathers information from both the client and the server, and the Response object sends, or resends, the information to the client by writing to the HTTP data stream.

Collection	Description
Cookies	Values of all the cookies to send to the browser.

Properties	Description
Buffer	Determines whether the page is to be buffered until complete
CacheControl	Determines whether proxy servers are allowed to cache the output generated by ASP
Charset	Appends the name of the character set to the content-type header
ContentType	HTTP content type (e.g. "Text/HTML") for the response
Expires	Number of minutes between caching and expiry, for a page cached on the browser
ExpiresAbsolute	Explicit date and/or time of expiry for a page cached on a browser
IsClientConnected	Indicates whether the client has disconnected from the server
PICS	Adds the value of a PICS label to the pics-label field of the response header
Status	Value of the HTTP status line returned by the server

Methods	Description
AddHeader	Adds or changes a value in the HTML header
AppendToLog	Adds text to the web server log entry for this request
BinaryWrite	Sends text to the browser without character-set conversion
Clear	Erases any buffered HTML output
End	Stops processing the page and returns the current result
Flush	Sends buffered output immediately
Redirect	Instructs the browser to connect to a different URL
Write	Writes variable values, strings etc. to the current page as a string

The Response interface elements can be divided into groups, like this:

Response Items	Description
Write, BinaryWrite	Inserts information into a page
Cookies	Sends cookies to the browser
Redirect	Redirects the browser
Buffer, Flush, Clear, End	Buffers the page as it is created
Expires, ExpiresAbsolute, ContentType, AddHeader, Status, CacheContol, PICS, Charset	Sets the properties of a page
IsClientConnected	Checks the client connection

The Application Object

Each application is represented by an instance of the Application object. This object stores variables and objects for application-scope usage. It also holds information about any currently-active sessions.

Collections	Description
Contents	Contains all of the items added to the application through script commands
StaticObjects	Contains all of the objects added to the application with the <OBJECT> tag

Methods	Description
Lock	Prevents other clients from modifying application properties
Unlock	Allows other clients to modify application properties

Events	Description
OnStart	Occurs when a page in the application is first referenced
OnEnd	Occurs when the application ends, i.e. when the web server is stopped

The Session Object

The Session object is used to keep track of an individual browser as it navigates through the web site.

Collections	Description
Contents	Contains all of the items added to the session through script commands
StaticObjects	Contains all of the objects added to the session with the <OBJECT> tag

Method	Description
Abandon	Destroys a Session object and releases its resources

Properties	Description
CodePage	Sets the codepage that will be used for symbol mapping
LCID	Sets the locale identifier
SessionID	Returns the session identification for this user
Timeout	Sets the timeout period for the session state for this application, in minutes

Events	Description
OnStart	Occurs when the server creates a new session
OnEnd	Occurs when a session is abandoned or times out

The Server Object

The main use of the Server object is to create components.

Property	Description
ScriptTimeout	Length of time a script can run before an error occurs

Methods	Description
CreateObject	Creates an instance of an object or server component
HTMLEncode	Applies HTML encoding to the specified string
MapPath	Converts a virtual path into a physical path
URLEncode	Applies URL encoding including escape chars to a string

The ObjectContext Object

When we use MTS (Microsoft Transaction Server) to manage a transaction, we have the functionality within our script to commit (or to abort) the transaction. This functionality is provided by the ObjectContext object.

Methods	Description
SetComplete	Declares that the script knows no reason for the transaction not to complete. If all participating components call SetComplete, then the transaction will complete. SetComplete overrides any previous SetAbort method that has been called in the script
SetAbort	Aborts a transaction initiated by an ASP

Events	Description
OnTransactionCommit	Occurs after a transacted script's transaction commits
OnTransactionAbort	Occurs if the transaction is aborted

Configuring IIS4

We shall now look at how you can configure the various options in IIS4. This is done via the Microsoft Management Console. This is intended as an aid to successfully host your finished web applications and configure IIS4 to perform at its best for your application.

Configuring Master Properties

We can configure the overall Web server properties by selecting the name of the computer, right clicking and selecting the Properties menu option.

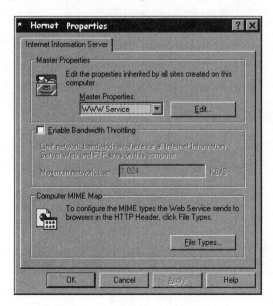

The different types are as follows:

Master Properties

Sets the default properties used by all new and current sites.

WWW Service Properties

Selecting WWW Service and the Edit button generates the default WWW properties – this is the same set of property sheets that we saw earlier when we inspected the properties of a directory.

FTP Service Properties

Selecting FTP Service and the Edit button generates the default FTP properties.

Bandwidth Throttling

> *Enable Bandwidth Throttling* – turns bandwidth throttling on / off for all Web and FTP sites – this enables bandwidth to be reserved and made available for other Internet services

> *Maximum network use* – specifies maximum bandwidth for all Web and FTP sites as a number of kilobytes per second (KBps)

Computer MIME Map

Sets the Multipurpose Internet Mail Extensions (MIME) mappings - these are names that identify the various file types that the Web service can return to browsers.

Configuring Web Site Properties

We can also configure properties for our specific web site:

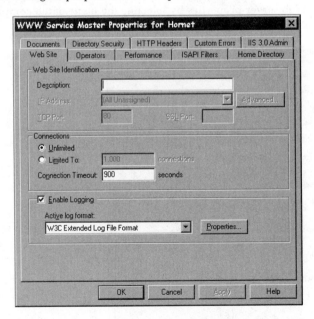

There are four main options that can be configured:

Web Site Identification

> *Description* – the name that appears in the MMC namespace

> *IP address* – the address of the Web Site

> *Port no* – the TCP port no ; Web browser defaults to port 80

Advanced Multiple Web Site Configurations

Selecting the Advanced button allows multiple identities to be configured for the site. Also, giving the site a Host Header Name enables multiple Web sites to be hosted on the same machine with the same IP address.

Connections

> *Unlimited / Limited to* – when enabled, specifies the maximum number of simultaneous connections to the site

> *Connection Timeout* – the time in seconds before an inactive user is disconnected

Logging

> *Enable Logging* – turns on / off the logging of web site access

> *Active log format* – formats available for logged information are: Microsoft IIS Log Format , NCSA Common Log File Format, W^{3}C Extended Log File Format and ODBC Data file

Configuring Operator Properties

The Operators dialog defines which Windows NT user accounts have access to operator functions for management of the Web site.

Configuring Performance Properties

The Performance dialog offers the following options:

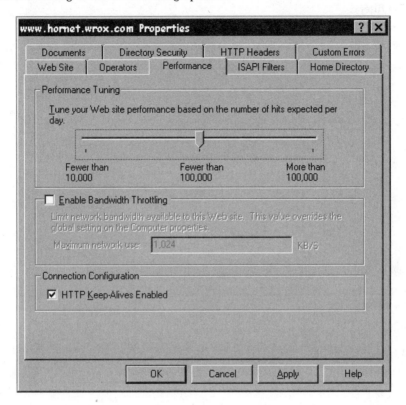

Performance Tuning

> ➢ *Number of expected hits per day* – by setting this to an appropriate value, IIS4 will adjust its internal parameters to provide optimum use of memory

Bandwidth Throttling

> ➢ *Enable Bandwidth Throttling* – turns bandwidth throttling on / off for this web site – this ensures that bandwidth is available for other Internet services

> ➢ *Maximum network use* – specifies maximum bandwidth for web site as the number of kilobytes per second (KBps)

Connection Configuration

> ➢ *HTTP Keep-Alives Enabled* - turns on / off the ability for the Web server to keep connections to the browser established thus improving performance

Configuring ISAPI Filters Properties

The ISAPI Filters dialog is used to add/remove ISAPI filters. It is also used to edit properties and enable/disable filters.

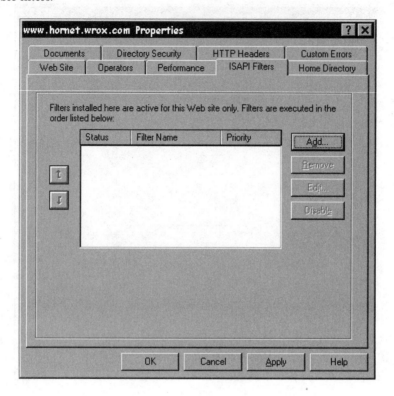

Configuring Home Directory / Virtual Directory / Sub Directory Properties

The Home, Virtual and Sub Directory all use the same dialog.

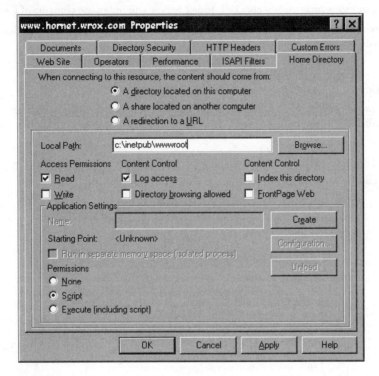

Since there are quite a few options we will look at them in more detail.

Resource Content Location

The directory may be one of:

- ➤ A physical directory located on the same computer as the Web server.
- ➤ A physical directory located on another networked computer (option disabled for sub directories) – referenced using the Universal Naming Conventions e.g.\\cobra\marketing.
- ➤ Located elsewhere and referenced by another URL – a request for this directory is then redirected.

Access Permissions

- ➤ *Read* – enables permission to read or download files.
- ➤ *Write* – enables permission to change files or upload files.

Content Control

> *Log access* – when checked, all accesses of Web resources are logged

> *Directory browsing allowed* – when enabled, a list of sub directories and files will be returned if no filename is specified in the URL (this is if no default document has been enabled)

> *Index this directory* – when checked, Index Server will index the contents of files in the directory

> *FrontPage Web* – when enabled, the directory will contain information such that the FrontPage explorer can handle Web site management tasks

Application Settings

Used to create applications and enable process isolation. The application permissions specify whether scripts (e.g. ASP files) or executables (e.g. .EXE & .DLL files) located in this directory may be invoked.

If the directory is the start point of an application, another set of property sheets for application configuration can be obtained by selecting the **Configuration** button.

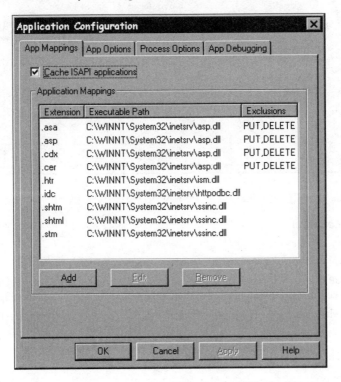

App Mappings

> *Cache ISAPI applications* – when enabled, ISAPI DLLs are cached; should only be disabled when developing/debugging

> *Application Mappings* – contains the mapping between file suffix in the URL and the ISAPI extension that will handle the request

App Options

> - *Enable session state* – turns on / off ASP creating sessions for each user accessing the application
> - *Session Timeout* – if session is enabled, this specifies a period of time that if no user activity occurs within, the session is deleted
> - *Enable buffering* – turns on / off the collection of ASP output before sending to the browser
> - *Enable parent paths* – turns on / off access to parent paths using the relative .. path notation
> - *Default ASP language* – language used if not specified within ASP script
> - *ASP Script timeout* – number of seconds an ASP script can run before an error is flagged

Process Options

> - *Write Unsuccessful Client Requests to Event Log* – when checked, client access failures are written to NT Event Log
> - *Enable Debug Exception Handling* – turns on / off detailed error messages being returned when a COM component fails
> - *Number of Script Engines Cached* – specifies the number of ActiveX Script engines to cache
> - *Script File Cache* – specifies the number of preprocessed ASP files to cache in order to improve performance.
> - *CGI Script Timeout* – amount of time a CGI process can execute before an error is flagged

App Debugging

> - *Enable ASP Server-Side Script Debugging* – turns on / off the ability to use the Script Debugger
> - *Enable ASP Client-Side Debugging* – ignored
> - *Send Detailed ASP Error Messages to Client* –turns on / off detailed error messages being returned when ASP errors occur
> - *Send Text Error Message to Client* – sends a fixed standard message for all ASP errors

Configuring Document Properties

The configuring Document Properties dialog allows you to specify the documents displayed when a user first goes to your site's home page:

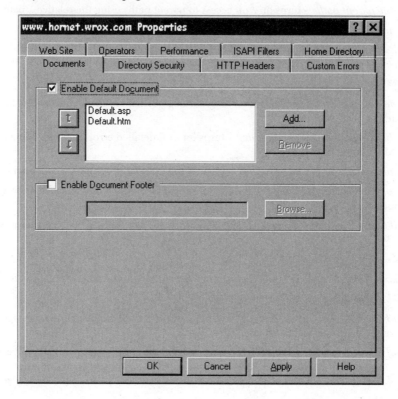

Default Documents

> ➤ *Enable Default Document* – turns on / off the use of a default document; this is the document that is sent if the URL omits a document name.

> ➤ *List of documents* – contains the list of possible default documents; the directory will be searched for one of these in the order that they appear in the list.

Document Footer

> ➤ *Enable Document Footer* – turns on /off the addition of a footer on every Web page

> ➤ *Filename* – full path and name of file containing the footer contents

Configuring Directory Security

The Directory Security dialog allows you to restrict access to certain addresses and domain names:

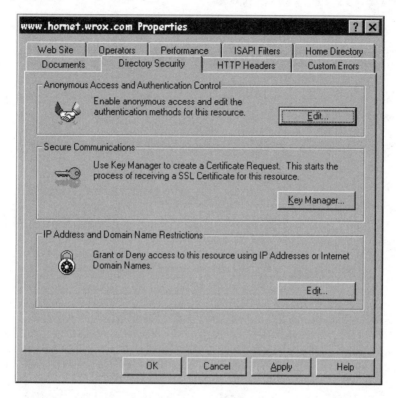

Anonymous Access / Authentication Control

Set authentication methods.

Secure Communications

Invokes Key Manager utility for handling digital certificates – these are needed to implement SSL

IP Address / Domain Name Restrictions

Grants and Denies access based on IP address or Domain Name of client

Configuring HTTP Headers

The HTTP Headers Dialog allows you to enable expiry of document content:

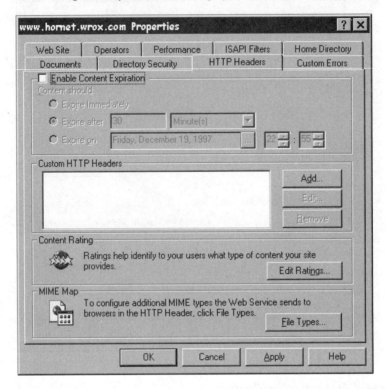

Content Expiration

Enable Content Expiry – when enabled, expiry information is included in data sent to the browser and stored with the item in the cache. The browser uses this information to decide whether to use cached files or request updates from the Web server. Content can expire:

> Immediately

> After a time period

> At a particular time/date

Custom HTTP Headers

This allows additional information to be appended in the HTTP response headers

Content Ratings

Used to rate Web content according to levels of violence, nudity, sex, and offensive language. This enables a Web browser to automatically reject information that is unacceptable to the user.

Mime Map

Sets the Multipurpose Internet Mail Extensions (MIME) mappings - these are names that identify the various file types that the Web service can return to browsers.

Configuring Custom Errors

The Custom Errors dialog allows you to display your own html files when a specified a HTTP error occurs:

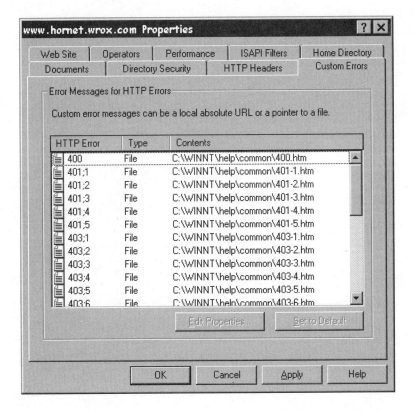

Error Messages

Allows the customization of the returned error text in any HTTP error responses.

ADO Remote Data Service (RDS) Reference

Introduction

The most common data-access technology used by Visual Basic and VBScript developers is Microsoft ActiveX Data Objects, or ADO. ADO is a set of ActiveX components that can be used to establish connections to a database and then either retrieve or change data. Its use in ASP-driven dynamic Web sites has made it the de facto standard for ASP developers.

ADO 1.5 saw the introduction of the Remote Data Service objects. These objects enable a remote client to connect to a database over the Internet. So, whereas ADO is primarily a server-side technology, RDS is primarily a client-side technology.

Typically, it is used for populating dynamic elements of a Web page without having to perform multiple round-trip calls to the server. For example, it's possible to create a list box on a HTML page that will instruct IE to ask RDS to connect to a remote server to get the data for that list. It's then possible to tie events into that list box such that when the selection changes, associated data is retrieved from the database and used to populate another list.

In a traditional ASP approach, the ASP developer would query the database and add the data for the list directly to the HTML to return to the browser. When the list box selection changes, IE would be instructed to re-request the page, where it's then the responsibility of IIS to build an entirely new page.

From a Web developer's perspective, RDS can only be used in IE4 and IE5 running on Windows platforms. This limits its usefulness to intranet and extranet scenarios – designing public sites that only work on specific browser versions is rarely a good call. But, if you do choose to deploy it, the benefit is substantially reduced load on both your Web server and reduced network traffic.

Those of you building custom front-ends using Visual Basic, or another language capable of handling ActiveX components, you have more freedom to adopt RDS because you can guarantee the capabilities of your audience's front end.

RDS is installed along with ADO 1.5 or higher. The ADO downloads can be found at `http://microsoft.com/data/`.

DataControl Object

The `DataControl` object is used to provide data access services to one or more elements on the page that can understand "data binding" – the name of the technology that enabled "data aware" page elements to retrieve data from a remote server using RDS.

Here's how we can create a `DataControl` object capable at connecting to the `SalesWeb` server over HTTP and fetch all of the rows in the `Customers` table. Notice that we're setting the ID of this object to `ADC1`.

```
<OBJECT CLASSID="clsid:BD96C556-65A3-11D0-983A-00C04FC29E33" ID="ADC1">
    <PARAM NAME="SQL" VALUE="Select * from Customers">
    <PARAM NAME="Connect" VALUE="DSN=MyDB;">
    <PARAM NAME="Server" VALUE="http://SalesWeb/">
</OBJECT>
```

We use three properties, `SQL`, `Connect` and `Server`, to tell the control where to get the data it needs.

Property: **SQL as String**	Tells the `DataFactory` object on the server what SQL statement it needs to execute.
Property: **Connect as String**	Tells the `DataFactory` object on the server what connection string it needs to use to connect to the database. In this example, we're using an ODBC data source called "MyDB", but this could be a connection string like `"Database=MyDB;UID=Who;PWD=Me"`.
Property: **Server as String**	Tells the `DataControl` object how to connect to the remote server. There are four different ways you can connect, but in this example we're connecting over HTTP.
	Over **HTTP:** VALUE="http://*webserver*/"
	Over **Secure HTTP:** VALUE="https://*webserver*/"
	Over **DCOM:** VALUE="*machinename*"
	In-process Server: VALUE=""

Once you have a `DataControl` object on your page, you can go ahead and associate any data aware page elements that you need with that object. Such as:

```
<TABLE DATASRC="#ADC1" border=1>
   <TR><TD><SPAN DATAFLD="Name"></SPAN></TD></TR>
</TABLE>
```

In that snippet of code, we create a table and tell it that its data source ("DATASRC") is the page element with the ID ADC1. (Note that you do need to precede the control name with a pound sign.) Because the TABLE element is data aware, it knows it needs to iterate through the Recordset that's returned and use the other elements up until the `</TABLE>` tag as a "template". To actually display some data, we use a SPAN inside of each table element and bind each SPAN to a field in the Recordset, in this case: Name.

Other Properties and Methods for DataControl

Moving Around the Recordset

Similar to the ADO functions you're familiar with, you can use `MoveNext`, `MovePrevious`, `MoveLast` and `MoveFirst` to move around a Recordset.

Sorting Values

Use these properties to sort the values in your Recordset. Both these properties are similar in nature to adding an `ORDER BY` clause to your SQL statement.

Property: **SortColumn as String**	The name of the column you wish to sort on.

Property: **SortDirection as Booleaní**	Set this value to True to sort in ascending order ("A...Z"), False for descending.

After you change these values, call the Reset method:

```
<SCRIPT LANGUAGE=VBSCRIPT FOR=RefreshButton EVENT=OnClick>
   DataControl.SortColumn = "City"
   DataControl.Reset
</SCRIPT>
```

> Use the DataControl.Reset method rather than the DataControl.Refresh method wherever possible. Reset will perform the operation on the already-fetched Recordset, whereas Refresh will re-request the Recordset from the server, using up expensive bandwidth.

Filtering Values

Use these properties to filter values in your Recordset. These properties are similar to adding a WHERE clause to your SQL statement.

Property: **FilterColumn as String**	The name of the column you wish to filter.

Property: **FilterCriterion as String**	The type of filter operation you wish to perform. This can be any one of: =, <, >, <=, >=, <>. Note, this type of filter cannot do wildcards, such as: `WHERE NAME LIKE 'TEMP%'`

Property: **FilterValue as String**	The value you wish to filter on.

Again, after you change these values, call the Reset method:

```
<SCRIPT LANGUAGE=VBSCRIPT FOR=RefreshButton EVENT=OnClick>
<!--
    DataControl.FilterColumn = "FirstName"
    DataControl.FilterCriterion = "="
    DataControl.FilterValue = "Brandon"
    DataControl.Reset
-->
</script>
```

Other Methods

These are the other miscellaneous methods the DataControl object has:

Method: **Refresh**	Tells the DataControl object to re-request the Recordset from the server.

Method: **Reset**	Performs a filter or sort operation on the Recordset already on the client.

Method: **Cancel**	Cancels any asynchronous retrieval or update operations that may be running.

Method: **SubmitChanges**	Tells the `DataControl` to send back to the server any changes to data in data aware page elements that have been made by the user.

"Method: **CancelUpdate**	Discards all of the changes that have been made by the user.

Method: **CreateRecordset**	Creates a new, empty Recordset that can be used to send data back to the server.

Other Properties

These are the other properties the `DataControl` object has:

Property: **FetchOptions** as Integer	Defines how fetch operations should be performed. Can be one of these values:	
	adcFetchAsync (Default)	Indicates the control will be returned to the client as soon as the request has been sent to the server. You can use the ReadyState property and onReadyState event to monitor the status of the Recordset.
	adcFetchUpFront	Indicates that as soon as data is requested, all of it will be returned before control is returned to the client.
	adcFetchBackground	Similar to adcFetchAsync, except that it if you request records beyond the extent of the Recordset held by the client, the DataControl object will wait until the relevant row has been returned. For example, if you ask for the last record in a Recordset using MoveLast with adcFetchAsync, you'll get the last returned row, irrespective of whether or not this is the last row in the server's set. adcFetchBackground will wait until the last row has been returned so you're guaranteed to get the right object.

Property: **ExecuteOptions** as Integer	Defines how update operations should be performed. Can be either of these values:	
	adcExecAsync (Default)	Indicates that operations will be asynchronous, i.e. the client will continue to do other stuff while the data operation is running.
	adcExecSync	Indicates that the client will wait until all data has been updated before performing other tasks.

Property: **Recordset** as ADODB.Recorset	This property represents the Recordset that the server has supplied. You can only directly access this property once ReadyState is either adcReadyStateInteraction or adcReadyStateComplete.

Property: **InternetTimeout** as Long	It can often take a long time to retrieve all of the values you require from the server. This property represents the number of milliseconds the client will wait before timing out an operation. By default, this is 300,000ms, or 5 minutes.	

Property: **ReadyState** as Integer	This property can be used to determine the status of the client/server communication operation. Use the onReadyStateChange event to efficiently see if the operation is still running, rather than periodically check this value.	
	adcReadyStateLoaded	The DataControl is ready to use, but no data has yet been returned from the server. You cannot use the Recordset property at this stage.
	adcReadyStateInteractive	Some of the rows have been retrieved from the server. The remaining rows are still being fetched.
	adcReadyStateComplete	All rows that were requested have been returned. You'll also see this state if the operation was cancelled because of an error.

Property: **Handler** as String	It's rare you'll need to use this property, but basically it allows developers to extend the functionality of the RDS.DataFactory object on the server. This is beyond the scope of this book, so see the Microsoft document for more information.	

Property: **URL** as String	Defines the URL of an ASP page that can be used to return a Recordset to the client. You can use this property rather than specifying a Web server, or DCOM-capable computer name, using the Server property.	

Write-only Property: **SourceRecordset** as Recordset	The functionality of this property is covered in the documentation for the DataSource object.	

Events

These are the events the `DataControl` object can fire.

onError	This event is fired when there is something wrong with the Recordset you have requested – for example if you have asked for a table that does not exist.	
	Scode as Integer	A status code for the error.
	Description as String	A human-readable description of the error.
	Source as String	The SQL query or command that caused the error
	CancelDisplay as Boolean	Set this to True if you handle the error yourself and don't want the message displayed to the user.
onReadyStateChange	This event is fired whenever the `ReadyState` property changes.	

DataControl Error Codes

These are the possible error codes the `DataControl` object can return through the `onError` event.

IDS_AsyncPending	0x800A1011	The operation could not be performed because an asynchronous operation is running.
IDS_BadInlineTablegram	0x800A1009	Bad inline `tablegram`
IDS_CantConnect	0x800A1003	The `DataControl` cannot connect to the specified server.
IDS_CantCreateObject	0x800A1004	The server cannot create the specific business object, usually the `DataFactory` object.
IDS_CantFindDataspace	0x800A1006	The `DataSpace` object that you've specified cannot be found.
IDS_CantInvokeMethod	0x800A1005	The method requested cannot be found in the business object.
IDS_CrossDomainWarning	0x800A1016	You are attempting to access a server found in another IE Trust Zone.
IDS_InvalidADCClientVersion	0x800A1010	The version of the RDS objects on the client is newer than the version on the server.

IDS_INVALIDARG	0x80071500	The parameters for the operation have not been correctly specified. Usually, this is because the Server or SQL properties haven't been set correctly before calling Refresh.
IDS_InvalidParam	0x800A1014	See IDS_INVALIDARG
IDS_NOINTERFACE	0x80071501	This error can occur when attempting to filter or sort on a Recordset type that doesn't support those operations.
IDS_NotReentrant	0x800A1015	The client is handling an event, and so another operation cannot begin.
IDS_ObjectNotSafe	0x800A1007	The object is not marked safe for initialization and scripting.
IDS_RecordSetNotOpen	0x800A1013	The Recordset object is currently not in an open state.
IDS_ResetInvalidField	0x800A1012	The SortColumn or FilterColumn does not exist.
IDS_RowsetNotUpdatable	0x800A1008	The Rowset cannot be changed.
IDS_UnexpectedError	0x800A10FF	Any other error.
IDS_UpdatesFailed	0x800A1002	The changes to the database could not be made.

DataSpace Object

The RDS.DataSpace object is a client-side object that can be used to communicate with a custom business object. So far, we've only seen the DataControl object that communicates with a DataFactory object on the server.

To create an instance of a DataSpace object on your page, use this:

```
<OBJECT ID="ADS" CLASSID="CLSID:BD96C556-65A3-11D0-983A-00C04FC29E36">
</OBJECT>
```

From this point, you can now call any properly configured object on your server and ask it to return a Recordset to you. For example:

```
<script language=vbscript for=refresh event=onclick>
<!--
    'Create an instance of the business object on the server
    Dim Business
```

```
   set Business = ADS.CreateObject("bitspub.site", _
    "http://SalesWeb/")

   ' Retrieve the Recordset
   Dim Recordset
   set Recordset = object.GetCustomers

   ' Set that Recordset as the source for a DataControl object
   ' with the ID "DataControl"...
   set DataControl.SourceRecordset = Recordset
-->
</script>
```

The DataSpace object only has a single method, and a single property.

Method: CreateObject(ProgID as String, Server as String)	Tells the DataSpace object which object to create on the server. It takes a ProgID (i.e. the name of the object), and a server. This server is similar to the DataControl.Server property. Possible values for Server are:

Over HTTP:	"http://*webserver*/"
Over Secure HTTP:	"https://*webserver*/"
Over DCOM:	"machinename"
In-process Server:	""

Property: InternetTimeout as Long	It can often take a long time to retrieve all of the values you require from the server. This property represents the number of milliseconds the client will wait before timing out an operation. By default, this is 300,000ms, or 5 minutes.

Configuring your Business Objects

RDS places some security around exactly which objects you can run on the server. To enable your objects to be created inside of RDS, you need to add the name of your object to a particular key in the registry.

You need to add your object to this hive of the Registry using REGEDIT.EXE:

```
HKEY_LOCAL_MACHINE
   \System
      \CurrentControlSet
         \Services
            \W3SVC
               \Parameters
                  \ADCLaunch
```

The figure below shows you what the Registry looks like with `MyBusiness.Object` added. There is no need to create any values inside this key.

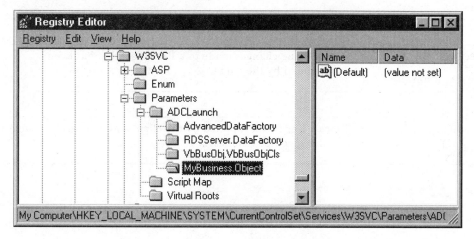

DataFactory Object

The `RDS.DataFactory` object is the server-side object that you can use to provide data access services to your client application.

The `DataFactory` object is supplied as a multi-use "business object" that can be used if you do not wish to roll your own objects in your application. Typically in 3-tier client/server applications, you define all of the objects in the business tier such that a method like "`GetCustomers`" encapsulates the SQL needed to generate a Recordset containing all customers. If you do not wish to go through that step, you can use the `DataFactory` object with a parameter set to the appropriate SQL statement. This will execute the statement on your applications behalf and return the data to you through a Recordset.

It's unlikely that as a VB developer you'll need to use this object directly. But, for completeness, this is a list of the six methods that this object supports. You can find more information on these at `http://msdn.microsoft.com/`.

Method:	Takes a Recordset and "flattens" it so it can be moved between processes or down a network link.
ConvertToString	

Method:	Creates a blank Recordset.
CreateRecordSet	

Method:	Executes the SQL statement the client has requested.
Execute	

Method:	Another way of executing the SQL statement.
Query	

Method:	Commits the changes made to a Recordset that has been manipulated by the client.
SubmitChanges	

Method:	Takes a Recordset supplied by the client and merges the changes into the specified database.
Synchronize	

Microsoft ActiveX Data Objects 2.0 Library Reference

In this section we will find the objects, methods, and properties necessary for ADO transactions using VB. This should aid the programmer when connections are to be made to a database from within a web application.

All properties are read/write unless otherwise stated.

Objects

Name	Description
Command	A Command object is a definition of a specific command that you intend to execute against a data source.
Connection	A Connection object represents an open connection to a data store.
Error	An Error object contains the details about data access errors pertaining to a single operation involving the provider.
Errors	The Errors collection contains all of the Error objects created in response to a single failure involving the provider.

Name	Description
Field	A Field object represents a column of data within a common data type.
Fields	A Fields collection contains all of the Field objects of a Recordset object.
Parameter	A Parameter object represents a parameter or argument associated with a Command object based on a parameterized query or stored procedure.
Parameters	A Parameters collection contains all the Parameter objects of a Command object.
Properties	A Properties collection contains all the Property objects for a specific instance of an object.
Property	A Property object represents a dynamic characteristic of an ADO object that is defined by the provider.
Recordset	A Recordset object represents the entire set of records from a base table or the results of an executed command. At any time, the Recordset object only refers to a single record within the set as the current record.

Command Object

Methods

Name	Returns	Description
Cancel		Cancels execution of a pending Execute or Open call.
CreateParameter	Parameter	Creates a new Parameter object.
Execute	Recordset	Executes the query, SQL statement, or stored procedure specified in the CommandText property.

Properties

Name	Returns	Description
ActiveConnection	Variant	Indicates to which Connection object the command currently belongs.
CommandText	String	Contains the text of a command to be issued against a data provider.

Name	Returns	Description
CommandTimeout	Long	Indicates how long to wait, in seconds, while executing a command before terminating the command and generating an error. Default is 30.
CommandType	CommandTypeEnum	Indicates the type of Command object.
Name	String	Indicates the name of the Command object.
Parameters	Parameters	Contains all of the Parameter objects for a Command object.
Prepared	Boolean	Indicates whether or not to save a compiled version of a command before execution.
Properties	Properties	Contains all of the Property objects for a Command object.
State	Long	Describes whether the Command object is open or closed. Read only.

Connection Object

Methods

Name	Returns	Description
BeginTrans	Integer	Begins a new transaction.
Cancel		Cancels the execution of a pending, asynchronous Execute or Open operation.
Close		Closes an open connection and any dependant objects.
CommitTrans		Saves any changes and ends the current transaction.
Execute	Recordset	Executes the query, SQL statement, stored procedure, or provider specific text.
Open		Opens a connection to a data source, so that commands can be executed against it.
OpenSchema	Recordset	Obtains database schema information from the provider.
RollbackTrans		Cancels any changes made during the current transaction and ends the transaction.

Properties

Name	Returns	Description
Attributes	Long	Indicates one or more characteristics of a Connection object. Default is 0.
CommandTimeout	Long	Indicates how long, in seconds, to wait while executing a command before terminating the command and generating an error. The default is 30.
ConnectionString	String	Contains the information used to establish a connection to a data source.
ConnectionTimeout	Long	Indicates how long, in seconds, to wait while establishing a connection before terminating the attempt and generating an error. Default is 15.
CursorLocation	CursorLocationEnum	Sets or returns the location of the cursor engine.
DefaultDatabase	String	Indicates the default database for a Connection object.
Errors	Errors	Contains all of the Error objects created in response to a single failure involving the provider.
IsolationLevel	IsolationLevelEnum	Indicates the level of transaction isolation for a Connection object. Write only.
Mode	ConnectModeEnum	Indicates the available permissions for modifying data in a Connection.
Properties	Properties	Contains all of the Property objects for a Connection object.
Provider	String	Indicates the name of the provider for a Connection object.
State	Long	Describes whether the Connection object is open or closed. Read only.
Version	String	Indicates the ADO version number. Read only.

Events

Name	Description
`BeginTransComplete`	Fired after a `BeginTrans` operation finishes executing.
`CommitTransComplete`	Fired after a `CommitTrans` operation finishes executing.
`ConnectComplete`	Fired after a connection starts.
`Disconnect`	Fired after a connection ends.
`ExecuteComplete`	Fired after a command has finished executing.
`InfoMessage`	Fired whenever a `ConnectionEvent` operation completes successfully and additional information is returned by the provider.
`RollbackTransComplete`	Fired after a `RollbackTrans` operation finished executing.
`WillConnect`	Fired before a connection starts.
`WillExecute`	Fired before a pending command executes on the connection.

Error Object

Properties

Name	Returns	Description
`Description`	String	A description string associated with the error. Read only.
`HelpContext`	Integer	Indicates the `ContextID` in the help file for the associated error. Read only.
`HelpFile`	String	Indicates the name of the help file. Read only.
`NativeError`	Long	Indicates the provider-specific error code for the associated error. Read only.
`Number`	Long	Indicates the number that uniquely identifies an `Error` object. Read only.
`Source`	String	Indicates the name of the object or application that originally generated the error. Read only.
`SQLState`	String	Indicates the SQL state for a given `Error` object. It is a five-character string that follows the ANSI SQL standard. Read only.

Errors Collection

Methods

Name	Returns	Description
Clear		Removes all of the Error objects from the Errors collection.
Refresh		Updates the Error objects with information from the provider.

Properties

Name	Returns	Description
Count	Long	Indicates the number of Error objects in the Errors collection. Read only.
Item	Error	Allows indexing into the Errors collection to reference a specific Error object. Read only.

Field Object

Methods

Name	Returns	Description
AppendChunk		Appends data to a large or binary Field object.
GetChunk	Variant	Returns all or a portion of the contents of a large or binary Field object.

Properties

Name	Returns	Description
ActualSize	Long	Indicates the actual length of a field's value. Read only.
Attributes	Long	Indicates one or more characteristics of a Field object.

Name	Returns	Description
`DataFormat`	Variant	Write only.
`DefinedSize`	Long	Indicates the defined size of the `Field` object. Write only.
`Name`	String	Indicates the name of the `Field` object.
`NumericScale`	Byte	Indicates the scale of numeric values for the `Field` object. Write only.
`OriginalValue`	Variant	Indicates the value of a `Field` object that existed in the record before any changes were made. Read only.
`Precision`	Byte	Indicates the degree of precision for numeric values in the `Field` object. Read only.
`Properties`	Properties	Contains all of the `Property` objects for a `Field` object.
`Type`	DataTypeEnum	Indicates the data type of the `Field` object.
`UnderlyingValue`	Variant	Indicates a `Field` object's current value in the database. Read only.
`Value`	Variant	Indicates the value assigned to the `Field` object.

Fields Collection

Methods

Name	Returns	Description
`Append`		Appends a `Field` object to the `Fields` collection.
`Delete`		Deletes a `Field` object from the `Fields` collection.
`Refresh`		Updates the `Field` objects in the `Fields` collection.

Properties

Name	Returns	Description
Count	Long	Indicates the number of Field objects in the Fields collection. Read only.
Item	Field	Allows indexing into the Fields collection to reference a specific Field object. Read only.

Parameter Object

Methods

Name	Returns	Description
AppendChunk		Appends data to a large or binary Parameter object.

Properties

Name	Returns	Description
Attributes	Long	Indicates one or more characteristics of a Parameter object.
Direction	ParameterDirectionEnum	Indicates whether the Parameter object represents an input parameter, an output parameter, or both, or if the parameter is a return value from a stored procedure.
Name	String	Indicates the name of the Parameter object.
NumericScale	Byte	Indicates the scale of numeric values for the Parameter object.
Precision	Byte	Indicates the degree of precision for numeric values in the Parameter object.
Properties	Properties	Contains all of the Property objects for a Parameter object.
Size	Long	Indicates the maximum size, in bytes or characters, of a Parameter object.

Name	Returns	Description
Type	DataTypeEnum	Indicates the data type of the `Parameter` object.
Value	Variant	Indicates the value assigned to the `Parameter` object.

Parameters Collection

Methods

Name	Returns	Description
Append		Appends a `Parameter` object to the `Parameters` collection.
Delete		Deletes a `Parameter` object from the `Parameters` collection.
Refresh		Updates the `Parameter` objects in the `Parameters` collection.

Properties

Name	Returns	Description
Count	Long	Indicates the number of `Parameter` objects in the `Parameters` collection. Read only.
Item	Parameter	Allows indexing into the `Parameters` collection to reference a specific `Parameter` object. Read only.

Properties

Methods

Name	Returns	Description
Refresh		Updates the `Property` objects in the `Properties` collection with the details from the provider.

Properties

Name	Returns	Description
Count	Long	Indicates the number of Property objects in the Properties collection. Read only.
Item	Property	Allows indexing into the Properties collection to reference a specific Property object. Read only.

Property Object

Properties

Name	Returns	Description
Attributes	Long	Indicates one or more characteristics of a Property object.
Name	String	Indicates the name of the Property object. Read only.
Type	DataTypeEnum	Indicates the data type of the Property object.
Value	Variant	Indicates the value assigned to the Property object.

Recordset Object

Methods

Name	Returns	Description
AddNew		Creates a new record for an updateable Recordset object.
Cancel		Cancels execution of a pending asynchronous Open operation.
CancelBatch		Cancels a pending batch update.

Name	Returns	Description
CancelUpdate		Cancels any changes made to the current record, or to a new record prior to calling the Update method.
Clone	Recordset	Creates a duplicate Recordset object from and existing Recordset object.
Close		Closes the Recordset object and any dependent objects.
CompareBookmarks	CompareEnum	Compares two bookmarks and returns an indication of the relative values.
Delete		Deletes the current record or group of records.
Find		Searches the Recordset for a record that matches the specified criteria.
GetRows	Variant	Retrieves multiple records of a Recordset object into an array.
GetString	String	Returns a Recordset as a string.
Move		Moves the position of the current record in a Recordset.
MoveFirst		Moves the position of the current record to the first record in the Recordset.
MoveLast		Moves the position of the current record to the last record in the Recordset.
MoveNext		Moves the position of the current record to the next record in the Recordset.
MovePrevious		Moves the position of the current record to the previous record in the Recordset.
NextRecordset	Recordset	Clears the current Recordset object and returns the next Recordset by advancing through a series of commands.
Open		Opens a Recordset.
Requery		Updates the data in a Recordset object by re-executing the query on which the object is based.
Resync		Refreshes the data in the current Recordset object from the underlying database.
Save		Saves the Recordset to a file.

Name	Returns	Description
Supports	Boolean	Determines whether a specified Recordset object supports particular functionality.
Update		Saves any changes made to the current Recordset object.
UpdateBatch		Writes all pending batch updates to disk.

Properties

Name	Returns	Description
AbsolutePage	PositionEnum	Specifies in which page the current record resides.
AbsolutePosition	PositionEnum	Specifies the ordinal position of a Recordset object's current record.
ActiveCommand	Object	Indicates the Command object that created the associated Recordset object. Read only.
ActiveConnection	Variant	Indicates to which Connection object the specified Recordset object currently belongs.
BOF	Boolean	Indicates whether the current record is before the first record in a Recordset object. Read only.
Bookmark	Variant	Returns a bookmark that uniquely identifies the current record in a Recordset object, or sets the current record to the record identified by a valid bookmark.
CacheSize	Long	Indicates the number of records from a Recordset object that are cached locally in memory.
CursorLocation	CursorLocationEnum	Sets or returns the location of the cursor engine.
CursorType	CursorTypeEnum	Indicates the type of cursor used in a Recordset object.

Name	Returns	Description
DataMember	String	Specifies the name of the data member to retrieve from the object referenced by the DataSource property. Write only.
DataSource	Object	Specifies an object containing data to be represented as a Recordset object. Write only.
EditMode	EditModeEnum	Indicates the editing status of the current record. Read only.
EOF	Boolean	Indicates whether the current record is after the last record in a Recordset object. Read only.
Fields	Fields	Contains all of the Field objects for the current Recordset object.
Filter	Variant	Indicates a filter for data in the Recordset.
LockType	LockTypeEnum	Indicates the type of locks placed on records during editing.
MarshalOptions	MarshalOptionsEnum	Indicates which records are to be marshaled back to the server.
MaxRecords	Long	Indicates the maximum number of records to return to a Recordset object from a query. Default is zero (no limit).
PageCount	Long	Indicates how many pages of data the Recordset object contains. Read only.
PageSize	Long	Indicates how many records constitute one page in the Recordset.
Properties	Properties	Contains all of the Property objects for the current Recordset object.
RecordCount	Long	Indicates the current number of records in the Recordset object. Read only.
Sort	String	Specifies one or more field names the Recordset is sorted on, and the direction of the sort.
Source	String	Indicates the source for the data in a Recordset object.

Name	Returns	Description
State	Long	Indicates whether the recordset is open, closed, or whether it is executing an asynchronous operation. Read only.
Status	Integer	Indicates the status of the current record with respect to match updates or other bulk operations. Read only.
StayInSync	Boolean	Indicates, in a hierarchical Recordset object, whether the parent row should change when the set of underlying child records changes. Read only.

Events

Name	Description
EndOfRecordset	Fired when there is an attempt to move to a row past the end of the Recordset.
FetchComplete	Fired after all the records in an asynchronous operation have been retrieved into the Recordset.
FetchProgress	Fired periodically during a length asynchronous operation, to report how many rows have currently been retrieved.
FieldChangeComplete	Fired after the value of one or more Field object has been changed.
MoveComplete	Fired after the current position in the Recordset changes.
RecordChangeComplete	Fired after one or more records change.
RecordsetChangeComplete	Fired after the Recordset has changed.
WillChangeField	Fired before a pending operation changes the value of one or more Field objects.
WillChangeRecord	Fired before one or more rows in the Recordset change.
WillChangeRecordset	Fired before a pending operation changes the Recordset.
WillMove	Fired before a pending operation changes the current position in the Recordset.

Method Calls Quick Reference

Command

Command.Cancel
Parameter = Command.CreateParameter(*Name As String, Type As DataTypeEnum, Direction As ParameterDirectionEnum, Size As Integer, [Value As Variant]*)
Recordset = Command.Execute(*RecordsAffected As Variant, Parameters As Variant, Options As Integer*)

Connection

Integer = Connection.BeginTrans
Connection.Cancel
Connection.Close
Connection.CommitTrans
Recordset = Connection.Execute(*CommandText As String, RecordsAffected As Variant, Options As Integer*)
Connection.Open(*ConnectionString As String, UserID As String, Password As String, Options As Integer*)
Recordset = Connection.OpenSchema(*Schema As SchemaEnum, [Restrictions As Variant], [SchemaID As Variant]*)
Connection.RollbackTrans

Errors

Errors.Clear
Errors.Refresh

Field

Field.AppendChunk(*Data As Variant*)
Variant = Field.GetChunk(*Length As Integer*)

Fields

Fields.Append(*Name As String, Type As DataTypeEnum, DefinedSize As Integer, Attrib As FieldAttributeEnum*)
Fields.Delete(*Index As Variant*)
Fields.Refresh

Parameter

Parameter.AppendChunk(*Val As Variant*)

Parameters

Parameters.Append(*Object As Object*)
Parameters.Delete(*Index As Variant*)
Parameters.Refresh

Properties

Properties.Refresh

Recordset

Recordset.AddNew(*[FieldList As Variant], [Values As Variant]*)
Recordset.Cancel
Recordset.CancelBatch(*AffectRecords As AffectEnum*)
Recordset.CancelUpdate
Recordset = *Recordset*.Clone(*LockType As LockTypeEnum*)
Recordset.Close
CompareEnum = *Recordset*.CompareBookmarks(*Bookmark1 As Variant, Bookmark2 As Variant*)
Recordset.Delete(*AffectRecords As AffectEnum*)
Recordset.Find(*Criteria As String, SkipRecords As Integer, SearchDirection As SearchDirectionEnum, [Start As Variant]*)
Variant = *Recordset*.GetRows(*Rows As Integer, [Start As Variant], [Fields As Variant]*)
String = *Recordset*.GetString(*StringFormat As StringFormatEnum, NumRows As Integer, ColumnDelimeter As String, RowDelimeter As String, NullExpr As String*)
Recordset.Move(*NumRecords As Integer, [Start As Variant]*)
Recordset.MoveFirst
Recordset.MoveLast
Recordset.MoveNext
Recordset.MovePrevious
Recordset = *Recordset*.NextRecordset(*[RecordsAffected As Variant]*)
Recordset.Open(*Source As Variant, ActiveConnection As Variant, CursorType As CursorTypeEnum, LockType As LockTypeEnum, Options As Integer*)
Recordset.Requery(*Options As Integer*)
Recordset.Resync(*AffectRecords As AffectEnum, ResyncValues As ResyncEnum*)
Recordset.Save(*FileName As String, PersistFormat As PersistFormatEnum*)
Boolean = *Recordset*.Supports(*CursorOptions As CursorOptionEnum*)
Recordset.Update(*[Fields As Variant], [Values As Variant]*)
Recordset.UpdateBatch(*AffectRecords As AffectEnum*)

Collaboration Data Objects for NT Server (CDONTS) Reference

What are CDONTS?

Collaboration Data Objects for NT Server (**CDONTS**) is a set of objects that provide lightweight messaging services to applications. For this book, the most relevant use of CDONTS is to provide our Web applications with services to send automated e-mails.

CDONTS is a subset of the Collaboration Data Object (CDO) library. The full CDO library lets applications communicate with Microsoft's flagship messaging system, Microsoft Exchange. Whereas CDO has access to all of the Microsoft Exchange features, such as scheduling, address books, stores, folders and e-mail, CDONTS is limited to only sending e-mail through the ubiquitous SMTP protocol.

> *A list of the objects, properties, and methods for the full CDO library is included at the end of this appendix.*

To use CDONTS from your Active Server Pages application, you'll need to make sure the Microsoft SMTP Service is installed and running on your computer. This service is installed along with IIS4 and is available on Windows NT Server only. When you're certain this service is installed and running, all you have to do is create the appropriate objects from your ASP code, or your business objects, and your outgoing mail will be sent through this standalone SMTP service.

To use CDONTS object from Visual Basic, you should include a reference to "Microsoft CDO for NTS 1.2.1 Library" by using the References dialog.

Object Reference

This is a list of the objects available to CDONTS developers.

The NewMail Object

There are two ways to send e-mail through CDONTS. The first method is the most straightforward and lets you send e-mail in about three lines:

```
set MyNewMail = CreateObject("CDONTS.NewMail")
MyNewMail.Send "fromsomeone@wrox.com", "tosomeone@wrox.com", _
            "Subject Line", "This is my exciting and informative message."
set MyNewMail = Nothing
```

The alternate method (covered in the next section) shows you how you use the Session object to gain finer control over the sending process.

The "Send" Method

As in the example above, you can perform the whole operation in a single line, if you want. The alternate method is to set properties on the object and then fire the Send command without parameters:

```
Dim newmail

Set newmail = CreateObject("CDONTS.NewMail")

newmail.From = "fromsomeone@wrox.com"
newmail.To = "tosomeone@wrox.com"
newmail.Subject = "This is my subject"
newmail.Body = "This is fascinating!"
newmail.Send

Set newmail = Nothing
```

Method: **Send**	Sends e-mail, either using the properties set on the object, or by populating optional parameters.	
	Optional **From** as String	The e-mail address of the sender.
	Optional **To** as String	Comma separated list of recipients.
	Optional **Subject** as String	The subject line to attach to the message.
	Optional **Body**	The text of the message. This can either be a String, or a reference to an IStream object.
	Optional **Importance** as String	The importance of the message. Possible values for this are covered in the documentation for the Importance property.

> In the Microsoft documentation, you will see references to using `IStream` objects to supply data to the CDONTS objects. Visual Basic is not capable at handling these objects, so we'll be ignoring references to them throughout this documentation.

Setting the Sender, Subject, Importance and the Recipients

The "`To`", "`CC`" (carbon copy) and "`BCC`" (blind carbon copy) properties on the NewMail object each work in the same way. Each of them takes a list of e-mail addresses separated either by a comma or a semicolon. (The documentation viewable in the Object Browser indicates that only a comma will work. This is not true - the properties will accept either.)

You can specify a display name for any address by using the syntax:

```
DisplayName<email@domain>
```

Like this:

```
newmail.To = "John Doe<john@wrox.com>;Ann Other<ann@wrox.com>"
```

Property (Write-only) **To, CC, BCC**	Used to specify recipients for the e-mail. Optionally, you can set the "To" recipients as a parameter on the "Send" method.	
	Recipients as String	A comma or semi-colon separated list of recipients, e.g. "first@wrox.com;to@wrox.com"

You can set the sender of the message using the "From" property. CDONTS only supports sending from a single address.

Property (Write-only)	Used to specify the sender for the e-mail.	
From	**From** as String	The e-mail address of the sender, e.g. "from@wrox.com"

You can set the subject of the message with the "Subject" property.

Property (Write-only)	Used to specify the subject of the e-mail.	
Subject	**Subject** as String	The subject, e.g. "Get rich quick with our scheme!"

You can set the importance of the message with the "Importance" property.

Property (Write-only)	Used to specify the importance of the e-mail.	
Importance	**Importance** as Long	One of these values:
	CdoLow	(0) Low importance
	CdoNormal	(1) Normal importance (Default)
	CdoHigh	(2) High importance

Specifing the Message to Send

To supply the text of the message, you can either use the Body property, or the Body parameter on the Send method.

This is an example of a VB object illustrating one method of building up the text of the message:

```
' Define somewhere to put the body text
Private m_body As String

' Public
Public Sub SendMail(recipients As String, subject As String)

    ' create the newmail object
    Dim newmail As newmail
    Set newmail = CreateObject("CDONTS.NewMail")

    ' put on a header...
    AddText "This is a list of all our customers..."

    ' build up the mail...
    Dim customers As Recordset
    Set customers = db.Execute("select * from customers")
    Do While Not customers.EOF
```

```
                ' add to the message
                AddText "Customer: " & customers("name")

                ' next
                customers.MoveNext

        Loop
        customers.Close
        Set customers = Nothing

        ' add a footer
        AddText "That's it!"

        ' send the mail
        newmail.Send "from@wrox.com", recipients, subject, m_body, CdoNormal

        ' cleanup
        Set newmail = Nothing

    End Sub

    Private Function AddText(buf As String)
        m_body = m_body & buf
    End Function
```

Property (Write-only)	Used to specify the complete body of the mail.	
Body	**Body** as String	The text of the message.

Sending HTML Mail

As more people start using HTML enabled mail clients, like Microsoft Outlook Express, organizations sometimes send out messages that use HTML to format the message to make them more appealing.

CDONTS supports sending mail in HTML format through the `BodyFormat` property.

```
    ' create the newmail object
    Dim newmail
    Set newmail = CreateObject("CDONTS.NewMail")

    ' tell it we're HTML mail...
    newmail.BodyFormat = CdoBodyFormatHTML

    ' format the text...
    Dim html
    html = "<HTML>"
    html = html & "<HEAD></HEAD>"
    html = html & "<BODY>"
    html = html & "<FONT COLOR=#800000 SIZE=5>"
    html = html & "Big red text!"
    html = html & "</FONT>"
    html = html & "<A HREF=""http://www.wrox.com/"">Wrox</A>"
    html = html & "<BODY>"
    html = html & "<HTML>"
```

```
' send the mail
newmail.Send "from@wrox.com", "to@wrox.com", "My Subject", html

' cleanup
Set newmail = Nothing
```

Property (Write-only)	Used to specify the format of the e-mail.		
BodyFormat	**BodyFormat** as Long	One of these values:	
		CdoBodyFormatHTML	(0) Use HTML mail for sending.
		CdoBodyFormatText	(1) Use plain text for sending. (Default)

Attaching Files

It's possible to attach files to your e-mail using the `AttachFile` and `AttachURL` methods.

The simplest to use is the `AttachFile` method. This takes a file name and an optional encoding method. The default encoding method is to use `UUEncode`. You can, however, specify that an attachment should be encoded using `"Base64"`. `UUEncode` will work in most cases, so it's usually not necessary to change this.

```
newmail.AttachFile "d:\ Brochure.pdf", "My File"
```

Method:	Attaches a file to the message		
AttachFile	**Source** as String	Fully qualified path to the file.	
	Optional **Filename** as String	Arbitrary name for the file.	
	Optional **Encoding** as Long	One of these values:	
		CdoEncodingUUencode	(0) Use UUEncode encoding. (Default)
		CdoEncodingBase64	(1) Use Base64 encoding.

The alternate method for sending attachments is to use the `AttachURL` method. This is an unusual method because you would assume it would send an Internet Shortcut to allow the reader to visit a URL by opening an attachment. Rather, it sends the attachment in the same fashion as `AttachFile`.

```
newmail.AttachURL "d:\inetpub\wwwroot\info.html", _
                  "http://www.wrox.com/info.html"
```

Method: **AttachURL**	Attaches a file to the message, but retains a reference to an URL where it originally came from.		
	Source as String	Fully qualified path to the file to attach.	
	ContentLocation as String	The absolute or relative URL that can be used to reference this URL later.	
	Optional **ContentBase** as String	A base of the URL that should be included if **ContentLocation** was a relative URL.	
	Optional **Encoding** as Long	One of these values:	
		`CdoEncodingUUencode`	(0) Use UUEncode encoding. (Default)
		`CdoEncodingBase64`	(1) Use Base64 encoding.

Using ContentBase and ContentLocation

If you choose to send mail in HTML format, you can optimize the process by globally defining the base of all the resource URLs, so that you just have to specify relative URLs in the message.

In an HTML file, you rarely specify absolute locations for images. In this example, `"index.html"` references an image in a folder immediately beneath the one containing `index.html`:

```
<img src="i/myimage.gif">
```

When we're building HTML mail, we don't want to have to absolutely define the paths, like this:

```
<img src="http://www.wrox.com/whereever/i/myimage.gif">
```

Use `ContentBase` to specify the server containing the content, `ContentLocation` to specify the folder:

```
' format the text...
Dim html
html = "<HTML>"
html = html & "<HEAD></HEAD>"
html = html & "<BODY>"
html = html & "<IMG SRC=""i/myimage.gif"">"
html = html & "<BODY>"
html = html & "<HTML>"

' specify the location...
newmail.ContentBase = "http://www.wrox.com/"
newmail.ContentLocation = "wherever/"
```

In this case, the image location will be resolved to:

```
http://www.wrox.com/wherever/i/myimage.gif
```

Property (Write-only)	Specifies the location of the server containing the resource.	
ContentBase	**URL** as String	The address of the server, e.g. "http://www.wrox.com/"

Property (Write-only)	Specifies the server folder containing the resource.	
ContentLocation	**Folder** as String	The name of the folder, e.g. "interesting/files/"

Miscellaneous Operations

The NewMail object also has a few methods and properties that don't fit into the above categories.

You can use the "Version" property to determine the installed version of CDONTS.

Property (Read-only)	Returns the value of the installed version of CDONTS, currently 1.2.1.
Version	

You can use the MailFormat property to set the encoding method for the mail. By default, this is text, but if you attach files with AttachFile or AttachURL and specify Base64 encoding, this property will automatically bet set to MIME.

Property (Write-only)	Used to specify the formatting for the message.		
MailFormat	**Format** as Long	One of these values:	
		CdoMailFormatMime	(0) Use MIME format.
		CDOMailFormatText	(1) Use text format. (Default)

You can use the Value method to specify headers for the mail in addition to the ones defined as part of the SMTP protocol. Some additional headers are widely understood by various messaging systems, such as "Reply-To". Limit the characters used in the value to letters, numbers and dashes.

Method:	Used to add additional headers to the message.	
Value	**Name** as String	The name of the header, e.g. "Reply-To", "Information"
	Value as String	The value to apply to the header, e.g. "fred@wrox.com" or "Interesting Message"

If you're sending mail to a different locale, you can use "SetLocaleIDs" to tell Windows NT to use different locale information. By default, CDONTS will use the locale information stored against the user running the operation (and in the case of ASP-driven sites with anonymous access, the default IUSER_machinename account). How to determine possible locale IDs is beyond the scope of this discussion, but you can find more information at http://msdn.microsoft.com/.

Method: **SetLocaleIDs**	Uses to specify an alternate locale ID to the one stored against the user originating the message.
	CodePageID as Long The new locale.

Usings the "Other" CDONTS Object Model

The NewMail object is a complete object for sending mails from your applications. However, you can use the other set of CDONTS objects to perform the same operations. Additionally, this other object model also lets you examine messages received by the SMTP server through the Inbox.

The full CDO object model does not have a NewMail object. To communicate with CDO you must establish a session with Microsoft Exchange through the Session object and perform all operations through that object. Mainly for compatibility, CDONTS also has a Session object with a limited subset of functionality. This section will take you through examples of using the CDONTS Session to perform similar functions to those we saw above.

The main purpose for this set of objects is to help developers who have already written CDO-enabled applications to port them to CDONTS, and to let CDONTS developers scale the applications to CDO.

The "Session" Object

The Session object is a cut down version of CDO's Session object. In full CDO, this object gives you access to all of the Microsoft Exchange folders available on the server. The session object of CDONTS lets you access the two CDONTS folders: Inbox and Outbox. As the only function of CDONTS is to send SMTP mail, none of the scheduling or other groupware functionality is available.

To create a session object, use this code:

```
Set Session = CreateObject("CDONTS.Session")
```

Or:

```
Dim Session as New CDONTS.Session
```

Logging onto the Session

Full CDO features a "Logon" method that connects the user to the required instance of Microsoft Exchange. CDONTS features the similar "LogonSMTP" method.

Method: **LogonSMTP**	Connects to the STMP service. This can either be on the local computer, another server on the network or a server elsewhere on the Internet.	
	Name as String	Arbitrary name for the session, e.g. "My SMTP Session"
	Server as String	IP address or NETBIOS name for the server, e.g. "127.0.0.1" (the local machine), or "STMPSERVER" or "smtp.wrox.com"

After you have completed your work with the server, you should call the "Logoff" method:

Method: **Logoff**	Disconnects the Session from the server.

Working with Folders

Full CDO heavily utilizes folders for its operation. CDONTS has only two folders: **Inbox** and **Outbox**.

Use the Inbox and Outbox properties to access the folders.

```
' create the newmail object
Dim session As New CDONTS.session

' logon to the server
session.LogonSMTP "My Session", "127.0.0.1"

' get the outbox folder...
Dim sendfolder As CDONTS.folder
Set sendfolder = session.Outbox

' now work with the folder...


' cleanup
session.Logoff
Set session = Nothing
```

Property (Read-only)	Description
Inbox	Returns a Folder object corresponding to the physical folder on disk that receives messages.
Outbox	Returns a Folder object corresponding to the physical folder on disk that spools messages for sending.

Use the `GetDefaultFolder` as an alternate method for accessing the `Inbox` and `Outbox` "Folder" objects. This method is supplied for compatibility with the full CDO library. In CDO, the method provides access to Calendar, Contacts, Journals, etc.

Method	Returns a Folder object for either the Inbox or the Outbox.	
GetDefaultFolder	**FolderType** as Long	Can be one of these values:
		`CdoDefaultFolderInbox` = 1
		`CdoDefaultFolderOutbox` = 2

Miscellanous Functions

You can use the "`Version`" property to determine the installed version of CDONTS.

Property (Read-only)	Returns the value of the installed version of CDONTS, currently 1.2.1.
Version	

Use the "`SetLocaleIDs`" method when sending mail to other locales:

Method:	Used to specify an alternate locale ID to the one stored against the user originating the message.	
SetLocaleIDs	**CodePageID** as Long	The new locale.

Use the "`Name`" property to return the name supplied when calling "`LogonSMTP`":

Property (Read-only)	Return the name of the session as specified in `LogonSMTP`.
Name	

Use the "`MessageFormat`" property to specify the default format for mails:

Property (Write-only)	Used to specify the formatting for the message.		
MailFormat	**Format** as Long	One of these values:	
		`CdoMailFormatMime` 0	Use MIME format.
		`CDOMailFormatText` 1	Use text format. (Default)

Standard Properties on CDONTS Objects

All of the CDONTS objects have these standard properties:

Property (Read-only)	Description
Session as CDONTS.Session	Returns the Session that owns the object.
Application as String	Returns the name of the application that owns the object. This always returns "Collaboration Data Objects for NTS version 1.2.1"
Parent as Object	The parent of the object. For example, a Folder object will return the Session as its parent. The Session object will return "Nothing" for its parent.
Class as Long	Returns a Long value representing the type of object. (Don't confuse this with a COM class.)
	AddressEntry CdoAddressEntry (=8)
	Attachment CdoAttachment (=5)
	Attachments Collection CdoAttachments (=18)
	Folder CdoFolder (=2)
	Message CdoMsg (=3)
	Messages Collection CdoMessages (=16)
	Recipient CdoRecipient (=4)
	Recipients Collection CdoRecipients (=17)
	Session CdoSession (=0)

The "Folder" Object

The Folder object provides programmatic access to Inbox and the Outbox. This, again, is a cut down version of the full CDO "Folder" object.

Its main function is to provide access to the "Messages" property, which in turn provides access to a collection of the messages in the folder. In the case of the Outbox, you can "Add" messages to this collection, which is how you actually send messages.

```
' get the outbox folder...
Dim sendfolder As CDONTS.folder
Set sendfolder = session.Outbox

' now get the messages collection from the folder...
Dim outgoing As CDONTS.messages
Set outgoing = sendfolder.messages
```

The "Name" property can be used to find the name of the Folder:

Property (Read-only)	Returns the name of the folder, e.g. "Inbox"
Name	

The "Messages" Collection Object

The Messages object provides access to all of the messages contained with a Folder. Again, this object is mainly here to provide compatibility with the full CDO object model. Because we usually use CDONTS for sending mail, most of the methods here are usually not required.

Creating a New Message

If you want to send a message, you need to use the Add method. This will return a Message object that you can then use to define the message. (The Message object is covered in the next section.)

```
' get the outbox folder...
Dim sendfolder As CDONTS.Folder
Set sendfolder = session.Outbox

' create a new message...
Dim newmessage As CDONTS.Message
Set newmessage = sendfolder.Messages.Add
```

Method:	Adds a new message to the folder and returns a Message object.		
Add	Optional **Subject** as String	The subject of the message.	
	Optional **Text** as String	The text of the message.	
	Optional **Importance** as Long	One of these values:	
		CdoLow	0	Low importance
		CdoNormal	1	Normal importance (Default)
		CdoHigh	2	High importance

Navigating the Message Collection

Although not necessary when sending messages, these methods and properties let you examine the state of the Messages collection:

Property (Read-only)	Description	
Count	Returns the number of messages in the collection.	
Item	Returns a Message from the collection.	
	Index as Long	A value between 1 and Messages.Count that indicates the required message.

You can move around the collection using the "GetFirst", "GetLast", "GetPrevious" and "GetNext" methods. These methods will return a Message object if the specified message was found, otherwise they will return Nothing. Note that calling GetNext before a call to GetFirst is not recommended.

Finally, you can delete all of the messages from the collection with the "Delete" method:

Delete	Deletes all of the messages from the folder, and hence deletes all the messages in the physical folder on disk.

The "Message" Object

Once you have created your new "Message" object through calling "Add" on the "Messages" collection, you can go ahead and configure the message and send it.

Setting the Sender, Recipients and Subject

Settings the sender of the message works slight differently than in the NewMail object. The Sender is determined by a combination of the Session name and the server name. For example, if you "LogonSMTP" to the Session like this:

```
session.LogonSMTP "From", "mail.wrox.com"
```

The "From" address will come out as:

```
from@mail.wrox.com
```

You can use the "Sender" property to examine what the sender of the message will be:

Property (Read-only) **Sender**	Returns an AddressEntry object relating the sender of the message

Setting the recipients for the message works differently than in NewMail too. Rather than specifying a string containing the e-mail address of the recipients, we use the RecipientsCollection and add Recipient objects to it using the "Add" method. Recipient objects can be "To", "CC" or "BCC". We'll be covering how to do this later in the "Recipients Collection" section.

To get the Recipients collection:

Property (Read-only) **Recipients**	Returns a list from the Recipients collection that can be used to manipulate the recipients on the object.

To set the subject, use the "Subject" property:

Property: **Subject**	Sets or gets the subject of the message, e.g. "Interesting Message Here!"

To set the importance, use the "Importance" property:

Property: **Importance**	Used to specify the importance of the e-mail.		
	Importance as Long	One of these values:	
		CdoLow 0	Low importance
		CdoNormal 1	Normal importance (Default)

Defining the Text of the Message

To define the text of the message, use the "Text" and "HTMLText" properties.

Both these properties can be read from and written to, unlike the Body property of the NewMail object, which is write-only.

To specify the text of the message:

```
newmessage.Text = "This is the start of the message."
newmessage.Text = newmessage.Text & "This is more text in the message."
```

You can send HTML format mail through the HTMLText property. You must instruct CDONTS to send the message in MIME format for this to work properly:

```
newmessage.MessageFormat = CdoMime
newmessage.HTMLText = "<HTML><HEAD></HEAD><BODY>"
newmessage.HTMLText = newmessage.HTMLText & "<B>Hello world!</B>"
newmessage.HTMLText = newmessage.HTMLText & "</BODY></HTML>"
```

Property	Description		
Text	Sets or gets the body of the message in plain text format.		
HTMLText	Sets or gets the body of the message in HTML format.		
MessageFormat	Sets or gets the message to send the format in. Can be one of these values:		
	CdoMime	0	Use MIME format.
	CdoText	1	Use plain text format. (Default)

Sending the Message

After you've properly configured the message, use the "Send" method to instruct CDONTS to send it. Unlike the "NewMail.Send" method, this method takes no parameters – everything must be configured using the properties of the Message.

Method:	Instructs CDONTS to send the message.
Send	

Sending Attachments

Sending attachments works in a similar manner to adding recipients to the message. The "Attachments" property returns an "Attachments" collection that can then be used to add attachments. This "Attachments" collection will be covered in a later section.

Property (Read-only)	Returns an Attachments collection.
Attachments	

Using ContentBase, ContentLocation and ContentID

Like in the NewMail object, if you choose to send mail in HTML format, you can optimize the process by globally defining the base of all the resource URLs. Unlike NewMail, however, these properties can be both read from and written to. See the description in the NewMail documentation above for more details.

Property	Description	
ContentBase	Specifies the location of the server containing the resource.	
	URL as String	The address of the server, e.g. "http://www.wrox.com/"
ContentLocation	Specifies the server folder containing the resource.	
	Folder as String	The name of the folder, e.g. "interesting/files/"

The ContentID method is not available on the NewMail object, mainly because it can only be examined for messages that have been received. It provides access to the "Content-ID" header in the received message. Note that not all mail servers add this header, so it may be blank.

Property (Read-only)	Used to examine the Content-ID header on the received message.
ContentID as String	

Deleting the Message

This operation is only valid when using the Inbox. If you want to "delete" a message that you haven't yet sent, simply don't call the "Send" method and delete any references to the object.

Method:	Removes the message from its parent's "Messages"
Delete	collection, and therefore from the physical folder on disk.

Miscellaneous Properties

Again, these properties are only valid when examining messages in the Inbox.

To see the size of the message, including attachments, use the "Size" property:

Property (Read-only)	Returns the size of the message, including attachments.
Size as Long	

To see the time the message was received or sent:

Property (Read-only)	Returns the time and date the message was received.
TimeReceived as Date	

Property (Read-only)	Returns the time and date the message was sent.
TimeSent as Date	

The "Recipients" Collection Object

The "Recipients" collection object provides access to the recipients of a message.

Adding a Recipient

To create a new recipient on the message, use the "Add" method. This code sample illustrates how to create a recipient in a single line, then a more verbose example on how to create a "CC" recipient by setting properties on the "Recipient" object that "Add" always returns.

```
' you can either give the name and address in the "Add" method...
Dim toRecipient As CDONTS.recipient
Set toRecipient = newmessage.recipients.Add("John Doe", "jdoe@wrox.com")

' or populate the new receipient object separately...
Dim ccRecipient As CDONTS.recipient
Set ccRecipient = newmessage.recipients.Add
ccRecipient.Name = "Ann Other"
ccRecipient.Address = "annother@wrox.com"
ccRecipient.Type = CdoCc
```

Method: **Add** as CDONTS.Recipient	Adds a new recipient to the collection and returns a Recipient object.	
	Optional **Name** as String	Specifies the given name of the recipient.
	Optional **Address** as String	Specifies the e-mail address of the recipient.
	Optional **Type** as Long	One of these values: CdoTo (=1) CdoCc (=2) CdoBcc (=3)

Navigating the Recipients Collection

You can find the number of recipients in the collection with the "Count" property:

Property (Read-only) **Count** as Long	Return the number of recipients.

You can access a given recipient using the "Item" property:

Property (Read-only)	Returns the given recipient as a Recipient object.	
Item as CDONTS.Recipient	**Index** as Long	A value between 1 and Recipients.Count that specifies the required recipient.

Deleting the Recipients

If you want to delete all of the recipients, use the "Delete" method. (You can delete individual recipients by calling the Delete method on the Recipient object.)

Method: **Delete**	Deletes all of the recipients in the collection.

The "Recipient" Object

The "Recipient" object provides information about a single recipient of the message.

You can get and set the given name, e-mail address and type of the recipient with the "Name", "Address" and "Type" properties:

Property	Description
Name as String	Sets or gets the given name of the recipient, e.g. "John Doe"
Address as String	Sets or gets the given e-mail address of the recipient, e.g. "john@wrox.com"
Type as Long	Sets or gets the given e-mail address of the recipient, which can be one of these values:
	CdoTo (=1)
	CdoCc (=2)
	CdoBcc (=3)

You can delete the recipient from the message's Recipients collection by using the "Delete" method:

Method: **Delete**	Deletes the recipient from the message's Recipients collection.

The "Attachments" Collection Object

The "Attachments" collection object provides access to the files attached to a message.

Adding an Attachments

To attach a new file to the message, use the "Add" method.

This sample creates a new attachment:

```
Dim attachment As CDONTS.attachment
Set attachment = newmessage.Attachments.Add("sales.pdf", _
  CdoFileData, "d:\salesinfo.pdf")
```

The method **Add** (as CDONTS.Attachment), adds a new attachment to the Attachments collection and returns an Attachment object.

Property (Optional)	Description
Name as String	The name of the attachment when it is received. Omitting this parameter will cause the name to be taken from the Source parameter.
Type as Long	One of these values: CdoFileData (=1) CdoEmbeddedMessage (=4)
Source as String	For an attachment using CdoFileData, this is the fully qualified path of the file to be attached.
ContentLocation as String	Used to specify the server for MIME attachments. (Typically used when attaching HTML files.)
ContentBase as String	Used to specify the folder for MIME attachments. (Typically used when attaching HTML files.)

The CdoEmbeddedMessage type is used when connecting to a Microsoft Exchange server. For SMTP mail, use CdoFileData.

Navigating the Attachments Collection

You can find the number of attachments in the collection with the "Count" property:

Property (Read-only)	Return the number of attachments.
Count as Long	

You can access a given attachment using the "Item" property:

Property (Read-only)	Returns the given attachment as a Attachment object.	
Item as CDONTS.Attachment	**Index** as Long	A value between 1 and Attachments.Count that specifies the required attachment.

Deleting the Attachments

If you want to delete all of the attachments, use the "Delete" method. (You can delete individual attachments by calling the Delete method on the Attachment object.)

Method: **Delete**	Deletes all of the attachments in the collection.

The "Attachment" Object

The "Attachment" object provides access to a single attachment to a message.

General Properties

We've examined some of the things we can do with the Attachment object thanks to the "Add" method on the "Attachments" collection object.

To get or set the name of the Attachment:

Property:	Sets or gets the name of the attachment. If this is omitted, the name will be taken from the source.
Name as String	

To get or set the source of the attachment:

Property:	Sets or gets the fully qualified file name of the file to be attached. Can be omitted if you intend to use the "ReadFromFile" method (see below).
Source as String	

To get or set the type of the attachment:

Property:	Sets or gets the type of the attachment. Can be one of these values:	
Type as Long	CdoFileData (=1)	Specifies that the attachment will be derived from a file.
	CdoEmbeddedMessage (=4)	Typically not used with CDONTS as it's usually used to connect to Microsoft Exchange.

Reading Attachments From Files

You do not have to specify the attachment as a file on disk through the "Source" property, or the "Source" parameter on "Attachments.Add". If you want, you can load the file directly into the Attachment through the "ReadFromFile" object. Internally, this is what CDONTS does when the message is sent.

```
Dim attachment As CDONTS.attachment
Set attachment = newmessage.Attachments.Add
attachment.Type = CdoFileData
attachment.ReadFromFile "d:\salesinfo.pdf"
```

Method:	Reads the data to be attached from a physical file on disk.
ReadFromFile	**Filename** as String The fully qualified name of a file.

This method is not supported if the attachment type is set to "CdoEmbeddedMessage".

If you are examining attachments from a received message, use the "WriteToFile" method to save the attachment's data to disk.

Method:	Saves the attachment's data to a file on disk.	
WriteToFile	**Filename** as String	The fully qualified name of the file you want to create.

This method is not supported if the attachment type is set to "CdoEmbeddedMessage".

Using ContentBase, ContentID and ContentLocation

You can find more information on these properties in the documentation for the "Message" object. Basically, when you attach a document that contains references to other resources, that resource can contain URLs relative to the document rather than fully qualified names (e.g. "i/hello.gif" as opposed to "http://www.wrox.com/i/hello.gif"). Usually, these documents are HTML documents.

ContentBase and ContentLocation are read-only properties that tell you how to interpret URLs embedded into the document.

Property (Read-only)	Returns the server that contains the resource.
ContentBase as String	

Property (Read-only)	Returns the folder on the server that contains the resource.
ContentLocation as String	

Some mail servers will create a "Content-ID" header in the message. CDONTS does not create such a header when it sends messages. You can find the Content-ID using the "ContentID" property:

Property (Read-only)	Returns the value in the Content-ID header, or a blank string if it was not specified.
ContentID as String	

Deleting an Attachment

To delete an attachment from the Attachments collection, use the "Delete" method.

Method: **Delete**	Deletes the attachment from the message's Attachments collection.

The "AddressEntry" Object

The "AddressEntry" object is used in only one place – it is returned from the "Sender" property on the "Message" object. This object has larger scope when using the full CDO object model.

You can determine the given name and e-mail address of the sender with the "Name" and "Address" properties:

Property (Read-only)	Description
Name as String	Returns the given name of the sender.
Address as String	Returns the e-mail address of the sender.
Type as String	Returns the type of address entry object. This is always "SMTP" when running inside of CDONTS.

With these objects, methods, and properties you should find it quite easy to create an e-mail client or otherwise deal with mail from within your VB applications.

The CDO MAPI Object

Included below is the full CDO set of objects, methods and properties if you wish to use this set instead of the CDONTS objects described above. The descriptions of each are omitted in this case. You need to reference the Microsoft CDO 1.21 Library to implement these objects in your VB projects.

Objects	Methods	Properties
AddressEntries	Add	Application
	Delete	Class
	GetFirst	Count
	GetLast	Filter
	GetNext	Item
	GetPrevious	Parent
	Sort	Session
AddressEntry	Delete	Address
	Details	Application
	GetFreeBusy	Class
	IsSameAs	DisplayType
	Update	Fields

Table Continued on Following Page

Objects	Methods	Properties
		ID
		Manager
		Members
		Name
		Parent
		Session
		Type
AddressEntryFilter	IsSameAs	Address
		Application
		Class
		Fields
		Name
		Not
		Or
		Parent
		Session
AddressList	IsSameAs	AddressEntries
		Application
		Class
		Fields
		ID
		Index
		IsReadOnly
		Name
		Parent
		Session
AddressLists		Application
		Class

Objects	Methods	Properties
		Count
		Item
		Parent
		Session
AppointmentItem	ClearRecurrencePattern	AllDayEvent
	CopyTo	Application
	Delete	Attachments
	Forward	BusyStatus
	GetRecurrencePattern	Categories
	IsSameAs	Class
	MoveTo	Conversation
	Options	ConversationIndex
	Respond	ConversationTopic
	Send	DeliveryReceipt
	Update	Duration
		Encrypted
		EndTime
		Fields
		FolderID
		ID
		Importance
		IsRecurring
		Location
		MeetingResponseStatus
		MeetingStatus
		Organizer
		Parent
		ReadReceipt

Table Continued on Following Page

Objects	Methods	Properties
		Recipients
		ReminderMinutesBeforeStart
		ReminderSet
		ReplyTime
		ResponseRequested
		Sender
		Sensitivity
		Sent
		Session
		Signed
		Size
		StartTime
		StoreID
		Subject
		Submitted
		Text
		TimeCreated
		TimeExpired
		TimeLastModified
		TimeReceived
		TimeSent
		Type
		Unread
Attachment	Delete	Application
	IsSameAs	Class
	ReadFromFile	Fields
	WriteToFile	Index
		Name
		Parent

Objects	Methods	Properties
		Position
		Session
		Source
		Type
Attachments	Add	Application
	Delete	Class
		Count
		Item
		Parent
		Session
Field	Delete	Applicaton
	ReadFromFile	Class
	WriteToFile	ID
		Index
		Name
		Parent
		Session
		Type
		Value
Fields	Add	Application
	Delete	Class
	SetNameSpace	Count
		Item
		Parent
		Session
Folder	CopyTo	Application
	Delete	Class

Table Continued on Following Page

Objects	Methods	Properties
	IsSameAs	Fields
	MoveTo	FolderID
	Update	Folders
		HiddenMessages
		ID
		Name
		Parent
		Session
		StoreID
Folders	Add	Application
	Delete	Class
	GetFirst	Count
	GetLast	Item
	GetNext	Parent
	GetPrevious	Session
	Sort	
GroupHeader		Application
		Class
		Count
		Level
		Name
		Parent
		Session
		Unread
InfoStore	IsSameAs	Application
		Clas
		Fields
		ID
		Index

Objects	Methods	Properties
		Name
		Parent
		ProviderName
		RootFolder
		Session
InfoStores		Application
		Class
		Count
		Item
		Parent
		Session
MeetingItem	CopyTo	Application
	Delete	Attachments
	Forward	Categories
	GetAssociatedAppointment	Class
	IsSameAs	Conversation
	MoveTo	ConversationIndex
	Options	ConversationTopic
	Reply	DeliveryReceipt
	ReplyAll	Encrypted
	Response	Fields
	Send	FolderID
	Update	ID
		Importance
		MeetingType
		Parent
		ReadReceipt

Table Continued on Following Page

Objects	Methods	Properties
		Recipients
		Sender
		Sensitivity
		Sent
		Session
		Signed
		Size
		StoreID
		Subject
		Submitted
		Text
		TimeCreated
		TimeExpired
		TimeLastModified
		TimeReceived
		TimeSent
		Type
		Unread
Message	CopyTo	Application
	Delete	Attachments
	Forward	Categories
	IsSameAs	Class
	MoveTo	Conversation
	Options	ConversationIndex
	Reply	ConversationTopic
	ReplyAll	DeliveryReceipt
	Send	Encrypted
	Update	Fields

Objects	Methods	Properties
		FolderID
		ID
		Importance
		Parent
		ReadReceipt
		Receipients
		Sender
		Sensitivity
		Sent
		Session
		Signed
		Size
		StoreID
		Subject
		Submitted
		Text
		TimeCreated
		TimeExpired
		TimeLastModified
		TimeReceived
		TimeSent
		Type
		Unread
MessageFilter	IsSameAs	Application
		Class
		Conversation
		Fields

Table Continued on Following Page

Objects	Methods	Properties
		Importance
		Not
		Or
		Parent
		Receipients
		Sender
		Sent
		Session
		Size
		Subject
		Text
		TimeFirst
		TimeLast
		Type
		Unread
Messages	Add	Application
	Delete	Class
	GetFirst	Count
	GetLast	Filter
	GetNext	Item
	GetPrevious	Parent
	Sort	Session
Recipient	Delete	Address
	GetFreeBusy	AddressEntry
	IsSameAs	AmbiguousName
	Resolve	Application
		Class
		DisplayType

Objects	Methods	Properties
		ID
		Index
		MeetingResponseStatus
		Name
		Parent
		Session
		Type
Recipients	Add	Application
	AddMultiple	Class
	Delete	Count
	GetFirstUnresolved	Item
	GetFreeBusy	Parent
	GetNextUnresolved	Resolved
	Resolve	Session
RecurrencePattern		Application
		Class
		DayOfMonth
		DayOfWeekMask
		Duration
		EndTime
		Instance
		Interval
		MonthOfYear
		NoEndDate
		Occurrences
		Parent
		PatternEndDate
		PatternStartDate

Table Continued on Following Page

Objects	Methods	Properties
		RecurrenceType
		Session
		StartTime
Session	AddressBook	AddressLists
	CompareIDs	Application
	CreateConversationIndex	Class
	DeliverNow	CurrentUser
	GetAddressEntry	Inbox
	GetAddressList	InfoStores
	GetArticle	Name
	GetDefaultFolder	OperatingSystems
	GetFolder	Outbox
	GetInfoStore	OutOfOffice
	GetMessage	OutOfOfficeText
	GetOption	Parent
	LogOff	Session
	LogOn	Version
	SetLocaleIDs	
	SetOption	

Microsoft Transaction Server Type Library Reference

This appendix should provide a list of the objects, methods, and properties which can be used within your programs to allow the programmer to make use of the Microsoft Transaction Server.

Global Methods

Name	Description
GetObjectContext	Obtains a reference to the IObjectContext that's associated with the current MTS Object
SafeRef	Used by an object to obtain a reference to itself that's safe to pass outside its context

Objects

Name	Description
ObjectContext	Provides access to the current objects context
SecurityProperty	Used to determine the current object's caller or creator
ObjectControl	Used to define context specific initialization and cleanup procedures and to specify whether or not the objects can be recycled

ObjectContext

Methods

Name	Returns	Description
CreateInstance	Variant	Creates an object using current object's context.
DisableCommit		Indicates that the object is not yet finished its work and any attempt to commit the transaction will force an abort.
EnableCommit		Indicates that the object is not yet finished its work but would allow the transaction to commit.
IsCallerInRole	Boolean	Returns TRUE if the caller's Userid is included in the identified role.
IsInTransaction	Boolean	Returns TRUE if this object context has an active transaction.
IsSecurityEnabled	Boolean	Returns TRUE if security is enabled.
SetAbort		Indicates that the object has completed its work and the transaction must be aborted.
SetComplete		Indicates that the object has completed its work and a transaction can be committed.

Properties

Name	Returns	Description	Type
Count	Integer	Get number of named properties.	Read only
Item	Variant	Get a named property	Read only
Security	SecurityProperty	Returns the security object	Read only

SecurityProperty

Methods

Name	Returns	Description
GetDirectCallerName	String	Returns the Name of the direct caller
GetDirectCreatorName	String	Returns the Name of the direct creator
GetOriginalCallerName	String	Returns the Name of the original caller
GetOriginalCreatorName	String	Returns the Name of the original creator

Constants

Error_Constants

Name	Value	Description
mtsErrCtxAborted	-2147164158	The transaction was aborted
mtsErrCtxAborting	-2147164157	The transaction is aborting
mtsErrCtxActivityTimeout	-2147164154	The activity timed out
mtsErrCtxNoContext	-2147164156	There is no object context
mtsErrCtxNoSecurity	-2147164147	There is no security context
mtsErrCtxNotRegistered	-2147164155	The context is not registered
mtsErrCtxOldReference	-2147164153	The context has an old reference
mtsErrCtxRoleNotFound	-2147164148	The role was not found
mtsErrCtxTMNotAvailable	-2147164145	The Transaction Monitor is not available
mtsErrCtxWrongThread	-2147164146	Execution on wrong thread

XactAttributeEnum

Name	Value	Description
adXactAbortRetaining	262144	Performs retaining aborts, so calling Rollback automatically starts a new transaction
adXactCommitRetaining	131072	Performs retaining commits, thus calling CommitTrans automatically starts a new transaction. Provider dependant.

Microsoft Message Queue Object Library Reference

This appendix lists the objects, properties, and methods available to the programmer to be able to implement the Microsoft Message Queue from within Web applications.

Objects

Name	Description
MSMQApplication	Obtains the machine identifier
MSMQCoordinatedTransactionDispenser	Use to obtain an MSMQ DTC Transaction Object (MSMQTransaction)
MSMQEvent	Allows implementation of a single event handler to support multiple queues
MSMQMessage	A message to be queued
MSMQQuery	Allow the querying of existing public queues
MSMQQueue	An MSMQ Queue
MSMQQueueInfo	Provides Queue Management
MSMQQueueInfos	Allows selection of public queues
MSMQTransaction	An MSMQ Transaction Object
MSMQTransactionDispenser	Used to create new MSMQ Internal Transaction Objects

MSMQApplication

Methods

Name	Returns	Description
MachineIdOfMachineName	String	Global function used to map a machine pathname to a unique identifier. For example, this identifier can be used to construct a format name for a computer so that its journal queue can be opened.

MSMQCoordinatedTransactionDispenser

Methods

Name	Returns	Description
BeginTransaction	IMSMQTransaction	Method used to obtain a new transaction from a transaction dispenser.

MSMQEvent

Methods

Name	Returns	Description
Arrived		User-defined method invoked when a message arrives at a queue.
ArrivedError		User-defined method invoked when an error is returned while reading messages asynchronously.

MSMQMessage

Methods

Name	Returns	Description
AttachCurrentSecurityContext		Method used to associate the current security context with a message.
Send		Method used to send a message to the destination queue. Can optionally be part of a transaction.

Properties

Name	Returns	Description	Type
Ack	Integer	Property indicating what kind of acknowledgement message is returned. Possible values defined by MQMSGACKNOWLEDGEMENT enumeration.	Read/Write
AdminQueueInfo	IMSMQQueueInfo	Property indicating the administration queue for the message.	Read/Write
AppSpecific	Integer	Property containing application-specific information.	Read/Write
ArrivedTime	Variant	Property indicating when the message arrived at its destination queue. Type is Variant Date.	Read only
AuthLevel	Integer	Property indicating the authorization level of a message. Possible values defined by MQMSGAUTHLEVEL enumeration.	Read/Write
Body	Variant	Property containing the message body. It is a Variant type and can contain any intrinsic type and persistent object.	Read/Write
BodyLength	Integer	Property indicating the length (in bytes) of the message body.	Read only

Table Continued on Following Page

Name	Returns	Description	Type
Class	Integer	Property indicating the class of message. Possible values defined by MQMSGCLASS enumeration.	Read only
CorrelationId	Variant	Property indicating the correlation identifier (array of bytes) of the message.	Read/ Write
Delivery	Integer	Property indicating the delivery mode of a message. Possible values defined by MQMSGDELIVERY enumeration.	Read/ Write
DestinationQueueInfo	IMSMQQueueInfo	Property indicating the destination queue of the message. Typically used when reading response messages, or messages in machine journals or dead-letter queues.	Read only
EncryptAlgorithm	Integer	Property indicating which encryption algorithm to use when encrypting the message body of a private message.	Read/ Write
HashAlgorithm	Integer	Property indicating which hash algorithm to use when authenticating the message.	Read/ Write
Id	Variant	Property containing the MSMQ-generated identifier (array of bytes) of the message.	Read only
IsAuthenticated	Boolean	Property indicating whether a message was or was not authenticated.	Read only
Journal	Integer	Property indicating journaling option for message. Possible values defined by MQMSGJOURNAL enumeration.	Read/ Write
Label	String	Property indicating the label of the message.	Read/ Write

Name	Returns	Description	Type
MaxTimeToReachQueue	Integer	Property indicating the amount of time MSMQ has to deliver the message to its destination queue.	Read/ Write
MaxTimeToReceive	Integer	Property indicating the amount of time the receiving application has to retrieve the message from its destination queue.	Read/ Write
Priority	Integer	Property indicating the priority level of a message. Range must be between MQ_MIN_PRIORITY and MQ_MAX_PRIORITY.	Read/ Write
PrivLevel	Integer	Property indicating the privacy level of a message. Possible values defined by MQMSGPRIVLEVEL enumeration.	Read/ Write
ResponseQueueInfo	IMSMQQueueInfo	Property indicating the response queue for the message.	Read/ Write
SenderCertificate	Variant	Property containing the security certificate of a message. Type is an array of bytes.	Read/ Write
SenderId	Variant	Property containing the sender identifier of the message. Type is an array of bytes.	Read only
SenderIdType	Integer	Property indicating what type of identifier is attached to the message. Possible values are defined by MSMQSENDERIDTYPE enumeration.	Read/ Write
SentTime	Variant	Property indicating when the message was sent. Type is Variant Date.	Read only

Table Continued on Following Page

Name	Returns	Description	Type
SourceMachineGuid	String	Property identifying the computer where the message originated.	Read only
Trace	Integer	Property indicating tracing option for message. Possible values defined by MQMSGTRACE enumeration.	Read/ Write

MSMQQuery

Methods

Name	Returns	Description
LookupQueue	IMSMQQueueInfos	Produces a collection of public queues that match a specified selection criteria. Queries the MSMQ information store.

MSMQQueue

Methods

Name	Returns	Description
Close		Method to close an open instance of a queue.
EnableNotification		Method to enable asynchronous notification of arriving messages. It can use the queue's implicit cursor. The user-defined MSMQEvent_Arrived event handler is invoked when a message arrives at the location specified by the optional Cursor parameter (default is first message in the queue), or a timeout occurs. The user-defined MSMQEvent_ArrivedError is invoked if the asynchronous message retrieval results in an error.
Peek	IMSMQMessage	Method to synchronously peek at the first message in the queue, regardless of the implicit cursor position. Optional parameters include ReceiveTimeout (default set to INFINITE), WantDestinationQueue (default set to False), and WantBody (default set to True).

Name	Returns	Description
PeekCurrent	IMSMQMessage	Method to synchronously peek at the current message in queue (message pointed at by the implicit cursor). The implicit cursor is not advanced. Optional parameters include `ReceiveTimeout` (default set to INFINITE) and `Transaction` (default set to MTS Transaction).
PeekNext	IMSMQMessage	Method to synchronously peek at the next message in the queue. When called, the implicit cursor is first advanced and then the message is returned. Optional parameters include `ReceiveTimeout` (default set to INFINITE) and `Transaction` (default set to MTS Transaction).
Receive	IMSMQMessage	Method to synchronously retrieve a message from a queue. It always removes the first message in queue regardless of the position of the implicit cursor. Optional parameters include `ReceiveTimeout` (default set to INFINITE), `Transaction` (default set to MTS Transaction), `WantDestinationQueue` (default set to False), and `WantBody` (default set to True).
ReceiveCurrent	IMSMQMessage	Method to synchronously remove the current message from the queue. Retrieves the message at the position pointed to by the implicit cursor. Optional parameters include `ReceiveTimeout` (default set to INFINITE) and `Transaction` (default set to MTS Transaction).
Reset		Method that resets the queue's implicit cursor to the beginning of the queue.

Properties

Name	Returns	Description	Type
Access	Integer	Property indicating the access mode of a queue. Possible values defined by `MQACCESS` enumeration.	Read only
Handle	Integer	Property indicating the internal MSMQ handle of an open queue instance. Useful for directly calling MSMQ APIs.	Read only
IsOpen	Boolean	Property indicating whether or not the queue object refers to an open instance of a queue.	Read only

Table Continued on Following Page

Name	Returns	Description	Type
QueueInfo	IMSMQQueueInfo	Property referring to an MSMQQueueInfo instance describing the queue.	Read only
ShareMode	Integer	Property indicating the share mode of a queue. Possible values defined by MQSHARE enumeration.	Read only

MSMQQueueInfo

Methods

Name	Returns	Description
Create		Method that creates a new queue. The PathName property is required to create a queue. The FormatName property is updated when the queue is created. Optional parameters include IsWorldReadable (default set to False) and IsTransactional (default set to False).
Delete		Method used to delete queue. The PathName property must be specified to delete a queue.
Open	IMSMQQueue	Method used to open a queue. The PathName property must be specified to open a queue. Parameters include Access (send, peek, or receive) and ShareMode (exclusive or all).
Refresh		Method used to refresh the properties of a public queue from the MSMQ information store.
Update		Method used to update the MSMQ information store with the public queue's current properties.

Properties

Name	Returns	Description	Type
Authenticate	Integer	Property that specifies whether or not the queue only accepts authenticated messages. If the authentication level of the message does not match the authentication level of the queue, the message is rejected by the queue. Possible values are defined by the MQAUTHENTICATE enumeration.	Read/ Write

Name	Returns	Description	Type
BasePriority	Integer	Property that specifies the base priority for all messages sent to a public queue. The queue's base priority has no effect on the order of the messages in the queue, or how messages are read from the queue.	Read/Write
CreateTime	Variant	Property that indicates the time and date when the queue was created. Type is Variant Date.	Read only
FormatName	String	Property that identifies the queue. The format name of a queue is generated by MSMQ when the queue is created, or generated later by the application.	Read/Write
IsTransactional	Boolean	Property indicating whether the queue is transactional or non-transactional. If the queue is transactional, all messages sent to the queue must be part of a transaction.	Read only
IsWorldReadable	Boolean	Property that indicates who can read messages in the queue. If False, then the queue has the default MSMQ security: all users can send messages to the queue but only the owner of the queue can read messages from it. Otherwise all users can read its messages.	Read only
Journal	Integer	Property that specifies if the messages retrieved from the queue are copied to the queue's journal queue. Possible values are defined by the MQJOURNAL enumeration.	Read/Write
JournalQuota	Integer	Property that specifies the maximum size (in kilobytes) of the journal queue.	Read/Write
Label	String	Property indicating the label of the queue.	Read/Write
ModifyTime	Variant	Property that indicates the time and date when the queue's properties were last modified. Type is Variant Date.	Read only
PathName	String	Property indicating pathname (physical location) of the queue.	Read/Write
PrivLevel	Integer	Property that specifies the privacy level that is required by the queue. The privacy level determines how the queue handles private (encrypted) messages. Possible values are defined by the MQPRIVLEVEL enumeration.	Read/Write

Table Continued on Following Page

Name	Returns	Description	Type
QueueGuid	String	Property indicating the identifier of the public queue.	Read only
Quota	Integer	Property that specifies the maximum size (in kilobytes) of the queue.	Read/Write
ServiceTypeGuid	String	Property identifying the type of service provided by the queue.	Read/Write

MSMQQueueInfos

Methods

Name	Returns	Description
Next	IMSMQQueueInfo	Method used to reset the implicit cursor to the start of a collection of queues produced by `MSMQQuery.LookupQueue`.
Reset		Method used to reset the implicit cursor to the start of a collection of queues produced by `MSMQQuery.LookupQueue`.

MSMQTransaction

Methods

Name	Returns	Description
Abort		Method used to abort an MSMQ transaction.
Commit		Method used to commit an MSMQ transaction.

Properties

Name	Returns	Description	Type
Transaction	Integer	Property that indicates the underlying "magic cookie" used by a transaction dispenser.	Read only

MSMQTransactionDispenser

Methods

Name	Returns	Description
BeginTransaction	IMSMQTransaction	Method used to obtain a new transaction from a transaction dispenser.

Constants

MQACCESS

Name	Value	Description
MQ_PEEK_ACCESS	32	Messages can only be looked at, and can not be removed from the queue
MQ_RECEIVE_ACCESS	1	Messages can be retrieved from the queue or peeked at.
MQ_SEND_ACCESS	2	Messages can only be sent to the queue

MQAUTHENTICATE

Name	Value	Description
MQ_AUTHENTICATE	1	The queue only accepts authenticated messages
MQ_AUTHENTICATE_NONE	0	The default. The queue accepts authenticated and non-authenticated messages

MQCALG

Name	Value	Description
MQMSG_CALG_DES	26113	Hashing algorithm used when authenticating messages
MQMSG_CALG_DSS_SIGN	8704	Hashing algorithm used when authenticating messages
MQMSG_CALG_MAC	32773	Hashing algorithm used when authenticating messages
MQMSG_CALG_MD2	32769	Hashing algorithm used when authenticating messages

Table Continued on Following Page

Name	Value	Description
MQMSG_CALG_MD4	32770	Hashing algorithm used when authenticating messages
MQMSG_CALG_MD5	32771	The Default. Hashing algorithm used when authenticating messages
MQMSG_CALG_RC2	26114	Hashing algorithm used when authenticating messages
MQMSG_CALG_RC4	26625	Hashing algorithm used when authenticating messages
MQMSG_CALG_RSA_KEYX	41984	Hashing algorithm used when authenticating messages
MQMSG_CALG_RSA_SIGN	9216	Hashing algorithm used when authenticating messages
MQMSG_CALG_SEAL	26626	Hashing algorithm used when authenticating messages
MQMSG_CALG_SHA	32772	Hashing algorithm used when authenticating messages

MQDEFAULT

Name	Value	Description
DEFAULT_M_ACKNOWLEDGE	0	Default value for the Acknowledgement property of a Message
DEFAULT_M_APPSPECIFIC	0	Default value for the AppSpecific property of a Message
DEFAULT_M_AUTH_LEVEL	0	Default value for the AuthLevel property of a Message
DEFAULT_M_DELIVERY	0	Default value for the Delivery property of a Message
DEFAULT_M_JOURNAL	0	Default value for the journal property of a Message
DEFAULT_M_PRIORITY	3	Default value for the Priority property of a Message
DEFAULT_M_PRIV_LEVEL	0	Default value for the PrivLevel property of a Message
DEFAULT_M_SENDERID_TYPE	1	Default value for the SenderId property of a Message
DEFAULT_Q_AUTHENTICATE	0	Default value for the Authenticate property of a Queue
DEFAULT_Q_BASEPRIORITY	0	Default value for the BasePriority property of a Queue

Name	Value	Description
DEFAULT_Q_JOURNAL	0	Default value for the Journal property of a Queue
DEFAULT_Q_JOURNAL_QUOTA	-1	Default value for the JournalQuota property of a Queue
DEFAULT_Q_PRIV_LEVEL	1	Default value for the PrivLevel property of a Queue
DEFAULT_Q_QUOTA	-1	Default value for the Quota property of a Queue
DEFAULT_Q_TRANSACTION	0	Default value for the Transaction property of a Queue

MQERROR

Name	Value	Description
MQ_ERROR	-1072824319	Generic error code.
MQ_ERROR_ACCESS_DENIED	-1072824283	Access to the specified queue or computer is denied.
MQ_ERROR_BAD_SECURITY _CONTEXT	-1072824267	Security context specified by PROPID_M_SECURITY_CONTEXT is corrupted.
MQ_ERROR_BUFFER_OVERFLOW	-1072824294	Supplied message body buffer is too small. A partial copy of the message body is copied to the buffer, but the message is not removed from the queue.
MQ_ERROR_CANNOT_IMPERSONATE _CLIENT	-1072824284	MSMQ information store server cannot impersonate the client application. Security credentials could not be verified.
MQ_ERROR_COMPUTER_DOES _NOT_SUPPORT_ENCRYPTION	-1072824269	Encryption failed. Computer (source or destination) does not support encryption operations.
MQ_ERROR_CORRUPTED_INTERNAL _CERTIFICATE	-1072824275	MSMQ-supplied internal certificate is corrupted.
MQ_ERROR_CORRUPTED _PERSONAL_CERT_STORE	-1072824271	Microsoft® Internet Explorer personal certificate store is corrupted.

Table Continued on Following Page

Name	Value	Description
MQ_ERROR_CORRUPTED _SECURITY_DATA	-1072824272	Cryptographic function (CryptoAPI) has failed.
MQ_ERROR_COULD_NOT _GET_ACCOUNT_INFO	-1072824265	MSMQ could not get account information for the user.
MQ_ERROR_COULD_NOT _GET_USER_SID	-1072824266	MSMQ could not get the specified sender identifier.
MQ_ERROR_DELETE_CN _IN_USE	-1072824248	Specified connected network (CN) cannot be deleted because it is defined in at least one computer. Remove the CN from all CN lists and try again.
MQ_ERROR_DS_ERROR	-1072824253	Internal error with MQIS.
MQ_ERROR_DS_IS_FULL	-1072824254	MSMQ information store is full.
MQ_ERROR_DTC_CONNECT	-1072824244	MSMQ cannot connect to the Microsoft® Distributed Transaction Coordinator (MS DTC).
MQ_ERROR_FORMATNAME _BUFFER_TOO_SMALL	-1072824289	Specified format name buffer is too small to contain the queue's format name.
MQ_ERROR_ILLEGAL _CONTEXT	-1072824229	The lpwcsContext parameter of MQLocateBegin is not NULL.
MQ_ERROR_ILLEGAL _CURSOR_ACTION	-1072824292	An attempt was made to peek at the next message in the queue when cursor was at the end of the queue.
MQ_ERROR_ILLEGAL _FORMATNAME	-1072824290	Format name specified is not valid.
MQ_ERROR_ILLEGAL _MQCOLUMNS	-1072824264	Indicates that pColumns is NULL.
MQ_ERROR_ILLEGAL _MQQMPROPS	-1072824255	No properties are specified by the MQQMPROPS structure, or it is set to NULL.
MQ_ERROR_ILLEGAL _MQQUEUEPROPS	-1072824259	No properties are specified by the MQQUEUEPROPS structure, or it is set to NULL.
MQ_ERROR_ILLEGAL _OPERATION	-1072824220	The operation is not supported on this specific platform.
MQ_ERROR_ILLEGAL _PROPERTY_SIZE	-1072824261	The specified buffer for the message identifier or correlation identifier is not the correct size.
MQ_ERROR_ILLEGAL _PROPERTY_VALUE	-1072824296	Property value specified in the PROPVARIANT array is illegal.

Name	Value	Description
MQ_ERROR_ILLEGAL _PROPERTY_VT	-1072824295	VARTYPE specified in the VT field of the PROPVARIANT array is not valid.
MQ_ERROR_ILLEGAL _PROPID	-1072824263	Property identifier in the property identifier array is not valid.
MQ_ERROR_ILLEGAL _QUEUE_PATHNAME	-1072824300	MSMQ pathname specified for the queue is not valid.
MQ_ERROR_ILLEGAL _RELATION	-1072824262	Relationship parameter is not valid.
MQ_ERROR_ILLEGAL _RESTRICTION_PROPID	-1072824260	Property identifier specified in MQRESTRICTION is invalid.
MQ_ERROR_ILLEGAL _SECURITY_DESCRIPTOR	-1072824287	Specified security descriptor is not valid.
MQ_ERROR_ILLEGAL _SORT	-1072824304	Illegal sort specified.
MQ_ERROR_ILLEGAL _SORT_PROPID	-1072824228	Property identifier specified in MQSORTSET is not valid.
MQ_ERROR_ILLEGAL _USER	-1072824303	User is not legal.
MQ_ERROR_INSUFFICIENT _PROPERTIES	-1072824257	Not all properties required for the operation were specified.
MQ_ERROR_INSUFFICIENT _RESOURCES	-1072824281	Insufficient resources to complete operation (for example, not enough memory). Operation failed.
MQ_ERROR_INTERNAL _USER_CERT_EXIST	-1072824274	Internal user certificate exists
MQ_ERROR_INVALID _CERTIFICATE	-1072824276	Security certificate specified by PROPID_M_SENDER_CERT is invalid, or the certificate is not correctly placed in the Microsoft® Internet Explorer personal certificate store.
MQ_ERROR_INVALID _HANDLE	-1072824313	Specified queue handle is not valid.
MQ_ERROR_INVALID _OWNER	-1072824252	Object owner is not valid. Owner was not found when trying to create object.
MQ_ERROR_INVALID _PARAMETER	-1072824314	One of the IN parameters supplied by the operation is not valid.

Table Continued on Following Page

Name	Value	Description
MQ_ERROR_IO_TIMEOUT	-1072824293	`MQReceiveMessage` I/O timeout has expired.
MQ_ERROR_LABEL_BUFFER_TOO_SMALL	-1072824226	Message label buffer is too small for received label.
MQ_ERROR_LABEL_TOO_LONG	-1072824227	Message label is too long. It should be equal to or less than
MQ_ERROR_MACHINE_EXISTS	-1072824256	Machine with the specified name already exists.
MQ_ERROR_MACHINE_NOT_FOUND	-1072824307	Specified machine could not be found in MQIS.
MQ_ERROR_MESSAGE_ALREADY_RECEIVED	-1072824291	Message pointed at by the cursor has already been removed from the queue.
MQ_ERROR_MESSAGE_STORAGE_FAILED	-1072824278	Recoverable message could not be stored on the local computer.
MQ_ERROR_MISSING_CONNECTOR_TYPE	-1072824235	Specified a property typically generated by MSMQ but did not specify `PROPID_M_CONNECTOR_TYPE`
MQ_ERROR_MQIS_READONLY_MODE	-1072824224	MQIS database is in read-only mode.
MQ_ERROR_MQIS_SERVER_EMPTY	-1072824225	The list of MSMQ information store servers (in registry) is empty.
MQ_ERROR_NO_DS	-1072824301	No connection with the Site Controller server. Cannot access the MQIS.
MQ_ERROR_NO_INTERNAL_USER_CERT	-1072824273	No internal certificate available for this user.
MQ_ERROR_NO_RESPONSE_FROM_OBJECT_SERVER	-1072824247	No response from MQIS server. Operation status is unknown.
MQ_ERROR_OBJECT_SERVER_NOT_AVAILABLE	-1072824246	Object's MSMQ information store server is not available. Operation failed.
MQ_ERROR_OPERATION_CANCELLED	-1072824312	Operation was cancelled before it could be started.
MQ_ERROR_PRIVILEGE_NOT_HELD	-1072824282	Application does not have the required privileges to perform the operation.
MQ_ERROR_PROPERTY	-1072824318	One or more of the specified properties caused an error.

Name	Value	Description
MQ_ERROR_PROPERTY _NOTALLOWED	-1072824258	Specified property is not valid for the operation (for example, specifying PROPID_Q_INSTANCE when setting queue properties).
MQ_ERROR_PROV_NAME _BUFFER_TOO_SMALL	-1072824221	The provider name buffer for cryptographic service provider is too small.
MQ_ERROR_QUEUE _DELETED	-1072824230	Queue was deleted before the message could be read. The specified queue handle is no longer valid and the queue must be closed.
MQ_ERROR_QUEUE_EXISTS	-1072824315	Queue (public or private) with the identical MSMQ pathname is registered. Public queues are registered in MQIS. Private queues are registered in the local computer.
MQ_ERROR_QUEUE_NOT _AVAILABLE	-1072824245	Error while reading from queue residing on a remote computer.
MQ_ERROR_QUEUE_NOT _FOUND	-1072824317	Public queue is not registered in MQIS. This error does not apply to private queues.
MQ_ERROR_RESULT _BUFFER_TOO_SMALL	-1072824250	Supplied result buffer is too small. MQLocateNext could not return at least one complete query result.
MQ_ERROR_SECURITY _DESCRIPTOR_TOO_SMALL	-1072824285	Supplied security buffer is too small.
MQ_ERROR_SENDER_CERT _BUFFER_TOO_SMALL	-1072824277	Supplied sender certificate buffer is too small.
MQ_ERROR_SENDERID _BUFFER_TOO_SMALL	-1072824286	Supplied sender identification buffer is too small to hold sender identification.
MQ_ERROR_SERVICE _NOT_AVAILABLE	-1072824309	Application was unable to connect to the Queue Manager.
MQ_ERROR_SHARING _VIOLATION	-1072824311	Sharing violation when opening queue. The application is trying to open an already opened queue that has exclusive read rights.
MQ_ERROR_SIGNATURE _BUFFER_TOO_SMALL	-1072824222	The signature buffer is too small.
MQ_ERROR_STALE_HANDLE	-1072824234	Specified handle was obtained in a previous session of the Queue Manager service.
MQ_ERROR_SYMM_KEY _BUFFER_TOO_SMALL	-1072824223	The symmetric key buffer is too small.

Table Continued on Following Page

Name	Value	Description
MQ_ERROR_TRANSACTION _ENLIST	-1072824232	Cannot enlist transaction.
MQ_ERROR_TRANSACTION _IMPORT	-1072824242	MSMQ could not import the specified transaction.
MQ_ERROR_TRANSACTION _SEQUENCE	-1072824239	Transaction operation sequence is incorrect.
MQ_ERROR_TRANSACTION _USAGE	-1072824240	Either the queue or the message is not transactional. Transaction messages can only be sent to a transaction queue, and transaction queues can only receive transaction messages.
MQ_ERROR_UNSUPPORTED _ACCESS_MODE	-1072824251	Specified access mode is not supported. Supported access modes include MQ_PEEK_MESSAGE, MQ_SEND_MESSAGE, and MQ_RECEIVE_MESSAGE.
MQ_ERROR_UNSUPPORTED _DBMS	-1072824302	Current version of Database Management System is not supported
MQ_ERROR_UNSUPPORTED _FORMATNAME_OPERATION	-1072824288	Requested operation is not supported for the specified format name (for example, trying to open a queue to receive messages using a direct format name).
MQ_ERROR_USER_BUFFER _TOO_SMALL	-1072824280	Supplied buffer for user is too small to hold the returned information.
MQ_ERROR_WRITE_NOT _ALLOWED	-1072824219	Write operations to MQIS are not allowed while an MSMQ information store server is being installed.

MQJOURNAL

Name	Value	Description
MQ_JOURNAL	1	when a message is removed from the queue it is stored in the queue journal
MQ_JOURNAL_NONE	0	The default. Messages are not stored in a journal queue when they are removed from the queue

MQMAX

Name	Value	Description
MQ_MAX_Q_LABEL_LEN	124	The maximum length of the queue label
MQ_MAX_Q_NAME_LEN	124	The maximum length of the queue name

MQMSGACKNOWLEDGEMENT

Name	Value	Description
MQMSG_ACKNOWLEDGMENT_FULL _REACH_QUEUE	5	Posts positive and negative acknowledgements depending upon whether or not the message reached the queue. This can happen when the 'time-to-reach-queue timer expires, or when a message cannot be authenticated
MQMSG_ACKNOWLEDGMENT_FULL _RECEIVE	14	Post a positive or negative acknowledgement depending on whether or not the message is retrieved from the queue before its time-to-be-received timer expires.
MQMSG_ACKNOWLEDGMENT_NACK _REACH_QUEUE	4	Posts a negative acknowledgement when the message cannot reach the queue. This can happen when the time-to-reach-queue timer expires, or a message can not be authenticated
MQMSG_ACKNOWLEDGMENT_NACK _RECEIVE	12	Posts a negative acknowledgement when an error occurs and the message cannot be retrieved from the queue before its time-to-be-received timer expires.
MQMSG_ACKNOWLEDGMENT_NEG _ARRIVAL	4	Indicates a negative message arrival
MQMSG_ACKNOWLEDGMENT_NEG _RECEIVE	8	Indicates a negative message receive
MQMSG_ACKNOWLEDGMENT_NONE	0	The default. No acknowledgement messages are posted.
MQMSG_ACKNOWLEDGMENT_POS _ARRIVAL	1	Indicates a positive message arrival
MQMSG_ACKNOWLEDGMENT_POS _RECEIVE	2	Indicates a positive message receive

MQMSGAUTHLEVEL

Name	Value	Description
MQMSG_AUTH_LEVEL_ALWAYS	1	The message must be authenticated when it arrives at the destination queue
MQMSG_AUTH_LEVEL_NONE	0	The default. The message does not have to be authenticated when it arrives at the destination queue

MQMSGCLASS

Name	Value	Description
MQMSG_CLASS_ACK_REACH _QUEUE	2	The original message reached its destination queue
MQMSG_CLASS_ACK _RECEIVE	16384	The original message was retrieved by the receiving application
MQMSG_CLASS_NACK_ACCESS _DENIED	32772	The sending application does not have access rights to the destination queue
MQMSG_CLASS_NACK_BAD _DST_Q	32768	The destination queue is not available to the sending application
MQMSG_CLASS_NACK_BAD _ENCRYPTION	32775	The destination Queue Manager could not decrypt a private (encrypted) message
MQMSG_CLASS_NACK_BAD _SIGNATURE	32774	MSMQ could not authenticate the original message. The original message's digital signature is not valid.
MQMSG_CLASS_NACK_COULD _NOT_ENCRYPT	32776	The source Queue Manager could not encrypt a private message
MQMSG_CLASS_NACK_HOP _COUNT_EXCEEDED	32773	The original message's hop count is exceeded
MQMSG_CLASS_NACK_NOT _TRANSACTIONAL_MSG	32778	A non-transaction message was sent to a transactional queue
MQMSG_CLASS_NACK_NOT _TRANSACTIONAL_Q	32777	A transaction message was sent to a non-transactional queue
MQMSG_CLASS_NACK _PURGED	32769	The message was purged before reaching the destination queue
MQMSG_CLASS_NACK_Q _DELETED	49152	The queue was deleted before the message could be read from the queue
MQMSG_CLASS_NACK_Q _EXCEED_QUOTA	32771	The original message's destination queue is full
MQMSG_CLASS_NACK_Q _PURGED	49153	The queue was purged and the message no longer exists
MQMSG_CLASS_NACK_REACH _QUEUE_TIMEOUT	32770	Either the time-to-reach-queue or time-to-be-received timer expired before the original message could reach the destination queue
MQMSG_CLASS_NACK _RECEIVE_TIMEOUT	49154	The original message was not removed from the queue before its time-to-be-received timer expired
MQMSG_CLASS_NORMAL	0	Indicates a normal MSMQ message
MQMSG_CLASS_REPORT	1	Indicates a report message

MQMSGCURSOR

Name	Value	Description
MQMSG_CURRENT	1	Notification starts when a message is at the current cursor location
MQMSG_FIRST	0	The default. Notification starts when a message is in the queue
MQMSG_NEXT	2	The cursor is moved, then notification starts when a message is at the new cursor location

MQMSGDELIVERY

Name	Value	Description
MQMSG_DELIVERY _EXPRESS	0	The default. The message stays in memory until it can be delivered
MQMSG_DELIVERY _RECOVERABLE	1	In every hop along its route, the message is forwarded to the next hop or stored locally in a backup file until delivered, thus guaranteeing delivery even in the case of a machine crash

MQMSGIDSIZE

Name	Value	Description
MQMSG_CORRELATIONID_SIZE	20	Size of CorrelationID byte array
MQMSG_MSGID_SIZE	20	Size of MessageID byte array

MQMSGJOURNAL

Name	Value	Description
MQMSG_DEADLETTER	1	If the message time-to-be-received or time-to-reach-queue setting expires, keep the message in the dead letter queue on the machine where time expired
MQMSG_JOURNAL	2	If the message is transmitted (from the originating machine to the next hop), keep it in the machine journal on the originating machine
MQMSG_JOURNAL_NONE	0	The default. The message is not kept in the originating machine's journal

MQMSGMAX

Name	Value	Description
MQ_MAX_MSG_LABEL_LEN	249	Maximum length of the message Label property

MQMSGPRIVLEVEL

Name	Value	Description
MQMSG_PRIV_LEVEL_BODY	1	The message is a private (encrypted) message
MQMSG_PRIV_LEVEL_NONE	0	The default. The message is a non-private (clear) message

MQMSGSENDERIDTYPE

Name	Value	Description
MQMSG_SENDERID_TYPE_NONE	0	SenderID is not attached to the message
MQMSG_SENDERID_TYPE_SID	1	The default. The SenderID property contains a SID for the user sending the message

MQMSGTRACE

Name	Value	Description
MQMSG_SEND_ROUTE _TO_REPORT_QUEUE	1	Each hop made by the original message generates a report that is recorded in a report message, which is sent to the report queue specified by the source Queue Manager
MQMSG_TRACE_NONE	0	The default. No tracing for this message

MQPRIORITY

Name	Value	Description
MQ_MAX_PRIORITY	7	Maximum queue priority
MQ_MIN_PRIORITY	0	Minimum queue priority

MQPRIVLEVEL

Name	Value	Description
MQ_PRIV_LEVEL_BODY	2	The queue accepts only private (encrypted) messages
MQ_PRIV_LEVEL_NONE	0	The queue accepts only non-private (clear) messages
MQ_PRIV_LEVEL_OPTIONAL	1	The default. The queue does not force privacy, and accepts both clear and encrypted messages

MQSHARE

Name	Value	Description
MQ_DENY_NONE	0	The queue is available to everyone for sending, peeking, or retrieving messages.
MQ_DENY_RECEIVE_SHARE	1	Messages can only be retrieved by this process.

MQTRANSACTION

Name	Value	Description
MQ_MTS_TRANSACTION	1	Specifies that the call is part of the current MTS transaction
MQ_NO_TRANSACTION	0	Specifies the call is not part of a transaction
MQ_SINGLE_MESSAGE	3	Sends a single message as a transaction
MQ_XA_TRANSACTION	2	Specifies that the call is part of an externally coordinated, XA compliant, transaction

MQTRANSACTIONAL

Name	Value	Description
MQ_TRANSACTIONAL	1	All messages sent to the queue must be done through an MSMQ transaction
MQ_TRANSACTIONAL_NONE	0	Default. No transaction operations can be performed on the queue

MQWARNING

Name	Value	Description
MQ_INFORMATION_DUPLICATE _PROPERTY	1074659333	Property already specified with same value. When duplicate settings are found, the first entry is used and subsequent settings are ignored.
MQ_INFORMATION_FORMATNAME _BUFFER_TOO_SMALL	1074659337	Supplied format name buffer is too small. Queue was still created.
MQ_INFORMATION_ILLEGAL _PROPERTY	1074659330	Specified identifier in property identifier array aPropID is not valid.
MQ_INFORMATION_OPERATION _PENDING	1074659334	Asynchronous operation is pending.
MQ_INFORMATION_PROPERTY	1074659329	One or more of the specified properties resulted in a warning. Operation completed anyway.
MQ_INFORMATION_PROPERTY _IGNORED	1074659331	Specified property is not valid for this operation (for example, PROPID_M_SENDERID is not valid; it is set by MSMQ when sending messages).
MQ_INFORMATION_UNSUPPORTED _PROPERTY	1074659332	Specified property is not supported by this operation. This property is ignored.

RELOPS

Name	Value	Description
REL_EQ	1	The default. Queue searching operator. Find only items that are Equal to the search string
REL_GE	6	Queue searching operator. Find only items that are Greater than or Equal to the search string
REL_GT	4	Queue searching operator. Find only items that are Greater Than to the search string
REL_LE	5	Queue searching operator. Find only items that are Less than or Equal to the search string
REL_LT	3	Queue searching operator. Find only items that are Less Than to the search string
REL_NEQ	2	Queue searching operator. Find only items that are Not Equal to the search string
REL_NOP	0	Queue searching operator.

Support and Errata

One of the most irritating things about any programming book is when you find that bit of code you've just spent an hour typing simply doesn't work. You check it a hundred times to see if you've set it up correctly and then you notice the spelling mistake in the variable name on the book page. Of course, you can blame the authors for not taking enough care and testing the code, the editors for not doing their job properly, or the proofreaders for not being eagle-eyed enough, but this doesn't get around the fact that mistakes do happen.

We try hard to ensure no mistakes sneak out into the real world, but we can't promise that this book is 100% error free. What we can do is offer the next best thing by providing you with immediate support and feedback from experts who have worked on the book and try to ensure that future editions eliminate these gremlins. The following section will take you step by step through the process of posting errata to our web site to get that help. The sections that follow, therefore, are:

- ➢ Wrox Developers Membership
- ➢ Finding a list of existing errata on the web site
- ➢ Adding your own errata to the existing list
- ➢ What happens to your errata once you've posted it (why doesn't it appear immediately)?

There is also a section covering how to e-mail a question for technical support. This comprises:

- ➢ What your e-mail should include
- ➢ What happens to your e-mail once it has been received by us

So that you only need view information relevant to yourself, we ask that you register as a Wrox Developer Member. This is a quick and easy process, that will save you time in the long-run. If you are already a member, just update membership to include this book.

Wrox Developer's Membership

To get your FREE Wrox Developer's Membership click on Membership in the navigation bar of our home site – `http://www.wrox.com`. This is shown in the following screenshot:

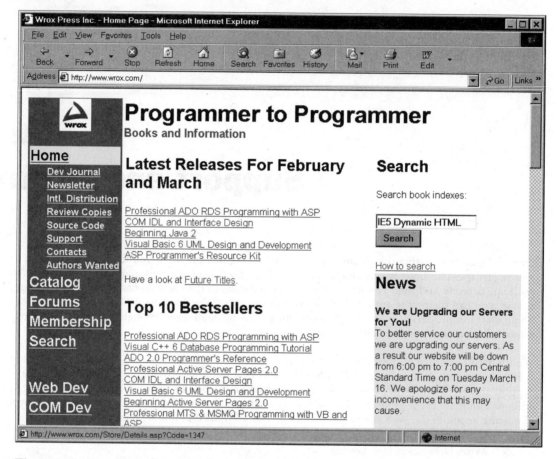

Then, on the next screen (not shown), click on **New User**. This will display a form. Fill in the details on the form and submit the details using the **Send Form** button at the bottom. Before you can say 'The best read books come in Wrox Red' you will get the following screen:

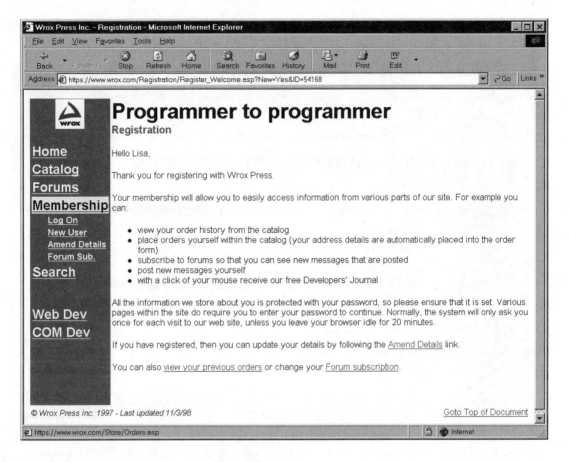

Finding an Errata on the Web Site

Before you send in a query, you might be able to save time by finding the answer to your problem on our web site – http:\\www.wrox.com.

Each book we publish has its own page and its own errata sheet. You can get to any book's page by clicking on Support from the left hand side navigation bar.

From this page you can locate any book's errata page on our site. Select your book from the pop-up menu and click on it.

Then click on **Enter Book Errata**. This will take you to the errata page for the book. Select the criteria by which you want to view the errata, and click the **Apply criteria...** button. This will provide you with links to specific errata. For an initial search, you are advised to view the errata by page numbers. If you have looked for an error previously, then you may wish to limit your search using dates. We update these pages daily to ensure that you have the latest information on bugs and errors.

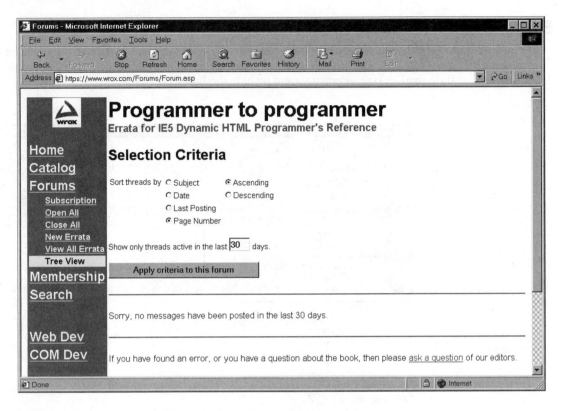

Adding an Errata to the Sheet Yourself

It's always possible that you may find your error is not listed, in which case you can enter details of the fault yourself. It might be anything from a spelling mistake to a faulty piece of code in the book. Sometimes you'll find useful hints that aren't really errors on the listing. By entering errata you may save another reader hours of frustration, and of course, you will be helping us provide even higher quality information. We're very grateful for this sort of advice and feedback. You can enter errata using the 'ask a question' of our editors link at the bottom of the errata page. Click on this link and you will get a form on which to post your message.

Fill in the subject box, and then type your message in the space provided on the form. Once you have done this, click on the Post Now button at the bottom of the page. The message will be forwarded to our editors. They'll then test your submission and check that the error exists, and that the suggestions you make are valid. Then your submission, together with a solution, is posted on the site for public consumption. Obviously this stage of the process can take a day or two, but we will endeavor to get a fix up sooner than that.

E-mail Support

If you wish to directly query a problem in the book with an expert who knows the book in detail then e-mail support@wrox.com, with the title of the book and the last four numbers of the ISBN in the subject field of the e-mail. A typical email should include the following things:

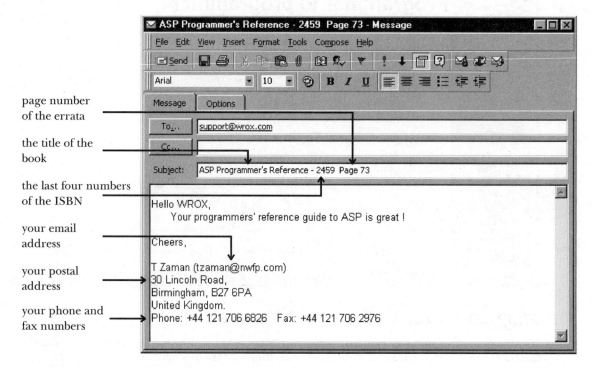

We won't send you junk mail. We need the details to save your time and ours. If we need to replace a disk or CD we'll be able to get it to you straight away. When you send an e-mail it will go through the following chain of support:

Customer Support

Your message is delivered to one of our customer support staff who are the first people to read it. They have files on most frequently asked questions and will answer anything general immediately. They answer general questions about the book and the web site.

Editorial

Deeper queries are forwarded to the technical editor responsible for that book. They have experience with the programming language or particular product and are able to answer detailed technical questions on the subject. Once an issue has been resolved, the editor can post the errata to the web site.

The Authors

Finally, in the unlikely event that the editor can't answer your problem, s/he will forward the request to the author. We try to protect the author from any distractions from writing. However, we are quite happy to forward specific requests to them. All Wrox authors help with the support on their books. They'll mail the customer and the editor with their response, and again all readers should benefit.

What We Can't Answer

Obviously with an ever growing range of books and an ever-changing technology base, there is an increasing volume of data requiring support. While we endeavor to answer all questions about the book, we can't answer bugs in your own programs that you've adapted from our code. So, while you might have loved the help desk systems in our Active Server Pages book, don't expect too much sympathy if you cripple your company with a live adaptation you customized from Chapter 12. But do tell us if you're especially pleased with the routine you developed with our help.

How to Tell Us Exactly What You Think

We understand that errors can destroy the enjoyment of a book and can cause many wasted and frustrated hours, so we seek to minimize the distress that they can cause.

You might just wish to tell us how much you liked or loathed the book in question. Or you might have ideas about how this whole process could be improved. In which case you should e-mail feedback@wrox.com. You'll always find a sympathetic ear, no matter what the problem is. Above all you should remember that we do care about what you have to say and we will do our utmost to act upon it.

Index

N

Name property
InternetExplorer object, 233
WebBrowser object, 233
NameInURL property
WebClass, 476
names
choosing
ActiveX DLLs, 341
Navigate method
InternetExplorer object, 217, 239
Web Browser Control, 85
WebBrowser object, 239
Navigate2 method
InternetExplorer object, 240
WebBrowser object, 240
NavigateComplete2 event
InternetExplorer object, 260
WebBrowser object, 260
navigation methods
InternetExplorer object, 239
WebBrowser object, 239
navigational properties
InternetExplorer object, 232
WebBrowser object, 232
NetShow Server
Windows DNA, 38
network address
IP address, 22
network folder
DHTML Application, example
deploying, 198
network traffic
reducing
RDS, 549
NewWindows2 event
InternetExplorer object, 262
WebBrowser object, 262
NextItem property
WebClass, 470, 478
No Compatibility
ActiveX DLLs, 342
Node Partial interface
AppendChild method, 584
DOM, 584
TransformNode method, 584
Xml property, 584
Non Internet Explorer
message board, 693

Non-repudiation
secure channels, 50
Notepad
HTML templates, developing, 498
NT Event log
ActiveX DLLs, 343
care in using, 344
n-tier client/server architecture
see multi-tier client/server architecture, 16
NumberOfReplies
stored procedures
message board, 639

O

Object Browser
ActiveX DLLs, 323
Authors.dll, 323
ObjectContext class
MTS, 409
ObjectContext object
ASP objects, 298, 311
SetAbort method, 298, 311
SetComplete method, 298, 311
objects
see also components
ASP objects, 311
events, 42
ingoing interface, 42
methods, 42
properties, 42
methods, 42
outgoing interface, 42
events, 42
properties, 42
ODBC
compared to OLEDB, 43
data source, creating
message board, 644
Office documents
loading
browser, 211
WebBrowser object, 211
Offline property
InternetExplorer object, 233
WebBrowser object, 233
OLE Commands
ExecWB method, 252

Q

Query method
 RDSServer.DataFactory object, 561
 syntax, 561
QueryKeyValue method
 registry class, 372, 376
QueryStatusWB method
 ExecWB method, 253
 InternetExplorer object, 251
 WebBrowser object, 251
QueryString collection
 Request object, 284
QueryValueEx method
 registry class, 376
QueueInfo object
 MSMQ, 415
 Open method, 415, 416
QueueMessage object
 MSMQ, 415
Quit method
 InternetExplorer object, 250
 OnQuit event, 263

R

RDBMS
 client/server computing, 14
RDO
 to be replaced, 44
RDS
 ADO, 44
 ADOR Recordset object, 550, 554
 advantages, 548
 architecture, 554
 compared to Expires property, 550
 data connection
  need not be permanent, 550
 DBMS, 555
 DCOM, 559
 DHTML, 551
 HTTP, 549, 550, 559
  advantages, 550
 HTTPS, 559
 information flow, 555
  RDSServer.DataFactory object, 572
 In-process, 559
 Internet wide access, 550
 introduction, 547
 multi-tier client/server architecture, 552, 553

 network traffic
  reducing, 549
 object model, 556
 overall picture, 571
 presentation, improving, 550
 RDS.DataControl object, 563
 RDS.DataSpace object, 556
 RDSServer.DataFactory object, 560
  information flow, 572
 server-side components, creating, 553
 structure, 551
 three-tier client/server architecture, 553
 using, 547
 writing code to, 551
RDS.DataControl object, 563
 ADOR Recordset object, 563
 Cancel method, 565
 CancelUpdate method, 565
 Connect property, 567
 CreateRecordset method, 565
 events, 570
 ExecuteOptions property, 567
 FetchOptions property, 568
 FilterColumn property, 569
 FilterCriterion property, 569
 FilterValue property, 569
 instantiating, 563
 InternetTimeout property, 568
 methods, 565
 Move methods, 565, 566
 MoveFirst method, 566
 MoveLast method, 566
 MoveNext method, 566
 MovePrevious method, 566
 onError event, 570
 onReadyStateChange event, 570
 properties, 567
 ReadyState property, 568
 Recordset property, 568
 Refresh method, 565, 566
 Reset method, 565, 566
 Server property, 569
 SortColumn property, 569
 SortDirection property, 569
 SourceRecordset property, 568
 SQL property, 569
 SubmitChanges method, 565
 URL property, 567
 using, 564